VICO AND MARX

VICO AND MARX:
Affinities and Contrasts

edited by
GIORGIO TAGLIACOZZO

HUMANITIES: NEW JERSEY

First published in 1983 in the United States of America by HUMANITIES PRESS INC.,
Atlantic Highlands, NJ 07716 and in Great Britain 1983 by THE MACMILLAN PRESS LTD.
London and Baskingstoke Companies and representatives throughout the world.

Library of Congress Cataloging in Publication Data
Main entry under title:

Vico and Marx, affinities and contrasts.

Includes index.
1. Vico, Giambattista, 1668–1744—Addresses, essays,
lectures. 2. Marx, Karl, 1818–1883—Addresses, essays,
lectures. I. Tagliacozzo, Giorgio.
B3583.V534   1982   195   82-18728
ISBN 0-391-02629-1

ISBN 0 333 35908 9 (Macmillan)

MANUFACTURED IN THE UNITED STATES OF AMERICA

Contents

Preface   **vii**

The Idea of "New Science" in Vico and Marx   1
  Peter Munz
Vico, Marx, Utopia, and History   20
  Alain Pons
Vico and Marx: Notes on a Precursory Reading   38
  David Lachterman
Ontological and Historiographical Construction in
Vico and Marx   62
  Leon Pompa
On "Making" History in Vico and Marx   78
  Terence Ball
Man Making History: The Role of the Plebeians
in Vico, the Proletariat in Marx   94
  Jeffrey Barnouw
The Question of Materialism in Vico and Marx   114
  George L. Kline
Vico and Marx: Human Consciousness and the Structure
of Reality   126
  Adrienne Fulco
Religion and the Civilizing Process in Vico and Marx   140
  Patrick H. Hutton
Vico and Marx: Notes on the History of the Concept
of Alienation   151
  Gustavo Costa
If a Science of Human Beings is Necessary, Can it
Also Be Possible?—A Paradox in Vico and Marx   163
  Hilliard Aronovitch
Vico, Marx, and Anti-Cartesian Theory of Knowledge   178
  Tom Rockmore
Scientific Knowledge in Vico and Marx   192
  Nikhil Bhattacharya
Vico and Marx and the Problem of Moral Relativism   206
  Lawrence H. Simon

Vico, Marx, and Heidegger   233
   Ernesto Grassi
Vico and Marx on Poetic Wisdom and Barbarism   251
   Donald Phillip Verene
Marx and Vico on the Oriental Mode of Production   263
   Emanuele Riverso
Naturalism in Vico and Marx: A Theory of the
Body Politic   277
   John O'Neill
Marx's Relation to Vico: A Philological Approach   290
   Arshi Pipa
Sorel, Vico, and Marx   326
   J. R. Jennings
Human Sciences and Philosophy of History Between
Vico and Marx (*Croce, Labriola, Sorel, and "Philosophy of History"*)   342
   Paolo Cristofolini
Vico and the Crisis of Marxism   352
   B. A. Haddock
From Vico's Common Sense to Gramsci's Hegemony   367
   Edmund E. Jacobitti
Vico and Marx after Nietzsche   388
   Allan Megill
Defense of Vico Against Some of His Admirers   401
   J. G. Merquior
Contributors   427
Name Index   431

Preface

On the eve of the Marx centennial—an anniversary occurring in an "Age of Disorientation," when established theories and ideologies have lost their firm hold on the minds of supporters and no clear alternatives have emerged—the importance of an assessment of Marx's thought in the light of Vico's, and of Vico's thought in the light of Marx's, is obvious if one considers:

a) *Marx's three well-known references to Vico* (in private letters to Lassalle and to Engels and in a footnote in *Das Kapital*) *and the interest in Vico of some eminent Marxist thinkers.*

b) *The existence of affinities—as well as contrasts—between the thought of Vico and that of Marx.*
The philosophical ideas of Vico and Marx have a comparable general setting, represented by the synthesis of philosophy and philology in Vico and the synthesis of theory and practice in Marx. They also have an analogous dominant focus on man in his concrete historical situation, and a similar encyclopaedic range. Furthermore, both Vico and Marx conceive human nature as changeable in the course of history, while maintaining that this does not obviate the need for the search and discovery of the law regulating change. Both hold—with different emphasis—that this law is dictated by the efforts of men to satisfy their material needs. Among the many contrasts between Vico and Marx perhaps the fundamental one is this: Vico is not a revolutionary author—his concept of the cyclical structure of time prevents him from thinking of history as having a final goal.

c) *The profound, implicit or explicit influence of Marx on much of contemporary humanistic and social scientific thought*—e.g. in the background of the Frankfurt School and of most Structuralist and Post-Structuralist scholars.

d) *The progressive increase in the past twenty years of the recognition of Vico as a seminal thinker in the fields of the humanities and the social sciences.*
Vico's ideas are in harmony with such basic features of advanced contemporary thought as "Anti-Cartesianism," an increasing recognition of the key philosophical importance of language, a growing presence of rhetoric and hermeneutics, a tendency of the humanities and the social science to converge, and a yearning for a unitary basis. The bibliography of writings

quoting Vico includes such authors as Derrida, Foucault, Frye, Bloom, Gadamer, Habermas, Toulmin.

e) *The fact that, in the various attempts so far to assess Vico's significance and possible influence, one key issue has been almost completely overlooked: the standing of Vico's thought in relation to the widespread influence of Marx, and the consequent need for a comparative assessment of the two thinkers.*

f) *The likelihood that counterposing Vico and Marx and pointing out areas of compatibility or incompatibility between them will suggest a matrix of novel questions and issues, opening new vistas in the humanities and the social sciences.*

The fragmentation of contemporary culture is the fundamental problem for the humanities and the social sciences in our time. If they cannot come to terms with this fragmentation, we are left without an intellectual center. Marx and Vico are both thinkers who provide a basis for holistic thought about culture. It is time that Marx was understood from a fresh viewpoint. Comparing Marx with Vico will let the thought of Marx appear in a new light. Both Marx and Vico are unique sources for finding the key to the unity of contemporary humanistic and social scientific thought.

This book is the outcome of an extensive canvassing in the USA and overseas of noted Vico and Marx scholars. Approximately one third of the scholars approached responded affirmatively. The large majority of these were Vico scholars. As I came to realize, the imbalance was due to the fact that, while Vico scholars (like most scholars in the humanities and social sciences today) are generally well acquainted with Marx's thought, very few Marx scholars are in a similar position with regard to Vico.

The reader may wonder why some specific topics and not others are covered in this book. The answer is the simple one of the availability of contributors and of their preferences. Perhaps it should be added that the few historical essays, included toward the end of the volume, were prepared in response to a clause in the initial letter of invitation, which extended the scope of the volume to such type of inquiry. Hopefully this book will be followed by another one which goes beyond the mere "affinities and contrasts" between Vico and Marx, to examine the lessons that the humanities and the social sciences can derive from such comparisons, both in their fundamental tenets and in specific areas.

An attempt has been made to arrange the papers that follow from the general to the specific and to keep the essays with similar concerns as near one another as possible. Since many different connections are possible between the subjects of these essays, no specific ordering along traditional headings has been attempted. Obviously the essays can and should be approached according to the order dictated by the reader's interest.

I want to express my heartfelt thanks to the distinguished scholars who have contributed to this volume and to Simon Silverman, Director of Humanities Press, who has believed in this project from its very inception.

Giorgio Tagliacozzo

Institute for Vico Studies, New York
September 1, 1982

To Missy

The Idea of "New Science" in Vico and Marx

Peter Munz

When, in the course of the seventeenth century, thoughtful men began to survey the scene of science and learning, it struck many that the attitude of the Renaissance and the Reformation to the past was no longer satisfactory. The view that the ancients had scaled the heights of human knowledge and that all that remained for the future was to restore and imitate the past—whatever that might precisely imply—could no longer make sense to people who had come across Descartes' mathematics, the science of Huyghens, not to mention Galileo, Kepler, and Newton. Starting more or less with Bacon's *The New Atlantis* (first published in 1627),[1] more and more thinkers took up the idea that the past, far from being perfect, was really something that ought to be overcome, jettisoned, despised, or at least neglected. It certainly ceased to be worthy of imitation.

The perspective that was thus shaped has become known as the Enlightenment, and to the Enlightenment we owe an enormous advance in knowledge, part of which depended in turn on the propagation of knowledge and the popularization of knowledge.[2] It affected every conceivable sphere, from education and psychology to society and the stars, from chemistry to biology and politics. But there re-

---

[1] "The very model of a wise government, then, is a society of scientists with leisure to accumulate knowledge and power to apply it to the public need, and the catalogue of wonders they have wrought reads like one of the crasser paeans to the American standard of living." Thus comments, on Bacon's *The New Atlantis,* C.O. Gillispie, *The Edge of Objectivity* (Princeton, 1960) p. 81. Similarly A. B. Ferguson, *Clio Unbound* (Durham, N.C., 1979), p. 406; P.M. Heimann, "The Scientific Revolution" in *The New Cambridge Modern History,* ed. P. Burke (Cambridge, 1979), vol. XIII, p. 261; R. Nisbet, *History of the Idea of Progress* (New York, 1980), p. 114; M. Horkheimer and T. Adorno, *Dialektik der Aufklärung* (Frankfurt, 1969), pp. 10-11. For Vico's critique of Bacon see Enrico de Mas. "On the New Method of a New Science," *Journal of the History of Ideas,* XXXII (1971), 86ff. J. C. Davis, *Utopia and the Ideal Society* (Cambridge, 1981), Chap. 5, however, sees *The New Atlantis* as an historical myth, not as the beginning of the Enlightenment.

[2] See R. Darnton, *The Business of the Enlightenment* (Cambridge, Mass., 1971).

2 *Vico and Marx*

mained one sphere where the Enlightenment remained notoriously deficient. The Enlightenment was unable to explain its own existence historically. One might describe this inability as a sort of in-built weakness. It was not that the men of the Enlightenment were not interested in the past. It was rather that the very notion of Enlightenment made a historical understanding of the past impossible and therefore proved a great handicap in one field and in one field only. The Enlightenment remained incapable of explaining how it had come into being.

Take the very image of "Enlightenment." It was derived from the observation that suddenly, on a dull day, the sun breaks through the clouds and turns darkness into light by dispelling the remaining clouds. Today we can, of course, explain the chain of events that brings about this natural phenomenon. In order to do so one has to have a great deal of knowledge about the behavior of sunlight—its ability to heat the earth rather than the air, the result of the reflection of these rays and the effect this reflection has on the air immediately adjacent to the earth, and so forth. As a poetic image, however, the phenomenon concentrates on the suddenness of light and as such emphasizes, not the chain of events leading up to it, but the splendor of light breaking in upon a dark world. With the advent of light, the gloomy mists that preceded it can be forgotten.

The poetic image apart, many thoughtful people nevertheless remembered that the darkness had been present. The traditional philosophies of history of the Middle Ages and the Renaissance were not really able to shed much light on the nature of that darkness. There were the usual Church histories derived from St. Augustine. But they were concerned with the fortunes of the Church and its relations to secular or human societies. Then there was the attitude of the Renaissance, with its worship of the ancients and its belief that one can learn lessons for this or that from the study of the past. Neither of the strands of thought was likely to shed much light on the new question of where the Enlightenment had come from and what had caused it.

Clearly, what was needed was a new science that would study the past as a chain of events leading up to the Enlightenment, so that the Enlightenment could be given an ancestry and made to appear more than a miracle. The miraculous had been extruded from all other thinking. It could not be allowed to retain its hold on our knowledge of history.

The thinkers who tried their hand at a new, non-Renaissance, view of the past can be divided into roughly three groups. There were, first, the philosophers who had no great interest in the past and simply formed the idea that the history of man was divided into two. There had been a state of nature—nasty or benign, as the case may be—and then there had been a state of civil society, characterized by commercial activity, scientific knowledge, and law. All the world, Locke said, had been like America. At some point or other, in some parts of the world, life had changed, and "America" had given way to civil society. He never expressed any interest in the question as to why this change had come about. Hobbes's vision of this one-time transformation was more pessimistic, more violent, and more ominous, but from the point of view of the historian, it was equally simple. These thinkers, perhaps more than the thinkers in the other two groups, were captive to Cartesian reasoning. We shall not come out as philosophers, Descartes had written, if we study Plato and Aristotle. If we read them, we shall not come out as scientists but as historians.[3] It does not help to remind ourselves that Descartes' argument was circular. What he was saying was that if we study history, we shall learn about history. Since we do not want to learn about history, there is no point in studying it. Hence the simple dichotomies of Locke and Hobbes and many other, minor thinkers sounded not only convincing but surprisingly adequate.

In the second group we find a number of mainly German writers like Lessing[4] and Herder.[5] These thinkers' interest in history was more genuine, and they tried to show that the coming of the Enlightenment

[3] *Philosophical Works*, trans. E. S. Haldane and G. R. T. Ross (Cambridge, 1911) I, p. 6. This and many similar statements by Descartes on the relationship of knowledge to history have been as influential and confusing as the famous dictum of Aristotle that poetry is preferable to history (*Poetics* [1451] A 36ff). Descartes' declaration is clear; Aristotle's distinction is difficult to interpret. Cf. Henry R. Immerwahr, *Form and Thought in Herodotus* (Cleveland, 1966), p. 4. Since history is part of our scientific knowledge of man, Descartes' view, though clear, is clearly absurd. At any rate, since the philosophy of science is deeply indebted to the history of science—for it is only from the history of science that we can learn about the criteria of truth, the relation of experiment to theory, and other such crucial matters—history is clearly relevant to our understanding of science. One need only look at one of the leading texts on physics, Leon N. Cooper, *An Introduction to the Meaning and Structure of Physics* (New York, 1968), to grasp that the best introduction to science is through its history.

[4] *Die Erziehung des Menschengeschlechts* (1778-79). M. H. Abrams, *Natural Supernaturalism* (London, 1971) pp. 237ff. reminds us that, if one includes Hegel's *Phenomenology* in this genre, one could also include other "educational travellers": Hölderlin's *Hyperion*, Goethe's *Faust*, the romances of Novalis. Whether we concentrate on historians or on poets, we have here the literature of the *Bildungsroman*.

[5] *Auch eine Philosophie der Geschichte* (1774). As the ironical title indicates, Herder wanted to make his own contribution to the evolution of cultural patterns, a subject on which both Voltaire and Montesquieu and many others had written. In the years 1784-91 Herder worked on, though never completed, *Ideen zur Philosophie der Geschichte der Menscheit*.

had been the result of a slow and gradual education of mankind. If one peruses these books today, one will be struck by the fact that they showed more Enlightenment than the simple dichotomists. But there were again enormous deficiencies in this kind of approach. First it depended on the simple assumption, much as the histories of the first group had, that mankind had started in a state of ignorance and savagery and gradually developed toward civilization. Second, in none of these books is there any clear information as to why this process had begun, how it had propelled itself forward and led to the state mankind found itself in. The authors of these books were gradualists rather than dichotomists. None of them, however, was really able to shed convincing light on the existence of the Enlightenment.

In the third group we find a large number of economists, sociologists, and historians who had perceived that the present state of civility, commerce, and science was the last stage of development in a series of stages. They tried to resolve the matter of providing a pedigree for the Enlightenment by dividing the past history of mankind into four stages. In the first stage people had been hunters; in the second stage, pastoralists; in the third stage, agriculturalists; and in the fourth and last stage, men of commerce.[6]

It is not easy to weigh the relative merits of the third group against those of the second group, though both were an improvement upon the merits of the first group. In the second group philosophers had placed emphasis on language and morals and culture. In the third group emphasis was put on the mode of subsistence and on economic activity in general. In the second group the story was one of gradual improvement rather than of abrupt changes. In the third group the emphasis was upon the hiatus. It seemed to the writers in the third group part of the Enlightenment to derive language and law, morals and art from the prevailing modes of subsistence, and, by comparison, it was supposed to be a lack of Enlightenment when the writers of the second group paid scant attention to the hard facts of economics and concentrated instead on language and culture. Concentrating on language and culture, one is predisposed to gradual change.[7] Concentrating on brute

---

[6] For these writers see Ronald L. Meek, *Social Science and the Ignoble Savage* (Cambridge, 1976).

[7] Because of his interest in language and culture rather than economics, Vico is regarded conventionally and, I believe, mistakenly as one of the precursors of the Romantic revolution against the Enlightenment. As such he appears, for example, in chap. I, iv, of F. Meinecke, *Die Entstehung des Historismus* (München, 1936). By contrast the Italian tradition, established

modes of subsistence, one is predisposed toward seeing abrupt changes. But in the long run neither approach was really enlightening because neither approach was able to explain the why and the wherefore of change.

It was left to Giambattista Vico to produce the new science required for the Enlightenment and to add our knowledge of history to our knowledge of all those fields in which Enlightenment had prevailed. With the true instinct of a really original thinker Vico confidently entitled his work—written in as great haste[8] as Kant's *Critique of Pure Reason*[9] and Hegel's *Phenomenology*[10]—*New Science*.

Like Kant's *Critique* and Hegel's *Phenomenology,* the work suffered from the haste with which it was composed. The obscurities in Vico's baroque Italian prose are daunting. He wrote without looking much at his notes, and so the shape of the work is lacking symmetry, even logic. If it is true, as Sir Isaiah Berlin once wrote, that Vico had not enough talent for his genius, the same could be said of both Kant and Hegel. Neither the *Critique* nor the *Phenomenology* is a literary masterpiece, and both are as tiresome to read as Vico's *New Science.* Moreover, living in Naples, Vico had to exercise much more restraint than either Kant or Hegel because he was determined not to fall foul of the Inquisition. Jena and Königsberg had problems with censors, but they could not be compared with the problems of the inquisitorial censoriousness of Italy, south of Rome.

Vico conceived three principles that informed his theory of history. They were all three interdependent. First, there had to be an account of development, a reason for development, and a logic of development. Second, if development is to be comprehensible, it has to center on philology—i.e., on human artifacts, especially those artifacts that are expressed in language. With unerring insight he perceived that only those things that are made by men can be intelligible to men. Things

---

by Croce and Gentile, has been to link Vico to Renaissance Humanism. See, e.g., E. Garin, "Vico and the Heritage of Renaissance Thought," in *Vico: Past and Present,* ed. G. Tagliacozzo (Atlantic Highlands, N.J.: Humanities Press, 1981), p. 100. In this essay I have eschewed both these classifications and regarded Vico at his face value as part of the Enlightenment. For important remarks on this topic, see Giorgio Tagliacozzo, "Vico filosofo del diciottesimo secolo (ma anche del nostro tempo)," in *Leggere Vico,* edited by Emanuele Riverso (Spirali Edizioni: Milano, 1982), pp. 45–55.

[8] M. H. Fisch and T. G. Bergin, eds., *The Autobiography of Giambattista Vico* (Ithaca, N.Y., 1944), p. 13.

[9] See Walter Kaufmann, *Discovering the Mind* (New York, 1980), vol. I, p. 181.

[10] See Walter Kaufmann, *Hegel* (New York, 1965), pp. 110-11.

that are not made by men can be described and classified but not understood. For true understanding is an ability to understand why something was made. If there is no intention, there can be no understanding. Understanding means the detection of the intention. Admittedly, as many critics ever since have pointed out, Vico's concept of understanding was limited and defined in terms of intentions, so that there is a certain circularity in his reasoning. There is no *prima facie* reason why one's knowledge of the stars and stones should not also be called understanding. But the problem has readily been solved by later thinkers who simply distinguished between two kinds of understanding.[11] There is, first, Vichian understanding, which amounts to empathy, to a grasp of what went on in the minds of the people who made the artifacts. Second, there is explanation, which is the sort of understanding we derive from Newton's laws, from quantum mechanics or molecular biology. The distinction is vital and profound and all-important. The difficulties surrounding it can easily be resolved by elucidation of what is meant by the distinction and of the nature of the material to which the two forms of knowledge can be applied. Human beings can be understood in a Vichian sense because they have intentions, be they conscious or unconscious, and insofar as they shape their lives and their societies, these lives and societies are artifacts informed by certain intentions. Atoms and stars, molecules and physical forces, are not artifacts. They are not conscious of themselves and have no intentions, not even unconscious ones. It is readily admitted that their behavior can only be "explained." But it is often and lamentably not equally readily granted that human beings and their artifacts should not be treated as if they had no intentions. On the contrary, the fact that many or most of these intentions are unconscious and not overtly "intended" has produced countless schools of social scientists and even psychologists who deal with human beings and their artifacts as if they were mindless stones and stars. What is more, such treatment—or ought one to call it "ill-treatment"—is frequently and paradoxically considered to be more "scientific" than any other treatment.[12]

---

[11] The *locus classicus* for the distinction is Max Weber, "Uber einige Kategorien der verstehenden Soziologie," *Logos* (1913), vol. 4. However, the distinction by itself does not prevent the emergence of endless problems. Cf. Peter Munz, "Humanism and the Social Sciences," in *The Reponsibility of the Academic Community in the Search for Absolute Values. Proceedings of the Eighth International Conference on the Unity of the Sciences,* Los Angeles, 1979 (New York: The International Cultural Foundation Press, 1980).

[12] The best exposition of this "confidence trick" played by social science, and its astonishing success, is W. Pelz, *The Scope of Understanding in Sociology* (London, 1974).

Finally, we come to Vico's third principle. The propulsion of development, Vico argued, derived from language and its artifacts. Since the use of language changes, the artifacts change. Therefore it follows that the modes of propulsion change. Thus we arrive at a clear formulation of the third principle: There is not only development, but development of the modes of development.

In early times, Vico argued, primitive men spoke in metaphors and became poets by force of circumstance. Abstract reasoning, the use of concepts, and the employment of literal, nonmetaphorical descriptions is made possible only after a long development. It is important to understand that Vico did not simply contrast concrete perception of particulars with abstract summaries of universal characteristics. Such a simple contrast suggests itself very readily to the modern mind and is frequently at the basis of much modern thinking about the perception, the reasoning, and the diction of primitive peoples and children.[13] Vico did not operate with such a simple contrast. Myths and symbols were for him "imaginative universals." He was well aware of the universal factor in all perception and did not use its absence as the distinguishing characteristic of primitive language and thought. When he maintained that primitive men use metaphors, he did not mean to imply that they were incapable of perceiving regularities, but that they were given to putting their perception of regularities into images. His use of the expression "imaginative universal" has an archaic ring. It might be fruitful to replace it by the expression "concrete universal," for an image is always concrete but not necessarily particular.[14]

The application of these three principles to history was the major content of Vico's great book. That content is sufficiently well known not to need more than the following summary glance.

---

[13] Vico displayed more logical precision here than almost anybody else who has written on this subject. Like Vico, Rousseau sensed that *tropes* precede abstract argument. But he never provided a logical clarification for his theory. Vico did. Later writers, with the exception of Hegel, have tended to confuse the issue by failing to understand that an image contains universals and therefore abstractions. An image, Vico said, though concrete and particular, does not exclude generalization. The opposite of an imaginative universal is not a particular image but a verbal universal (= concept). The major writers who follow Vico's distinction are not always equally clear. Lucien Lévy-Bruhl, Ernst Cassirer, and Jean Piaget sometimes write as if primitive thought was specially connected with particulars and sophisticated thought with universals. Vico's ingenious insight concerns, however, especially the fact that images are universals, even though concrete or particular, and that the whole contrast between primitive and nonprimitive thought depends on the degree of verbalization and not on the degree of universalization. The argument that the distinction between "primitive" and "modern" depends not on universalization but on verbalization is at the root of C. Lévi-Strauss' *La Pensée Sauvage* (Paris, 1961).

[14] Cf. Peter Munz, *The Shapes of Time* (Middletown, Conn., 1977) pp. 128ff.

Mankind's history began with very primitive but well-ordered societies in which men were capable of speech. The growth of population and the disasters of the flood dispersed the members of these societies. We get, as the next stage, an age of brutes living in the vast forests. Here was genuine savagery, and men forgot the speech and the customs of their ancestors. This bestialization occupied roughly two centuries. Then the awareness of thunder terrified men to seek shelter and build retreats where their families could find protection and privacy. Being settled, they cleared forests and developed burial customs, morality, and religious rituals. They were ruled by monarchic, "Cyclopean" fathers. This was the age of the gods.

In the age of the gods there were serfs who challenged the privileges of the "fathers." In order to protect their privileges the "fathers" formed alliances—a patrician order. This was the age of the heroes. In this age there was much conflict between the lower classes and the upper classes. Eventually, the lower classes revolted successfully and extorted concessions. New rituals appeared. The new rituals were enshrined as laws; laws were written in prose; prose generated argument; argument led to questions, philosophy, skepticism, and egalitarianism until, in the end, the subversion of the old authoritarian customs produced atomization, destructive individualism, and social collapse.

Reading and rereading the *New Science* it is difficult to form a clear and consistent idea of Vico's ultimate views. In many passages he writes as if there were some special virtue in tradition and authority and as if the next stage, based on argument and leading to destructive egotism, were to be deplored. At other times he holds out the hope that some superhuman statesman, a sort of Augustus, might arise to prevent the collapse of egalitarian philosophy and science-based society. In some places he writes as if the circularity of this development were inevitable, and in others he is a little uncertain as to whether the collapse of the philosophy-based society would lead to the first age of innocence, as had prevailed before the flood, or whether it would lead back to the age of the brutes. Some interpreters think that his first age of innocence was merely a forced concession to the inquisitors, who would not have tolerated a history that did not begin with a sort of society one finds in *Genesis;* others take the first stage seriously but believe that it was the one age that would not recur and that the *ricorsi* would always lead back to the age of the brutes and that the development would take up from there, and so forth. There is, finally, also a problem connected with

Vico's theory of metaphor. Sometimes he writes as if the use of metaphor was "forced" on primitive people by their mode of existence;[15] in other places he writes as if the use of metaphor simply went hand in hand with their way of life[16] and was thus expressive or indicative of it.

These questions must be resolved, if indeed they can be resolved, by Vico scholars. One might be satisfied with the general impression that Vico himself was a little unclear about these details because he wrote in a hurry.[17] In any case these details are no more vital or disturbing than the many unclarities one finds in Kant's *Critique* and Hegel's *Phenomenology* written under similar pressure by a power of similar originality.

The points that really matter are that the whole of this history was informed by the three principles. Vico did not start with a state of nature that had to be improved but with a state of nature that in its own way was quite satisfactory. By contrast, he places the age of the brutes second. That age is not the original condition of men but a secondary phenomenon, a breakdown of human nature. Obviously it is most unproductive and undesirable but contains the conditions from which the first stage of consciously intended civilization derives. So, though undesirable, it has its important function. Unlike many early historians and anthropologists, Vico did not consider this state to be the natural condition of mankind, but to be the result of the breakdown of a more natural condition. He therefore believed that the growth of civilization is not an alternative to the state of nature but follows upon the breakdown of a natural situation. Thus he criticized and avoided the simple dichotomy between nature and artifice and introduced a realistic theory of human development.[18] Finally, we can see how the use of language is in every case the molding principle. The manner in which language is used, poetically or as prose, metaphorically or rhetorically, is the principle that determines the social structure of every stage. In this way he exemplifies his insight that not only do we have change, but

[15]*The New Science of Giambattista Vico,* trans. T. G. Bergin and M. H. Fisch (Ithaca, N.Y., 1968), par. 378.

[16] *Ibid.,* par. 405, ad finem.

[17] Some of these inconsistencies and unresolved arguments are so deeply embedded in the text that even so acute an interpreter as Isaiah Berlin, *Against the Current* (New York, 1980), p. 103, fails to notice, e.g., that Vico seems uncertain whether later forms of civilization are better or worse than, or equivalent to, earlier forms.

[18] See Peter Munz, "Early European History and African Anthropology," *New Zealand Journal of History* 10 (1976), p. 44.

the method of change is itself subject to change. He does not assume
that human nature is given and that all subsequent change has to be
interpreted as derived from human nature. He argues instead that
human nature is itself subject to constant changes and that these
changes of the changes provide the inner momentum that determines
the forms societies have taken.[19]

Here, in outline, we have the new science required by the Enlightenment.[20] It may have been less optimistic than the ordinary view the
Enlightenment took of itself. It was part of the Enlightenment to
believe that in future there would always be change toward even more
Enlightenment. Such optimism, be it in the form put forth by Locke, or
by Lessing, or by Adam Smith, was anything but enlightened, however,
for it was always based on a neglect of history in general and on a failure
to apply Vico's three principles. Vico, on the other hand, with the help
of his three principles, was able to make the Enlightenment truly
enlightened because he provided a historical explanation for it. At the
same time, making it truly enlightened, he also departed from the
prevailing optimism. Knowing and analyzing history in a fashion far
more sophisticated than the authors in any of the three groups described above had been able to do, he showed that if history is subject to
enlightened analysis, it could be added to all the fields that had been
enlightened by the Enlightenment. The price was an outlook somewhat
less sanguine than the simple theory of progress which had really been
derived from the notion that, as the sun breaks through the clouds, so
the Enlightenment had simply dispelled the superstition and darkness
of the past forever. Vico's pessimism is no disadvantage. After all, a
genuine pessimist is a well-informed optimist.

[19] See Peter Munz, *The Shapes of Time* (Middletown, Conn., 1977) p. 189ff.
[20] It has appeared to many readers that Leon Pompa, *Vico* (Cambridge, 1975) and Isaiah
Berlin, *Vico and Herder* (New York, 1977), are in disagreement as to whether Vico's "new
science" was scientific knowledge or "inner historical knowledge." To me the disagreement, if
there is one, is minimal. In Vico's mind his new science was historical knowledge and, as such,
a scientific contribution to knowledge. At the same time, since the modes of change that have
prevailed are all modifications of the human mind, this scientific historical knowledge must
be, as Berlin says, an inner historical knowledge, a sort of human autobiography. The point
Vico is making is precisely that scientific knowledge of history is an inner historical knowledge. Vico's contribution to the Enlightenment was the proposal that scientific knowledge of
man's past is a recapitulation of man's awareness. If it is anything else, we might have said, it is
not scientific—as the absurd historical dichotomies between the state of nature and the
sudden onset of civil society so amply proved.

This, then was the new science: the addition of history to the many fields studied and understood by the Enlightenment.[21]

The concept "new science" can be and was easily misunderstood. For Vico it was the application of human reason—duly qualified by his appreciation that when the subject matter is human artifacts, there is a form of understanding different from the form that must prevail when the subject matter is stones and stars—to the past. In this way Vico had dispelled darkness and explained the past and its relation to the present. There were and are other ways of dispelling darkness. Instead of applying reason to the phenomena—i.e., to the appearances—as Vico did, one can seek to dispel darkness by lifting the veil. One of the oldest traditions says in so many words that the darkness is caused by the appearances that hide, like a curtain, the reality that lies behind them. This tradition is older than Plato but received its clearest formulation in Plato's philosophy of knowledge.[22] The idea that darkness can be dispelled by the lifting of a veil that hides the truth is, of course, appealing as well as compelling. We know of masks and *personae*, of roles and pretensions. Why should the world of nature as it appears to us not also be such a mask, and why should we not think of science as an "unmasking" that discovers the reality *behind* the appearances. There is no reason why the discovery of the reality behind the appearances should not be considered a "new science." When Newton showed that color is an optical phenomenon best analyzed with the help of a prism, one could, although one should not, say that with the help of a prism he managed to lift the curtain and show us what color *really* is.[23]

Such a non-Vichian conception of "new science" received, within a quarter of a century of the composition of the *Scienza nuova*, a powerful, though not intended, new lease of life through the work of Kant. In the

[21] "The understanding of human nature requires an understanding of historical origins. 'The science of humanity' involves not only a recognition of ideas, but also of the way in which these ideas come to light. It is in the realities of history that clear ideas grow from inchoate origins." Patrick H. Hutton, "Vico and the French Revolution," *Journal of the History of Ideas*, 37 (1976): 253.

[22] K. R. Popper, *The Open Society and Its Enemies* (London, 1945), vol. II, sec. ii, pp. 8ff, was the first to draw attention to the important consequences of the fact that for Plato the search for knowledge was not a search for the regularities in phenomena but a search for the hidden essences of phenomena.

[23] It is worth noting that in part Goethe's misguided objection to Newton was based on the thought that Newton was an "essentialist"—a scientist who sought truth by searching for what light "really" is, as distinct from light as it appears to the human eye.

Critique of Pure Reason Kant argued that behind the appearances that
alone we can know there must be an unknown and unknowable reality
of which the appearances are appearances. It would be absurd, he
reasoned, to imagine that there are appearances but nothing the appearances are appearances of.[24] Since this conclusion was not central to
Kant's argument and purpose, there have been interpreters who have
refused to take Kant's distinction seriously. But Kant himself took it
seriously enough to spell it out in full in his preface to the second
edition. It is true that for Kant the existence of a reality behind the
appearances was tangential and that it played a major role only in his
ethics. It is also true that his first major critic, Hegel, showed very
reasonably that there is no total dichotomy between appearance and
reality, at least not as far as the evolution of human consciousness is
concerned. Following upon Hegel, though neither inspired by him nor
aware of the similarities[25] between his and their arguments, we find
that contemporary evolutionary epistemologists have interpreted Kant
for their own purposes. Kant simply took it for granted that the categories of perception, which filter reality so that we only know of it as it
appears molded by these categories and by the forms of our understanding, are simply there—part of human nature. But if one considers
evolutionary adaptation, one can easily see that they are there because
they are successful adaptations of the nervous system to "reality." In
this way Kant has become the great precursor of modern evolutionary
epistemology, which, of course, plays down the distinction between
appearance and reality. Evolutionary epistemology says that the appearances mediated through the categories of our understanding cannot be all that different from the "reality" alleged to be behind these
appearances, because if they were, the human nervous system would
make too many mistakes in its perception of the world we live in, and if
it did, it could not have survived for long.[26] In evolutionary epistemology, as in Hegel, the original Kantian dichotomy between reality and
appearance is eroded, is played down, and eventually ceases to be
absolute.[27]

---

[24] Preface, second edition, XXVII.

[25] Konrad Lorenz, *Behind the Mirror* (London, 1977), pp. 8 ff., is quite unaware that his
criticism of Kant's dichotomy was anticipated by Hegel.

[26] See D. T. Campbell, "Evolutionary Epistemology," in P. A. Schilpp (ed.), *The Philosophy
of Karl Popper* (La Salle, Ill., 1974) pp. 441-47.

[27] In the end Schopenhauer remained the only true Kantian. Using a Latin translation of
the *Upanishads,* and giving ontological teeth to Kant's distinction, he produced a very

In spite of these reinterpretations of Kant's fundamental distinction, the idea that the "new science" consists in unveiling the reality behind the appearances has retained a powerful hold. When we now turn to Marx, we find that for him the "new science" consisted precisely in such an unveiling. Marx argued that religion and culture, language and law, art and the state, are so many appearances of a true reality, the mode of production. Changes in the appearances, he concluded, derive from changes in the reality.[28]

There is no doubt that such and all other forms of unveiling are always enlightening. Both Nietzsche and Freud, to mention only the most famous of the unveilers, have helped us to see more clearly the things that do not meet the eye—at least not at a first glance. The trouble caused by such unveiling does not lie in the unveiling itself. Our knowledge is enriched through Marx's insistence that the mode of production in feudalism was functionally related to the religious beliefs and the artistic productions of the feudal age. Trouble arises as soon as one insists, as Marx did, that the things unveiled are the only true and ultimate reality and that the rest is appearance, superstructure, and therefore derivative or secondary.[29] If one believes in "unveiling," it is important to stipulate that the things behind the veil in turn veil further things and that, moreover, they in turn veil the thing that was unveiled as much as the first thing veiled the second. Every unveiling discloses something and newly disguises something. Every new revelation conceals something that had been open. There is always a loss as well as a gain.

---

formidable argument that everything we know is an "appearance" of the reality, which he described as "Will."

[28] There have been countless revisions of the initial Marxist dogma, including attempts by Marx himself, by Engels, and by Georg Lukács, emphasizing that Marx really saw society as an interacting whole and that in this whole material factors were more important than ideal ones, but not ultimately causal, let alone primary. Against all these attempts, G. A. Cohen, *Karl Marx's Theory of History* (Princeton, 1978), p. 134, has reestablished that Marx really meant what he said: The productive forces are the reality that determines the production relations (i.e., relations between classes and ownership of the means of production) and, in turn, the superstructure (i.e., law, politics, religion, ideas, etc.). My emphasis here is on the difference between Vico's evolutionism and Marx's "essentialism." Marx and Vico have really nothing in common, and it can be no accident that Marx mentioned Vico only once in all his published writings. See Eugene Kamenka, "Vico and Marx," in *Giambattista Vico: An International Symposium*, eds. G. Tagliacozzo and Hayden V. White (Baltimore, 1969), pp. 137 ff.

[29] It is an important principle in all theory of knowledge that one ought not to accord privileged or prior ontological status to the thing unveiled. If one does, the unveiling obscures and does not reveal. Cf. Peter Munz, *When the Golden Bough Breaks* (London, 1973) chap. X, and p. 86f. for Freud's own understanding of this principle.

To Kant the distinction between reality and appearance was peripheral and simply followed his argument. Since he was concerned with knowledge, and since knowledge was always knowledge of the appearances, the nature of the reality behind the appearances was of no consequence. For Hegel the dichotomy between appearance and reality was less absolute than it was for Kant. Modern evolutionary epistemologists have followed Hegel. Why did Marx revert to the crudest possible interpretation of the dichotomy, and why did he persuade himself that the reality behind the appearances could be known with such certainty? Nietzsche may have been right in his demonstration that if one unveils Christian love, one discovers the slave's resentment of his master. Freud may have been right in insisting that if one unveils a man's political ambitions, one will discover his unresolved Oedipus conflict. But Marx insisted dogmatically that if one unveils the religion of the feudal age, one will find that it is no more and nothing but an ideology designed to make the reality of feudal exploitation palatable. This sort of "new science," examined critically, was not really a new science at all but an attempt to end all further scientific inquiry. Marx's dogmatism compares very unfavorably with Vico's rationalism. Marx had a simple rule of thumb based on his "I know better." With this rule he was able to expose what went on in a feudal society or in the Roman Empire, as distinct from what people who experienced feudalism or the Roman Empire really thought. Vico's rationalism, by contrast, was avowedly tortuous. He warned us that "it is only with the most agonizing effort that we can even attempt to enter the mentality of the primitive savages."[30]

It may seem incongruous to compare Vico and Marx, especially if the comparison is in favor of Vico. Marx seems so utterly modern. He writes about politics and economics, about Napoleon III and the class struggle. Vico is obviously old-fashioned. He wore the clothes of the ancien régime and wrote in baroque Italian about Homer and the Law of the Twelve Tables. And yet, when one considers what Vico meant by "new science" and how in Marx's mind the search for new science was turned into a search for an illusory reality, one can see that modernity does not necessarily depend on the clothes a man is wearing.

How did Marx manage to persuade himself that an unmasking of this type was enlightening? Like Vico, Marx realized that a science of

[30] I. Berlin, *Against the Current* (New York, 1980), p. 98. See also G. Steiner, *After Babel* (Oxford, 1975), p. 76.

history must account for change and that it must do so in a manner more sophisticated and realistic than had been possible for the natural law historians of the Enlightenment or for the philosophical historians who had seen change as the result of an educational process. The mere distinction of four stages of development—hunting, pastoralism, agriculture, and commerce—was by itself also insufficient unless one could show how the functioning of any one stage was productive of the next stage.

This critique of earlier theories of history was common to Vico and Marx. However, as we have seen, Vico identified language as the agent of change. Language was a human creation, and in following its career one could understand how change had come about. Focusing always on something we can really understand (language), there was no need for him to declare dogmatically that language is the essence of man and the reality behind the various appearances such as law and state, religion and art. Vico's reason for suggesting we start with language was not that he believed language to be the reality that determined the shape of the appearances, but that he believed the argument that language is something we can understand because its operations are something we can feel our way into.[31]

Marx, on the other hand, considered that the agent of change is the mode of production. In every mode, he argued, there are losers—i.e., people who are underprivileged. Eventually they build up their strength and overthrow the prevailing mode. Unlike language, the mode of production is not something that can be understood in Vichian terms. The mode of production does not center upon the human mind but upon the material conditions, natural resources, and human hunger. If one takes language as the agent of change, one can intuitively feel one's way along the career of language and use it to explain change. But if one takes material conditions as the agent of change, one can explain change only by a further postulate—that is, by the claim that these material conditions are the *essence*, the genuine reality of which

---

[31] Vico's examples of such "feeling one's way into languages" may strike us as forced and archaic. But the archaism of his examples should not obscure the importance of the method. When he writes that the history of the word *lex* tells us how life in the forests was followed by life in huts and eventually by life in cities—(*The New Science of Giambattista Vico*, trans. T. G. Bergin and M. H. Fisch [Ithaca, 1968], p. 78)—our modern critical faculties may do a double take. But this cannot obscure that "Vico knows, this is one of his great clairvoyances, that man enters into active possession of consciousness, into active cognizance of reality, through the ordering, shaping powers of language"—G. Steiner, *After Babel* (Oxford, 1975), p. 75.

religion, culture, politics, and language as well as art are the *ap-pearances*. The enlightenment that results from such a claim is not at all enlightening because such a claim can only be justified dogmatically. It is striking that Marx never bothered to justify this dogmatic claim. Like other dogmatists he presumably imagined that it was self-evident. Marx simply regarded "production" as more real than politics or religion.[32]

Needless to say, Marx was not the first materialist. Talking of language, we may choose Turgot as an example. In 1750 he wrote that different languages arose because hunters "would have few words, very vivid, not closely linked together, and progress would be slow. The shepherd, with his peaceful life, would construct a gentler and more refined language; the husbandman, one that was colder and more coherent."[33] While this argument may not throw much light on the origins of languages, it clearly sets out that languages are the secondary effects of modes of material subsistence. Even so, Turgot saw no need to describe the modes of subsistence as "primary" or as the reality behind the appearances. But then he was not concerned with an explanation of change and of how hunters had become pastoralists. Using a Vichian method in order to explain change, one would concentrate on the modifications within the human mind—i.e., on the changes of languages that have made the world of the societies in question. In this way one can understand the changes in question as the products of human minds. To explain change by this method there is no need to designate one side of the equation (social form = language) as real and the other as appearance. This is not so if one uses the Marxist method. If one wants to explain the changes in question by deducing them from the material circumstances, one must persuade oneself that the material circumstances are a reality of which the languages (for example) are the appearances. One can then seek the reasons for the change in the material circumstances and deduce the change in languages accordingly. In short, a materialist who wants to explain change has to assume that change is inherent in the material circumstances, that these circumstances are the reality, and that all the rest—language, religion, law, politics—are appearances of these changes. If one is not a materialist, one can explain change in many different ways and never be obliged to see any particular kind of change as the reality behind the appearances.

[32] This point is well made by W. H. Shaw, *Marx's Theory of History* (Stanford, 1978).
[33] G. Schelle ed., *Oeuvres de Turgot* (Paris, 1913), vol. I, p. 172.

Marx's implicit conclusion was to wipe out Vico's distinction between genuine understanding (*verum et factum convertuntur*) and ordinary explanation. For Marx there was only one kind of understanding—the kind we can have not only of men but also of stars and rocks. The observer stands outside and treats human beings as if they were stones. He makes assertions about them, completely oblivious of the fact that human beings, unlike stones, can also make assertions about themselves and, ideally, even about the observer. Human beings can therefore be understood through the establishment of a dialogue with them.[34] The insight into this possibility lies at the heart of Vico's method. Not so for Marx. He refused to make any distinction between human beings and stones and prided himself that such a refusal was the true mark of objective science. Always making assertions about human beings from the outside, as if they were no different from inanimate matter, he devised a special technique for dismissing the subject matter's protestations. Should the object of knowledge protest that Marx's dogma of economic determinism or of the primacy of the mode of production is wrong, at least in his (the object's) case, Marx recommended that such protestation be dismissed as an example of ideology, delusion, class bias, etc. One must, I suppose, be grateful for small mercies. At least Marx realized that men are not like stones in that they could contradict the assertions of an observer, and he therefore acknowledged the need for a special technique for dismissing such counterassertions.[35]

---

[34] See Peter Munz, *The Shapes of Time* (Middletown, Conn., 1977), pp. 79ff., for an elaborate treatment of the rules of such dialogue.

[35] A contemporary school of Marxists plead that history should be written from below, i.e., from the perspective of the inarticulate and illiterate masses. See, for example, J. Chesneaux, *Pasts and Futures* (London, 1978). The idea of such a project is, without doubt, important. If it could be carried out, it would be of extreme value. But the idea is a contradiction in terms. Where there is illiteracy and absence of records, history cannot be written. If it is written nevertheless, in the absence of records, it could mean only one thing: The historian is free to impose his views on the object he is writing about without fear of contradiction and without the need for dialogue. By contrast, Vico held "that the application of present ideas [e.g., the class struggle] to past peoples assumed the character of 'conceits.' "—B. A. Haddock, "Vico's Discovery of the True Homer," *Journal of the History of Ideas* XL (1979): 598. Vico's distinction is of vital importance in modern psychiatry. See R. D. Laing, *The Divided Self* (London, 1960). Laing is unfortunately unaware of Vico, but his argument that classical psychiatry "assumed the character of conceits" in brushing aside what the patient said because he is classified as "insane" and his plea for listening to the patient *before* classifying him, have a true Vichian ring. Existentialist psychiatry, from L. Binswanger to Rollo May and R. D. Laing is Vichian. (See Rollo May, "Comment on Professor Giorgi's Paper," in G. Tagliacozzo, M. Mooney and Donald P. Verene, eds., *Vico and Contemporary Thought*, Baltimore, 1979, Vol. II, pp. 79-80). For the methodological link between historical explanation and psychiatric classification see Peter Munz, *The Shapes of Time* (Middletown, Conn., 1977), pp. 318-19.

The final question in the comparison between Vico's "new science" and Marx's "new science" is therefore the question why Marx thought it worth while to have recourse to such a dogmatic postulate. The question is doubly important; for Marx's "new science," which consisted in the unveiling of the reality behind the appearances, was in the end self-defeating. A "new science" that is based on dogmatism is really part of the obscurantism it sets out to destroy. Why, then, did Marx embark on an argument that was self-defeating because ultimately unenlightening?

The answer must be sought in the different response of Vico and Marx to the phenomenon of change. Vico accepted change and, as we have seen, came to a final conclusion that was less than optimistic. There are *corsi* but there are also *ricorsi,* he argued. Marx also accepted that there is change and that we must study it. But he wanted to study it because he wanted to abolish it. Unless one can understand change, he reasoned, one cannot stop it. Now the striking peculiarity of Marx's historical thought is precisely his deep and ultimate desire to stop change. He said that so far philosophers had only studied change. The time has come, he concluded, to stop change. He did not put it in these terms. What he said was different. He said that so far philosophers have only interpreted the world; the time has come to change it. But what he meant is quite clear. The world that philosophers had interpreted was the world that was always changing. When he added that the time has come to *change* that world, he could only mean that the time has come to stop it from changing.

Most of his interpreters are agreed that Marx acted from the highest ethical motives.[36] The world as it is changing is not all that beautiful and good—at least not for the vast majority of mankind. The determination to change it was, therefore, theoretically entirely laudable. But if the changes one wants to bring about are to give more than temporary relief—and Marx was certainly thinking of something more splendid and durable than mere temporary relief to some people—the change envisaged must be a change that produces permanence and stability and ceases to be subject to further change. It was this ultimate and

---

[36] Today there are many Marxists and neo-Marxists who think there is merit in proving that Marx had no ethical concerns at all and that the scientific status of Marxism depends on the demonstration that he had none. The scientific status of Marxism is so weak that it would not matter if one could prove that he was devoid of ethical interest. It is therefore preferable to remain with the old version that he was prompted by his humanitarianism and his ethical passion to find a science that might ameliorate the sufferings of mankind.

inevitably and ineradicably utopian element in Marx's attitude to change that forced the dogma of materialism on him. That dogma asserts that the material conditions of production are the ultimate and real reality. Vico, prepared to accept chance, *ricorsi* as well as *corsi,* did not have to seek shelter behind such a dogma or behind any dogma. His new science provided a historical explanation of the Enlightenment, and he was content to resign himself to the conclusion that the Enlightenment was likely to give way to a new course of barbarism. Marx's "new science" consisted in the discovery that behind all culture and law there was a hard reality, the material modes of production. He did of course provide an explanation of sorts for the emergence of the Enlightenment. But since he was unable to resign himself to the thought that the Enlightenment might not continue, he turned Enlightenment into something very unenlightening—that is, into the attitude: I know better than you, for I have discovered the ultimate truth. Such an attitude may have superficial similarities with "new science," but it is, in the last analysis, a new dogmatism.

Vico, Marx, Utopia, and History

Alain Pons

In his conclusion to the *Scienza nuova* Vico places his theory of history under the patronage of Plato, who "conceives a fourth kind of commonwealth in which good honest men would be supreme lords. This would be the true natural aristocracy." Now, "this commonwealth conceived by Plato was brought into being by providence from the first beginnings of nations..." (*N.S.*, par. 1097).[1]

This assimilation of the entire history of nations to the "fourth kind of commonwealth," or "aristocracy"—that is, the "government of the best," in Plato's opinion—has troubled several commentators[2] and demands a clear explanation. Vico reinterprets in his own way the Platonic dualism: Man consists of one spirit and one body, of an informative principle and of an indeterminate and rebellious matter. Christianity, with the dogma of the Fall, does nothing but transpose in religious terms this duality defined by Plato in metaphysical as well as moral terms. Justice, which is order, reigns in man when his spirit commands his bodily passions and appetites. Vico also accepts the political projection of this dualism at the level of the city. The just city is a city commanded by men who are masters of themselves and for whom the practice of wisdom is the only occupation. These, according to Plato, are "the philosophers." To accept the Platonic dualism is to reject the point of view of those who reduce man to one or the other of the components that constitute him, whether it is the Stoics, "who seek the mortification of the senses" and who "chain themselves to fate," or the Epicureans, "who make the senses the criterion" and "abandon them-

[1] The translations of Vico are from the Bergin and Fisch edition, except for the last, which is from Vico's *Practic of the New Science*, translated by T.G. Bergin and Max H. Fisch, in G. Tagliacozzo and D. P. Verene (eds.), *Giambattista Vico's Science of Humanity* (Baltimore: Johns Hopkins Press, 1976), pp. 451-54.

[2] In particular Nicola Badaloni, in his Introduction to Vico, *Opere filosofiche* (Florence: Sansoni, 1974), p. XLIX.

selves to chance" (*N.S.*, par. 130). No social life can develop from such principles, and that is why Stoics and Epicureans "should be called monastic and solitary philosophers" (*N.S.*, par. 130). Vico, therefore, refuses ascetic or hedonistic cities. The monastic orders, like the Solitaires of Port-Royal, for example, follow the rules of asceticism, but as their name itself shows, they do not constitute real communities and are just simple gatherings of loners. Accordingly, it is absurd to want to found, even in one's imagination, cities where everyone could be pleased, as in Rabelais' Abbaye of Thélème, or where "the passionate attraction" would reign, as in Fourier's Phalanstère. "Anarchy or the unchecked liberty of the free people" could not be a positive social ideal. It leads to a state of "bestial solitude," because when it reigns, "scarcely any two would be able to agree, since each follows his own pleasure or caprice" (*N.S.*, pars. 1102, 1106).

The only "political philosophers" are, therefore, the Platonists, who recognize the existence of passions but state that "human passions should be moderated and made into human virtues" (*N.S.*, par. 130). But if Plato has a vision of human nature and a conception of the city that corresponds to the truth, he leaves whole the problem of the effective realization of this just city. He writes in *The Republic*:

> Our city and our constitution are not idle chimeras, and even if their realization is difficult, it is nevertheless possible, but only when we will see as heads of the city one or more philosophers.... No republic will reach perfection before this small number of philosophers will be forced by Fate ($\tau \acute{\nu} \chi \eta$) to take care of the city or before the hereditary kings, by divine inspiration ($\vartheta \varepsilon \hat{\imath} \alpha$ $\varepsilon \pi \acute{\imath} \pi \nu o \iota \alpha$), are seized by true love for the true philosophy.

In Vico's opinion, if Plato recognizes the existence of a certain divine providence, he strangely restricts its action, since he is waiting for the salvation of chance or of an inspiration the light of which would sporadically fall on certain privileged mortals. This perspective is discouraging. The utopians, from Thomas More on, will refuse to question themselves further on the conditions of realization of this just city, and by a literary artifice will suppose that the possible has been realized already, beyond the common space of man, beyond time and history. From this point on they will be able to deal descriptively, not only normatively or optatively, with "the best kind of republic," the one where wisdom is in power. With the thought of the Enlightenment the

Platonic city will be reintegrated into time as representing the goal
aimed at by the historical process, a goal that philosophical and scientific progress allows the hope of realizing in the more-or-less near
future.

The two illusions, of the classical utopia and of a utopia of progress,
are rejected by Vico, for they both rest on a more fundamental illusion
concerning the nature and power of philosophy. Plato is himself responsible for this illusion as he identifies the reign of wisdom with the
power of the philosopher-kings or that of the king-philosophers. But
Vico asks, "What can philosophy do for man?" Many things, but not
everything. It "considers man as he should be" (*N.S.*, par. 131), which
signifies that it "does not abandon him in his corruption" but "raises
and directs weak and fallen man." In this way philosophy is "useful to
the human race" (*N.S.*, par. 129). But how can this usefulness of philosophy be effectively manifested? In two ways: first, by individual conversion, which will transform a man who is immersed in matter and who is
rolling in the "dregs of Romulus" (*N.S.*, par. 131) into a sage whose
spirit will command his body. However, few men are capable of this
conversion. Plato has commented, and Vico has repeated with greater
insistence as a Christian, on the profound corruption of human nature:
"Philosophy can bring aid to very few men...the generic character of
men cannot...bring it about that every individual's mind should command and not serve his body" (*N.S.*, pars. 18, 131). To imagine, as in the
"progressive" utopias, that one day humanity will only consist of wise
men is idle fancy. A city of wise men would in any case not be a city. As a
political organization the city takes into consideration the disparity of
elements of which it is composed and, therefore, of the relationships of
command and of obedience, without which justice would have nothing
to which to apply itself.

However, since it is unable to convert the majority of men to wisdom,
cannot philosophy govern the city for the good of all through the
intermediary of an elite of philosophers who would have traced a plan
of it by studying the divine model and who would enforce the strict
application of the rules of justice? Such is the second solution, that of
Plato, if one interprets it literally. But for Vico this solution is totally
unrealistic, not because there is little probability that one day the
philosophers will be made kings or that the kings will become philosophers, but because the role of philosophy is not to govern. "Philosophy
considers man as he should be" (*N.S.*, par. 131); but to govern one must

consider men as they are. There is no doubt that Vico belongs in thought to the family of Machiavelli, who writes in *The Prince:*

>...it has seemed to me more suitable to follow the actual truth of the thing rather than its imagination. Many have imagined Republics or Principalities which were never seen nor recognized as true ones. But there is such a great distance between the kind that one lives as compared to the kind one should live, that the one who will leave what is being done for what is to be done rather learns to lose himself than to preserve himself."

Vico is also very close to Spinoza, who begins his *Political Treaty* by criticizing philosophers who "conceive of men not as they are but as they wish them to be," from which it results "that the political system to which they have given birth must be considered as an idle fancy or as a system to be established in an utopia or in the golden age of poets, where one has no need of it whatsoever." Like these men Vico refutes all utopias that consider man to be naturally good—or in any case morally neutral and malleable to the whim of an inspired legislator who presides at the foundation of all utopian cities. Philosophy, by itself, has no hold on the real, on the social, or on the political. It announces what should be but is incapable of incarnating it in the being that resists. This is an old idea of Vico's, which can be found in the *Inaugural Orations* and in particular in *De studiorum ratione* (chap. VII), where the *doctus imprudens* is opposed to the *vir sapiens* whose *prudentia* is capable of bearing in mind the *anfractuosa vitae*. The *doctus imprudens* is the one who transfers the scientific mode of judgment into the aspects of life that have to do with prudence, i.e., civil affairs. "They judge human actions as they should have been, but they are for the most part performed blindly. In fact, most men are not directed by reflection, but rather by desire and chance." The figure of the *doctus imprudens* who judges human actions "as they should have been" is undoubtedly that of the philosopher, who in common opinion is inept as to political practice. It is known that Socrates and Plato desperately fought against this popular prejudice, but Vico, as in all his work, sides with common sense.

In addition to these arguments against the possibility that philosophy would ever be directly in power, there is a more original, more typically Vichian one. Philosophers, in fact, as the *Scienza nuova* teaches, are latecomers in the city, because philosophy itself appears only when the city, constituted long before, has reached its democratic form. This corresponds, in the development of humanity, to the age of the completely developed reason and reflection. Must we, then, suppose that until this time men had been completely abandoned to themselves and given totally to their passions? But how did they come out of their original state of bestiality, and how did they create cities? Because cities must already exist in order that the philosophers might think of "the just city." The argument attains utopia not only in the classical form, which expressly refuses to bear in mind history, but also in its "progressist" form, which does not take real history too seriously and disqualifies the past by reducing it to the only dimension of the future in which the being and the must-be will join. The realization of the just city could not be the work of the philosophers. To believe this is to fall victim to the *"boria de' dotti"* (*N.S.*, par. 124) and to admit implicitly that this realization will never come to be (u-topia) even if it was to be in the ever-escaping future.

However, what philosophy cannot do, legislation is able to attain.

> "Legislation considers man as he is, in order to turn him to good uses in human society. Out of ferocity, avarice, and ambition, the three vices which run throughout the human race, it creates the military, merchant, and governing classes, and thus the strength, riches, and wisdom of commonwealths. Out of these three great vices, which could certainly destroy all mankind out of the face of the earth, legislation makes civil happiness" (*N.S.*, par. 132).

The postulate of the existence of providence, which assures that human history is intelligible, that it has meaning and value, and that it is not handed over to chance, takes on then a precise meaning. Divine providence "is a divine legislative mind. For out of the passions of men each bent on his private advantage, for the sake of which they would live like wild beasts in the wilderness, it has made the civil institutions by which they may live in human society" (*N.S.*, par. 133). We have no more to deal with a vague and abstract theodicy. If things are at all times as they should be, it is not only in virtue of the principle of "the best possible of worlds." The Augustinian metaphor of the earthly city takes on all its significance: The ideal republic where wisdom reigns is no longer to be sought after in a utopic "elsewhere"; it is *present already*, always, as in all moments of history as in their totality. Recalling Ranke's formula, all generations are equally close to God. For Vico the different forms of government that succeed one another in a determined order throughout the historical course of nations represent, each one, the best that could possibly exist at the precise moment each appears. To put it more concretely, since legislation signifies command, power exercised by those who represent the spirit over those who incarnate the passions, "divine providence has ordered human institutions with this eternal order: that, in commonwealths, those who use their mind should command and those who use their body should obey." (*N.S.*, par. 18).

The Platonic dream of seeing the best reach power, or of seeing those who hold power become the best, is therefore permanently fulfilled. It is always the best who hold the power; it is always "the true, natural aristocracy" that has commanded, commands, and will command in this "fourth kind of commonwealth," which is nothing but the history of nations as "ordered" and directed by legislative providence.

This affirmation can bring about debatable interpretations and utilizations, especially if it is noted that Vico constantly identifies the "honest men" and "the good men," who are the "supreme lords" in this "fourth kind of republic" (*N.S.*, par. 1097), with "the strong." However, Vico's summary, in his conclusion of the *Scienza nuova* (*N.S.*, pars. 1097-1108), of his conception of the evolution undergone by all nations, in light of the principle according to which in commonwealths it is always the "strong" who have control over "the weak," permits the ambiguities to dissipate.

The main ambiguity could come from the use of the word "nature" in the expression "true natural aristocracy." It would be a serious contradiction to believe that for Vico, as for Callicles, or for a certain Nietzschism, there are "by nature," in the absolute, strong and weak men and that the former are eternally destined to command the latter. The dichotomy supposes a radical and definitive opposition between *physis* and *nomos*, between nature and history, an opposition that is at the antipodes of Vichian thought. In Vico's works what is natural is what is born in its time, in the time to which it has been assigned, within the course of things such as has been ordained by providence. The notion of "true natural aristocracy" is therefore entirely historical and, we will add, dialectical. "True" and "natural" have the same meaning—they portray what must be at a given time. "Aristocracy," therefore, is not the specific property of a class, and it must not be identified with those who were at a certain time its representatives. What Vico calls "true nobility" (*N.S.*, par. 18) is the characteristic of those who in the aristocratic commonwealths of antiquity, or in the modern feudal systems, performed the "heroic" virtues necessary in their epoch for the conservation of humanity and civil happiness. Nothing leads us to believe that for Vico the Neapolitan barons, his contemporaries, the descendants of feudal nobility, maintained titles that allowed them to exercise power in the "human times" of early-eighteenth-century Naples.

"Strength" is therefore a virtue that signifies the domination of the spirit over the body. It takes on different shapes and is incarnated in different social classes according to the different stages of historical evolution. All these groups, it must be noted, are minorities inasmuch as the wise and the temperate are always the least numerous. At the beginning of everything there is the small number of *bestioni* of gigantic stature, whom thunder stops in their bestial wandering. They are "strong," not because of their stature, but because of an already spiritual strength and because the fear of a divine power gives them the strength to tame the "wandering Venus" and to found families. Solitary rulers of these "economic commonwealths" constituted by the families, they learn to make use of human liberty by directing the movements of corporal instincts. These "fathers," pious and chaste, are by far "the best" by sex, age, and virtue. They assure the safeguarding of humankind with the only means that at that time are efficacious: They kill wild beasts, cultivate the earth, and plant seeds.

It is also they who, by welcoming the weak, wandering, and solitary in search of a refuge against "the robust violent men" (the strength must not be associated with physical robustness or with violence), and by accepting them as *famuli,* create this class division, which will give birth to civil order and which will be the motor behind its evolution. In creating orders to resist rebel *famuli,* these "fathers," as a matter of fact, found "cities, that men might live secure from the unjust and the violent." (*N.S.,* par. 18). The civil order that then replaces the natural order is still nearer to the latter, and it is by lineage, sex, and virtue that these nobles, "the heroes," are distinguished. They define themselves as "the best" in relation to the plebeians, who do not have the right to contract religious marriage and who therefore remain within natural order.

It is useless to insist on these well-known texts. It is known how, according to Vico, there will appear within these aristocratic commonwealths the kings, who are the more courageous and robust. They are chosen from among the nobles to organize in an orderly fashion the nobility as well as to direct the fight against the rebellious *famuli.* Later on, when the plebs understands that it is of a human nature equal to that of the nobles, it then demands equal rights. However, remarks Vico, "since in due time the peoples were to become sovereign, providence permitted a long antecedent struggle of plebs with nobility over piety and religion..." (*N.S.*, par. 1101). We see there the interesting idea of a preparation that providence imposes on those destined to assume historical reponsibilities and of a necessary maturation for the passage from one social and political formation to another. In the popular commonwealths that succeed to the aristocratic commonwealths the plebs has therefore become capable and worthy of the sharing of power. "The best" are still those who govern, but they are henceforth chosen according to the censuary system. The democratic states, which correspond to a stage of advanced economic development, demand that "the industrious and not the lazy, the thrifty and not the prodigal...—in a word the rich with some virtue or semblance thereof and not the poor with their many shameless vices"—govern them (*N.S.*, par. 1101).

This principle of government of "the best" is found at the ultimate stage of the course followed by the nations. When democracy degenerates into anarchy, providence proposes three remedies (*N.S.*, par. 1103). First, the appearance of a monarch who monopolizes the power and who, in spite of his unlimited sovereignty, is confined "within the natural order of keeping the peoples content and satisfied with both their religion and their natural liberty" (*N.S.*, par. 1105). This is, in Vico's opinion, the most natural as well as the best outcome. Then comes the conquest by natural right, by better nations—"he who cannot govern himself must let himself be governed by others...The world is always governed by those who are naturally fittest" (*N.S.*, par. 1105). And finally the extreme remedy: men having been led back to a state of primal simplicity, which will permit them to rediscover the foundations of justice, piety, faith, and truth. This is a radical way to lead the strong and the best back to power, thus giving to human affairs a new beginning for a new *corso* (N.S., par. 1106).

The cities founded by Lycurgus, Solon, and the Roman Decemviri (cities that, one must note, served as models and as favorite historic references for the utopians) are of little importance, according to Vico, in comparison with "the great city of nations founded and governed by God," in comparison with "the universe of people, which was ordered by such institutions and secured by such laws that even in its decay it assumes those forms of states by which alone it may everywhere be preserved and perpetually endure" (*N.S.*, par. 1107). The *Conclusion* of the *Scienza nuova,* therefore, picks up what had been affirmed since the beginning of the work: in the origins of all human institutions "one can trace the eternal plan (*pianta*) of commonwealths, on which states...must take their stand..." (*N.S.,* par. 18). The word plan (*pianta*) is to be emphasized because it denotes the drawing, the preconceived organization, and also the stem and the root. The utopians design their ideal cities according to plans considered rational, but the real cities naturally take root in history, and the plan that leads to their development was not designed by man but by God.

It would seem arbitrary to compare the great Vichian city of nations, governed by providence, with history conceived according to the principles of Marx's materialistic science—the same Marx who criticizes in this way, in *The Poverty of Philosophy,*[3] all those who resort to the notion of providence: "providence and providential aim, this is the great word which is used today to explain the progression of history. In fact, this word explains nothing. It is at the most a declamatory form, a method, the same as any other to paraphrase facts." We will try to prove, without multiplying the oratorical precautions, that such a comparison is not devoid of pertinence. We will see that the conception that Marx has of communism and his criticism of utopian socialism rests on a dialectic of the normative and the real, of the necessity-to-be and the being, of the ideal and empirical, which constantly evokes the way in which Vico has tried to solve the Platonic aporias of the ideal city.

The essential objection that Marx has always made to utopia is that men have drawn from their imagination the depiction of the future societies without understanding that "the conditions of the proletarian emancipation are given by history" (*Manifesto of the Communist Party*).[4] In *The Civil War in France* (1871) he specifies:

> The working class....does not have ready-made utopias ready to be introduced by decree to the people. It knows that to realize its own emancipation and with it the higher living standard to which today society irresistibly tends by virtue of its economic development, it must pass through long fights, by a whole series of historic procedures which will completely transform men and circum-

---

[3] Karl Marx, *Misère de la philosophie,* in Marx, *Oeuvres. Economie,* Vol. I (Paris: Gallimard, Bibliothèque de la Pléiade, 1965), p. 87. [It should be noted that, to avoid discrepancies between the author's quotations from Marx and Engels and his own text, all those quotations in this essay are translations from the French text used by the author. Tr.].

[4] Karl Marx, *Manifeste du Parti communiste,* in Marx, op. cit., p. 191.

stances. It needs not realize any ideal but only liberate the elements of the new society carried in its womb by the crumbling old bourgeoisie.[5]

Utopian socialism, according to Marx, no matter how right are its critical analyses and how deep are the solutions that it proposes, is by definition condemned to impotence. Always arising from the reflection of isolated thinkers, "fortuitous discovery of such and such genius," it considers its problems solved by supposing, as Cabet does, that a wise legislator gave the utopian city his laws. If it is further preoccupied with the conditions permitting its realization, like Fourier, it expects everything from the "conversion" of an enlightened capitalist and from the contagious effect of a successful first experience. We are always dealing with Plato, his philosopher-kings and his king-philosophers, his "chance" or his "divine inspiration." For Marx, on the contrary, communism is not a desirable ideal, as it is for classical utopia, nor is it the result of a historical process, as it is for the "progressist utopia": Communism *is* that historical process itself in its making. The texts of the *1844 Manuscripts* are formal. If "communism is the resolved enigma of history and [if] it acknowledges itself as this solution," it is because "the entire movement of history is...on the one hand the real act of procreation of this communism—the birth certificate of its empirical existence—and on the other hand it is for its thinking conscience the understood and known movement of its becoming."[6] Further on one reads:

"Just as atheism, the suppression of God, is the advent of theoretic humanity, communism, the abolition of private property, is...the advent of practical humanism....But atheism and communism are not an escape, an abstraction, the loss of an objective world engendered by man.... They are rather, for the first time, the concrete becoming, the realization become real for man of his essence and of his essence as real essence."[7]

[5] Karl Marx, *La guerre civile en France* (Paris: Editions sociales, 1952), p. 53.

[6] Engels-Marx, *La première critique de l'économie politique,* translated by K. Papaioannou, U.G.E. 10/18 (Paris, 1972), p. 229.

[7] ibid., pp. 292-3.

The German Ideology is even more categoric: "communism is for us neither a *state* which must be created nor an *ideal* upon which reality must regulate itself. We define communism as the *real* movement which abolishes the actual state. The conditions of this movement result from actually existing premises."[8]

It is of course impossible not to refer to Hegel in order to understand this effort to surpass the alternative between utopia and the deterministic vision of the historic process, identified by a series of natural events over which men have no control. This alternative, which is normatively and ethically speaking that of practical reason, and descriptively speaking that of theoretical reason and science, leads back finally to the alternative between liberty and necessity.[9]

The two terms of this alternative were stated by Hegel in the famous formula of the Preface of *Principles of the Philosophy of Right:* "what is rational is real, and what is real is rational." Two opposite interpretations of this formula are possible. On the one hand the submission to the fact, "the sanctification of all that exists" (Engels, *Ludwig Feuerbach and the End of the Classic German Philosophy*),[10] and on the other hand the revolt in the name of critical reason against the existing world, disqualifying and relegating to the unreal all that which does not correspond to the exigencies of this reason. However, both of these two interpretations, which have been those of the Hegelian right and left respectively, suppose a suprahistoric reason that is situated above its objects and that simultaneously renders itself impotent in relation to them. They do not keep in mind the essential character of the dialectical thought of Hegel, which is to postulate the final identity of subject and object. There is not, for Hegel, a subject immobile and identical to itself, which would judge a changing object, i.e., the world. It is the world itself that judges itself in each of its acts: "the history of the world is the tribunal of the world."

According to Kolakowski's writings, "Marx never abandoned faith in the final identity of subject and object, and without this faith all that he wrote is unintelligible."[11] It is this faith that forces him very early to

[8] Karl Marx-Friedrich Engels, *L'Idéologie allemande* (Paris: Editions sociales, 1968), p. 64.

[9] On this aspect of Marx's thought see in particular Leszek Kolakowski, *L'anti-utopie utopique de Marx*, in *L'esprit révolutionnaire* (Bruxelles: Editions Complexe, 1978). My analysis of Marx's thought is largely inspired by this impressive study.

[10] Friedrich Engels, *Ludwig Feuerbach et la fin de la philosophie classique allemande* (Paris: Editions sociales, 1966), pp. 10-11.

[11] op. cit., p. 121.

abandon the idea, found among the young Hegelians of the left, of a philosophy whose sole mission would be to criticize and to judge reality, social and political life. Philosophy, according to him, must annihilate itself by incarnating itself in the life of reality. It is not a question, therefore, of pronouncing moral judgments on the world and opposing to what it is what it should be, by tracing the plan of the utopian societies. Neither is it a question of, in the name of social and historical science, describing this world from a "positive" point of view. It must be brought to consciousness by "expressing" the real and revolutionary movement that is at work within it. "The working class," as Marx says in the above-quoted passage, "needs not realize an ideal, but only to liberate the elements of the new society."

The distinction between normative and positive, between liberty and necessity, annihilates itself in such a perspective, since the normative is inscribed in the reality in terms of its vocation. The real is not what is empirically given, neither is it what, according to moral standards, should be arbitrarily decreed as absolute. The real—more real than what one sees and more real than what results from value judgments—is the vocation of history to the creation of a society without classes, vocation that incarnates itself in each of the stages of historical development. This reality can only be seen from within the action itself which allows participation to this incarnation. Whence the privilege of the proletariat, in whom, inasmuch as it constitutes the universal class, the identity of historical comprehension and the revolutionary action working to abolish the society of classes is realized.

It is therefore justifiable to see with Kolakowski in this reality—more real than the real, which is at the basis of all the movement of history and at the same time gives it life and meaning—a kind of Platonic *hyperousia,* at which level temporal distinctions disappear.[12] For Marx as for Hegel, the difference between predicted future and wanted future is erased inasmuch as the future is known in the act itself that produces it. The future is *already there,* existing from an existence that is more eminent than the empirical world, which is incessantly crumbling. It is significant that Marx, when he speaks of communism, always speaks of it in the present tense. We see here the expression of a certitude in the fact that a certain order of things, desired or foreseen, corresponds also to the exigencies of man as man and realizes not what empirical individuals demand, but what was demanded by the *eîdos* of humanity. The

[12] op. cit., p. 123.

"science" of "scientific socialism" has no other role but that of extricating the laws of this hyperreal reality, and as all sciences, it announces the results in the present and does not prophesy.

Must one attribute to a common Platonism, admitted by Vico and affecting Marx by the intermediary of Hegel, the striking resemblances that exist between their two visions of history—i.e., the refusal of the normative separated from the world, which represents the impotence of philosophy to transform the world, and the certitude that this normative is already integrated in the tissue of the world, in the course of history, and that the must-be and the being coincide? This certitude derives in Vico's writings from an explicit act of faith in providence; Marx claims to be based on science. For Vico, as we have seen, the integration of the value and the norm in the historical course of nations is interpreted in the sociopolitical domain by the principle of the best—namely, it is the best who always, by definition, command. Could we not relate this idea to the one so often expressed by Marx and Engels, according to which "all situations that have followed one another in history are nothing but transitory stages in the endless development of human society...each stage being necessary and consequently legitimate for the epoch and for the condition to which it owes its origin?"[13] Engels adds that "this dialectical philosophy dissolves all the notions of absolute definitive truth and of absolute states of humanity which correspond to it...It also has, it is true, its conservative side; this philosophy recognizes the legitimacy of certain stages of development of knowledge and society for their time and their conditions."[14] This insistence on the term "legitimacy" is revealing: It shows to which degree the normative penetrates what wishes to be a purely scientific theory of history.

If each stage is necessary and "legitimate," none can be omitted, none can be crossed faster than one should. "A social formation never disappears before all possible productive forces that it is capable of holding have been developed." (Marx, Preface to *Contribution to the Critique of Political Economy*).[15] It is already what Vico remarked when dealing with Roman history, which is for him the archetype of the course followed by all nations: "the Romans proceeded with even steps, being ruled by

[13] Engels, op. cit., p.13
[14] op. cit., p. 14.
[15] Préface to *Contribution à la critique de l'économie politique* in Marx, *Oeuvres*, op. cit., Vol. I, p. 273.

providence through the medium of vulgar wisdom. Through all the forms of civil states, in the natural order which has been demonstrated by so many proofs in this work, they persisted in each until it was naturally succeeded by the next" (*N.S.*, 1088).

Within these social formations that succeed each other, the political power belongs, according to Marx, to the dominating economic class. However, if this domination is, by definition, the result of exploitation of man by man, it is not condemned in the name of morality. If there is a condemnation it is written in history, which in turn will destroy this domination by annihilating the conditions that gave birth to it. We know the pages where Engels, in the *Anti-Dühring,* justifies ancient slavery by the weak development of productive forces and by the necessity, for the development of intellectual history, of the existence of a leisure class. We also know that no one praised the bourgeoisie more highly than Marx and Engels in the *Manifesto,* and that no one insisted as much on the aspect that was beneficial, in the last analysis, of the domination exerted by the bourgeoisie, in so far as it prepared and made possible, by the unprecedented development of the productive forces it allowed, the domination of the proletariat, i.e., of the universal class that will abolish the society of classes and will destroy the roots of all domination. It is not due to its moral worthiness, acquired by its suffering, that the proletariat will accede to power and will exert its provisional dictatorship; it is because the proletariat is the only class capable of picking up the torch from the hands of the faltering bourgeoisie. The problem of the "political capacity of the working class," which tormented the "utopian socialists," does not pose itself for Marx. This capacity is written in history as well as was that of the rising bourgeoisie to substitute its power for that of the nobility. Let us go further still. Vico, following Plato, admits as permanent truth that the power was, is, and will be exercised by the little number of the "strong." As far as the past is concerned, Marx would readily agree, but not for the future that will succeed the revolution. Communist society will be a society without classes, therefore without domination. But the dictatorship of the proletariat, even if transitory and even if for the first time in history representative of the majority over the minority, does it not have characteristics of "the government of the best"? And the proletariat, a vague entity, should it not be "constituted into a class" and organized? We are not far from the Leninist notion of "class party," proletarian elite, spearhead of the revolution, "collective prince," as Gramsci wanted it. History has shown that a society "without classes" could easily secrete its "elites of power."

However, a fundamental difference exists between Vico and Marx. The Vichian commonwealth, "the great city of nations," has no end—or, rather, has an end only in itself, which is reached at every moment. The theme of *corsi* and *ricorsi* does not signify a relapse into ancient naturalism, but a tentative of escape from the aporias of the eschatological perspective of history, as well as from those of political and social utopianism. The old question of knowing which is the best political regime loses its meaning. Each regime has its qualities, which correspond to the necessities of the providential order. This does not impede Vico from having his preferences, whether acknowledged or secret. The "divine" and the "heroic" periods and their corresponding familial and aristocratic regimes fascinate him. He dedicates to them the greater part of the *Scienza nuova,* because these are the founding periods, when human institutions arise thanks to the "heroic" reclaiming of the libidinous "great forest." As to monarchy, in which, according to a *lex regia,* the cycle of types of government finds its end and its temporary rest, we know, from the *De studiorum ratione,* how Vico conceives of it. We also know the role he would like to see being played there in the midst of jurists and "court philosophers," intellectuals prepared for the exercise of politics. In a rarely quoted passage of the *Pratica della Scienza nuova* (N.S., par. 1410), Vico still further specifies what for him is a society where the spirit commands, which is the opposite of a society at the mercy of matter and chaos:

> Those who are the form and mind of this world of nations, in respect of form's property of being perfection, are the men who can counsel and defend themselves and others, and these are the wise and the strong. In respect to activity, the industrious and diligent men. In respect of being luminous, the men adorned with praise in private life and with glory in public. In respect of indivisibility, the men who in every pursuit of profession are engaged with all their powers and with all propriety: the knight in knightly arts, the scholar in studies of the sciences, the statesman in the practices of the court, and every artisan in his own craft."

It would be possible, if one wanted, to find in this text the elements of a Vichian utopia. One would note then that, for Vico, one of the essential conditions for the good order of the city is the division of labor and specialization, each man having to apply himself totally in his own art. It is the opposite of what Marx expects of communist society:

> In a communist society, where everyone does not have an exclusive sphere of activity but can perfect himself in the branch which is pleasing to him, society regulates general production, which creates for me the possibility of today doing one thing, tomorrow another, of hunting in the morning, fishing in the afternoon, raising animals at night, doing "criticism" after resting, as I please, without ever becoming hunter, fisherman or "critic." (*The German Ideology*).[16]

For Vico, as for Plato, such a dispersion of activities, far from being a manifestation of human fullness, would betray the mobility, the characteristic instability of the anarchical man, of the "multicolored" man, said Plato, "given to changing and contradictory instincts." But we are not dealing with a utopia: Vico points out, immediately after the several lines quoted above, that he has just given the definition of that toward which the world of nations, since its beginning, has been striving; and it is this effort (*sforzo*) that counts more than the result.

Can we say as much of Marx? It has often been remarked that, for him, the way—in other words, the revolution—tends to become the end; and that the end, the installation of communist society, after all, interests him little. But this goal, communism, has existed since his first works; it is defined as the end of history or rather of that which will appear as a "prehistory," where necessity used to reign and which will have to give up its place to true history, where liberty will rule and where men, fully consciously, will make their own history. Even if Marx, due to his horror of all vulgar "utopisms," due to his rejection of all purely theoretical viewpoints, and due to the trust he puts into practice, always refuses to outline the organization of the communist society of the future, he tells us in the *Manuscripts* of 1844 what communism is, "true appropriation of human essence by man and for man, therefore complete comeback of man for himself as social man, that is human, conscious comeback, which unfolded by conserving all the richness of the previous development."[17] Even if he later uses a more sober style and abandons the philosophical coquetteries borrowed from the young

---

[16] *L'Idéologie allemande*, op. cit., p. 63.
[17] *La première critique de l'économie politique*, op. cit., pp. 228-29.

Hegelians, he never renounces that definition of communism, which in all his texts will always be characterized by "the free development and the self-realization of the individual," "the setting in movement in different directions of the multiple predispositions of men," personal liberty made possible in and by the community, the mastery acquired by men of their own socialization....

Communism is, therefore, an end aimed for by all of history, a state that completes all that precedes it and that realizes all the potentials history carried in its womb. Historical time is linear, irreversible, and organized in function of an eschatological perspective, that which Vico, with his conception of an "ideal, eternal history," explicitly refutes. But communism, for Marx, is also a return, "return of man for himself, as a social man, that is human," says the text quoted above. In *Poverty of Philosophy* Proudhon is criticized because he ignores that "all history is but a continuous transformation of human nature,"[18] but this does not mean that human nature does not exist. There is a human nature that is a "social nature of man," which is discussed starting already with the *Critique of Hegel's Philosophy of Right,* which Marx will never renounce and without which the theory of alienation would have no meaning. The primitive unity of the individual and the community, which has been lost, will be found again and raised to a higher level thanks to the long detour of history which is alienation, loss of oneself and of others, separation, suffering, but also preparation for reconciliation. There again, we are not dealing with a theme appropriate to the texts of Marx's youth, marked by Hegelianism. In *Wages, Prices and Profits* (1865), he notes that

> the pretended primitive accumulation signifies nothing but a series of historical processes ending in the dissociation of the primitive unity which existed between the worker and his work tools.... The separation between the worker and his work tools, once established, this state of things will subsist and pursue itself at an increasing speed, until a new revolution, turning inside out the system of production, will come to overthrow it and to restore the primitive unity under a new historical form.[19]

In a letter to Engels (March 25, 1868), he speaks of a reaction "which corresponds to the socialist orientation," and which "consists in looking

[18] *Oeuvres,* op. cit., vol. I, p.111.
[19] *Oeuvres,* op. cit., vol. I, p. 510.

beyond the middle ages toward the primitive ages of each people." One is then "completely surprised to discover the most new in the most ancient." We could also quote a rough copy of a letter to Vera Zassoulitch (1881),[20] where he announces that the present crisis of capitalism will end by a return of modern society to a superior model of an archaic type of property and communal production.

We can therefore affirm that, for Marx, there is a certain circularity in the historical process. This circularity orients the Marxist eschatology, gives it in some way its guarantee. As in Hegel, the Iliad, the departure for conquest, by last analysis, reveals itself to be an Odyssey, a return home. In this lies the assurance that the adventure finishes well, and that the communist city is already there, has been there, and that only a little patience is needed to see its empirical realization.

The confidence of Marx in history, of which he is persuaded to have pierced the enigma and of mastering the science, is filled with pride. The Marxist hero par excellence is Prometheus. By finding his true alienated nature, man will pass from the reign of necessity to the reign of liberty; he will become a god or rather comprehend that the only god, in final analysis, is man. Here lies the only utopia, but it is of the size of this antiutopian thinker. Vico's confidence is more humble. It does not rely on a "violence done to weak and decadent human nature," and it needs faith in providence to justify itself. The *Scienza nuova* does not teach men that they are gods who ignore themselves, nor does it teach them to build a city of Gods; it only helps them, with strength and wisdom, to follow their profession of men.

Translated by Donatella Lorch

---

[20] *Oeuvres*, op. cit., vol. II, pp. 1559 ff.

Vico and Marx: Notes on a Precursory Reading

David Lachterman

I

Affinities and disparities between two seriously thoughtful writers, whether of the same or of different ages, are always difficult to gauge, especially when what is at stake are questions of substance and not merely the seeming exactitudes of *Quellenforschung*. This fundamental difficulty is only compounded when each of the two thinkers has himself been the topic of innumerable, widely divergent interpretations—something that has surely happened in the cases of Vico and Marx. These obstacles give the issue of their possible philosophical kinship both its poignancy and its elusiveness.

Several notable interpreters, for different reasons and with different emphases, have seen in Vico a precursor of some of Marx's central claims or insights.[1] In this essay I want to explore a number of the more prominent discrepancies between Vico and Marx, in the hope that the landscape of their relation might continue to be fully and provocatively charted.

The natural starting point of such an inquiry is, I think, Marx's unique reference to Vico in a work published during his lifetime, since

[1] For example, B. Croce, *The Philosophy of Giambattista Vico*. trans. R. G. Collingwood (Oxford, 1913), p. 243, and I. Berlin, *Vico and Herder* (N.Y., 1977), p. 120, n. l. See also E. Grassi, "Marxism, Humanism and the Problem of Imagination in Vico's Works," in *Giambattista Vico's Science of Humanity,* ed. Tagliacozzo and D. P. Verene (Baltimore, 1976), pp. 275-94 [Tagliacozzo/Verene I]; John O'Neill, "On the History of the Human Senses in Vico and Marx," *Social Research,* 43 (1976): 838-44 (reprinted in *Vico and Contemporary Thought,* ed. G. Tagliacozzo, M. Mooney and D. P. Verene (Atlantic Highlands, N.J., 1980) [Tagliacozzo/Verene II]; L. H. Simon, "Vico and Marx: Perspectives on Historical Development," *Journal of the History of Ideas,* 42 (1981): 317-31. Mention should also be made of Max Horkheimer, *Die Anfänge der bürgerlichen Geschichtsphilosophie* (Stuttgart, 1930), the work that sparked interest in Vico among the members of the "neo-Marxist" Frankfurt School, and J. Habermas, "Between Philosophy and Science: Marxism as Critique," in *Theory and Practice,* trans. J. Viertel (Boston, 1973), pp. 195-252.

this reference not only puts the question of their *historical* affiliation on a firm documentary footing, but also allows us to appraise Marx's implied *philosophical* interpretation of Vico.[2]

This unique reference occurs in a footnote to volume I of *Capital,* in a section devoted to "The Development of Machinery." (The significance of this locale will emerge in what follows.) The salient portion of the note reads:

> Darwin has directed interest upon the history of natural technology, that is, upon the formation of the organs of plants and animals as instruments for the production of their lives. Doesn't the history of the formation of the productive organs of social man, the material basis of every particular social organization, deserve the same attention? And wouldn't such a history be easier to furnish, since, as Vico says, human history is distinguished from natural history by the fact that we have made [*gemacht*] the former, but not the latter? Technology discloses man's active relation to nature, the immediate process of producing his life, his social life-relations and the mental [*geistige*] conceptions that stem from these.[3]

At first blush Marx seems to have hit the mark. He effectively echoes what Vico himself called "the first incontestable principle of our science" (*N.S.,* par. 1108),[4] namely, that "men themselves have made [*hanno...fatto*] this world of nations," together with the crucial implication of this principle, that "men could have attained knowledge of this civil world since they made it," whereas they did not themselves make the natural, external world (*N.S.,* par. 331). Put slightly differently, Marx seems to have captured in this one, very economical allusion to Vico the twin, if not identical, bases of the latter's thought: (1) Man makes his

[2] Marx also referred to Vico by name in two letters written in 1862, one to Lassalle, the other to Engels. See E. Kamenka, "Vico and Marxism," in *Giambattista Vico. An International Symposium,* ed. G. Tagliacozzo and H. V. White (Baltimore, 1969), pp. 137-43 [Tagliacozzo/White].

[3] *Das Kapital,* Book I. sec. IV, Chap. 13, n. 89, in *Marx-Engels Werke* (Berlin, 1956 ff.), vol. 23, pp. 392-93. (All references to the German texts of Marx will be to this edition [*MEW*], unless otherwise noted. Translations are mainly my own, although standard English translations will usually be cited as well. Here, *Capital,* ed. F. Engels (N.Y., 1967), vol. I, p. 372, n. 3.)

[4] References to the *New Science* (1744) are to the paragraph numbers used by Nicolini and by Bergin and Fisch in their English translation; these are enclosed in square brackets in the body of the text or are cited in the notes.

own history, and (2) only what has been made by an agent can be fully known by that agent—*verum et factum convertuntur*—the thesis argued in the earlier *De antiquissima* and powerfully at work in the *New Science*, although verbally latent.[5] I want to try to show that this initial look of congeniality is in many ways a mirage.

Marx situates his appreciation of Vico in a setting dense with conceptual commitments and implications of major importance to his own systematic thinking. First, nature itself has a technology—that is, it *produces* (e.g., the organs of plants and animals) after the fashion of an artisan. Marx hereby erases or, perhaps, sublates the premodern distinction between what comes to be by nature and what is made to come into being by art, *techné*.[6] Second, human technology, over the course of its historical development, has furnished men with an increasingly skillful capacity to preserve and even to enhance their lives as *productive* agents.[7] Third, human social and cultural accomplishments derive from, and are to be explicated in terms of, modes of *production*, the manifold ways in which human beings technically encounter and act

[5] Cf. J. Habermas, op. cit., p. 247. Guido Fassò, "The Problem of Law and the Historical Origin of the *New Science*," in Tagliacozzo/Verene I, pp. 3-14, argues that the principle *verum et factum convertuntur* was not the historical cause of the *New Science*, although it was most probably its logical cause. (The historical cause was, according to Fassò, Vico's turn to the philosophy of law.) One might qualify this somewhat by pointing to the discussion of *verum* and *certum* in the first book of "Il Diritto Universale," *Opere giuridiche*, ed. P. Cristofolini, (Florence, 1974), p. 35, in which Vico asserts that the mind gives birth (*gignit*) to the truth and that "authority," the mainstay of the *certum*, "is itself a part of reason." On the further relations between *De antiquissima* and *Il Diritto Universale*, see Biagio De Giovanni, "Riflessione sulla critica della coscienza pura nel 'Diritto Universale,'" *Annali della Facoltà di Giurisprudenza* (Bari), 17 (1962): 79-121.

[6] See, for example, *Das Kapital*, ed. cit; I, p. 196 (English, p. 181). The *locus classicus* is Aristotle, *Physics* II 1, 192b 12ff. but even in *De partibus animalium*, where Aristotle is sometimes thought to have conflated *physis* and *techné* (cp. M. Fisch, "Vico and Pragmatism," in Tagliacozzo/White, p. 404), the distinction is maintained along with the parallelism of the terms distinguished (cf. 639b15-21 and 641b10-15). On the relations between these see Karl Ulmer, *Wahrheit, Kunst und Natur bei Aristoteles* (Tübingen, 1953), and Gian Arturo Ferrari, "L'officina di Aristotele: natura e tecnica nel II libro della 'Fisica'," *Rivista critica di storia della filosofia*, 32 (1977): 144-73. On the tensions between ancient *techné* and modern technical production see M. Heidegger, "Die Frage nach der Technik," in *Die Technik und die Kehre* (Pfullingen, 1962), pp. 5-36.

[7] Cf. John McMurtry, *The Structure of Marx's World-View* (Princeton, 1978), p. 71: "Technology is, in a word, the Marxian Providence." On the other hand, Marx on occasion was acutely sensitive to the conflicts between technological progress and human enhancement. "At the same pace that mankind masters nature, man seems to become enslaved to other men or to his own infamy.... All our invention and progress seem to result in endowing material forces with intellectual life, and in stultifying human life into a material force." Speech at the Anniversary of the People's Paper [1856], in *Selected Works in Two Volumes* (Moscow, 1955), I, p. 359.

upon nature.[8] The central point at which these three primary themes meet is the notion of *production*; to shift to a Marxian metaphor, production is the "lightning-rod" that carries the diverse energies of his thought to their common ground.

We can now formulate the question of Marx's appropriation of Vico as follows: Is the 'making' of history technical production for Marx and Vico alike? Are *fare* and *machen/produzieren* convertible concepts? To answer, we begin by bringing at least the main features of Marx's concept of production into clearer relief.[9]

1. Production is neither a simple physiological process—the expenditure of physical labor-power—nor a narrowly economic affair—the making of articles of consumption and exchange.[10] These and other phenomenal instances of production are so many ontic hieroglyphs that must be deciphered if we want to reach the ontological significance they carry: For Marx to be at all (*to on hē on*) is to be either a producing or a produced being.[11] "As individuals express [*äussern*] their lives, so are they. What they are thus coincides with their production, both with *what* they produce as well as with *how* they produce."[12] And "...this activity, this continuing sensuous working and creating, this production [is] the basis of the entire sensuous world, as it now exists."[13]

2. Marx tries to capture the foundational role of production in the language of "objects" and "subjects." "Production thus not only creates

---

[8] The best-known statement of this theme is in the Preface to *A Critique of Political Economy, MEW* 13, p. 8 (English, *Early Writings*, trans. R. Livingstone and G. Benton (N.Y., 1975), pp. 425-26.

[9] The following synopsis is based upon a forthcoming study "Marx's Concept of Production: The Paradox of Labor and the Enigma of Praxis." In addition to the works cited in footnote 11 *infra*, I have been helped by G. Lukács, *Zur Ontologie des gesellschaftlichen Seins* II.1 (Darmstadt: Neuwied, 1972) and Pierre Livet, "Temps de travail, acte réflexif, force productive," *Revue de métaphysique et de morale*, 86 (1981): 54-68.

[10] On the insufficiency of the simple physiological view see *Das Capital* I, ed. cit., p. 58 (English, p. 44), and *Die Deutsche Ideologie, MEW* 3, pp. 21, 37. On the inadequacy of a simple economic or utilitarian explanation see *Grundrisse*, trans. M. Nicolaus (N.Y., 1973), pp. 88-100, esp. p. 94: "Consumption as urgency, as need, is itself an intrinsic moment of productive activity."

[11] The most helpful or challenging accounts of Marx's ontological commitments may be found in Kostas Axelos, *Alienation, Praxis and Techné in the Thought of Karl Marx*, trans. R. Bruzina (London, 1977), esp. pp. 123-42; 215-68; Gerard Granel, "L'ontologie marxiste de 1844 et la question de la 'copure,' " in *L'Endurance de la pensée* (Paris, 1968), pp. 267-317; Michel Henry, "Le concept de l'être comme production," *Revue philosophique de Louvain*, 73 (1975): 79-107 and Karel Kosik, *Die Dialektik des Konkreten* (Frankfurt a.M., 1967), esp. pp. 184-211. (See also the references in notes 20-21, infra.)

[12] *Die deutsche Ideologie*, ed. cit. p. 21.

[13] Ibid., p. 44.

an object for the subject, but also a subject for an object."[14] The encounter between subject and object brought about by production is, however, more complex still, since each term of this relation is also transformed into its categorial opposite. For an agent to introduce into the world an object that was not previously there in the form given to it by his labor is for him both to convert his *subjective,* fluid activity into immobile being or *objectivity and* to put his subjective stamp on this newly present object.[15]

> This *form-giving* activity [sc. of labor] consumes the object and consumes itself, but it consumes the given form of the object only in order to posit it in a new objective form, and it consumes itself only in its subjective form as activity. It consumes the objective character of the object—the indifference toward the form—and the subjective character of activity; forms the one, materializes [*materialisiert*] the other.[16]

3. This continual interplay of "objectification" and "subjectification" is nonetheless geared toward the affirmation of the productive prowess of the agent. Human labor is best characterized as *Selbstbetätigung* and *Selbstbestätigung,* an activation or actuation of the self that confirms, substantiates its power to transform the materials of external nature into products suiting its own needs and intentions.[17] By "objectifying"

---

[14] *Grundrisse,* trans. M. Nicolaus, p. 92. That Marx continues to use the vocabulary of "subject" and "object" in the *Grundrisse* is one sign among many that no deep rupture separates his earlier from his later thinking. *Pace* M. Henry, op. cit., p. 100, Marx never discards Hegelian dialectic as the armature of his own thinking. See Terrell Carver, "Marx and Hegel's Logic," *Political Studies,* 24 (1976): 57-68; André Doz, "Analyse de la marchandaise chez Marx et théorie de la mesure chez Hegel," in *Le logique de Marx,* ed. J. D'Hondt (Paris, 1974), pp. 91-103, and J. O'Malley, "Marx's Précis of Hegel's Doctrine of Being in the Minor Logic," *International Review of Social History,* 22 (1977): 423-31.

[15] *Das Kapital* I, p. 195 (English, p. 180): "Was auf seiten des Arbeiters in der Form der Unruhe erschien, erscheint nun als ruhende Eigenschaft, in der Form des Seins, auf seiten des Produkts." Cf. *Grundrisse,* ed. cit., p. 300.

[16] *Grundrisse,* p. 301. Cf. *Das Kapital* I, p. 195: [Die Arbeit] ist vergegenständlicht, und der Gegenstand ist verarbeitet."

[17] See "Ökonomische-philosophische Manuskripte," *MEW* Ergänzungsband I, pp. 578-79 for an instance of this alliterative pun (English, *Early Writings,* pp. 389-91.) Compare, also, *Die deutsche Ideologie,* pp. 71-72, for additional remarks on *Selbstbetätigung.*

[17] These needs are not constant or fixed. "The production of new needs is the first historical deed" (*Die deutsche Ideologie,* p. 28; cf. *Grundrisse,* pp. 91-92). Furthermore, conscious intentions or imaginative projects are at the heart of Marx's artisanal or artistic model of production. (See *Das Kapital* I, p. 193 (English, p. 178) on "the worst of architects" and "the best of bees" and *Ökon.-phil. Manuskripte,* pp. 516-17 (*Early Writings,* pp. 328-29), where man,

himself in this fashion man constantly bears witness to his subjective agency; by appropriating nature, making it his own, man comes into *his* own.[18] Man "actively and actually reduplicates himself....and he can therefore contemplate himself in a world he has himself created [*in einer von ihm geschaffenen Welt*]."[19] The products of properly human, unalienated labor "would be so many mirrors from which our essence [*Wesen*] would shine back to us."[20] Man is, therefore, the productive measure of all things, and all of his works are self-portraits. His knowledge is always self-knowledge, embodied in the objects he has caused to be present in the world.[21]

4. Production is, of course, a social, not a purely individual process. This has two primary consequences. First, man as a "generic being" [*Gattungswesen*] produces universally, free of the constraints of immediate needs as well as of standards limited by his own biological constitution.[22]

---

unlike the other animals, is said to "produce according to the laws of beauty." On the other hand, it must be observed that this artisanal model plays a "regulative," not a historically constitutive, role in Marx's analysis of past and present social incarnations of productive labor. This difference between Marx's regulative and constitutive ideas of productive labor might go some way toward explaining the roots of Hannah Arendt's influential criticism of the primacy of labor over work (*The Human Condition* [Chicago, 1958], pp. 79-174, esp. p. 99, n. 36). In *Die deutsche Ideologie* Marx and Engels distinguish between "the actual process of production" and "the material production of immediate life" (p. 37 and cf. ibid. pp. 67-68). See the assessments of Arendt's critique by M. Bakan, "Hannah Arendt's Concepts of Labor and Work," and B. Parekh, "Hannah Arendt's Critique of Marx," in *Hannah Arendt: The Recovery of the Public World*, ed. M. A. Hill, (N.Y., 1979), pp. 49-100.

[18] Appropriation (*Aneignung*) must be distinguished from property (*Eigentum*) or "having." See *Ökon.-phil. Manuskripte*, p. 537, 540 (*Early Writings*, pp. 349, 352).

[19] Ibid., p. 517 (*Early Writings*, p. 329).

[20] "Auszüge aus James Mills Buch 'Élémens d'économie politique,' " *MEW* Erg.-Bd. I, p. 463 (*Early Writings*, p. 278). Marx's use of the motif of self-mirroring is one more symptom of his allegiance to several of the keynotes of Fichte's thought. See, e.g., "Einige Vorlesungen über die Bestimmung des Gelehrten" (*SW* VI, p. 304): "All of the concepts in the Ego should be given an expression, a counterpart [*Gegenbild*] in the Non-Ego." Other aspects of the relation between Fichte and Marx have been studied by J. Habermas, *Erkenntnis und Interesse* (Frankfurt a. M., 1968), pp. 36-59, and Tom Rockmore, "Fichte's Idealism and Marx's Materialism," *Man and World*, 8 (1975): 189-206; "Activity in Fichte and Marx," *Idealistic Studies*, 6 (1976): 191-214.

[21] Despite his emphasis on self-activity, on living labor as subjectivity (cf. *Grundrisse*, p. 272), the subject, for Marx, necessarily shows, and thus knows, itself *only* in the form of objects (see *Ök.-phil. Manuskripte*, pp. 577-79; *Early Writings*, pp. 389-90). The "metaphysical" source of this commitment may be traced back to Schelling's (and Feuerbach's) search for a positive ground of the real that is prior to, not the outcome of, reflection (ibid., p. 570; English p. 381). This search for positivity is also at the root of Marx's critique of Hegel's philosophy of nature (ibid., pp. 587-88; English, pp. 398-400). On this entire matter see Manfred Frank, *Der unendliche Mangel an Sein. Schellings Hegelkritik und die Anfänge der Marxschen Dialektik* (Frankfurt a. M., 1975). pp. 207-32.

Second, the *human* activity of production is not consummated straight-
away or naturally; it is an historical process, in the course of which the
full array of human abilities and force progressively displays itself.[23]
Accordingly, and in terms reminiscent of his reference to Vico, Marx
calls "the history of industry,...the *open*-book of *man's essential powers,*
human psychology present in sensuous form."[24]

5. Although he sometimes writes as though nature and man were
equal partners in the process of production—when, for example, he
uses the term *Stoffwechsel,* "exchange of matter" or "metabolism"—
Marx's more consistently sustained view is that external, nonhuman
nature is man's "inorganic body," "the workshop of his powers," and,
finally, "the domain of his will."[25] Nature is indefinitely malleable and
thus is at man's productive disposal. Marx cites with approval Descartes' self-revealing promise in the Sixth Part of the *Discourse on
Method, viz.,* that the "infinity of artifices" made possible by the new
sciences will promote men into the role of "masters and possessors of
Nature."[26] The conquest of nature through human production is "the
true resurrection of Nature," the continual reanimation of its corrupti-
ble materials through "labor...the living, form-giving fire," the gift of
Prometheus. The *telos* of production, "the fully-achieved unity of man's
essence with the essence of Nature," depends decisively on the human
factor. Only when nature "appears as his [man's] work and his actuality," only when it is made to put to work its "human essence," will "the
natural essence of man" be fully and transparently manifest in the
external world.[27]

[22] It is the great merit of Lucio Colletti, "The Concept of the 'Social Relations of Production,'" in his *Marxism and Hegel* (London, 1979), pp. 199-248, to have brought out the pivotal
distinction between the human genus and the other living *species.* See Marx's own account in
Ök.-phil. Manuskripte, pp. 516-17; English, pp. 328-329.

[23] Ibid., p. 579; English, p. 391.

[24] Ibid., p. 542; English, p. 354.

[25] See *Das Kapital* I, p. 192 (English, p. 177) and *Grundrisse,* p. 489 (*Stoffwechsel*); *Ök.-phil.
Manuskripte,* p. 516 (English, p. 238) and *Grundrisse,* p. 488 (inorganic body) and ibid., p. 497
(workshop, domain of will). On this complex theme see Alfred Schmidt, *The Concept of Nature
in Marx,* trans. B. Fowkes (London, 1971), pp. 76-93. Part of the complexity stems from
Marx's equivocal notion of man's genesis as "creatio aequivoca" (*Ök.-phil. Manuskripte,*
pp. 544-46; English, pp. 356-58). Cf. John F. Crosby, "Evolutionism and the Ontology of the
Human Person: Critique of the Marxist Theory of the Emergence of Man," *Review of Politics,*
38 (1976): 208-43.

[26] *Das Kapital* I, p. 411, n. 111; English, p. 390, n. 1. Cf. R. Kennington, "Descartes and
Mastery of Nature," in *Organism, Medicine and Metaphysics,* ed. S. F. Spicker (Dordrecht, 1978),
pp. 201-23 and Lawrence Berns, "Francis Bacon and the Conquest of Nature," *Interpretation,*
7 (1978): 1-26.

[27] See, respectively, *Ök.-phil. Manuskripte,* p. 538 (English, p. 350); *Grundrisse,* p. 361 ("das

6. Marx does not so much demolish the Aristotelian distinction between *praxis* and *poiesis,* despite what has frequently been argued; rather, he subordinates the former to the latter, thereby inverting their places in the Aristotelian hierarchy.[28] Even when labor is no longer alienated, but can occur in a manner adequate to man's nature, when it is free and no longer necessitous, production remains the matrix of social interactions.[29] Language, the exchange of telling speeches, cannot lay claim to any autonomy, any transcendence of the fulfillment and creation of needs:

> Thus, men begin effectively by appropriating certain things in the external world as means of satisfying their own needs, etc.; later they came also to give them a verbal designation according to the function they seem to fulfill in their practical experience, that is, as means of satisfying these needs...[30]

II

In light of these fundamental characteristics of the Marxian concept of production we can now approach our earlier question concerning the relation of *fare* and *produzieren* in a more adequate and determinate

---

lebendige gestaltende Feuer, die Vergänglichkeit der Dinge, ihre Zeitlichkeit als ihre Formierung durch die lebendige Zeit" [Berlin, 1953, p. 266]); *Ök.-phil. Manuskripte,* p. 538 (English, p. 349); ibid., p. 517 (English, p. 329) and *ibid.,* p. 543 (English, p. 355).

[28] See, e.g., Manfred Riedel, *Theorie und Praxis im Denken Hegels* (Frankfurt a.M., 1965), p. 220. On the relation of this Aristotelian distinction to the modern political economists' discrimination between productive and unproductive labor, see Solange Mercier Josa, "Après Aristote et Adam Smith que dit Hegel de l'agir?" *Les études philosophiques* (1976), pp. 330-50. For further reflections on Marx's relation to the Aristotelian understanding of civic praxis, cf. C. Castoriadis, "From Marx to Aristotle, from Aristotle to Us," *Social Research,* 45 (1978): 667-738 and H. Mansfield, Jr., "Marx on Aristotle: Freedom, Money and Politics," *Review of Metaphysics,* 34 (1980): 351-68.

[29] See "Auszüge aus James Mill...' " ed. cit., pp. 462-63 (English, pp. 277-78), where mutual human recognition and friendship stem from unalienated production, and compare *Wage-Labor and Capital,* in *K. Marx. Selected Writings,* ed. David McLellan (Oxford, 1977), p. 256. Marx's refusal to give praxis any independent role is also treated in J. Habermas, "Labor and Interaction: Remarks on Hegel's Jena 'Philosophy of Mind,' " in *Theory and Practice,* cit. supra, pp. 168-70, and Louis Dupré, "Marx's Critique of Culture and Its Interpretations," *Review of Metaphysics,* 34 (1980): 91-121.

[30] "Comments on Adolph Wagner," in *Selected Writings,* ed. D. McLellan, cit. supra, p. 582. Cf. M. Henry's remark "La vie [*sc.* de la production] est une vie invisible et silencieuse" op. cit., p. 106. Alan Blum, *Theorizing* [London, 1974], pp. 250-65, makes a very ingenious attempt to interpret the Marxian notion of production as a "metaphor for speaking.")

way. What is it that is "made" in Vico's eyes? Who are its "makers"? What is the manner of their "making"? Where, lastly, does Vico's "epistemological" principle—*verum et factum convertuntur*—fit within this triad of questions? In what domains, by whom and in what manner is this principle evidenced and substantiated?[31]

Since to answer these associated questions in full would no doubt amount to interpreting the whole of Vico's *oeuvre*, all I can hope to do here is to sketch the primary contours of the issues they bring into play.

Vico's governing aim is to bring to light the principles, the fateful starting points, from which "humanity" inexorably and invariably developed, at least among the profane nations.[32] He sets out to demonstrate how the proper being of humans is the necessary consequence of the way they come into being, of their genesis. A thing's *nature* is the manner of its birth (*nascimento*); alternatively expressed, the elements of its full-fledged actuality are ingredient in its original state, without being patently at work from its very start. Thus, Vico is intent on unfolding the causally necessary and sufficient conditions for the emergence of civility, the *mondo civile* both in its generic inclusiveness and in its particular realizations (the individual gentile nations).[33] To carry through this intention he has not only to identify nature with genesis, but also to break down the putative barriers separating nature from custom. The customary, far from being at odds with human nature, will turn out to be the sole medium of its expression.[34] Human

[31] In addition to the well-known studies of Arthur Child and Karl Löwith, several recent studies illuminate aspects of this principle: B. De Giovanni, " 'Facere' e 'factum' nel *De antiquissima*," *Quaderni Contemporanei*, 2 (1968): 11-35; G. Severino, "Il 'verum-factum' vichiano come struttura originaria dei principi e delle modificazioni della storicità," *Giornale critico della filosofia italiana*, 51 (1972): 525-54; F. Fellmann, *Das Vico-Axiom: Der Mensch macht die Geschichte* (Freiburg/Munich, 1976); James C. Morrison, "Vico's Principle of *Verum* is *Factum* and the Problem of Historicism," *Journal of the History of Ideas*, 39 (1978): 579-95, as well as the papers by Stephan Otto cited in note 57 infra.

[32] In *Il Diritto universale* Vico claimed that his synthesis of philology and philosophical science (*Opere giuridiche*, ed. cit., p. 401) would allow him to "demonstrate the principles of Christian theology" (ibid., p. 5). On the motives and ironies of his later restriction of the "new science" to the history of the gentile nations, see F. Nicolini, *La Religiosità di Giambattista Vico* (Bari, 1949), and J. C. Morrison, "Vico and Spinoza," *Journal of the History of Ideas*, 41 (1980): 49-68.

[33] Efforts to analyze more fully Vico's conception of scientific explanation and methodology have been made by Leon Pompa, *Vico: A Study of the New Science* (Cambridge, 1975); W. H. Walsh, "The Logical Status of Vico's Ideal Eternal History," Tagliacozzo/Verene I, pp. 141-53, and E. McMullin, "Vico's Theory of Science," *Social Research*, 43 (1976): 450-80 (repr. in Tagliacozzo/Verene II, pp. 60-90).

[34] See N.S., par. 309, and particularly the phrase "i naturali costumi." Cf. J. C. Morrison, "Vico's Doctrine of the Natural Law of the Gentes," *Journal of the History of Philosophy*, 16 (1978): 47-60.

practices, however divergent in their particular details, however much exposed to what Vico earlier called the "oblique and uncertain path of the things men do" (*agendorum obliqua et incerta...iter*), will be shown to have pervasively common sources and institutional forms. At the level of the generative principles and the constitutive elements of human action, then, the Aristotelian distinction between what can and what cannot be otherwise drops from view.[35]

Most of these programmatic intentions are already crystallized in Vico's synopsis of the first version of the *New Science,* at the start of Book IV:

> This is the universal language of the universal law of the peoples, observed in this great city of the human race; the language that unfolds the ways [*guise*] in which all the parts composing the entire economy [*iconomia*] of the nature of nations were born...this language [i.e., The New Science] discovers the eternal properties of the times themselves and of the manners [*guise*] of their birth...and from the nations' first births it leads them, according to the natural progression of human ideas, through an uninterrupted succession of affairs [*cose*]...[36]

The *New Science,* accordingly, is meant to be a "philosophy of humanity," that is, a theoretical account of the uniform historical process of humanization.[37]

How does this summary help us toward an answer to the questions originally addressed to the meaning of 'making'? "*Fatti*" (and its accompanying verbs *fare, criare, generare*) plays a threefold role in the *New Science.* It can designate, first of all, the deeds, the *feats* of nascent human beings. In the second place it can refer to the poetic renditions and recollections of those feats, to their *fabulation,* as we might call it. Finally, the *New Science,* both text and content, is itself a *fatto,* the narrative generation and, thus, explication of the feats and fables

---

[35] *De nostri temporis studiorum ratione* (*Opere filosofiche,* ed. P. Cristofolini [Florence, 1971], p. 811; English, *On the Study Methods of Our Time,* trans. E. Gianturco [Indianapolis, 1965], p. 35.) Vico, it must be noted, never confuses a theoretical science of the invariant principles of human institutions and their development with a suppositious *science* of the contingent actions of individuals or nations. Rhetoric, not science, addresses itself to this contingent realm. Compare his distinction between the maker (*faber*) and the man of prudence (*prudens*) in *De antiquissima,* ibid., p. 119.

[36] *Opere filosofiche,* ed. cit., p. 304.

[37] Ibid., p. 338.

through which a certain natural species becomes the race of human beings. The *New Science* is the *formulation* of the history of (gentile) humanity.

Let me try to throw some light on each of these facets of Vico's notion of "what is made" and its "making."

Vico's historical agents start out, not as humans, but as prehuman beasts, feral giants; consequently, not everything they do counts as a *human* deed *sensu proprio. Le cose umane,* "human institutions," as the English translators render his lapidary phrase, come onto the scene only when those prehuman agents subdue and then begin to transform their bestial passions and proclivities—in other words, when they are forced to put a check on their "ferocious freedom" [*la libertà inferocita*— *N.S.,* par. 338]. It is the mind—or, more exactly, mind under the aspect of will—that imposes this check on the body and thereby generates the customs and laws that will over time, and time and again, give these creatures their human status.[38]

In the first version of the *New Science* Vico asserted that "the human will is...the maker [*fabbro*] of the world of nations."[39] This thesis has to be supplemented by the recognition that it is only when will comes under the dominion of inchoate mind—when, in other words, such "prehuman" passions as ferocity, avarice, and ambition are tempered by the force of regulative custom, that the will begins to be genuinely human.[40]

Vico has at least two complementary ways of formulating this key point. The body on its own lacks the capacity to move itself *ad libitum;* in the physical terminology Vico took over from Hobbes and Leibniz and reelaborated in *De antiquissima,* the body is the physical seat of a trans-physical *conatus* or endeavor.[41] The *direction* in which a body moves— that is, its inclination to bestial or human passions—is imposed by the will, since "bodies are by nature necessary agents" (*N.S.,* par. 340). A second articulation of the same point occurs in *Il Diritto Universale,*

---

[38] Although Vico's terminology is not perfectly consistent, it does appear that "mind" (*la mente*) is the more comprehensive term, embracing both "intellect" and "will." Thus, the first men had minds (*N.S.,* par. 378) and thoughts (ibid. 340), but did not yet employ intellect (ibid. 363). (The dichotomy of *mente/intelletto* and *animo/volontà* in *N.S.,* par. 364 is, however, inconsistent with this.)

[39] Ed. cit., p. 189.

[40] These three vices or passions are the sources of the three classes of the 'Platonic' commonwealth (*N.S.,* par. 131-32). Consequently, for Vico, ambition (*thymos*) and not *eros* is the root of wisdom.

[41] See *De antiquissima,* ed. cit., pp. 85-97.

where Vico gives as the "two principles of humanity" shame [*pudor*] and freedom [*libertas*] and then relates these as form to matter. (Liberality is the joint issue of shame and freedom; it is "the virtue directing and perfecting human *ingenium*.")[42]

We can conclude that the "free will" that makes the civil world is the will apt to humanize the prehuman, corporeal passions, to transform them into virtues. For instance, thanks to the restraints of the will, "the giants gave up the custom of wandering through the great forest of the earth and habituated themselves to the quite contrary custom of remaining settled and hidden for a long period in their caves (*N.S.*, par. 388).

Hence the feats of men, the *fatti* studied and ordered in the *New Science*, are not any and all acts performed by the primordial giants and their human descendants; rather, only those acts that take on the force of custom and law fall within the compass of Vico's account. "Making," in this context, is a matter of *neutralizing* the prehuman nature of those physical creatures who supply the "raw material" of civilization. The world so made is the realm of recurrent and binding social practices— e.g., the taking of auspices, solemnization of marriage, burial rites— that hold primeval barbarism at bay, at least for some time.

The transformation of the body accomplished through the restraint and redirection of its passions is, however, only a necessary, not a sufficient, condition for the fashioning of the civil world. Minds must likewise be given a properly human cast; ideas must be implanted in the minds of prehuman giants and early men that will persuade them to sense and imagine the world in a manner suited to their unfolding civil condition.[43] For Vico it is above all language that brings into relief and fixes in memory the humanity of *le cose umane*. Hence the "master-key" of the *New Science:* "the early gentile peoples...were poets, who spoke in poetic characters" (*N.S.*, par. 34). Hence, Vico's often repeated claim, "Poetry founded gentile humanity" (*N.S.*, par. 214). "Humanity is most powerfully bound up with languages."[44]

[42] *Opere giuridiche*, ed. cit., pp. 401-3. Cf. the discussion of shame and freedom in B. De Giovanni, "Riflessione..." cit. supra (n. 5), pp. 107-10.

[43] The "whole of economic doctrine," for Vico, consists in these two forms of "education." (*N.S.*, par. 520). The point of the fathers' work and industry is to assure a patrimony for their sons, in case the institutions of civil life should fail or fall (*N.S.*, par. 525).

[44] *Opere giuridiche*, p. 401. For ampler studies of Vico's theory of language, see A. Pagliaro, *Altri saggi di critica semantica* (Messina & Florence, 1961), pp. 299-474; G. Cantelli, "Myth and Language in Vico," Tagliacozzo/Verene I, pp. 47-63, and Michael Mooney, "The Primacy of Language in Vico," *Social Research*, 43 (1976): 581-600 (repr. in Tagliacozzo/Verene II, pp. 191-210).

The poets, then, or the nations construed as collective poets, are the most potent and influential "makers" or "creators" of the civil world. Vico takes pains to emphasize the original Greek sense of "poets"—"the creators," those who create things by imagining them, that is, by fashioning their sensuous or corporeal images, whether in words or in another medium.[45]

It is vital to grasp here that originative poetry, for Vico, is not self-expression but *fabulation,* the crafting of image-laden tales by virtue of which poets and their audiences alike are brought under the yoke of humanizing customs. Originative poetry speaks to its auditors—indeed, gives them voice—at the level appropriate to their stage of development—"the senses are its [*sc.* nascent humanity's] sole way of knowing things" [*N.S.*, par. 374]. Thus the three labors [*lavori*] of great poetry are "to invent sublime fables suited to the popular understanding; to perturb to excess, in pursuit of the end proposed; and to teach the vulgar to act virtuously, just as they [*sc.* the poets] have taught themselves." (*N.S.*, par. 376)

Poetry here assumes the role assigned earlier to the will—namely, the inculcation of the virtues, now with the aid of sublime and perturbing fables. What is the status of the fable, and what is the operation of that "most corporeal imagination" [ibid.] through which the poets and poetic peoples transform themselves from bestiality to humanity?

Near the start of his discussion of "Poetic Logic" Vico tries to convince us that *mythos* and *logos, fabula* and *favella* are semantic kinsmen. Their kinship runs even deeper: "*logos* or *verbum* also meant deed [*fatto*] to the Jews and signified thing [*cosa*] to the Greeks" (*N.S.*, par. 401). These etymological lucubrations give us reason for saying that a poem, a poetic fable, is itself a deed, a thing made or created by human ingenuity. By exciting and sustaining in memory the most perturbing but also most humanizing passions—e.g., fear, shame and wonder—poetry succeeds in checking the prehuman or dehumanizing passions. It is the endeavor that directs feral bodies and ferocious minds toward the shapes proportioned to "civil beauty."[46] In the earlier *Il Diritto Univer-*

---

[45] *N.S.*, par. 376. According to Vico all the other human arts are derived from poetry; their products are "in a certain way real poems" (*N.S.*, par. 217), that is, they have the character of an external object (*res*). The shield of Achilles seems to be Vico's favored example of such a "real poem" (*N.S.*, par. 794).

[46] *N.S.*, par. 565.

sale (but not, surprisingly, in the *New Science,*) Vico pointed out that *nomos,* for the Greeks, meant both law and song.[47]

Still lacking the faculty of ratiocination, the poets went about their civilizing tasks on the strength of their "most corporeal imaginations." I do not need to dilate at length on the central place of imagination in Vico's account of the origins of the civil world.[48] It is sufficient here to refer briefly to his theory of imaginative/fantastic genera or universals as the fruits of mythopoetic endeavor. The poets fashion characters— the gods and heroes of the gentile nations—by imaginatively projecting their own bodies, senses, and passions onto the natural world; like children they animate the inanimate in order to hold converse with it. They invest what is nonhuman, the cause of their wonder, with "substantial being" (*l'essere di sostanze—N.S.,* par. 375); that is, they give to the figments of fantasy sensuous and active bodies. They make the world in their own corporeal image and likeness. The naming and depicting of these imaginative genera gives birth to the civil world in accordance with the principles that *name =nature* and *nature =birth* (e.g., the institution of the auspices comes to be when the "voice" of thunder is given the name of "Jove").[49]

Making, in this, its second aspect, is thus mythopoiesis, the verbal crafting of a fabulous world. What cognitive credentials do these first two modes of making carry for Vico? It might seem initially surprising, given the customary association of man's making of the civil world with the convertibility of *verum* and *factum,* that Vico repeatedly stresses that the "making" of the world in the human image, whether in feats or fables, is an act of epistemic self-deception.

> ...man in his ignorance makes himself the rule of the universe, for in the examples cited he has made of himself an entire world. So that, as rational metaphysics teaches that man becomes all things by understanding them...this imaginative metaphysics shows that man becomes all things by *not* understanding them...and perhaps the latter proposition is truer than the former, for when man understands he extends [*spiega*] his mind and embraces

---

[47] *Opere giuridiche,* p. 403. Cf. *N.S.,* par. 433, where Vico aligns *nomisma* (money) with *nomos.*

[48] See D.P. Verene, *Vico's Science of Imagination* (Ithaca, 1981).

[49] *N.S.,* pars. 174, 494.

[*comprende*] the things, but when he does not understand he
makes the things out of himself and becomes them by transforming himself into them (*N.S.*, par. 405)

Vico plays here on Aristotle's theme that in knowing "*nous* is somehow
the intelligibles" in order to suggest that in *bodying* forth their passions
and senses men, although indeed fashioning a "world" that mirrors
them, fail to come rationally to grips with the world "as it is." Under the
guises of primordial human action and originative human poetry, *factum* is not convertible with *verum*, but is its distorted, anthropomorphic
image.

III

It is only when we bring into view the third facet of making that its
reciprocity with "the true"—i.e., the synonymy of *facere* and *verare*—is
perspicuously illuminated. The relevant *factum* in this final instance is
the *New Science* itself, and Vico is "*il miglior fabbro.*"[50]
Vico himself guides us to this speculation in various ways. First, he
endorses a portion of Aristotle's theory of science by requiring that
scientific knowledge be grounded upon universal and eternal principles.[51] The relation between the principles of the civil world and their
consequences in the history of all the gentile nations must allow one to
conclude that "the course of the institutions of the nations had to be,
must now be, and will have to be such as our Science demonstrates"
(*N.S.*, par. 348). Neither the bestial vagabonds nor their poets proceeded *ex principiis;* the former enacted what became natural customs
in opposition to their passionate intentions; the latter, not having the
use of rational understanding, registered the decisive civil principles
(e.g., marriage and burial) in their utterances and strengthened the
force of humanizing customs by shaping their own and their auditors'
minds, without knowing in advance what they were doing. "Thus it was
fear that created [*finse*] gods in the world; not fear awakened in men by
other men, but fear awakened in men by themselves" (*N.S.*, par. 382).

---

[50] On the *New Science* as a "construction" see D. R. Kelley, "Vico's Road: From Philology to
Jurisprudence and Back," Tagliacozzo/Verene I, p. 29, and J. C. Morrison, "Vico's Principle...", cit. supra, p. 590, n. 49.
[51] *N.S.*, par. 163.

Secondly, the principles from which the "eternal recurrence" of the same *cose umane* stem are generative principles, *archai* at once formal and efficient.[52] The particular materials assembled by *"la storia certa"* (*N.S.*, par. 358) or philology furnish strong evidence of the operation of these principles, but they are not reflectively derived from them. To grasp these materials "scientifically" is to see how they are inevitably effected, "made," once one begins with their originative causes. It is in light of this conception of science that Vico invites his readers to regard the text of the *New Science* as the generation *ex principiis* of the "ideas, customs and deeds of mankind" (*N.S.*, par. 368): "And history cannot be more certain than when he who makes [*fa*] the things also narrates them" (*N.S.*, par. 349). In coming to recognize the necessary and unitary links between the eternal principles of humanity and the multiplicity of historical phenomena, the reader of Vico's work "will experience in his mortal body a divine pleasure as he contemplates in the divine ideas this world of nations in all the extent of its places, times and varieties" (*N.S.*, par. 345). What the earliest poets could do directly to, and by means of, the bodily senses Vico promises to do indirectly via the rational mind.

Finally, and most revealingly, Vico stresses both the analogy and the disanalogy between making in geometry and making as it figures in the generative narration of the "ideal eternal history." The geometer and the historian alike make or construct a world for themselves; however, "the orders [or: institutions] having to do with human affairs have more reality than do points, lines, planes and figures" (*N.S.*, par. 349). This combination of emphases has been the source of interpretive confusion, particularly when Vico's much-abbreviated account of geometry in paragraph 349 of the *New Science* is amplified by the more detailed treatment in *De antiquissima*. The primary source of confusion arises, in my judgment, from the ultranominalist or fictionalist construal most often given to the theory of geometrical constructions in the latter work.[53] If this construal is accepted, then we would also have to concede that the "geometrical paradigm" underlying Vico's defense of the equa-

---

[52] Vichian "principles" (e.g., religion, marriage, burial) both give the civil world and the human soul their form (cf. *N.S.*, pars. 520, 1109) and generate an "infinite number of civil effects (*N.S.*, par. 264). His thinking hews closely to the notion of "genetic definition" promoted by Hobbes and Spinoza, *Cf.* Franco Biasutti, *La dottrina della scienza in Spinoza* (Bologna, 1979), pp. 103-27.

[53] See, among others, Croce, op. cit., pp. 8-13; I. Berlin, op. cit., p. 21; A. Corsano, *Giambattista Vico* (Bari, 1956), p. 112.

tion of *verum* and *factum* in *De antiquissima* has lost much, if not all, of its relevance by the time he conceived the "new science" of *le cose umane*, since these are palpably "real," not "figmental." On the nominalist interpretation man's creative power in mathematics gives him only a "trifling divinity" (*una divinità di burla*), in Croce's engaging phrase. The "making" exhibited in the *New Science* would, therefore, differ significantly from the concept of making in *De antiquissima*.

Since I have attempted to refute this interpretation in detail elsewhere, let me simply offer synopses of some cardinal points.[54]

1. In the first four chapters of *De antiquissima* Vico is wrestling with geometry's proper relationship to metaphysics, on the one hand, and to physics, on the other. Neither Descartes nor Aristotle grasped these relationships correctly; only "Zeno," Vico's *persona* in the text, discovered the right way of "descending from metaphysics to physics" *by means of geometrical constructions,* especially the construction of the geometrical point, the image or simulacrum of the metaphysical point. (Both, for example, are unextended sources of extension.[55]) The Euclidean definition of this geometrical point is said to be "nominal" only to avoid confusing what it defines with any item (*res*) in the *physical* world, any extended body. Vico's rejection of a *rival* definition of point—"a minimum particle divisible infinitely" [*minima...particula in immensum dividua*]—makes it clear that arbitrary linguistic conventions cannot settle the issue of the true status of mathematical entities.[56] The criterion Vico invokes is, instead, the *congruity* of geometrical formations with their metaphysical originals, a congruity assuring that human science is proceeding *ad scientiae divinae instar*—"on the model of divine science."[57]

2. The relation between divine and human science is also secured by Vico's endorsement of synthetic geometry in place of Cartesian, ana-

---

[54] "Vico, Doria e la geometria sintetica," *Bollettino del Centro di Studi Vichiani,* 10 (1981): 10-35, and "Vico, Nominalism and Mathematics" (forthcoming).

[55] See Risposta (1711), *Opere filosofiche,* ed. cit., p.158 (metaphysics, geometry, and physics); p. 137 (metaphysical and geometrical points); and *De Antiquissima,* p. 91 (extension and its ground).

[56] Ibid., p. 89.

[57] On the analogy between divine and human making and its implications for Vico's "transcendental" grounding of historical science, see Stephan Otto, "Die transzendentalphilosohische Relevanz des Axioms 'verum et factum convertuntur.' Überlegungen zu Giambattista Vico's 'Liber metaphysicus,'" in his *Materialien zur Theorie der Geistesgeschichte* (Munich, 1979), pp. 174-96 and "Imagination und Geometrie: Die Idee kreativer Synthesis," *Archiv für Geschichte der Philosophie* 63 (1981), pp. 305-24.

lytical geometry. Only the first version of geometry yields cognitive transparency both in its operation (*opus*) and in its products (*opera*). It can do so because synthetic construction and demonstration begin from elemental *genera* or *forms*, the Vichian equivalents of Platonic *eidē*, interpreted as generative exemplars.

> Geometry [*sc.* synthetic geometry]...teaches how to compose the elements from which the truths it demonstrates are formed [*formantur*]. The reason it teaches how to compose the elements is that man has within himself the elements it teaches.[58]

Hence, mathematics, contrary to vulgar opinion, is *causal* knowledge; that is, it demonstrates how a complex structure necessarily follows from its elements, which the mind arranges and combines. Causal knowledge is "productive" or "creative" in just this sense: it is

> knowledge of the genus or mode through which a thing comes to be; by means of this knowledge, when the mind knows this mode it makes the thing, since the mind contains its elements.[59]

It is in *this* setting—the defense of synthetic geometry—that Vico asserts and explicates the identity of "the true" and "the made."

In his first reply to the critics of *De antiquissima* Vico gives his fullest account of the stages involved in the mental operation by which "the true" is made:

> ...the true, indeed unique cause is that which [a] contains within itself the elements of the things it produces [*produce*] and [b] arranges these elements and [c] forms and understands their guise [*la guisa*] and [d] by comprehending it, sends forth the effect [*manda fuori l'effetto*]."[60]

The effect, the man-made truth, in the case of geometry is an image or sequence of images mimicking *in time* the order and arrangement of

[58] *De antiquissima*, p. 77.
[59] Ibid., p. 63.
[60] Risposta (1711), p. 136.

those genera or eternal ideas in the Divine Intellect through which it *instantaneously* gives birth to Divine Truth.[61]

3. This exposition of the procedure of synthetic geometry shows unmistakably, I think, that Vichian making is *neither* a *creatio ex nihilo,*[62] since the mind has the relevant elements in it from the start, *nor* the arbitrary, spontaneous fashioning of an external, physical object that was not previously in the world in that shape. Instead, "making" is a mental operation through which already existent elements, themselves the images of divine generative archetypes, are set in order in a decorous array. In different language, we might say that Vichian making, in this mathematical format, is the "schematizing" of eternal ideas by the faculty of "productive imagination."

On this interpretation of the "geometrical paradigm" we can now begin to understand why Vico describes rational, intellective truth as truth "generated by the conformation of the [human] mind with the [eternal] order of things"[63]; why, furthermore, it is the business of *ingenium* to seek "the well-proportioned measure of things" (*rerum commensus*). "Human science consists in nothing else than in making [*efficere*] things correspond to themselves in a beautiful proportion."[64] Passages such as these from *De antiquissima* and *Il Diritto universale* should remove the sting from the otherwise baffling statements in the final text of the *New Science*: "the intellect on the other hand [is] a passive power subject to the truth" (*N.S.,* par. 388) and "when man understands he extends, or spreads out [*spiega*] his mind and embraces things" (*N.S.,* par. 405). It is by taking the measure of things as they are (i.e., in the Vichian analogue of the *kosmos noetos*), not by making itself their sole measure, that the intellect learns to evolve within itself a world of mental forms congruent and commensurate with, but not identical to, the metaphysical and physical realms.

The "geometrical paradigm" molded in *De antiquissima* and the two *Risposte* remains visible at work in the *New Science*, but *not* when Vico treats the feats or the fables of men in the ages of the gods and the

---

[61] *De antiquissima,* p. 67.

[62] Contrary to R. G. Collingwood, *the Idea of History* (Oxford, 1946), p. 65: "The fabric of human society is created by man out of nothing..." In the *New Science* Vico is always careful to qualify the assertion that man makes or generates his own human form (both mental and physical); cf. *N.S.,* par. 520—"s'incominciò a menar fuori *in un certo modo* la forma dell'anima umana"—and par. 692—"s'abbiano essi *in un certo modo* generato e prodotto la propria lor forma umana." (My emphases.)

[63] *Il Diritto universale,* ed. cit., p. 35.

[64] *De antiquissima,* p. 117.

heroes, since in both cases *homo non intelligendo fit omnia,* i.e., neither his operations nor his products are cognitively transparent to him. Moreover, this geometrical paradigm has not been simply converted into the quasi-demonstrative scaffolding supporting the discursive and rhetorical edifice of the "new science."[65] Instead, it shows up in Vico's central attempt to exhibit the order and configurations of *le cose umane* as they unfolded, and will always unfold, in time from the event of their genesis, their birth in a certain guise, until their dissolution and, perhaps, rebirth. His enterprise follows closely, although not always explicitly or unwaveringly, the sequence of stages of "production" previously cited from the first *Risposta:* the mind, once it has attained the level of science, arranges the elements and principles it contains within itself—i.e., the "modifications of the mind," which are not changes, but the generative modes out of which the "customs, laws and ideas" of the gentile nations arise in a well-ordered sequence.[66]

The scientific mind, or rational metaphysics, then gives commensurate form to these elements and grasps their *guises,* the patterns exemplified by what originates and develops from them. Having grasped these guises and their relations to their consequences, the mind then "sends forth the effect," in this case the text and speech of the *New Science.* "By the force of order we understand the truth of things."[67] By demonstrating, bringing to light in an ordered way, the causes from which the *fatti* in the first two senses necessarily stem, Vichian science redeems the promise conveyed by the geometrical paradigm, that "demonstration" is the same as "operation." Or, in the language of the *New Science,* paragraph 349:

> Indeed, we make bold to affirm that he who meditates this Science narrates to himself this ideal eternal history so far as he

[65] In the second Risposta (1712) Vico satirizes those who vaunt the geometrical method of axioms, etc., comparing them to an inept painter who has to write under his indistinguishable images "this is a lion" or "this is a satyr"(p. 165).

[66] The meaning of *modificazioni* is quite ambiguous. In the first Risposta (1711) Vico treats "generi o guise o modificazioni o forme" as synonyms (p. 136). This suggests that "modification" has the same exemplary and generative function as the eternal and intellectual genera (see p. 52 above). On one occasion (*N.S.,* par. 1096) Vico gives fairly clear evidence of the Spinozistic provenance of his usage: "the identity in substance of the understanding and the diversity of its modes [*modi*] of unfolding, explicating itself [di spiegarsi]..." The ambiguity is very likely due to Vico's attempt to assimilate the temporal to the eternal and vice versa. (For another interpretation of "modifications" see E. Severino, *op. cit.,* pp. 536-37.)

[67] *Il Diritto universale,* p. 41.

himself makes it for himself by that proof "it had, has and will have to be."

Knowledge of the productive guises from which the sequence of human feats and fables was, and always will be, univocally initiated furnishes a clear glimpse of what "the 'moving image of eternity,' or the image of eternity imprinted on time, look like."[68]

Vico, however, does not totally discard the earlier procedure of "imaginative metaphysics" when he sets into motion his rational narration. On the contrary, the text—the *fatto* that *is* the "new science"— brings sensory fantasy and geometrical reason into a kind of discursive equilibrium: both "the true" and "the certain" (or, particular), both science and consciousness, have to be given their due weight if the "new science" is to succeed in integrating all of the productive faculties or operations of which man is capable.[69] Accordingly, Vico interweaves a rational with an imaginative account of the course and recourse of the nations, in much the same spirit in which he had earlier claimed that synthetic geometry, although the work of rational industry, nevertheless reinforces the imagination, "the eye of *ingenium*," by rendering it adept at the construction of sensory or mental forms.[70]

This interweaving of reason and fantasy begins at the start of the *New Science*, where Vico places a hieroglyphic and heroic emblem of his own devising so as to allow his reader to "grasp the idea of this work before reading it and, after having read it, to commit it more easily to memory with the help that fantasy supplies" [*N.S.* 1]. He furthers this plan by fashioning his own "imaginative genera" in imitation of the theological and heroic poets. "Divine Providence" may well be the foremost of these.[71] In sum, Vico's own *factum*, finally coincident with *verum*, is simultaneously an ingenious and an intellectual deed of speech, inciting and appealing to both the senses and the mind. "To sum up, a man is properly only mind, body and speech and speech stands as it were

---

[68] Vittorio Mathieu, "Truth as the Mother of History," Tagliacozzo/Verene I, p. 117. Cf. A. Robert Caponigri, *Time and Idea* (Notre Dame, 1953), *passim*.

[69] Cf. D. P Verene, *Vico's Science of Imagination*, cit. supra, on "recollective fantasy."

[70] Indeed, although in *N.S.*, par. 699, memory, imagination, and *ingenium* are assigned to the "primary operation of the mind," Vico's account of *ingenium* in *De antiquissima* brings it into close approximation to *scientia:* e.g., "*Ingenium* is given to man for the sake of knowing or making [ad sciendum seu faciendum]", p. 131; cf. p. 117.

[71] Cf. J. C. Morrison, "How to Interpret the Idea of Divine Providence in Vico's *New Science.*" *Philosophy and Rhetoric*, 12 (1979): 256-61.

midway between mind and body" (*N.S.*, par. 1045). His knowingly crafted *factum* is a *formulation,*

> which, like light, of itself informs [*informa*] in all the minutest parts of their surface the opaque bodies of the facts [*fatti*] over which it is diffused, in just the way all of this was designed in the "Elements."(*N.S.*, ibid.)

IV

It is time to draw up a short balance sheet of those differences between Marxian and Vichian thought that should have come into the open in the first three sections of this study.

1. Marx places Vico's insight under the rubric of "a history of [human] technology," because for him it is in this history that man's essential powers come to display themselves. They do so, as we saw, inasmuch as *production,* the bringing forth of a new object into the world in a subjectively intended shape, *is* the vehicle of human self-activation and self-confirmation. Technical production leads both to the subjectification—i.e., the conquest of nonhuman nature—and to the objectification—i.e., the naturalizing of human beings—individually and in their social ensemble. The self-creation of man transforms nature into an image, a mirror, of humanity.

For Vico, in contrast, the origin of human history does not lie in technical production, nor is its *telos* the conquest of external nature.[72] Men make their own history by slowly building, through their feats and fables, a civil world of customs and rituals that tame and humanize their prehuman, ferocious passions. For long periods of this history an anthropomorphic projection of human bodies and passions onto external nature promotes the taming of these passions; man makes himself "the rule of the universe" only in virtue of his ignorance.

2. For Marx knowledge is *embodied* in the objects man artfully produces in order to fulfill and extend his needs as a generic, universally competent, being. The identity of *verum* and *factum,* in Vico, is not accomplished by prephilosophical deeds and speeches; it is secured only when one succeeds, under the guidance of the geometrical para-

---

[72] Cf. F. Fellmann, op. cit., p. 70.

digm, in reconstructing, regenerating those complex deeds out of the elemental principles of the mind.

3. Vichian recollection of the elements of universal history is most attentive to what men have said—*logos* is a *fatto*, as we recall—while Marx's productive agents are in principle silent. The gap that separates Marx and Vico in this regard is measured by the distance between manufacture and mythopoiesis, a factory and a fable.

4. For Marx, *praxis*—human action and interaction—is permanently embedded in technical production, his oracular remarks about "the realm of freedom" and the "absolute movement of becoming" notwith-standing.[73] For Vico, the rational governance of human practices—the institutions, laws, and rituals of "the great city of the nations" (*N.S.*, par. 1107)—both draws its lessons from and underlies the recollective syn-thesis of universal history formulated in the *New Science*. In the "*Pratica della Scienza nuova*," the suppressed finale of his *magnum opus*, Vico revivifies the idea of a "Platonic" commonwealth to which he had already made frequent reference. The civil world made by man should, at its acme, exhibit the same rule of body by mind, of passion by wisdom, ideally in force in the "form of man" itself.[74] Vico's "*Pratica*" strives to educate the educators by rejuvenating a language suited to the "heroic mind."[75] Instead of substituting a philosophy of history for a political theory, he undertakes to sustain the latter by unifying philoso-phy and eloquence.[76]

[73] *Das Kapital* III [MEW 25], p. 828, and *Grundrisse*, p. 488. (I deal with these texts in the forthcoming paper mentioned supra, n. 9).

[74] See *Practic of the New Science*, trans. Bergin and Fisch, in Tagliacozzo/Verene I. pp. 451-454. This is not the place to deal more extensively with Vico's "Platonism." Suffice it to say that his claim that the best commonwealth started coming into being from the earliest age of gentile humanity, hence that it did not depend on philosophical wisdom, is at odds with Socrates' arguments and allusions in *The Republic* (cf. *N.S.*, par. 1097). Moreover, Vico praises the commonwealth formed by "cyclopean family discipline" as "happier than the common-wealth conceived by Plato" (*N.S.*, par. 523). One might guess that Vico's allegiance is more to *The Laws* than to *The Republic*. (On the form and matter of man see Pratica, *N.S.*, par. 1408-10.)

[75] See his final inaugural oration "De mente eroica," translated in *Social Research*, 43 (1976): 886-903 (repr. in Tagliacozzo/Verene II, Part II, pp. 228-245). The motif of a reversion to the "age of heroes" is sounded on more than one occasion in Vico's writings; cf. his letter to Father Giacco (*Opere* [Ricciardi], p. 118), where he says that the first version of the *New Science* "filled me with a certain heroic spirit." Cf. A. M. Jacobelli, "The Role of the Intellectual in Giambattista Vico," Tagliacozzo/Verene I, pp. 417-21, and M. Mooney, op. cit., pp. 597-600 (repr. in Tagliacozzo/Verene II, pp. 191-210).

[76] Contrary to the arguments of Hannah Arendt, op. cit., p. 373, n. 62 and Alain Pons, "Prudence and Providence," Tagliacozzo/Verene I, pp. 431-48. On Vico's own view political science is "the science of commanding and obeying in states" (*N.S.*, par. 629), and eloquence is its indispensable instrument.

5. Marx, disdaining the possibility of modern myths—"...is Achilles possible when powder and shot have been invented?"—resuscitates an ancient fable.[77] Prometheus is "the noblest saint and martyr in the philosophical calendar."[78] Marx's Prometheus is not the bound and lacerated victim of Zeus, but the bringer of stolen fire and, thence, of the productive arts, the arts by which men eventually conquer nature. "Labor is the living, form-giving fire." Prometheus with his flame makes the world a "dwelling in the light" for completely humanized man.[79] Above all, Prometheus, who declares his hatred for all the gods, represents the elevation of "human self-consciousness to the highest divinity."[80]

In Vico's works "Orpheus" and "Heracles" are the focal myths. Orpheus is "the first founder of humanity," who with his lyre tamed the beasts and made them obedient to him; Heracles is "the first subduer of the lands," who set fire to the primeval forest in order to clear a space for the auspices. Similarly, Orpheus stands for "the Greeks recently *brought back* from their bestial way of life to humanity," while Heracles is the imaginative universal embracing "the heroes who first founded civic communities."[81]

These focal myths make visible the union of persuasive song and heroic "labors," a union perhaps even more necessary when the nations are on the brink of returning to barbarism, this time a "barbarism of reflection" that would render men more inhuman than the original beasts.

We might conjecture, in closing, that unbridled technicism, the boundless Promethean conquest of nature, when paired with the loss of religion among the peoples (*N.S.*, par. 1109), could well produce a "barbarism of reflection" from which even Vico's Orphic charms provide no recourse.

[77] *A Contribution to the Critique of Political Economy,* trans. S. Ryazanskaya (Moscow, 1970), p. 216.

[78] *MEW* Erg.-Bd. I, p. 263. (From Marx's notes for his Dissertation).

[79] Ibid., p. 548 (English, p. 359).

[80] Ibid., p. 262. On the Prometheus theme in Marx see T. K. Simpson, "Prometheus Unbound," *The St. John's Review,* 31 (1980): 55-63.

[81] *Opere giuridiche,* p. 911; pp. 847-49; *N.S.*, par. 539-40.

Ontological and Historiographical Construction in Vico and Marx

Leon Pompa

I

Marx's explicit references to Vico are relatively few and suggest that Marx saw Vico as a kindred spirit rather than as someone who exerted any powerful influence upon the development of his own thought. This, at any rate, is the view taken, I think rightly, by some commentators.[1] In the present essay, however, I shall argue that, although there are some resemblances between Vico's and Marx's accounts of the nature of the historical world, there are underlying differences that suggest it is misleading to see any strong affinity between them. I shall then proceed to argue that these differences in their theories about the nature of the historical world leave Vico in a position to offer a more defensible account of the nature of historical knowledge than Marx.

II

Although Marx's only reference to Vico in his published work was in a footnote to *Capital,* it is of sufficient length to allow one to conjecture how Marx saw the affinity between Vico and himself. I shall begin my account by discussing some points in this passage:

A critical history of technology would show how little of the inventions of the eighteenth century are the work of a single individual. Hitherto there is no such book. Darwin has interested us

---

[1] See, for example, E. Kamenka, "Vico and Marxism" in *Giambattista Vico: An International Symposium,* ed. G. Tagliacozzo and H. V. White (Baltimore: Johns Hopkins University Press, 1969).

in Nature's Technology, i.e., in the formation of the organs of plants and animals, which organs serve as instruments for sustaining life. Does not the history of the productive organs of man, of organs that are the material basis of all social organisation, deserve equal attention? And would not such a history be easier to compile, since, as Vico says, human history differs from natural history in this, that we have made the former but not the latter? Technology discloses man's mode of dealing with Nature, the process of production by which he sustains his life, and thereby also lays bare the mode of formation of his social relations and of the mental conceptions that flow from them. Every history of religion even, that fails to take account of this material basis, is uncritical. It is, in reality, much easier to discover by analysis the earthly core of the misty creations of religion, than, conversely, it is to develop from the actual relations of life the corresponding celestialized forms of those relations. The latter method is the only materialistic, and therefore the only scientific one. The weak points in the abstract materialism of natural science, a materialism that excludes history and its process, are at once evident from the abstract and ideological conceptions of its spokesmen, whenever they venture beyond the bounds of their own speciality.[2]

If we consider the context of general theory in which the reference to Vico is made, we shall see that it does indeed contain an explicit enough account of Marx's general metaphysical doctrine for us to be able to infer part of what he took Vico to be saying. For that purpose the following claims are of importance:

1. Technology is a social or communal product.
2. Technology is the material basis of social organization.
3. Since, as Vico says, human history differs from natural history in that we have made the former but not the latter, a critical history of human technology ought to be easier to compile than one of nature's technology.
4. A history of technology would lay bare man's productive forces, and the social relations and mental conceptions that, in turn, flow from them.

[2] *Capital.* vol. 1. p. 372, n. 3. Quotation from *Karl Marx,* ed. Z. A. Jordan (Exeter: Nelson University Paperbacks, 1972), p. 201.

5. By way of example, a history of religion ought to proceed by showing how the conceptions of religion develop from the actual (i.e., the historically determinate) relations of life or social relations.

6. The only acceptable scientific method is one that can do this in such a way as to show how concrete historical conceptions develop from a concrete materialistic set of social relations.

A brief comparison of the above passage, in which Vico is mentioned, with another in which he is not, will help to clarify the sense in which Marx believed that Vico's doctrine—that the difference between the human and the natural world lies in the fact that man has made the former and not the latter—was compatible with his own claims. For this purpose the well-known passage from the Preface to *A Contribution to the Critique of Political Economy* will suffice:

> In the social production of their life, men enter into definite relations that are indispensable and independent of their will, relations of production which correspond to a definite stage of development of their material productive forces. The sum total of these relations of production constitutes the economic structure of society, the real foundation, on which rises a legal and political superstructure and to which correspond definite forms of social consciousness. The mode of production of material life conditions the social, political and intellectual life process in general. It is not the consciousness of men that determines their being, but, on the contrary, their social being that determines their consciousness.[3]

In this passage Marx makes the same fundamental claim about the determining relationships between the forces of production, the relations of production and social consciousness, which was given in 4 above and which supports the claims of 5 and 6 below. No specific mention is made, it is true, of technology, but it is not difficult to see that the claim stated in 2 constitutes one possible specification of the constitution of the material productive forces. It should be noted, however, that even those commentators most wedded to the technological interpretation of the productive forces rarely claim that technology, in its narrowest sense, can comprise them in their entirety. There must, indeed, be some sort of relationship between the technology of a society and the other material resources available to it, since the technology under

---

[3] Jordan, op. cit. p. 198.

discussion is a determinate technology, shaped so as to utilize the material resources of a society at a determinate stage in history in the most fruitful way, and one that will change when those resources are exhausted or transformed. Accordingly I shall assume that Marx is here talking about technology as the means whereby, at a determinate stage in the development of human skill, man can most fruitfully transform the materials of production that are available to him in such a way as to sustain the needs of life.

We may now combine the two passages to obtain the following series of propositions, which I set out in a different order.

a. Technology is a human and social product.

b. Technology, in its wider sense, is the main constituent of the forces of production.

c. The forces of production determine the relations of production.

d. The relations of production determine the mental conceptions involved in human consciousness.

e. A critical history of any mental conception, e.g., that of religion, ought to show how its determinate historical phases are explained by determinate phases of social relationships which are, in turn, themselves explained by determinate developments in the material basis, i.e., in technology.

f. Since, as Vico says, man makes human but not natural history, it ought to be easier to compile a technological history of man than of the natural world of plants and animals.

It is apparent that in *f* Marx took himself to be in agreement with Vico about something very important. For, in the above set of propositions *a-d* delineates a series of determining relationships, from the forces of production to human conceptions; *e* asserts that a critical history of a higher-level phenomenon should show how its determinate phases relate to the determinate phases of more fundamental phenomena; while *f* asserts that since, as Vico agrees, man makes human but not natural history, a history of human technology, the most fundamental level of all, ought to be easier to compile than a history of natural technology. Thus the agreement Marx finds with Vico concerns a condition for writing the history of that area of human practice that governs all others and by which they will be explained.

To ascertain the degree of agreement more precisely, it is useful to turn to the passage from Vico that Marx probably had in mind:

But in this dense night of darkness, which enshrouds earliest antiquity so distant from us, appears the eternal light, which never sets, of this truth which is beyond any possible doubt: that the civil world itself has certainly been made by men, hence its principles can, because they must, be rediscovered within the modifications of our own human mind. And this must give anyone who reflects upon it cause to marvel how the philosophers have all earnestly endeavoured to attain knowledge of the natural world which, since He made it, God alone knows, and have neglected to meditate upon this world of nations, or civil world, knowledge of which, since men had made it, they could attain.[4]

Vico here makes two assertions: that man can know the civil or historical world and God the natural world, and that because man has made the historical world, its principles can be rediscovered within our own human mind and lead us to knowledge of that world. It is clear that in this second assertion Vico implies a distinction between two kinds of making or construction: man's ontological construction of the historical world—i.e., of the institutions, languages, events, and other elements that constitute it—and man's epistemological or historiographical construction of that world—i.e., of our historical knowledge of the things that constitute it. If, for convenience, the expressions "ontological construction" and "epistemological" or "historiographical construction" are used to designate these two kinds of making, Vico's claim may be expressed by saying that because men are responsible for the ontological construction of the past, its principles must lie in the modifications of our mind, and because this is so, its epistemological construction is possible. The second claim therefore presupposes the first.

Comparing *f* above with this passage, it will be seen that Marx explicitly agrees with Vico about the ontological construction of the world and adduces this as a reason why we should find its historiographical construction at least "easier" than that of the natural world, for the ontological construction of which we are not responsible. He does not, it is true, explicitly refer to Vico's other claim, that it is because men construct the past ontologically that the modifications epistemological construction requires must remain in their minds. This may suggest that he saw his agreement with Vico extending only to the question of the ontological construction of the past. But if this were the case, his own position would be seriously deficient, for the fact that man was

---

[4] *The New Science* of 1744, (hereafter *N.S.*[3]) par. 331, my translation.

responsible for the ontological construction of the past world would not, just of itself, provide a reason why men should later find the history of the human past easier to construct than that of the natural past. This would hold even if we understood Marx's claim in the light of his doctrine of the *objectification of human species life.* For the fact that men transform the natural world by objectifying themselves would still provide no reason why men should later find it easier to write the history of that world than of the animal world, since, in virtue of historical change in man, that world might be quite unlike the world of the historian.

This suggests that in the above passage Marx must agree with Vico to the extent of seeing a connection between ontological and historiographical construction, but leaves it an open question whether he agrees with Vico in connecting the two via Vico's doctrine of the modifications of the human mind. Since it would force matters to try to extract more from these passages alone, I shall proceed, in the next two sections, to make some further independent points about ontological construction in Marx and Vico.

III

The first aspect to be noted about Marx's account of ontological construction is the discontinuous nature it ascribes to human consciousness as it is created in history. This follows from the fact that since human conceptions exist to satisfy needs within the economic structure—and these, in turn, to satisfy those of the forces of production—when the development of the latter within a given set of economic relations is wholly exhausted, and after a period of social revolution, a new technology will emerge, requiring a new set of economic relations and giving rise to a new form of consciousness.[5] Thus the difference between the attitudes, feelings, and beliefs that constitute the consciousness of the feudal lord and those that constitute that of the industrial capitalist are to be traced to the technology of the hand mill

[5] The passage from the *Preface* quoted above continues:
"At a certain stage of their development, the material productive forces of society come in conflict with the existing relations of production or—what is but a legal expression for the same thing—with the property relations within which they have been at work hitherto. From forms of development of the productive forces these relations turn into their fetters. Then begins an epoch of social revolution. With the change of the economic foundation the entire immense superstructure is more or less rapidly transformed."

and the steam mill, respectively, and to the different economic structures they require.[6] That is to say, they are not to be traced to an
historical development of the concepts themselves which structure
those attitudes and beliefs. But since the sequence of technologies is
itself discontinuous, for one never replaces another until its total possibilities have been exhausted, so in the superstructure the replace-
ment of one set of ideas by another is discontinuous in the sense that
this change is not to be explained by men's critical consideration or
evaluation of the ideas themselves but by these ideas being required for
the functioning of some new set of economic or social practices.

Two points follow from this feature of Marx's theory. First, there is
little or nothing that is fixed or constant in the human nature created in
history. Certainly there is no constant core of human ideas or of economic relations or even of technological skill. The only constant that is
allowable in Marx's scheme is what is required for man to be a technologist—i.e., a desire to transform the materials of nature in such a way as
best to satisfy his own material needs.

The second point is that, just as there is no constancy in human
nature in history, so also the human natures that are created are
discontinuous. For, as we have seen, the human conceptions, social
practices, and other traits that comprise a large part of human nature
at any given time do not develop, in accordance with some principle,
from their own earlier states, but are in effect simply supplanted by new
and different practices and conceptions when a new technology replaces an outworn one.

The other feature that must be noted in Marx's account of the
ontological construction of the past is the importance in it of the distinction between appearance and reality. We cannot, Marx tells us, take the
beliefs of, for example, religion at their face value; or, to put this
otherwise, we cannot accept the evaluation put upon them by those
whose beliefs they were.[7] The same is true not only of all elements in the
superstructure, which are ideological, but of many in the economic

---

[6] "The handmill gives you society with the feudal lord; the steam-mill, society with the
industrial capitalist.

"The same men who establish their social relations in conformity with their material
productivity, produce also principles, ideas and categories, in conformity with their social
relations." *The Poverty of Philosophy,* p. 105. Quotation taken from Jordan, op. cit., p. 186.

[7] "Just as our opinion of an individual is not based on what he thinks of himself, so can we
not judge of such a period of transformation by its own consciousness..." The *Preface,* Jordan,
op. cit., p. 198.

structure such as, at a certain stage in history, the concepts of bourgeois economics themselves. This is not, however, something accidental. It is, on the contrary, quite necessary, for these phenomena would be unable to perform their necessary functions were they not disguised in certain determinate ways. The practices of religion, therefore, are carried out in a context of beliefs accepted as true even though they are wholly false, if not totally unintelligible, considered from the Marxist viewpoint. But they must be accepted as true if they are to fulfill their necessary function. The whole point, then, of the critical history of religion that Marx calls for in *e* above is that it will be critical in the sense not only of relating a determinate religion to a determinate set of productive forces and relations of production, but that, in so doing, it will distinguish appearance from reality by showing how such a religion can perform its necessary function only by adopting a certain appearance.

In the case of technology, on the other hand, this is not so. Technology is the most basic expression of man's real—i.e., material—nature. Unlike religion or law, it presents itself as it is, not so much because it cannot do otherwise but because there is no need, in order that it function correctly, for it to do otherwise. There is a close relationship, therefore, between the basically materialist nature of Marx's ontology and his use of the distinction between appearance and reality. For although, for Marx, all phenomena are material in nature, the real are those that present themselves as such, which they do when, as in technology, they are directly related to the natural world, and the apparent are those that do not present themselves as such, which occurs when, as in religion, they are more indirectly related to the natural world.

IV

Turning now to Vico, it will be seen that despite certain resemblances between his and Marx's accounts of the ontological construction of the past, there are crucial and fundamental differences.[8] I shall start from their common use of the notion of class struggle. Whether or not in stating that "the history of all hitherto-existing society is the history of

---

[8] The account offered below is in no sense exhaustive. There are many further points, both of resemblance and difference, worthy of further fruitful study.

class struggles"[9] Marx was deliberately exaggerating for rhetorical effect,[10] the importance of the notion in his account of history is too well established to require further comment. Vico is generally given credit for having anticipated Marx in this, although he does not use the expression "class struggle" itself. Nevertheless the ascription is correct, for the whole of Vico's account of the sequence of changes whereby the early "fathers" progressively surrender their almost total ownership of their dependents or, what is the same thing, the family, and then the *famuli,* and progressively win the aspect of legal status that, when gained, constitutes the basis of citizenship and hence of the city, is an account of class struggle.[11]

It should be noted also that Vico insists that in the course of this struggle, where it is access to what is judged "right" that is at issue, what is judged "right," "due," or "just" is intimately connected to the needs and utilities that men feel in certain determinate historical situations.[12]

Further, Vico insists that one aspect of this struggle is an attempt to wrest control of the law from those who would abuse it for purposes of exploitation.[13]

These resemblances conceal, however, more important differences. The first may be noted by recalling Vico's denial that utility is the *basis* of the law. Utility, he avers, is the occasion but not the cause of the just, i.e., of what men aim at by way of justice. The cause, he tells us, is the eternal idea of justice,[14] an idea that he goes on to identify with an appropriately specified concept of equity, which is progressively discovered by man as, in the course of history, the human mind itself develops. Thus, in connection with the immutability of law, he writes:

> ...the natural law of the gentes is an eternal law which traverses time. But just as within us lie buried a few seeds of truth, which are

[9] *Manifesto of the Communist Party,* I. Jordan, op. cit., p. 161.

[10] Discussed in *Philosophy and Public Affairs* by R. W. Miller, "The Consistency of Historical Materialism" (Summer 1975), and S. Moore, "A Consistency Proof for Historical Materialism" (Spring 1976).

[11] The account is, of course, further continued as Vico traces the struggle between the lords and the plebs in the cities.

[12] *N.S.*[3] par. 141, 341.

[13] Vico does not use the term "exploitation," but he does maintain that the law provides advantages for some at the expense of others and that this is partly what the struggle is about.

[14] "...the cause of the just is not variable utility [itself] but eternal reason which, in immutable geometric and mathematical proportions, distributes the variable utilities upon the occasion of different human needs" (The *New Science* of 1725 [hereafter *N.S.*[1]] par. 41. My translation); "...the natural law is, in truth, eternal in its idea..." (*N.S.*[1], par. 21).

cultivated gradually from childhood until, with age and through [various] studies, they develop into the fully clarified notions which belong to the sciences, so, as a result of [human] sin, within mankind were buried the seeds of justice, which, as the human mind develops gradually according to its true nature from the childhood of the world, develop into demonstrated maxims of justice.[15]

Precisely the same is true also of human religious belief. Thus, the occasions of the determinate phases through which, according to Vico, the idea of God must develop, are the needs that arise in the progressively humanized world man creates, but the cause is the eternal idea of God, present as an innate idea at every stage of history, but developing from the status of a superstitious belief to that of a demonstrated truth as the human mind becomes increasingly rational.[16]

In allowing utility as the occasion of the introduction of a new content into the law or into religious belief, Vico might seem fairly close to Marx's notion that the content of these ideas is to be explained by some social function that they exist to satisfy. But in asserting that utility is nevertheless not their cause, he is clearly making a very different claim. For what this amounts to is that it is the idea itself, in its final form, that is the cause of the different developmental phases revealed in its prior history.

Before proceeding further, however, something must be done to dispel at least some of the mystery that must attach to the suggestion that an idea in a later stage of development can be a cause of its own history. The first point to note is that although Vico claims that the eternal idea of, e.g., God, is the cause of the determinate forms that idea takes in history, he cannot mean that it is the whole cause. For he certainly allows that part of the reason it exists in a particular form is that it satisfies certain social needs. This, indeed, is what he means when he says that utility is the occasion but not the cause of particular views of justice. There would appear, therefore, to be two causal factors at work here—utility and the eternal idea. Vico's way of expressing

---

[15] *N.S.*,[1] par. 49. It is worth recalling that in the *Preface* Marx, with Hegel in mind, expressly rejects the idea of a development of the human mind as an explanatory principle: "My investigation led to the result that legal relations as well as forms of state are to be grasped neither from themselves nor from the so-called general development of the human mind."

[16] *N.S.*,[3] par. 385.

himself may now be rendered less mysterious if we treat this as a way of saying that although considerations of utility—socially grounded utility, that is—are among the occasions that move men to act and that must be satisfied by any new institutional arrangements they make, as revealed in the phases of the class war, they do not wholly determine these new arrangements. The latter are underdetermined by utility—or, to put it otherwise, the demands of utility could be satisfied by other arrangements. A further reason is therefore required to explain the development of the particular set of arrangements adopted, and this is to be found in a certain *ideal* that, in the course of their history, men are progressively developing.

To mention an ideal as a cause is, of course, to differentiate Vico sharply from Marx, for whom ideals cannot be other than material factors that, for various reasons, can fulfill certain necessary functions only by masquerading as ideals. The difference between the two is, however, even sharper than this, for Vico is committed not only to the causal efficacy of ideals but also to their objectivity, a position for which he argues by trying to establish the identity of the ideals that occur at the corresponding stages in the sequence of institutional developments all nations must undergo.[17] Thus the only ideals that can count for Vico are those that will be able to be seen as helping to lead to the construction of a society such as that in which the historian finds himself, which, in Vico's own case, would be a society of sufficient conceptual development to be able to produce the criteria of rationality satisfied by his own science. Vico does indeed claim that reason has here developed to the point of being able to grasp the real natures of things, implying that some ultimate criterion has been satisfied. It is not necessary, however, to go the whole way with Vico and accept that the concepts to which he here appeals must satisfy some ultimate criterion of rationality. His position would lose none of its strength if we accept that we must take the concepts of morality, truth, and knowledge present in our own society as the results of a process of historical development in which men have adjusted their practices not only merely to suit the demands of utility, but also to satisfy, in ways that ever more closely approximate our standards of rationality, ideals only partially satisfied in their earlier arrangements. Thus it is not required that we view our present standards of justice or of science as rationally ultimate and wholly beyond improvement. It is required, however, that we view them as the

[17] Cf. *N.S.*,[1] par. 55-56.

result of a process of ontological construction in which men, while trying to satisfy the needs and utilities of their time, should do so in accordance with a desire to satisfy more rationally ideals that their earlier arrangements can be seen only to approximate.

Essentially, then, for Vico the ontological construction of the world is a response to the utilitarian needs of the situation, a response that is conditioned also by the ideals we develop in the light of our understanding of their own past history.[18] For Marx, on the other hand, ideality never has more than a functional role to play, a role that it can play, moreover, only insofar as, in dressing itself as ideal, it disguises its functional character.

V

It is possible now to relate these features of ontological construction in Vico and Marx to their accounts of epistemological construction. We may start from the fact that in both accounts of ontological construction there is a distinction between appearance and reality. For Marx, for example, religion, in the sense of a body of belief with claims to truth value, is a wholly false, but functionally necessary appearance of something else: wishes, needs, and desires that cannot fail to arise in certain economic circumstances. For Vico, on the other hand, although the beliefs of religion, as they have appeared in the past, are largely false— men believed that the world was a vast living god, which was false that it was[19]—they are not wholly false. For there is a truth in religious belief, and the history of religion is the history of the way in which men have come to understand this truth. And the same difference, of course, applies to both thinkers with regard to the concepts of law and of morality.

This distinction between appearance and reality is fundamental in understanding Marx's epistemology. For the task of science, as he conceives it in *Capital,* is precisely to expose the reality that underlies the appearances, whether the latter are taken to be the beliefs of religion or morality or feudal or bourgeois economics themselves. Thus, in a world in which reality revealed itself as it is—as it always

---

[18] The case of common law, which develops in accordance with principles only to be detected by looking at precedents, but not determined by them, would be an example of this model.

[19] *N.S.,*[3] par. 375-80.

does, for example, at the level of the forces of production and as it would in the communist state—there would be no need for science. But to know the history of any precommunist society we require a science that can operate theories involving the distinction between appearance and reality. And, applied to the religions of the past, such a science would give us that critical and materialistic history of religion Marx called for in *e* above.

It is clear, however, that if a scientific history is one in which things are shown to be what they are—i.e., realities as realities and appearances as appearances—at least two requirements must be satisfied. The first will be that of offering a description of the phenomena in question, be they "realities" or "appearances" according to Marx's distinction, in the terms in which they were originally understood—i.e., in terms that can be applied without invoking the distinction between reality and appearance. Let us, for convenience, call this a "first-order interpretation." We shall thus come to know how historical agents saw themselves and lived out their lives. The second requirement will then be to show how, given a theory involving the distinction between appearance and reality, some of the facts established by first-order interpretation are to be classified as "real" and others as "appearance," in such a way that we can see how the one set of facts, the "real" facts, can explain the nature and occurrence of the others, the appearances. It follows, therefore, that in taking the task of science to be that of exposing the reality that underlies appearance, Marx has propounded a concept of science that, when applied to history, turns out to produce explanatory theories; as such, it presupposes another kind of science which will produce a theory of first-order interpretation. For without the latter we would be unable to acquire the data the former is to explain. Yet Marx shows no recognition of this fact.

It may seem that this reveals only that the theory is deficient rather than that it is seriously defective. But the fact that the predicament is graver than this becomes apparent if we ask about the nature of the categories of interpretation needed to provide an objective account of the illusions of the past seen, as Marx's theory of explanation requires, not as illusions but as realities by the agents who entertained them. Could they, for example, be categories of historical interpretation that were "pure," in Kant's sense? It is difficult to see how Marx could accept this possibility, given his view of the social and historical grounding of categories. If not, could they be socially grounded categories that somehow escaped the constraints of their origins? Clearly they could not be categories peculiar to any historically determinate era, for these could not be applied to a past in which, we are told, no conceptions are common to our own. But could there not be some categories common to all historical eras? Here, Marx's appeal to Vico in *e* above might suggest that this is possible. For the claim that we can write the history of human technology more easily than that of natural technology because we have made the former suggests, in turn, a reason why this should be so: We are ourselves makers of technology. But, by a parity of reasoning, would we not then need to have engaged in all those activities the history of which we want to write, which are allegedly so different from, and discontinuous with, our own historically local activities? Again this does not seem an option open to Marx. Could such a theory of interpretation rest upon some presuppositions about the constancy of human nature, as Hume thought?[20] If the analysis of ontological construction given in the foregoing section is correct, this is equally unacceptable, since in Marx's account of ontological construction the only constraints in human nature are those required for man to be a technologist. Finally, we may ask, could it rest upon a theory of the continuity, rather than of the constancy, of human nature? But this is again impossible because, according to the analysis offered in the foregoing section, Marx offers a discontinuous theory of human nature. There would simply be no continuity between our nature and that of people in the past, knowledge of which we could use in trying to interpret their activities.

The difficulty, then, is that Marx's theory of explanation presupposes a first-order theory of interpretation, but his account of ontological construction is such that we cannot derive a set of categories adequate to such a theory of interpretation. The difficulty may be stated in the form of a dilemma: First-order interpretations may stand on pure categories, but this is impossible because all categories are socially and historically grounded categories; or these interpretations may stand on socially and historically grounded categories, but this is also impossible because such categories are neither the same as, nor historically continuous with, those of the agents of the past whose practices we need to interpret.[21]

---

[20] See *An Enquiry Concerning Human Understanding*, sec. VIII, esp. par. 65 ff.

[21] I assume here that such a first-order interpretation can capture the world as it was for past historical eras only if it utilizes the same categories as were proper to those eras. Whatever difficulties there may be about showing that one is indeed using the correct categories, such an enterprise is intelligible only if it is possible, in principle at least, to have access to those categories. It is this, I claim, that is made impossible by Marx's account of ontological construction.

VI

In this concluding section I shall maintain that Vico offers a more fruitful approach to the solution of these difficulties because he has a more adequate grasp than Marx of the need for our theories of ontological and epistemological construction to be accommodated to each other. In allowing that a history of human technology ought to be easier to write because we are ourselves producers of technology, Marx shows some awareness of this need. If the points made in Part IV in connection with Vico are correct, however, there are two requirements here. The historian must not only use his knowledge of what it is to be a producer of technology, in order to understand its purposes, characteristic features and so on, but he must view his present technology as a continuous and to some degree rational development from past technology, thus allowing that some purposes, characteristic features, and so on are transtemporally predicable. Marx can perhaps concede this in the case of technology, since in his account it is an absolute material necessity that man be a technologist. Thus we can interpret a past activity as a form of technology only on the assumptions that it satisfies our concept of technology and that, in writing its history, we can see it as a part of a process whereby our own technology, to which that concept is appropriate, has come into being.[22] But in any other sphere of human activity things are wholly different. On Marx's account changes in religion are not determined by new ways in which men might try to think about God or to satisfy their religious needs, but by new non-religious needs that arise at the behest of change in the economic structure. Similarly, changes in the economic structure are not determined by what goes on in that structure, but by new needs of the forces of production that it exists to satisfy. There can therefore be no internal coherence to a history of religion or of law or of economic practice, if by this it is meant that the causes of change in these areas of activity lie, at least partly, in the capacity that historical agents have to reflect upon them and ask themselves how well they satisfy certain ideal aims. But if we are to think of activities under descriptions that do not imply some

[22] Even in the sphere of technology, however, this possibility would be open to Marx only if different successive technologies are not wholly discontinuous with each other but are connected by some such principle as shared aims or common functions, so that, no matter how widely the conditions in which different technologies operate may differ, it will be intelligible to take one as a "development" of another. What is required, therefore, is a conception of ontological construction that allows for a transhistorical concept of technology.

or other ideal aims, what could entitle us to take certain activities of successive historical periods and describe some of them as "legal" and others as "religious"? Our procedure here would be entirely arbitrary.

Vico avoids these difficulties, however, because the insight that Marx was able to accept only in the case of technology is fundamental to his conception of anything that can count as a part of human history and be known as such. What Marx would allow in the case of technology must apply also to religion, law, languages, economic practices, and so on, if we are to be able to think of their past as parts of human history. This means not merely that the historian must have antecedent insight into these areas of human activity through his understanding of them as grounded in his own society, but that he must also have a conception of the ontological construction of the past, which will allow him to take them, and hence his understanding of them, as the product of past reflection[23] on these activities.[24] If there is to be knowledge of the human past *as* human, we must both use knowledge of the modifications of the human mind in constructing that knowledge and, at the same time, insist that that knowledge be used to provide a coherent and continuous account of the development of those same modifications. The reason why Vico is able to offer a more satisfactory framework for a first-order theory of interpretation than is Marx is thus that he has grasped the necessity to adjust our accounts of ontological and historiographical construction in such a way as to meet this requirement.

It would seem, then, that while Marx agreed with Vico in seeing a connection between ontological and historiographical construction, he did not see the necessity to connect them by means of a doctrine of the modifications of the human mind as historical products, and to that extent he had a less satisfactory conception of what it is for man to be an historical being. Had this not been so, he would have been in a better position to explain why it should be easier to compile a history of human technology than of natural technology, although the account he would then have compiled would have been very different.

[23] Reflection is not, of course, the *occasion* of the change. It is the reason why we accept that change rather than another.

[24] This is offered only as a necessary and not a sufficient condition of historical knowledge. I do not intend to impute to Vico the view that an historian of religion must attend only to religion as it develops through different historical periods. This would be wholly foreign to Vico, who lays great stress on certain pervasive ideas belonging to different historical periods, which color and unify the institutions of each period. In emphasizing that it is a necessary condition, however, I do want to insist that it would not be sufficient to view the "religion" or "law" of an historical period as though it were something that could be understood utterly and completely in terms of its place in the totality of practices of that period. This would be equally foreign to Vico's conception of historical development.

On "Making" History in Vico and Marx

Terence Ball*

In their eagerness to discover intellectual influences upon, and theoretical connections between, thinkers of different ages, commentators
too often mistake passing references or resemblances for the real
thing. This is notoriously the case with Marxists and Marxologists who
attempt to trace the sources of Marx's ideas. As often as not old myths—
that Marx was, for example, a socialist Darwinist whose concept of class
struggle stemmed from Darwin's "struggle for existence"—have
merely been perpetuated and embellished instead of being critically
reconsidered. I have attempted elsewhere to expose the errors and
exaggerations of a "Darwinian" reading of Marx;[1] here I shall suggest
why a Vichian reading of Marx, or a Marxian reading of Vico, is equally
unsatisfactory. Marx and the Marxists—like so many others—have in
certain respects misappropriated Vico. This misappropriation rests, I
believe, upon a misrepresentation, or at any rate a misunderstanding,
of Vico's views and in particular of his central doctrine that we have a
special sort of knowledge of what we ourselves have made.

In working my way toward this conclusion I shall make use of a series
of intertwining arguments. I shall begin by examining, and distinguishing between, several sorts of supposed "connections" between
Vico and Marx. Then I shall consider some of the more obvious, though
often overlooked, differences between the two thinkers. This in turn
leads me to inquire into a nonobvious but, I believe, crucial difference
between Vico and Marx—namely, their very different conceptions of
what is involved in "making" history and human society. Vico's doctrine

*Author's Note: The central ideas and arguments advanced in this essay grew out of
stimulating conversations with Sir Isaiah Berlin, James Farr, B. A. Haddock, and Giorgio
Tagliacozzo. I should like to thank them for forcing me to clarify my ill-formed ideas, and to
exempt them from any blame or responsibility for the final result.

[1] See my "Marx and Darwin: A Reconsideration," *Political Theory*, 7 (November 1979):
469-83.

that we can know civil society because we ourselves have made it rests, I contend, upon a communicative conception of making (as when we "make" an agreement or "make sense"), while Marx's version of this doctrine relies upon "making" in the technical-productive sense of fabrication or manufacture and applies, moreover, not only to human society but to nature as well. The upshot of my several arguments is that the distance between Marx and Vico is vaster than has heretofore been believed.

I

The idea that Vico was something of a proto-Marxist, or Marx a latter-day Vichian, appears to owe more to later Marxists than to Marx himself. Marx seems not to have read Vico before 1862 or thereabouts, well after the groundwork of his system has been laid, and even then he made remarkably few references to "the old Neapolitan."[2] Marx's "favorite occupation," he confessed, was "book-worming";[3] it was apparently in the course of pursuing this occupation that he came across Vico's *New Science,* immediately read—or rather, devoured—it, and thereupon recommended it enthusiastically to Ferdinand Lassalle. Warning that the original would be hard going, not merely because it was written in Italian but, worse yet, in the "very tricky Neapolitan idiom" (*sehr verzwicktem neapolitanischen Idiom*), Marx accordingly recommended the 1844 French translation, from which he quotes several snippets "to whet your appetite."[4] He adds that he has tried but failed to find Vico's juridical writings.[5]

Like most of Vico's readers, Marx was impressed by Vico's originality and erudition and half-amused by his more bizarre flights of philological fancy.[6] But one aspect of Vico's thought impressed Marx greatly: the

[2] Marx to Engels, April 28, 1862, in Marx and Engels, *Werke* [hereinafter *MEW*] (Berlin: Dietz Verlag, 1972), vol. 30, p. 228. See also Eugene Kamenka, "Vico and Marxism," in *Giambattista Vico: An International Symposium,* ed. Giorgio Tagliacozzo and Hayden V. White (Baltimore: Johns Hopkins University Press, 1969), esp. p. 138; and Martin Jay, "Vico and Western Marxism," in *Vico: Past and Present,* ed. Giorgio Tagliacozzo (Atlantic Highlands, N.J.: Humanities Press, 1981) vol. II, pp. 195-212.

[3] Quoted in David McLellan, *Karl Marx: His Life and Thought* (London: Macmillan, 1973), p. 457.

[4] Marx to Ferdinand Lassalle, April 28, 1862, *MEW,* vol. 30, p. 622. [This letter is extensively discussed by Arshi Pipa in his essay, *Marx's Relation to Vico: A Philological Approach,* in the present volume, pp. 290-325. Ed.]

[5] Ibid., p. 623.

[6] Marx to Engels, April 28, 1862, *MEW,* vol. 30, pp. 227-28.

idea that men make their own history and can, accordingly, know it in a way that they do not—indeed, cannot—know what they have not made. In an "important footnote"[7] to *Capital I* Marx writes:

> Darwin has interested us in the history of Nature's Technology, i.e. in the formation of the organs of plants and animals, which organs serve as instruments or production for sustaining life. Does not the history of the productive organs of man, of organs that are the material basis of all social organization, deserve equal attention? And would not such a history be easier to compile, since, as Vico says, human history differs from natural history in this, that we have made the former, but not the latter?[8]

Marxists and Marxologists have made much—indeed, perhaps too much—of this passage. A mere three sentences, tucked away in a single footnote in a book of 800-plus pages, and appearing to occur almost as an afterthought or embellishment to the text, hardly suffices to show that Marx owed a great intellectual debt to Vico. And yet for nearly a century, Marxists and Marxologists have insisted that Marx's reference to Vico points to a profoundly important connection between the two thinkers.

Claims about the existence of such a connection generally take one of two forms, some commentators contending that the link is one involving direct influence, and others making the less precise claim that there are deep-seated thematic affinities between Vico and Marx. A claim of the former sort is advanced by M. Rubel, who maintains that Marx's "Promethean vision of history" derives in large part from his reading of Vico.[9] Such a claim seems scarcely plausible, considering

---

[7] Max Harold Fisch, Introduction to *The Autobiography of Giambattista Vico* (Ithaca, N.Y.: Great Seal Books, 1963), p. 104.

[8] Marx, *Capital* (New York: International Publishers, 1967), vol. I, p. 372.

[9] Maximilien Rubel, *Karl Marx: Essai de biographie intellectuelle* (Paris: M. Rivière, 1957), p. 315. In a similar vein, Shlomo Avineri writes of Marx's "indebtedness to Giambattista Vico" for having been "the first to have suggested that man creates himself by his own work." See Avineri, *The Social and Political Thought of Karl Marx* (Cambridge: Cambridge University Press, 1970), p. 77. Actually Avineri is mistaken on both counts. If my arguments are correct, Marx owed no significant debt to Vico. Nor was Vico the first to suggest that man creates himself by his own work. Long before Vico, Cicero wrote: "...by the use of our hands, we bring into being within the realm of Nature, a second nature for ourselves" (*De Natura Deorum,* II, 60). But Cicero—like Aquinas and Marx, but unlike Vico—conflates the crucial classical distinction between making or producing (*poiesis*) and acting (*praxis*). See section III of the present essay.

that Marx arrived at his vision of history well before he had read Vico and that Hegel, in any event, lay closer to hand. Nor is Rubel alone in insisting that such a connection exists. Christopher Lasch, who takes the title of his book—*The World of Nations*—from Vico, writes that "Vico's principle [that we can understand the world of nations because we ourselves have made it] provides an indispensable support for the Marxian critique of political economy."[10] Yet Lasch's claim is no more plausible than Rubel's, and again for much the same reason: The main lines of Marx's critique of political economy were laid down in the *Grundrisse* of 1857/8—five years *before* Marx's book-worming led him to Vico's *New Science*. The real or imagined "support" provided by Vico was doubtless welcome, but it was hardly "indispensable." Otherwise Vico would, one might think, merit more than a minor footnote in Marx's magnum opus.

If claims about direct Vichian influences are easily countered, another sort of claim is difficult to formulate precisely, much less to criticize or confute. I mean, of course, the claim that there are affinities, elective or otherwise, between the two thinkers, and that the historian of ideas has only to point these out. Doubtless there are parallels and resemblances, some of them quite striking, between Vico and Marx. But these do not, I think, go very deep, nor are they especially impressive when considered in the light of the vast and profound differences between the two thinkers. This sweeping claim I cannot, for want of sufficient space, substantiate here. Instead I shall, in the sections following, focus upon several striking differences. I want to focus in particular upon Marx's and the Marxists' understanding—or rather, as I maintain, their misunderstanding—of Vico's view that we can know human history because we ourselves have made it. For it is this Vichian doctrine, more than any other, that Marx and later Marxists—including Marx's son-in-law Paul Lafargue, Georges Sorel, Antonio Labriola, and Leon Trotsky—seized upon and interpreted as an anticipation of the materialist conception of history.[11]

---

[10] Christopher Lasch, *The World of Nations* (New York: Knopf, 1973), p. 312.

[11] See Paul Lafargue, *Karl Marx: His Life and Work* (New York: International Publishers, 1943), p. 15, and *Le Déterminisme Économique de Karl Marx* (1907), 3rd. edn. (Paris: Marcel Giard, 1928), ch. 3, "Lois historiques de Vico," pp. 24-33; Georges Sorel, "Étude sur Vico," *Devenir Social*, 2 (Oct.-Dec. 1896), *passim;* Antonio Labriola, *Essays on the Materialist Conception of History*, first publ. 1896 (New York: Monthly Review Press, 1966), esp. pp. 120-21, 163, 215-18, and 232-33; and Leon Trotsky, *My Life* (New York: Pathfinder Press, 1970), pp. 119, 122, for an account of the impact of Labriola's *Essays*, which Trotsky read in a French translation during his first imprisonment in 1898.

Consider the case of Sorel. His study of Vico led him to embrace a peculiarly Vichian version of Marxism in the waning years of the nineteenth century.[12] Two Vichian doctrines he found especially attractive. The first was the notion of *ricorsi,* those periodic revivals of ethical energy and enthusiasm that precede and announce new epochs. The second—and for our purposes more pertinent—is Vico's notion that men make their history. An engineer by profession, Sorel was particularly impressed by the idea that man *makes* the social world no less than the engineer constructs bridges and dams. These two elements he brings together in a peculiar and novel way. The next *ricorso* would, he hoped, be brought about by, and reveal, a new kind of hero uniquely suited to the peculiarities and possibilities of a new age. For Sorel, as Hughes remarks, "craftsmen and technicians—the heroes of the machine age—offered the loftiest contemporary examples of morality."[13] In Sorel's hands Durkheim's notion of "mechanical solidarity" receives a quite literal twist. For he believed, as Berlin observes, that "Machinery is a social cement more effective...than even language" and that "the factory should become the vehicle of the social poetry of modern producers."[14] (There are echoes here of Marx's celebration of the factory as the schoolroom of revolution.)[15] Sorel ranks, in Berlin's judgment, as "one of the few perceptive readers [of Vico] in the nineteenth century."[16] Doubtless this is in some respects entirely correct. But it is, I believe, apt to be misleading in another, long-overlooked sense. For, I shall argue, Sorel—like Marx before him—had in one crucial respect misread Vico and, having misunderstood his meaning, went on to misinterpret him as something of a proto-Marxist.

Very simply, both Sorel and Marx misunderstood what Vico meant in saying that we *make* the social world. They understood Vico to mean "making" in the technical sense of construction, fabrication, production, or manufacture; but in fact, as I shall argue, Vico harks back to the classical distinction between the *technè* of the craftsman and the *praxis* of

---

[12] Sorel, op. cit. See also George Lichtheim, *From Marx to Hegel* (New York: Herder and Herder, 1971), pp. 101, 111; H. Stuart Hughes, *Consciousness and Society: The Reorientation of European Social Thought, 1890-1930,* rev. ed. (New York: Vintage Books, 1977), chap. 5, esp. pp. 171-72; and Isaiah Berlin, "Georges Sorel," in his *Against the Current: Essays in the History of Ideas,* ed. Henry Hardy (New York: Viking, 1980), pp. 296-332.

[13] Hughes, op. cit., p. 172

[14] Berlin, *Against the Current,* p. 308.

[15] In the *Communist Manifesto.* See Marx and Engels, *Selected Works,* in one volume [*MESW*] (New York: International Publishers, 1968), pp. 43-46.

[16] Berlin, *Against the Current,* p. 301.

communicating members of historically situated communities. The sort of "making" to which Vico refers is not the technical-productive activity of *homo faber* but the "practical" creativity of communicating citizens. Before making (*sic*) this argument regarding a nonobvious difference between Vico and Marx, however, I should first like to bring out some of their more obvious differences.

II

Two differences between Vico and Marx are crucial, and too obvious to be missed. The first is that Vico was a devout Christian and Marx an atheist.[17] Anyone wishing to connect Marx's thought to Vico's must somehow bridge this chasm between them. Some commentators have accordingly suggested that Vico was not such a devout Christian after all; that he kept God in his system only because he feared the fires of the Inquisition; and that his references to divine providence are merely metaphorical. Thus James Morrison, for example, maintains that "The idea of divine providence is for Vico simply a metaphor for the irony of history."[18] And Edmund Wilson says that "In the Catholic city of Naples, in the shadow of the Inquisition, Vico had to keep God in his system,"[19] the implication being that he would, if he dared, remove Him entirely—as though Vico could say of God, as Laplace did, "*Je n'ai pas eu besoin de cette hypothèse.*"[20] If Vico were the secular thinker that Messrs. Morrison and Wilson portray, it would of course be easier to reconcile his thought with Marx's. But Vico was not a secular thinker. God was not, for Vico, a hypothesis, much less a dispensable one, nor

---

[17] Interestingly, Marx denied that he was an atheist, inasmuch as atheism is, strictly speaking, the denial of something unreal, i.e., God. See Marx, *The Economic and Philosophic Manuscripts of 1844* (New York: International Publishers, 1964), pp. 145-46. Suffice it to say that he was at any rate an unbeliever.

[18] James C. Morrison, "How to Interpret the Idea of Divine Providence in Vico's New Science," *Philosophy and Rhetoric*, 12 (Fall 1979): 256-61, at 259. For another argument to the effect that Vico did not actually mean what he said, see Frederick Vaughan, *The Political Philosophy of Giambattista Vico* (The Hague: Martinus Nijhoff, 1972), *passim*. Dr. Vaughan, a disciple of the late Professor Leo Strauss, follows his mentor in elevating the mere possibility that an author who feared persecution might write cautiously and circumspectly into an all-pervasive principle of textual interpretation. See Leo Strauss, *Persecution and the Art of Writing* (Glencoe, Ill.: Free Press, 1952), *passim*.

[19] Edmund Wilson, *To the Finland Station* (New York: Anchor Books, 1953), p. 467.

[20] Legend has it that this was Laplace's reply when Napoleon asked where God belonged in his *Système du Monde* (1796). See Alexandre Koyré, *From the Closed World to the Infinite Universe* (Baltimore: Johns Hopkins University Press, 1957), p. 276.

were his references to divine providence merely metaphorical. As Professor Fisch remarks, Vico's theory of divine providence "is not merely a presupposition of [his] science but an integral part or 'principal aspect' of it"—an "article of faith," in short, which animates his thinking and gives coherence to his system.[21]

A second important difference between Vico and Marx can, I think, be traced to the first. Marx is a monist and Vico a dualist—as much of a dualist, indeed, as his *bête noire* Descartes ever was, although, as Berlin notes, his dualism "stretches across a different part of the metaphysical map."[22] As an atheist and an avowed opponent of all dualisms Marx could hardly have accepted Vico's version of the doctrine that we know what we ourselves have made. For this epistemological doctrine, as Vico formulates it, points to an irreducible ontological dualism—to a division, that is, between that which God has made and that which man has made. "Natural history" is the story of what God has made—namely, nature—and "human history" is the story of what man has made—namely, civil society or "the world of nations." Because one has a special knowledge—knowledge *per caussas* (*sic*), "through causes"—of what one has made, God alone has an intimate "maker's knowledge" of nature.[23] Such a knowledge of nature is not open to man, for he merely takes nature as he finds it; because he did not create it, nature remains opaque and not fully accessible to man's intelligence. It is, however, quite a different matter with human society; for, since man himself has made it, he has a quasi-divine knowledge of its structure, purpose, and operation. In a famous and oft-quoted passage Vico is quite explicit about the divine origin of this ontological and epistemological dualism:

---

[21] Max Harold Fisch, Introduction to *The New Science of Giambattista Vico* [*N.S.*] (Ithaca, N.Y.: Cornell University Press, 1968), p. xxxii. The author of the *Scienza nuova* was, as Berlin rightly remarks, "a pious if peculiar Christian": *Vico and Herder* (New York: Viking, 1976), p. 70.

[22] Berlin, *Vico and Herder,* p. 121.

[23] The phrase belongs to Professor Jaakko Hintikka. See his "Practical vs. Theoretical Reason—An Ambiguous Legacy," in *Practical Reason,* ed. Stephan Körner (Oxford: Blackwell, 1974), chap. 3. Dr. Andrew Harrison, in *Making and Thinking* (London: Harvester Press, 1978), p. 152, attributes the phrase to Vico—mistakenly, I believe. Unfortunately, both Hintikka and Harrison—like most modern writers, including Marx—confuse and conflate the "practical" knowledge of the actor (or doer) with the "technical" knowledge of the producer. The result, so far as their reading of Vico is concerned, is little short of disastrous. For Hintikka, like Marx, maintains that men have an ever-increasing "maker's knowledge" of nature—a view rightly attributable to Marx but *not* (*pace* Hintikka, pp. 87-88) to Vico! See sections III and IV of the present essay.

But in the night of thick darkness enveloping the earliest antiquity, so remote from ourselves, there shines the eternal and never failing light of a truth beyond all question: that the world of civil society has certainly been made by men, and that its principles are therefore to be found within the modifications of our own human mind. Whoever reflects on this cannot but marvel that the philosophers should have bent all their energies to the study of the world of nature, which, since God made it, He alone knows; and that they should have neglected the study of the world of nations, or civil world, which since men had made it, men could come to know.[24]

This arresting passage contains the most succinct statement of Vico's version of the medieval doctrine (traceable to Aquinas and, before him, to St. Augustine) of *verum et factum convertuntur*—that knowledge and creation are one.[25] Just as God can know nature because He has made it, so men can know civil society because they have made it.

I turn now to the central contention of this essay: that Vico and Marx meant very different things by "making"; that Vico meant making in a communicative sense, while Marx referred to making in the nature-transforming technical sense of fabrication, production, or manufacture; and that in terms of the classical distinction, drawn by Aristotle, between acting (or doing) and making, Vico relies implicitly upon the former and Marx explicitly upon the latter.[26] I shall begin with a digression upon the distinction drawn by "the master of them that know."[27]

III

Aristotle drew a distinction among *theoria, poiesis,* and *praxis,* linking these with three categorially distinct kinds of knowledge and three

---

[24] *N.S.,* par. 331.

[25] See Karl Löwith, " 'Verum et factum convertuntur': le premesse teologiche del principio di Vico e le loro conseguenze secolari," in Antonio Corsano et al., *Omaggio a Vico* (Naples: Morano, 1968), pp. 73-113.

[26] I therefore disagree with Berlin's passing remark that Vico "does not distinguish, as Aristotle did, between 'doing' [or acting] and 'making'; nor, for his purposes, was this necessary": *Vico and Herder,* p. 107, n. 1.

[27] *'l maestro di color che sanno:* Dante's paean to Aristotle (*Inferno,* Canto IV, 130-31). On the connection between Vico and Dante see Glauco Cambon, "Vico and Dante," in Tagliacozzo and White, op. cit., pp. 15-28.

corresponding ways of life (*bioi*).[28] *Theoria* is the activity of contemplating what is immutable, eternal, and divine; "theoretical knowledge" is the certain knowledge (*episteme*) of these unchanging objects and relations, and the *bios theoretikos* is the way of life devoted to this solitary pursuit. *Poiesis* is the productive activity of the craftsman or artisan; his knowledge is "technical" and is shown in the particular skill or *technè* with which he transforms natural materials into humanly useful objects or artifacts. *Praxis* is the communicative activity of the citizen; his "practical" knowledge (*phronesis*) is the knowledge of men like himself—of their thoughts, ambitions, and aspirations, their hopes and their fears—and is acquired in and through his actions and interactions with them. Unlike the craftsman, who works with tangible materials, those who pursue the *bios politikos* "work" with words: speech (*lexis*) is their medium, and rhetoric their art. Rhetoric, the political art par excellence, appeals quite literally to common sense—that is, the sense and sensibilities shared in common by an assembly, or indeed a whole people—which the Romans later termed the *sensus communis*.[29]

In the transition from pagan polis to Christian cosmopolis, however, several significant changes were wrought in Aristotle's distinction. The most important of these, for our present purposes, concerns the curious conflation of "practical" and "productive" activities (so that one could, for example, henceforth speak of making a pot as a "practical" task). The case of Aquinas is perhaps especially instructive. St. Thomas was certainly well acquainted with the distinction between *poiesis* and *praxis,* and when commenting on Aristotle he renders these as *factio* and *actio,* respectively. But, as Lobkowicz notes,

> when he is not commenting on Aristotle and speaks in general about human actions, he continually illustrates *actio,* the medieval counterpart to *praxis,* by activities of production. This is more than a conceptual sloppiness, of which St. Thomas can hardly be accused. It is a consequence of, among other things, the idea,

---

[28] Aristotle in, e.g., *Nichomachean Ethics*, Book VI, secs. 4-5. See, further, Nicholas Lobkowicz, "On the History of Theory and Praxis," and my "Plato and Aristotle: The Unity Versus the Autonomy of Theory and Practice," both in *Political Theory and Praxis: New Perspectives,* ed. Terence Ball (Minneapolis: University of Minnesota Press, 1977).

[29] Vico, *N.S.,* pars. 142, 145, 311. On the meaning and significance of the *Sensus communis,* particularly for Vico, see Hans-Georg Gadamer, *Truth and Method,* trans. G. Barden and J. Cumming (New York: Seabury Press, 1975), pp. 19-29; and John Michael Krois, "Vico's and Peirce's 'Sensus Communis'," in *Vico: Past and Present,* ed. Tagliacozzo, op. cit., Vol. II, p. 58-71.

which is foreign to the Greeks, that God has created the world
and, to that extent, can be understood *mutatis mutandis* as producer...this leads to an immense increase in the value of *poiesis*
and eventually to a disappearance of the distinction between
praxis and *poiesis*.[30]

In Marx's writings, as I shall suggest presently, this distinction disappears completely—so completely, indeed, that *praxis,* as he uses the
term, refers to the technical transformation of nature through productive labor. In Vico's *New Science,* by contrast, the classical distinction
between *poiesis* and *praxis* is obscured but not, I think, obliterated.

The classical distinction between acting (or doing) and making is
obscured in Vico's *New Science* in much the same way, and for much the
same reason, I suspect, as it is obscured in Aquinas. For if man is
godlike in his ability to know what he has made, and if God's creation of
the natural world falls under the heading of *factio* (the medieval counterpart of *poiesis*), then man's creation and knowledge of the civil world
must likewise be technical or "poetic" in character. And indeed, Vico is
etymologically explicit on this score. The wisdom of our distant ancestors he terms "poetic," not merely because their metaphysics—their
attempt to understand the world—was couched in the language of
poetry, but because those who made it "were called 'poets,' which is
Greek for 'creators.'"[31] The *word* to which he refers is clearly *poiesis,* or
making; however, I want to suggest, the *concept* to which he implicitly
refers is not *poiesis* but *praxis*.[32]

Poiesis originally referred, as we have seen, to the class of technical-
instrumental activities aimed at producing tangible objects like pots
and chairs, while *praxis* had to do with the intangible but socially
indispensable "practical" activities of communicating and making
sense together. Yet "poetic" knowledge or wisdom, as Vico understands
it, has no connection with *poiesis* in the classical sense, for it is not
concerned with the transformation of natural substances into tangible
objects or artifacts. Poetic metaphysics is not an attempt to "make" in

---

[30] Lobkowicz, op. cit., pp.22-23.

[31] *N.S.,* par. 376.

[32] Other writers—notably Dr. Haddock—have similarly suggested that Vico does not
mean "making" in the technical-instrumental sense. See B.A. Haddock, "Vico on Political
Wisdom," *European Studies Review, 8* (1978): 165-91, at 181; Berlin, *Vico and Herder,* pp. xvi,
107; and Fisch, Introduction to *N.S.,* p. xl. They do not, however, follow this up in the way I
attempt to do in section III of the present essay.

the sense of fabrication or manufacture, but rather to create meaning and to make sense of an otherwise puzzling world.

In our collective attempt to make sense together we create the world in which we live—the world of nations. Societies are the communicative creations of their members, past and present.[33] Political systems and codes of law, like epic poems, are not the inventions or fabrications of any individual but are instead the communicative creations of an entire people. They arise from the daily discourse of a people seeking some sense of shared meaning; and, being unable to credit their own collective genius, they conceive of these ingenious creations as the "products" of heroic and godlike individuals—of Homer, of Solon and Lycurgus, of Romulus.[34] But in fact it is the whole people, speaking and acting together, who create poems and polities. It is they, Vico suggests, who have (or rather *can* have) a special insight into, and knowledge of, their own creation and who are in this respect godlike.

Two questions arise here. First, how can a person or a people be said to "make" or "create" anything "communicatively"? Second, in what sense is such a creation, and their knowledge of it, godlike? For surely, it will be objected, God did not create the world of nature as man creates the world of nations—that is, by communicating or interacting with other creatures like himself. Or, to put it another way: If *praxis* refers to communicative action or interaction among equals, then surely God—who is unique and therefore without equals—does not, and indeed cannot, engage in *praxis*. He can engage in *poiesis*, however, which involves no other beings like Himself. I shall consider the second question first.

First, God did create the world of nature in a distinctly "communicative" sense. For He created it ex nihilo and—more significantly still—by the Word. "In the beginning was the Word, and the Word was with God, and the word was God.... All things were made by Him..."—and made,

---

[33] Cf. Dewey's observation that "Society not only continues to exist...*by* communication, but it may fairly be said to exist *in*...communication. There is more than a verbal tie between the words common, community, and communication. Men live in a community in virtue of the things which they have in common; and communication is the way in which they come to possess things in common...."—John Dewey, *Democracy and Education* (New York: Macmillan, 1916), pp. 4-5. In emphasizing the twin notions of community and communication, Dewey was reiterating a theme advanced by the long-neglected American philosopher, Charles Sanders Peirce, who has been resurrected more recently by Professor Jürgen Habermas. My very great debt to Habermas (and thence to Peirce) should be sufficiently evident throughout the present essay.

[34] *N.S.*, Bk. III, esp. sec. II; pars. 414-17, 423, 469, 561-62, *et seq.*

moreover, by the spoken word: "And God said, Let there be light: and there was light."[35] And God in this way created the world of nature—the sun, the moon and the stars, dry land and oceans, plants and animals. Finally he created "in his own image" a communicating creature: man.

Now, just as the Word of God created the world of nature, so do the words of man create the world of nations. The creators of this world are also godlike, inasmuch as they create it ex nihilo and by the word. We live, after all, in a world of words: These are the "materials" from which society is "made." Vico, whose academic specialty was rhetoric, was greatly impressed by the creative power of language. By their utterances men create their world—as when we "create" obligations by "making" promises.[36] By means of language we not only name, denote, or describe; we also perform the actions and perpetuate the practices upon which society depends.[37] So powerful and pervasive is this feature of language that our ancestors were led to believe that the very words used in performing actions—promising, blessing, forgiving, etc.—were themselves magical.

Because the world of nations is conceptually and communicatively constituted, it differs radically from the world of nature, and the human sciences must perforce differ in principle from the natural sciences. The natural scientist may in some (admittedly problematic) sense refer to or describe a preexisting world: stars and galaxies, for example, existed before the concepts of 'star' or 'galaxy' existed. But

---

[35] John, I, 1-3; Genesis, I, 1-27.

[36] It is perhaps significant that we do not speak of (say) promising in the "technical" idiom: We do not, for example, speak of producing or manufacturing promises and obligations. We should hardly know what to think of someone who purported to "fabricate" or "manufacture" promises (are these, we might ask, false or fictitious promises?). This is not mere word play; it provides a conceptual clue and serves—in the truest Vichian sense—to remind us of a truth so obvious as to be overlooked. We can only begin to understand the sense in which "making" promises and "creating" obligations *differs* from other sorts of making by noting what we do (and do not) ordinarily say. Ordinary language is a repository of common sense, that is, of the shared sense and sensibility that constitutes what the Romans called the *sensus communis* and what we are apt to call "culture" or "tradition." The modern resuscitator of this view is of course Ludwig Wittgenstein. See Emanuele Riverso, "Vico and Wittgenstein," in *Giambattista Vico's Science of Humanity*, ed. Giorgio Tagliacozzo and Donald Phillip Verene (Baltimore: Johns Hopkins University Press, 1976), pp. 263-73; and Stuart Hampshire, "Vico and the Contemporary Philosophy of Language," in *Giambattista Vico: An International Symposium*, eds. Tagliacozzo and White, op. cit., pp. 475-481.

[37] Cf. Berlin, *Vico and Herder*, pp. 50-51; and Hannah Arendt, *The Human Condition* (Chicago: University of Chicago Press, 1958), pp. 236-47. Arendt, in particular, stresses the socially constitutive character of such "performative" utterances as promising and forgiving.

our social and political concepts do not describe or denote or refer to a preexisting world; they actually *constitute* that world. Promises and obligations did not exist before the concepts of 'promise' and 'obligation.' Our social and political concepts are themselves constitutive of social reality; they figure in the creation and maintenance of the world in which we live and act. If shared meaning and social order is conceptually or communicatively constituted, then it cannot, Vico reasoned, be imposed from without; it cannot, that is, be the product of a solitary lawgiver—a Solon or a Lycurgus or a Draco—whose laws and precepts would quite literally be incomprehensible and meaningless unless couched in the terms of an already-existing common sense, i.e., the communicatively constituted *sensus communis*.[38]

The "master key" of Vico's new science is to be found in tracing the modifications of the human mind so as to dispel the myths and mystifications that prevent our seeing our own creations for what they are. Human history is the story of changing concepts or ideas; it is the story of the human mind's successive self-modifications. The secrets so long kept from ourselves can be unlocked and revealed, to be sure, but only with the greatest difficulty. For this a special method is required. The method, unique to the human sciences, is imaginative reconstruction—*fantasia*—or simply, as Vico says elsewhere, "reflection."[39] It is only by reflection or imaginative re-creation that we are able to acquire knowledge per caussas of our own collective creation.

Our godlike character is revealed only in our communicative creations, i.e., in our *praxis*. Our technical transformations of the natural world, by contrast, yield no special or privileged knowledge. The secrets and the essential structure of nature must remain forever opaque to us. The world of nature, being God's creation, is fully meaningful only to Him. The world of nations, by contrast, is our own collective creation and is, accordingly, as meaningful to us as nature is to God.

In thus distinguishing between natural history and human history, Vico renders unto God what is God's and unto man what is man's. And never the twain shall meet. This, as we shall now see, is a far cry from Marx's conception of "making" history and his monistic view of the relation between man and nature.

[38] Vico, *On the Study Methods of Our Time,* trans. Elio Gianturco (Indianapolis: Bobbs-Merrill, 1965), chap. 7, rebukes Descartes—with his "theoretical" notion of solitary, dispassionate and disconnected egos—for his lack of "common sense." Cf. Arendt, op. cit., p. 283; and Jürgen Habermas, *Theory and Practice,* trans. John Viertel (Boston: Beacon Press, 1973), pp. 43-46.

[39] *N.S.,* pars. 338, 378, and 236.

IV

Human history is for Marx the story of the self-transformation of the human species, of the unfolding and development of dormant human powers through the nature-transforming medium of man's own labor. "The writing of history," says Marx, "must always set out from these natural bases [*natürlichen Grundlagen*] and *their* modification in the course of history through the action of men."[40] The "modification" of which Marx speaks is not Vico's "modifications of our own human mind,"[41] but rather our successive modifications of the natural environment and, in consequence, of our social organization and our ideological self-conceptions. Thus, by "the action of men" (*Aktion der Menschen*) Marx understands, not action or *praxis* in the classical communicative sense, but *poiesis*—that is, nature-transforming labor or "production."[42]

Ironically, the assimilation of "practical" to "productive" activities begun by the Christian Schoolmen was carried by Karl Marx to its logical conclusion. For Marx *praxis* becomes synonymous with material and thence mental "production." "Men," says Marx, "begin to distinguish themselves from animals as soon as they begin to *produce* [*produzieren*] their means of subsistence," and their "mode of life" is determined or shaped (*bedingt*) by the requirements of material production. "What they are, therefore, coincides with their production, both with *what* they produce and with *how* they produce. The nature of individuals thus depends on the material conditions determining their production."[43] In the course of producing their material means of subsistence men unwittingly "produce" conceptions or ideas, e.g., political theories, laws, morality, religion and metaphysics—"ideologies," in short—which serve to explain and justify successive social formations as natural, normal, and necessary.[44] The ideology of primitive producers assumes the form of "natural religion," or nature-worship, in which the powers of nature are personified as alien divinities, whimsical, capricious, and cruel. Like Vico's *grossi bestioni,* Marx's primitive

[40] Marx and Engels, *The German Ideology* (New York: International Publishers, 1963), p. 7.
[41] *N.S.,* par. 331.
[42] See, e.g., Lobkowicz, op. cit.; Kostas Axelos, *Marx, Penseur de la Technique* (Paris: Editions de Minuit, 1969), esp. chap. 7; Arendt, op. cit., chap. 3; Habermas, op. cit., chap. 1, and his *Knowledge and Human Interests,* trans. Jeremy Shapiro (Boston: Beacon Press, 1971); chap. 3.
[43] Marx and Engels, *The German Ideology,* p. 7.
[44] Ibid., p. 14.

producers stand in awe of an alien nature, which they try to render less alien and more comprehensible by anthropomorphizing it.[45]

Marx's account of primitive ideology bears, at first glance, a striking resemblance to Vico's account of poetic wisdom. On closer inspection, however, the resemblance proves superficial if not illusory. For whereas nature is, in Vico's view, rendered (illusorily) comprehensible by way of anthropomorphic concepts and categories, it is, on Marx's account, rendered *actually* comprehensible. For, as men work to transform nature, it becomes less and less alien to them; they begin, haltingly at first, and later in an almost torrential rush of human invention and technological innovation, to dominate nature, to harness its powers for human ends. Nature ceases to be alien; it becomes "humanized nature." Nature "in itself" (*an sich*) ceases to exist, and is replaced by a humanized nature existing "for man." Nature—and man himself—become at last a human creation, and God is revealed as an outworn and outmoded ideological fiction. The truth, disclosed to human beings as through a glass darkly, though with increasing clarity, is that man is the active subject and nature the passive predicate, the inert material upon which man stamps the unique and unmistakable mark of his own personality (a relationship still obscured, admittedly, under the conditions of capitalist production). In Marx's view "the entire so-called history of the world is nothing but the creation of man through human labor, nothing but the emergence of nature for man, so he has the visible, irrefutable proof of his birth through himself, of the process of his creation."[46] So complete is this humanization of nature, says Marx, that man can no longer be "considered to be distinct from nature. For...nature, the nature that preceded human history, is not by any means the nature in which Feuerbach lives, nor the nature which today no longer exists anywhere (except perhaps on a few Australian coral-islands of recent origin)..."[47]

The Vichian distinction between man and nature, between "human" and "natural" history, is for Marx scarcely more than a convenient figure of speech. Nature can hardly have been created by God, for God does not exist; or rather, He exists only as a human creation, a projection onto the heavens, as it were, of man's heretofore alienated

[45] Ibid., p. 19.

[46] Marx, *Economic and Philosophic Manuscripts of 1844* (New York: International Publishers, 1964), p. 145.

[47] Marx and Engels, *The German Ideology*, p. 37.

powers.[48] As man comes to dominate nature, to remake it in his own image, he becomes increasingly aware of his own human powers, until at last he recognizes that the nature he knows is his own creation. "Man is the supreme being for man."[49] "Naturalism" and "humanism" then become interchangeable expressions, and "natural science" identical with "the science of man." "History itself," says Marx, "is a real [actual, *wirkliche*] part of natural history—of nature developing into man. Natural science will in time incorporate into itself the science of man, just as the science of man will incorporate into itself natural science: there will be *one* science."[50]

The distance between Marx's views and Vico's could hardly be greater. Whatever else he might have been, Marx was surely no Vichian.

[48] An idea borrowed, of course, from Feuerbach. See Ludwig Feuerbach, *Preliminary Theses on the Reform of Philosophy* (1842) in *The Fiery Brook: Selected Writings of Ludwig Feuerbach* (New York: Anchor Books, 1972), pp. 153-73, and *The Essence of Christianity*, trans. George Eliot (New York: Harper & Row, 1957), esp. pp. 274-75

[49] Marx, *Critique of Hegel's "Philosophy of Right,"* trans. Joseph O'Malley (Cambridge: Cambridge University Press, 1970), p. 137.

[50] Marx, *Economic and Philosophic Manuscripts*, p. 143. Marx's remarks should not, however, be interpreted in light of the later—and in many respects antithetical—"unity of science" program propounded by the Logical Positivists, whose views, ironically, are closer to those of Engels than to those advanced by Marx. See my "Marx and Darwin," op. cit., esp. pp. 470-72; and James Farr, "Marx and Positivism," in *After Marx*, eds. Terence Ball and James Farr (forthcoming, 1983).

Man Making History:
The Role of the Plebeians in Vico,
the Proletariat in Marx
Jeffrey Barnouw

"**A**s Vico says, human history differs from natural history in this, that we have made the former, but not the latter." This reference to Vico in a subordinate clause in a footnote to *Capital,* the only mention of him in the writings (other than letters) of Marx, alludes to the passage in the *New Science* where this "truth beyond question" is taken to show that man can gain a knowledge of the "civil world" more certain than his knowledge of nature could ever be. Marx draws on Vico to support his view that the history of technology is the indispensable and assured basis for an understanding of the social development of man.[1]

Without implying that Vico influenced Marx, we may take this allusion as an invitation to explore some correspondences between the two. The present essay will consider the relation between (1) the development of technology, in the broad sense of man's means of coping practically with nature in his collective struggle for life and commodious living—and it is the history of technology in this sense that is the topic of Marx's footnote—and (2) the historical course of class struggle within society as the two principal factors in Vico's and Marx's constructions of human history that led them to claim that man makes his own history.

Bound up with this claim is the further idea that man himself is made through his own practical activity, that he makes himself—indirectly—through history. For both Vico and Marx the idea that man becomes human in the course of, and by means of, history implies (3) a development of the self-awareness of men as makers of the historical world, a growing awareness *in* their participation in society which itself contrib-

---

[1] Karl Marx, *Capital, A Critique of Political Economy,* trans. Samuel Moore and Edward Aveling (New York: Modern Library, n.d.), p. 406. Giambattista Vico, *The New Science,* trans. Thomas G. Bergin and Max H. Fisch, (Ithaca, N.Y.: Cornell University Press, 1968), p. 96, henceforth cited within my text by paragraph number, as here (*N.S.,* par. 331).

utes to and alters the constitution of that world. Progress in the self-consciousness of men as social-practical beings is driven by material pressures impinging on consciousness—in effect, the forces involved in (1) and (2).

Moreover, for Vico as well as for Marx, (1) seems to be understood as largely determining (2). This means that society is seen as the organization of a collective effort to secure life and its enjoyment by coping with and harnessing nature, and that class struggle is a function—and dysfunction—of that social-practical relation to nature. This reading of Marx is not original, nor has it gone uncontested. The present essay is meant to contribute to the interpretation of Marx by calling attention to the similar configuration of ideas in Vico. This may help overcome an unnecessarily narrow understanding of the "technological" dimension of society, which has lent support to an artificial and invidious contrast with social practice considered as "human interaction." Conversely, the comparison with Marx should serve to emphasize the significance of Vico's achievement.

The idea that man makes history and is made by it refers to (1) metabolic interaction with nature through means sustained by society, and (2) interaction between classes that reflect society's specific relation to nature. Both these factors can in turn be seen to promote (3) the growth of men's understanding of their involvement in these social processes. This understanding can affect the character of their involvement and thus the makeup of the social-historical world; and this growth of social self-awareness, finally, is mirrored in the epistemology of such constructions of history.

Not only is the historian able to interpret human history more insightfully than natural history because the former has in some sense been made by men, but also, as Vico, at least, goes on to suggest, (4) the historian, in construing history, makes it. Introducing large-scale conceptual simplifications and stylizations in one's account of—and accounting for—historical developments is fabrication that does not so much falsify as complement and complete man's history-making practice.

The problem of how social or human science is related to ongoing social practice must arise in this context (though it cannot be dealt with here.) Does scientific knowledge of society continue to draw on, and feed back into, civil knowledge, or *prudentia*? Is human science essential to the enlightenment of self-interest, or must social, practical self-awareness grow directly from engagement in one's own partialities and

concerns? Vico and Marx alike seem finally to have concluded overtly
that a science of the civil world cannot take on the role of guiding civil
life.[2]

Across the gap that supposedly preserves the integrity of practice as
well as of theory by keeping them discrete, however, an undeniable
influence is exerted on social reality, at least by Marx's would-be science. The historian's own making of history by construction, in terms of
technological advance, class struggle, social self-awareness, or whatever, is implicated in the practical process of history. I am not concerned
here with the class or party bias that may be intrinsic to any interpretation of history, but rather with the countervailing *parti pris* of the
historian for human solidarity.

What is most deeply problematic about the idea that man is the
maker of history is not the shifting and elusive senses of "making," but
the very notion of "man"—Marx's "we"—since this assumes a universality of reference that is not borne out by "human" history insofar as it
must be read as a story of class struggle. Vico and Marx agree in seeing
class struggle—civil conflict, which should not be taken to mean simply
revolution or civil war—as the means by which man paradoxically
becomes aware of his common humanity. A striking parallel here is that
both thinkers conceive it to be the role of a particular but "universal"
class to make history human, a story whose practical subject is man in a
full sense.

The primary meaning that Vico gives to man's "making history" in
the passage alluded to by Marx is that human institutions derive from
the activity of men and thus must reflect principles present in (but not
to) their minds. An awareness or deliberate intention relevant to the
result need not have been involved originally. Indeed, Vico clearly
implies that the principles were not applied or acted on consciously to
begin with, but are nonetheless accessible to the historian in his own
mind, to draw on in interpreting what has resulted from past activity.
The Vichian historian seeks to understand customs, institutions, and
laws by construing their origins as responses to situations of necessity or
utility, taking into account the historical and thus changing character of
conceptions and perceptions of need and use. This reference to practi-

[2] I discuss this with respect to Vico in "The Critique of Classical Republicanism and the
Understanding of Modern Forms of Polity in Vico's *New Science*," *Clio,* 9 (1980): 393-418, and
in a review of *Giambattista Vico's Science of Humanity,* ed. Giorgio Tagliacozzo and Donald
Phillip Verene, in *Eighteenth-Century Studies,* X, 3, (Spring 1977): 384-88, particularly regarding Vico's fragment, "Pratica."

cal constraints is crucial to what I have called "Vico's pragmatist construction of human history."[3]

Vico's approach thus both stresses an historical "primacy of the practical" (in a sense quite different from Kant's ethical conception) and recognizes that thinking and acting practically only became possible through a long disciplining of the human mind in collective (and often socially antagonistic) experience. Marx's reference to Vico appears in the context of an argument that is akin to Vico's orientation. In the footnote Marx points to the need for a critical history of technology and to the incentive provided by Darwin's idea of a "history of natural technology," that is, the formation of organs of plants and animals as the productive instruments that sustain their life. Would not a history of the formation of the productive organs of social man, "the material basis of all particular social organization," be as worthy of attention? Marx asks rhetorically. Would it not also be easier to provide than the history of natural technology? he adds, citing Vico's idea that we ourselves have made human history.

As Marx continues, it is clear that the making involves technology, but it is not clear just how. "Technology reveals man's relation (*Verhalten*) to nature, the immediate productive process of his life, and thus also of his social conditions of life [*gesellschaftlichen Lebensverhältnisse*] and the intellectual ideas that flow from them." The key to "the sole materialist and therefore scientific method" is to trace intellectual and ideological forms in their derivation from "this material basis" as articulated in the "real conditions of life."[4]

Technology is apparently a key element and thus an index of the state of "productive forces" in a society, which ultimately determine its "production relations" (including class relations), as Marx suggested in striking terms in the *Poverty of Philosophy:* "Social relations are intimately bound up with productive forces. In acquiring new productive forces men change their mode of production; and in changing their mode of production, their manner of making a living, they change all their social relations. The windmill gives you society with the feudal lord; the steam mill, with the industrial capitalist."[5] This concluding

---

[3] Jeffrey Barnouw, "The Relation between the Certain and the True in Vico's Pragmatist Construction of Human History," *Comparative Literature Studies,* 15 (1978): 242-64.

[4] *Capital,* p. 406. I have altered the translation somewhat. Cf. *Das Kapital,* Marx-Engels *Werke,* vol. 23 (Berlin: Dietz, 1962), pp. 392-93.

[5] *Writings of the Young Marx on Philosophy and Society,* ed. and trans. Loyd D. Easton and Kurt H. Guddat (New York: Anchor, 1967), p. 480. Cited below as "*Writings.*"

encapsulation, with its drastic oversimplification, may seem to deprive all social efforts toward change, and particularly class struggle, of any real significance. Interpreters who stress the importance of class struggle in Marx's view of history are therefore often inclined to minimize or deny what they see as technological determinism. But as G. A. Cohen, one of the most recent and thoroughgoing exponents of "a 'technological' interpretation of historical materialism,"[6] has argued, the explanatory power of "class struggle" is limited in that the strength and success of a particular class at a given time depends on the character of the productive forces at that point. The class that prevails in each case is that best fitted "to preside over the development of the productive forces at the given time," Cohen writes, adding, "Hence Marx frequently allows that a dominant class promotes not only its own interests but, in so doing, those of humanity at large—until its rule becomes outmoded, and it becomes reactionary—and he gives no explanation of class supremacy which is not founded on the productive needs of the relevant age."[7]

To place class struggle within the context of the development of productive forces, which after all are social human powers, is not to deny its significance but to understand it more fully. For Marx class struggle is the indispensable means of breaking through production relations that have come to hamper the development of human productive forces: "the historical development of the antagonisms, immanent in a given form of production, is the only way in which that form of production can be dissolved and a new form established."[8]

The particular historical role that Marx claims for the proletariat must be looked at in this light. But we will turn first to Vico, in order to see how his conception of human history as determined by necessity and utility—that is, first by primitive mythopoeic perceptions of need and use—is linked to his understanding of the importance of class

---

[6] G. A. Cohen, *Karl Marx's Theory of History. A Defence* (Princeton: Princeton University Press, 1978), p. 29, cf. chap. vi *passim*. In the 1890s Georges Sorel brought Vico and Marx together, or rather treated them in parallel, in terms of an approach "positing technology as the foundation of all conceivable ideologies," in "Etude sur Vico," *Devenir Social,* 2 (1896): 785-817, p. 813, as quoted in James H. Meisel, *The Genesis of Georges Sorel* (Ann Arbor, Mich.: George Wahr, 1951), p. 69, cf. 68-75. Sorel overemphasizes Vico's cyclism, which he rejects, at least until his syndicalist period, when he embraces it as a catastrophic primitivism, a *ricorso* from bourgeois decadence. Sorel embraced "a new barbarism" in Vico's name, and Marx's as well!

[7] Cohen, *Karl Marx's Theory of History,* p. 149.

[8] Quoted from *Capital* in Cohen, p. 146.

struggle in the history of man. At the same time we will have to attend to the role of the historian who makes history significant by reading it in terms of such conceptions.

The Role of the Plebeians in Vico

Vico understands "humanity" in one sense as a character of civil life arising in and through history, but he also maintains that the historian can somehow span the entire development and enter to some extent into the minds of the primitive "heroes" who preceded and then resisted the coming of the age of "men." A psychological affinity that links the historian with the pre- "human" underlies—i.e., is an even more fundamental premise than—the hypothesis of an heroic age in which strictly human modes of thought and motivation had not yet arisen. On the one hand, then, Vico takes "human" in an ideal-typical (if not historical-teleological) sense, as the third stage of a schema of development that outlines how man made himself through civil institutions, while on the other hand he takes "human" in an implicitly normative sense that cannot be seen as exhaustively exemplified in past history, and which exerts its own pressure in his treatment of developments within the "age of men" and particularly its modern European version.[9]

The certainty of historical and civil knowledge that derives from man's making history himself depends on this psychological continuity of humanity in the larger sense that embraces the historian and the hero. In the passage Marx alludes to, Vico expresses amazement "that the philosophers should have bent all their energies to the study of the world of nature, which, since God made it, He alone knows; and that they should have neglected the study of the world of nations, or civil world, which, since men had made it, men could come to know" (*N.S.*, par. 331). In a closely following passage, however, Vico extends the idea of "making history" by taking the constructive procedure of the natural scientist as a model for his own approach.

The first indubitable principle posited above [*N.S.*, par. 331] is that this world of nations has certainly been made by men, and its guise must therefore be found within the modifications of our

[9] See the essay cited in note 2 above. In his introduction to *The New Science* p. xix, Fisch points out that a lost early draft seems to have borne the title *New Science concerning the Principles of Humanity*.

own human mind. And history cannot be more certain than when
he who creates the things also narrates them. Now, as geometry,
when it constructs the world of quantity out of its elements, or
contemplates that world, is creating it for itself, just so does our
Science. (*N.S.*, par. 349)

The rationality or truth of natural science, as Vico had argued in his
earlier work *De antiquissima Italorum sapientia,* was achieved through the
introduction of man-made fictions such as the dimensionless point in
the mathematical construction of nature as a system of laws.[10] In the
New Science it is by interpreting civil development in terms of an "ideal
eternal history" that man is to gain demonstrative knowledge of the
man-made world. Bringing to full awareness the unintended achievement of early anonymous founders of institutions, it is the historian
who makes history by construing it rationally.

For Vico there is no tension between understanding institutions in
the light of the modifications of our own human mind and explaining
them in terms of the ideal eternal history, since these procedures are
intimately related parts of a single method.[11] The ideal eternal history
provides the framework for analyzing the parallel development of civil
society in different nations. It is a grandiose abduction that could not
have been arrived at by induction, yet can be refined and elaborated by
many partial insights at various points through empirical study of
institutions, and Vico evidently thinks of it as being verified by the sense
it makes of particular relations and situations in civil history.[12]

The core of the ideal eternal history consists in the (in some sense
necessary) transition from the heroic to the human age and the continuation of the same social (and increasingly political) process within
the age of men in the form of class struggle between the patricians and
the plebeians. An epitome of Vico's overall conception of his historical
process can be found in his view of Solon, largely arrived at by analogi-
cal inference from Roman history to Greek. "Solon must have been a
sage of vulgar [as opposed to learned, conceptually articulate] wisdom,
party leader of the plebs in the first times of the aristocratic commonwealth at Athens,...unless, indeed, Solon was [a poetic character stand-

---

[10] Cf. Jeffrey Barnouw, "Vico and the Continuity of Science: The Relation of His Epistemology to Bacon and Hobbes," *Isis,* 71 (1980): 609-20.

[11] See *N.S.*, pars. 342, 347-48, 374. Cf. the essay cited in note 3 above.

[12] See *N.S.*, par. 114, which should be referred back to *N.S.*, par. 105, the paragraph taken
as a point of departure in the essay cited in note 2 above.

ing for] the Athenian plebeians themselves" (*N.S.*, par. 414). The basis of this assertion seems to be the association of Solon with the maxim "Know thyself" (cf. *N.S.* 416, 424). Its meaning for the plebeians in the primitive aristocratic Athenian commonwealth exemplifies what "was universally the case in all the heroic commonwealths":

> The heroes or nobles, by a certain nature of theirs which they believed to be of divine origin, were led to say that the gods belonged to them, and consequently that the auspices of the gods were theirs also. By means of the auspices they kept within their own orders all the public and private institutions of the heroic cities. To the plebeians, whom they believed to be of bestial origin and consequently men without gods and hence without auspices, they conceded the use of natural liberty.... Solon, however, had admonished the plebeians to reflect upon themselves and to realize that they were of like human nature with the nobles and should therefore be made equal with them in civil rights. (*N.S.*, par. 414)

In connecting the admonition "Know thyself," taken as a generic social and human self-recognition, with a "poetic character," or imaginative universal who stands for the plebeians themselves, Vico nicely suggests the nonconscious nature of their urge for equality. In his interpretations of Roman history Vico avoids any suggestion that the plebeians were or could have been motivated by an explicit ideal of equality or understanding of rights. As we shall see, it was precisely pursuit of the particulars at stake in the class struggle at each stage that led to the opening up of consciousness. The very conception of law and the awareness of a universal human nature were by-products of conflicts over privilege and prerogative.

In the scope of a short essay it would be impossible to trace in any detail what is in effect one of the three or four major themes of the *New Science*: the development of law from primitive, punctilious particularity ("the certain") to open-minded, flexible universality ("the true"),[13] which is at the same time the story of the class struggle between patricians (originally the "heroes") and plebeians (the "humans," first in a derogatory sense.) But it is important in the present context to recognize how this class struggle is related to the even broader perspec-

---

[13] See the essays cited in notes 2 and 3 above.

tive of man's struggle with nature to secure the basis of life and eventually of civil and civilized life.

Vico sees the city as emerging from the cultivation of land, *urbs* originally meaning the curved moldboard of the plough (*N.S.*, par. 16). Ploughed lands were thus the first altars (*N.S.*, par. 15), tended by nobles who had descended from the gods.

> To these altars then, the impious-nomadic-weak, fleeing for their lives from the stronger ["godless" wanderers, i.e., "Hobbes's violent men" (*N.S.*, par. 553, cf. par. 179)], came seeking refuge, and the pious-strong killed the violent among them and took the weak under their protection. Since the latter brought with them nothing but their lives, they were accepted as *famuli* and given the means of sustaining life. The family took its name principally from these *famuli*, whose status roughly approximated that of the slaves who came later with the taking of prisoners in war. (*N.S.*, par. 18)

Vico writes that with this arrangement "divine providence ordered human institutions" according to the principle "that, in commonwealths, those who use their minds should command and those who use their bodies should obey" (*N.S.* 18). But the effect of civil institutions is in part discipline and development of the use of the mind.

Already the granting of asylum to the *famuli* was implicitly a sort of contract, one of submission, but the *famuli* achieved tenuous recognized status through the agrarian contests in which they mutinied and laid claim to the lands they worked. The nobles, "to content the revolting bands of *famuli* and reduce them to obedience, granted them an agrarian law, which is found to have been the first civil law born in the world" (*N.S.*, par. 25). It is crucial to understand what constrained the nobles to this concession. "Because they had need of others to serve them," Vico explains, "by a common sense of utility the heroes were constrained to satisfy the multitude of their rebellious clients" (*N.S.*, par. 597).

Vico suggests that the force of the revolt imposed a "necessity" on "the heroic fathers in the state of families, as a result of which the commonwealths were born" (*N.S.*, par. 583), but this is in line with his idea that the strong only "yield, from necessity or for utility, as little as they can and bit by bit" (*N.S.*, par. 261). This commonwealth marks the beginning of fiefs and a feudal system based on a mixture of domination and mutual benefit. It is the labor power of the *clientes* or *famuli* that makes them necessary to their masters, whose "common sense of utility" leads them to grant natural or "bonitary" ownership of the lands to their serfs, while retaining civil or "quiritary" ownership for themselves.

> This law was dictated by the following natural law of the *gentes*: since ownership follows power, and since the lives of the *famuli* were dependent on the heroes who had saved them by granting them asylum, it was lawful and right that they should have a similarly precarious ownership, which they might enjoy as long as it suited the heroes to maintain them in possession of the fields they had assigned to them. Thus the *famuli* merged to form the first plebs of the heroic cities, in which they had none of the privileges of citizenship. (*N.S.*, par. 597).

Lacking written language, this first civil order was founded not on statutory law but on feudal custom, and "fiefs were the first origins of all the laws that grew up later among all nations both ancient and modern" (*N.S.*, par. 67, cf. 262f.). The status of the *famuli*, or first plebeians, was only secured by "the natural obligations said to be *de iure naturali gentium* [according to the natural law of the *gentes*], which Ulpian further specified as *humanarum*" (*N.S.*, par. 582), "human," that is, "as distinguished from that of the barbarous *gentes* that had preceded them," but also in contrast to the (in a laudatory sense) inhuman rigors of the heroic civil law reserved for the patricians.

As the weak *socii* of the heroes, "the second comers, since they came out of a necessity of saving their lives, gave a beginning to society in the proper sense, with a view principally to utility, and consequently base and servile" (*N.S.*, par. 555). Here Vico characterizes the humans from the noble point of view, ironically anticipating, in different ways, Hegel, Nietzsche, and Hannah Arendt, with an undercurrent of solidarity with the perspective of base utility that the later thinkers did not share. But by attending to the crucial function of labor, of servile engagement with necessity, one might project an ideal lineage from Vico, through Hegel's dialectic of master and slave in the *Phenomenology*, to Marx.

After the plebs themselves had gained quiritary ownership of their fields in the second agrarian law, which was conceded by the nobles in the Law of the Twelve Tables (*N.S.*, par. 598), a further stage in their class struggle was reached with the conflict over the *connubium*, or right of marriage. Vico's interpretation of this turning point, which differed materially from his Roman sources such as Livy, has not been accepted by later scholarship. At the beginning of Book IV Livy dramatizes what was at stake in the *Lex Canuleia* (445 B.C.) as the legalization of intermarriage between the nobility and the commons, which the senatorial party objected to because it would lead to contamination of noble blood and loss of noble privilege, particularly the hereditary right of "taking the auspices."

Vico reconstructs the issue rather as a plebeian claim to the same right of marriage recognized by law and religion that the nobles already enjoyed. He says the plebeians had come to realize that civil ownership of land was of limited value where it could not be passed on to heirs, and heirs were only possible where marriage had legal status and fatherhood was officially ascertained (*N.S.*, pars. 110, 567, 587, 598).[14] A by-product was that, in participating in the marriage rites, the plebeians would break the noble monopoly of the auspices which were the source of all Roman law, private and public. "Then, in the course of human desires, the plebeians went on to secure from the fathers the communication of all those institutions of private law which depended upon the auspices" (*N.S.*, par. 110).

The struggle over the *connubium* exemplifies Vico's point that the axiom, "the weak want laws; the powerful withhold them," "is the torch of the heroic contests in the aristocratic commonwealths, in which the nobles want to keep the laws a secret monopoly of their order" (*N.S.*, pars. 283-4). In breaking through the privacy of "law" maintained as privilege, the plebeians in effect, though not in conscious intent, opened the way for the development of law in the strict sense—i.e., law that must be both accessible and the same for all. This progress was implicit in the plebeian acquisition of civil ownership of land, since that could not depend on the (good) will of the nobles. "For, as long as the nobles retained the royal power of taking them back again, the ownership could not continue certain unless the law granting it was fixed eternally on a public tablet, determining the rights that had been uncertain and making manifest those that had been secret" (*N.S.*, par. 612). This public determination of the laws removed them from the

---

[14] The *Oxford Classical Dictionary* (Oxford: Clarendon Press, 1968), p. 163, art. 'Canuleius,' includes a hint of Vico's version together with Livy's: "*Lex Canuleia*...allowed intermarriage between patricians and plebeians, probably by recognizing the legitimacy of children of plebeian mothers..."

essentially arbitrary sphere of what was "certain" in the rigid noble code.

The plebeians continue here to be motivated by perceptions of their own utility. They are no more capable of a conception of abstract or common good at this stage than the patricians (whose "res publica" is, as Vico argues,[15] the crassest of private interests, which seems objective only to primitive minds still incapable of universals). But the pressure the plebs exert to share in noble rights and in the nobles' access to the "law" leads finally, with the Publilian Law (339 B.C.), to the transformation of the commonwealth from an aristocratic to a popular constitution (*N.S.*, pars. 104, 112-3, 612).

This means that law must be laid down in "human language using words agreed upon by the people,...a language whereby the people may fix the meaning of the laws by which the nobles as well as the plebs are bound" (*N.S.* 32). Such law is the formal guarantee of equality. "In virtue of this sovereignty over languages and letters, the free peoples must also be masters of their laws, for they impose on the laws the senses in which they constrain the powerful to observe them, even against their will" (*N.S.*, par. 936, cf. par. 953). In this way the plebeians bring themselves, and constrain the patricians, to a recognition of their common humanity.

One could say, though Vico does not use such terms of providential purpose here, that it was the historical role of the plebeians, in their class struggle with the patricians, to bring about "human governments, in which, in virtue of the equality of the intelligent nature which is the proper nature of man, all are accounted equal under the law" (*N.S.*, par. 927). Vico treats this practical problem of the universality of human nature, or equality of man, mainly with reference to the classical world and only occasional allusions to European feudalism. He seems to have regarded aristocracy as economically vestigial and does not anticipate the emergence of a modern plebeian class. But his treatment of classical class struggle prefigures, in several ways, Marx's idea of the proletariat.

The Role of the Proletariat in Marx

The concept of the proletariat is introduced into Marx's universe of discourse in the conclusion of his 1843 article, "Toward the Critique of

---

[15] See the essay cited in note 2 above.

Hegel's Philosophy of Law: Introduction." He is arguing that in the
German social and economic context what is utopian is not "radical
revolution, universal human emancipation," but rather "the partial,
the merely political revolution" in which part of civil society would
emancipate itself and attain universal supremacy and then undertake
the emancipation of the whole "but only on the condition that the whole
of society is in the same position as this class, for example, that it has or
can easily acquire money and education."[16]

This latter stipulation is ironical, its point aimed back at the bourgeoisie, which Marx sees as having missed its moment to play a revolutionary role in Germany. "No class in civil society can take this role
without arousing an impulse of enthusiasm in itself and in the masses,
an impulse in which it fraternizes and merges with society at large,
identifies itself with it, and is experienced and recognized as its *general
representative*." German society has still not reached the stage of development of the French in 1789, but the economic ascendancy of the
middle class is such that it necessarily creates an antagonist that can act
as a universal class, because social oppression has been concentrated in
it. The positive possibility of German emancipation lies "in the formation of a class with radical chains,...a class that is the dissolution of all
classes,...a sphere that can invoke no traditional title but only a human
title,...the proletariat."

The working class appears here like a deus ex machina to resolve the
impasse of German philosophy as well as of German society. "As philosophy finds its *material* weapons in the proletariat, the proletariat finds
its *intellectual* weapons in philosophy.... Philosophy cannot be actualized without the transcendence of the proletariat, the proletariat
cannot be transcended without the actualization of philosophy."[17]
Revolution is to be made possible by the enlightenment of the people
and must be "based on the theory proclaiming that man is the highest
essence of man."

Nothing, it would seem, could be farther from Vico's tendency to see
not only enlightenment but social emancipation as byproducts emerging from class struggle that is motivated by practical necessity and
particular goals. Marx's treatment of these ideas in 1843 is influenced,
however, by his use of France as a foil to "show up" Germany. In France
every class is "politically idealistic and experiences itself first of all not

[16] *Writings*, p. 260. I omit most of Marx's frequent typographical emphases.
[17] Ibid., pp. 263-64.

as a particular class but as representing the general needs of society," whereas in Germany no class "has any need or capacity for general emancipation until it is forced to it by its immediate condition, by material necessity."[18] This sarcastic and scornful view of the peculiarly German situation will gradually become the general model of revolutionary motivation for Marx, absorbing and giving a new function to its opposite, as Marx grows both more skeptical of and historically insightful about "politically idealistic" pretensions or assumptions concerning "the general good."

In *The German Ideology* (1845-46) a distinctly different argument is made: "that every class striving to gain control [*Herrschaft*]—even when such control means the transcendence of the entire old form of society and of control itself—must first win political power in order to represent its interest in turn as the universal interest." The claim to objectivity is now clearly seen as masking "real struggles between the different classes."[19] The appearance of representing the common good is in turn needed for the newly ruling class to achieve its own interest: "Each new class which displaces the one previously dominant is forced, simply to be able to carry out its aim, to represent its interest as the common interest of all members of society."[20]

In each successive cycle, what seemed the common good to revolutionary enthusiasm turns out to be a class interest, but this does not mean that it was originally projected hypocritically or cynically, as a gloss on the preceding generalization suggests: "the illusion of *common* interests (in the beginning this illusion is true)." Rather, the shift of perspective from general to particular, from shared concerns to divisive ones, is built into the historical dynamic of revolution. It is only the logic of their social and economic situation that makes the case of the proletariat different in this respect. Their universality as a class is based in the presumptive circumstance that in revolution they will transcend the status of a class, that they will necessarily overcome class society.

Already the notion of "radical chains" points in a different direction from that of the overt argument of the 1843 essay. It may be, as Shlomo Avineri has suggested, that Marx originally wanted to supplant Hegel's candidate for "universal class," the bureaucracy that supposedly stood

[18] Ibid., p. 262.
[19] Ibid., p. 425.
[20] Ibid., p. 439.

for the universality of the state, itself an embodiment of "the good of the whole," over against the divisive partial interests that characterize society.[21] But this negative pedigree hardly accounts for the historical role that is assumed by the proletariat in Marx, which is to lead *through* the clash of interests and beyond it rather than rising above and containing it.

The Feuerbachian theory of man as the highest essence of man, which was to provide the intellectual foundation and weapon of proletarian revolution in 1843, is significantly transformed in the following year through Marx's turn to radical economic theory. Man's "essence" is now recognized as being what he has made and can make of himself, by his labor, in and through society and history. In the "Economic and Philosophic Manuscripts" Marx writes, "the entire so-called world history is only the creation of man through human labor and the development [*das Werden*] of nature for man," a proof of man's self-production and consequently of "the essentiality [*Wesenhaftigkeit,* "autonomous substantiality"] of man in nature," which dispels the alienated and alienating notion of "an alien being or essence beyond man and nature."[22]

Human nature is acquired over countless generations in practical interaction with a natural world that in a sense is made by human labor in the same process. "This production is his active species-life. Through it nature appears as his work and his actuality. The object of labor is thus the objectification of man's species-life: he produces himself not only intellectually, as in consciousness, but also actively in a real sense and sees himself in a world he made."[23] It is in the context of this idea of the social and historical self-creation of man through labor

---

[21] Shlomo Avineri, *The Social and Political Thought of Karl Marx* (Cambridge: Cambridge University Press, 1971), chap. 2.

[22] *Writings,* p. 314. The translation unaccountably has "essential dependence" for *Wesenhaftigkeit.*

[23] Ibid., p. 295. Cf. p. 309, "...not only the five senses but also the so-called spiritual and moral senses (will, love, etc.) in a word, *human* sense and the humanity of the senses come into being only through the existence of *their* object, through nature *humanized.* The development of the five senses is a labor of the whole previous history of the world." For Vico's view of the physical self-making of man see *N.S.,* pars. 367-68, 520, 524, and 692. In Marx see too the critique and conversion of Hegel's alleged view of labor as the essence of man, *Writings,* pp. 322, 324-25, 327. Joseph J. O'Malley, "History and Man's 'Nature' in Marx," in *Marx's Socialism* ed. Schlomo Avineri (New York: Atherton, 1973), pp. 80-100, pp. 84-5, quotes this from *Capital:* "By acting on the external world [*die Natur auBer ihm*] and changing it, [man] at the same time changes his own nature. He develops his slumbering powers and compels them to act in obedience to his sway."

that Marx now analyzes the radical chains of the proletariat in terms of "alienated labor." It is only in *The Germany Ideology,* however, that Marx considers the relation of class struggle to man's struggle with nature.

In a passage from the opening section which anticipates the terms of the foonote in *Capital* where Vico is mentioned, the science of history is claimed to be the only science. "It can be divided into the history of nature and that of man. The two sides, however, are not to be seen as independent entities."[24] The interaction of man and nature, most often simply excluded from human history, thereby encouraging the misleading opposition of nature and history, is rather to be taken as the persisting basis of human history.[25]

Men first distinguished themselves from animals by beginning "to produce their means of subsistence," and from then on what they are "coincides with what they produce and how they produce." This means that

the entire internal structure of the nation itself depends on the stage of development achieved by its production and its domestic and international commerce. How far the productive forces of a nation are developed is shown most evidently by the degree to which the division of labor has been developed....The different stages of development in the division of labor are just so many different forms of ownership.[26]

The German Ideology goes on to provide a capsule history of forms of ownership, from tribal through communal and state and then estate (or feudal) ownership to private property, an outline that shows notable correspondences with Vico's views.

The basic premise of this history of property relations is that "the social structure and the state continually evolve out of the life-process [*Lebensprozess*] of definite individuals,...as they work, produce materially, and act under definite material limitations, presuppositions, and conditions independent of their will."[27] Class divisions and class struggle are

[24] *Writings,* p. 408.
[25] Ibid., pp. 432-33. For a divergent view see Bernard Gendron, "Marx and the Technological Theory of History," *The Philosophical Forum,* VI, 4, (Summer 1975): 397-421. Opposition to the "technological theory" often depends on too narrow a construction of "technology."
[26]*Writings,* p. 410.
[27] Ibid., pp. 413-4.

expressions of tensions in the social production of the means of living, and they also provide a way, as we shall see, for society to change the forms governing its own sustenance and reproduction.

This *Lebensprozess* links natural history with human history. "Real, positive science" is simply the presentation (*Darstellung*) of this life-process in which men both take on and create particular social and cultural forms. The positivity or objectivity of science is not gained through abstraction from practical aims or interests. Marx rather emphasizes its involvement in the historical life-process: it is not presuppositionless, but takes the real conditions of production and development as its premises.[28] Science cannot be conceived as relating to an independent, unchanging reality because the world surrounding man

> is not something directly given and the same from all eternity but the product of industry and of the state of society in the sense that it is a historical product, the result of the activity of a whole succession of generations, each standing on the shoulders of the preceding one, developing further its industry and commerce, and modifying its social order according to changed needs. Even the objects of the simplest "sensuous certainty" are given to him only through social development, industry, and commercial relationships.[29]

The emergence of the proletariat as "a class which has to bear all the burdens of society without enjoying its advantages," and which in virtue of this situation becomes the potential agent of emancipation for society as a whole, is presented here as a conclusion from "the conception of history" sketched above.[30] "This conception of history depends on setting forth the real process of production, starting from the material production of unreflective [*unmittelbaren*] life, and to comprehend the form of interaction [or commerce (*Verkehr*)] connected with this and created by this mode of production...as the basis of all history."[31]

The particular terms of the social historical life-process determine the "role" of the proletariat. The communist revolution is not another

---

[28] Ibid., p. 415.
[29] Ibid., p. 417.
[30] Ibid., p. 430.
[31] Ibid., p. 431, translation altered.

redistribution in the division of labor; on the contrary, it is necessarily "directed against the preceding mode of activity, does away with labor," in the sense of alienated labor, "and abolishes class rule along with the classes themselves, because it is accomplished by the class which society no longer recognizes as a class."[32]

This must be understood as a revolution of society itself, allowing the productive forces to expand beyond the limits imposed by private property and class division. Not only does the revolution depend essentially on material preconditions, without which the propagation of revolutionary ideas is immaterial; the revolution is moreover a liberation *through* and *of* technology and productivity: "slavery cannot be abolished without the steam engine and the spinning jenny.... 'Liberation' is a historical and not a mental act. It is effected by historical conditions, by the development of industry, commerce, agriculture, transportation."[33]

The dynamism of civil development seems to derive, for Marx, from its core in technology: "That kind of labor which from the beginning required a machine...turned out to be most capable of development."[34] It is only this dynamism of productive forces—recognized as human powers—that is capable of breaking through the class structures and restrictive production relations of bourgeois capitalism. Here a fundamental conception of Marxism is enunciated: revolutions result from the "contradiction between the productive forces and the form of interaction."[35] (From another angle this means: "No antagonism, no progress.... Till now the productive forces have been developed by virtue of this system of class antagonisms."[36])

[32] Ibid., p. 432. The polemic thrust against the young-Hegelian claims for the revolutionary role of self-consciousness should not obscure the fact that the role of the proletariat involves consciousness of their situation, i.e., of their misery and its cause and remedy, though not in the form of a theory of history.

[33] Ibid., p. 437. The manuscript breaks off after "transportation."

[34] Ibid., p. 447.

[35] Ibid., p. 454. The term "form of interaction" (*Verkehrsform*) is later replaced in Marx's technical vocabulary by "relations of production" (*Produktionsverhältnisse*).

[36] Marx sees this as "the law that civilization [i.e., the advance of human culture] has followed up to our days"—quoted from *The Poverty of Philosophy* in J. B. Sanderson, *An Interpretation of the Political Ideas of Marx and Engels* (London: Longmans, Green, 1969), p. 27. Sanderson also quotes on p. 22 a passage (from the paragraph used as a motto and focus by Cohen, see notes 6 and 7 above,) from *Preface to the Critique of Political Economy:* "No social order ever perishes before all the productive forces for which there is room in it have developed; and new, higher relations of production never appear before the material conditions of their existence have matured in the womb of the old society itself." In the same vein Cohen, p. 146, cites the maxim from *Capital:* "the historical development of the antagonisms, immanent in a given form of production, is the only way in which that form of production can be dissolved and a new form established."

This fundamental contradiction at the same time assumes "second-ary forms" (*Nebengestalten*), including "collisions of various classes." "From a narrow point of view one can isolate one of these secondary forms and consider it the basis of these revolutions,"[37] but this only perpetuates illusions arising from the limited perspectives of historical agents themselves. Marx's basic position that "all collisions in history"—including the struggle of the proletariat with bourgeois capitalism—"have their origin in the contradiction between the productive forces and [prevailing production relations]," in effect makes class conflict a vehicle for the radical structural adaptations of "man's" metabolic relations with nature.

As a complement to the conception of alienated labor or the "radical chains" of the proletariat, it is implicit in Marx's conception of the proletariat as a "universal class" that its capacity to represent human society derives positively from its immersion in production, for if any-thing could be said to constitute the transhistorical essence of man for Marx, it is need and productivity.[38] Without this positive sense of the meaning of (nonalienated) labor for human fulfillment, it would make little sense to claim that in the emancipation of the proletariat "is contained universal human emancipation."[39]

To those who would argue that this projects a demeaning view of man, the mature Marx provided an answer in a passage where he first grants that "the ancient conception, in which man always appears...as the aim of production, seems very much more exalted than the modern world, in which production is the aim of man and wealth the aim of production," and then responds,

> In fact, however, when the narrow bourgeois form has been peeled away, what is wealth, if not the universality of needs, capacities, enjoyments, productive powers etc., of individuals, produced in universal exchange? What, if not the full develop-ment of human control over the forces of nature—those of his own nature as well as those of so-called "nature"? What, if not the absolute elaboration of his creative dispositions, without any pre-conditions other than antecedent historical evolution—i.e., the

[37] *Writings*, p. 454. "Narrow" is less derogatory than the original *borniert*.

[38] See the essay by O'Malley cited in note 23 above.

[39] *Writings*, p. 299. See also the utopian anthropology of freely productive man, rich in the wealth and quality of his needs, ibid., pp. 308, 312, 325-26.

evolution of all human powers as such, unmeasured by any previously established yardstick—an end in itself?[40]

From *The German Ideology* on, Marx, like Vico in 1744 and earlier, maintained a conception of the dynamics of class struggle and in particular of the 'role' in history of the respective lower class, the working class, that took its meaning from its position in a larger view of man making himself and his world through his own labor, at first indirectly and inadvertently, but then with increasing awareness and—conceivably—with correspondingly greater control and responsibility.

Vico was understandably more cautious in his references to the conditions of his contemporary world, which on the whole he did not regard as in need of political or social revolution. The 'last recourse' of providence faced with an "ultimate civil disease" shows a drastic logic vaguely akin to the 'radical chains' model of revolution in Marx. But this is not a correlation I would like to make. Marx's idea of the (socioeconomic) historical necessity of proletarian revolution has the weakness of a 'worst case' hypothesis where other courses of historical development are clearly conceivable, while in Vico the *ricorso* from the barbarism of reflection is only the most extreme of three alternative paths that history could take, and it has been given undue importance in the secondary literature.[41]

What has been underestimated, and what this essay has concentrated on, is the vivid sense, common to Vico and Marx, of civil history as the open-ended realization of human potentialities, in which need and use, or labor and productivity, are of fundamental importance. The division and conflict of classes is an aspect of this history that they both did much to illuminate. But whether such conflict was seen as feeding into civil evolution or erupting in revolution, its ultimate fruits were claimed, by the theories of Vico and Marx, for society as a whole, for man.

---

[40] *Pre-Capitalist Economic Formations,* trans. Jack Cohen (New York: International Publishers, 1965), pp. 84-85. This text is a section of the *Grundrisse.*

[41] *N.S.,* pars. 1103-6, and see the essay cited in note 2 above, pp. 410-14.

The Question of Materialism in Vico and Marx

George L. Kline

I

This essay is in part an attempt to remove a common, but baseless assumption—namely, that as ontologists Vico the "idealist" is to be contrasted to Marx the "materialist." I do not deny that Vico's ontology is, in a suitably qualified sense, idealistic. But I find it to be closer to Hegel's "objective" idealism than to either the "subjective" idealism of Berkeley or the "transcendental" idealism of Kant.

I do deny, however, that Marx, even the youngest Marx, was a philosophical materialist, i.e., a thinker who develops or defends a materialist ontology, asserting the ontological primacy of matter and explaining whatever appears to be nonmaterial (thoughts, feelings, values, ideals, structures, laws) as manifestations, functions, or relational properties of "matter in motion." I do not, of course, deny that *Engels*—as well as Plekhanov, Lenin, and all contemporary Marxist-Leninists—were and are philosophical materialists, that they developed, or at least defended, a materialist ontology. But I reject their unanimous claim that in so doing they were following *Marx's* ontological lead.

Furthermore, I do not deny that Marx's own theory of social structure and historical development lays central stress upon economic factors. I do deny that the theoretical priority of "the economic" entails, or supports, a materialist ontology. But I recognize that the claimed linkage of economism and philosophical materialism is given a certain surface plausibility by Marx's own careless usage of the ambiguous adjective *materiell* ('material').

II

In the *De antiquissima Italorum sapientia* Vico makes a sweeping and surprising claim: "All the errors in philosophy spring from [the use of] homonyms or, in common language, equivocal terms" (*Omnes in philosophia errores ab homonymis, vulga aequivocis, nascuntur*). He goes on to define 'equivocal terms' concisely as "words common [i.e., applicable] to more than one thing" (*voces pluribus rebus communes*).[1] Vico's own examples are not overly convincing, partly because none of them involves a categoreal term.[2] Thus he points out that the Latin adjective *certum* has two distinct meanings: (1) *exploratum* ('tested', 'secure') or *indubium* ('undoubted', 'indubitable'), and (2) *peculiare* ('particular') (I, 147). In fact, the English term 'certain' behaves much like the Latin *certum:* We may refer to proofs or claims as 'certain', i.e., 'secure, tested, indubitable', but also to 'certain (i.e., 'particular') proofs or claims'. It seems unlikely, however, that the surface ambiguity of *certum* and other terms of the same type has generated much philosophical confusion.

Although Vico's charge is surely overstated, he has put his finger on an important and insufficiently noted source of philosophical misunderstanding. *Marx's* terminological equivocations have caused untold hermeneutical trouble. This is especially true of his careless and uncritical use of the equivocal term *materiell* in writings both early and late—a carelessness that he has in common with Feuerbach. This has been exploited by Marxist-Leninists to support their claim that Marx himself was a philosophical materialist. Elsewhere[3] I have distinguished six distinct theoretical or systematic senses of this term as used by Marx, only the first of which—a usage that is relatively infrequent in Marx's writings—has any bearing whatever on the question of a materialist ontology.

---

[1] References to the Latin text of *De antiquissima Italorum sapientia* (1710) will be given by volume and page number of the *Opere*, ed. G. Gentile and F. Nicolini (Bari: Laterza, 1914), vol. I. Here: I, 146. References to the Italian text of the two *Risposte* (1711, 1712) will be to the same edition, given as, e.g., "*Prima risposta:* I, 211." References to the *Scienza nuova* will be by section number. All translations from *De Italorum sapientia*, the two *Risposte*, and Italian secondary sources are my own unless otherwise identified. The translation of the *Scienza nuova* is that of Bergin and Fisch, with occasional minor revisions.

[2] I am unaware of any evidence that Vico considered the adjective *materiale* or the noun *materia* to be equivocal terms. Similarly with his own key terms—*verum, factum, caussa, negotium:* He seems not to have recognized that they are equivocal, even if harmlessly so, i.e., that they have different systematic and nonsystematic senses but not, like Marx's *materiell,* several distinct systematic senses as well.

[3] See my essay, "The Myth of Marx's Materialism," forthcoming in *Annals of Scholarship* (1983) and in *The Varieties of Contemporary Marxism: Essays in Honor of J. M. Bocheński*, ed. T. J. Blakeley and J. J. O'Rourke (Dordrecht: D. Reidel, 1983). The remainder of this section represents a considerably abridged version of secs. II and III of that paper.

A thinker who is developing or defending a materialist ontology will tend to use the noun 'matter' at least as frequently as the adjective 'material'. It is a striking fact that whereas Engels, et al., make copious use of the noun—in such expressions as 'matter in motion' and 'the forms, properties, and relations of moving matter'—Marx himself rarely uses the noun *Materie,* and never in expressions of this type, the sole, and partial, exception being his dissertation of 1841. There, in expounding and analyzing the positions of Democritus and Epicurus, Marx occasionally uses the nouns *Materie* and *Materialität.* On the other hand, he often contrasts the *Materie* with the *Form* of the Democritean atoms, thus slipping into the quite different sense of 'matter' as equivalent to 'content'.[4]

The six meanings of 'material' as used by Marx follow, in roughly systematic order, identified by subscript numerals: 'material$_1$' = 'physical', 'spatio-temporal'; 'material$_2$' = 'biological', 'physiological'; 'material$_3$' = 'sensuous', 'sensual'; 'material$_4$' = 'economic'; 'material$_5$' (or 'materialistic$_5$') = 'acquisitive', 'consumption-oriented'; 'material$_6$' = 'related to content' (contrasted with 'formal'), in German: *inhaltlich.*

The last sense ('material$_6$') is not often used by Marx, and when it is it generates no significant problems. I shall not pause over it except to note a curious connection between 'material$_3$' and 'material$_6$'—namely, that in the Kantian tradition, in which, at least terminologically, both Feuerbach and Marx stood, the sensuous element in experience is called 'material$_6$'. This is because the senses supply the "matter" (i.e., content) of experience in contrast to the understanding, which supplies the categories (i.e., forms). But neither 'material$_3$' nor 'material$_6$' has anything to do with a materialist$_1$ ontology.

Materiell in the sense of 'material$_3$' was much used by Feuerbach and by the young Marx under Feuerbachian influence. It is this usage that generates the misidentification of 'materialism$_3$' with 'sense-datum empiricism' and permits Feuerbach to make grotesque claims such as: since there is no such thing as "immaterial$_3$" (i.e., 'nonsensual') love, "love is materialism$_3$" (*Liebe ist Materialismus*). In fact, this amounts to little more than a conventional denial of "Platonic" love and a common-sense assertion that sensuality is an uneliminable ingredient in love between the sexes. Marx does not often use the term as loosely as this,

[4] Karl Marx, "Ueber die Differenz der demokritischen und epikureischen Naturphilosophie," in *Frühe Schriften,* ed. H.-J. Lieber and P. Furth (Stuttgart: Cotta, 1962), I, 40, 44-45, 48, 50, 54-57, 65-67.

although in one place he makes the parallel claim that the "beloved is *a sensuous/sensual object*" (*die Geliebte ist* sinnlicher Gegenstand) and that "love...is...a *materialist*" (*Die Liebe...ist ein...*Materialist), when he means to say, with Feuerbach, simply that all love has a sensuous-sensual component.[5]

Marx undertakes to reduce what he calls *das Geistige* to *das Materielle;* but this means not "spirit to matter" or "mind to body," but rather "the superstructural to the substructural," i.e., cultural and ideological factors to economic ones. Here, in other words, Marx characteristically uses *materiell* in the sense of 'material$_4$'. Indeed, all of his works, both early and late, are filled with such expressions as '*material* forces of production', '*material* conditions', '*material* relations', '*material* activity', '*material* process', and '*material* life'. In almost all such cases he means 'material$_4$': These expressions could be translated without semantic loss into '*economic* forces of production' (or 'forces of *economic* production'), '*economic* conditions', '*economic* relations', '*economic* activity', etc. However, in a few cases Marx exploits a second or third sense— 'material$_1$' or 'material$_2$'—or shifts from one sense to another, sometimes within a single paragraph.[6]

I claim that there is nothing peculiarly material$_1$—or for that matter material$_2$ or material$_3$—about *economic* institutions, activities, or relations. This is true even in the case of the economic institution upon which Marx focused his analysis: the mid-nineteenth-century steam-powered, partially automated factory or mill. Now a factory or mill—or a bank, insurance company, or stock exchange (to mention three other peculiarly economic— "material$_4$"—institutions)—is no more and no less "physical" or involved with the "biological/physiological" or "sensuous/sensual" than any other social or cultural institution. Institutions whose primary function is noneconomic, such as universities, churches, professional societies, symphony orchestras, also require buildings and artifacts, including furniture, tools, and instruments, and, of course,

[5] "Die heilige Familie," IV, 3, in *Frühe Schriften*, I, 685. Emphasis in the original.

[6] Thus, in the famous footnote to *Capital* that contains the only reference to Vico in a work published during Marx's lifetime, there is a semantic slide from 'material$_4$' in the expression *materielle Basis* to 'materialistic$_1$' in *materialistische Methode*. Marx uncritically assumes that there is something peculiarly material$_1$ (i.e., 'physical', 'spatio-temporal') about technology. What he calls a 'materialistic$_1$ method' is one that takes the historical development of *technology* adequately into account in explaining the history of a superstructural element like religion. At the same time this is a 'materialistic$_4$ method', i.e., one that takes the history of the *economy* into account in explaining the development of religion. See *Marx-Engels-Werke* (East Berlin: Dietz, 1962), vol. 23, pp. 392-93 n. 89.

human beings, in order to function. In this respect a factory (or a bank, insurance company, or stock exchange) is no different. *All* such institutions are *social;* all are established and maintained by concerted human purpose, intelligence, inventiveness, conscientiousness. There is nothing peculiarly material$_1$—or material$_2$ or material$_3$—about any of this.

I shall mention but not discuss[7] two further factors, internal to Marx's thought, that have facilitated the misinterpretation of his position as a philosophical materialism: namely (1) his exclusive stress on the production of *goods* and virtually total neglect of economic *services,* and (2) his economic reductionism. I simply note that while all materialist ontologies—emphatically including that of Engels—are reductionist, not all reductionist positions amount to or entail materialist ontologies. Those positions (like Engels') that *do* might be characterized as "transcategoreally" reductionist. They typically reduce what is human to something non- or subhuman, e.g., intentional or purposive actions to (manifestations of) physiological or biochemical events. Marx's characteristic reduction, in contrast, is "intracategoreal": it reduces one human level to another, viz., cultural-ideological factors to economic ones. Such a position, I would argue, neither entails nor offers significant support for a materialist ontology.

III

I want now to sketch just enough of Vico's early—undeveloped, obscure, yet tantalizing—ontology to permit some comparison with Marx's position and to prepare the ground for a few concluding comments concerning the mature systems of the two thinkers.

Vico's stress on *origins* anticipates both Hegel and Marx but also echoes—at least in part—themes in Spinoza. Vico defines science as "knowledge of genesis, of the way in which a thing comes to be" (*cognitio generis, seu modi, quo res fiat*) (I, 132). Thus, one of his—implicit if not explicit—reasons for rejecting a materialist ontology[8] is that the atoms

---

[7] For details see my essay, "The Myth of Marx's Materialism," especially secs. II and III.

[8] I agree with Croce's remark that, although there is a "theologian Vico, an agnostic Vico," etc., there is never a "materialistic Vico" and that Vico's early metaphysics "shows the same aversion to materialism and the same love for idealism which inspire the...New Science" (*The Philosophy of Vico,* trans. R. G. Collingwood, [New York: Macmillan, 1913], pp. 136-37, 142). Vico focuses his critique of materialism on Epicurus' notion of the atom as a *simplex corpus extensum* (I, 154)—in other words, as Croce puts it, "matter [i.e., 'body' = *il corpo*] already formed and divided into ultimate particles" (Croce, op. cit., p. 137).

of the materialists are "eternal"; they neither come to be nor develop. As Whitehead has noted in another connection, the matter of the seventeenth-century materialists, conceived as an "ultimate substance" or "aboriginal stuff," is "incapable of evolution."[9] It is subject neither to genesis nor to development; hence in Vichian terms it is cognitively opaque.

Vico thus had good reason for proceeding from his study of geometry, a discipline that can trace the genesis of (constructed) mathematical entities and relations[10] to the "new science" of history, a discipline that can, with greater subtlety and depth, trace the origin and development of the institutions[11] of human society.

Vico's rather harsh strictures against Spinoza, mainly directed at his metaphysical determinism, his criticism of the Bible, and his political theory, should not be permitted to obscure Vico's closeness to Spinoza's

[9] A. N. Whitehead, *Science and the Modern World* (New York: Macmillan, 1926), p. 157. Gentile, earlier, had made a similar point, characterizing the changeless "matter" of the eighteenth-century philosophical materialists as "inerte,...sempre identica a sè stessa, senza storia" (Giovanni Gentile, "La filosofia di Marx: Studi critici" [1899], *Opere* [Florence: Sansoni, 1959], vol. 28, pp. 164, 162).

[10] As Vico puts it, in mathematics *dum mens cognoscit modum, quia elementa componit, rem faciat* ("whenever the mind knows the way [in which a thing comes to be], in putting together the elements [of the thing], it is making the thing" (I, 132)). The looseness of George Mora's English version of this key passage ("the mind 'properly arranges the elements of the known thing and, at the same time, makes the thing'" appears to be the result of his having worked from Nicolini's very free Italian version, which reads: "la mente, nell'atto stesso in cui viene a conoscere codesta guisa [sc., the way—*modus*—a thing comes to be], dispone ordinatamente gli elementi della cosa conosciuta e, insieme, la fa" (*Opere*) [Ricciardi], p. 249). See George Mora, "Vico, Piaget, and Genetic Epistemology," in *Giambattista Vico's Science of Humanity*, p. 378 n. 47.

[11] The Latin *res* has approximately the same range of meanings ('thing', 'affair', 'institution') in the *De Italorum sapientia* that the Italian *cosa* has in the *Scienza nuova*. English translators have tended to obscure Vico's terminological consistency, rendering *res* as 'object' or 'thing' and *cosa* as 'institution'. I don't deny that 'institution' carries some of the right connotations for the Vichian *cosa*. But I share Salomone's uneasiness, not just for the reason he gives—that *cosa* has a wider meaning than 'institution'—but also because of the loss of semantic continuity between such early expressions as *cognitio generis, seu modi, quo res fiat* (I, 132; emphasis added) and such late ones as *Natura di cose altro non è che nascimento di esse*...(par. 147; emphasis added). This last is, of course, translated by Bergin and Fisch as "The nature of *institutions*..." (emphasis added). See A. William Salomone, "Pluralism and Universality in Vico's *Scienza Nuova*," in *Giambattista Vico: An International Symposium*, p. 525 n. 23.

   The translation of *cosa* as 'institution' also muffles the clear echo of Spinoza's *Ordo et connexio idearum idem est, ac ordo et connexio rerum* (*Ethics*, II, 7; emphasis added) in Vico's *L'ordine dell'idee dee procedere secondo l'ordine delle cose* (par. 238; emphasis added). Nicolini further confuses the issue by misidentifying the Spinoza reference as *'Etica*, I, prop. 7' (*Opere* [Ricciardi], p. 458 n. 2).

theory of mental activity. For example, Spinoza's rules for constructive
definition are quite Vichian.[12] A circle, Spinoza insists, is to be defined
as "a figure *described* by any line one end of which is fixed, the other
movable" (*figuram, quae* describitur *a linea quacunque, cujus alia ex-
tremitas est fixa, alia mobilis*).[13]

Spinoza likewise defines 'idea' in such a way as to bring out its active
character as a *mentis conceptus* ('conception of the mind'), which in turn
is an *actio mentis* ('action of the mind').[14] He further characterizes an
idea as a *cogitationis conceptus* ('conception of thought'), *modus cogitandi*
('mode [or 'way'] of thinking'), and *ipsum intelligere* ('[active] understanding itself').[15]

Vico's early ontology, the theory of "metaphysical points" and *conatūs*,[16] although compact, even laconic, in its formulation and puzzling
in some of its details, is an impressive intellectual achievement. It
scarcely deserves Croce's stern indictment as "fantastic and arbitrary"
or justifies his claim that "we must deny all value to Vico's cosmology."[17]
After all, even Croce admits that "we cannot deny its dynamic nature as
opposed to the mechanicism [*meccanicismo*] of contemporary [viz., Carte-
sian] philosophy."[18]

Vico's intention, at least, is reasonably clear. He wants to replace the
unsatisfactory Cartesian physics, with its unrelated categories of extension and motion. His "Zenonian" doctrine specifies the metaphysical

---

[12] Phrases such as *ut demonstratio eadem ac operatio sit, et verum idem ac factum* (I, 150) are ably
glossed by Giuliani: "The definition...is an act of human creation.... Vico's reflection on the
definition appears to be the point of departure of his principle that the human mind
participates in a creative manner in the real" (Alessandro Giuliani, "Vico's Rhetorical Philosophy and the New Rhetoric," trans. S. Rotella, in *Giambattista Vico's Science of Humanity*, p. 41).
Lachterman adds that Descartes must also be given his due: "l'accento vichiano sull'oper-
azione e costruzione matematica...riprende un motivo introdotto per la prima volta da
Descartes nella sua difesa dell'analisi come *ars inveniendi*" (David R. Lachterman, "Vico,
Doria e la geometria sintetica," trans. B. Arcangeli, *Bollettino del Centro di Studi Vichiani*, 10
[1980]: 21 n. 36).

[13] Benedict de Spinoza, "Tractatus de intellectus emendatione," in *Opera*, ed. J. van Vloten
and J. P. N. Land (The Hague: Nijhoff, 1914³), I, 29. Emphasis added.

[14] *Ethics*, II, def. 3 and explanation.

[15] *Ethics*, II, 38n. and 43n. Unfortunately, the standard Stirling-White translation changes
Spinoza's participles and infinitives into nouns, thus obscuring his stress on mental *activity*.
Modus cogitandi becomes 'mode of *thought*' and *ipsum intelligere* becomes '*intelligence* itself'
(emphasis added).

[16] Unlike Spinoza, in whose mature system the key term *conatus* is always used in the
singular, Vico regularly uses the term in the plural (*conatūs*), e.g., in the expression *ex
simplicibus punctorum conatibus* (I, 163).

[17] Croce, op. cit., pp. 141, 142.

[18] Ibid., p. 142.

points, with their *conatūs*, as the ground which brings together the disjoint Cartesian categories. He calls this unifying ground an "indivisible potentiality for extension and motion" (*indivisibili extensionis motusque virtute*) (I, 153).[19]

A particular extended thing, we might say, is for Vico not a passive Cartesian *res extensa* but rather an active "Zenonian" *res extendiens*.[20] The ontological ground of a thing's activity-of-extending is the unextended metaphysical point, an "indivisible point of conation," a "potential of extension," which is metaphysically real. Like the Pythagorean One, which, though not itself a number, generates number, it, though not itself extended, generates extension.[21]

Cartesian dualism is avoided by "taking the substance of bodies to be incorporeal, the causes of motion to be motionless." God creates extended bodies "from points that are unextended...but endowed with infinite power of extension [i.e., extend*ing*]."[22]

More generally, in interpreting the *conatus* as "nature *in fieri*," and identifying reality with force, Vico has discovered the "metaphysical significance of action" and reduced "human thought itself to a *facere*."[23] Croce sums up the matter quite nicely, although in this instance Collingwood's generally accurate and readable English translation contains several misleading renderings of key terms. Conation, Croce says, is:

> the indefinite energy [i.e., 'infinite potency' = *indefinita virtù*] and attempt [i.e., 'effort' = *sforzo*] on the part of the universe to bring into being [i.e., 'bring out' = *mandar fuori*] and sustain each particular

[19] Vico himself provides the Italian equivalent of this Latin expression: *l'indivisibil virtù dell'estensione e del moto* (*Prima risposta*: I, 213). See David R. Lachterman, "Vico, Doria e la geometria sintetica," pp. 13, 15. (As the result of a typographical error the Latin term *indivisibili* appears, confusingly, as *invisibili* on p. 15.) See also the characterization of the *conatus* as *la possibilità del moto* in Nicola Badaloni, *Introduzione a G. B. Vico* (Milan: Feltrinelli, 1961), p. 343. I prefer the terms 'potentiality' and 'potency'. Vico refers to the "*virtù o potenza di estensione e di moto*" (*Seconda risposta*: I, 265; emphasis added), and speaks of "una indefinita virtù o uno sforzo dell'universo a mandar fuori e sostener le cose particolari tutte" (*Prima risposta*: I, 210). The expression *mandar fuori* suggests Hegel's conception of nature as the *Entäusserung des Geistes* ('externalization of the spirit').

[20] Although Vico does not himself use the active participle *extendiens*, he does characterize the essence of body as "una indefinita virtù di mantenerlo disteso" (*Prima risposta*: I, 210).

[21] Yvon Belaval, "Vico and Anti-Cartesianism," trans. E. Gianturco, in *Giambattista Vico: An International Symposium*, p. 86.

[22] Max H. Fisch, "Vico and Pragmatism," in *Giambattista Vico: An International Symposium*, p. 410.

[23] Badaloni, op. cit., p. 343.

thing. The existence of matter [i.e., 'body' = *corpo*] is nothing but an indefinite power [i.e., 'infinite potency' = *indefinita virtù*] of keeping the universe extended, which underlies all extended objects [i.e., 'things' = *cose*].[24]

IV

There is what one might describe as a partial convergence between the mature theories of Vico and Marx, in the sense that both of them come to develop "Hegelian" or at least "quasi-Hegelian" general theories of social structure and historical change. These positions could be called "social ontologies" or "ontologies of social being" (on the model of Georg Lukács' *Ontologie des gesellschaftlichen Seins*), but I am doubtful that such labels would more accurately describe Vico's or Marx's position than would the blander label: "general theories of social structures and institutions, viewed in their historical origins and development."

In my judgment Vico comes closer than Marx does, not only to Hegel but also to the truth in these matters, when, for example, he identifies the three fundamental institutions among the *cose umane civili* (par. 570) as religion, marriage, and the burial of the dead (e.g., par. 333), stressing that each of these institutions and practices is attended by a solemnity that has legal as well as linguistic and cultural dimensions. It is just these linguistic and cultural dimensions that are conspicuously absent from Marx's general account of the "forces and relations of economic production" as well as from his special analysis of "alienated labor" (see p. 124 below).

There are striking similarities between the positions of Vico and Marx on a number of points, some of which are pursued by other contributors to the present volume. I wish rather to stress certain differences, which cluster around the principle of *verum = factum*, broadly conceived.

Without making explicit reference to Marx, Amerio has sketched out one important difference. He justly notes that the Vichian *factum* (or *facere*) is not to be interpreted either—as Croce, among other "ideal-

---

[24] Croce, op. cit., p. 139. For Vico nature is not "matter" or "matter in motion" but "*motion*": "Natura est motus; huius motus indefinita movendi virtus conatus; quam excitat infinita mens in se quieta, Deus" (I, 161). Elsewhere he makes clear the categoreal distinction between God and nature, insisting that "*in natura non si dia quiete*, perché gli sforzi sono la vita della natura, e'l conato non è quiete" (*Prima risposta:* I, 211).

ists," has done—as a constructing or positing by (either finite or infinite) mind; or, as the positivists (and, we might add, Marx) have done, as a making or producing "in the physical and material sense" (*nel senso fisico e materiale*). The criterion of the true, Amerio insists, is not the "capacity to produce the object" (*capacità di fabbricare l'oggetto*).[25]

This point is persuasively developed by Lachterman, who draws a sharp distinction between the Marxian sense of the verbs *machen* and *produzieren*, on the one hand, and the Vichian sense of the verb *facere*, on the other. For Marx, making or production is the "arbitrary, spontaneous fashioning of an external, physical object which was not previously in the world in that shape." In contrast, for Vico, making is a "mental operation through which already existent elements, themselves the images of divine generative archetypes, are set in order in a decorous array."[26] The term 'mental' is perhaps too restrictive, too "Crocean"; the term 'cultural' would better bring out the Vichian point that what has been "made"—the *factum*—is not just ideas or concepts, but institutions, social structures, forms of life; in short, *le cose umane civili*.

For Marx, in any case, the Vichian *factum* is *toto caelo* distinct from *das Gemachte* ('what has been made'), *das Produzierte* ('what has been produced'), *das Vergegenständlichte* ('what has been objectified', i.e., 'produced as an object'), and even from *das Verwirklichte* ('what has been actualized'). If, in a weak moment, Marx were to transpose Vico's *verum = factum* into the key of political economy, he would have to say *Das Wahre ist die Ware* ('the true is the commodity')! Such a transposition would amount to no more than a graceless and wholly unserious play on words, even though *die Ware* is indeed that species of the genus *das Gemachte/Produzierte/Vergegenständlichte/Verwirklichte* upon which Marx focuses his theoretical attention.

Lachterman's summary of the relevant differences is both lucid and eloquent:

> For Vico, in contrast [sc., to Marx], the origin of human history does not lie in technical production, nor is its *telos* the conquest of external nature. Men make their own history by slowly building,

---

[25] Franco Amerio, *Vico* (Brescia: La Scuola, 1945²), pp. 53-54.
[26] David R. Lachterman, "Vico and Marx: Notes on a Precursory Reading," this volume, p. 56.

through their feats and fables, a civil world of customs and rituals that tame and humanize their pre-human, ferocious passions.[27]

The Vico-Marx opposition, which places "fables, customs, and rituals" on Vico's side and "technical production" along with the "conquest of external [nonhuman] nature" on Marx's, leads to another important but generally unnoticed difference.

Vichian recollection of the elements of universal history [Lachterman asserts] is most attentive to what men have *said*...,while Marx's productive agents are in principle *silent.* The gap that separates Marx and Vico in this regard is measured by the distance between manufacture and mythopoiesis, a factory and a fable.[28]

I would add to this penetrating comment only the marginal gloss that the "silence" of Marxian producers is not a *Stille* but a *Schweigen,* not noiselessness but nonspeaking. Such a withdrawal from, or suspension of, language (along with myth, fable, ritual, etc.) is of course entirely compatible with the obtrusive presence of "noise" in and around the process of production.

Marx's neglect of the role of language in the historical process—like his assignment of a derivative and subordinate role to culture and the arts—is, I suspect, a corollary of his neglect, in the celebrated analysis of alienation (*Entfremdung*) in the Paris Manuscripts of 1844, of the linguistic, literary, and cultural dimensions of alienation, precisely those dimensions that Hegel, in the *Phenomenology of Spirit* of 1807, had made central.[29]

For Marx, alienation is an economic, social, and—to a degree—psychological phenomenon. But it is not in any sense a linguistic phenomenon; it does not in any way involve language, myth, or fable. Marx's striking insensitivity to the power—both constructive and destructive—of national and ethnic traditions is, I suspect, a special case

---

[27] Ibid., p. 59.

[28] Ibid., p. 60. Emphasis added. The Vichian historical "recollection" appears close to the Hegelian *Erinnerung,* which is both recollection and internalization. Cf. the parallel between Vico's *mandar fuori* and Hegel's *entäussern* (note 19 above).

[29] See my article, "The Existentialist Rediscovery of Hegel and Marx," in *Phenomenology and Existentialism,* ed. E. N. Lee and M. Mandelbaum (Baltimore: Johns Hopkins University Press, 1969[2]), pp. 132-33.

of his broader blindness to the linguistic, mythical, and "symbolic" dimensions of human existence. Vico's theory can account, as Marx's cannot, for the undiminished pull, in the closing decades of the twentieth century, of religious, national, and ethnic loyalties.

More generally, Vico, in stressing the role of language, myth, fable, and other cultural factors in human history seems to me to stand measurably closer to Hegel—as well as to the truth concerning human institutions (*le cose umane civili*)—than does Marx.

Vico and Marx: Human Consciousness and the Structure of Reality

Adrienne Fulco

I

The historical theories of Vico and Marx share many ideas in common. In the formulation of their theories both thinkers began by rejecting the prevailing philosophical doctrines of their own times on epistemological and methodological grounds. Vico, in his confrontation with the Cartesian rationalists, and Marx, in his break with the German Idealists, offer strikingly similar arguments: The focus of philosophy must be shifted away from the realm of abstract concepts that are far removed from human reality and instead become oriented toward the concrete world of man. Both Vico and Marx turned to human history in their efforts to establish explanations and principles regarding the nature of human activity and experience, and both understood the pivotal category in all such explanations to be human consciousness. Consciousness, including its birth, growth, and development, is regarded as the central structural, interpretive, and transformative force governing all human endeavor. It is what structures reality and gives shape to the world. As such, consciousness provides the cementing link between being and knowledge, between activity and thought, between ontology and epistemology. The purpose of this paper is to discuss the Vichian and Marxian notions of consciousness and to consider some important similarities of, and differences between, their positions.

On the most basic level Vico and Marx share the belief that consciousness is man's distinguishing characteristic, the essential core of his humanity. For both Vico and Marx, consciousness in its most general form is the capacity all men have for becoming aware of themselves and the world around them. But consciousness is not merely a property of mind—it is an activity that has a definite social character. Both Vico and Marx assert that men become aware of themselves and of nature collectively rather than individually, that whatever knowledge is achieved by men is likewise a social product. Both thinkers explain the social nature of man and the social nature of human knowledge in terms of the origin and development of consciousness so that the epistemological problem is inextricably tied to the problem of human nature: Ultimately, what man *is* cannot be divorced from what man knows and the means by which he arrives at knowledge.

Vico, in response to the philosophical heritage of the seventeenth century, comes to his theory of consciousness—as well as to his theories of history, language, society, and politics—as a consequence of his attempt to refute the Cartesian theory of knowledge.[1] However, he never identifies his theory of consciousness as such; for him it remained embedded in the larger problem of knowledge that he addressed. On the other hand, by the time Marx wrote in the mid-nineteenth century, the concept of consciousness had achieved an independent status in Hegel's thought, and epistemological problems were recognized as having a direct relationship to both social philosophy and the philosophy of history. Marx was therefore able to consider the problem of consciousness as a primary component of his scientific examination of man and society.

II

Vico comes to the problem of consciousness in the course of his exploration of the nature of the primitive mind and the origins of language. Having made the discovery that, contrary to the view of prevailing theories, the first men who founded civil society were not sages endowed with esoteric wisdom, but "poets who spoke in poetic characters,"[2] Vico attempts to reconstruct primitive man's experience of the world. Abandoning philosophy's traditional preoccupation with characterizing mind's essence, Vico turns to an explanation of mind's primary function, the interpretation of the world. His discussion of the interpretive function of mind entails an examination of mind's concrete expression in human language, which Vico regards as the hitherto untapped repository of human history. He insists on a return to

---

[1] There is a large literature on Vico's criticisms of Descartes. See, for example, in G. Tagliacozzo and H. White, eds., *Giambattista Vico: An International Symposium* (Baltimore: Johns Hopkins University Press, 1969), the following: Yvon Belaval, "Vico and Anti-Cartesianism," pp. 77-92, and Isaiah Berlin, "A Note on Vico's Concept of Knowledge," pp. 371-77.

[2] Giambattista Vico, *New Science* (Ithaca: Cornell University Press, 1968), par. 34.

the point when "men began to think humanly" in order to differentiate
between the *origins* of human language and thought and all subsequent
developments.[3]

According to Vico language is the creative expression of mind in the
sense that by means of language men assign names to things, thereby
investing them with meaning. It is his belief that the actual assigning of
names to things is accomplished by human speech, which over time
undergoes changes and transformations. He contends that human
speech has always assumed two forms, poetry and prose. But in contrast to more traditional views, Vico claims that poetry, not prose, was
the original form of human speech because poetry issues from imagination, which Vico believes to be the primary form of human thought.
It is for this reason that he insists that the founders of civil society were
"poets who spoke in poetic characters."[4] On the basis of his study of
ancient law, poetry, and etymology Vico concludes that the thoughts of
primordial man consisted of "certain imaginative genera (images for
the most part of animate substances, of Gods or heroes, formed by their
imagination) to which they reduced all the species or all the particulars
pertaining to each genus."[5] In other words, in Vico's view primitive man
"attributed senses and passions...to bodies, and to bodies as vast as sky,
sea, earth."[6] The attribution of human passions that arises out of sense
experience of the outside world is always expressed initially in figura-
tive language, or tropes. The creation of figures of speech is the first
human attempt to make sense out of the unknown world that is external
to human beings, the first attempt to establish a relationship between
man and his environment.[7] In effect, the unknown is made intelligible
by attributing to it characteristics known to, and felt by, man. Vico says
that "...when [man] does not understand he makes the things out of

[3] Ibid., par 338.
[4] Ibid, par. 34.
[5] Ibid., par. 35.
[6] Ibid., par. 402.
[7] On Vico's use of tropes see Hayden White, *Tropics of Discourse* (Baltimore: Johns Hopkins
University Press, 1978), pp. 204-17. White says, "Vico argues that all figures of speech may be
reduced to four modes or tropes: metaphor, synecdoche, metonymy, and irony...[And] he
makes of metaphor a kind of primal (generic) trope, so that syndecdoche and metonymy are
viewed as specific refinements of it, and irony is seen as its opposite....The theory of
metaphorical transformation serves as a model for a theory of the autotransformation of
human consciousness in history." (pp. 204-5)

On Vico's use of tropes see also Michael Mooney, "The Primacy of Language in Vico," in
Vico and Contemporary Thought ed. G. Tagliacozzo, M. Mooney, and D. Verene (Atlantic
Highlands, N.J.: Humanities Press, 1980), pp. 191-210.

himself and becomes them by transforming himself into them."[8] Ignorant and fearful, but endowed with a powerful imagination, primitive "man made himself an entire world."[9]

Essentially what Vico describes is the process by which ignorance simultaneously gives rise to knowledge and consciousness, a process whereby the unknown gradually becomes intelligible to man. The role of language in this process is twofold: It is both the demonstration of man's capacity to make his own world and the means by which he documents, stores, and passes on the record of his creative activity and the transformations it undergoes. One of the most significant conclusions that can be drawn from Vico's theory of the origin of consciousness is the *collective* nature of the process. Consciousness is not simply a state of mind achieved by individuals, it is a *social product*, a set of shared perceptions about the nature and structure of reality. Consciousness comes about because on the most fundamental level men are continually involved in the enterprise of interpreting and giving meaning to their activity and their surroundings, and language is the collective means with which men concretize and share those interpretations. And, according to Vico, just as language arises out of the human *need* to structure and interpret the world, so, too, all human institutions are likewise the product of collective, shared perceptions.

Vico maintains that there are three primitive social institutions shared by every nation on earth: religion, marriage, and burial of the dead. Each of these institutions is rooted in human need and in the collective action of the community that brought them into being. Vico believes that religion is the most basic of all human institutions and the source of all morality, a claim he was certainly not the first to make. His originality lies in his assertion that man actually brings God into being as a way of rendering the unknown intelligible. He postulates that the first men, who were "immersed in the senses" and "without the power of ratiocination," wandered the earth in a solitary fashion, much like the beasts.[10] What caused the first men to renounce their solitary existence was the appearance of a thunderclap and lightning bolt in the sky that so frightened them that they attributed enormous powers to the sky, calling it "Jove."[11] Prior to this first collective act of naming the

---

[8] Vico, *New Science,* op. cit., par 405.
[9] Ibid.
[10] Ibid., par 378.
[11] Ibid., pars. 378-79.

fearful object external to themselves, men were hardly distinguishable from beasts. But in this moment of shared apprehension they attributed to the sky powers over themselves and the world around them, thus giving birth to human consciousness. For Vico, the moment of the creation of religion is the prototype for the creation of all human institutions. All emerge out of sense experience and the need to render the unknown intelligible. It is for this reason that Vico says that "the order of ideas follows the order of institutions."[12] The first human institutions were formed, not on the basis of ideas arrived at rationally, but on the basis of spontaneous collective action. Only after the institutions come into being do men develop "ideas" about them.

Vico argues that even though institutions arise spontaneously, they conform to a definite pattern of development both within any particular nation and across the entire human race. It is the existence of this discernible pattern of development that accounts for the uniformity, continuity, and totality of human history. The most general form the pattern takes is the division of human history into three ages or periods—the age of the gods, the age of the heroes, and the age of men. Each period is meant to define an entire cultural epoch in which all phases of life are worked out in accordance with a specific way of viewing and structuring reality, a particular attitude of human consciousness. Furthermore, according to Vico, the entire pattern is subject to the guidance and intervention of "divine providence," the force that "without human discernment or counsel, and often against the designs of men...has ordered...the human race."[13] For Vico, the creative activity of man giving meaning to his world must be placed within the context of the "hidden" activity of divine providence.

The age of the gods, the earliest cultural epoch and the one in which consciousness is actually born, is characterized by man's immersion in his senses so that reality consists of the attribution of physical sensations to the outside world. As the age of the gods gives way to the age of the heroes, man's capacity to distinguish between his own feelings and things external to him grows, and reality is perceived in increasingly abstract terms. Finally, in the age of man reason as such comes into being and becomes the faculty of mind with which man structures his

---

[12] Ibid., par. 238.

[13] Ibid., par. 342. On Vico's notion of divine providence see James C. Morrison, "How to Interpret the Idea of Divine Providence in Vico's *New Science*," *Philosophy and Rhetoric*, 12 (1979): 256-61. It should be pointed out that for Vico divine providence always works in conjunction with concrete human needs.

world and understands himself. Each age is dominated by a particular capacity of mind that gives consciousness and, ultimately, reality its shape. The distinctions between the three broad epochs are of less importance than is Vico's bold assertion that the manner in which men structure reality varies according to their needs and perceptions, and that as those needs and perceptions change, the structure of reality and human consciousness itself are both transformed,

III

Whereas Vico never specifically identifies the concept of consciousness as such, Marx discusses the role of consciousness as a discrete component in his theory of history. In his early works, particularly the preface to the *Critique of Political Economy* and the *German Ideology,* Marx rejects the idealist and materialist conceptions of his predecessors and reconsiders the relationship between human ideas, material production, and the structure of reality.[14] Marx's point of departure is Feuerbach's distinction between the consciousness of man and the consciousness of animals. Feuerbach had argued that only man has the capacity to become aware of himself both as an individual and as a member of the human species. Only man comes to know that he shares something in common with other members of his species. Accepting this distinction, Marx identifies man as a "species-being" who possesses a "species-consciousness."[15] To say that man has species-consciousness is to say that man is able to become aware of his relationships with other human beings. As Kathleen Bulmash argues, "What the concept of species-being meant to convey, more than anything else, was an awareness of man's nature as essentially historical and essentially social..."[16]

Furthermore, the context within which men become aware of one another is that of their concrete human activity, which is labor. Marx says, "Man makes his life activity itself the object of his will and of his

[14] For recent interpretations of Marx's rejection of both idealism and materialism, with specific reference to positivist readings of his epistemology, see Kathleen Bulmash, *The Marxist Concept of Community* (unpublished Ph.D. thesis), City University of New York, 1978, Alan Swingewood, *Marx and Modern Social Theory* (New York: John Wiley, 1975, Melvin Rader, *Marx's Interpretation of History* (New York: Oxford University Press, 1979), and Shlomo Avineri, *The Social and Political Thought of Karl Marx* (Cambridge: Cambridge University Press, 1968).

[15] Karl Marx, *The Economic and Philosophical Manuscripts of 1844* in *The Marx-Engels Reader,* ed. Robert Tucker (New York: W.W. Norton, 1972), p. 72.

[16] Kathleen Bulmash, *Marxist Concept of Community,* op. cit., p. 202.

consciousness. He has conscious life activity...[which] directly distinguishes man from animal life activity."[17] Marx inverts the idealist
position, which made human activity a function of consciousness and
thought, maintaining that

> the production of ideas, of conceptions, of consciousness is at first
> directly interwoven with the material activity and the material
> intercourse of men, the language of real life.... Men are the
> producers of their conceptions, ideas, etc.—real, active men, as
> they are conditioned by a definite development of their produc-
> tive forces and of the intercourse corresponding to these, up to the
> furthest forms.[18]

For Marx, then, activity is prior to thought, and men produce their
ideas in the course of their life activity. Life activity is itself social:
"Consciousness is therefore from the very beginning a social product
and remains so as long as men exist at all."[19] Consciousness is rooted in
human nature because it arises only "from the need, the necessity of
intercourse with other men."[20] According to Marx the consciousness
that originally distinguishes man from the animals serves two functions. On the one hand, it is

> merely consciousness concerning the immediate sensuous en-
> vironment and consciousness of the limited connection with other
> persons and things outside the individual who is growing self-
> conscious. At the same time it is consciousness of nature, which
> appears to men as a completely alien, all powerful and unassail-
> able force, with which men's relations are purely animal and by
> which they are overawed like beasts; it is thus a purely animal
> consciousness of nature (natural religion.)[21]

This original form of consciousness, which permitted men to become
aware of both themselves and nature, Marx refers to as "sheep-like or
tribal consciousness."[22] The significance of this original form of con-

---

[17] Karl Marx, *The Economic and Philosophical Manuscripts of 1844,* op. cit., p. 62.
[18] Karl Marx, *The German Ideology* in the *Marx-Engels Reader,* op. cit., p. 118.
[19] Ibid., p. 118.
[20] Ibid.
[21] Ibid.
[22] Ibid.

sciousness is that with it men became aware of the necessity of associating with others, and it therefore constitutes "the beginning of the consciousness that [they] are living in society at all."[23] To acquire the consciousness that men live in society with each other is thus the first step in the structuring of reality. Whereas animals merely respond reflexively to instinctual demands, man becomes aware of his own "life process," of his own social existence, and on the basis of this awareness he gives form and meaning to his activity.

So, although consciousness initially serves the positive purpose of making men aware of their social nature, the history of mankind is the record of his "estrangement" from his original condition. At the same moment that man became aware of his social nature he also experienced his natural surroundings as "alien." Thus, at the very beginning consciousness also separated man from nature, making him aware that he is independent of it. It is for this reason Marx says that when men first felt "overawed" by the "powerful and unassailable force" of nature, they created religion to overcome the feeling of estrangement or alienation. Estrangement of another sort arose as human productive activity increased, and a division of labor, first within the family, then within the larger community, occurred. The division of labor had two important consequences for the development of consciousness. First, the division of labor brought about the unequal distribution of the products of labor so that property came into being. Ultimately, property relations evolved to the point that classes were created, and some individuals in society were able to "dispose of the labor-power of others."[24] Depending upon the distribution of property, different individuals achieved different relationships to the actual material conditions of life. So the second consequence of the division of labor is that because "the nature of individuals...depends upon the material conditions determining their production,"[25] the consciousness of individuals and of classes in any society varies according to the particular relationships to the modes of production. For Marx, the division of labor necessarily undermines the original social condition of man: "The division of labor implies the contradiction between the interest of the separate individual...and the communal interest of all individuals who have intercourse with one another."[26]

[23] Ibid.
[24] Ibid.
[25] Ibid.
[26] Ibid.

An analysis of the actual relationships between individuals and the modes of production—i.e., an analysis of the specific relationships brought about by the division of labor—reveals that men structure reality according to those relationships. In the preface to *Critique of Political Economy* Marx says:

> In the social production of their life, men enter into definite relations that are indispensable and independent of their will, relations of production which correspond to a definite stage of development of their material productive forces. The sum total of these relations of production constitutes the economic structure of society, the real foundation, on which rises a legal and political superstructure and to which correspond definite forms of social consciousness...It is not the consciousness of men that determines their being, but, on the contrary, their social being that determines their consciousness...[27]

For Marx, although consciousness is originally shared, the fact that different groups in society have related differently to the modes of production means that each group ultimately acquires its own unique view of reality. By virtue of their differing interpretations of reality men become separated, "estranged" from each other and from the social community. Thus the division of labor becomes a division of consciousness, and for this reason each class in society develops a consciousness of its own which expresses its own particular interests.

The significance of the development of a divided consciousness is that according to Marx, "The ideas of the ruling class are in every epoch the ruling ideas, i.e. the class which is the ruling *material* force in society is at the same time its ruling *intellectual* force."[28] Particular class consciousness thus affects the entire social order: "The class which has the means of material production at its disposal, has control at the same time over the means of mental production, so that thereby, generally speaking, the ideas of those who lack the mental production are subject to it. The ruling ideas are nothing more than the ideal expression of the dominant material relationships."[29] This power of the ruling class to

---

[27] Karl Marx, Preface to *Critique of Political Economy* in the *Marx-Engels Reader,* op. cit., pp. 4-5.
[28] Karl Marx, *The German Ideology,* op. cit., p. 136.
[29] Ibid.

enforce its view of reality on all of society has two important results. First, to the extent that the ideas of the ruling class dominate, the ruling class is able to recognize its own interests and to become conscious of them. But, on the other hand, to the extent that the ruling class "is compelled merely in order to carry through its aim, to represent its interests as the common interest of all society,"[30] its consciousness must be regarded as "false" and therefore identical with "ideology." According to Marx, "in all ideology men and their circumstances appear upside-down as in a *camera obscura*."[31] In their effort to universalize their own exclusive point of view the ruling class actually distorts reality. Moreover, not only does it distort reality, but it falsifies knowledge itself, using knowledge to serve its own particular interests.

The problem of "false" consciousness and ideology is a central issue in Marx's concept of historical change. Each new ruling class "achieves its hegemony only on a broader basis than that of the class ruling previously."[32] The basis continues to broaden until in capitalist society there exists the possibility of abolishing class antagonisms entirely, and in so doing abolishing "false" consciousness and ideology as well. Marx believes that his analysis of capitalist society demonstrates that with the appearance of the proletariat as a class that is truly universal by virtue of its relationship to the mode of production, the possibility exists for overcoming the need to distort reality. The proletariat is the only class in human history that does not need to oppress other members of society, and so it does not falsely universalize its own interests. For the first time the interests of the ruling class are truly the universal interests of all. As the proletariat becomes aware of its position and of its true interests, it comes to realize that it must overthrow the remaining fetters of capitalism. As the proletariat comes to this awareness, it develops a revolutionary consciousness which is the prerequisite for human freedom. For Marx, as consciousness transcends the limitations of any particular, partial view of reality, it provides the impetus to willful revolutionary change.

IV

The most significant difference between the Vichian and the Marxian notions of human consciousness stems from their conceptions of the

---

[30] Ibid., p. 138.

[31] Ibid. p. 118. It is Engels who actually coins the phrase "false" consciousness in 1893, according to Martin Seliger. See his *The Marxist Conception of Ideology: A Critical Essay* (London: Cambridge University Press, 1977), p. 30.

[32] Karl Marx, *The German Ideology*, op. cit., p. 138.

relationship between knowledge and reality and from their basic epistemological views. For Vico, man is continually engaged in the process of interpreting and reinterpreting his relationship to others and to his natural surroundings. The process is creative because according to Vico the fundamental human activity is that of rendering the world intelligible. It is only in the process of bringing reality into being that men know anything—about themselves, each other, or nature. Thus, as men structure their world, they express that structure in language that is a collective human product. Language allows men both to concretize their apprehension of reality and to share their understanding and their knowledge with each other. Knowledge is itself therefore a social product. But Vico also believes that although men structure reality continually, the way in which they do so changes according to concrete circumstances. Therefore, men's notion of reality, their consciousness of themselves, their surroundings, and their relationships to others, also varies and undergoes change. They are responsible for that change because it is the product of their activity. Vico recognizes that all change entails the struggle between groups of individuals whose concrete situations differ enough for each to attempt to impose its own view of reality on the rest of the community. The group that succeeds legitimizes its point of view in the law and political and social institutions. Yet, despite Vico's belief in the necessity of concrete human struggle, he does not claim that reality itself becomes bifurcated. Although each social class may have its own perception of the meaning of social life, on the most fundamental level consciousness is *shared* because language is the collective product of the entire community. For Vico, language is the living testimony to the ongoing creative aspect of human activity.

Marx, on the other hand, emphasizes the extent to which reality and truth are ultimately in opposition to one another. For Marx, because the struggles that characterize human history necessarily presuppose a divided perception of reality (growing out of the division of labor), and so a divided consciousness, knowledge itself comes to be regarded as one-sided, distorted, and ideological. Even though Vico argues that men are often unaware of the true intentions of divine providence, that their actions have unintended consequences, he does not claim that men's consciousness of reality as such is faulty. The fact that men lack historical insight or perspective does not mean that their capacity to structure reality is impaired. Vico recognizes that men are not omniscient and that their consciousness of their actions is never total. Since in Vico's view consciousness mediates between men's relationships with each other and with nature according to their inventive and creative activity, consciousness can never contradict reality. The fact of particular interests or conditions does not negate the essentially *collective* activity of interpreting and reinterpreting the world.

Vico's thought is dialectical in the sense that it attempts to "reflect the real movement of phenomena" and to demonstrate "their interconnectedness and unity."[33] However, unlike Marx, Vico does not attempt to reveal the internal contradictions of these phenomena. As Hayden White points out, Vico's dialectic "is not a dialectic of the syllogism (thesis, antithesis, synthesis) but rather the dialectic of language and the reality it seeks to contain."[34] This is perhaps the crux of the difference: Although Vico recognizes that history is transformed by real struggles between real men, those struggles are not based upon a principle of contradiction, in the sense of reality confronting illusion. Any contradictions that arise come from the opposition between human intention and the work of divine providence. On the most general level, then, human reality remains intact. For Marx, however, it is reality and illusion that are the true opponents in history, and so history becomes the struggle of reality freeing itself from illusion, true consciousness freeing itself from ideology.

Given the fact that Vico does not regard human consciousness as being in fundamental opposition to reality, his theory posits no notion of false consciousness, alienation, or ideology. He agrees with Marx that the ruling class will impose its view of reality on the entire community in order to dominate and to maintain its ascendant position, but consciousness itself remains a collective product, coming into being in the context of a larger scheme devised by divine providence. As Shlomo Avineri points out, for Marx, "...getting acquainted with reality constitutes shaping and changing it. Epistemology ceases to be a merely reflective theory of cognition, and becomes the vehicle for shaping and moulding reality."[35] The same point applies equally to Vico. However, Avineri also argues that

Marx's epistemology conceals an internal tension. It tries to solve the traditional epistemological problems, but it tacitly holds that human consciousness could operate according to the new epis-

---

[33] Alan Swingewood, *Marx and Modern Social Theory*, op. cit., p. 32.
[34] Hayden White, *Tropics of Discourse*, op. cit., p. 209.
[35] Shlomo Avineri, *The Social and Political Thought of Karl Marx*, op. cit., p. 68.

temology only if the obstacles in its way in present society were
eliminated. Hence Marx's epistemology is sometimes divided
against itself: it is both a description of consciousness and a vision
of the future.... [The] imperfect modes of consciousness will exist
as long as bourgeois society continues to exist.[36]

Underlying Marx's desire to permit consciousness to coincide with
reality is his belief that "The philosophers have only *interpreted* the
world, in various ways; the point, however is to change it."[37] For Marx,
human knowledge and human history have a *purpose:* to permit men to
go beyond the mere understanding of reality and to willfully change it.
Underlying the notion that men can willfully change their world is the
idea that they can change it for the better. Once consciousness arrives at
the point at which men are able to perceive reality correctly, they
become able to change the social order so that freedom and equality
come into being for all men.[38] Thus the ultimate end of both consciousness and history is human freedom. This is not to say that Marx was a
determinist who believed that his communist vision would necessarily
come about. Nonetheless, his very idea of a communist society posits a
world that is qualitatively better than that which preceded it because,
for the first time, human freedom can be actualized.

In sharp contrast to this view Vico believes that the designs of divine
providence will always remain hidden from man. Consequently, man is
incapable of *willfully* changing history. Moreover, Vico does not claim
that either consciousness or history has any particular goal or end. As
Hilliard Aronovitch has remarked, "Vico denies that history ever comes
to fulfillment: he denies that men ever come to a stage in which sources
of essential divisiveness within and between them are overcome."[39] For
Vico, the *ricorsi* of human history always include the possibility of a

[36] Ibid. p. 69.

[37] Karl Marx, *Theses on Feuerbach* in the *Marx-Engels Reader,* op. cit., p. 109.

[38] Bertell Ollman says, "In his most explicit statement on this subject, Marx calls man's
freedom 'the positive power to assert his true individuality'. This 'true individuality' is man at the
height of his powers and needs, thoroughly and intensively cooperating with his fellows, and
appropriating all of nature. Free activity is activity that fulfills such powers, and freedom,
therefore, is the condition of man whose human powers are thus fulfilled; it passes beyond the
absence of restraint to the active unfolding of all his potentialities." (*Alienation: Marx's Conception of Man in Capitalist Society* [Cambridge: Cambridge University Press, 1971], p 117.)

[39] Hilliard Aronovitch, "Vico and Marx on Human Nature and Historical Development," in
G. Tagliacozzo, ed., *Vico: Past and Present,* vol. II, (Atlantic Highlands, N.J.: Humanities Press,
1981), p. 54.

descent into a stage of barbarism, and so there can be no end to human struggle. According to Vico struggle and conflict among men are permanent features of the human condition. Aronovitch says, "For Vico there can be no...unity to the various faces human nature has shown. In both the individual and the group some basic human attitudes and endeavors will come at the cost of others, and there will always be conflict."[40] In other words, for Vico, the fact that consciousness is the shared product of the community does not mean that the real, concrete differences between men will eventually disappear. Vico clearly distinguishes between a consciousness that is a shared social product and a consciousness that is essentially the *same* for everyone. This is perhaps the crux of the difference between Vico and Marx: For Marx, consciousness provides the means to overcoming the split between reality and illusion. The transcendence of that split in turn allows for the existence of a free social order in which the fundamental antagonisms among men have been eliminated. Vico, on the other hand, regards consciousness as the means by which men structure reality but without any final end in view. For Vico, consciousness does not develop in opposition to reality, nor does the future hold the prospect of a social world free from conflict. Although consciousness is social, it is not identical for all men. As human history unfolds, consciousness does not move in any one direction but remains the most basic connective link between men.

Ultimately, Vico's theory of consciousness suggests a less optimistic evaluation of the human condition than does that of Marx. Despite Vico's enthusiasm for the creative and innovative means by which men structure reality, he did not believe that men could consciously intervene in the unfolding of history so as knowingly to *make* a revolution. Men structure their world according to the concrete needs of their situations, but they lack the capacity to direct change itself, and the course that human consciousness takes is beyond the province of human design. Vico's thought does not conform to the Enlightenment ideal of progress, which was part of Marx's intellectual inheritance. As Sir Isaiah Berlin points out, Vico's thought is not progressive in nature, and "there is no vision of the march of mankind toward final perfection, whether inspired by a conscious realization of it...or driven by hidden but beneficient forces."[41]

[40] Ibid., p. 56.
[41] Sir Isaiah Berlin, "Vico and the Ideal of the Enlightenment," Tagliacozzo, Mooney, and Verene, eds., op. cit., vol. I, p. 262.

Religion and the Civilizing Process in Vico and Marx

Patrick H. Hutton

Neither Marx nor Vico is thought of primarily as a philosopher of religion. In Marx's case the judgment is readily understandable. Insofar as he studied religion at all, he did so to expose the nature of its illusions. The religious question, while it served as a point of departure in his early writings, proved to be a passing interest in his intellectual journey toward a more exclusive preoccupation with economic issues. It was Marx's belief that the advance of civilization toward communism would render the religious question obsolete. The topic of religion all but disappears from the writings of his mature years.[1]

Vico, in contrast, took the religious question more seriously. In the *New Science* he underscores the significance of the role of religion in the civilizing process and of divine providence in guiding that process to fulfillment. While scholars agree about the depth of Vico's insights into the anthropology of religion, his doctrine of providence has proved more controversial. Vico alludes to providence as a kind of lord of history, the guarantor of the process by which man builds his civilization. The meaning of this doctrine is sufficiently ambiguous that some scholars have discounted its significance. They argue that Vico's homage to providence was only a ruse to stave off criticism by the ecclesiastical censors. Others reinterpret the meaning of providence for the modern age. They contend that Vico's providence was a metaphor for the irony implicit in an historical process in which men's short-range intentions realize an unsuspected long-range end.[2] But the ef-

---

[1] On Marx's religious views see Kostas Axelos, *Alienation, Praxis, and Techné in the Thought of Karl Marx*, trans. Ronald Bruzina (Austin: University of Texas Press, 1976), pp. 159-73; Hans Küng, *Does God Exist?*, trans. Edward Quinn (New York: Doubleday, 1980), pp. 217-61; Saul K. Padover, ed., *Karl Marx on Religion* (New York: McGraw-Hill, 1974), pp. ix-xxviii; Charles Wackenheim, *La faillite de la religion d'après Karl Marx* (Paris: Presses Universitaires de France, 1963).

[2] For a critical evaluation of the literature on Vico's idea of providence see James C. Morrison, "How to Interpret the Idea of Divine Providence in Vico's *New Science*," *Philosophy and Rhetoric*, 12 (1979): 256-61.

fect of desacralizing Vico's providence is to secularize his theory of civilization. In such a view Vico's discussion of the making of man's rational humanity overrides his equally compelling emphasis on rebirth and redemption through a return to sacred origins. This secular reading of Vico favors a linear conception of the civilizing process, and hence obscures the cyclical conception implicit in his discussion of the *ricorsi*: the repetitive pattern of genesis and growth civilizations follow independent of their place in the chronology of world history. Religious understanding in Vico's work is thereby reduced to his discussion of religious anthropology, with no concession to the view that Vico's theory of civilization itself might have religious implications. Without entering the debate about the status Vico assigns God in the *New Science,* this essay will examine Vico's use of the term "providence" as it relates to man's faith in his own creativity.

Despite their opposing views about the authenticity of religious expression, Vico and Marx offer conceptions of the role of religion in the civilizing process that provide some striking parallels. Both explain religious need in terms of human alienation and religious origins in terms of man's mythic projection of his feelings of insecurity. Both argue that religious statements serve as indices to the development of human consciousness. Most important, both describe a creative process in which man's hope in his future possibilities enables him to transform present realities. This last topic constitutes the heart of this essay. It is their discussion of the nature of man's belief in his own creativity, with all of the imperatives that such belief implies (the call to courage, the demand for risk, the willful affirmation of the prospect of self-transcendence), which suggests that the atheist Marx and the theist Vico share a common theological ground.

Vico's conception of the role of religion in the civilizing process is based upon a theory of interpretation. While modern scholars label this theory hermeneutics, Vico entitled it divination,[3] which means literally the power to fathom the unknown—"to understand what is hidden from men—the future—or what is hidden in them—their consciousness."[4] Man's urge to create civilization begins with his efforts to interpret the meaning of natural phenomena: to find a pattern

---

[3] For the relationship between Vico's theory of religion and the new hermeneutics see W. Taylor Stevenson, *History as Myth; The Import for Contemporary Theology* (New York: Seabury, 1969), pp. 55-57, 94-107.

[4] *The New Science of Giambattista Vico,* 3rd ed. (1744), trans. and ed. Thomas G. Bergin and Max H. Fisch (Ithaca: Cornell University Press, 1961), pars. 342, 365, 382, 437, 508. Hereafter cited as *N.S.*

underpinning the chaos that renders life uncertain and precarious. At the dawn of civilization primitive man is filled with awe and wonder at a world he does not understand. Lost in ignorance, he experiences existential terror; feeling powerless, he seeks to explain the power of natural phenomena. The first civilized institutions, Vico explains, were the auspices by which man interpreted natural phenomena as signs of divine favor or disfavor.[5] Man's entry into civilization, therefore, is at its most fundamental level an act of interpretation.

Vico's theory of interpretation is integrally related to one of imagination. Man explains the world by drawing upon the creative resources of his own mind. The images with which he makes sense of the world are the bodily images with which he is most familiar. In the civilizing process man creates a human world by describing natural phenomena in anthropomorphic terms. Nature, Vico explains, is nothing more than the names that man has applied to phenomena apart from himself.[6] In this way man humanizes the natural world as he interprets his experience. In his descriptions he assigns not only human forms but human powers. For nature as primitive man understands it is alive with unknown (divine) powers. The thunderbolt becomes Jove; the earthquake, Neptune; the water spring, Diana; the earth, Cybele. The divinities proliferate as human experience widens. The map of human knowledge charts a theogony through which man comes to understand his own power to cope with the world.[7] In his effort to master his environment he reaches deeper into himself. In the process the human imagination unfolds. Human creativity, therefore, is at its source religious in character. Religion serves as the foundation for all human knowledge.

Nor does the religious need disappear as human experience, originally strange and terrifying, becomes familiar. As man comes to comprehend his human powers, his perception of the religious question changes. Vico plots a movement in the civilizing process from transcendent to immanent conceptions of God. The all-powerful God that primitive man worshipped in poetic images yields place to modern man's rational recognition of his own godlike powers.[8] Man's sense of the presence of God nonetheless endures. Despite the widening

---

[5] *N.S.*, pars. 189, 339, 367, 375, 381-82, 391, 447.
[6] Ibid., pars. 236, 331, 376, 429, 433, 484, 494.
[7] Ibid., pars. 193, 317, 377-81, 392, 402, 502, 528, 579, 634.
[8] Ibid., pars. 366, 385, 916-18, 1043.

boundaries of human knowledge the unknown future continues to awaken awe and curiosity. The images that man assigns to the unknown change, but the religious quest for meaning remains the same. Truth, Vico explains, is always perceived "under masks."[9] The unknown can only be understood in human images. Religion is a human resource and belongs to human culture.

Religious understanding in the civilizing process involves more than the creation of images of divinity. Man's efforts to fashion a human world take place in time. Hence his images of his experiences are woven into narratives, or myths. Myths tell stories that reveal the creative ways in which man has responded to the problems he has encountered in becoming aware of his world. Not only does he assign divine forms to worldly phenomena, he also defines life activity in terms of divine archetypes of human behavior. Vico recounts the myths that gave meaning to the formative civilizing experiences through which man made sense of his human nature: his suffering (through religious rites), his sexuality (through marriage), his mortality (through ceremonial burial).[10] For this reason myth provides a true account of the genesis of civilization—not a history of specific events, but a model of the type of experience with which all societies must come to terms in the civilizing process. Myth reveals man not as historical actor but as religious seeker who in the course of making his civilization asks the same questions about his nature and destiny. Although myths recount human experiences embedded in the past, their religious significance lies in the meaning they assign to the future: the unknown toward which man risks his creativity in his quest for self-understanding.

If myth reveals man's quest for meaning, history reveals the meaning of that quest. Herein Vico introduces his notion of providence.[11] He avoids all discussion of God's nature or purposes, since these lie outside the ken of human understanding. Rather he uses the term to signify that man's faith in God is the basis of his faith in his own creativity. The creation of history is a risk for man in that it is an act of faith in the face of an unknown future. Not only does man believe in God, he seeks to imitate him. Herein lies the religious significance of Vico's theory of mimesis. Man as creator imposes aesthetic form upon chaos. In this affirmation he acts as if he believes in a larger harmony. Mimesis, Vico

[9] Ibid., par. 1036.
[10] Ibid., pars. 333-37, 401-02.
[11] Ibid., pars. 133, 136, 312, 328, 341-44, 385.

explains, originally meant mimicking. In mimicking the sights and sounds of nature, man mimics what he believes to be God's own creativity.[12] The risk of creativity is undertaken in the faith that there is a divine order whose harmonies are mirrored in the human order fashioned in the civilizing process. There is thus a correspondence between man's faith in the harmony of God's eternal plan and the harmony of the aesthetic images that man himself creates. The study of history reveals that correspondence. Man pursues his own purposes in fashioning the human world, but in the process he unwittingly serves God's larger plan for the preservation of the human race on earth.

If Vico's concept of mimesis suggests a link between religion and aesthetics, his concept of wisdom suggests another between religion and social convention. Wisdom means knowledge of the way.[13] As a concept it conveys a mixture of practicality and piety. In a practical sense wisdom means the use of myth as constructive knowledge for dealing with the world. Man believes in myths for the practical truths they provide. Myth records creative improvisation with life experience, improvisation that in turn becomes the basis of custom and in time the foundation of law. The institutions that shape human lifestyles are no more than applied mythology, i.e., the regular patterns through which life activities are formalized. But in its pious meaning the concept of wisdom implies not only knowledge of, but reverence for, the way. The wisdom that Vico had in mind is the "common sense" of ordinary people to believe in the myths, to follow the rituals they suggest, to remain loyal to the social conventions they describe. For wisdom is the imitative side of creativity. Imagination is the gift of a few; imitation the lot of the many. Wise men imitate the myths of the elite of genius for the psychic as well as the practical security they offer.

Vico's concept of wisdom also sheds light upon the limits of religious belief. Just as consciousness is modified in the civilizing process, so too is man's capacity to believe. In broad terms the civilizing process is marked by a movement from belief to skepticism. In his ignorance and naiveté primitive man was given to credulity. He "no sooner imagines than he believes."[14] In a world as yet undefined he was able to let his imagination run free. The active use of imagination was an affirmation of his faith in the future. But as creative innovation becomes common

---

[12] Ibid., pars. 204, 225-29, 348, 447, 565-66, 590, 1032.

[13] Ibid., pars. 350, 362-65, 398, 948.

[14] Ibid., par. 376.

knowledge, as challenge becomes routine, myth loses its power to inspire commitment. Belief gives way to doubt; poetry is reduced to prose. As his consciousness becomes more complex and rational, man loses his capacity to accept the common wisdom. Wisdom may offer certain knowledge of the past, but it cannot provide man with certainty about the future. The creative use of myth is limited to the time in which it provides direct insight into human problems. The creation of a new reality through mythic improvisation raises new problems, problems that old myths cannot solve. New realities demand new visions of the world. The religious sense of wisdom for Vico lies in man's capacity to grasp the moment when old myths must be abandoned. It is as if man is condemned to renew continuously his creative response to life. In his creativity man seeks harmony. But to stay immersed in the harmony he has already created would be a denial of the process that makes him human—his capacity to imagine other worlds.

In the last analysis Vico's theory of civilization is founded upon a theology of human choice whether or not to create for the future. For the creation of civilization fulfills a need that does not disappear. The historical pattern of the rise and fall of civilizations possesses for Vico a certain logic: Enthusiasm ordinarily gives way to inertia; imagination to imitation; inventiveness to routine-mindedness. But from a theological perspective the choice between creativity and resignation is always open to man. Man can always transcend the particular stage of history in which he finds himself to begin the creative process once more. The religious significance of Vico's doctrine of the *ricorsi* may be interpreted in this way. Throughout the history of the rise and fall of civilizations man ceaselessly repeats the process of creativity and regeneration in his search for a form of redemption that transcends historical realities.[15] In such a vision providence is not a force that intervenes to determine the course of history, but a hidden presence that serves as the inspiration for man's radical freedom to create anew.

Marx was an atheist, but his interest in the anthropology of religion was his route to intellectual discovery. Like Vico, Marx understands religion as an expression of man's fear of a world he does not understand. God is an anthropomorphic projection of man's feelings of insufficiency.[16] For Vico, this notion had positive implications. Religious

---

[15] Ibid., pars. 349, 915, 1043, 1096, 1106-10.

[16] Karl Marx, *Toward the Critique of Hegel's Philosophy of Law* (1843), in *Writings of the Young Marx on Philosophy and Society*, ed. and trans. Loyd D. Easton and Kurt H. Guddat (New York: Doubleday, 1967), p. 250. All references to Marx's writings will be to this anthology.

belief is an act of affirmation in which man defines the images through which he subsequently interprets the world. Profane knowledge always has its sacred origins, for religious understanding is the deep source of the human sciences. But Marx had no corresponding interest in imagination as the essential mode of human creativity. Myths, which for Vico were the imaginative building blocks of the structures of perception, were for Marx only hollow fantasies that obscure the nature of reality. Because he had so little interest in the nature and function of imagination, he was unable to grasp its significance in the formation of human institutions. The notion of man as a form-maker who draws the structures of perception from the depths of his own psyche was one he never explored. The formation of structures in Marx's theory of civilization is tied to productive, not mental processes. For this reason Marx was unable to take the act of mythmaking seriously. Myths create not a way of seeking truth but a fictitious world of illusion. In his religions man employs myths to create a spiritual (i.e., nonexistent) reality in resignation to what he perceives to be the obstacles of the phenomenal world. Hence, in Marx's view, religion is an expression not only of fear but of weakness, and the emancipation from religious belief represents man's first step in the historical process of self-discovery.[17]

The key to creativity for Marx lies not in *mythopoesis* but in *praxis*. Praxis means free, self-fulfilling activity in the phenomenal world.[18] It is based upon Marx's proposition that man creates his own nature through his labor in the world. Man's nature is not an essence but an activity, and that activity involves "the ensemble" of his productive and social relationships.[19] The notion of praxis, moreover, is designed to overcome the distinction between thought and action by revealing them to be two aspects of the same dynamic process. Man shapes his thought as he shapes his environment. Herein there are certain affinities with Vico's conceptions. Both Marx and Vico argue that knowing and acting are moments of the same process of creative improvisation and that man's consciousness of the world is forged out of his attempts to change it. For Marx, as for Vico, man humanizes nature. But the emphasis in Marx is upon its appropriation rather than its interpretation. Marx's

---

[17] Ibid., pp. 248-51, 257-58.

[18] For Marx's concept of praxis see especially Shlomo Avineri, *The Social and Political Thought of Karl Marx* (Cambridge: Cambridge University Press, 1970), pp. 139-49.

[19] Marx, *Economic and Philosophic Manuscripts* (1844), pp. 294, 308-10; *Theses on Feuerbach* (1845), pp. 400-02.

conception of creativity turns upon a theory of work in which man's productive labor determines the structure of his thought.[20]

While he scorned religion as such, Marx's theory of praxis does have its religious implications.[21] In the first instance his precept that human understanding must be a "sensuous perception" suggests the religious awe he felt about the material reality of the human condition. In this respect he was deeply influenced by Ludwig Feuerbach's doctrine of human suffering. Despite his criticism of Feuerbach for his efforts to define man as an essence, Marx accepts Feuerbach's conception of man as a being burdened by his material condition. Man suffers in the sense that he is immersed in the texture of sense experience and bound by the realities of his material needs. The flight into spirituality for Marx, as for Feuerbach, represents man's refusal to accept the limits set by the material condition of his nature. The sensuous experience of the phenomenal world is the source of man's alienation, but it is also the only meaningful focus for human endeavor. Transforming that reality provides man with his only route to salvation.[22]

In this respect Marx's doctrine of praxis also involves a direction of intention. In dealing with the realities of the world man calculates his future possibilities. For Marx, as for Vico, man creates in the present as if the future holds out larger prospects. The future is a realm where the contradictions of present experience will be overcome. In this way Marx blends materialism and prophecy. In realizing his humanity man will fashion a world in which his capacity for free, spontaneous, self-fulfilling activity will be matched by a capacity to understand the world in its transparency, i.e., as it really is.[23] Thus Vico the mythmaker and Marx the demythologizer both argue that man's quest for self-transcendence is based upon his quest for a vision of the world that will enable him to grasp the meaning of the human condition in its totality.

This quest for a synthetic vision of man's humanity unfolds for both Marx and Vico through the historical process. There are certain sim-

---

[20] Marx, *Economic and Philosophic Manuscripts*, pp. 311-12; *The German Ideology* (1845-46), pp. 422-23, 437. For a comparison of Vico's and Marx's conception of work see Ernesto Grassi, "Marxism, Humanism, and the Problem of Imagination in Vico's Works," in *Giambattista Vico's Science of Humanity*, ed. Giorgio Tagliacozzo and Donald Phillip Verene (Baltimore: Johns Hopkins University Press, 1976), pp. 286-94.

[21] Cf. Karl Löwith, *Meaning in History* (Chicago: University of Chicago Press, 1949), pp. 33-46.

[22] *Toward the Critique of Hegel's Philosophy of Law*, p. 250; *Economic and Philosophic Manuscripts*, pp. 288-93, 303, 316, 325-27; *German Ideology*, pp. 418-19.

[23] *Economic and Philosophic Manuscripts*, pp. 303-07, 314; *German Ideology*, pp. 414, 427-32.

ilarities between Marx's stage theory of historical development and
Vico's civil theology of divine providence. Both philosophers believe
that historical knowledge enables man to transcend the limits of understanding imposed by his immediate experience. Both argue that men,
in pursuing their immediate interests, further the larger goal of mankind: the discovery of their rational humanity. For Marx, that goal is
achieved through the creation of a society in which man's need for self-
expression will be reconciled with his way of life, a goal to be realized at
a particular moment in history. What for Marx is a condition of progress, however, is for Vico one of repetition: man's quest for self-
understanding is an ongoing process of rediscovery and reaffirmation.
Man's need for self-transcendence requires a continual return to
origins.

For this reason each plots different landmarks in surveying the
broad pattern of historical development. For Vico, the capacity for
synthetic vision was the privilege of the poets of antiquity, who perceived the world in whole and harmonious images. The primordial
origins of civilization represent the sacred ground where the forms of
human consciousness were first defined. Throughout history, Vico
contends, consciousness-raising has involved the modification and refinement of these first poetic formulations. For Marx, however, there is
no ancient poetic sage who prepares the way for the modern rational
philosopher. Consciousness-raising is a matter of rational recognition
rather than imaginative interpretation. What for Vico had been a
matter of poetic divining becomes for Marx one of rational forecasting.
The will to transform society for the future is based upon a rational
calculation of present possibilities. For Vico, emotional expression establishes the preconditions for rational reflection. For Marx, in contrast, the rational understanding of present forms of experience
inspires the emotions needed to construct a different future. Marx's
praxis, it is clear, involves an enthusiasm of reason rather than of
wonder.[24]

For Vico, man's humanity is identified with the process of creating
civilization, whereas for Marx it is projected upon a civilization not yet
achieved. Understandably, Marx is reluctant to delineate the nature of
the classless society in which man will fully realize his creative potential. To know the future, after all, is to create it. In place of Vico's
sublime memories of the poets of antiquity, Marx provides shadowy

---

[24] *Toward the Critique of Hegel's Philosophy of Law*, p. 257.

prophecies of the activities of a new kind of worker. If the elect for Vico is the poet-founder of antiquity, the elect for Marx is the proletariat of the industrial age, who, by virtue of the nature of its alienation from its work, will for the first time in history dare to undertake a total reconstruction of society. In contrast with Vico's identification of aesthetics with primordial origins, Marx identifies aesthetics with future fulfillment. His vision of the classless society is presented as an aesthetic tableau of a world in which one can "hunt in the morning, fish in the afternoon, breed cattle in the evening, criticize after dinner...."[25]

There was a time when the religious appeal of Marx's theory was derived from the prophecy it foretold. Nineteenth-century Marxists, caught up in the notion that Marxism was a science of society, were prepared to accept Marx's predictions as the inevitable denouement of a law of history. There is a certain irony in the fact that Marx, who had so little use for myth, should have bequeathed to his followers in the late nineteenth century a doctrine that was to operate as a powerful mythology. But for all of Marx's insights into the economic foundations of nineteenth-century industrial society, the pattern of historical development that he anticipated has not come to pass. Yet, even though the economic realities he analyzed and the forms of social conflict he described have been superseded, his insights into the nature of human alienation and creativity remain useful. If his specific critique is no longer relevant, his method remains a powerful tool of analysis. For this reason the interest in Marx in recent decades has assumed a new direction. Marxist studies today are characterized by a fuller appreciation of the elements of human volition and creativity in historical development. While a reading of Marx in the nineteenth century focused upon his economics, a reading in the present age is as likely to deal with his conception of culture.[26]

Some Marxist scholars, while sympathetic to Vico, might nonetheless wish to situate his intellectual contribution permanently in an earlier age. It could be argued that Vico's depiction of providence, the hidden God who reigns over history without intruding therein, was typical of the half-emancipated intellectual of the early Enlightenment. Yet Vico's theory of religion is distinctly modern in its definition of religion

---

[25] Ibid., pp. 263-64; *German Ideology,* pp. 425, 436, 439, 467.

[26] George Lichtheim, *Marxism: An Historical and Critical Study* (New York: Praeger, 1961), pp. 393-406; Leszek Kolakowski, *Main Currents of Marxism,* trans. P. S. Falla (Oxford: Clarendon, 1978), vol. III, pp. 253-530.

as a hermeneutic task. His insight into the workings of the imagination through which man continuously interprets his own creativity addresses an aspect of human experience that Marx never adequately investigated. Vico's work complements rather than anticipates that of Marx. As Marxist scholars reinterpret Marx for the contemporary age, they would do well to take cognizance of Vico's understanding of the role of the imagination in forecasting a future whose possibilities unfailingly inspire religious awe.[27]

[27] The twentieth-century Marxist intellectuals who come closest to reiterating Vico's religious sense of forecasting are Lucien Goldmann, *The Hidden God,* trans. Philip Thody (London: Routledge & Kegan Paul, 1964), pp. 89-102, and Ernst Bloch, *Man on His Own; Essays in the Philosophy of Religion,* trans. E. B. Ashton (New York: Herder & Herder, 1971), pp. 147-240.

Vico and Marx:
Notes on the History of the
Concept of Alienation
Gustavo Costa

T he idea of alienation or estrangement (*Entfremdung* or *Entäusserung*) has a long history, encompassing the fields of Christian theology, Roman law, political science, philosophy, and psychology.[1] We know that Karl Marx's *Economic and Philosophic Manuscripts of 1844* (first published in 1932) played an essential part in the vogue that alienation has continued to enjoy since the 1940s. On the other hand, Vico's contribution to the development of that idea in the eighteenth century has not been assessed. Yet the Italian philosopher entertained original views on alienation, and helped Marx in shaping some of his opinions. Marx's admiration for Vico is a well-known fact, and was pointed out by Max Harold Fisch in the introduction to the English translation of the Vichian autobiography. On April 28, 1862, Marx mentioned the *New Science* in two letters: one addressed to Ferdinand Lassalle and another to Engels. In 1867 Marx referred to the Vichian masterpiece in a footnote in his *Capital.*[2] Although Marx did not quote Vico in reference

[1] In this paper it would be impossible to give a complete bibliography on alienation. See particularly the following studies: S. Avineri, *The Social and Political Thought of Karl Marx* (Cambridge, 1968), pp. 96-123; R. Schacht, *Alienation* (Garden City, N.Y., 1970); I. Mészáros, *Marx's Theory of Alienation* (London, 1970); P. Masterson, *Atheism and Alienation: A Study of the Philosophical Sources of Contemporary Atheism* (Dublin, 1971), pp. 79-98; B. Ollman, *Alienation: Marx's Conception of Man in Capitalist Society* (Cambridge, 1976); P. M. John, *Marx on Alienation: Elements of a Critique of Capitalism and Communism* (Calcutta, 1976); W. M. LeoGrande, "An Investigation into the 'Young Marx' Controversy," *Science and Society*, XLI, 2 (Summer 1977): 129-51; I. Feuerlicht, *Alienation from the Past to the Future* (Westport, Conn., 1978); J. R. Stanfield, "Marx's Social Economics: The Theory of Alienation," *Review of Social Economy*, XXXVII, 3 (December 1979): 295-312. LeoGrande's article has been the object of an interesting polemic: see E. K. Hunt, "A Comment on William LeoGrande's Approach to the 'Young Marx'," *Science and Society*, XLII, 1 (Spring 1978): 84-89; W. M. LeoGrande, "Marx, Feuerbach, and the Essence of Man: A Reply to E. K. Hunt," Ibid., XLII, 2 (Summer 1978): 211-18.

[2] *The Autobiography of Giambattista Vico*, trans. M. H. Fisch and T. G. Bergin (Ithaca, N.Y., 1975), pp. 104-5; B. Croce and F. Nicolini, *Bibliografia vichiana* (Naples, 1947-48), II, pp. 713-15; A. Jacobelli Isoldi, "Vico e Marx," *Giornale Critico della Filosofia Italiana*, XXX, S. 3, V (1951): 69-102, 228-53.

to the idea of alienation, I intend to demonstrate in this paper that the Italian philosopher deserves a place in the history of this idea, and that he should be considered, along with thinkers like Rousseau, Schiller, Fichte, Hegel, Feuerbach, Hess, and Bruno Bauer, in any study concerning the genesis of Marxian alienation.

The concepts of alienation that were familiar to Vico belonged to two different spheres: Christian theology and Roman law. Theological alienation, an essential feature of Judeo-Christian tradition, is the basis of the development of pagan civilizations, created by the giants, descendants of the Jews, who had lost all knowledge of the true God and, because of this, had regressed to a bestial state.[3] Seen from this point of view, the history of the gentiles is the sum of their efforts to overcome, without the help of Revelation, the dire consequences of their complete estrangement from God. In other words, theological alienation, affecting all pagan civilizations, is the implicit presupposition of the *New Science*. In addition to this kind of religious estrangement, Vico had in mind the juridical estrangement when, depicting the alienated condition of the plebeians in primitive society, he maintains that they had no property right but were themselves the property of the heroes or noblemen.[4] In dealing with this aspect of ancient history, Vico relates the juridical to the social aspect by showing how the oppressed plebeians fought against the noblemen in order to improve their status. Both kinds of alienation developed by Vico appealed to Marx's mind: the theological, because it led to a God entirely created by man, which the German thinker could easily understand in the light of Feuerbach's philosophy, and the juridical, because it was the mainspring of a social struggle that seemed to confirm materialist dialectics.

Marx's letter to Lassalle proves that in 1862 he had read the *New Science* in the French translation published by Princess Cristina di Belgioioso in 1844, and that he was looking for other Vichian works. In fact, Marx recommends to Lassalle the Belgioioso version, asserting that the *New Science* "is written not merely in Italian but in a very complicated *Neapolitan* idiom."[5] This view derives from the long introduction (a real monograph on Vico) that Princess Belgioioso had written under the influence of the historian François Mignet: "Ajoutons

---

[3] G. B. Vico, *La Scienza nuova, giusta l'edizione del 1744*, ed. F. Nicolini (Bari, 1928), I, pp.141-42 (par. 369).

[4] Ibid., I, pp. 269-70 (par. 582).

[5] K. Marx and F. Engels, *Werke* (Berlin, 1961-   ), 30, p. 622; *The Karl Marx Library*, VII, *On History and People*, ed. S. K. Padover (New York, 1977), p. 311.

encore que son italien n'est guère qu'un dialecte napolitain rattaché au latin, ce qui forme un langage inintelligible au premier coup d'oeil, pour tout autre que pour un latiniste de la ville de Naples."[6] Marx's adherence to Princess Belgioioso's introductory essay obliges us to view the Vico-Marx relationship in the larger frame of the fortunes of the *New Science* in the nineteenth century, since Princess Belgioioso mentions two major contributions that marked a new epoch in the history of Vichian studies: Jules Michelet's free translation of the *New Science* and of other Vichian works, and Giuseppe Ferrari's edition of the complete writings. Princess Belgioioso passes a harsh judgment on Michelet—who "n'a voulu donner ni une traduction exacte, ni même une analyse sévère de Vico"[7]—but shows a high opinion of the Ferrari edition: "Cette édition, qui est sans contredit la meilleure de toutes, est accompagnée de notes explicatives qui aident à l'intelligence du texte."[8] She mentions also Ferrari's essay in French, *Vico et l'Italie*, a controversial piece of Vichian scholarship.[9]

Princess Belgioioso's remarks probably had the effect of inducing Marx to shun the Michelet translation, which probably was already known to him, and to seek the Ferrari edition (containing also an Italian version of Ferrari's essay on Vico) in order to read the philosopher's juridical works. In 1862 Marx had not yet done so, because he wrote to Lassalle: "Up to now I have not been able to lay my hands on his juridical works proper."[10] However, Marx may well have been able to consult the book before the year 1867, when he published his *Capital*. The Ferrari edition was probably available at the British Museum, whose librarian, the Italian patriot Antonio Panizzi, could not have

[6] *La Science nouvelle par Vico; traduite par l'auteur de l'Essai sur la formation du dogme catholique* (Paris, 1844), pp. cxvi-cxvii. See Croce and Nicolini, *Bibliografia*, II, pp. 549-50. A similar view of Vico's style has been expressed by modern scholars such as F. Flora and M. Fubini: see G. Mastroianni, "Vico e Marx nella *Bibliografia Vichiana*," *Società*, VIII (1952): 522-23. On the Belgioioso-Mignet relationship see Y. Kibiehler, *Naissance des sciences humaines: Mignet et l'histoire philosophique au XIXᵉ siècle* (Paris, 1973), pp. 7-8, 215-24; B. A. Brombert, *Cristina: Portraits of a Princess* (New York, 1977), pp. 108-55.

[7] *La Science nouvelle*, pp. cxvii-cxviii. On Michelet see Croce and Nicolini, *Bibliografia*, II, pp. 525-38. An anonymous reviewer of the Belgioioso translation defended Michelet, asserting that the French historian "had already given to the French public all that is, at present day, at all worth having of Vico" (*Foreign Quarterly Review*, XXXIV [1845]: 291). This review has been attributed to Thomas Adolphus Trollope (1810-92): see *The Wellesley Index to Victorian Periodicals, 1824-1900*, ed. W. E. Houghton (Toronto, 1966-79), II, pp. 168-69.

[8] *La Science nouvelle*, p. cxvii. On Ferrari see Croce and Nicolini, *Bibliografia*, I, pp. 140-46.

[9] Ibid., II, pp. 590-94; F. Brancato, *Vico nel Risorgimento* (Palermo, 1969), pp. 128-35. On Ferrari's essay see footnote 46 below.

[10] Marx and Engels, *Werke*, 30, p. 623; *The Karl Marx Library*, VII, p.312.

failed to order it,[11] and at the University of London Library.[12] At the
British Museum Marx could also consult the Michelet and the
Belgioioso translations, although he seems to have possessed the former, judging from a letter of Paul Lafargue to Engels (February 6,
1884).[13] It remains a mystery whether Marx first became acquainted
with the *New Science* through Michelet or through Princess Belgioioso.
But we can assume that Marx's interest in Vico, originally kindled by
Michelet, was refreshed by the Belgioioso translation. It is also possible
that Lassalle's book, *Das System der erworbenen Rechte* (1861), revived in
Marx the memory of Vico, whose philosophy was already familiar to
him. Indeed, all passages quoted in his letter to Lassalle deal with
Roman law and reflect Vico's original interpretation of Roman history,
an important aspect of the *New Science* that could not escape Marx's
attention, since Princess Belgioioso had insisted on it, pointing out
Vico's originality vis-à-vis Niebuhr.[14]

Marx considered particularly relevant to the topic treated by Lassalle
a corollary of the *New Science*, Book 4, demonstrating "That the Ancient Roman Law Was a Serious Poem, and the Ancient Jurisprudence
a Severe Kind of Poetry, within Which Are Found the First Outlines of
Legal Metaphysics in the Rough."[15] In addition to this title summariz-
ing the content of the corollary, Marx quotes a passage from it (par.
1036) in which Vico undermines the foundation of Roman law by
showing its essentially poetic inspiration: "In conformity with such
natures, ancient jurisprudence was throughout poetic. By its fictions
what had happened was taken as not having happened, and what had
not happened as having happened; those not yet born as already born;
the living as dead; and the dead as still living in their estates pending
acceptance."[16] Marx also transcribes a passage from the *New Science*,
Book 2 (par. 513), which confirms the mythic character of ancient

---

[11] *British Museum, Catalogue of Printed Books* (London, 1881-1900), Vercamer-Victori, col.
373. On Panizzi see Croce and Nicolini, *Bibliografia*, II, p. 570; E. Miller, *Prince of Librarians:
The Life and Times of Antonio Panizzi of the British Museum* (Athens, Ohio, 1967).

[12] *Catalogue of the Library of the University of London* (London, 1876), p. 741. The Ferrari
edition is also listed in *Catalogue of the London Library* (London, 1913-14), II, p. 1191.

[13] F. Engels and P. et L. Lafargue, *Correspondance*, ed. É. Bottigelli (Paris, 1956), I,
pp. 168-69.

[14] *La Science nouvelle*, pp. cxii-cxiii. Marx maintains the same view on the Vico-Niebuhr
relationship; see Marx and Engels, *Werke*, 30, p. 623.

[15] *The New Science of Giambattista Vico* [hereafter *N.S.*], trans. T. G. Bergin and M. H. Fisch
(Ithaca, N.Y., 1968), p. 386. See *La Science nouvelle*, p. 363; Marx and Engels, *Werke*, 30, p.
622.

[16] *N.S.*, p. 390. See *La Science nouvelle*, p. 367; Marx and Engels, *Werke*, 30, p. 622.

legislation, implicitly limiting its validity to a particular phase (the heroic one) of social development: "*Heri* had this same meaning in Latin, whence *hereditas*...the heir...in inheriting represents the defunct paterfamilias."[17] It is evident that Marx viewed the *New Science* as a philosophy of property, following Vico's suggestion according to which he intended to write "a philosophy of authority...taking the word 'authority' in its original meaning of property."[18] Such a philosophy of property traced the early history of society as a tension between the privileged heroes and the oppressed slaves, whose condition was vividly described by Princess Belgioioso: "Ainsi donc pour eux, point de mariage, point de famille, point de nom; point de propriété, de contrat, d'acquisitions, d'échanges."[19] Indeed, Marx could read in the *New Science* a radical example of social alienation, founded not on Hegel's idealistic premises, but on the autonomous existence of real objects and a real social structure, where the plebeians were originally regarded as enemies. In fact, the heroes swore eternal hate against the plebs, as Michelet noted in his Vichian translation.[20]

Someone may argue whether Vico's view first lent support to Marx's criticism of Hegel and then to the dramatic shift that his idea of alienation allegedly underwent in 1845-46, when estrangement founded on human essence and considered as a contradiction between existence and essence was replaced by estrangement founded on an alien power dominating man.[21] Whatever the case, Marx could not fail to realize that the *New Science* contains an anthropological as well as an historical philosophy, and that its view of history, fashioned after a spiral pattern, binds the future of man to a rigid system of recurrent stages of civilization. Moreover, Marx was certainly aware that Vico's historical theory rests on a complete ignorance of the Industrial Revolution and of its economic and social consequences. In fact, Marx, who had probably read the Michelet translation before writing the *Economic and Philosophic Manuscripts of 1844*, asserts in the latter a philosophy of history completely different from the Vichian one, because it combines the Judeo-Christian eschatology with the modern myth of progress leading to a new Golden Age. In other words, Marx felt that Vichian thought was incomplete and needed a radical revision: the events

[17] Ibid., p. 174. See *La Science nouvelle,* pp. 171-72; Marx and Engels, *Werke,* 30, p. 622.
[18] Ibid., p. 120 (par. 386). See *La Science nouvelle,* p. 108.
[19] Ibid., p. lxxviii.
[20] *Oeuvres choisies de Vico,* trans. J. Michelet (Paris, 1835), I, p. xxxiii.
[21] LeoGrande, "An Investigation," pp. 143-49.

analyzed in the *New Science* proved that history led nowhere, but repeated itself indefinitely, unless the pessimistic idea of historical recurrence was replaced with the optimistic one of a final regeneration brought about by communism, viewed as "the riddle of history solved" and "the complete return of man to himself as a *social* (i.e., human) being—a return become conscious, and accomplished within the entire wealth of previous development."[22] Marx was encouraged to insert a final stage into the spiral pattern of the *New Science* because he realized that Vico, having flourished before the age of capitalism, does not take it into account. If the Italian philosopher was able to find himself at ease with the classical scheme of ascent, decline, and fall, Marx, aware of the abyss dividing the preindustrial from the industrial age, had by necessity to switch from a static to a revolutionary vision of human destiny.

The considerable change brought about by the Industrial Revolution was apparent to Marx even in the more traditional field of agriculture, which was radically transformed by modern capitalism: "The power of industry over its opposite is at once revealed in the emergence of *agriculture* as a real industry, while previously it left most of the work to the soil and to the *slave* of the soil, through whom the land cultivates itself."[23] It was exactly this preindustrial stage of agriculture, the only one that Vico considered possible, that warranted the Vichian concept of alienation. But Marx saw in contemporary Europe a unique kind of estrangement caused by the modern economic system, in which "the extension of products and needs falls into *contriving* and ever-*calculating* subservience to inhuman, unnatural and *imaginary* appetites."[24] Modern history does not hold to the rigid pattern of development and

[22] K. Marx, *Economic and Philosophic Manuscripts of 1844,* trans. M. Milligan (New York, 1973), p. 135. For the background of Vico's historical thought see G. W. Trompf, *The Idea of Historical Recurrence in Western Thought: From Antiquity to the Reformation* (Berkeley and Los Angeles, 1979). My interpretation of Marx's historical thought is founded on the following studies: K. Löwith, *Meaning in History* (Chicago, 1960), pp. 33-51; M. Eliade, *Le mythe de l'éternel retour: archétypes et répétition* (Paris, 1949), pp. 219-20; R. C. Tucker, "Marx and the End of History," *Diogenes,* 64 (Winter 1968): 165-74; F. E. Manuel and F. P. Manuel, *Utopian Thought in the Western World* (Cambridge, Mass., 1979), pp. 697-716. Among recent studies dedicated to Marx's vision of history see particularly W. H. Shaw, *Marx's Theory of History* (Stanford, Calif., 1978); C. Lefort, "Marx: From One Vision of History to Another," *Social Research,* 45, 4 (Winter 1978): 615-66; M. Rader, *Marx's Interpretation of History* (New York, 1979); D. R. Gandy, *Marx and History: From Primitive Society to the Communist Future* (Austin and London, 1979).

[23] Marx, *Economic and Philosophic Manuscripts,* p. 123.

[24] Ibid., p. 147.

decay set by Vico. We do not have a prearranged recurrence of events where the positive is strictly intertwined with the negative and barbarism itself is a beneficial force, despite its cruelty and its superstitions. Instead of this we have an anomalous, malignant cycle, combining all negative aspects of the various stages of civilization and therefore leading mankind to ruin. Barbarism comes back accompanied by ecological disaster in a new destructive guise that Vico did not even suspect: "Man returns to a cave dwelling, which is now, however, contaminated with the pestilential breath of civilization, and which he continues to occupy only *precariously,* it being for him an alien habitation which can be withdrawn from him any day."[25] Indeed, according to Marx, "man is regressing to the *cave dwelling...*in an estranged, malignant form."[26] The recourse of barbarism is not a palingenesis of mankind, purging itself of the corruption inherent in a previous decadent age (as Vico viewed it), but a mixture of old and new evils without any benefit: "The crudest *methods* (and *instruments*) of human labor are coming back: the *treadmill* of the Roman slaves, for instance, is the means of production, the means of existence, of many English workers."[27]

That Marx found Vico's spiral system deficient is attested by his letter to Engels, where he alludes to the *New Science*, Book 2 (paragraph 445), according to which German is "a living heroic language." Marx observed that, if Vico read Austrian or German newspapers like the *Presse* or the *National-Zeitung,* he would retract this judgment.[28] This is more than a passing criticism on a particular point of Vico's thought: it is a radical rejection of an abstract scheme superimposed upon an historical material not sufficiently digested. Vico had wonderful insights into the early history of Greek and Roman civilizations, but he was unable to understand contemporary life because he was bound by his philosophy to recognize in present events the pattern of past events. Vico founded the continuity between past and present in the structure of human mind, revealed by Locke in his *Essay Concerning Human Understanding.* In fact, according to the *New Science*, Book 1 (paragraph

---

[25] Ibid., p. 148. See *Marx and Engels on Ecology,* ed. H. L. Parsons (Westport, Conn., 1977), p. 205 and *passim.*

[26] Marx, *Economic and Philosophic Manuscripts,* p. 155.

[27] Ibid., p. 149.

[28] *N.S.,* p. 148; Marx and Engels, *Werke,* 30, pp. 227-28. This passage proves that "Marx's letters show at every turn his concern for, and his sensitivity to, literary style"—S. S. Prawer, *Karl Marx and World Literature* (Oxford, 1976), p. 207.

331), "the world of civil society has certainly been made by men," and in view of this, "its principles are...to be found within the modifications of our own human mind."[29] Marx accepted from Vico the principle that men make their own history, but he did not call attention to the permanent structure of the human mind (as Vico had done). Marx preferred to stress the concrete historical conditions inherited from the past, as appears from *The Eighteenth Brumaire of Louis Bonaparte* (1852): "Men make their own history, but they do not make it just as they please; they do not make it under circumstances chosen by themselves, but under circumstances directly found, given and transmitted from the past."[30] No matter how strong the influence of historical conditions may be, the recurrence of past events is not possible because history is not a spiral, repeating itself ad infinitum. What at first sight seems a return of past figures and facts is a mere illusion, fostered by the creators of new history, who "anxiously conjure up the spirits of the past to their service and borrow from their names, battle slogans and costumes in order to present the new scene of world history in this time-honored disguise and this borrowed language."[31]

Although he rejected Vico's spiral pattern, Marx did not want to dispose of Vichian social alienation. But if the present phase of history has nothing to do with the preceding ones, having completely different economic and social features, the Vichian idea of a radical alienation, recurring at different times under analogous circumstances, is no longer tenable. In view of this Marx transferred Vico's concept of estrangement to modern times, viewed as a unique, anomalous, and malignant course of history, initiated by the Industrial Revolution. This is apparently what Marx did in the *Economic and Philosophic Manuscripts of 1844,* centered on the idea of social alienation, quite different from Hegel's ontological and Feuerbach's religious estrangement. Marx maintained the same attitude in the *Grundrisse* (1857-58), where he treats estrangement in the context of the accumulation of capital, caused by the dissolution of earlier modes of production, when the free workers, possessing only their labor capacity, "confront all objective conditions of production as *alien property,* as their own *not-property.*"[32]

---

[29] *N.S.*, par. 331, p. 96.

[30] K. Marx, *The Eighteenth Brumaire of Louis Bonaparte* (New York, 1935), p. 13.

[31] Ibid. A French scholar has recently warned that it would be wrong to attribute to Marx "quelque nietzschéisme ou vichisme secret s'imposant malgré lui"—P.-L. Assoun, *Marx et la répétition historique* (Paris, 1978), pp. 14-15.

But ancient history does not show such dissolution, which cannot be brought about by the mere presence of monetary wealth. The ancient world did not end its history with free labor and capital, and therefore ignored true alienation, because "the dissolution of the old property relations...instead of leading to industry...led in fact to the supremacy of the countryside over the city."[33] Even in the *Grundrisse,* as he had already done in the *Economic and Philosophic Manuscripts,* Marx implicitly criticizes the idea of an eternally recurrent alienation held by Vico, substituting for it a concept of estrangement founded on an exceptional course of history, without parallel in the ancient civilizations, which postulates a radical solution, able to create a new economic and social order.

In *Capital* (1867) Marx confirms his admiration for Vico: "as Vico says, human history differs from natural history in this, that we have made the former, but not the latter."[34] Marx refers to the *New Science,* Book 1 (paragraph 331), where the so-called *verum/factum* principle is clearly stated: "Whoever reflects on this cannot but marvel that the philosophers should have bent all their energies to the study of the world of nature, which, since God made it, He alone knows; and that they should have neglected the study of the world of nations, or civil world, which, since men had made it, men could come to know."[35] Marx could not miss this passage, because Princess Belgioioso amply commented on it: "Nous ne connaissons que ce que nous avons fait, dit Vico, l'esprit ne connaît qu'en créant: *le critérium du vrai, c'est de l'avoir fait.*"[36] But Princess Belgioioso elaborated on the Vichian reference to God, while Marx preferred to ignore it, giving a wholly secular interpretation of Vichian thought, which was followed by Antonio Labriola in his essay *In Memory of the Communist Manifesto* (1895): "And had not Vico already recognized that Providence does not act in history from without? And this same Vico...had he not reduced history to a process which man himself makes through successive experimentation consisting in the invention of language, religion, customs and laws?"[37] In other

---

[32] K. Marx, *Grundrisse: Foundations of the Critique of Political Economy (rough draft),* trans. M. Nicolaus (Harmondsworth, 1973), p. 502 (Notebook V).

[33] Ibid., p. 506.

[34] K. Marx, *Capital: A Critique of Political Economy,* trans. S. Moore and E. Aveling (New York, 1970), I, p. 372, n. 3.

[35] *N.S.,* p. 96.

[36] *La Science nouvelle,* p. lv.

[37] A. Labriola, *Essays on the Materialistic Conception of History* (New York, 1966), p. 76.

words, Marx viewed Vico as a forerunner of Feuerbach and bequeathed this arbitrary image of the author of the *New Science* to the Marxian school of thought. He was therefore ready to accept the allegedly antimetaphysical inspiration of Vichian philosophy, throwing away "the ideal eternal history traversed in time by every nation in its rise, development, maturity, decline, and fall."[38] Marx read in the *New Science* Feuerbach's religious alienation, but he did not accept Vico's idea of a recurring social alienation.

Discussing the greed for surplus labor, Marx asserts that, whenever the means of production are monopolized by a part of society, "the laborer, free or not free, must add to the working-time necessary for his own maintenance an extra working-time in order to produce the means of subsistence for the owners of the means of production, whether this proprietor be the Athenian καλὸς κάγαθός, Etruscan theocrat, civis Romanus, Norman baron, American slave-owner, Wallachian Boyard, modern landlord or capitalist."[39] This passage from *Capital* seems a concession to Vico because it apparently equates the ancient, the medieval, and the contemporary world. Had this been the real intention of Marx, the Vichian concept of alienation no longer would have proven to be an embarrassment to him. But Marx had a completely different view: he considered the surplus labor of ancient history much more limited than the one experienced after the advent of the industrial era, because in antiquity the use value of the product predominated over its exchange value, while in his times it was the other way around. In view of this the modern series of events has nothing to do with the past, contrary to Vico's opinion. The validity of Vichian thought is undermined by modern economic and social facts that never took place in antiquity or in the Middle Ages and were, therefore, completely unknown to Vico. Marx admits that "in antiquity over-work becomes horrible...when the object is to obtain exchange value in its specific independent money-form; in the production of gold and silver."[40] But Marx insists on the fact that such cases were absolutely exceptional in antiquity, while they are quite normal in modern times: "as soon as people, whose production still moves within the lower forms of slave-labor, corvée-labor, &c., are drawn into the whirlpool of an interna-

---

[38] *N.S.*, p. 79 (par. 245). On the Feuerbach-Marx relationship cf. R. Mondolfo, "Feuerbach e Marx," in *Umanismo di Marx: Studi filosofici 1908-1966* (Turin, 1968), pp. 8-78; R. C. Tucker, *Philosophy and Myth in Karl Marx* (Cambridge, 1972), pp. 95-105 and *passim*.

[39] Marx, *Capital*, I, p.235.

[40] Ibid.

tional market dominated by the capitalistic mode of production, the sale of their products for export becoming their principal interest, the civilized horrors of overwork are grafted on the barbaric horrors of slavery, serfdom, &c."[41] We are in a new phase of history which cumulates the horrors of civilization with those of barbarism. In view of this Marx simply transposes alienation from a recurrent stage of history to a new historical reality different from the one described by Vico. This solution, adopted by Marx in the *Economic and Philosophic Manuscripts* and in the *Grundrisse,* appeared still satisfactory to the author of *Capital,* who equated social and religious alienation in his theory of the "Fetishism of commodities."

In order to explain "the Fetishism which attaches itself to the products of labor, so soon as they are produced as commodities," Marx refers the reader to religious experience: in "the mist-enveloped regions of the religious world...the productions of the human brain appear as independent beings, endowed with life, and entering into relation both with one another and the human race. So it is in the world of commodities with the products of men's hands."[42] The concept of religion underlying Marx's position is Vichian thought interpreted in the light of Feuerbach's philosophy. On one hand, primitive men created a complex mythology, starting with the figure of Jove, "an image so popular, disturbing, and instructive that its creators themselves believed in it, and feared, revered, and worshiped it in frightful religions";[43] on the other hand, modern men are making new idols that condition modern mentality so that "a definite social relation between men...assumes, in their eyes, the fantastic form of a relation between things."[44] Vico did not even suspect any parallelism between religious and economic facts because he did not live in England, where modern capitalism first developed, but in the Kingdom of Naples. In Italy the phenomenon of the dissolution of serfdom and of the transformation of the serf into a free proletarian took place in the Middle Ages (almost exclusively in the northern and central regions of the peninsula), but this was reversed at the end of the fifteenth century by the radical change in world trade caused by the geographic discoveries: as a conse-

---

[41] Ibid., I, p. 236.

[42] Ibid., I, p. 72. On the relevance of the concept of fetishism in Marxian thought see H. Lewin and J. Morris, "Marx's Concept of Fetishism," *Science and Society,* XLI, 2 (Summer 1977): 172-190.

[43] *N.S.,* p. 118 (paragraph 379).

[44] Marx, *Capital,* I, p. 72.

quence of this, the "laborers of the towns were driven *en masse* into the country, and gave an impulse, never before seen, to the *petite culture*, carried on in the form of gardening."[45]

In conclusion, Marx dealt with Vico as any original thinker is expected to deal with his predecessors: he systematically betrayed him. Marx found in Vico many exciting ideas concerning ancient society and particularly the representation of the alienated slave, which provided gist to Marx's views about social estrangement. But Marx could not fail to notice that Vico's penetrating insights were buried under a mass of antiquated lore, organized in a rigidly repetitive structure. Despite Princess Belgioioso's brilliant defense of the author of the *New Science*, Marx came to share Ferrari's severe judgment: "Il y a peu de grands hommes qui aient eu plus de génie que Vico; il y a peu d'hommes qui aient systématisé un plus grand nombres d'erreurs; les plus sublimes vérités de la *Science nouvelle* se trouvent enveloppées d'absurdités."[46] The Italian philosopher cared more for his system of thought than for concrete reality, and he did not admit any radical change for worse or for better. Vico's "ideal, eternal history" is essentially retrospective and does not admit any palingenetic hope. The future of Europe appeared to Vico a recourse of past events, as Ferrari noted in his essay: "Qu'arrivera-t-il de l'Europe? Ici Vico se tait; mais l'histoire idéale est là comme une triste prédiction applicable à toutes les histoires...on voit bien que Vico prédestine l'Europe au même sort que Rome."[47] On the contrary, Marx believed that the destiny of Europe was set on a completely new course by the Industrial Revolution, which caused an unprecedented social alienation, similar to the religious one, and became the prophet of a new age, terminating the estrangement of mankind. Paradoxically, the founder of historical materialism proved to be closer to the Judeo-Christian tradition, strictly related to the Golden Age myth, than the author of the *New Science*, a book meant to be an apology for Christianity.

[45] Ibid., I, p. 716n.
[46] G. Ferrari, *Vico et l'Italie* (Paris, 1839), p. 477.
[47] Ibid., p. 352.

If a Science of Human Beings Is Necessary, Can It Also Be Possible?–A Paradox in Vico and Marx   Hilliard Aronovitch

There is a paradox at the center of Vico's conception of a science of the human world; essentially the same paradox is present in Marx. After stating the paradox generally, I shall bring it out in each thinker, showing the moves or assumptions each makes in the unsuccessful attempt to resolve it. The paradox can be avoided, but at the price of a deep pessimism about the project of a human science. My conclusion will be on the side of such pessimism, and while thus not pleasing, it should at least stand as plain and not paradoxical.

The general terms of the paradox can be quickly sketched thus: On the one hand, we can be sure a science of the human world is *possible* because that world has been made by human beings, and what human beings have themselves made must be especially intelligible and transparent to them; on the other hand, we see that a science of the human world is *necessary* because at the prescientific, commonsense level that world continually appears to us as opaque and illusion-ridden, which is to be expected since what is done and made by human beings is typically unwitting and tangled. In other words, the thing that makes a human science possible—the special intelligibility of the human world to us (humans)—is the very opposite of what makes a human science necessary—the special unintelligibility or opacity of the human world to us (humans). Hence, insofar as a human science seems possible, it appears unnecessary, and insofar as it seems necessary, it appears impossible. Moreover, both the claim about the possibility of a human science and the claim about its necessity derive from the same initial premise—the human world (unlike the natural) has been made by humans, and that affects its knowability for humans—but on the one side it is then held that the knowability is affected for the better, and on the other side that it is affected for the worse.

Separated as Vico and Marx are in their respective contexts and commitments— Vico an eighteenth- (and in a sense seventeenth-) century Italian, who was at first a Cartesian and then an anti-Cartesian, and who was always a committed Catholic and mostly a political conservative; Marx a nineteenth- (unquestionably nineteenth-) century German who began as an almost-Hegelian and became an anti-Hegelian, and who was from first to last an atheist and political revolutionary—both men nonetheless banked on the possibility of a science of the human world and labored to construct it. And for both the starting point was the distinctiveness of the human world in comparison with the natural world. Though Marx read Vico too late in his career to have been influenced by him, he testifies to the shared starting point in the one published mention he makes of Vico: "Would not such a history [that of human technology] be easier to compile than natural history since, as Vico says, human history differs from natural history in this, that we have made the former but not the latter?"[1]

I

The doctrine in Vico to which Marx refers is that of the *verum-factum* principle, according to which one can definitely know the truth only about what one has made. When Vico enunciated this principle in *De antiquissima*, he took it to apply principally to mathematics, which he regarded as a purely human construction, by contrast with physics, whose subject matter—the natural world—was the work of God and as such susceptible of being truly known only by Him. With his major work, the *New Science*, Vico extended the *verum-factum* principle to human history and society, thus making the human domain capable of being the subject of a science, i.e. "the new science." Vico says it is

> a truth beyond all question: that the world of civil society has been made by men, and that its principles are therefore to be found within the modifications of our own human mind. Whoever reflects on this cannot but marvel that the philosophers should have bent all their energies to the study of the world of nature, which, since God made it, He alone knows; and that they should have neglected the study of the world of nations, or civil world, which since men had made it, men could come to know.[2]

[1] *Capital,* trans. S. Moore and E. Aveling (Moscow: Progress, 1954), vol. I, p. 352n.
[2] *The New Science of Giambattista Vico* [hereinafter *N.S.*], trans. Thomas Bergin and Max H. Fisch (Ithaca: Cornell University Press, 1968), par. 331.

In a restatement of the principle Vico says

> that this world of nations has certainly been made by men, and its
> guise must therefore be found within the modifications of our
> own human mind. And history cannot be more certain than when
> he who creates the things also narrates them.[3]

Notice that it is not being claimed that being the creator of something
guarantees or makes it automatic that you will know it with certainty,
only that being the creator makes such knowledge possible. That,
however, is precisely the possibility-claim that makes up one side of the
paradox. Still, we need to consider (1) what Vico means by true knowledge—or scientific knowledge, assuming that is what he is here talking
about, and (2) why such knowledge of things should be specially or
uniquely accessible to their creator(s). Unfortunately, it is not possible
to consider fully in this paper either of these matters, not to mention
both; fortunately, the essentials on each will do.

Genuine knowledge for Vico is scientific in being knowledge that
penetrates to the causes or roots of things, and so takes us below the
level of surface seemings. By "causes" Vico means conditions of origination and development, not Humean causes, that is, merely conditions that regularly precede their effects. In Vico causes are conditions
that generate their effects and do so necessarily. That is why to know
something, for Vico, is one and the same as knowing the causes of it in
the sense of knowing how it came to be what it is. *Scienza,* scientific
knowledge, is thus knowledge of things in and through knowledge of
their generating causes. Knowledge of this sort definitely involves
knowledge of regularities, or rather laws, and Vico often identifies
scienza by contrasting it with *coscienza,* which is only knowledge (actually
just awareness) of particulars. But the reason that laws or generalized
knowledge are marks of science for Vico is that the truth about how
things originate, develop, and come to be what they are is spelled out in
that way.

> We explain the particular ways in which things first came into
> being; that is to say, their nature, the explanation of which is the
> distinguishing mark of science. And finally these origins are con-
> firmed by the eternal properties the institutions preserve, which

[3] Ibid., par. 349.

could not be what they are if the institutions had not come into being just as they did...[4]

At the risk of oversimplification we can, then, put together everything we have been saying in this paragraph into an extended equation: Genuine knowledge, for Vico = science = knowing the causes of things = knowing the conditions of their origination and development = knowing the laws characterizing their origin and development. But more important for us than any of these equivalent ideas is a further one that must be included among them. For Vico, scientific knowledge, as just spelled out, goes beyond or beneath the mere appearances of things and the variety of them as particulars; it uncovers the reality of things. Philology and history, Vico insists, leave us only with a

> deplorable obscurity of causes and almost infinite variety of effects which philosophy has had almost a horror of treating; and which philosophy reduces...to the form of a science by discovering in it the design of an ideal eternal history traversed in time by the histories of all nations.[5]

The story that science tells about human affairs is not at all written on the surface of them; on the surface there is no coherent story in human affairs; there is somewhere there a story to be told, but it takes the special knowledge of science to tell it.

Its message does not matter for us in this essay, but the manner of arriving at it does. From the above albeit abbreviated account of what Vico means by a science we can see why Vico should have thought that the (scientific) knowledge of something is specially or uniquely possible to its creator(s). The reason is that the creator seems specially and perhaps uniquely in a position to know what went into the thing. Granted, Vico owes an explanation of why he counts us latecomers in history as creators of it or as embodying the nature of its creators sufficiently so that we can know how and why they made the past as they did. I believe, though, that the required explanation can be found in Vico—and anyway, it is not at issue here.[6] Let it be conceded that we can

[4] Ibid., par. 346.
[5] Ibid., par. 7.
[6] See my "Vico and *Verstehen*" in *Vico: Past and Present,* ed. G. Tagliacozzo, (Atlantic Highlands, N.J.: Humanities Press, 1981), vol. I, pp. 215-26.

somehow substitute ourselves for, or put ourselves in the place of, those other humans, even those in the remote past, and so know their doings and makings as well as, and maybe even better than, they did. The issue remains as to why that knowledge must take the form of science, where that means going beyond common sense, using categories and forms of explanation not used by (pretheoretical) common sense. Of course we can answer: because that is what is required to know things truly, as was before explained. But why should knowledge of the human world have to take the form of science as the *unveiler of appearances*? Why couldn't knowledge of human things, even showing the causes of them, etc., consist simply of pretheoretical common sense? The answer to *that* is: because, as Vico insists, what human beings do and make is almost invariably cloaked by unconscious motivation; what appears to be the basis or motive for something, for some thought or deed or institution, is so often very different from the real basis or motive. Vico theorized, for example (along lines now familiar from Freud), that our ancestors living in family-based societies fashioned the figure of Jove out of "the reigning fathers," and that there thus arose "fear of the divinity, the cult of which is the first fundamental basis of commonwealths"; and such cults and commonwealths thus emerged, though "men's intentions were quite otherwise" than to form them.[7] In these and other major social developments the wrinkle is not just in the emergence of consequences other than anticipated ones; that wrinkle is surely there as a constant and complicating factor of human affairs, but the further, more disturbing factor consists of the undercurrent of motivations, a level of motivation of which agents are systematically unaware. The existence of such undercurrents makes it necessary that science see and see through the surface of human affairs, if it is to give the true generating conditions of them. A central quality that the human world has because of being made by humans—the opaque quality due to things having been unconsciously motivated—necessitates a scientific knowledge of it that transcends common sense.

But then, is what is necessary really possible, and if so, how? With the answer to this question we shall see that the promised paradox is securely in place and that it is only by a large dose of faith that Vico can pretend it is not. The problem just being posed was: What basis does Vico have for believing that the cloak of unconscious motivation that covers human phenomena and makes them unknowable to common

---

[7] *N.S.*, par. 629.

sense can be stripped away by a science? The "solution," for Vico, was there from the start and even explicitly laid out by him: The role of providence in history assures that there is an underlying rhyme and reason to human action and historical development. So when explanations of history exhibit the relevant rhyme and reason—whatever it may be, and the sort is already specified in the conception of providence— they can be taken as showing the true causes and natures of things. Vico repeatedly characterizes science as the proof of providence, as deserving the title of true knowledge just to the extent that it provides that proof; that is, to the extent it uncovers the appearances of things to show the hidden hand of God. In one of the very first paragraphs of the *New Science* Vico proclaims:

> It will be shown in the present work that...law exists in nature. The conduct of divine providence in this matter is one of the things whose rationale is a chief business of our science, which becomes in this aspect a rational civil theology of divine providence.[8]

The (quasi-Cartesian) role of providence as an epistemological guarantor of historical explanations is stated even more explicitly later in the text:

> Our new Science must therefore be a demonstration, so to speak, of what providence has wrought in history, for it must be a history of the institutions by which, without human discernment or counsel, and often against the designs of men, providence has ordered this great city of the human race.[9]

And:

> The decisive sort of proof in our Science is therefore this: that, since these institutions have been established by divine providence, the course of the institutions of the nations had to be, must now be, and will have to be such as our science demonstrates...[10]

---

[8] Ibid., par. 2.
[9] Ibid., par. 342.
[10] Ibid., par. 348.

There is nothing really remarkable in the fact that Vico believed in divine providence or even in the fact that he made it an essential part of the science he was trying to build, and one would be very wrong to suppose that Vico's conception of science can be articulated with providence omitted or somehow secularized.[11] The inclusion of providence in Vico's program for a human science, however, does not at all resolve the paradoxical clash between the contention about the possibility of a human science and the contention about its necessity. On the contrary, the claims about providence only reinforce the paradox, and for reasons quite apart from general doubts about the existence of God. For one thing, as always with claims about providence's guiding hand, even if we are prepared to believe in it, there are the unsolvable difficulties as to exactly when and how providence is at work. Consequently, to allege that we can know we have penetrated the appearances of human history when our account shows how providence is at work in it is to argue in a circle. The circle is a very vicious one at that, for it can plausibly be suggested that in selecting a particular explanation as the explanation that shows the hand of providence we have ourselves been deluded by unconscious motives (wishing that something be providential when it is not.) And besides, if the working of providence in human affairs is our basis for believing that we can somehow know the real truth about them, then human affairs are *not* after all made by human beings, at least not wholly and not in the most significant respects. And if that is so, then how can Vico, given his central, *verum-factum* principle, suppose that *human beings* can know the "human" world? Must he concede that, after all, history like nature is knowable only by God? But what sense, then, can it make for Vico to write his book? He cannot overcome the paradox of the possibility versus the necessity of a human science except at the cost of complete incoherence. The paradox of course has its own price of incoherence for Vico's system, but not as high a price as when one tries to deny the paradox with the help of providence.

II

If we move now to Marx, we shall see that it is not just Vico's endeavor to construct a human science (with, as one might be tempted to think,

[11] I myself made just that supposition in "Vico and Marx on Human Nature and Historical Development," in G. Tagliacozzo, ed., op. cit., vol. II, pp. 47-57. Cf. L. Pompa, *Vico* (Cambridge: Cambridge University Press, 1975), pp. 51-61.

its seventeenth-century idiosyncracies) that suffers from such deep difficulties.

We have already seen that Marx agrees with Vico as to the distinctiveness of the human world versus the natural world and as to the implication that a science of the human world should be more readily feasible than a science of nature. There is not in Marx a labeled doctrine that parallels the *verum-factum* principle in Vico, but Marx obviously thought in terms of such a principle from the start. One of the main things Marx appropriated from Hegel, and used in his critique of traditional materialism, was the idea that the human world is the ongoing creation of human beings, and not of purely natural (or divine) forces. Marx writes that "the science of man is therefore itself a product of man's establishment of himself by practical activity."[12] He means that the content of the science of man is simply the story of the human making of the human world; and Marx elsewhere underscores that "all mysteries which mislead theory into mysticism find their rational solution in human practice and the comprehension of this practice,"[13] which is to say that the special content of a human science, human *praxis*, makes that science eminently intelligible to human beings. The possibility of a human science is guaranteed by the fact that the science is about human *praxis*, the world (insofar) as humanly made.

But what then does Marx mean by "a science," whether of the human or of the natural world? What kind of knowledge of the human world are we being guaranteed? Like Vico, Marx unquestionably identifies scientific knowledge with causal knowledge, and he too thinks of causes as generating conditions that are essential to, and constitute, what they generate. It is this conception of causes that leads Marx to say, for example, both that production determines consumption as well as that "production is also immediately consumption" and even "consumption is also immediately production."[14] Science is about causes, for Marx, but evidently not Humean ones. The basic causes of origination and development are, as in Vico, spelled out in laws. There is great controversy over what Marx's view is of the scope and force of these laws, but there is no doubt he holds that the discovery and articulation of such laws are essential earmarks of science.

[12] *Economic and Philosophic Manuscripts of 1844,* in *The Marx-Engels Reader,* ed. R. Tucker (New York: W. W. Norton, 1978) 2nd ed., p. 91.

[13] *Theses on Feuerbach,* in Tucker, op. cit., p. 145.

[14] *The Grundrisse,* as in Tucker, op. cit., p. 228-29.

I wish to draw attention, however, to a related aspect of science as Marx conceives of it. It is the aspect of science, that we have already seen was central for Vico, as a form of knowledge that delves beneath or behind the appearances of things. Some sentences from Kolakowski's recent study of Marx, with the quotation from Marx they contain, clearly reveal the importance of that aspect to Marx:

> The phenomenon of profit must be explained on the assumption that all commodities are sold at their true value. This sounds paradoxical, but as Marx observes in *Wages, Prices and Profit*, "it is also a paradox that the earth moves around the sun and that water consists of two highly flammable gases. Scientific truth is always paradoxical if judged by everyday experience which catches only the delusive appearances of things"[15]

Marx in effect makes it a rule: "If there were no difference between essence and appearance, there would be no need for science."[16] Of what sort, though, is this gap between essence and appearance in human affairs? How and why does it arise? The general and familiar answer for Marx is that the gap has a systematic character and basis: Human affairs are governed by unconscious motivations rooted in the productive needs of a society and the particular class interests associated with them. This claim about unconscious motivation is of course not—any more than the corresponding claim in Vico was—a psychological one alleging a general tendency of people or of some people to be especially selfish and then given to rationalizing away that fact about themselves; rather, the claim is a sociological one about how the social roles and institutions in which people act and live affect them, and affect them in ways of which they may be systematically unaware. So it is that "an epoch imagines itself to be actuated by purely political or religious motives, although religion and politics are only forms of its motives...[17] Marx concludes this statement by emphasizing that generally "the historian accepts this opinion," that is, the systematically deluded opinion that a society or a social class has of itself and its times (and indeed of history as a whole). But the susceptibility of historians to the "illusion of

[15] L. Kolakowski, *Main Currents of Marxism*, trans. P.S. Falla (Oxford: Clarendon Press, 1978), vol. I, p. 275.

[16] Cited in G. A. Cohen, *Karl Marx's Theory of History: A Defence* (Princeton: Princeton University Press, 1978), p. 326.

[17] *The German Ideology*, in Tucker, op. cit., p. 165.

the epoch" further testifies for Marx to the need for a genuinely scientific, demystifying account of the human world. Marx aimed in the whole corpus of his writing to supply just such an account. But what made him believe that he, or anyone, could provide that kind of thorough and final unraveling of the tangle of history and human perceptions?

The question is not, what made Marx in the first place think that a science of the human world is possible? We have already seen that Marx, like Vico, took it from the start that a human science was possible because he held that the humanly made world, above all, must be intelligible to human beings. But we have now found in Marx, as we did in Vico, the view that the human world regularly gives rise to distorted and deluded conceptions of itself such that if it is to be made intelligible, the intelligibility will have to come in the form of a science, a systematic unveiling of illusions. So the question now is, how could Marx have persisted in thinking that what is necessary is after all possible? In other words, the paradox has again taken concrete shape, and the question is why Marx did not see it, or if he did, why he thought he could resolve it or get around it. The problem I am thus posing for Marx is much harder than one that is commonly posed and with which it may be confused. It is often asked how Marx could have thought, could have dared to think, that he was seeing straight while claiming everyone else was seeing crooked. That problem could perhaps be answered adequately if it could be shown that Marx was just smarter than everyone else, or knew more, or happened to hit on the right angle for seeing things. But, by Marx's own reckoning, such factors will not suffice to explain how he could claim that he or anyone could come to see not merely straighter and better than everyone else but in a radically new and different way, as science—and not mere, though maybe well-honed, common sense—sees.

Science, as we have it in the developed form of physics and chemistry, breaks through the appearances of everyday life by means of technical concepts, special instruments, and established laws that it builds on. Certainly science even at its best is far from error-free; I am not suggesting the contrary, nor did Marx. But science, on the other hand, is also very different in kind and level from the best wisdom of the man on the street or in the market, for that wisdom is always still specially liable, or anyway immeasurably more liable than science, to be caught up in surface illusions. The liability is there because everyday wisdom is gleaned from, and articulated in terms of, how things seem to be.

Science hardly takes things as they seem even to the ordinarily astute eye. It is science in that quite strict sense Marx believed necessary in human affairs because of how specially illusory he believed the appearances of history and society to be. But if, for Marx, science in the sense specified is necessary for the reason specified, how can it still be thought possible and even already in essence attained by him?

The core of the explanation is that Marx was convinced that history had taken a new turn with the emergence and development of capitalism and the working class. The turn consists of the beginning of a new way of fashioning social events and institutions, a way that for the first time in history is self-conscious and rational and that has its culmination in socialism. To grasp the issues here properly we must first get straight on a matter in Marx that is often not adequately understood. It is often thought that according to Marx the big and decisive break in the pattern of social and historical development is to come with the end of capitalism and/or the implementation of socialism. Unquestionably that break is a major one in Marx's schematization of development. He speaks of it as marking the transition from the realm of necessity to the realm of freedom and even as the passage out of the "pre-history" of mankind.[18] However, seen from another perspective in Marx that break is really just the final act of a new historical departure that occurred earlier, somewhere in the middle or late stages of the development of capitalism. This new departure consists of the gradual coming together of the working class as a revolutionary agency and, as part of this, the emergence of a collective awareness of the true workings of capitalism and its limits. Early in his career Marx had proclaimed that "when the proletariat announces the *dissolution of the existing social order,* it only declares the *secret of its* own existence."[19] Marx holds and must hold that already within capitalism the workers come to see the world in its true light. That occurs because in struggling to transform capitalism they begin to fashion the world in precisely the collective self-conscious manner that eliminates the illusions that otherwise attend human action. Marx's own theory is to be nothing more, though nothing less, than the articulation of what is happening in human history and of the new type of consciousness that has arisen. This means that Marx's claim to be presenting a science of the human world is grounded in his

---

[18] *Capital,* vol. III, as in Tucker, op. cit., p. 441.
[19] *Contribution to the Critique of Hegel's Philosophy of Right: Introduction,* in Tucker, op. cit., p. 65. (Emphasis in the text).

conviction that for the first time that world has begun to be truly transparent, devoid of illusion and mystification. Marx's point about the possibility of a human science, that the possibility rests on the intelligibility to humans of what they themselves make, has its payoff here. When the making is of the requisite sort, a science comes about. But is the paradox thus resolved? Has it been shown that Marx can simultaneously uphold the possibility and the necessity of a human science and even maintain sensibly (whether or not in the end correctly) that the science is actual or quickly becoming so?

It should be evident that the paradox has not been resolved or avoided and that Marx has just been made to dance from one side of it to the other. When we began to explain how he might cope with it, what seemed especially in jeopardy was the *possibility* of a human science, given the compelling Marxian case for the opacity of the human world and for the need to have something more than commonsense knowledge to make it intelligible. Then the possibility of a human science was restored to the favored position, and Marx was permitted to allege that the science had in fact come about in his writings—only to have that science be suddenly unnecessary and even pointless. For if the inception of the science coincides with, and is a consequence of, the world's having suddenly begun to be transparent, devoid of illusions, then the science is stillborn. If the function of science is systematically to extend and to correct common sense, then Marx's science seems to lose its essence and function as science from the moment it becomes actually possible to elaborate it. Marx's writings could still perhaps claim for themselves a useful and even valuable role: By carefully spelling out how the world was now coming to be seen and altered, they might further that vision and transformation—but not by virtue of being *scientific* writings. We need only remember here that the works of poets and novelists and also of wise social critics can help us see afresh and even change ourselves or the world accordingly, without any suggestion of a science having to enter into the matter. I shall return to this line of thought presently, but we still have to fill in here the final chapter in our account of Marx. Marx's views on the relation between science and a socialist society give proof that he cannot escape the paradox in question.

Marx actually comes to the conclusion that in a socialist society there can be no meaningful need or role for a human (or social) science. G. A. Cohen has intriguingly explored this theme in an appendix to his recent book defending Marx's theory of history. Cohen contends that "for Marx, socialism and social science are incompatible—as socialism develops, social science must wither away."[20] Cohen argues, though, that Marx did not distinguish as he should have between science as a corrective on (the illusions of) common sense and science as an extension of (the limitations of) common sense. Cohen finds unacceptable the thesis of the "withering away of social science" when applied to science in the latter sense but not when applied to science in the former sense. I would maintain, however, that the prospect of everyday knowledge of social life being essentially correct, free from illusion, is as thoroughly implausible as is the prospect of such knowledge ever being complete. Whether or not a human science is possible for us, there would always be much need for it in both regards; in fact the two regards seem hardly separable, for any significant addition to my knowledge of what I and others are doing will require me to reconceive these things and perhaps also the motives or purposes of them. If Cohen's hopes for everyday consciousness under socialism are millennial, Marx's hopes are all the more so. Moreover, that millennialism in Marx testifies to how deeply at odds was his view of the possibility of a human science with his view of its necessity. And Cohen seems not to see that the problem, indeed the paradox, has been there all along, even before the question arises over what the coming of socialism means for the science that Marx thought he was building.

III

A final comment on Cohen will lead us to our own conclusion. Cohen maintains that "it is reasonable to find the need for a science of society intrinsically regrettable" even when that science is needed just to supplement and not also to correct common sense.[21] He says:

I believe that it is desirable for a person to understand *himself* without relying upon theory. For there is a sense, difficult to make clear, in which I am alienated from myself and from what I do to the extent that I need theory to reach myself and the reasons governing my actions.[22]

[20] G. A. Cohen, op. cit., p. 326.
[21] Ibid., p. 342.
[22] Ibid., p. 343.

This provocative thought is a tempting one to accept, but it is nonetheless mistaken, I believe. What is regrettable is not that we need a human science but that we need it and seem ever unable to attain it. And the error of Vico and Marx lay in overestimating the ease of attaining it—indeed, in taking as the guarantee of its possibility what appears to be the prime obstacle in its way, namely, that the science is about ourselves.

I must be content in this quick conclusion to suggest far more than I have space to support, but suggestiveness may be just what is useful at this stage. I do not wish to claim that a science of human beings is an impossibility, only that there are major difficulties to be overcome if it is to be achieved, and that we seem sadly far from being in a position to overcome them. A central difficulty has been explored by Charles Taylor in his illuminating essay "Interpretation and the Sciences of Man."[23] Taylor stresses that "man is a self-interpreting animal" and that in the quest for a human science "that of which we are trying to find the coherence is itself partly constituted by self-interpretation."[23] This complex process becomes an especially entangled one, I would stress, because of interests and unconscious motivations affecting social agents and scientists seeking to comprehend them; and because, of course, social scientists are themselves social agents whose activity affects and is affected by the activity of other social agents and is itself part of what is to be understood. No current methods or models for the social sciences seem to promise a way out of this morass. Certainly the actual achievements of these sciences are entirely unimpressive.

It would be seriously wrong, however, to infer that we don't need a human science or that if we do, it is regrettable; at the same time it is a mistake to think that we are entirely at sea without one. Vico and Marx were right about the necessity of a human science. Such a science is necessary precisely because our everyday, commonsense knowledge is seriously incomplete and flawed; it often fails us to the point where we become sure that we had been taking for real what is not. Yet to regret, as Cohen does, that human self-knowledge should stand in need of completion, not to mention correction, through theory is essentially to wish that we be less complex, less deep, less rich beings than we are. It is, in effect, to wish for an almost inhuman simplicity and straightforwardness to personal and social life, which appears far from what Marx had in mind in his actual sketches of socialism. The real regret, again, is that we should be creatures whose complexity is such that it would take

---

[23] *Review of Metaphysics*, XXI, 1 (September 1976): 16

a science to understand us truly and that that science continues to evade us, though we have no reason to think it impossible.

Without a science there is still surely much that we can discover and confirm about ourselves and society. And what we learn about different types of people, programs, and even patterns of social development can be very valuable, all the more so if we are candid about its not having the backing of specialized concepts and high-level laws. Such candor will enable us to count for its full worth what seems wise and right in Vico, Marx, and others, while remembering that no one of us is likely soon to put aside seeing through a glass darkly.

Vico, Marx, and Anti-Cartesian Theory of Knowledge

Tom Rockmore

As the aim of this paper is to compare the positions of Vico and Marx through their relation to Descartes and Cartesianism, we can begin with a comment on their respective understanding of the relation of knowledge and history. It is well known that for Descartes, knowledge of experience, which, under proper conditions, is incorrigible, is separate from history, which he regards as a mere *fabula mundi.* But for both Vico and Marx, from different perspectives, knowledge necessarily leads to the historical process. Indeed, Marx may have been partially influenced by Vico on this point, for he remarks in *Capital,* in a passage on the history of technology,: "And would not such a history be easier to compile since, as Vico says, human history differs from natural history in this, that we have made the former but not the latter?"[1] This passage echoes Vico's fundamental epistemological claim, *"verum et factum convertuntur."* But although both theories of history have received attention in a large literature, quantitatively greater for Marx and probably qualitatively better for Vico, less attention has so far been devoted to the epistemological views that mandate the turn to history, and almost none to the relation between the two views on this point. Accordingly, the aim of the present essay is less the interpretation of each position in isolation, although that cannot be wholly neglected, than the comparative study of two similar but independent reactions against the Cartesian epistemology and the subsequent unrelated turn to history.

Different positions can be compared in a variety of ways, but as a general rule it would appear that the comparison cannot be wholly independent of the kind of relation that can be demonstrated between the views in question. In the present case comparison hinges on an understanding of the genesis of the relation between two positions whose similarity is mediated, not by the influence, either indirect or

[1] Karl Marx, *Capital* (New York, 1906), p. 406.

direct, of one thinker upon the other, but rather in some other, more general, and basically different manner. For although Marx does mention Vico in the passage quoted as well as in several other places, and seemed to appreciate the latter's thought, the earliest reference by name does not occur until 1862, and it does not appear that he would have been familiar with the *New Science* before about 1850, when, on even the most generous interpretation, the main lines of his own position were already in place.[2] It follows that Vico can hardly have contributed directly to the formation of the Marxian position. Nor can Vico's influence be shown to impact on Marx's view indirectly through the mediacy of other positions that can be held to have influenced it.

Although neither a direct nor indirect influence of Vico's thought on the constitution of Marx's view can either be demonstrated or held to exist, there is nonetheless a remarkable series of parallels between the two positions. The parallels can be developed on a number of levels, including, but not limited to, those of the respective conceptions of civil society, subjectivity, historical knowledge, and the emphasis on practice as opposed to theory. In each of these areas and in others as well a deep and substantive similarity between the two positions can be detected— though this should not be taken as an assertion of complete agreement—which seems inexplicable in terms of more usual modes of explanation through direct or indirect influence.

But it seems entirely possible that another form of influence can be adduced. Indeed, it is the thesis of this paper that the parallels to be discussed below arise through, and can be understood in terms of, the relation of both thinkers to the modern philosophical tradition, and in particular to Descartes and Cartesianism. In this respect Lukács is partially correct in his famous claim, uncritically repeated in almost identical terms by Horkheimer, that in ways consistent with the respective positions the whole of modern philosophy has been preoccupied with the problem of the distinction between the history of man, which we have made, and the history of nature, which we have not.[3] But the strength of this unusual insight into the structure of modern philosophy is considerably vitiated by the regrettable confusion of the equally

---

[2] For speculation as to when Marx read Vico see B. Croce, *Bibliografia Vichiana*, ed. F. Nicolini (Naples: R. Ricciardi, 1948), vol. 2, p. 714.

[3] George Lukács, *History and Class Consciousness* (Cambridge, Mass.: M.I.T. Press, 1973), p. 112; Max Horkheimer, *Traditionelle und kritische Theorie* (Frankfurt/Hamburg, 1970), pp. 71-72.

fundamental confusion between the Cartesian and anti-Cartesian sides of the philosophical tradition.

Despite the confusion inherent in the formulation of his claim, Lukács is correct in implying the existence of a basic affinity in the post-Cartesian stage of the philosophical tradition, beginning with Vico, among those who hold, against Descartes, that the condition of knowledge is that we are in some sense the producers of what we can and in fact do know. An example of someone who holds a similar view, uninfluenced either directly or indirectly by Vico, is Kant who, in the introduction to the second edition of the *Critique of Pure Reason*, formulates the claim, which follows from his celebrated Copernican Revolution, that reason can have insight only into that which it produces according to a plan of its own.[4] But the similarities among those who hold this view against Descartes are due neither to the influence of Vico's position, which was only understood much later, nor to mere chance resemblance. On the contrary, they are the product of a joint, but independently achieved, common stance to a basic philosophical option, a turning point in the modern tradition of philosophy in terms of which conceptual roads tend to divide. Indeed, according as one or another branch of this conceptual road is followed, there is an observable tendency to draw together or drive apart otherwise unrelated and disparate positions.

A cardinal example of a conceptual turning point in the history of philosophy is the role of the Cartesian position in the constitution of the modern tradition. Research in this century has exposed stronger links between Descartes' position and earlier thought, especially Augustine's, than previously suspected, and this in turn weakens the extent to which Cartesianism may fairly be said to usher in a wholly new philosophical moment or to constitute an unprecedented new beginning. Descartes' position continues to be recognized as a fundamental element, however, perhaps the most basic building block of the modern philosophical world view. Much of the modern philosophical tradition, to be sure, consists in a series of attempts to reject the Cartesian framework by a host of important thinkers often incorrectly thought to be united mainly, if not only, by that goal. On the contrary, to the extent that Descartes' thought is indeed central to the evolution of the later philosophical tradition, acceptance or rejection of it has the effect of creating strange conceptual bedfellows, such as Peirce and Heidegger,

---

[4] I. Kant, *Critique of Pure Reason*, p. B xiii.

often ignorant even of one another's existence. But in retrospect much of the strangeness is dissipated when the underlying reasons for the observable relations between such apparently disparate views is made manifest, for they are precisely related through their prior relation to Descartes.

Another example of such an association, mediated through the position of a third thinker, is the relation of Vico and Marx. The former, of course, is known widely, although perhaps not widely enough, as one of the first and most significant of Descartes' critics, although the extent and depth of his firsthand knowledge of that view are not altogether clear. The latter is more famous for a variably defined set of doctrines, collectively known as Marxism, which are always invoked in his name, but whose relation to his own position is often tangential at best. Their intellectual backgrounds are, to be sure, widely disparate. Vico, as is well known, was influenced mainly by Plato and Tacitus, Grotius and Bacon. The influences on Marx's position stem mainly but not exclusively from the German philosophical tradition, including Hegel, to a lesser extent Fichte, but also Aristotle. But despite the differences, and they are real, there is an important point of intellectual contact in terms of which a series of interesting similarities, some of which will be discussed here, can be seen to arise. Although this point has not often been made, no doubt because following Marxist dogma there is a widespread tendency, among Marxist and non-Marxist commentators, to view Marx's thought as sui generis and hence unrelated to the philosophical tradition, in a sense his entire position is based on the rejection of the Cartesian philosophy, particularly its doctrine of subjectivity and knowledge. Since it is from this perspective that Marx arrives at a theory of history and knowledge surprisingly like that of the *New Science*, it seems entirely possible to view the relation between the two positions, including their similarities and differences, as the result of their respective critical reactions to Descartes and Cartesianism.

Although the relation of both thinkers to each other is, as already mentioned, mediated through their independent, critical relation to a third thinker, it should immediately be noted that there is more than one way to be critical of a body of thought. Vico was one of the original critics of Descartes, although his criticism is often apparently formulated in terms of his understanding of Cartesianism. Marx, on the other hand, has almost nothing directly to say about Descartes, if indeed he says anything at all, though he does have more to report about Descartes' intellectual heirs, particularly Hegel. But insofar as Hegel sees his own position, not wholly erroneously, as the culmination of the Cartesian impulse in philosophy, Marx's critical response to modern philosophy, especially to Hegel's thought, can be understood in relation to the Cartesian dimension intrinsic to the recent tradition.

As has already been emphasized, Vico's relation to Cartesianism is less to the wider doctrine than to the original position from which it springs. The relation is complicated by several factors, including the imperfect state of his knowledge of Descartes' view as well as its initial acceptance and later rejection in his thought. Vico's criticism, which interests us here, is diffuse, touching on a wide variety of topics in Descartes' position. In order to sharpen the focus, and keeping in mind the present concern with epistemology, it seems best here to concentrate initially on the main objections raised, perhaps in clearest form, in his *De antiquissima Italorum sapientia*.

In this work Vico attacks the Cartesian position at three main points—concerning the cogito, the proofs of God, and the criterion of clear and distinct ideas. It has often been stressed that these criticisms follow from Vico's famous claim that we can only know what we make. But in view of the widespread anti-Cartesian character of much of modern philosophy, not enough attention has been given, I believe, to the way in which later discussion, through ignorance, repeats Vico's largely unknown, pioneer efforts.

The Cartesian reliance on the cogito must be rejected since my self-awareness is insufficient to defeat the skeptic who will readily concede it, but who will not admit that from my own consciousness any cognitive conclusions can be drawn. Although Vico here evidently relies on his conviction that mere awareness of a result is insufficient for a claim of knowledge if we are not also cognizant of its causal origins, the objection has a modern ring. In a sense it anticipates Husserl's later claim that once Descartes regresses into the cogito, he cannot return to the world, since from knowledge of essence one cannot make any existential inferences at all.

Vico further rejects the a priori Cartesian proofs for the existence of God with the remark that they are the result of an impious curiosity. Although this kind of comment has no more than rhetorical weight, the objection nonetheless is meaningful if to know is to make. Since God is not produced or otherwise caused as a result of such proofs, but only known, it follows that neither God nor any other possible object of cognition can be known on an a priori basis. The result, then, of this line of argument is to reject the utilization of an a priori approach to the proof of God's existence in terms of a general objection to all claims for nonexperiential knowledge. It is perhaps worth noting that, although Kant, for instance, maintains a similar point, his well-known criticism of the ontological argument, which rests on a narrower ground concerning its intrinsic validity with respect to the problem of predication, is considerably less general and hence weaker than Vico's point.

In analogous fashion Vico also opposes the Cartesian criterion of clarity and distinctness. The objection here is twofold. On the one hand, if we again appeal to Vico's prior epistemological conviction, mere clarity and distinctness is, as he points out, insufficient to support a claim for knowledge, unless we also make what we know, in which case the criterion is superfluous. This criterion is also insufficient, as he points out, for purposes of Descartes' own argument, since it does not permit him to defeat skepticism. Because of perceptual relativity, what is clear and distinct to one observer may well be less so, indeed insufficiently so for cognitive purposes, to someone else. Vico here puts his finger on the problem of subjectivity in perception so dear to recent English philosophy. Thus, although Descartes' apparent intention is to eliminate all subjectivity through the appeal to wholly objective perception, he is himself forced to admit, in his response to Arnauld, that indubitability means only that he himself cannot imagine how the perception in question could in fact be doubted, a point that has recently been echoed in another context by Gadamer.

Although there is an enormous body of literature concerning Marx's position, the extent to which an anti-Cartesian stance is intrinsic to his thought has, to the best of my knowledge, not as yet been explored at any depth. This oversight is quite simply due, in part because of Marx's own self-misunderstanding as well as the interpretative pressure exerted by his followers, to the general reluctance to recognize the philosophical status of his view. Nonetheless, it is not difficult to discern anti-Cartesian currents within his overall position.

There is, to be sure, the often-mentioned emphasis on the relation of theory to practice, which has assumed the status of an imprecise slogan in the discussion. This doctrine is difficult to interpret since Marx does not say much about it, but rather, as it were, exhibits it in his writings. Certainly, it has often been misunderstood in the anti-intellectual stress on practice as opposed to theory by many of his followers, so often reproduced by politically neutral Marx exegetes, as well as in the unfortunately widespread tendency to ignore the Aristotelian component of his understanding of practice. But for present purposes it is

perhaps most important to note his insistence on the practical or experiential evaluation of theory as well as his criticism of Hegel's alleged
attempt to resolve the problem of alienation solely on the theoretical
plan. This stress on the intrinsically and necessarily practical relation
of theory to the world in which we live is obviously diametrically opposed to the Cartesian understanding of knowledge as a wholly theoretical process.

The view of theory as intrinsically related to practice rests on a notion
of the subject that is fundamentally unlike—indeed, the direct obverse
of—the Cartesian spectator of all that is. One of the most widely known
aspects of Marx's thought is his attention to work as the predominant
form of human productive activity in capitalism. Through work, Marx
suggests in quasi-idealistic fashion, man literally produces his product,
his social relations, his entire social context, and himself as a worker.
But work is merely one aspect of man's activity, as Marx indicates in his
view of what may be called free human activity, which will, he believes,
be made possible as the result of the transition from capitalism to
communism, and through which man will be able to produce himself as
a fully individual human being. Marx's idealist emphasis on man as a
basically active being, whose present passivity is linked to a transitory
historical stage, is strictly opposed to the Cartesian spectator view of
subjectivity. Perhaps the closest analogy to Marx's view at this point is
the understanding of human being in pragmatism.

There is a further, anti-Cartesian dimension to Marx's position that
has been widely ignored—and, indeed, perhaps obscured by the Marxist claim regarding its scientific and, by implication, nonphilosophic
status. Descartes' emphasis on the cogito as the *fundamentum incon-
cussum* was later attacked from different perspectives, and has more
recently become an explicit issue in the widespread revolt against
foundationalism. At least one facet of this revolt was, however, anticipated by Marx in his little studied comments on epistemology in the
introduction to the *Grundrisse*. Here he argues in effect that a "linear"
theory of knowledge is not possible because experience must be interpreted in terms of categories that, although a priori with respect to that
which they are employed to construe, from another perspective are
seen to emerge from experience. Although he is dealing in this passage
only with the Hegelian system, Marx's adoption here of a "circular"
theory of knowledge clearly belongs in the ranks of the hermeneutical
approach as old as Aristotle and currently popular among the post-
Husserlian phenomenologists opposed to Cartesianism.

If we turn now to comparison, we can immediately note that Vico and Marx attack the Cartesian edifice at different points. Vico's criticism is mainly directed at the epistemological presuppositions of the putatively universal Cartesian methodology. The consequence of this critique is to return, in modified fashion, to the Aristotelian view that theory is dependent on, and limited by, its object. Marx's objections are directed more to the Cartesian concept of subjectivity and its associated view of knowledge. For if one substitutes an anti-Cartesian understanding of subjectivity, a radically different view of knowledge must be maintained.

Although the angle of criticism of the Cartesian view is dissimilar, there are a number of parallels between the two views that arise from their independent assaults on the Cartesian framework. For as is the case for any well-articulated body of thought, the Cartesian world-view is constructed of a series of conceptually interrelated building blocks upon each of which the entire theory stands or falls. To the extent that each of the basic doctrines is essential to the entire theory, denial of any of them will cause the position to collapse. Conversely, insofar as criticism emanates from a self-consistent theory, regardless of the perspectival differences from which objections to a third position might arise, the mere fact that both positions serve as points of departure for objections to the same, third body of thought, and hence that each maintains theses opposed to it, will serve to bring about a positive resemblance between the positions on the basis of which the criticism is launched.

From the epistemological perspective the central similarity between the positions of Vico and Marx, as mediated through their relation to Cartesianism, is their respective relativization of the famous Cartesian ontological distinction between subjectivity and objectivity, terms that differ not in degree but in kind. This distinction is basic to the Cartesian epistemology, for it is in virtue of the belief that the world is already there and fully constituted independent of us that we can pretend to knowledge through a concept of the subject as the mere spectator of all that is. In terms of this strategy it is perfectly reasonable to shift attention from the subject to the object, as Descartes does, since the knower can reasonably be reduced to a mere epistemological function whose only role is to provide a wholly unbiased account of the purely given. Precisely this inference was indeed drawn by the English empiricists, who, since they accepted broadly the Cartesian ontological distinction, were able to approach epistemology, as is still the case in that part of the tradition, mainly through the restricted entry afforded by the problem of veridical perception.

But either on the arid, abstract plane of Cartesian metaphysics or on the more concrete level of the world in which we live, there are finally only two ways to understand this relation: either objectivity is independent of subjectivity or it is not, although the manner of the dependency may vary considerably. Now if the ontological distinction is relativized, there is no independent given to be known precisely because what we know is in some sense dependent upon us who know it. Otherwise stated, for both Vico and Marx an ontological dependency of subjectivity and objectivity replaces the Cartesian view of their independence as a condition of knowledge. But if that which we know is to depend upon us, the rules of the Cartesian epistemological game become substantially altered in several ways. To begin with, the subject cannot be passive on pain of there being neither knowledge nor a world to be known. Secondly, knowledge depends on subjectivity, since the limits of what can be known are circumscribed by what can be and is made by us. More generally, the nature of knowledge depends on a conception of the knower as actor whose activity manifests itself both on the epistemological and ontological planes, basically unlike the Cartesian view. Further, since the object is no longer already constituted prior to, and apart from, its encounter with subjectivity, but rather is produced by the subject, knowledge is no longer conceived of under the sign of eternity but in time.

In practice both Vico and Marx relativize the Cartesian ontological distinction through a shift to the temporal, social world and hence to history, although neither draws the full implications of that shift as clearly as I have tried to draw them here. Consistent with his view that we know what we make, Vico turns his gaze from nature, which is indeed wholly constituted prior to its relation to us and hence unknowable by man, to the problem of history. With the exception of a single reference in the *Paris Manuscripts,* Marx is also disinterested in the problem of natural knowledge. This is true even if some of his disciples have made claims for dialectical knowledge of nature through the extension of a dialectical method, which Marx has never been shown to use or even to formulate, to nature and the related, but abortive attempts to constitute dialectical versions of natural science. Engels has further claimed, in the spirit of the assumed distinction between nonideological science and ideological philosophy, that the contribution of Marx's view, or historical materialism, was to expel philosophy from the realm of history.[5] But if we deny the Marxist presupposition of the incompatibility of science and philosophy, which runs counter to the traditional claim for philosophy as the science of sciences, a basic parallel between the positions of Vico and Marx emerges, since as a result of their respective criticisms of Descartes and the Cartesian world-view, both thinkers turn independently to the elaboration of a philosophical science of history.

The respective views of the science of history are similar—indeed, in some respects strikingly so—despite the conceptual independence of their origins. Both stress genetic explanation according to which, for both Vico and Marx, what is must be understood as the latest stage of a developmental process. Both also share an emphasis on civil society and its analysis in terms of class structure. Both insist on the concept of an overriding historical structure whose agency is partially human and partially extrahuman, whether in Vico's concept of providence or in Marx's view of the causality of capital. Both further make claims for a necessary relation of knowledge to practice—in Vico's position in the connection of philosophy and philology, and in Marx's thought in the view of the practical evaluation of theory. And there are other similarities in terms of which this list could easily be extended.

But as is often the case in comparing two similar positions, the dissimilarities are more interesting than the resemblances. The emphasis on similarities between the two positions, each of which could in turn be developed in detail, should not be permitted to obscure the numerous ways in which they differ, although it should not therefore be thought that all differences are equally significant. If we turn now to direct comparison, we can note that both views are of approximately equal explanatory richness and self-consistency. And although the canons of historical scholarship have undergone revision since Vico's time to a degree that would render much of the detail of his view literally unacceptable on merely historical grounds, a related comment can also be made for Marx's position. It would, I submit, be naive for anyone now to accept without qualification the view of the proletariat found in his writings, although this concept is rightly regarded as one of the pillars of his overall position. But there are, I believe, further differences between the two positions that will allow us to distinguish them at least relatively, if not absolutely.

---

[5] Friedrich Engels, *Ludwig Feuerbach and the Outcome of Classical German Philosophy* (New York: International Publishers, 1941), p. 59.

One such difference concerns the type of historical model each employs. Vico favors a circular view in which history is held to advance before collapsing back upon itself, whereas Marx employs a quasilinear model in which each successive moment is further advanced from a teleological perspective than its predecessor. In a real sense for the former we are eternally caught up within, and hence condemned to, history, whereas the latter holds open at least the possibility, if not the certainty that his political epigones have too often asserted, of an historical escape from history. But although one may therefore be thought of as presenting a politically conservative view that in the final analysis emphasizes the fundamental lack of historical change, and the other can be seen as stressing the concept of historical advance in progressive fashion, from the philosophical perspective a choice between them on political and hence prephilosophical grounds, although perhaps strategically necessary, would be unjustified.

Another, perhaps more significant way to differentiate the two positions is in respect to their views of historical knowledge. Just as the similarity between the two positions can be understood in terms of their resistance to Cartesian philosophy, so their differences can also be grasped in the same manner. This point can be made in terms of two central elements of the Cartesian view, namely the concepts of system and certainty. Following Plato Descartes restates the relation of the argument to the premises from which it derives in his appeal to a quasigeometrical form of philosophical science as well as in his reproduction of the metaphor of the tree of knowledge implicit in Plato's position but rendered explicit by Aristotle. Descartes further preserves the Platonic insistence that knowledge in the full sense, or science, is not mere opinion but self-validating, hence indubitably true as an integral part of his own response to Pyrrhonism.

It is interesting, in view of their criticism of Descartes and his tradition, that both Vico and Marx attempt to give systematic form to their respective views of the science of history. The Vichian explanatory framework is both ideal, since there is a single specifiable historical structure that must necessarily be followed by every nation, and eternal, since it is wholly deducible as a series of a priori or timeless truths from prior axioms. The axioms themselves are neither deducible nor demonstrable a priori, nor are they inductive generalizations. Rather, as Pompa has suggested,[6] they arise from various sources, including

[6] Leon Pompa, *Vico: A Study of the New Science,* (Cambridge: Cambridge University Press, 1975), p. 110.

Vico's own observations concerning the universal criteria of social life (*N.S.*, par. 334)[7] and his reading of classical authors.

Vico's formulation of a theory of historical explanation upon first principles that are neither a priori nor a posteriori is extremely modern, correctly anticipating by several centuries the central consequence of Quine's attack on Kant's analytic-synthetic distinction, which had not as yet even been formulated. The result is a general historical framework that has a double status. As ideal, it is located beyond experience in a way that permits interpretation of the full range of historical phenomena without denying the wealth of experience. But as real, that framework is verified in experience through the reciprocal relation of philosophy and philology, or the science of history (*N.S.* 140). Marx also offers a systematic account. But in virtue of the idealist nature of his conception of system, his discussion has a reductionist tinge in terms of which some forms of experience, allegedly derivative, are to be understood not in terms of themselves or an external, ideal framework, but rather through other experiential modes that are allegedly prior and from which, in the final analysis, all other types of social experience can be said to derive.

Marx's view of system is quasirationalist, but its proximate source lies in the idealist tradition. In the period following the publication of the *Critique of Pure Reason* it was widely held that although the conclusions were correct, they needed to be reformulated in more rigorous fashion. The basic idealist concept of system, in which the entire theory derives in quasigeometrical, rationalist fashion from an initial, self-evident premise, was originally stated by Reinhold, later utilized by Fichte in his important, early work, and accepted as paradigmatic by Schelling and Hegel.

Marx echoes this idealist, quasirationalist understanding of system in his well-known insistence on the explanatory priority of the economic dimension of social life. The advantage of this approach is that further forms of social life can be understood in terms of political economy in general, which in turn can be grasped through the unanalyzed concept of private property, whose genesis Marx claims to explain through the concept of labor. But the difficulty of this strategy is that in attempting to explain all other dimensions of social life in terms of its economic component—and that in terms of private prop-

---

[7] I shall refer to the *New Science* in parentheses in the text as N.S., followed by paragraph number.

erty—Marx is required to reduce the former to the latter and the latter to merely one of its dimensions. Otherwise stated, Marx's idealistic view of systematic historical explanation introduces a reductionistic dimension to his position lacking in Vico's own position.

But although Marx's historical reductionism is a disadvantage with respect to Vico's view, he seems to understand more clearly than does Vico that the traditional concept of knowledge cannot be defended on the plane of human history. Although Vico denies that man can know nature, his view remains Cartesian in his apparent belief that knowledge in the full and traditional sense is possible in respect to human history. He draws, to be sure, a distinction between conscience and knowledge (*N.S.*, par. 137), according to which the former is the result of philology (*N.S.*, par. 138-9) and the latter corresponds to the Aristotelian view of knowledge, which derives from philosophy (*N.S.*, par. 163). But he then proceeds to blur this distinction in several ways, such as the fundamental claim that we know what we make (*N.S.*, par. 331) and the further claim, twice stated in identical terms, that we can know human history through study of the modifications of our human mind (*N.S.*, pars. 331, 349). The inference, which is clear, is that although we cannot know nature, we can, through knowledge of the human psyche, achieve on the plane of history, which we make, a form of knowledge akin to that attainable by God as the author of nature. Thus, although Vico perhaps never directly states this claim, his view seems to commit him to the belief that even though there is a difference in object from nature to history, the degree to which knowledge is in fact possible is not itself basically different in the two realms.

Vico's insistence on the difference between historical and natural forms of knowledge is indeed an important insight, as Berlin has recently emphasized,[8] since he thereby anticipates the nineteenth-century emphasis on *Verstehen,* which is still with us in the hermeneutical movement. But Vico fails to go far enough in drawing the consequences of his distinction, a mistake perhaps also present among some students of hermeneutical phenomenology, perhaps because he did not fully realize the significance of it. In particular he remains too Cartesian in his belief that historical knowledge differs from natural knowledge mainly in terms of object, but not in kind. In this respect a relative advantage of Marx's view, although not of the non-Marxian Marxist insistence on apodictic knowledge of history, is that he sees

---

[8] Isaiah Berlin, *Vico and Herder* (New York: Viking Press, 1976).

more clearly than does Vico that if knowledge is in some sense understood as the result of human activity on the plane of society, the quasi-Cartesian claim to apodicticity is indefensible in the historical domain.

I would like to conclude with an historical observation. The burden of this paper has been to compare Vico and Marx in terms of their criticism of Descartes and Cartesianism. But if, as I believe, Vico and Marx can be understood as two thinkers striving to burst the bounds of the Cartesian framework, their attempts have a wider significance in terms of the traditional conception of philosophy. For Descartes, despite his undoubted, although often exaggerated, claim to originality, is in many ways a traditional philosopher, especially as concerns his contemplative theory of epistemology, which is as old as the Platonic tradition. But in their rejections of the spectator view of subjectivity in favor of a conception of man as active, Vico and Marx reject at the same time the traditional understanding of epistemology, in the Greek sense of *epistēmē*, reproduced in Descartes' conception of philosophical science, for a view of man that acts and knows not absolutely, but in a finite sense. Hence a further result of their independent assaults on the Cartesian edifice is that both Vico and Marx participate in the shift away from the traditional conception of epistemology, which was begun by Plato and continued by Descartes, in the direction of a broadly pragmatic theory of knowledge.

Scientific Knowledge in Vico and Marx

Nikhil Bhattacharya

I

There exists a dominant and a minority tradition about knowledge in modern philosophy. The dominant one is well known. Beginning in earlier roots, it is developed by Descartes and subsequently splits into the two branches of British Empiricism and Continental Rationalism. Since the history of epistemology, as is endlessly repeated in our classrooms, is interminably focused on the relatively minor points of difference between these twin subtraditions of the dominant tradition, epistemological options appear to be exhausted by them. For philosophers for some time modern epistemology has begun with Descartes and, through the evolving dialogue of Locke and Leibniz, Berkeley and Hume, has come to rest with Kant. Twentieth-century philosophy of science, despite great concentration on technicalities, has oscillated from the neo-Humean stance of the logical empiricists to the neo-Kantian one of Popper.[1]

The minority tradition began with the work of Francis Bacon.[2] It was developed further by Bacon's secretary, Thomas Hobbes, particularly after the latter's discourses with Galileo. Hobbes's work evoked a strong positive response from Giambattista Vico.[3] The tradition languished, with occasional distant echoes in the work of the Romantics and Hegel, and reappeared in a strong form in the epistemological perspective of Karl Marx. Understandably, by way of the Hegelian connection, resonances of this tradition can be seen in the work of American Pragma-

---

[1] N. Bhattacharya "Popper's Theory of the Rationality of Science," *The Southern Journal of Philosophy* 16 (1978): 139-53.

[2] F. Bacon. *Novum Organum.* Book I.

[3] See Leon Pompa's Introduction to *Vico: Selected Writings,* ed. and trans. L. Pompa (Cambridge: Cambridge University Press, 1982), p. 11.

tists, particularly John Dewey.[4] But strictly speaking it is only Marx's work—somewhat casual and aphoristic though its tenor might be on epistemological questions—that is the latest version of this minority tradition.

What exactly is the minority tradition? Before we examine it, there is a question we have to face. Is there indeed such a deviant tradition in epistemology? And if there is, why then have we not heard more about it?

In the dominant tradition the cognitive enterprise has two bases. The first is that which our senses encounter—call it the S-component. This is the input into our cognitive systems from the outside. The second consists of the ways in which the S-component is processed by the remainder of our cognitive equipment. Whether this is called the "mind" or "reason" or by no such traditional name matters little. Let us call it the M-component. All the intramural battles within the dominant tradition, that of "empiricism" versus "rationalism" or contemporary variants thereof,[5] are squabbles about the relative roles played in the acquisition of knowledge by the S- and M-components.

Now what is important to realize about the dominant tradition is this. It is tacitly assumed that the S- and M-component model of the formation of knowledge is *complete*. That is, not only are the S- and M-components involved in the cognitive process, *but nothing else is*. Any act of acquisition of knowledge can be reduced, without remainder, to an S-component and an M-component.

If one recognizes this implicit presupposition of the dominant tradition, the difficulty about acknowledging the existence of any minority tradition about knowledge becomes clear. For either such a model is a bona fide theory of knowledge, in which case it is reducible to an S-M model, or else it is not so reducible, in which case it is not a proper theory of knowledge at all. For what else could be involved in the cognitive universe besides an S- and an M-component? Given such a premise, there can be no minority tradition in the theory of knowledge.

But suppose we assume that both components, though necessary, are insufficient in providing us with a theory of knowledge. However counterintuitive it may appear, the minority tradition begins with just

---

[4] N. Bhattacharya "John Dewey's Philosophy of Science," *The Philosophical Forum* 7 (1977): 105-25; A. Child *Making and Knowing in Hobbes, Vico, and Dewey* (Berkeley, 1953).

[5] N. Bhattacharya "Popper's Theory of the Rationality of Science," *The Southern Journal of Philosophy* 16 (1978): 139-53.

such an assumption. The premise here is that the acquisition of knowledge demands a third factor besides the basic ones of sensation and mind. The psychomental processes and structures can and do give rise to *opinion*. But by themselves they can neither provide nor guarantee *knowledge*. For this a third factor is necessary. But what on earth can such a new factor be?

It was Francis Bacon who first attempted to draw a distinction between the S-M model of knowledge and an alternate three-component one. He called the first *Anticipations of Nature,* "as a thing rash and premature,"[6] and the alternative *Interpretation of Nature.* The psychomental model can at best generate belief but not knowledge: "Anticipations are a ground sufficiently firm for consent; for even if men went mad all after the same fashion, they might agree one with another well enough."[7] As for the third component, it is the work of human hands. The way to arrive at knowledge of nature is "from works and experiments to extract causes and axioms and again from those causes and axioms new works and experiments, as a legitimate interpreter of nature."[8] Knowledge of nature involves not only cognitive but *physical* effort as well: Towards the effecting of works, all that man can do is to put together or put asunder natural bodies. The rest is done by nature working within."[9] So it is with an experiment. Ensembles of physical bodies have to be constructed to bring about specific effects and outcomes. It is such *productions* that both generate and test our knowledge.

Why is this third factor necessary? Because the traditional two are inadequate for the purpose of attaining a knowledge of nature: "The subtlety of nature is greater many times over than the subtlety of the senses and understanding; so that all those specious meditations, speculations and glosses in which men indulge are quite from the purpose, only there is no one to observe it."[10]

Nature must be viewed as if it were an agent that produces "works" or "fruits." Some of these "fruits" are beneficial for us—we live on them. To know nature at all we have to know nature as artificer, as the producer of "works." Unless we know the *acts* of nature, to engage in a random voyeuristic contemplation of the effects that nature produces around us is to court radical incomprehension. True, "senses and un-

[6] *Novum Organum,* Book I. Aphorism xxvi.
[7] Ibid., Book I. Aphorism xxvii.
[8] Ibid., Book I. Aphorism cxvii.
[9] Ibid., Book I. Aphorism iv.
[10] Ibid., Book I. Aphorism x.

derstanding" provide experience of a sort. But not all sorts of experience can produce knowledge. In particular, to acquire knowledge of nature we need a *specific sort* of experience, structured in a precise way, that is more than the simple concatenation of "senses and understanding."

Bacon, in the eyes of the careless reader, is vaguely perceived to be one of the crude and well-meaning proto-empiricists.[11] Bacon is aware, however, that he is attempting something quite different from the dominant tradition, and warns us to try to understand the difference: "Even to deliver and explain what I bring forward is no easy matter; for things in themselves new will yet be apprehended with reference to what is old."[12] But is there indeed a difference? Bacon claims that our knowledge is based on experience. So, in one form or another, does the dominant tradition. It is in defining what constitutes experience that the difference seems to lie. But can such a purported difference survive scrutiny?

For Bacon's sense of experience the S- and M-components are not enough for knowledge. One needs a component of constructive work—call it the C-component—both to produce the specific type of experience that leads to knowledge, as well as to test it. To an S-M theorist the C-component might appear redundant. For whatever we may do with our hands, the information must come to us by sensory channels and undergo the processing of reason. So it seems that Bacon's S-M-C theory can indeed be reduced to an S-M theory. Bacon does not accept such a reduction.

Why not? Because the object of our knowledge, the natural world, has surface appearances determined by inner workings that are not available to the senses, nor given a priori to reason. To know something is to know what to expect of it, and one cannot know what to expect unless one knows the inner causes that produce the surface effects: "It is a correct position that 'true knowledge is knowledge by causes.'"[13] An S-M theory must, understandably, abandon the search for causal knowledge, as in their variant ways both Hume and Kant would do. And how may we have knowledge of causes?

[11] For the popular misconception see for instance H. L. Finch, "Introduction," *The Complete Essays of Francis Bacon.* (New York: Washington Square Press, 1963), pp. ix-xx. The most flagrant example of thus misreading Bacon is, of course, K. R. Popper, *Conjectures and Refutations* (New York and Evanston: Harper Torchbooks 1963), pp. 4-5, 12-18 and passim.

[12] *Novum Organum.* Book I. *Aphorism* xxxiv.

[13] Ibid., Book II. Aphorism ii.

Assuming that like causes have like effects, the only way we may lay claim to causal knowledge is by the production of appropriate effects. This demands mental and physical alterations of existing sensible circumstances, to explore what causal chains might be at work: "For I am building in the human understanding a true model of the world, such as it is in fact, not such as a man's own reason would have it to be; a thing which cannot be done without a very diligent dissection and anatomy of the world."[14] It is thus the construction of such models of causal natural processes that we must engage in. Our experiments are our attempts to isolate and identify causal chains in nature. The validity of such models that we construct is given by the results of such experiments—whether we can indeed produce the effects we want: "Truth therefore and utility are here the very same things: and works themselves are of greater value as pledges of truth than as contributing to the comforts of life."[15]

Experimental science is not reducible to a science of mere observation and inference. True, we evaluate the results of our experiments by senses and by reason. But Bacon's S-M-C model is a two-tier model. From preliminary observation and reasoning we construct a mental model of what actually happens causally in nature. Once we have done this, we physically construct an experiment to try to reproduce nature's work—the C-component. Of course we use S- and M-components of our cognitive apparatus to do so. But these two components are here no longer used to decide what might be occurring in nature. They are used simply to decide whether the experiment works or not: "For the sense by itself is a thing infirm and erring; neither can instruments for enlarging or sharpening the senses do much; but all the truer kind of interpretation of nature is effected by instances and experiments fit and apposite; wherein the sense decides touching the experiment only, and the experiment touching the point in nature and the thing itself."[16] Experiments, the work of human hands, thus cannot be replaced by simple observations and their processing, which leads to random, arbitrary, and unreliable generalizations—not knowledge.

But Bacon is not blind to the problems of the experimental method. The working of an experiment, the reliability of a practice, is no certain guarantee that truth has been arrived at in the attempt to discern how

[14] Ibid., Book I. Aphorism cxxiv.
[15] Ibid.
[16] Ibid., Book I. Aphorism l.

nature works. There are too many unknowns in nature. What Bacon does recommend is a future history of natural science: "I propose to establish progressive stages of certainty."[17] Continual use of the experimental method, with time, would make our models more accurate. To undertake the Baconian regimen in science and technology is immediately to embrace a history of science, where "gradual steps"[18] lead to more certain knowledge.

As we might expect, such a theory of natural science is embedded in a metaphysical framework. Bacon felt little need to clarify the premises of this framework, so that there remains a measure of confusion in it.[19] There are three types of agents in the world: God, nature, and man. Ultimately nature and nature's works—for nature is a productive agent—is the work of God. But the day-to-day operations of the universe are the work of nature. It is nature whose causal chains of action we must uncover in order to harness it. Our task is to construct suitable modifications of nature so that, working within those constrained channels, *nature* provides us with fruits. Proximately there are two agents, man (to constrain nature) and nature (to do the work). Theoretically there is a remote agent, God, who created both nature and man. But Bacon makes no serious attempt to understand the relation of the constructive activities of each agent—though in producing new inventions man is supposed to act like God.[20]

II

Vico's central contribution to epistemology and the philosophy of science is a sharpening and refinement of Bacon's S-M-C model of knowledge.[21] To begin with, Vico defines the relationship between human and divine activity much more precisely than Bacon does, which has important epistemological consequences.

In the history of modern philosophy God has played an all-important role in theories of knowledge. All-seeing and all-knowing by definition, such a cognitive subject provides absolute standards for knowledge,

[17] Ibid., Preface.
[18] Ibid., Book I. Aphorism xxii.
[19] Ibid., Book I. E.g. Aphorisms i, iv, xxiii, xciii.
[20] Ibid., Book I. Aphorism cxxix.
[21] For Bacon's influence on Vico see M. H. Fisch's Introduction to *The Autobiography of Giambattista Vico*, trans. M. H. Fisch and T. G. Bergin (Ithaca, N.Y.: Cornell University Press, 1963), passim.

against which human knowledge claims are to be measured. What God knows are eternal apodictic truths. Human cognitive endeavors attempt to reproduce this feat. In case we are tempted to feel superior to such a theocentric epistemology, we must recall Dewey's analysis, that contemporary epistemologies work precisely within the framework, with the same notions of divine knowledge, as the ineluctable standard, while politely omitting any mention of God.[22]

Both the dominant S-M tradition and the rebel S-M-C tradition took God's knowledge as paradigmatic. They also viewed humans as beings created in God's image. The difference lay in how God's activity was viewed. The S-M theorists basically saw God as an ideally rational voyeur. The S-M-C theorists centered on God's activity of constructing the universe. To the S-M theorist God was all-knowing by virtue of a perfect sensory apparatus and perfect reason. To the S-M-C theorist God was all-knowing because he was all-powerful. It was out of his power expressed in concrete creative outcomes that his knowledge arose, and the power was the testament of the knowledge. So Bacon could equate knowledge with power.

Vico focused on precisely what God's constructive activity consisted of—that is, what precisely was the character of the C-component in the S-M-C model. His answer was simple. God's knowledge was a product of his power, which was also its warranty—and this power was the power to create ex nihilo. In contrast, the shortcomings of our knowledge-claims arise from the fact that, in general, we cannot create ex nihilo.[23]

This specification of the C-component could immediately solve a serious problem that dates back to Plato. The problem is about the relationship of mathematical knowledge to that of the empirical sort.

The shortcomings of our knowledge-claims about the empirical world are well known. Equally well known is the success of our knowledge-claims in mathematics. How is such a disparity to be explained?

It is at this point that the S-M tradition has a tendency to split into two or more subtraditions, depending on how seriously one takes this disparity. To Locke and Hume, for instance, the problem is inconsequential. A mathematical statement is in a different class than is an empirical

[22] N. Bhattacharya, "John Dewey's Philosophy of Science," *The Philosophical Forum* 7 (1977): 105-25; see also N. Bhattacharya, "Psychology and Rationality: The Structure of Mead's Problem," *The Philosophical Forum* 10 (1979): 112-38.

[23] For a detailed discussion of Vico's theory of natural science see N. Bhattacharya "Knowledge *per caussas*: Vico's Theory of Natural Science," in G. Tagliacozzo, ed., *Vico: Past and Present* (Atlantic Highlands, N.J.: Humanities Press, 1981), vol. I, pp. 182-97.

one. Epistemology is simply not concerned with the former because no S-component is involved.

From a Platonic or a Cartesian S-M perspective, however, there is a serious problem at issue. Mathematical results, by virtue of their apodicticity, are paradigmatic in epistemology. Empirical judgments simply fail to meet the standard, and this must be because of some inherent problem in the S-component. Even Kant's attempt to mediate between the two extremes (by bringing both sorts of knowledge-claims under the umbrella of "synthetic" judgments) is forced to a fundamental distinction between the two: that of a priori and a posteriori judgments.

Thus, on the S-M model our theories of knowledge have two distinct components that cannot be harmonized with each other: how we know a priori truths and how we know a posteriori ones—if indeed we know them at all.

Vico's S-M-C model, with the specific definition of the paradigmatic C-component as being creation ex nihilo, dissolves such a dichotomy. The difference between mathematical and empirical judgments becomes one of degree rather than a qualitative one, and thus allows an integral theory of knowledge. For in mathematics we know with certainty because mathematical entities are *entirely* our own creations. In the natural world we are unable to create ex nihilo. The degree of our knowledge in the empirical domain thus depends on the degree to which we are involved in constructing the state of affairs about which we make knowledge-claims.

If we use the degree to which we construct something as a measure of the degree of our knowledge about it, we get an epistemic scale for the sciences. This is possibly the most significant consequence of Vico's theory of science, as well as the least appreciated. For Vico can answer a question that no other philosophy of science has been able to confront. The question is quite simple. Why is it that our knowledge-claims in physics and chemistry seem so much more reliable than those in biology or physiology?

On the simple S-M model of the dominant tradition there is no answer to the question. For all of these examples we have physical sensations that we mentally process. Were this all, as the dominant tradition would have it, the only possible reason for the discrepancy would be the hypothesis that nature is inexplicably perverse in one domain and not in another. The character of this perversity is usually summed up by claiming that some systems are more "complex" than others. However, no specific meaning is attributable to such a notion of "complexity." Vico would replace such a notion by what might be called "degree of production." Physics is epistemically sounder than physiology because in the former we have had a greater hand in producing what we experiment on than in the latter. This is the character of "experimental physics which today is practiced with great profit to humanity, because from this metaphysics we can consider true in nature that to which we make something similar through experiments."[24] The way to a sounder physiology is not more painstaking observations by themselves, but the attempt to *construct* physiological systems in the laboratory.

But Vico, unlike Bacon, is pessimistic about the scope of human knowledge in natural science. This is understandable, for his notion of constructive activity, unlike Bacon's, is quite precise and specific. Since its paradigm is creation ex nihilo, the gap between God and man renders experimental science feeble in possibility. But, as in the case of mathematics, mental creation is the domain in which humans can lay claim to valid knowledge: "Since human knowledge is purely theoretical, the more physical a science is the less certain it is. For instance mechanics is less certain than geometry and arithmetic, because it involves motion effectuated in and through machines, physics is less certain than mechanics..."[25] Though he has noted the great development of experimental physics in his time, he does not seem to see much future in it. After all, the material world is created by God and not by man.

III

There are two major modifications that Karl Marx would attempt to introduce into the S-M-C model as developed by Vico.[26] From the

[24] G. Vico. *De antiquissima Italorum sapientia.* trans. Lucia Palmer (Ithaca, N.Y.: Cornell University Press, in press), p. 159. Page references in *De antiquissima* refer to the typescript. The corresponding passage in the Italian translation by Fausto Nicolini appears in *Vico: Opere* (Milano: Ricciardi, 1953), p. 307. A partial translation of *De antiquissima Italorum sapientia (On the Ancient Wisdom of the Italians)* is included in *Vico: Selected Writings,* ed. and trans. L. Pompa, pp. 47-78.

[25] *De antiquissima,* p. 27 (p. 255 of the Nicolini translation). On 'the origin and order of sciences' according to Vico, see Attila Fáj, "Vico as Philosopher of Metabasis," in *Giambattista Vico's Science of Humanity,* ed. G. Tagliacozzo and D. P. Verene (Baltimore: Johns Hopkins University Press), 100-109.

[26] The statement does not assume direct influence. The question is discussed by Fisch in the Introduction to *The Autobiography of Giambattista Vico* (p. 104) and by Eugene Kamenka in "Vico and Marxism," in *Giambattista Vico: An International Symposium,* ed. G. Tagliacozzo and H. V. White, (Baltimore: Johns Hopkins University Press, 1969), 137-43.

standpoint of epistemology Marx's effort is somewhat disappointing. He deals with the problem en passant, here and there, in the midst of other discussions. But however incomplete his work on the problem, there is a distinct and coherent core version of the S-M-C model that Marx has to offer.

The first alteration consists of Marx's hypothesis that human creativity is the only kind of creativity that exists: There is no divine model with which to compare and contrast it. It is not difficult to grasp how someone as seriously influenced by Feuerbach as Marx was, might dissolve the divine model of creative activity. Marx's response was to claim that creative activity was *essentially* a trait of human nature. It is the human being whose very mode of existence is to transform the environment he lives in: "He opposes himself to Nature as one of her own forces, setting in motion arms and legs, head and hands, the natural forces of his body, in order to appropriate Nature's productions in a form adapted to his own wants. By thus acting on the external world and changing it, he at the same time changes his own nature."[27] Given this, following Feuerbach, one can understand how humans may well project an ideal creator who creates everything ex nihilo.

But the essence of human existence is nonetheless creative in bringing about circumstances that are not present. Even without God and the divine standard the S-M-C model holds, and human knowledge has to come from this constructive activity. Explaining the Marxian perspective, Engels points out that

Natural science, like philosophy, has hitherto entirely neglected the influence of men's activity on their thought; both know only nature on the one hand and thought on the other. But it is precisely *the alteration of nature by men,* not solely nature as such, which is the most essential and immediate basis of human thought, and it is in the measure that man has learned to change nature that his intelligence has increased.[28]

Not only are knowledge-claims the outcome of our transformative activity on nature, their validation is the consequence of our ability to produce things.

[27] K. Marx, *Capital* (New York: International Publishers, 1967), vol. I, p. 177.
[28] F. Engels, *Anti-Düring* (New York: International Publishers, 1939), p. 172.

Marx's second point of departure stems from his explicit dein-dividualization of the C-component. Construction is a social activity. Inasmuch as for Marx such activity is the basis on which the S- and M-components are dependent, the entire epistemological model becomes social and not individual.

Is this a different perspective from that of Vico? It might not seem so. After all it was Vico who attempted, through philology, to characterize the cognitive world of a "nation," and who argued for the dependence of the very nature of consciousness on the epoch of social history. Marxian dependence of the cognitive superstructure on the social infrastructure is presaged in "the course of ideas is determined by the course of things."[29] Nevertheless, inasmuch as God is the paradigmatic cognitive subject, Vico's epistemological model is based on the individual as the cognitive subject.[30] I want to suggest that Marx's version of the S-M-C model is more explicitly based on social practice.

For the human constructive activity the transformation of what exists is social. It is the outcome of the productive labor of society. Man's basic relationship to his environment is a productive one. It is not essentially as a voyeur but as a laborer that he encounters nature. It is this switch from the dominant tradition of human voyeurism to the fundamental role of transforming nature that deindividualizes epistemology. For while sensation is private, labor is social: "The production of life, both of one's own in labor and of fresh life in procreation, now appears as a double relationship: on the one hand as a natural, on the other hand as a social relationship. By social we understand the cooperation of several individuals, no matter under what conditions, in what manner and to what end."[31] The social character of productive labor is nothing fortuitous:

Man is a *zoön politikon* in the most literal sense: he is not only a social animal, but an animal that can be individualized only within society. Production by a solitary individual outside society—a rare event, which might occur when a civilized person who has already absorbed the dynamic social forces is accidentally cast into the

[29] See the discussion in Kamenka, p. 138.

[30] Thus Arthur Child is correct in saying that for Vico "the historian does not know in his generic character but as the particular man he is," in *Making and Knowing in Hobbes, Vico, and Dewey* (Berkeley: University of California Press, 1953).

[31] K. Marx, *The German Ideology* (New York: International Publishers, 1939), p. 50.

wilderness—is just as preposterous as the development of speech without individuals who live *together* and talk to one another.[32]

The epistemological consequences of such a position are serious. Bacon had seen natural science as a social activity, both in its method and its consequences. So, if more implicitly, had Vico. Marx goes a step further to claim human consciousness itself as a social product.

The S-M tradition in epistemology is based on the individual as the cognitive subject. As long as we believe that cerebral processing of sensations is the way we come to know, this seems the natural and obvious assumption to make. But if we think that productive labor is the appropriate and legitimate basis for knowledge, we can no longer treat the isolated individual as the cognitive subject. For "production is always appropriation of nature by an individual within and with the help of a definite social organization."[33] Somehow society has to enter the problem.

Traditional theory has assumed that we are a world of isolated individuals, with our individuated consciousnesses. There is no reason to assume this, for it is a historically dated model: "It is on the contrary, the anticipation of "bourgeois society" which began to evolve in the sixteenth century and in the eighteenth century made giant strides towards maturity. The individual in this society of free competition seems to be rid of natural ties etc."[34] Beginning with isolated individuals is the understandable oddity of an epoch, even if we have tenaciously clung to such models. "The solitary and isolated hunter or fisherman, who serves Adam Smith and Ricardo as a starting point, is one of the unimagined fantasies of eighteenth century romances à la Robinson Crusoe."[35] It is this peculiar cultural tradition to which the S-M tradition in epistemology has fallen victim. But Marx, alas, goes no further. Just how the perceptions of the individual depend on society remains unclear.

Marx's second contribution to the minority S-M-C tradition, as we have said before, is his suggestion that the S-M-component is in some way a product of the C-component. That is, what we perceive and how we think are somehow a direct consequence of our material productive

[32] K. Marx, *Introduction to the Critique of Political Economy* (New York: International Publishers, 1970), p. 189.
[33] Ibid., p. 192.
[34] Ibid., p. 188.
[35] Ibid.

activity: "The production of ideas, or conception, of consciousness, is at first directly interwoven with the material activity and material intercourse of men, the language of real life. Conceiving, thinking, the mental intercourse of men, appear at this stage as the direct efflux of their material behavior."[36] Unfortunately, Marx makes no attempt to go beyond the rhetoric in clarifying the precise relation between material productive activity and consciousness.

Thus the history of our opinions and knowledge of nature is a consequence of our economic history. Looking back at the past, Vico has seen distinctly different social modes of perceiving the world. He classified such modes as belonging to distinct epochs of history.[37] Marx's strategy attempts to remove such ad hoc divisions from history by making our perceptions and beliefs dependent on the C-component, our constructive material activity. Needless to say, individual acts of material construction are undertaken in the light of existing perceptions and beliefs—which emerge from a prior history of constructions.

Vague and quite ill-defined, this is where the S-M-C model of knowledge and science stands today. Vico himself, despite the important analysis in *On the Ancient Wisdom of the Italians,*[38] had little serious interest in natural science:

> A short time after this he learned of the growing prestige of experimental physics, for which the name of Robert Boyle was on everyone's lips; but profitable as he thought it for medicine and spagyric, he desired to have nothing to do with this science. For it contributed nothing to the philosophy of man and had to be expounded in barbarous formulas, whereas his own principal concern was the study of Roman laws, the main foundations of which are the philosophy of human customs and the science of the Roman language and government, which can only be learned in the Latin writers.[39]

Marx's comments are vague, aphoristic. It has been over a century since the model has been seriously worked on. Its proponents have their

---

[36] K. Marx, *German Ideology*, p. 47.

[37] The *New Science of Giambattista Vico*, trans. T. G. Bergin and M. H. Fisch (Ithaca, N.Y.: Cornell University Press, 1958), par. 31.

[38] See N. Bhattacharya "Knowledge *per caussas,*" in G. Tagliacozzo, ed., *Vico: Past and Present*, I, 182-97.

[39] *The Autobiography of Giambattista Vico*, op. cit., p. 128.

differences, explicit and implicit, about what precisely constitutes constructive activity—the C-component of the model. How this constructive activity relates to the sensation component is also unclear, and generally covered by unfortunate metaphors. But this alternative theory of knowledge is the only one that incorporates the all-important idea of experimental and theoretical modeling in a theory of science. It also is the only theory of knowledge we know of that links scientific activity with what else happens in society. Bacon feels that the constructive activity, in order to be successful, has to be a collective social effort, which a well-meaning government can undertake. It *should* be social, because the individual sensory-mental processing of information from nature is extremely unreliable.[40] Intersubjective cross-checking is essential. For Marx all such activity—in fact, all the components of the model—is necessarily social, though precisely *how* is uncertain.

It would be a mistake, I think, to continue to ignore the S-M-C model in epistemology and the philosophy of science. The model has its share of problems. But such problems may well remain more by virtue of our prolonged neglect than anything else.

---

[40] *Novum Organum.* Book I. Aphorism LIIIff.

Vico and Marx and the Problem of Moral Relativism

Lawrence H. Simon

I

Ever since Thrasymachus's challenge to Socrates that justice is the interest of the stronger, moral philosophers have attempted to found ethics on reason rather than mere physical power. To accept Thrasymachus's position, to concede that might makes right, it is felt, is to surrender the ethical dimension of human life and thus to acknowledge that force of muscle rather than force of argument is the final arbiter of human conflict. To admit this seems to reduce human beings to the level of other animals and to rob us of the use of that distinctively human faculty, reason, in the vital arena of conflict resolution.

Relativism, it is often thought, renders us incapable of using reason in this same fashion. In ethics, for instance, we often feel, following Kant, that if moral principles are rational, then they must be the same, and found to be rational in the same way, for all people. But ethical relativism implies that this is not the case, that moral principles are not the same for all people. Hence, given this Kantian view of rationality, if ethical relativism is true, moral principles are not rational. But if they are not rational, then reason cannot be used as the final arbiter of moral disagreement. Human conflict involving ethical issues could thus only be settled by force, whatever the appearance of rationality there may be, and we are back to Thrasymachus.

The position that holds for the universality of reason and its centrality in human life is frequently identified with the Enlightenment. As Patrick Gardiner has recently characterized it, the Enlightenment standpoint held as a central presumption "...that human beings are endowed with a common nature, a set of mental attributes and powers which remain broadly constant from age to age and milieu to milieu. The faculty of reason was accorded a pre-eminent position amongst these...."[1]

---

[1] Patrick Gardiner, "German Philosophy and the Rise of Relativism," *Monist* 64 (April 1981): 139.

The tradition that is seen in opposition to the Enlightenment stand-point is often said to be historicism, which has been characterized by Isaiah Berlin as the "belief in the unique character and indispensability, and above all, validity at its own stage of development, of each of the phases through which mankind has passed and will pass...."[2] If the Enlightenment standpoint stresses the universal features of human life, the historicist standpoint focuses on the particularities that differentiate one culture, epoch, or age from another. The key to understanding human life and history is seen to reside, not on the abstract level of shared characteristics, the historicist would argue, but on the concrete level of difference where the richness and diversity of human existence can be exhibited.

The move from historicism to relativism is fairly direct. If each age of human existence has a unique character that includes, among other things, principles and values that guide its social behaviors, and if there are no universal principles or values over and above the particular ones manifested in each age, then it seems illegitimate to measure the achievements or failures of one age by the values of another. An age can only be assessed in terms of its own values. To pretend that there is an absolute standard is, on this view, to mistake for a universal what is in fact the expression of a particular age. In particular, one cannot make ethical judgments across ages without stretching the scope of the validity of ethical values beyond its limit.

Vico and Marx are generally taken to be in the historicist tradition. Central to the projects of both are theories of historical development that mark off human history into definite stages. Both Vico and Marx are concerned to understand these stages in terms of what is specific to each. At least in regard to this sensitivity to historical difference, they both seem in opposition to the Enlightenment tradition.[3] If Vico and Marx qualify, at least initially, as historicists, are they also moral relativists? Is it the case that neither allows for transhistorical standards with which one can measure and assess the practices of different societies at different stages of historical development? What are the types of moral judgments, if any, that have validity across societies and

[2] Isaiah Berlin, *Vico and Herder: Two Studies in the History of Ideas* (London: Hogarth, 1975), p. 72.

[3] I do not wish to imply here that Marx is in any simple sense an opponent of the Enlightenment. In many ways he is also its child and heir. The Enlightenment and anti-Enlightenment strands in Marx's thought are complex and at times conflicting. Vico is more comfortably placed in the anti-Enlightenment tradition, although even this raises difficulties since Vico's work predates the high points of the Enlightenment.

stages of development? Do the theories of Vico and Marx agree on these matters?

If one surveys the literature on Vico and Marx one will find conflicting answers to these questions. Let me, however, cite just two sources as examples. In a recent book on Marx's theory of history Melvin Rader writes:

> Many of Marx's references to morality are hostile. He calls into question bourgeois morals by depicting them as a reflection of the interests of a privileged class. This relativistic interpretation of morality is a critical weapon of great potency, but it would be a mistake to classify Marx as no more than a relativist. His theory of alienation and its overcoming and his faith in progress imply objective standards.[4]

There are elements of relativism in Marx, Rader recognizes, but in the end Marx is not to be classified as a moral relativist. Likewise, in a discussion of Vico's theory of cultural understanding, Isaiah Berlin writes:

> There is no need to compare and grade on some single scale of merit each cultural phase and its creations and forms of life and action; indeed, it is not possible to do so, for they are evidently incommensurable...This is not relativism, for we are able not merely to record but to understand the outlooks of other societies, however imperfectly, without assimilating them to our own; nor is it the old absolutism whereby we can pronounce their works to be superior or inferior to each other, or to our own, by the use of some unaltering criterion valid for all men, everywhere, at all times.[5]

Vico seems to be a relativist, but not in a simple or straightforward way.

In order to be clearer about the question of whether either Vico or Marx is a moral relativist, more precision must be introduced into the discussion. It is necessary to ask first what is meant by moral relativism. This question is not an easy one to answer, for the concept of moral

---

[4] Melvin Rader, *Marx's Interpretation of History* (New York: Oxford University Press, 1979), p. 52.

[5] Sir Isaiah Berlin, "Vico and the Ideal of the Enlightenment," *Social Research* 43 (Autumn 1976): 650 (reprinted in *Vico and Contemporary Thought*, ed. G. Tagliacozzo, N. Mooney and D. P. Verene [Atlantic Highlands, N.J., 1980], p. 260).

relativism is complex and controversial. I will examine in detail the position of one contemporary moral philosopher in an effort to clarify the concept. In so doing I do not claim that I will exhaust all senses of the concept or speak to all the issues that enter into the debates concerning moral relativism. Rather, I will attempt to gain in precision what might be lost in breadth. I will then discuss the views of Vico and Marx on the nature of morality and assess their positions on the question of moral relativism.

II

Most commonly, moral relativism is taken to be the view that there is no set of basic moral beliefs or values that can be objectively and rationally justified such that everyone is obliged to accept it. In other words, it is the claim that there are basic moral conflicts that are not rationally resolvable. The opponent of the relativist, then, is the objectivist, who believes that there are objectively correct moral beliefs and values that are universally applicable and rationally defensible. In this paper I shall not be concerned with the question of whether moral relativism in any of its forms is a true doctrine—that is, whether it correctly describes the nature of morality and moral judgments. Rather, my concern is only to establish that the doctrine can be stated in a coherent and philosophically interesting manner.

There are three constraints that must initially be placed on any form of moral relativism if it is to yield an interesting doctrine. These constraints are that the doctrine put forth a philosophical thesis, that the doctrine give an account of the possibility of real moral disagreement, and that the thesis be coherent in the sense of not leading to an inconsistency. The first constraint is meant to rule out of consideration a form of relativism that is often referred to as descriptive relativism. This is the doctrine that "...the *basic* ethical beliefs of different people and societies are different and even conflicting."[6] This form of moral relativism involves an empirical claim that in itself does not offer a philosophical thesis, although it is often mistakenly thought to do so. It makes no philosophical claim of the relevant sort because it does not as such speak to the problem of the validity or correctness of the different sets of basic ethical beliefs that different people might hold. If true,

---

[6] William K. Frankena, *Ethics*, 2nd ed. (Englewood Cliffs, N.J.: Prentice-Hall, Inc., 1973), p. 109.

descriptive relativism establishes only that there exists a diversity of moral views; but this state of affairs is compatible with only one of the views being objectively correct. Thus, to satisfy the first constraint the doctrine must involve a normative thesis concerning the correctness of one or more of the sets of moral beliefs.

The second constraint is meant to ensure that the phenomenon of real moral disagreement is not lost. The danger is that if moral judgments are relativized, then two judgments that appear to conflict will turn out not to do so. Thus in certain situations where people mean to be morally disagreeing with each other, they will not really be doing so. Yet moral disagreement seems to be a phenomenon with which we are all familiar. A relativistic theory that rendered such a phenomenon a mere pseudoissue would seem to be unacceptable. Thus the relativist must provide an account of the nature and scope of moral disagreement.

Once an account of real moral disagreement is given, another danger presents itself—the threat of inconsistency. The problem here is that if there is a genuine disagreement, and if we want to be relativists, then we have to admit the possibility that two conflicting moral judgments, "X is right" and "X is wrong," are both correct (true, valid). But this conclusion is logically inconsistent. A given action X cannot both be really right and really wrong. If a doctrine of relativism leads to this conclusion, it can easily be dismissed as incoherent. Thus the third constraint, that of coherence, is imposed.

Gilbert Harman in a series of recent articles defends a plausible doctrine of moral relativism.[7] In particular he distinguishes three versions of the doctrine which, although they do not necessarily imply one another, can be put together in the context of a larger moral theory.[8] The three forms of relativism Harman discusses are normative moral relativism, moral judgment relativism, and meta-ethical relativism. I will discuss each version of relativism in turn and then briefly indicate the type of moral theory in which all three could coexist.

Normative moral relativism is the thesis that different people (or societies) can hold different moral norms or values and hence be

[7] "Moral Relativism Defended," *Philosophical Review* 84 (January 1975): 3-22; "Relativistic Ethics: Morality as Politics," *Midwest Studies in Philosophy,* vol. III: *Studies in Ethical Theory* (1978): 109-21; "What Is Moral Relativism?" *Values and Morals,* ed. Alvin Goldman and Jaegwon Kim (Dordrecht, Holland: D. Reidel, 1978); pp. 143-61; see also Harman's book, *The Nature of Morality* (New York: Oxford University Press, 1977).

[8] Harman, "What Is Moral Relativism?" Harman discusses the possibility of accepting any one of these versions while rejecting the other two on pp. 148-49.

subject to different moral obligations. Frankena defines it as the principle that

> what is right or good for one individual or society is not right or
> good for another, even if the situations involved are similar, mean-
> ing not merely that what is thought right or good by one is not
> thought right or good by another…, but that what is really right or
> good in the one case is not so in another.[9]

This doctrine is not to be confused with the thesis that to judge something right or wrong is to make it so, or that something is right or wrong only if a person thinks it so. There may be factors of a rational or empirical sort that must be taken into consideration, factors that limit accounts of what can be moral despite what people think to be the case. What normative moral relativism does imply is that there is no set of moral beliefs or values that issues in a set of moral demands such that all human beings are morally obliged to do certain things on pain of being irrational. This last claim involves a certain view of moral obligation and a substantive claim about moral demands. The view of moral obligation that is required to support normative moral relativism is sometimes called an internalist account.[10] This account postulates an internal connection between obligation and motivation. A person is thus morally obliged to do something (morally ought to do it) only if the person has a compelling reason to do it. The moral "ought," according to Harman, "is used to speak of things an agent has moral reasons to do…."[11] According to Harman an agent has moral reasons to do something only if the agent accepts certain relevant moral demands concerning that action. But moral demands, on this view, "have to be acceptable to those to whom they apply…."[12] Therefore, a person is morally obliged only to do those things that follow from the moral demands he or she accepts.

Normative moral relativism does not follow from this view of moral obligation alone, for it may be that all agents have compelling moral reasons to do the same things—that is, all agents submit (or ought to

---

[9] Frankena, p. 109.

[10] See Harman, "What Is Moral Relativism?" pp. 152-53, and William K. Frankena, "Obligation and Motivation in Recent Moral Philosophy," *Perspectives on Morality*, ed. K. E. Goodpaster (Notre Dame: University of Notre Dame Press, 1976); pp. 49-73.

[11] Harman, "Relativistic Ethics: Morality as Politics," p. 111.

[12] Harman, "What Is Moral Relativism?" p. 152.

submit, on pain of irrationality) to the same moral demands. Thus
Harman argues for a strong substantive claim that there are no moral
demands that everyone has reason to accept; "...for any such demand,
someone might fail to accept it without being ignorant of relevant facts,
without having miscalculated, without having failed to see the consequences of his or her opinions, and without being in any way irrational."[13] The success of his argument requires that we accept that
neither philosophy nor psychology has been able to disprove his claim
about moral demands. For my purposes I need not evaluate this argument here, for the coherence (as opposed to the truth) of normative
moral relativism requires only that the argument be plausible.

Normative moral relativism holds, then, that all people need not be
subject to the same ultimate moral demands. Harman states this doctrine as a conclusion derived from two assumptions. The first assumption "says, roughly, that a moral demand applies to someone only if it is
rational for that person to accept that demand." The second assumption "says, roughly, that it can be rational for different people to accept
different moral demands 'all the way down.' Together these assumptions logically imply, roughly, that different people can be subject to
different moral demands 'all the way down.'"[14]

The second form of moral relativism, moral judgment relativism, is
the view that "moral judgments implicitly refer to one or another
person, group, or set of moral demands...."[15] It is a claim about the
logical form of moral judgments to the effect that all such judgments
implicitly include phrases such as "according to the moral demands I
accept..." or "according to the moral system of society X...." The obvious objection to moral judgment relativism is that it fails to satisfy our
second constraint. That is, moral judgment relativism appears to render real moral disagreements as merely apparent disagreements. As
Harman states it, "If two people—even two relativists—disagree about
whether it is morally wrong to cause pain and injury to animals, they
really do disagree and are not just talking past each other—the one
saying that causing pain and injury to animals is wrong in relation to
our morality, and the other saying it is not wrong in relation to [for
example] Hopi morality."[16]

[13] Harman, "Relativistic Ethics: Morality as Politics," p. 110.
[14] Harman, "What Is Moral Relativism?" pp. 155-56.
[15] Ibid., p. 148.
[16] Ibid., pp. 157-58.

Harman's suggestion for getting around this objection involves a modification in the normal understanding of the usage of moral terminology. This modification has to do with what Harman calls the claim of universality, which is, in his opinion, part of the "naive view" of morality.[17] The claim of universality holds that moral demands "are supposed to be accepted as demands on everyone; they are to have universal application."[18] Harman argues that if we otherwise have reason to accept relativism, then the claim of universality must be loosened. Instead of ranging over everyone, moral judgments should be understood to range over just those people who accept the morality accepted by the speaker. If S says to P, "Action X is wrong; you morally ought not do it," this moral judgment, properly relativized, is to be taken as implying that both S and P accept the moral demand that one ought not do action X. If it turns out that P does not accept the same morality as S (or a morality that does include the same relevant moral demand), then on Harman's proposed modification, S, in making the above moral judgment, is involved in a misuse of moral language.

A relativist can make moral judgments in relation to moralities he or she (or the audience) does not accept, but it is a misuse of moral language—even when it has been relativized—to do this without making it clear that one is doing so. It is, furthermore, always a misuse of language to make a moral judgment about an agent in relation to a morality not accepted by the agent."[19]

The upshot of Harman's proposal is to clarify and restrict the nature of moral disagreement in the context of a relativist theory. Genuine moral disagreement can only occur in relation to a shared morality or set of moral demands. In particular, I cannot say of you that you ought morally to do X unless you share the relevant moral demands with me. And I cannot engage in a genuine disagreement over whether you should do X with a third person unless all three of us share the same morality. If you share the relevant moral demands with the third person but not with me, then I am out of order, morally speaking, to make my moral judgment of you, while the third party with whom I am in ostensible disagreement is not really disagreeing with me. In such a

[17] Harman, "Relativistic Ethics: Morality as Politics," p. 109.
[18] Ibid.
[19] Harman, "What Is Moral Relativism?" p. 158.

case I cannot really intend to disagree once the implicit references are made clear.

The third form of moral relativism Harman presents is meta-ethical relativism. This version of relativism concerns the justification of moral judgments. As Frankena states it, it is the view that "in the case of ethical judgments, there is no objectively valid, rational way of justifying one against another; consequently, two conflicting basic judgments may be equally valid."[20] As Harman points out, this view requires that there be at least two judgments involved, that both be about the same particular case, and that it be the case that they not only conflict but are both correct. This version of relativism seems immediately to run up against our third constraint, that of coherence. If two judgments genuinely conflict, and both are correct, then the relativist seems to be committed to a contradiction (X is wrong, and X is not wrong), hence to have fallen into logical inconsistency.

It might seem that the above discussion of the modification of the principle of universality might be helpful here. Genuinely disagreeing judgments about what an agent morally ought or ought not do, I said, could only be properly made against the background of a shared morality. But in such a situation it is difficult to see how more than one of the judgments could be correct. From a given set of moral demands, if they are consistent, only one of the judgments should be correctly derivable. On the other hand, if two correct judgments appear to conflict over what one ought or ought not morally to do, then it would seem that they must start from different moral demands. In that case there would be no genuine disagreement.

In his attempt to solve this problem, Harman says the following:

> ...we should count a nonrelativistic moral judgment right if the corresponding relativistic moral judgment is right made in relation to the morality accepted by the person making the non-relativistic moral judgment. The relativist can intelligibly suppose that really conflicting nonrelativistic moral judgments are both right in this sense.[21]

He goes on to conclude that meta-ethical relativism is "a thesis about nonrelativistic but not relativistic moral judgments."[22] What he seems

[20] Frankena, *Ethics*, p. 109.
[21] Harman, "What Is Moral Relativism?" p. 160.
[22] Ibid.

to have in mind in this difficult statement is a situation with two people operating out of different moralities, but each accepting the principle of universality. If the first person says "X is right" and the second "X is wrong," and they both mean their judgments to have universal applicability, then each intends his or her respective judgment to be in disagreement with the other. From the point of view of the relativist each judgment could still be correct if it is correct in relation to the moral system of the person making the judgment.

Harman makes another distinction that can help us clarify this confusing idea. The distinction is between two forms of moral judgments, inner and non-inner. An inner moral judgment is intended to supply an agent with moral reason to do or not do something and can properly be made "only about those who are assumed to accept (or have reasons to accept) the moral demands on which the judgments are based."[23] Inner moral judgments generally take the form of moral "ought" statements (S morally ought do X), but other moral judgments can be considered inner if they presuppose a shared universe of moral demands and hence reasons. Thus, "It was morally wrong of S to do X" is an inner moral judgment. Harman argues that judgments of a situation as right or wrong, or judgments that something ought or ought not be done, where the agents involved do not share the morality of the speaker, are properly understood as not using the moral "ought." Rather, these judgments use what Harman calls the evaluative (or normative) "ought." This "ought" expresses a preference or dissatisfaction on the part of the speaker in the sense that he/she feels that it would be better if a certain situation or action did (did not) occur. What the evaluative "ought" does not do is provide agents who do not share the morality of the speaker with moral reasons to do anything.

Not all moral judgments, however, are inner. "One can judge that certain outsiders are good or bad or evil from the point of view of one's morality even if they do not share that morality, just as one can judge that outsiders are friends or enemies."[24] These latter forms of moral judgments are non-inner moral judgments. They do not assume that the agent(s) addressed share(s) the same set of moral demands as the speaker, and thus they are not properly intended as such to supply moral motivation. It should be noticed that one cannot necessarily infer

[23] Harman, "Relativistic Ethics: Morality as Politics," p. 115. Also see discussion in "Moral Relativism Defended," pp. 4-11.
[24] Ibid., p. 116.

from a non-inner moral judgment to a corresponding inner one. That is, from "That situation is not good (unfair, evil, etc.)," one cannot infer "S morally ought not bring that situation about" except in the case where S shares the same morality as the speaker. In all other cases, given Harman's system, we can regret that the situation exists and even say that it ought not exist, where the "ought" is the evaluative "ought." What we cannot do is blame a person in the sense of saying he or she was morally wrong in bringing about the situation.

This distinction provides us with another way of understanding how two moral judgments about the same particular case can be conflicting yet both be correct at the same time. If properly relativized, two inner moral judgments either do not really conflict or, if they do conflict, cannot both be correct. However, this does not seem to be the case with non-inner moral judgments. Two non-inner judgments can both be correct, relative to their respective moralities, and yet predicate conflicting moral properties (good and evil) of the same thing.

A final point about Harman's position that is worth noting is the type of overall moral theory that he favors, one that would accommodate his versions of moral relativism. The type of theory espoused by Harman is a form of social-custom theory. Such theories "say that morality derives from the rules or customs that society enforces in a certain way, a way that may be specified differently in different theories."[25] This form of theory makes morality into an entirely social affair; there is no morality prior to the formation of society and the establishment of the appropriate social arrangements. As Harman states it, "Morality is constituted by the rules, whatever they are, that society enforces. There is no prior morality. If society were to enforce different rules, what is right and what is wrong would change."[26] It should be noted that while this sort of theory of morality is thoroughly conventional, it does not follow that, if it were true, there would be no constraints on moral systems that could be adopted by human societies. It might turn out that any successful human society would have to recognize certain rules or practices—for instance, truth telling—as primary and hence incorporate these practices into its moral rules. This is a question that has to do with the nature of human beings and social life. Also, a social-custom theory of morality in no way precludes the possibility of our providing a functionalist and/or historical account of actual moral systems. In fact, one

[25] Harman, *The Nature of Morality*, p. 93.
[26] Ibid., 94.

might argue that it facilitates such accounts. These points again will be relevant in the discussion of Marx and Vico.

Harman, then, has outlined three versions of moral relativism—namely, normative moral relativism, moral judgment relativism, and meta-ethical relativism—that seem to be acceptable, given our initial three constraints. Again, my primary interest is not whether relativism in the three versions presented by Harman is the correct view of morality or moral judgment. My concern is to establish a coherent and at least initially plausible theory of moral relativism in order better to focus the discussion of Marx and Vico. However, it is necessary to say something in consideration of the truth of moral relativism in order to appreciate more fully the positions of Marx and Vico. In doing so I will use a discussion of moral relativism by Philippa Foot.[27]

As I stated at the beginning of my discussion, at the core of the relativist position is the claim that there is no set of basic moral beliefs or values that can be objectively and rationally justified such that everyone, regardless of time and place, is obligated to accept these beliefs and values on pain of irrationality. If there were such a set of shared values or standards, then normative moral relativism would not be true, for everyone would have compelling reasons to accept the same moral reasons and be thus subject to the same moral demands. Likewise, if such a shared set of standards existed, then these standards would play a crucial role in the justification of moral judgments, thus falsifying the central claim of meta-ethical relativism that such a justificatory procedure does not exist. As we have seen, it is important to Harman's argument that he deny that there is a set of moral demands that everyone has reason to accept.

In her discussion Foot is not so much concerned to answer the question of the truth of moral relativism as to explore various considerations surrounding this question. Are moral judgments, she queries, analogous to judgments of taste? Relativism seems true in the realm of taste. This is so in part because it seems that "some rather general judgments of taste [can] be identified through any amount of variation in the application of the key concepts through the relevant domain."[28]

There appears to be little constraint on what can pass as delightful seasonings on food or correct color coordination or styles of personal

---

[27] Philippa Foot, "Moral Relativism," Lindley Lecture, The University of Kansas, April 19, 1978.

[28] Ibid., p. 14.

beauty. In the realm of morality, however, this open variation does not seem to be acceptable, and so there seem to be limits on relativism. According to Foot certain judgments and forms of behavior, e.g., the Nazis' treatment of the Jews, are morally indefensible, and no code that did not condemn them could be considered a correct or true moral code.

Being able to delineate in some general sense the realm of morality does not, however, settle the issue.

> Even if the fact that it is morality that is in question gives us some guaranteed starting points for arguments about moral right and wrong, how much is this going to settle? Are there not some moral matters on which, even within our own society, disagreement may be irreducible? ...May there not be places where societies simply confront each other, with no rational method for settling their differences?[29]

Moral relativism is not true, Foot argues, to the extent that we can employ what she calls, borrowing the term from Bernard Williams,[30] the substantial sense of "true." According to Foot, " 'True' and 'false' get a substantial use where there are objective criteria, or at least methods of some kind of settling disputes..."[31] Such methods or criteria require, in part, that there be some shared standards governing the moral realm. To the degree that there are such standards we can resolve moral disagreements objectively and rationally. We come back to the question, then, is there a set of moral standards that all human beings, simply in virtue of being human, are rationally compelled to accept? Secondly, if such standards exist, can they be specified sufficiently so as to settle the wide range of particular and often radical moral disputes?

At this point in her discussion Foot draws back from making any pronouncements on the truth or falsity of moral relativism. There are certain prior questions that must be answered and certain concepts that must be better understood before we will be in a position to decide on the issue of moral relativism, she argues. In particular we need to

---

[29] Ibid., p. 15.

[30] See Bernard Williams, "Consistency and Realism," *Problems of the Self* (Cambridge: Cambridge University Press, 1973), esp. pp. 202-203.

[31] Foot, "Moral Relativism," p. 16.

better understand human nature and what it means for human beings to flourish. Although Foot does not explicitly say this, I would argue that central to these concerns is the issue of the conditions under which human beings can fully develop themselves as humans and the relation of social institutions to this process. These sorts of considerations, I will indicate below, have a point of resonance in Vico's theory.

III

In order to answer the question of whether Marx or Vico is best construed as a moral relativist, it is necessary first to examine their views on the nature and function of morality. I will look at each in turn, beginning with Marx.

What are Marx's views on morality? This question is ambiguous and needs to be broken down into the following two questions: How does Marx understand the nature of morality, and in particular, does he think that there is a universal, objectively true set of moral standards? Secondly, what are Marx's own moral views, especially as revealed in the type of criticism he makes of capitalism? There has been an extended and heated debate in the recent literature over these questions.[32] The debate has focused on the question of whether Marx condemns capitalism as unjust. If Marx does so condemn capitalism, that would be evidence both of Marx's own moral views and of the sorts of judgments that he thinks morality can be used to support. On the other hand, if Marx does not condemn capitalism as unjust, then his not doing so when one expects him to would constitute evidence of his views on the nature and limits of moral judgment. Central to this debate is the issue

---

[32] For various aspects of this debate see Allen W. Wood, "The Marxian Critique of Justice," *Marx, Justice, and History,* ed. Marshall Cohen, Thomas Nagel, and Thomas Scanlon (Princeton, N.J.: Princeton University Press, 1980), pp. 3-41; Ziyad I. Husami, "Marx on Distributive Justice," *Marx, Justice, and History,* pp. 42-79; George G. Brenkert, "Freedom and Private Property in Marx," *Marx, Justice, and History,* pp. 80-105; Allen W. Wood, "Marx on Right and Justice: A Reply to Husami," *Marx, Justice, and History,* pp. 106-34; Richard J. Arneson, "What's Wrong with Exploitation?" *Ethics,* 91 (January 1981): 202-27; Hilliard Aronovitch, "Marxian Morality," *Canadian Journal of Philosophy,* X (September 1980): 357-93; Kai Nielsen, "Marxism, Ideology, and Moral Philosophy," *Social Theory and Practice,* 6 (Spring 1980): 53-68; Nancy Holmstrom, "Exploitation," *Canadian Journal of Philosophy,* VII (June 1977): 353-69; William Leon McBride, "The Concept of Justice in Marx, Engels, and Others," *Ethics,* 85 (April 1975): 204-18; Derek P. H. Allen, "Is Marxism a Philosophy?" *Journal of Philosophy,* LXXI (October 10, 1974): 601-12; Allen Buchanan, "Exploitation, Alienation, and Injustice," *Canadian Journal of Philosophy,* IX (March 1979): 121-39; Allen W. Wood, *Karl Marx* (London: Routledge and Kegan Paul, 1981).

of the relation of morality to ideology in Marx. If morality is merely ideology, and if ideology as part of the superstructure of a society is produced as a function of the economic structure of the underlying mode of production, then there is no independent and external moral position from which to judge a mode of production or some part of it (such as wage labor) as immoral. On this reading of Marx he cannot, consistent with his own theory, condemn capitalism and the exploitation of wage labor as unjust. If, however, one finds in Marx evidence that he does morally condemn capitalism, then, it is usually argued, he does ascribe such condemnation to a moral theory that affords him an external perspective from which to make such judgments. In this case it is necessary to interpret Marx's views on the nature of morality so as to allow morality to be more than mere ideology.

I cannot, within the limits of this paper, enter into this debate. It is a complex problem that raises a number of difficult issues and requires a careful reading of a number of controversial passages in Marx.[33] Rather, I will simply state that I find most convincing the position that Marx does not condemn capitalism as unjust and in general as immoral, that in effect his condemnation of capitalism does not involve considerations of strict morality, and that morality is best understood in Marx as part of the ideological structure of a society. In presenting Marx's views on morality, therefore, I will be assuming the correctness of this position and follow the arguments of the person I consider its most cogent expositor, Allen Wood.

In order to understand Marx's views on the nature of morality, one has to locate them in the context of his general theory of society. According to Marx societies are to be distinguished in terms of the different social forms they embody. Crucial to the identification of the social formation of a society is the economic structure that forms its core. According to G. A. Cohen, "The economic structure of a society is the entire set of production relations obtaining in it."[34] The economic structure patterns the relations that human beings enter into as they

---

[33] The key texts in Marx around which the debate centers include *Capital*, trans. Samuel Moore and Edward Aveling, vol. 1 (London: Lawrence and Wishart, 1970), pp. 176, 194, 582-84; *Capital*, ed. Frederick Engels, vol. 3 (New York: International Publishers, 1967), pp. 339-40; and "Critique of the Gotha Programme," *Karl Marx: The First International and After,* ed. David Fernbach (New York: Vintage Books, 1974), pp. 339-59.

[34] G. A. Cohen, *Karl Marx's Theory of History: A Defence* (Princeton, N.J.: Princeton University Press, 1978), p. 77. Cohen's book is, in my opinion, the clearest analytic treatment of Marx's theory of society and history that exists. Allen Wood offers a related view in *Karl Marx.*

utilize the available forces of production to produce the goods necessary to sustain their existence. The underlying dynamic of history is the
development of the productive forces. As these forces develop, they
come into contradiction with the existing, prevailing relations of production. The dialectic of history is such that at these points of contradiction the relations of production are dismantled and new ones are put
into effect, thus creating a new economic structure that facilitates the
further development of the productive forces. That is, the economic
structure functions to allow the further development of the productive
forces, and the historical existence of a particular economic structure at
a given time is determined (and functionally explained) by the level of
the productive forces that obtain at that time. This relationship is what
Marx refers to when he speaks of "relations of production which
correspond to a definite stage of development of their material productive forces."[35] What is called the superstructure consists of the noneconomic institutions of society and is generally taken to include
political and legal structures, morality, religion, philosophy, and culture in general. Just as the economic structure corresponds (is functionally related) to the existing level of the productive forces, so the
superstructural elements correspond to the economic structure. That
is, the superstructure functions to help sustain and stabilize the existing economic structure, and the existence of a particular superstructural form can be explained in terms of its ability to fulfill this task.

Given this brief and overly simplified summary of Marx's theory of
society, how is morality to be understood? Morality, and specifically
standards of justice and right, are part of the superstructure. The
content of morality is determined by the functional relation sketched
above. Since every social formation—or, to mention another term that is
sometimes used in this context, every mode of production—has a different economic structure, it would follow that we would expect every
social formation to include a different morality functionally related to
the economic structure. Morality, then, is relative to the social form or

---

[35] Karl Marx, "Preface to *A Critique of Political Economy,*" *Karl Marx: Selected Writings,* ed.
David McLellan (Oxford: Oxford University Press, 1977), pp. 388-92. Cohen's book consists,
in the main, of an extensive explication of the "Preface." He successfully demonstrates that
the "Preface," if properly interpreted, contains a consistent and possible theory of history,
and he offers compelling reasons to think that his interpretation is true to Marx's own
understanding of his project. Whether the interpretation of Marx Cohen puts forth can
make sense of all of Marx's texts, and whether one can find other theories of history (or parts
of such theories) in Marx, are further matters.

mode of production. To say that a given action or institution is moral is thus to say something about the relation of that action or institution to the prevailing economic structure. Specifically in terms of justice,

> When Marx says that a just transaction is one that corresponds to the prevailing mode of production, he means...that it is one which plays a concrete role in this mode, one which functions as an actual moment in the productive process. Just transactions "fit" the prevailing mode, they serve a purpose relative to it, they concretely carry forward and bring to actuality the process of collective productive activity, of human individuals in a concrete historical situation.[36]

For Marx, given this function of moral norms to sanction the existing social and economic relations, "what is right and just simply *is* what performs this function at this time...."[37] There are no absolute or eternal principles, no independent, objective moral position from which to appeal. To apply the moral standards that fit one mode of production to actions or institutions of another mode of production is to misapply them.

One might object here that displaying the social function of morality and even explaining the content of morality according to the canons of historical materialism is not the same as justifying a particular moral code. I think, and Wood seems to agree, that this objection has merit. To explain and to justify are not the same. Marx provides no arguments to show that there is no objective, true morality that is independent of historical situation. Marx clearly thinks, however, that there is no such morality and that all attempts to supply one—Kantian, Christian, utilitarian, or what have you—fail to provide a rational grounding for such a morality. As Wood puts it, "Marx's view is that once we come to see what the appeal of moral and religious ideas really rests on, we will no longer be in thrall to them, and we will at last be in a position to recognize...that they have no firmer foundation than the one Marx's theory gives them."[38]

---

[36] Wood, "The Marxian Critique of Justice," p. 15.

[37] Wood, *Karl Marx*, p. 149.

[38] Wood, "Marx on Right and Justice: A Reply to Husami," p. 129. Also see Wood, *Karl Marx*, pp. 144-45.

If this view of the nature of morality is the one that Marx held, should we conclude that Marx is a relativist? Opinions differ here. Brenkert, who agrees in the main with this interpretation, concludes that "Marx's views on justice, then, do seem to be what might be called relativistic."[39] According to Marx, Brenkert argues, "we cannot apply our moral principles of justice to other historical epochs."[40] Wood, on the other hand, argues that "Marx's concept of justice is not relativistic."[41] Marx's concept of justice, Wood maintains, affords a clear decision procedure. Anyone using it would reach the same conclusion concerning the justice or injustice of an action or institution in a particular society. The decision procedure, of course, is to see whether the action or institution in question corresponds to the prevailing mode of production in the requisite way. Brenkert and Wood reach opposite conclusions, in part, at least, because they invoke different senses of relativism. In order to clarify the issue, I will return to Harman's analysis to see how Marx fares in relation to the three forms of relativism discussed above.

Is Marx a normative moral relativist? Normative moral relativism, it will be remembered, is the doctrine that all people need not be subject to the same ultimate moral demands, that different people or societies can be subject to different moral demands. It is fairly clear, then, that the answer to the question is yes. Marx holds that different social formations give rise to different moral systems and people are subject to just those moral demands that follow from the moral system that fits the social formation to which they belong. According to Marx people do not choose which moral demands they are subject to in the fashion implied by Harman in his theory. Morality is a function of a society's economic structure, not of people's immediate choices. Still, according to Marx, there is no transhistorical, objective set of moral demands to which all people, regardless of their place and time, are subject.

Is Marx, then, a moral judgment relativist? As Harman explicates it, this form of relativism is a thesis about the logical form of moral judgments—in particular, moral judgments that are intended to supply an agent with moral reasons to do or not do something. The thesis holds that all such judgments make implicit reference to some system of morality or set of moral demands. As clarified by Harman, this form

[39] Brenkert, p. 92. It should be noted that Brenkert goes on to argue, in opposition to Wood, that freedom is a moral good, and as such, the concept of freedom affords Marx a basis for a transhistorical, nonrelativistic moral theory.

[40] Ibid., p. 93.

[41] Wood, *Karl Marx,* p. 131. Also see Wood, "The Marxian Critique of Justice," p. 18.

of relativism stipulates that inner moral judgments can properly be
made only about persons who share the same morality as the speaker.
Marx, it would seem, is also a moral judgment relativist. Marx does not
discuss the logical form of moral judgments. Given his views on the
nature of morality, however, it is plausible to conclude that he would
agree that moral judgments are relative in this way and that their use
should be restricted in the manner suggested by Harman. It would
make no sense to Marx for a member of a capitalist society to tell an
ancient Roman slaveholder that he morally ought to manumit his
slaves. The slaveholder is morally obliged only to follow the moral
canons appropriate to his mode of production, and according to the
morality of ancient slave society, slavery is morally acceptable.

Lastly, is Marx a meta-ethical relativist? This version of relativism, as
I interpret Harman, allows that two non-inner moral judgments can
both be correct, relative to their respective systems of morality, and yet
predicate conflicting moral properties of the same thing. The situation
is complicated here. The member of capitalist society can correctly
judge that slavery is morally wrong and the ancient Roman slaveholder
can judge, equally correctly, that slavery is morally acceptable. Yet
given Marx's understanding of morality, the member of a capitalist
society cannot say that slavery was wrong in ancient slave societies, nor
could the Roman slaveholder say that slavery would be morally acceptable in capitalism. In this regard Wood is right. If properly relativized
to a concrete historical situation, two conflicting moral judgments cannot both be correct. The only moral judgment that can apply, according
to Marx, is the one that follows from the morality corresponding to that
historical situation. Thus, if morality is understood as Marx understands it, two conflicting moral judgments about the same historical
particular cannot both be correct. I conclude, then, that Marx is a
normative moral relativist and a moral judgment relativist, but not a
meta-ethical relativist.

One last point concerning Marx needs to be raised. It should be
impossible for Marx, given his view on the nature of morality, to morally
condemn capitalism. The only standards for such an evaluation available to him as a member of a capitalist society are those that functionally fit the capitalist mode of production. But the standards
applicable to capitalism are standards that make capitalist transactions
come out as just. Yet Marx clearly is critical of capitalism and does
condemn it. Furthermore, it seems equally obvious that Marx feels that
communism is preferable to capitalism. On the above reading of Marx's

views on the nature of morality, however, he cannot claim, as one might otherwise expect, that communism is morally preferable to capitalism. Each social formation can be judged only by the moral norms that correspond to it. Communism does not offer a higher form of morality and justice, only a different form. These conclusions seem paradoxical, if not inconsistent. How are we to understand them?

In order to solve this problem, Wood introduces a distinction between moral and nonmoral goods.[42] Moral goods are things such as justice, right, virtue, and duty. Nonmoral goods include freedom, health, happiness, self-actualization, prosperity, and community. This distinction is controversial, and even more controversial, perhaps, are decisions about whether to place certain items in one list or the other or perhaps both. But it is a distinction that moral philosophers use, and as Wood argues, while Marx never explicitly draws the distinction, "it is not implausible to suppose that Marx observes it...."[43] Given this distinction, we can say that Marx's condemnation of capitalism rests on the fact that it deprives people of nonmoral goods such as freedom and happiness that, given the historical realities, they could otherwise have and want to have in greater measure. Furthermore, the content and measurement of nonmoral goods is not relative to a specific mode of production. Nonmoral goods have to do with the needs, interests, and potentialities of human beings as they develop from one social form to the next. They are grounded in Marx's philosophical anthropology, and because of this theoretical status nonmoral goods do not bear the same relation to a particular social form as do moral goods.[44] Thus there is no contradiction in Marx saying both that capitalism is to be condemned for alienating and oppressing people and depriving them of happiness, security, etc., and that one cannot morally condemn capitalism for being unjust. Likewise, Marx can base the claimed superiority of communism on the fact that it affords a greater degree of nonmoral goods while consistently holding that communist society is not morally superior to capitalism.

[42] See Wood, *Karl Marx*, pp. 126-30, and "Marx on Right and Justice: A Reply to Husami," pp. 121-23. Also see Brenkert, pp. 93-95. For an argument against differentiating freedom from happiness using the distinction between moral and nonmoral goods, see Arneson, pp. 217-21.

[43] Wood, "Marx on Right and Justice: A Reply to Husami," p. 122. As Wood notes, philosophers with as different moral theories as Kant and Mill invoke such a distinction. For a discussion of the distinction by a contemporary moral philosopher see Frankena, *Ethics*, p. 62.

[44] For an elaboration of this point see Wood, *Karl Marx*, p. 128, Wood, "Marx on Right and Justice: A Reply to Husami," p. 122, and Brenkert, pp. 94-98.

IV

Turning to Vico, we must, as we did with Marx, place his views on the
nature of morality in the context of his theory of society. Vico's theory of
society has two important dimensions, historical and sociological. The
historical dimension is encapsulated in his theory of "the ideal eternal
history traversed in time by every nation in its rise, development,
maturity, decline, and fall."[45] According to the ideal eternal history, all
gentile societies pass through three different stages of development:
the age of the gods, the age of heroes, and the age of men. The growth
of a society from its rise to its fall is plotted through these three stages.
Central to Vico's theory is the proposition that there is a stage in the
development of the human mind that corresponds to, and is characteristic of, each of the three stages of social development. It is the
development of the human mind and the form of the human nature
thus expressed, through the stages of mythico-poetic, heroic-poetic,
and finally rational thought, that is the underlying driving force of
history. The human mind, and human nature in general, however, only
exist within, and as expressed by, social institutions, and the growth of
the mind is stimulated and channeled by the developing social institutions, which are themselves products of human activities. As Pompa
summarizes this point,

> the fundamental cause of historical change is human nature as it
> develops in historico-sociological conditions. The human nature
> from which all else "arises" is not something which can exist, or
> even be thought of as existing, separately from the network of
> human institutions....It is not something over and above the
> customs and laws of men. It is expressed in them. Their history is
> its history.[46]

From a sociological point of view the key to understanding society is
the idea that each stage of social development embodies what Vico

[45] Giambattista Vico, *Scienza nuova seconda, Opere,* ed. Fausto Nicolini (Milan and Naples:
Riccardo Ricciardi, 1953), par. 245. Also see pars. 35, 349, and 393. The English translation is
The New Science of Giambattista Vico, trans. T. G. Bergin and M. H. Fisch (Ithaca, N.Y.: Cornell
University Press, 1968). Henceforth citations to this work will be to *N.S.* followed by the
paragraph number common to both the Italian and English texts.

[46] Leon Pompa, *Vico: A Study of the 'New Science'* (Cambridge: Cambridge University Press,
1975), p. 124.

refers to as a modification of the mind.[47] The modification of mind and related form of human nature shape all the core institutions of the society and thus unify the society into a coherent whole. The institutions represent the solutions the society has devised to the problem of satisfying the various shared interests and needs of the members. Both the nature of the needs and interests and the type of institutional solutions are understood in the terms of the particular cast or modification of mind available to the members of the society. That the members of a society share an outlook that allows them to construct social solutions to their immediate problems is captured by Vico in his concept of the common sense of an age.[48] Common sense is the shared collective outlook, operating on the level of unreflective judgment, consisting of commonly held beliefs and values that are expressed in both the thought and practices of the members of a society. Morality is one aspect of the common sense of an age, and the specific form of morality in a society is a function of the modification of mind informing that society and embodied in its institutions.

In order to focus on Vico's views on morality, I will examine paragraph 341 of the *New Science,* which is found in the section on method. Vico begins the paragraph by stating that at the core of human beings is a corrupted or bestial nature that causes them to be totally self-interested—in Vico's words, puts them "under the tyranny of self-love." As such, Vico's first men—really presocial, protohuman feral giants—are incapable of acting out of a concern for justice, where justice means taking an interest in the well-being of at least some other human beings. Vico then goes on to explain how a sense of justice or morality develops historically, given this initial fact "that man in the bestial state desires only his own welfare;"

> having taken wife and begotten children, he desires his own welfare along with that of his family; having entered upon civil life, he desires his own welfare along with that of his city; when its rule is extended over several peoples, he desires his own welfare along with that of the nation; when the nations are united by wars, treaties of peace, alliances, and commerce, he desires his own

[47] *N.S.,* par. 148.
[48] See *N.S.,* pars. 142, 348. The concept of common sense is more complex than indicated here. It involves at least two levels, what Pompa calls absolute common sense and relative common sense. What I discuss here is the latter. See Pompa's careful discussion in chapter 3 of *Vico.*

welfare along with that of the entire human race. In all these circumstances man desires principally his own utility. Therefore it is only by divine providence that he can be held within these institutions to practice justice as a member of the society of the family, of the city, and finally of mankind. Unable to attain all the utilities he wishes, he is constrained by these institutions to seek those which are his due; and this is called just.[49]

This paragraph indicates the complexity of Vico's thinking on morality. Morality is basically an extension of self-interest. As man, through involvement in developing social institutions, comes to appreciate the fact that he shares a common identity of interest with certain other humans, he develops the ability to act in the interests of these others and keep his own immediate self-interest in check. This ability to consider the welfare of others is the core of justice. In the first stage of human history, the age of the gods, considerations of justice extend over the members of one's family. In the second stage, the age of heroes, the scope of justice is widened to include the members of one's city-state. In the third age, that of men, there is a realization that all human beings share basic interests, and a sense of universal justice is achieved. At each stage self-interest is involved, but self-interest expanded to include the interests of others—and so not narrow self-interest in the sense of egoism. Presumably at each stage those actions that would be considered just or unjust, moral or immoral, change, or rather, increase in number. In the first age one could be rude or hostile toward a person who is not a member of one's family, even rob or assault him, without violating one's moral principles. In the second age this sort of behavior would be ruled out in relation to one's fellow citizens, and finally in relation to all other human beings. The nature and implementation of just authority and law would likewise vary.

Vico thus is saying that morality is relative to historical stages; in other words, morality, as an aspect of common sense, is a function of the structure of society and the corresponding modification of the mind. However, as mentioned above in the discussion of Marx, it is one thing to explain why morality has the content it does at various points in history and quite another to justify a particular code of morality as correct for a particular stage of social development. In fact, Vico sometimes talks as if the moral code of the age of men is superior to earlier

[49] *N.S.*, par. 341.

ones and somehow privileged. The human nature of the third age, he says, is "intelligent and hence modest, benign, and reasonable, recognizing for laws conscience, reason, and duty."[50] The law of this age is "dictated by fully developed human reason."[51] And the jurisprudence of the age of men "looks to the truth of the facts themselves and benignly bends the rule of law to all the requirements of the equity of the causes."[52] This form of jurisprudence is superior to both divine and heroic jurisprudence because it looks to the true while they can attain only the certain.[53] From these and other remarks it appears that Vico is arguing that the correct set of moral principles is that which accords with the rational and truly human common sense of the age of men. Thus, while we can understand the morality of previous ages and understand how and why people in those times acted as they did, we cannot morally justify their actions when they violated the principles of the third age. If this interpretation were accepted, then Vico would not be a moral relativist.

I wish to resist this interpretation, however. First of all, the superiority of the morality and justice of the age of men depends on the fact of the general superiority of that age, given Vico's organic view of society. But there is reason to believe that Vico has reservations about the age of men, morally and otherwise. It does, after all, have the potential to descend into a barbarism of reflection and finally end in a *ricorso*.[54] Also, there is reason to believe that Vico actually preferred the heroic age to the age of men. The heroic mind is poetic, not caught up in abstract thought, and, as Vittorio Mathieu points out, "has not lost touch with divine inspiration."[55] In the end, however, I think that this line of argument is inconclusive. The real point has to do with the nature and purpose of morality in relation to the human nature, interests, and capacities of people at each of the stages of history. Morality is part of the institutional structure of a society and in turn is an expression of the basic human nature and common sense of the people of that society. Morality, that is, is very much embedded in

[50] *N.S.*, par. 918.

[51] *N.S.*, par. 924.

[52] *N.S.*, par. 940.

[53] *N.S.*, par. 941.

[54] See my paper "Vico and Marx: Perspectives on Historical Development," *Journal of the History of Ideas* XLII (April-June 1981): 317-31 for a discussion of this point.

[55] Vittorio Mathieu, "Truth as the Mother of History," *Giambattista Vico's Science of Humanity*, ed. Giorgio Tagliacozzo and Donald Phillip Verene (Baltimore: Johns Hopkins University Press, 1976), p. 123.

society, and the principles and values of a particular morality only make sense within the context of the society of which it is a part. To import a moral code from one society and use it to make moral judgments in another is, for Vico as I read him, to risk losing the sense of morality as well as to ask people to do or not do things that they might well not understand. This is the sense of incommensurability I think Berlin has in mind in the quotation given at the beginning of the paper. Vico sees morality as an intrinsic part of society, and a moral system cannot be abstracted from its particular context.[56] Moral systems can be judged as fitting or unfitting for a particular form of society, but they cannot be judged as better or worse than one another.

Given this reading of Vico's views on the nature of morality, is Vico a moral relativist according to the theories of Harman? Like Marx, Vico would seem to be a normative moral relativist. People are subject only to the moral demands of their age. While the members of a society at a latter stage of social development might be able to understand the moral code and behavior of the people of an earlier stage, they would not be able to make moral sense of the earlier code. They would look upon it as a primitive and unsatisfactory code of morality and not feel subject to its moral demands. The people of the earlier stage, meanwhile, could not understand the morality of a latter stage if presented with it, nor would they feel any compulsion to follow the moral demands of the more developed society. There is, then, for Vico no set of specific moral demands that all people are subject to regardless of their historical and social location. It follows that Vico would also be a moral judgment relativist. If morality is part of the common sense of an age, then inner moral judgments can only be understood in reference to the modification of mind of that age. What people take to be morally acceptable or unacceptable, and hence the moral demands they feel obligated to follow, is part of their common sense. Moral reasons function as reasons to act only within the framework of a particular modification of mind. Since inner judgments are properly taken as presenting moral reasons, they can only fulfill this function in reference to a specific system of morality that is, in turn, an expression of a modification of the mind.

Lastly, is Vico a meta-ethical relativist? Again, as was the case with Marx, Vico's theory could allow that two non-inner moral judgments

[56] I do not think that the same considerations apply to the status of cognitive knowledge or science in Vico. That is, in my reading of Vico, he is not a cognitive relativist even if he is in certain respects a moral relativist. This point, however, cannot be developed here.

both be correct, relative to their respective systems of morality, yet predicate conflicting moral properties of the same thing. But if the object under moral scrutiny is described in a manner proper to its specific historical and social location—that is, if the object is described as an object within a society at a certain stage of development—then the only moral judgments that could be applied are those that follow from the common sense of that stage. Two conflicting moral judgments could not both be correct. At least one of the judgments, that which followed from the morality of a different age from that of the object being judged, would have no real application. If this is the case, then Vico, like Marx, is best construed as not being a meta-ethical relativist.

One final point concerning Vico should be made, if only briefly. In my discussion of Foot I noted that she feels that the truth of moral relativism depends on whether or not there are shared standards governing the moral realm. In order to decide if there are such standards, she argues, we need to investigate further human nature and the idea of a proper human life. Vico's theory, as I have interpreted it, allows for an irreducible variation in moral standards. Vico would therefore resist the idea that there are shared standards of the type Foot requires if moral relativism be false. However, Vico does not allow for an unlimited degree of moral variation. In particular, Vico holds that a precondition of human life is the containment of the bestial passions that lie at the core of our natures. Such containment is a prerequisite for the possibility of cooperative social activity. Without cooperative activity, a society could not maintain even a semblance of coherence and order necessary for its continued existence. Human, as opposed to bestial, history in such circumstances would be impossible. In order to solve the problem of converting our bestial passions into some form of moral virtues, Vico argues, three social institutions are necessary: religion, marriage, and burial rites.

it must have been dictated to all nations that from these three institutions humanity began among them all, and therefore they must be most devoutly guarded by them all, so that the world should not again become a bestial wilderness. For this reason we take these three eternal and universal customs as three first principles of this Science.[57]

[57] *N.S.*, par. 333.

I cannot discuss here the nature, status, and justification of these three institutions and principles within Vico's theory.[58] The general point, however, is that all human societies must include some form of religion, marriage, and burial rites; the specific form of each in a given society depends on the modification of mind prevailing in that society. That this is the case for Vico follows from his analysis of human nature and the nature of a properly human life.

What I wish to suggest in conclusion is that Vico's discussion of these three institutions and the role they play in human life can serve as a starting point for the type of analysis that Foot argues we need if we are to answer the question of the truth of moral relativism. Vico's theory, as we have seen, requires that there be a certain amount of variation in the specific form these three institutions can assume, corresponding to the different ages or forms of society. Yet, because some form of these institutions is necessary in all human societies, given the important function they fulfill, there is a limit on what can count as a human moral system. For instance, according to Vico, a system that permitted total sexual promiscuity is not a possible human system of morality. Given Vico's sensitivity to historical difference, however, this limitation on moral systems does not take us very far. He remains a moral relativist in the ways discussed above. Nonetheless, if the search for shared moral standards is to succeed, then the problem of historical similarity and difference must be faced. Vico's rich and suggestive discussion in the *New Science* presents us with precisely this challenge.

In summary, the theories of Vico and Marx appear to have a similar structure in regard to the problem of moral relativism. The forms of moral relativism my analysis has uncovered in their thought can be seen as an expression of their historicist tendencies, as an appreciation of an irreducible element of historical particularity. However, the social theories of both thinkers provide not only explanations of the nature and function of morality, but also an account of what moral judgments have justified applicability in a given concrete context. This last move prevents Vico and Marx from being full-blown moral relativists and thus keeps their theories from falling into the dangers many find there.

---

[58] For discussions see my "The Problem of Historical Knowledge: Epistemology in the 'New Science' of Giambattista Vico" (Ph.D. diss., Boston University, 1980), chap. IV, and Pompa, op. cit., chap. 3.

Vico, Marx, and Heidegger

Ernesto Grassi

I

To bring together Vico, Marx, and Heidegger may seem arbitrary. There is a certain parallelism in the thought of Vico and Marx, one that also requires that their thought be kept distinct. The present volume arises out of a recognition of this. But why should Heidegger be included in this discussion? One could also engage in a discussion of the relationships between existentialism and Marxism, but it is not evident that Heidegger would necessarily be a part of this discussion.

The purpose of this essay is not only to demonstrate the importance of Vichian thought in the investigation of the relation between Marxism and Heideggerian existentialism, but further to point out how within this problem Vichian thought assumes a central role and with it the humanistic tradition to which Vico belongs.

What unites these three thinkers is their point of departure, even though it is done in different speculative keys. They share in the negation of traditional metaphysics. Vico begins with a negation of the metaphysic that deduces reality from a first truth according to the scheme of Cartesianism, in function of which the humanistic tradition is refuted. Marx begins with a negation of Hegelian speculative idealism, which dialectically deduces reality and historicity a priori. Heidegger refutes the preeminence of the problem of the true as the essence of Western metaphysical thought, arriving at the radical thesis of the end of this tradition.

Vico substitutes for critical philosophy, Cartesian rationality, his theory of imaginative universals (*universali fantastici*) as the source of historical becoming. Marx sees in work—as the mediation of reality—the root of historicity. Heidegger replaces traditional metaphysics, which begins from the problem of the true, with an ontology of unconcealedness (*Unverborgenheit*) in which imaginative thought—in fact, poetry—assumes a preeminent philosophical function. A first ascertainment follows from this that until now, as far as I know, has not been brought to light. Vichian thought—in which the humanistic philosophical tradition culminates—reveals the original function of the poetic word, thus disclosing a thesis parallel to that of Heidegger, which from his perspective expresses a refutation of humanistic thought. This refutation is contained in his famous letter to Beaufret, which was first published by me.[1]

In order to comprehend the import of this problem it is necessary to retrieve the speculative origin of the Heideggerian thesis of the preeminence of the poetic word over the rational word, which is rooted in his theory of the ontological difference between Being (*Sein*) and beings (*Seiendes*).

Two questions arise here. Does there exist a theoretical connection between Heidegger's ontological difference and Vico's theory of the imaginative universal? What are the consequences arising from this with regard to the conception of Marx?

II

It should be stressed that Cartesian metaphysics does not surpass the scheme of traditional thought; in it the preeminence of the problem of the true ultimately holds sway, and philosophy is conceived as rational deduction from a "first" truth. From this perspective the Cartesian claim to refutation of traditional philosophizing—I refer to Descartes' beginning in his *Meditations* from a new first truth, namely the *cogito ergo sum,* as the foundation of metaphysical deduction—reveals itself as specious; metaphysics maintains its traditional deductive character and moves exclusively within the limits of the problem of the true.

Marx criticizes and refutes Hegel's metaphysical dialectical thought, but he stops within the scheme of traditional thought. The theory of work as the mediation of nature always presupposes as its initial point of departure the reality of beings (i.e., nature, man, history, and sociality). Vico and Heidegger pose their problem much more radically. In what original realm does the significance of work, sociality, and the historicity of man appear? To this question Vico responds with the original function of the imagination (*fantasia*) and with the ingenious act (*ingegno*). Heidegger radically distinguishes the problem of Being

[1] Martin Heidegger, *Brief über den Humanismus* (Bern: Francke, 1947; 2nd ed., 1954).

and of its unconcealedness (as the sole sphere in which questions can arise concerning beings) from work and sociality. It is this thesis that leads Heidegger to the affirmation of the originality of the imagination, of metaphorical thought as against rational thought.

It is precisely because of this thesis that Heidegger affirms the end of Western metaphysics which always moves within the problem of the true and, hence, by means of the rational word. For Heidegger Western metaphysics has ignored the question of the unconcealedness (*Unverborgenheit*) of Being.

In the collection *On Time and Being*, in the essay "The End of Philosophy and the Task of Thinking,"[2] Heidegger categorically affirms that philosophy ends in the present epoch. [3] He explains, however, that with this assertion he does not intend to make a purely negative judgment, but to show that Western thought arrives at the completion of a whole epoch of thought. Thus, he asserts: "The end of philosophy is the place, that place in which the whole of philosophy's history is gathered in its most extreme possibility."[4]

In the following considerations I shall refer to the thesis that Heidegger developed in his *An Introduction to Metaphysics*[5] and in the volumes *Vorträge und Aufsätze*[6] and *On the Way to Language.*[7]

Western thought—which begins with the Platonic-Socratic and not with pre-Socratic thought—begins with the problem of beings (*Seindes*) such as inorganic nature, plants, animals, and man, as given. From this premise the necessity of formulating the question concerning the relation between beings and thought follows. And from this, within the realm of traditional philosophy, the preeminence of the problem of logical truth is derived.

Heidegger shows how a more original problem thus comes to be completely ignored—rather, placed into oblivion. This is the problem of unconcealedness (*Unverborgenheit*), the opening (*Offenheit*) of the clearing (*Lichtung*) as the realm in which beings originally appear. I do not know of a more appropriate term for the word *Lichtung*. Vico speaks

[2] Martin Heidegger, "The End of Philosophy and the Task of Thinking," *On Time and Being,* trans. Joan Stambaugh (New York: Harper & Row, 1972).
[3] Ibid., p. 56.
[4] Ibid., p. 57.
[5] Martin Heidegger, *An Introduction to Metaphysics,* trans. Ralph Manheim (New Haven: Yale University Press, 1976).
[6] Martin Heidegger, *Vorträge und Aufsätze* (Tübingen: Nesk Pfullingen, 1967).
[7] Martin Heidegger, *On the Way to Language,* trans. Peter Hertz (New York: Harper & Row, 1971).

of the light (*luce*) that man realizes in clearing the trees from the forest. In French there is a word that is perfectly adequate—*clairière* ("clearing," "glade"). To make clear (*lichten*) is to make something free (*leicht*), to liberate from the trees a certain space in the forest. The realm of freedom that is thus generated is the clearing (*das so entstehende Freie ist die Lichtung*). Clearing, in the sense of liberation and opening, has nothing to do either linguistically or from the objective point of view with the adjective "luminous" or "clear." Light never creates in a forest the clearing I am talking about, for light presupposes the act of clearing (*Das Licht, setzt dieses, die Lichtung voraus*). The act of clearing (*öffnen*) is the freedom that distinguishes light and dark: "The clearing is the opening for any presence or absence."[8]

As a consequence of this the problem of the *lumen naturale*, presupposed by the metaphysical tradition, is not an original problem, for the light breaks through only where the forest is cleared. Only within the realm of the clearing are things, humans, the divinities, the arts, and with them the historicity of existence (*Da-sein*) and the problems that concern it, able to appear.

The preeminent and original problem is not that of the true—as the relation between beings and thought, that is, between subject and object—but that of unconcealedness. (This problem is original also in the narrow historical sense insofar as it was the problem of the pre-Socratics. Heidegger demonstrates this with his interpretation of the fragments of Heraclitus and Parmenides.)

At this point the necessity of posing the problem of the original process—that is, the how and when, and in function of what beings appear (*phainesthai*)—manifests itself. Only in the light of this problem is it possible to understand why Heidegger has translated the Greek word *aletheia* as unconcealedness (*Unverborgenheit*) rather than, traditionally, as truth:

> It is not for the sake of etymology that I stubbornly translate the name *aletheia* as unconcealment, but for the matter which must be considered when we think that which is called Being and thinking adequately. Unconcealment is, so to speak, the element in which Being and thinking and their belonging together exist. *Aletheia* is named at the beginning of philosophy, but afterward it is not explicitly thought as such by philosophy. For since Aristotle it

[8] Martin Heidegger, "The End of Philosophy and the Task of Thinking," p. 65.

became the task of philosophy as metaphysics to think beings as such onto-theologically.[9]

These indications reveal how the Heideggerian term of the fundamental problem of the clearing, of the original opening in which beings appear, has been forgotten by Western metaphysical thought. This problem, however, coincides with the thought of Vico in the *New Science*,[10] in which there appears, surprisingly, even the term "light" (*luce*) as a clearing in the forest (*schiarita nel bosco*), the only realm within which beings, the city, the temple, and man in his humanity are able to appear.

III

It must now be made clear in function of what reflection Heidegger proclaims the necessity of affirming the preeminence of the unconcealedness of Being over that of the "truth" of beings. This is the central point of Heidegger's thought, which demonstrates the actuality of the Vichian thesis according to which it is the imagination (*fantasia*), the poetic, metaphorical word, that, as a result of anguish arising from the human experience of its own alienation from nature, establishes the human world by lighting the sacred flame in order to clear the forest (the labor of Hercules), thereby delimiting the realm (place) of human institutions.

The ontological difference between Being and beings—by virtue of which alone it is possible to comprehend the Heideggerian thesis of the preeminence of the poetic, metaphorical, and imaginative word—is rooted in the following argument. Nature, plants, animals, and man are forms of beings. We say of all beings that they *are*. Thus we say that man *is*, the animal *is*, and so on. The essence of a being appears only in the light of the clarification of what we intend with the verb "to be," for it is in function of "to be" that the singular being is able to appear in its signification.

This argument of Heidegger (given in the text of a course he held in 1941 in Freiburg, and which has yet to be published) demonstrates that every attempt to logically—that is, rationally—identify Being carries

[9] Ibid., pp. 68-69.

[10] Giambattista Vico, *The New Science*, trans. Thomas Bergin and Max Fisch (Ithaca, N.Y.: Cornell University Press, 1968), p. 11, par. 16.

with it a logical contradiction. Here it will suffice to indicate the central points of Heidegger's argument.

The Being that is expressed in the verb "is" is to be understood as the term that is most fundamental to every affirmation concerning beings. At the same time, however, this expression is the most obscure term, for every attempt to define it—insofar as it becomes an object of a determination—necessarily reduces it to a being. Furthermore, it is the most general and most empty term, otherwise it would not be able to apply to every being. At the same time it alone is unique, for it gives of its essence to every determinate being. Being is the foundation of all of our affirmations, for each one finds repose in it. But Being reveals itself as a foundation on which we cannot rely because it escapes us. Every attempt to define it necessarily reduces it to a being, thus changing its nature as Being.

The signification of Being is the most forgotten, because all of our problems regarding beings already presuppose it. Nonetheless, as the presupposition of every affirmation, it is the condition for every adjective concerning beings. As such, the meaning of Being must always be present, always be remembered. In short, the affirmation of Being appears as a necessary reality, for it is the condition of every affirmation concerning beings. At the same time, however, it is liberator, for it is the foundation of all determinations of beings, opening the possibility of the distinction between subject and object by virtue of which the subject is able to arrive at its own identification.

As a function of the impossibility of defining Being by means of rational thought—which is valid within the realm of beings—the necessity of distinguishing the problem of Being from that of beings follows. Heidegger develops this thesis in *Der Satz vom Grund.*[11] The traditional interpretation of the logical axiom *nihil est sine ratione* affirms that it presides within the thinkability of beings to draw beings out of the realm of vacillating opinion (*doxa*) by giving them reasons. By doing this one stops, fixes, and identifies the singular being by means of the rational process whereby the rational word is the only adequate expression. Thus the principle of sufficient reason comes to be the canon that presides over the thinking of beings (*Satz vom Grund als Grundsatz des Seienden*).

According to Heidegger the principle of sufficient reason is to be understood in a more profound way:

---

[11] Martin Heidegger, *Der Satz vom Grund* (Tübingen: Nesk, Pfullingen, 1958).

Only being has a ground, and indeed necessarily so. It *is* only as grounded. Being [*Sein*], however, because itself the ground, remains without ground. Insofar as Being, itself the ground, grounds, it allows the being to be a being at any given time.[12]

In other words, the principle of sufficient reason, as the word for Being, is not able to signify the reason of Being. If we were to interpret the term Being in this sense, we would equivocate the identification being with Being. Only to beings does there belong a reason or an explanation.

This renders comprehensible why Being is not rationally identifiable and why every traditional metaphysic that begins with a first being in order to deduce the significance of beings is not an original metaphysic. At this point we arrive at the Heideggerian thesis that the logical word is not originally open to Being and, therefore, does not disclose the realm within which beings and their related problems are able to originally appear.

IV

It is precisely at this point that the essential dialogue between the thought of Vico and of Heidegger, and the amazing contemporary relevance of the former, is revealed. We refer, in the first place, to Heidegger's thesis of the preeminence of the poetic word in its function of disclosing Being. In his work *On the Way to Language* Heidegger affirms: "Language is the House of Being"[13] (*Die Sprache ist das Haus des Seins*). Man finds his existential subsistence in the word, for as Heidegger asserts: "There is no thing where the word is absent"[14] (*Kein Ding ist, wo das Wort fehlt*).

Beginning with his interpretation of the fragments of Parmenides and of Heraclitus, and with the chorus of Sophocles' *Antigone* (developed in his *An Introduction to Metaphysics*), as in his interpretation of Hölderlin and Trakl, Heidegger categorically affirms that the poet projects (*stiftet*); that is, he finds the place and time of existence (*Dasein*). Marcuse, for example, did not accept this thesis, for since he did

---

[12] Martin Heidegger, "The Principle of Ground," trans. Keith Hoeller, in *Man and World*, vol. 7, no. 3 (The Hague: Martinus Nijhoff, 1974), pp. 217-18.

[13] Martin Heidegger, *On the Way to Language*, p. 63.

[14] Martin Heidegger, *Unterwegs zur Sprache* (Tübingen: Nesk, Pfullingen, 1965), p. 165.

not go back to the ontological difference we mentioned before, thus retaining Heidegger's *Being and Time* as a fundamental point of departure for all of our modern thought, he could only think of the Heideggerian thesis concerning the function of the poetic word as a mystical aberration deprived of rigorous philosophical content.

In his interpretation of the chorus of Sophocles' *Antigone* Heidegger says: "Man, in *one* word, is *denotation,* the strangest. This one word encompasses the extreme limits and abrupt abysses of his being. Such being is disclosed only to poetic insight."[15] Out of the terror of confronting Being, by means of the poetic word, the polis emerges as the opening within which historicity appears. Thus, Heidegger asserts:

> The polis is the historical place, the there *in* which, *out of* which, and *for* which history happens. To this place and scene of history belong the gods, the temples, the priests, the festivals, the games, the poets, the thinkers, the ruler, the council of elders, the assembly of the people, the army and the fleet.[16]

With this thesis of the preeminence of the poetic word Heidegger makes it clear that only art renders possible the original appearance of beings: "It is through the work of art as essent being that everything else that appears and is to be found is first confirmed and made accessible, explicable, and understandable as being or not being."[17]

What value do these affirmations of Heidegger have with regard to the comprehension of Vico's contemporary relevance? Vico retrieves the elements of humanistic thought. In his *New Science* Vico does not develop an anthropology; he addresses the question of the unconcealedness in which only man and his history are able to appear. He is concerned with this question as a function of a twofold problem. On the one hand, he poses the problem of the light (*luce*) (Vico uses this term *before* Heidegger) in which human history arises; on the other hand, he poses the problem of the original function of the imaginative word.

In the terror that seizes man in the experience of his own alienation from nature, he creates and establishes the first human place in his historicity, the mark (*segno*) of imaginative activity (*fantasia*) and ingenuity (*ingegno*). As Vico asserts:

[15] Martin Heidegger, *An Introduction to Metaphysics,* p. 149.
[16] Ibid., p. 152.
[17] Ibid., p. 159.

...the first cities, which were all founded on cultivated fields, arose as a result of families being for a long time quite withdrawn and hidden among the sacred terrors of the religious forests. These [cultivated fields] are found among all the ancient gentile nations and, by an idea common to all, were called by the Latin peoples *luci,* meaning burnt lands within the enclosure of the woods.[18]

For Vico, thanks to the imaginative word, the human world arises as an expression of the original attempt to explain the terror of confronting the power of Being which manifests itself in beings. Hence his insistence in emphasizing that philosophers and philogists, in their search for a first philosophy, for explaining the coming into being of the order of human sociality, should have begun instead with poetic wisdom (*sapienza poetica*), and not with a rational first philosophy.

The thought of Vico is animated by a persistent reference to myth. Thus he refers to the myth of Hercules, which is a symbol and metaphor of the existential realization of man in his rising from the woods, from nature, and with his burning a place in the forest; the myth of Cadmus, which is a metaphor for the transformation of nature by means of human work and social labor; the myth of Daphne and Apollo, who transforms Daphne into a tree—the forever green laurel—a symbol of the vitality of the human generation, the genealogical tree.

The essence of Vico's thought is not understood by those who limit themselves to uncovering the function of the imaginative universals as a substitution for rational concepts. Nor is the essential problem of Vico merely history, as is usually assumed. The essence of Vichian thought emerges by recognizing—which is rarely done—that the problem of Vico is the realm within which man appears in his concrete and total realization. In other words, Vico has recognized that it is not beings (i.e., nature, man, or his creations) which are to be considered the essential subject matter of a new science. With this insight he has hit upon a completely new way of confronting traditional metaphysics. That is to say, for Vico the problem of the true is subordinate to the problem of the appearance of human reality. The bursting forth of Being in human historicity from time to time, always in new forms, realizes itself originally in the poetic, imaginative word (*parola fan-*

---

[18] Giambattista Vico, *The New Science,* par. 16.

tastica) in function of which the world appears in its human significance. Vico's problem is that of what opens the realm of human
sociality, and he identifies this original opening with the metaphorical,
mythic word.

V

We affirmed that the thought of Vico represents the philosophical
culmination of the humanistic tradition. The importance and validity
of this thesis is able to appear only if we consider the problems to the
solution of which the humanists principally dedicated their efforts.

Among the major humanists who devoted themselves to uncovering
the origin and function of imaginative thought, later reached by Vico,
was A. Mussato (1261-1329), the major representative of prehumanistic
thought. In his *Epistole,* and precisely in chapters IV, VII and XVIII,[19]
he proclaims the preeminence of poetic thought, and with a fertile
imagination he calls poetry *alterna philosophia, divina ars* and *theologia
mundi.*[20] To poetry there belongs a sacred function, not because it is
concerned with religious theses that conform only to Christian theology, but because it originally makes reality manifest in its concreteness
and, from time to time, differentiates the structure of history. To this
reality belong the various conceptions of divinity, different forms of
sociality, and even various forms of obscenities (*Interdum sacrae monu-
menta Minervae/incidit officiis atque Venus apta meis*).[21] With poetry one is
not concerned with truth, only with revealing beings in their historicity.
Mussato insists, for instance, upon the variety and ever-new represen-
tations of divinity. Consequently, God is not to be identified with the
singular conceptions of divinity that appear and disappear from time
to time in history, but with the imaginative power of manifestation in
function of which the historicity of the divine discloses itself in various
modes as the historicity of Being.

In the poetic mythology of ancient Greece Jove strikes the giants with
his own lightning. In the *Old Testament* God strikes man with the mal-
ediction of the confusion of languages (*Confundit lingua Deus hic, qui
fulmine jecit, qui Deus est nobis, Jupiter ille fuit*).[22] In Greek mythology the

---

[19] A. Mussato, "Tragoediae duae, alia autoris poemata, Epistulae nimirum, Soliloquia,
Eclogae et Fragmenta," *Epistole* (Venice, 1636).

[20] Ibid.,*Epistole,* XVIII, 61A and VII.

[21] Ibid., *Epistole,* VII, 44B.

[22] Ibid., *Epistole,* IV, 41A.

gods swear their allegiance to the Styx in a manner analogous to Christ's affirming that the baptismal water is the sacrament for one's entrance into eternal life (*in Baptismi nostrae numen consistere vitae*).[23] Likewise, says Mussato, the poets of antiquity "*sumpsere Deum, verumque bonumque in re corporea, tamquam Deus esset in illa.*"[24]

It is from here that Mussato's thesis derives—which we find also in Vico—that the poets revealed the secrets to the first men (*tecta quidem primae fudere nigmata Genti*) insofar as with their poetic words (metaphors) they were able to supersede the reality of the senses. Thus, the ancient poets came to be called prophets[25] (*Hique alio dici coeperunt nomine vates*). Because the poets speak through images (*figmenta*), the significance of which is metaphorical, their words are enigmatic (*Nigmate maiori mystica Musa docet*).[26] With this transposition—through the veil (*velame*), the sensible crust (*corteccia sensibile*)—poetry reveals Being.

These enunciations of Mussato provoked the indignation of a Dominican preacher, Giovannino da Mantova, who attempted to demonstrate the absurdity of a Christian wanting to reduce theology to poetry. In fact Mussato's thesis reverses the medieval *topos* of the close connection between poetry and theology and thus invalidates the thesis of E. R. Curtius, according to which only the traditional position of medieval thought is recognizable in Mussato's affirmation.

Boccaccio, recovering Mussato's thesis in the *Genealogia Deorum*, tried to defend Latin mythology by searching below the veil of the poetic fable to its hidden truth. He says: "*fabula est exemplaris seu demonstrativa sub figmento locutio.*"[27] In order to comprehend the significance of Boccaccio's thesis, the following must be kept in mind. The *exemplaris locutio* obtains a function in rhetoric analogous to logical induction. To induce does not mean here to extract the common element from the multiplicity; rather, it means to bring back the multiplicity to that unity which gives it a sense and as a function of which it "illuminates" itself with a significance. The corresponding *demonstrativa locutio* of which Boccaccio speaks in his definition of fable does not therefore have a rational, logical character. The fable is a disclosing. It allows one to see, by means of the fabulous "exemplary image," the place and time in which men, things, and institutions appear. This

---

[23] Ibid., *Epistole*, XVIII, 60F.
[24] Ibid., *Epistole*, XVIII, 60 F.
[25] Ibid., *Epistole*, 44C.
[26] Ibid., *Epistole*, IV, 41A.
[27] G. Boccaccio, *Genealogia Deorum* (Bari: Laterza, 1951), p. 706.

vision is an appearance that comes in an easy and immediate fashion essentially diverse from the proceedings mediated by the rational process. Because of this the fable evokes a world, an institution, which it manifests immediately. This is why Boccaccio is able to affirm: *"non erit supervacaneum fabulas edidisse."*[28]

In order to confirm his own thesis, Boccaccio indicates that the Old as well as the New Testament utilize the metaphorical fable. Thus, for example, Moses perceives God in a burning bush, Christ appears as a lamb and as a dragon.[29] This recognition of the value of the imaginative world leads him to the thesis that "not only is poetry theology, but theology is poetry."[30] Unlike Mussato, however, Boccaccio then realizes the consequences of a similar thesis from a Christian standpoint. In fact he abandons the thesis of poetry as theology in order to differentiate the true poetry from the false. He identifies the true with Christian theology, i.e., with a thing (*res*) outside of, or above, historicity. He recognizes that with his intention to legitimize poetry—indicating ancient myths as *velamina* of truth—he runs the risk of also relativizing the truth of Christianity. So he renunciates both the preeminence of poetry over theology and their identity. This movement signifies a return to dogmatic thinking and to the main lines of traditional metaphysics with the preeminence of the problem of the true.

More radical is the thesis of C. Salutati (1331-1406). In his *De Laboribus Herculis*[31] human historicity, with all of its religious, social, political, and ethical elements, manifests itself through poetry. Poetry is what diverts bestial man from the world of sense.[32] With this thesis Salutati discloses the original function of poetry.[33] Below the crust or veil of poetry, the always different sense of the real is concealed. When Salutati speaks of truth in this connection, however, he does not mean logical truth, but the historical manifestation of the human world. Thus he says:

> The far-seeing prophets (*Vates*) considered from the height of their ingenuity (*ingenii altitudine*) a threefold reality with which they adorned history as with lumination (*quibus sua poemata quasi*

[28] Ibid.

[29] G. Boccaccio, *Vita di Dante* (Florence: Barbera, 1837), pp. 5-6.

[30] Ibid., p. 59.

[31] C. Salutati, *De Laboribus Herculis,* ed. B. L. Ullmann (Zurich, 1951).

[32] Ibid., p. 7.

[33] Ibid., p. 8.

luminibus exornarunt): God, the world, and living things (*deum, mundum et animantia*). They did this in order to express with beings and in beings, the totality of that which we call living beings (*ut per illum omnia et in illo omnia quae animalia dicimus esse dicantur*).[34]

Within the open realm of the poetic word the gods, things, and living beings appear with a signification that corresponds to the epoch. It is a unique and indivisible God that, in different forms, manifests itself in various times and places. Thus Salutati asserts:

Since they [the poets] acknowledged that God as architect of the world had realized everything with total wisdom...and since this wisdom is nothing other than the divinity itself, they gave different names to God.... Thus, no one is able to doubt that, even with so large a number of divinities, the poets did not think of many divinities, but of the same God with regard to his different functions, places and times (*non de pluribus sed de uno sensisse*).[35]

It is therefore within the realm of the poetic word that the dialogue between thing (*res*) and word (*verba*) is dealt with, not in the realm of metaphysics or in a theory of knowledge as that sought by Cassirer.

This speculative tradition arises again in Vico, who recapitulates and reemploys it in his theory of the function of the imagination. It is therefore necessary to review the negative judgment which holds that humanism was devoid of an affirmative philosophy of its own and that such a philosophy only surfaced later, at the end of the fifteenth century, with the return of traditional metaphysics in its Platonic, Neo-Platonic, and Aristotelian forms. Kristeller, for example, holds that the philosophy of humanism can be identified with this form of thought only.

It is not necessary to continue referring to the humanists in order to illustrate the tradition that culminates in Vico. We shall note only how G. Pontano (1426-1503) in his dialogue *Egidio*[36] affirms the wonder (*meraviglia*), the amazement (*stupore*), and the terror (*spavento*) as sources of poetry that awaken the passions of the spirit and allow "the

---

[34] Ibid., vol. II, p. 587.
[35] Ibid., vol. II, p. 588.
[36] G. Pontano, "Egidio," in *Dialoghi*, ed. G. Previtera (Florence: Sansoni, 1943).

thing to spring forth as it is" (*ut qualis res ipsa esset*).[37] The poetic word is not therefore subjective and arbitrary, but—as says Pontano: "that which is inherent to the thing" (*rebus ipsis inhaerens*).[38] Thus the poetic word is not to be understood as a resemblance to things (*at noster nulla huiusmodi similitudine usus*).[39] By means of the word of the poet the thing itself appears in itself and becomes modeled in the verse (*velletque rem ipsam ut admirabilem, ut horroris plenam verbis suis ante oculos ponere animisque infigere ac tubae suae canorem tenere*).[40]

VI

The preceding indications reveal the relevance of Vichian thought, rooted in the humanistic tradition that Heidegger—paying attention only to the traditional sense of humanism—has refuted. Heidegger maintains that humanism is not an original type of thought and that it stops within the metaphysical tradition of beings without posing the problem of Being as original unconcealedness of Being. Let us recall the antihumanist position of Heidegger expressed in his *Letter on Humanism*: "Humanism does not pose the problem of the relation of Being with the essence of man. Humanism precludes even the possibility of this problem which—given its metaphysical provenance—it ignores and does not understand."[41]

We shall now articulate the differences among the three thinkers discussed in this paper. First, Marx and Vico. Marx refutes the metaphysical apriorism of Hegelian idealism; that is, the attempt dialectically to deduce the historical concreteness of man. Let us recall Marx's fundamental argument agains Hegel: "Hegel uncovered only the abstract logical expression of the unfolding of history which, as such, is not yet the true history of man."[42] For Marx, Hegel's attempt consists in his effort logically to deduce concrete reality, which he identifies with the outcome of a dialectic of ideas. He points out that by developing history as an outcome of the dialectic of ideas, Hegel does not consider

[37] Ibid., p. 70.
[38] Ibid., p. 69.
[39] Ibid., p. 69.
[40] Ibid., p. 73.
[41] Martin Heidegger, *Brief über den Humanismus* (Bern: Francke, 1947; 2nd ed., 1954), pp. 63-64.
[42] Karl Marx, "Oekonomische-philosophische Manuskripte 1844, Kritik der hegelschen Dialektik und Philosophie," in *Karl Marx, Friedrich Engels Werke* (Berlin: Dietz, 1973-74), p. 570.

historical, social, and political events as fruits of the actuality of concrete men within clearly defined situations. As Marx asserts:

> Since *the* truth, like history, [for Hegel] is an ethereal subject separate from the material "Mass," it does not address itself to empirical man but to the "depth of the soul"...it does not touch man's *gross body* which may dwell in the depths of an English cellar or in the height of a French attic, but "forces" itself "on and on" through his idealistic intestines.[43]

In this way men are reduced to predicates, to symbols and instruments of a dialectic of ideas about which it is not known by whom it is really thought. For Marx the development of human history is not to be found in the dialectic of abstract ideas, but in the transformation of nature by human work, through which existing beings fulfill their needs. By affirming that work is the primary root of historicity, Marx presupposes man and nature as given things. From this he derives the preeminence of work as the original mediation of nature, with the consequent vision of work as a way to fulfill human needs understood in their biological and anthropological significance (i.e., nutrition, reproduction, social realization).

Marx's affinity with Vico, therefore, is that Vico also rejects any metaphysic that, beginning with a first truth, proposes to deduce reality a priori. This is the meaning of his polemic against Cartesian thought. The radical difference between Vico and Marx is that Vico investigates the realm within which history arises, a realm that unveils itself in the function of the imagination (*fantasia*). While for Marx the root of historicity is work, for Vico it is imaginative ingenuity (*ingegnosa fantasia*) that opens the possibility of the unfolding of history. It is in function of imaginative ingenuity that different conceptions of work, of the importance and purpose of work, and correspondingly the structure of society, its economy, its politics, and its institutions arise. Thus, for Vico the imagination is not a superstructure. The loss of the conscience of the originality of Being as it is realized through a fertile imagination alienates man from his own root. This estrangement leads to the barbarism of reason (*barbarie della riflessione*).

---

[43] Karl Marx, "The Holy Family," in *Writings of the Young Marx on Philosophy and Society,* trans. L. Easton and K. Guddat (Garden City, N.Y.: Doubleday, 1967), p. 377.

Vico does not begin with beings as already given—that is, with man, his history, or his social institutions. He begins, rather, with imaginative signs (*segni fantastici*), with imaginative universals (*universali fantastici*) that are the basis of the humanization of nature. Thus, he says: "...the first men of the gentile world conceived ideas of things by imaginative characters...they expressed themselves by means of gestures or physical objects which had natural relations with the ideas."[44] And further:

> From these first men, stupid, insensate, and horrible beasts, all of the philosophers and philogians should have begun their investigations of the wisdom of the gentiles; that is, from the giants.... Hence poetic wisdom, the first wisdom of the gentile world, must have begun with a metaphysics not rational and abstract like that of learned men now, but felt and imagined as that of these first men must have been, who, without power of ratiocination, were all robust sense and vigorous imagination. This metaphysics was their poetry, a faculty born with them...born of their ignorance of causes, for ignorance, the mother of wonder, made everything wonderful to men who were ignorant of everything.[45]

What are, then, the identities and differences among Heidegger, Marx, and Vico? First, their identities. All three agree in the rejection of traditional metaphysics as a point of departure for the conception of existence (*Da-sein*). We have already referred to Heidegger's critique and his thesis of the end of Western philosophy. It is necessary to recognize the problem of *aletheia* as a problem of the unconcealedness of Being as it is distinguished from the problem of the truth of beings (the ontological difference). The logical problem of the true presupposes the solution to the problem of the manifestation of truths—that is, how and where and in what original form Being reveals itself. It presupposes the problem of the opening (*Offenheit*), of the clearing (*Lichtung*) by virtue of which man emerges and delimits, within the darkness of the forest of nature, the place and time of his own existence. Conjoined to this affinity between Heidegger and Vico is their affirmation of the preeminence of the poetic word as a consequence of the demonstration of the limits of the rational word, as well as the

---

[44] Giambattista Vico, *The New Science*, pars. 374-75.
[45] Ibid.

function of the imagination, within the realm of which the significance of work is brought to light differently each time.

But what is the essential difference between Heidegger and Marx; and what are the critical implications of the former with respect to the latter? It was G. Petrovic, with his work, *The Language of Heidegger,*[46] who masterfully illuminated this problem for the first time.

With his theory of alienation Marx indicates the uprootedness of Western man. He recognizes this, as Heidegger does, but without recognizing its true cause. The turning upside down of philosophy, which Marx believed to have accomplished with his critique of Hegel, does not surpass the scheme of traditional thought that begins with the problem of beings and the reciprocal relation between man and nature. Heidegger remarks that Marx supposed to have uncovered the "human man," as he appears in the realm of the social, by identifying humanity and sociality. This, according to him, would be so because in this way the fulfillment of man's immediate biological and anthropological necessities (i.e., nutrition, reproduction, and sociality) would be assured to him.[47] With this, however, Marx does not overcome the sphere of an anthropologism that Heidegger characterizes as a humanism which inevitably leads—as it has already—to a consumptive and technological ideal—common to the Marxist and capitalist societies.

Petrovic summarizes and acutely interprets the essence of Heidegger's critique of this conception of Marx: "With his humanism Marx attempts to overcome metaphysics. But, since every metaphysics is a humanism and every humanism is a metaphysics, Marx also remains (for Heidegger) within metaphysics."[48] By metaphysics is meant the thought that originates from the problem of the true—that is, the relation between beings. Speaking of Marx's theory, Heidegger points out that the essence of materialism does not consist in the affirmation that all is material, "but rather in a metaphysical determination according to which all that which is in being constitutes the material of work....The essence of materialism is hidden in the essence of technique."[49]

[46] G. Petrovic, *Der Spruch Heideggers,* published in a volume celebrating the eightieth birthday of Heidegger (Frankfurt, 1970), p. 426.

[47] Martin Heidegger, *Platons Lehre von der Wahrheit* (Bern: Francke, 1947).

[48] G. Petrovic, *Der Spruch Heideggers,* p. 61.

[49] Martin Heidegger, *Platons Lehre von der Wahrheit,* p. 88.

How are we to understand this thesis? Only the clearing (*Lichtung*) of Being can guarantee to man the approach of Being itself, which is the essential condition of existence (*Da-sein*). To begin exclusively from the problem of beings implies the estrangement (*allontanamento*) from Being, an estrangement that is the true source of uprootedness (*Heimatolosigkeit*)—the oblivion of Being (*Seinsvergessenheit*) peculiar to Western man.

But what is the relation between this thesis and the emergence of the technological and consumptive ideal—be it Marxist or capitalist—of the Western world, which Heidegger refers to? If the problem of Western philosophy is that of beings, the specific theme of any investigation is their identification by rational definition, a definition carried out by means of traditional logic (i.e., the principle of sufficient reason). Rendering reason foundational to every singular being, the fixation of everything to calculation and availability comes to be presupposed. Consequently, the preeminence of the problem of the relation between subject and object—both types of beings—follows. From this the urgency of the domination of objects by the subject also follows. The latter is alienated from the question of Being, which implies that man, "having strayed from the truth of Being…continually returns himself to himself as a rational animal."[50]

The identity of logical thought with the consequent availability of beings is the premise of technological thought as calculation, as domination of beings. Hence, the preeminence of the problem of consumption follows. This is the social ideal of Marxist and capitalist consumptionism. According to Vico the preeminence of the problem of the true is the source of the "barbarism of reflection."

Translated by Joseph Vincenzo

[50] Ibid., p. 89.

Vico and Marx on Poetic Wisdom and Barbarism

Donald Phillip Verene

In his footnote to Vico in the thirteenth chapter of *Das Kapital*, "Maschinerie und große Industrie," Marx connects Vico's conception of history to a conception of the history of technology. Marx says that John Wyatt, with the production of his spinning machine in 1735, began the Industrial Revolution of the eighteenth century. This beginning took place "without a word." Wyatt's program, Marx says, was to produce a machine "in order to spin without fingers." To this point Marx adds his footnote:

> Even before him [John Wyatt], if also very much unperfected, machines for roving [the process of forming slivers of wool or cotton] had been employed, probably first in Italy. A critical history of technology [*Technologie*] would show how little any of the inventions of the eighteenth century was the work of a single individual. No such book has yet been published. Darwin has aroused our interest in the history of natural technology, that is in the development of the organs of plants and animals as productive instruments sustaining the life of these creatures. Does not the history of the productive organs of man in society, the organs which are the material basis of every kind of social organization, deserve equal attention? Since, as Vico says, the essence of the distinction between human history and natural history is that the former is made by man and the latter is not, would not the history of human technology be easier to write than the history of natural technology? By disclosing man's dealings with nature, the productive activities by which his life is sustained, technology lays bare his social relations and the mental conceptions that flow from them. Even all history of religion that is abstracted from this material basis is—uncritical. It is in fact much easier to find through analysis the earthly core of misty religious formations, than conversely, to develop its lauded, heavenly forms

from particular existing life forms. The latter is the only materialistic
and thereby scientific method. One sees readily from the abstract
ideological presentations of its spokesmen, as soon as they venture
out of their specialities, the defects of abstract natural scientific
materialism, which excludes the historical process.[1]

The age of technological life begins with the machine employed as
the means of production rather than with the body and the tool as an
extension of the body. This transformation does not take place in
thought but directly in the field of human activity. It takes place
"without a word," anonymously, through the mechanization of part of
the spinning process, "probably first in Italy." At the same time that
John Wyatt introduces the definitive version of the spinning machine
(1735), Vico introduces the definitive version of the *Scienza nuova*
(1730). The spinning machine establishes machines as a means of
production and defines the basis of modern life. Vico in his conception
of history defines the basis for understanding it. Technology is prominent in modern life. It is the form of modern life. But the Vichian
principles through which it could be understood have no prominence
in modern thought. In Marx's view both the spinning machine and the
principles with which to understand its history arise from Italian soil.

Because of the work of Darwin, Marx says, we have a picture of
natural technology—the ways in which organisms sustain their life in
relation to their surroundings. The historical understanding of how we
as humans sustain our life is possible because we produce our world.
Through our relationship to our natural surroundings we make an
historical world for ourselves. If we understand this process of technology between man and his surroundings, this sphere of activity, we will
also understand the mental conceptions, the *Vorstellungen,* that flow
from them. In this way Marx points to Vico's sense of "making"—men
make their world through their actual activity, and because of this they
can intellectually make a knowledge of this world. The forms of human
society and human conceptions are connected to the modes of activity

[1] Karl Marx, *Das Kapital: Kritik der politischen Ökonomie,* vol. 1 (Berlin: Dietz Verlag,
1973), pp. 392-93. My translation.
    See also Max Harold Fisch, "Vico's Reputation and Influence: In the Marxist
Tradition," in *The Autobiography of Giambattista Vico,* trans. Max H. Fisch and Thomas G.
Bergin (Ithaca, N.Y.: Cornell University Press, 1975), pp. 104-7. I have added my
translation of the parts of the footnote that Fisch omits in his quotation of it.

man devises in response to his surroundings. His surroundings are a world that is not of his making.

If religion is to be understood as a form of human activity, Marx says, it must not simply be related back to human needs: It must itself be understood as generated from particular life forms that occur through the technological relationship between man and his surroundings. This is a materialistic and scientific understanding, not in the sense of matter causing the life forms, but in the sense of understanding religion as a secondary product of the activity through which men make their life in common. What must be understood is the actual course of these commonalities that arise through the productive relationship between man and surroundings. To come to such activities with ideological principles is to produce abstract metaphysical understanding. Genuine understanding requires seeing historical process as grounded in the way men make their common world from their surroundings and that we see this as an historical process. To do otherwise is to have a science of words, an ideology, to have materialism as a religion.

Marx had read Vico's *Scienza nuova* by 1862, when he wrote of it to Lassalle and Engels. He perhaps read it earlier, prompted by the event of its French translation by Princess Belgioioso in 1844. If he read it this early, Marx's attention would have been called to Vico's conception of history at the time when he was discovering his own materialist conception of history.[2] His footnote to Vico in *Das Kapital* (1867) is the one place he remarks on this conception in his published works. Marx takes up the topic of machinery and large industry; he begins by discussing the development of machines and calls to mind the classic beginning point of the Industrial Revolution—Wyatt's spinning machine. He then thinks how this sense of beginning is artificial, how such inventions are in a sense anonymous, not the work of any single individual. He then thinks on Italy, on the Italian roving machines, and then on Vico. He places Vico's thought in a new light: the *Scienza nuova* in relation to machines.

I have for some time thought that Vico's conception of *generi intelligibili*, of intelligible universals, together with his general conception of the third age of his *storia ideale eterna*, ideal eternal history, contains the basis for a theory of modern technological society. Vico does not

---

[2] Eugene Kamenka, "Vico and Marxism," in *Giambattista Vico: An International Symposium*, ed. Giorgio Tagliacozzo and Hayden V. White (Baltimore: Johns Hopkins University Press, 1969), p. 139.

himself discuss the technology of machines. I agree that if the history of human technology is to be written, it is Vico who provides the proper basis. The question I would like to raise in this paper is: How are Vico's and Marx's basic sensibilities to history aligned or not aligned? I do not speak on this as an expert on Marx. My emphasis is on Vico, and ultimately my own sensibilities are more Vichian than Marxian. My view of Vico here depends upon a total view of his thought that I have worked out elsewhere.[3] What can be learned by bringing Vico and Marx together concerning the form of the modern world?

I wish to focus the discussion that follows on two passages. The first is from Marx's introduction to the *Grundrisse,* the second from Vico's conclusion to the *Scienza nuova.* My aim is not to prove something about these two thinkers, but to bring forth something of the orientation of each thinker in problematic form, to contrast their senses of history.

Marx says in the *Grundrisse*:

About art it is well known, that certain golden ages stand by no means in relationship to the general development of society, and thus to the material basis, as it were, to the skeleton of its organization. For example the Greeks in comparison to the moderns or even Shakespeare. In regard to certain forms of art, e.g., even the *epos,* it is recognized that they can never be produced in their world epoch making, classical form at the point at which the production of art as such enters; thus within the domain of art itself certain significant forms are possible only at an undeveloped stage of artistic development. If this is the case in the relationship of various types of art within the sphere of art itself, it is certainly less remarkable that it is the case in the relationship of the whole of art to the general development of society. The difficulty exists only in the general apprehension of these oppositions. Once specified, they are explained.

Let us take, for example, the relationship of Greek art and then that of Shakespeare to the present. It is well known that Greek mythology is not only the arsenal of Greek art, but its ground. Is the perception of nature and the social relationships that lie at the basis of Greek imagination [*Phantasie*] and thereby Greek mythology possible with spinning machines and railways and locomotives

[3] Donald Phillip Verene, *Vico's Science of Imagination* (Ithaca, N.Y.: Cornell University Press, 1981).

and electric telegraphs? Where does Vulcan stand against Roberts and Co., Jupiter against the lightning rod, and Hermes against the *Crédit Mobilier*? All mythology overcomes, commands, and forms natural forces in imagination [*Einbildung*] and through imagination [*Einbildung*]; it disappears thus with the actual mastery of these forces. What becomes of *fama* next to Printinghouse square? Greek art presupposes Greek mythology, that is, nature and social forms, themselves already manufactured in an unconscious artistic way through common imagination [*Volksphantasie*]. That is its material. Not every random mythology, that is, not every random unconscious artistic elaboration of nature (included under this, all objectivity, hence society). Egyptian mythology could never be the soil or the womb of Greek art. But in any case a mythology. Hence in no case does a social development that excludes all mythological relation to nature, all mythologizing relationship to it, require from the artist an imagination [*Phantasie*] independent of mythology.

From another side: is Achilles possible with powder and lead? Or, the *Iliad* at all with the printing press and even the printing machine? Do not singing and reciting and the muse necessarily cease with the printer's bar, hence do not the conditions of epic poetry necessarily disappear?

But the difficulty of understanding this does not lie in the fact that Greek art and *epos* are tied to certain forms of social development. The difficulty is that they still furnish us artistic enjoyment and hold good in a certain respect as a norm and unattainable model.

A man cannot become a child again or he becomes childish. But must he not delight in the naïveté of the child and must he not endeavor on a higher stage to reproduce its truth? Does not the nature of the child, in its own character, revive in each epoch the truth of nature? Why should the historical childhood of humanity, where it most beautifully unfolds as a never returning stage, not exert eternal charm? There are ill-bred children and precocious children. Many of the ancient peoples belong in this category. The Greeks were normal children. The charm of their art for us does not stand in opposition to the undeveloped stage of society from which this art grew. It is rather its outcome, and inseparably connected with it is that the immediate social conditions under which it originates, and alone could originate, can never recur.[4]

[4] Karl Marx, *Grundrisse der Kritik der politischen Ökonomie*, 2. Auflage (Berlin: Dietz Verlag, 1974), pp. 30-31. My translation.

Vico says in the *Scienza nuova*:

But if the peoples are rotting in that ultimate civil disease and cannot agree on a monarch from within, and are not conquered and preserved by better nations from without, then providence for their extreme ill has its extreme remedy at hand. For such peoples, like so many beasts, have fallen into the custom of each man thinking only of his own private interests and have reached the extreme of delicacy, or better of pride, in which like wild animals they bristle and lash out at the slightest displeasure. Thus no matter how great the throng and press of their bodies, they live like wild beasts in a deep solitude of spirit and will, scarcely any two being able to agree since each follows his own pleasure or caprice. By reason of all this, providence decrees that, through obstinate factions and desperate civil wars, they shall turn their cities into forests and the forests into dens and lairs of men. In this way, through long centuries of barbarism, rust will consume the misbegotten subtleties of malicious ingenuities [*ingegni maliziosi*] that have turned them into beasts made more inhuman by the barbarism of reflection than the first men had been made by the barbarism of sense. For the latter displayed a generous savagery [*una fierezza generosa*], against which one could defend oneself or take flight or be on one's guard; but the former, with a vile savagery [*una fierezza vile*], under soft words and embraces, plots against the life and fortune of friends and intimates. Hence peoples who have reached this point of reflective malice [*riflessiva malizia*], when they receive this last remedy of providence and are thereby stunned and brutalized, are sensible no longer of comforts, delicacies, pleasures, and pomp, but only of the sheer necessities of life. And the few survivors in the midst of an abundance of the things necessary for life naturally become sociable and, returning to the primitive simplicity of the first world of peoples, are again religious, truthful, and faithful. Thus providence brings back among them the piety, faith, and truth which are the natural foundations of justice as well as the graces and beauties of the eternal order of God.[5]

[5] Giambattista Vico, *La scienza nuova seconda*, vol. 4 of *Opere di G. B. Vico*, 8 vols. in 11 (Bari: Laterza, 1911-41), par. 1106. The passage is from *The New Science of Giambattista Vico*, trans. Thomas G. Bergin and Max H. Fisch (Ithaca, N.Y.: Cornell University Press, 1968). I have made several changes in the translation for emphasis. Citations that follow in the text are to the paragraph numbers common to the Laterza edition and the Bergin and Fisch translation.

Where did Marx get his sense of the contrast between the classical world and the technology of machines that brought on the Industrial Revolution? Perhaps it was in Trier, the city of his birth and early years, where he could walk from the Porta Nigra, the old surviving gate of the Roman city of Treveris, to the *Zollkran,* the customs crane on the banks of the Mosel, a part of eighteenth-century ingenuity in which heavy men could be placed in two squirrel cages and whose movement provided the power to unload the barges of goods. In Marx's trinity of natural forces of power, *Tier, Wind und Wasser,* animal, wind, and water, the *Tier* here was man. Porta Nigra against the *Zollkran,* Vulcan against Roberts and Co., Jupiter against the lightning rod.

Where did Vico get his picture of the "ultimate civil disease" of society, his third age of ideal eternal history, the age in which men have lost their sense of the gods and can think only in human terms? This third age is marked by a malicious ingenuity, a vile ferocity or savagery. This is a barbarism of reflection (*barbarie della riflessione*). It is a product of a reflective intellect that has reached the level of malice, a *riflessiva malizia.* In this ultimate state of Vico's third age men are like those of the lowest level of Dante's *Inferno,* the final pit of treachery, those who violate humanity itself by poisoning common confidences that are necessary for human society. They turn their *ingegno* into *insidia,* into "plots against the life and fortune of friends." They live like "wild beasts," like the three beasts that block Dante's way to the *dilettoso monte* at the beginning of the *Divina commedia*—the *lonza, leone,* and *lupa.* They deal in lust, greed, and trickery, perversions that distort the faculties necessary to the *sensus communis* (pars. 141-45) upon which truly human society depends. This third age is Vico's own, and it is, as Marx points out, also the age of the technology of the machine.

I wish to seek out, in the two quoted passages, Vico's and Marx's senses of poetic wisdom and barbarism. These are Vico's terms, not Marx's, yet they represent ideas that have a sense in Marx. *Sapienza poetica,* poetic wisdom, is Vico's term for the barbarism of sense (*barbarie del senso*), which has a generous savagery rather than the vile savagery of the barbarism of reflection. *Sapienza poetica* designates the first two ages of the *storia ideale eterna,* the ages of gods and of heroes. In these ages men thought in terms of *universali fantastici,* imaginative universals, or poetic characters. They formed all the forces of nature as gods—thunderous sky as Jove, earth as Cybele, the sea as Neptune (par. 402). Marx says, "All mythology overcomes, commands, and forms natural forces in imagination and through imagination." Greek art presupposes that nature and social forms are manufactured first in *Volksphantasie.*

Vico's barbarism of sense refers most directly to the very first stage of *sapienza poetica,* where men formed the world through their senses, where they forged a *topica sensibile,* sensory "topics" (par. 495), places in the immediacy of their flow of sensations from which to form images of the world with their power of *fantasia,* their varicolored imagination. Men formed physical places for themselves by their labor in clearing the forests, space in which to create common bonds through what Marx would call their productive relation to their surroundings. Vico's barbarism of reflection refers most directly to the very endpoint of the third age, in which men have completely lost their *fantasia* and their original sense of productive labor as communal bond. As Marx says, mythological structuring of natural forces "disappears with the actual mastery of these forces." For Vico, this mastery is a loss of the memory of *fantasia* as well as its power, a loss of the Herculean sense of the labor of clearing the forests. It is a descent into the lowest circle of the *Inferno.*

In Vico's conception of *storia ideale eterna* each form of social life is accompanied by a specific form of thought. The thought of the third age is a mentality that abstracts genera from sense particulars. The *generi intelligibili* of this age are like the class concepts of Aristotelian logic—they abstract common properties from sense particulars. The sensible world is understood at a distance. All in the sensible world is transformed by the concept, and what can be known of the sensible world is what can be known by placing a sense particular in relation to a concept. The concrete formation of the world through the image accomplished in earlier ages through *generi fantastici* is lost. In this age the power of *fantasia,* of imagination, is confined to art and the sphere of feeling. This sphere is the holdover in consciousness of the original *sapienza poetica*—except that here the *sapienza,* the wisdom, has been separated from *poetica.* The poet is no longer a maker (Latin, *poeta;* Greek, *poietes*). The poet does not make a truth of the senses or the image. Truth is associated only with the power of the concept, of intelligibility in the sense of the abstract symbol. Wisdom itself is lost. In its place stands intellect or, in Vico's terms, reflection. The original forest of actual trees that was the surrounding of the first men is now replaced by a forest of the intellect, of ingenuity (*ingegno*) separated from its original bond with memory (*memoria*) and imagination (*fantasia*) (pars. 699 and 819). In this barbarism of reflection there is a forest of the concept. The intellect is without place, without *topos.*

Labor and life activities also become abstract. The passions no longer have a role in forming the surroundings. They lose their connections with the necessities of life, including the necessity of a *sensus communis.*

The *sensus communis* as the basis of social relationship is replaced by techniques of social order. The passions become refined and "delicate"; they turn inward and produce a kind of monadic individualism. Instead of being a driving force in the formation of life through *fantasia*, the passions become directed toward plots against the well-being of others. Ingenuity is cut off from its role in grasping metaphorical relationships or identities within the world of sense and becomes the basis of schemes of power over others. It is a world of malicious ingenuities and vile savagery because the sense of the world itself has been lost. Man has lost contact with his body and his senses because he has begun to employ the power of the intellect in the field of human action. It is a world in which machines as the means of production make sense.

Marx's undeveloped passage from the *Grundrisse* is in many ways quite close to Vico. Marx makes a distinction between art as directly connected to a mythological base, which can occur in "world epoch making, classical form," and art as such that occurs at a later stage of development. This is like the distinction between art as *sapienza poetica*, which is tied to the world-making power of myth, and art as it becomes limited to its own sphere of reality, separated from *sapienza*. In Marx's view the technology of machines and their world makes the world of poetic making impossible: "Do not singing and reciting and the muse necessarily cease with the printer's bar, hence do not the conditions of epic poetry necessarily disappear?"

Marx like Vico associates the mentality of the *epos* and the myth with that of the child. In Vico's view the first men, who thought and acted in terms of poetic characters, were the children of the human race. Marx's conception of *Volksphantasie* reminds one of Vico's conception of *fantasia* as the basis of the *sensus communis* of the human race. Marx knows that once the language of the *epos* is lost, it does not return. It is lost as the child is lost to the adult. Although ancient peoples are all children of the human race, there are different kinds of children. Vico understands each nation to be a different version of humanity, but each nation develops ultimately in accordance with the general principles of humanity expressed in the conception of *storia ideale eterna*. Vico and Marx both hold that certain forms of thought arise only in connection with certain social conditions. For both Vico and Marx, "men make their own history," and they make it through a transformation of their surroundings.

These are all points of comparison, but there is a fundamental difference. This difference lies in Vico's and Marx's perception of the historical process and the place art occupies in this process. To speak generally, Vico's view of history is mythic and tragic; Marx's view is rationalistic and progressive.

Is the walk between the Porta Nigra and the *Zollkran* the origin of Marx's dialectic, his first dialectical act? The Porta Nigra and the other Roman remains in Trier are reminders of the aesthetic forms of the past, but they were grounded in a form of slave society, as were the art forms of Greece. The *Zollkran* is a symbol of the present technology of machines and modern economy, even though patterned on the earlier *alter Kran*. Where is the art of the machine? There is no room for *epos* or *fama* in the society of business and the printing press. Yet the forms of Greek art, like the life of the child, hold out their attraction, show us a picture of humanity. The technology of machines replaces *Volksphantasie* as the means for transforming the forces of nature. But the products of this unconscious, communal power of imagination—the forms of ancient art—remain. Is there a form of poetic making that is not directly or indirectly always an attempt to tap the original world-making of the myth? If history is to be made by men so that the capitalist form of the technology of machines is overcome by a truly humanistic society, from where will the norm for the human issue?

For Marx, history has a future; for Vico, it does not. Marx and James Wyatt and the mechanical inventors of the eighteenth century have in common their desire to build better. For Vico, the study of history results in heroic education, in the heroic mind, as he calls it in *De mente heroica*.[6] In Vico's view men make history, but they do not change it. The course of the three ages is ever-present; it is the presence of providence. Vico, sitting at his desk, which he mounted like an altar, in his communal living room and study in Naples, is a tragic figure. "Mastro Tisicuzzo," Mr. Bag of Bones, who desires to learn the shape of providence in the social bodies of history—the nations. In the midst of the *Inferno* of the "ultimate civil disease" choice is an illusion. The origins of society catch up with it, and it is brought down. The world of necessities emerges once again—now differently, but things begin over.

In this state of ultimate civil disease the memory of Achilles can be kept alive, and in so doing memory itself is kept alive. The third stage of society is marked by loss of memory and the emphasis on intellect, on

---

[6] Giambattista Vico, *De mente heroica*, in *Opere*, vol. 7, pp. 3-20. "On the Heroic Mind," trans. Elizabeth Sewell and Anthony C. Sirignano, in *Vico and Contemporary Thought*, ed. Giorgio Tagliacozzo, Michael Mooney, and Donald Phillip Verene (Atlantic Highlands, N.J.: Humanities Press, 1979), pp. 228-45.

abstract ingenuity. When the memory of Achilles as a *universale fantastico* is kept alive, a sense of place, of the origin of society, can be opposed to the placeless and memoryless field of modern rationalized life. This is an heroic act because it keeps open the possibility of self-knowledge. But it does not keep open the possibility of changing events, of building the future. History is not a nightmare, but it is a tragedy.

Vico's ancient art of self-knowledge presupposes a beyond to history that attempts to appear in history and that men attempt to form. This is clear from the light from the triangular eye in the frontispiece of the *Scienza nuova*. I do not think Marx and Vico differ on religion as much as it might seem on first glance. For Vico, as for Marx, forms of religion are tied to forms of society. Religion is an agency of social control. In Vico's view the formation of the thunderous sky as Jove leads to the science of divination. The actions of the divine, his signs, must be understood. This power to read the signs of Jove is used by the first families as part of their power over those who are without lineage and names.

It is Marx's and Vico's sense of "surroundings" that ultimately divides them. In Marx's view man makes his history by the technologies he evolves in relation to his surroundings. His social forms and patterns of thought are interconnected with this. But what surrounds history? What of this sense of "surrounding"? What surrounds history for Vico is the divine. The divine is always within history in a tragic way because it remains a surrounding never realized as such in history but seen only in its reflection as the *storia ideale eterna*. Alienation, for Marx, can attend man's relationship to his surroundings. Art, poetic making, is part of the productive activity within a given epoch. Alienation is within the world. For Vico, the world itself is alienation. History is the tragic cycle, the labor of the negative. At the endpoint of the *corso* providence begins again to display to the human the necessities of human life. We are never at home in history.

Attention to the original mythic sense of the symbol gives Vico this sense of history. The myth is always trying to bring forth the reality of the god, who becomes hero and then degenerates into man. The sense of the primordial gives Vico a sense of the ultimate in history, a sense of dissolution in history that is at a particular point not correctable. Marx begins not with the god but with the man-god. He stays with the man-god, the maker of truth out of immediate surroundings. The machine placed in the hand of the man-god gives history a future. The origin, the child, cannot recur. Marx does not have the primordial scene before his mind as he works; he has the future. Vico has always the primordial scene before his mind—the world-shaking force of Jove as the sky itself that speaks only through the mute signs. In the barbarism of reflection this fear is lost. There is no primordial scene behind the project of human action toward the future.

Vico's and Marx's conceptions of history and the relation of history to poetic making cannot be resolved into a common perspective. When Marx's connection of Vico with the technology of machines is further connected with Vico's sense of the third age of ideal eternal history, it suggests a way to expand Vico's "ultimate civil disease," the *ultimo civil malore,* into a theory of our present time. It is a time in which the *sapienza poetica* is lost, like childhood is lost, and men "live like wild beasts in a deep solitude of spirit and will." In the end Marx has no sense of tragedy. His sense of the providential is no more than hope for the future. The belief in progress is still there in Marx's sense of history. Although Marx was well read in ancient poetry and deeply sensed the contrast between its world and the modern world of machinery, he failed to learn the truth of poetic wisdom. He failed to take seriously the truth that myth teaches—that what is begun at a point of origin in human affairs cannot be reversed. The conditions of an origin finally work themselves out as determinations of an end. Marx failed to grasp the truth that Vico grasped in his theory of ideal eternal history—that civilizations and peoples really do have origins, and rise, and fall in history. And they do this without regard to the conceptions and plans their citizens may have to reform their social order so as to make their culture eternal and to put an end to history.[7]

[7] This paper was written in Trier and in Italy. I wish to thank John Krois, University of Trier, for the conversations we had about it.

Marx and Vico on the Oriental Mode of Production

Emanuele Riverso

Marx on Precapitalist Economy

Bertell Ollman opens his book on *Alienation* by stating that "'Marxism' is essentially Marx's interpretation of capitalism, the unfinished result of his study into how our society works, how it developed, and where it is tending."[1] Marx devoted most of his lifelong work to problems related to the means, the modes, and the relations of production, hoping to construct a theory of capital that would clarify the nature and origin of capitalist production and capitalist society. His inquiry was historically oriented; that is, the nature of capital was explained in terms of its origin. In this sense Marx stands in agreement with Vico that "the nature of institutions is nothing but their coming into being at certain times and in certain guises."[2]

There are two ways in which a system of social structures might be genetically explained. One way is to uncover a process of reproduction through which the structure is generated along the span of its existence. The second way is to retrace the stages of social organization that have chronologically preceded the structure's appearance. Both types of explanations are historical, since the process by which a social structure is perpetuated is not less historical than the process by which it was created. The *historicism* of Marx dealt with the nature and origin of capital by employing an analysis of both processes. However, Marx's thought eventually took the shape of a theory that dwells more on the capitalist accumulation of an age than on either the modes of production by which it was preceded or the roots it shared with antiquity.

---

[1] Bertell Ollman, *Alienation. Marx's Conception of Man in Capitalist Society* (Cambridge: Cambridge University Press, 1971), p. ix.
[2] *The New Science of Giambattista Vico,* translated by Thomas G. Bergin and Max H. Fisch (Ithaca, N. Y.: Cornell University Press, 1968; hereinafter *N. S.*), par. 147.

All of this was a consequence of the urgency of Marx's enterprise. He felt pressed by the task of producing a set of suitable notions that would constitute a fresh interpretation of social and economic structures.[3] Kolakowski remarks that "Marx regarded the works of the classic British economists as a model of unprejudiced analysis endeavouring without sentiment to discover the actual mechanisms of social life. He understood, indeed, that their doctrine was grounded in economic liberalism and the belief that it was 'natural' for owners of land and capital to be rewarded for their share in production."[4] Since Marx rejected such grounds, he felt obliged to reanalyze the nature of capital, and in his widely read works on the critique of political economy[5] and on capital[6] he developed the view that the exchange-value of an article is wholly supplied by, and should be measured in terms of, the amount of labor that went into its production. The capital that is invested in the production is not a separate source of value deserving a reward of its own; it is the result of an accumulation of surplus value that the capitalist deducted from what is properly due the workers as compensation for their labor.

Since the wage system is an element of the capitalist mode of production, capital, in some form or another, should have existed from the outset. The accumulation of surplus value explains the reproduction and increase of capital, but it does not explain how capital and capitalist society first appeared. An explanation of these latter would entail an inquiry into the organization of society and the modes of production that conceivably preceded, prepared, and finally brought forth both the capitalist accumulation and the related form of society. Marx certainly appreciated the weight of this question and tried to sketch an inquiry into precapitalist society, availing himself of the reports of ethnologists and historians of his time. Evidence of his interest in this field can be found both in the *Grundrisse*[7] and in his ethnological notebooks.[8]

[3] Cf. V. L. Allen, *Social Analysis. A Marxist Critique and Alternative* (London and New York: Longmans, 1975).

[4] Leszek Kolakowski, *Main Currents of Marxism*, trans. P. S. Falla (Oxford: Clarendon Press, 1978), vol. 1, p. 270.

[5] Karl Marx, *Zur Kritik der politischen Ökonomie*, in Karl Marx and Friedrich Engels, *Werke* (Berlin: Dietz Verlag, 1963-68), vol. 13.

[6] Karl Marx, *Das Kapital*, vols. 23, 24, and 25 of Karl Marx and Friedrich Engels, *Werke*.

[7] Karl Marx, *Grundrisse der Kritik der politischen Ökonomie*, ed. by Imel (Moscow: Marx-Engels-Lenin Institute, 2 vols., 1939-41; hereinafter *Grundrisse*).

[8] Karl Marx, *The Ethnological Notebooks*, ed. Laurence Krader (Assen: Van Gorgum, 1974[2] (1971[1]))

Vico's Ethnological Interest

Marx's ethnological interests parallel Giambattista Vico's concern with the early forms of society found in those ages that preceded what Vico called the "age of men." Vico realized that the more developed forms of culture could only be explained in terms of their birth in the more primitive forms of social life. However, since Vico lived one and a half centuries before Marx, he could not utilize the reports of explorers of the eighteenth and nineteenth centuries. These reports contained growing information about the forms of culture in Eastern countries. To be sure, by the end of the seventeenth century the learned men of Western Europe were acquainted with the existence of peoples and tribes on the American continent, in Africa, in East Asia, and in eastern countries of Europe that were bearers of religious, moral, and social customs deeply different from those of the Christian world.

Vico was careful to acquaint himself, as best he could, with the basic nature of these differences. The fact that he understood such differences is particularly evident in the second edition of his *New Science*. In the *Principi di Scienza Nuova* (1744) references are made to Hugo van Linschooten (Ugone Linschotano), whose *Intinerarium Indicum* on the populations of Guinea had been published in the Hague in 1699, and to José Acosta, author of *Historia natural y moral de las Indias* (Medina del Campo, 1591), a work that described the life of the indigenes of Peru and Mexico. Vico also refers to Thomas Harriot, who published *A Brief and True Report*—in London in 1588—on the Indians of Virginia, and to Richard Withbourne (Riccardo Waitbornio), whose *Discourse* (London, 1620) gave information on the kingdom of Siam. *The New Science* also includes allusions to Joost Schouten (Giuseffo Scultenio), whose *Beschrijvinge van den Conigricks Siam* (*Description of the Kingdom of Siam*) had appeared in 1636,[9] to Johannes van Laet, who composed a *Description of New India,* where information is presented about the inhabitants of East India known by Dutch merchants and explorers,[10] to Marc Lescarbot, who in *De Francia nova* had reported on the Indians of North America, and to Gonzalo Fernández de Oviedo y Valdés, whose *De Historia Indica* gave accounts of the human victims sacrificed by the aborigenes of America.[11]

---

[9] *N. S.*, par. 337.
[10] Ibid., par. 435.
[11] Ibid., par. 517.

Vico did not feel obliged to refer over and over again to contemporary sources that he conceivably judged less reliable and authoritative than the classical ones. He generally preferred to take into account the life of the Indians of America and of the peoples of East Asia with no indication of sources.[12] Unfortunately, the information he could attain on such civilizations hardly touched the real structures of social and economic life; it usually just skimmed the surface, pointing out only that which could impress or startle European readers with its strangeness. Also, the languages of these populations were not well known, and religious prejudices prevented explorers and writers from fully appreciating the behavior and beliefs of cultures other than their own. Thus the reports were too untrustworthy to be of great anthropological interest. But what weighed most against the usefulness of the reports was the fact that the civilizations they endeavored to illustrate had no place on the evolutionary path followed by Mediterranean civilizations.

Vico would have profited from fresh information about the life of the people that lived or had lived in West Asia, particularly in the Fertile Crescent, Egypt, Anatolia, Iran, Turkestan, and the Indian peninsula. Unfortunately, in the seventeenth century the political conditions of those lands made such information difficult to get. The Ottoman Sultanate, which extended from the Balkans to the Red Sea, along with Mesopotamia and North Africa, formed a legitimate barrier between Western Europe and the Orient. Hence there were few cultural and commercial exchanges between the West and the East. Yet Vico realized that he could not ignore the life and civilizations that had flourished in the lands of Western Asia. He knew that the social structures, beliefs, and traditions of these cultures could not be viewed as silly or unworthy of attention. Although he rejected the humanistic doctrine of *Prisca Theologia*,[13] which made some exceptional men of old into the first teachers of all the wisdom that flowed through the generations of men, Vico endorsed the view that ancient deep wisdom (*sapere riposto*)—as a popular endowment (*sapienza volgare*)—came from the East and was carried by Phoenicians to the Egyptians and Greeks.[14] He used to refer

[12] *Princìpi di una scienza nuova intorno alla natura delle nazioni per la quale si ritruovano i princìpi di altro sistema del diritto naturale delle genti* (*Scienza nuova prima*, 1725; hereinafter *Princìpi di una scienza nuova*), in Giambattista Vico, *Opere Filosofiche* a cura di Paolo Cristofolini (Firenze: Sansoni, 1971), pp. 246, 258, 313; *New Science* (1744), pars. 170, 375.

[13] E. Riverso, "Vico and the Humanistic Concept of Prisca Theologia," in Giorgio Tagliacozzo, ed., *Vico: Past and Present* (Atlantic Highlands, N.J.: The Humanities Press, 1981), vol. I, pp. 52-65.

[14] *N. S.*, chronological table and par. 57ff.

to Assyrians and Chaldeans—without clearly distinguishing between them[15]—as remarkable for their wisdom and political achievements. It might also be noted that he respected the Egyptians for their knowledge.[16] Similarly, Vico respected the Arabs for their language, even though he misunderstood the role of the Arabic article.[17]

The Concept of *Oriental* and *Asiatic*

Before proceeding further in this inquiry, it will be of use to consider how, in the span of time separating Vico from Marx, the category of *oriental* or *Asiatic* was defined to such a point that Marx could mention the "Asiatic mode of production" by referring only to the approximate geographical region in which Vico had located the preparatory stages of human civilization. It need not be said that the Orient here refers to more than simply the direction of the sunrise; it is rather than part of Asia that is related to the eastern shores of the Mediterranean Sea. This is due to the fact that the word "Orient" got an absolute denotation before the sphericity of the earth became a commonsense notion. In the Middle Ages the representatives of an Iranian school of Shi'ism led by Shihâboddin Yahyâ Sohrawardî qualified their wisdom as *oriental (ishrâcî)*.[18] They took Iran as the true Orient (Ishrâq), giving it a meaning that was at once geographical, metaphysical, and mystic. This view reached the scholars of Western Europe during the Renaissance. The eastern shores of the Mediterranean Sea were under the sway of Arabian culture and Ottoman Sultanati; at this time the Orient came to include all of *Dar al Islâm* (the house of Islâm) from the Maghrib to the Atlantic shores of Morocco, and from the Indian lands of Mughal Sultanate to the mouths of the Ganges.

At the beginning of the nineteenth century thinkers began to speculate about the possibility of retracing the common lines of those ancient social structures that were still alive in these lands. Vico had been interested in the wisdom and the political achievements of Orientals,[19]

---

[15] *The Autobiography of Giambattista Vico,* trans. Max H. Fisch and Thomas G. Bergin (Ithaca, N.Y.: Cornell University Press, 1963; hereinafter *Autobiography*), p. 142; *Principi di una scienza nuova,* pp. 179, 240, 245.

[16] *Autobiography,* p. 148; *Risposta di Giambattista Vico all'articolo X del tomo VIII del "Giornale de'letterati d'Italia,"* in *Opere Filosofiche,* pp. 147-48; *Principi di una scienza nuova,* in *Opere filosofiche,* p. 208.

[17] *N. S.,* par. 462.

[18] Sh. Y. Sohrawardî, *Oeuvres philosophiques et mystiques,* Bibliothèque Iranienne 2 (Teheran-Paris: 1952), I, Prolegomènes p. 22, text pp. 9, 298.

[19] *N. S.,* pars. 48, 55.

and had credited Nino—a presumed king of Chaldea—with bringing
about the beginning of universal history. In Vico's words: "avendoci
Nino dato il primo incominciamento della storia universale."[20]

Following the sociological bent of his time John Stuart Mill showed
an interest in "oriental society."[21] But thereafter, as it gained more
frequent use by scholars, the category of "oriental" or "Asiatic" turned
into a simple abstraction. It became a concept used to refer to humans
that were living under despotic governments with stagnating econo-
mies. "Orientals" were considered to be people located in a stage of
development more primitive than that of the peoples of Western Europe. Vico, however, was too sophisticated to resort to such an abstraction; his references to eastern civilization were much more guarded
and articulate, even though his sources were older and less reliable.

Marx, on his side, realized, or at least guessed, that the abstract
conception of oriental culture was tainted, and shrank from any endeavor that would attempt a full treatment or description of it. He
rather tried to analyze the particular conditions of social and economic
nature that could be supposed to have contributed to the existence of a
system in which the capitalist form of production and accumulation was
foreshadowed. What is important for our inquiry is that Vico and Marx,
although undeceived by any fictitious category, both looked to the same
geographical area for premises that would support an historical understanding of the fully developed stages of mankind. Was Marx in any
way oriented or stimulated in this respect by the thought of Vico? Or
was his interest in the Orient simply a part of the general European
trend to look eastward for the explication of what happens in the West?
These questions will likely remain unsolved, since it is not yet known to
what extent Marx was acquainted with Vico's work. It would, however,
be profitable to consider some other more penetrating questions: Why
did Vico and Marx study the Orient? What did they discover in the
Asiatic civilization? How did they relate Eastern life to that of the West?
In what ways are their inquiries similar? How are they different? These
questions lead us to the core of the topic of this essay.

Vico's Method of Inquiry

The Marxian concept of *mode of production* encompasses the whole of
a social system looked at from an economic perspective. Therefore, a

[20] Ibid., par. 55.
[21] John Stuart Mill, *Principles of Political Economy* (London: Lubbock's Hundred Books,
1948), I, p. 50.

description of the mode of production of a given society would include the type of authority whose power grants both the organization and the distribution. Although he did not stress economic concerns, Vico did not omit such elements when outlining or discussing the life of a people or nation. Vico understood social structure as a product of human will. Although variable in each man, human will is nonetheless determined by the wisdom of mankind together with the human utility or necessity, which are common to all particular natures of men. Human necessity and utility are the sources of the natural law of mankind.[22] The "wisdom of mankind" (*sapienza del genere umano*), which operates according to divine providence, is a metaphysical notion used by Vico as a means of clarifying his concept of *ideal eternal history*.[23]

Human will refers to the entire spectrum of human choices. Although on a small scale such choices are unpredictable, on a large scale, under the pressure of utility, such choices acquire an oriented frequency that reflects the immanent providence or wisdom of mankind and brings about the laws of the various peoples—that is, their social and political structures. This means that in Vico's view history is the formation of both nations and their structures as they result from human choices, choices that are in turn determined on a large scale by needs and utility. According to this view the social and political structures created by the laws are answers of the human will to the pressures produced by needs and utilities. The homogeneity of the most fundamental needs and utilities is a product of the universality and immutability of the natural law on which the different evolutionary stages of mankind are based and on which the more specific laws of particular nations are grounded.[24] The *useful* is something material that can satisfy some need or wish: "utilitates autem quae cupiditatem cient, corpore constant."[25] Justice or equity is the *equality of the useful* among

[22] *Princìpi di una scienza nuova*, pp. 189-90: "Il fabbro poi del mondo delle nazioni...egli e' l'arbitrio umano, altramente ne' particolari uomini di sua natura incertissimo, però determinato dalla sapienza del genere umano con le misure delle utilità o necessità umane uniformemente comuni a tutte le particolari nature degli uomini; le quali umane necessità o utilità, così determinate, sono i due fonti che i giureconsulti romani dicono di tutto il diritto natural delle genti."

[23] Ibid., pp. 207, 336 ("Tavola delle discoverte generali," I); *N. S.*, par. 393. See Leon Pompa, *Vico. A Study of the 'New Science'* (Cambridge: Cambridge University Press, 1975), pp. 97-128.

[24] Giambattista Vico, *De universi iuris uno principio et fine uno* (hereinafter *De uno principio*) in Giambattista Vico, *Opere giuridiche. Il diritto universale* a cura di Paolo Cristofolini (Firenze: Sansoni, 1974), I, XLIV, pp. 57-59.

[25] *De uno principio*, I, XLIV, pp. 57-59.

men.[26] The natural sociability of men simply means that "men are destined by nature to share with each other according to the demands of equity. Society is a community of utilities" (commonwealth).[27] Vico, therefore, was more interested in the use value of goods than in their exchange value. Marx, on the other hand, placed his emphasis on the exchange value of goods, which he thought to be measurable in terms of the quantity of labor needed for their production.

Vico's Perception of Oriental Achievements

According to Vico the Orientals created the first significant forms of social life. This was because they were successful in establishing the sense of justice, as an equality of utilities, that could be achieved by men whose actions were not guided entirely by reason.[28] Their achievements were brought westward; but the evolutionary stages of mankind, although the same in both western and eastern lands—"onde si demostra che gli stessi principi ebbero le genti latine che i greci, i fenici, gli egizi e i popoli d'Oriente"[29]—were not simultaneous, since the Orientals had reached the age of heroes while the Western countries remained in the age of gods.[30] This accounts for the greater antiquity of the Egyptian Hercules when compared with the Western Hercules.[31] The appearance of Hercules stands at the dawn of the heroic age, since Hercules represents all of the heroic labor required to achieve the first socio-political organization of men.[32] The bestial stage, in which barbaric human beings wandered through the wilderness of wood-clad mountainsides, was first surmounted in the Orient, when families began to unite into republics and then developed a measure of stability through marriage.[33] It was also at this time that the first relations of production were fixed, as heroes took possession of lands and began to defend their crops against robbers and other individuals who had

[26] Ibid., p. 59.
[27] "Igitur homo natura factus ad communicandas cum aliis hominibus utilitates ex aequo bono. Societas est utilitatum communio, aequum bonum est ius naturae: igitur homo est natura socialis."—(*De uno principio*, I, XLV, p. 59. See also ibid. I, XXIV, p. 51).
[28] *De uno principio*, I, XLIII, p. 57.
[29] *Principi di una scienza nuova*, p. 319
[30] Ibid.: "Per quello che sopra ragionammo del propagamento delle nazioni, mentre copre l'età degli dèi a' greci, le turbolenze eroiche d'Egitto, di Fenicia, di Frigia, vi spingono le loro nazioni con Cecrope, Cadmo, Danao, Pelope nelle marine."
[31] Ibid., p. 323
[32] Ibid., pp. 324-25 and (Tavole delle tradizioni volgari, XV) 333; *N. S.*, pars. 82, 196.
[33] *N. S.*, par. 11.

perhaps not yet transcended the bestial stage.[34] The achievements of the heroic age spread westward, as oriental heroes built ships and sailed toward the shores of Greece and Italy.[35] As a consequence the Romans were able to obtain a heroic or aristocratic social organization and were able to produce heroic laws that were enforced in the barbarian countries of the West.[36]

The heroic way of life changed into a civil one when the feudal and harshly aristocratic control of production in estates owned by a small number of families was attacked by rioting mobs of *clientes*—that is, laborers oppressed by hard work in the fields of their masters. According to Vico this mutiny of the *clientes* created the first monarchy. The lands at this point were partly distributed among the *clientes,* as the society developed a two-class structure—patricians and plebeians, aristocrats and populace—in which citizens remained divided but enjoyed the same basic rights and shared more equitably in the goods produced by labor.[37] This transformation of heroic society into civil society was essentially a reshaping of social structures, a transformation brought about through the modification of both the relations and the modes of production. As laborers on their own estates the *clientes* became free producers. This initially occurred in the Orient, when Nino founded the first monarchy and opened the flow of universal history.[38] It was still a largely despotic and uncouth form of monarchy, but it was this form of monarchy, and its mode of production, that came to be known as the oriental structure of society; it paved the way for the more refined forms of sociopolitical organization that flourished in the Western lands of Greece, Rome, and, after the *barbaries* of the Middle Ages, in the civilized countries of modern Europe.

Marx's Conception of the *Oriental Mode of Production*

The gulf between Vico's thought and that of Marx is mostly a consequence of a suggestion made by Adam Smith[39]—and discussed and

---

[34] *Principi di una scienza nuova,* pp. 314-15; *N. S.,* pars. 553-69. The division of fields, Vico says, was first made with the help of religion and by the use of religious persuasion, which made fierce people acquiesce in keeping the boundaries fixed and abandon the *bestiale comunione* of nomadic and uncouth life; so agriculture was the form of production that first caused people to become sedentary and submit to despotic sovereigns supported by religious authority. See also *Principi di una scienza nuova,* p. 214.

[35] *N. S.,* par. 22. According to Vico in the Bestial Age there were no ships, and human beings wandered only by land.

[36] *Principi di una scienza nuova,* p. 327; *N. S.,* par. 27.

[37] Ibid., p. 224; *De uno principio,* I, CV-CIX, pp. 127-31.

[38] *N. S.,* par. 55.

[39] Adam Smith, *An Inquiry into the Nature and Causes of the Wealth of Nations,* ed. R. H.

stressed by David Ricardo[40]—that *value in use* should be distinguished from *value in exchange* and that the latter is measured in terms of the labor needed for its production or "the toil and trouble of acquiring it."[41] While Vico was unconcerned with the quantity of labor and conceived of the relations and *modi* of production with a view to the goods given or taken in use by different social groups, Marx examined the exploitation of labor in different social forms, forms that gave rise to the precapitalist accumulation in Asiatic societies and to the capitalistic one in the western world.

Capitalistic exploitation and accumulation are the products of wage labor, but what about precapitalistic accumulation? Marx had set to work upon such a theme by presupposing a certain equivalence among the slave relation prevailing in ancient Greece and Rome, the servile relation of the Middle Ages in the West, and the type of relation prevailing in the oriental kingdoms.[42] Therefore he was inclined to see the capitalistic accumulation as foreshadowed, in a particular way, by the despotism of these monarchies.

The fundamental character of this despotism was not for Marx what it was for Vico. For Vico, it was the achievement of a balance between aristocracies and the plebeians; for Marx, it was the consequence of having a monarch as the higher proprietor of the soil and of having a regime that granted the monarch exclusive possession of the surplus product of the lands labored on by his subjects, subjects who lived in small communities with no private property.[43] The accumulation of this surplus product—the same as the accumulation of the product of slave labor and of servile labor—ended in the stockpiling of treasures, properties, and riches, which became capital as soon as they were employed, through the wage system, in the exploitation of labor.[44]

Campbell, A. S. Skinner, and W. B. Todd. Glasgow Edition of the Works and Correspondence of Adam Smith (Oxford: The Clarendon Press, 1976) pp. 44-45.

[40] David Ricardo, *The Principles of Political Economy and Taxation* (London: Dent & Sons, 1973)

[41] Adam Smith, op. cit., p. 47.

[42] Karl Marx, *Grundrisse*, pp. 187-88, 363-76, 389.

[43] "In asiatischen Gesellschaften, wo der Monarch als der exclusiver Besitzer des Land-surplus products erscheint, entstehe ganze Städte, die au fond nichts als wandelnde Lager sind, durch den Austausch seiner Revenue mit den free hands, wie Steuart sie nennt. In diesem Verhältnis ist nichts von Lohnarbeit, obgleich es in Gegensatz zur Sklaverei und Leibeigenschaft stehen kann, nicht muss, denn unter verschiedenen Formen der Gesamt-organisation der Arbeit wiederholt es sich immer"—*Grundrisse*, p. 371.

[44] *Grundrisse*, p. 364.

In Vico the relations of production—typified by those oriental societies that were emerging from a heroic stage into a civil one—rested mainly on the transformation of *clientes* into small landowners. In Marx, however, the *oriental mode of production* does not admit of private property, lands owned by the individuals living on them. The owner of the lands is the community, the local village, which represents the monarch, who is in fact the overarching authority and ultimate proprietor of the soil.[45] The surplus product extorted from the community by the monarch was not intended as a payment for the administrative or protective role exerted by him; it was conceived simply as a rent paid to the overall proprietor merely because he owned the lands in question. As a consequence this form of land rent can be conceived as the first instance of gratuitous subtraction of the product of labor from laborers who were free in themselves. In the exploitation of bound labor—slavery and serfdom—the proprietor possesses everything that is produced by the laborers.

The subtraction of surplus value from workers in the wage system was foreshadowed by this form of land rent. According to Marx the life of villages in the oriental or Asiatic society, where monarchs extort rent and give nothing in exchange, makes each village into a rather self-enclosed economic unity. This, for example, explains their backwardness and fragility.[46] As Lawrence Krader has pointed out, the authority of the monarch in such a society was conceived of by Marx as a personification of the higher regional community that is the State: "the inference is the following: in the absence of private property, the community is the proprietor of the land; the State is recognized as proprietor, and hence is a higher community...The State exists as a Person, and the surplus labor is made over to it in the form of tribute and in the form of labor in common for the actual despot and for the God."[47]

Marx's Ethnological Interest

Marx's conception of the structure and historical place of Eastern society did not spring full grown from his fantasy: It was the product of his vast historical and ethnological knowledge. Like Vico, Marx was

---

[45] Ibid., pp. 375-95.
[46] Lawrence Krader, *The Asiatic Mode of Production* (Assen: Van Gorcum, 1975), pp. 131-32.
[47] Ibid.

ready to borrow whatever information he could from classical or modern sources. His research into the Danubian principalities, his study of the Slavic, Germanic, Irish, Indian, Chinese, and South Asian peasant communities, his correspondence with Vera Zasulich,[48] the ethnological data enclosed in *Capital,* the introduction he prepared to the *Critic of political Economy,*[49] and the *Grundisse,* all show that he was well acquainted with the ethnological literature of his time. Of particular interest, however, are the *Notebooks* he wrote between 1880 and 1882, wherein he comments on the ethnological works of Morgan, Phear, Maine, and Lubbock.[50] He both quoted from and critically reviewed these works, which were among the most important anthropological works of the day. As Krader put it,

> the notebooks are not to be regarded as fortuitous agglomerations; they stand as nodal points in which ideas related to each other were explored in various studies, perhaps not as lines of association in general, but in particular. Starting from the study of primitive society, they lead to the evolution of society and, to judge by their juxtaposition, to the problems of colonialism and technological progress in agriculture.[51]

Vico did not accept the views on evolution sometimes suggested by his sources, but he did use their reports in formulating his *New Science* on the *Common Nature of Nations.* Marx, too, did not endorse as scientific the speculative side of the doctrines of Lubbock, Morgan, etc.—doctrines that concealed a self-satisfaction with the form of civilization attained by the bourgeois society of the nineteenth century and that insinuated a justification of colonialist exploitation of Eastern and primitive nations.

[48] Karl Marx, *Correspondence with Vera Zasulic* in *Marx-Engels Archiv,* 1926, I, pp. 309-42 (D. Rjazanov, ed.).

[49] The Introduction to *Zur Kritik der politischen Ökonomie,* written in 1857, was not published by Marx with the *Kritic,* but appeared for the first time in *Neue Zeit,* March 1903, by the cares of Karl Kautsky.

[50] Karl Marx, *The Ethnological Notebooks,* op. cit. The works studied by Marx include Lewis Henry Morgan, *Ancient Society* or *Researches in the Lines of Human Progress from Savagery through Barbarism to Civilization* (1877); John Budd Phear, *The Aryan Village in India and Ceylon* (1880); Henry Summer Maine, *Lectures on the Early History of Institutions* (1875); John Lubbock (Lord Avebury), *The Origin of Civilization and the Primitive Condition of Man: Mental and Social Conditions of Savages* (1870).

[51] Lawrence Krader, Introduction to K. Marx, *The Ethnological Notebooks,* op. cit., p. 7.

Marx's study and discussion of the work of ethnologists was ended by his death in 1883, but the notebooks he left behind show how his views on the subject were still in flux. Since he had abandoned the Hegelian view that anthropology was ultimately a speculative science, he was ready to improve and retouch his matter-of-fact conception of the historical development of mankind.

Conclusion

The comparison of the ethnological interests of Vico and Marx—at least, as sketched in this essay—needs to be expanded in a more detailed manner. However, the goal here has been merely to shed some light on features of their thought that are useful in understanding their respective positions and methodologies. Both agree on the importance of ethnological inquiries for the historical understanding of the human world. Both endorse the view that the understanding of the human world should rest on an examination of the material conditions that in different ages determined the satisfaction of fundamental needs. Both looked to oriental countries for the socioeconomical conditions that prepared the way for the evolutive stage reached by mankind in modern times. Both are oriented toward an anthropology based on facts and not, as had been the case for Marx in his younger years, on abstract speculations. Both agree that the truly human stage of development is reached only within the particular collectivities where conflicting interests of groups and the mediating role of the state emerge. They disagree on the final destination of this conflicting condition. Such a condition, according to Marx, should be overcome in a stage of reconciliation; according to Vico it should evolve into more and more refined forms of civil life, so that the *aequum* as *aequalitas utilitatum* might be better achieved.

Vico's view is likely to appear much less abstract and utopian than that of Marx. The fact that Vico's thought is more concrete is illustrated by the fact that Vico was more interested in the enjoyment of goods (*utilitates*) than in the labor and instruments employed in their production: use value is undoubtedly more concrete than exchange value, especially when this latter is conceived abstractly as "labor."[52] Yet the

---

[52] Bertell Ollman (*Alienation,* op. cit., p. 174) suggests that it was not the fault of Marx but of society (the capitalist society) to have taken the labor in abstract; be that as it may, the methodology of Marx is deeply conditioned by the use of this abstraction.

notion of exchange value is the pillar supporting the entire Marxian system. The role of the oriental or Asiatic form of society, as a precursor to the modern age of the West, is treated differently by Vico than it is by Marx. The latter focuses on the productive activity and its conditions and makes all other sides of life dependent on it. Vico, however, by stressing the organization of justice and the enactment of laws, paints a more balanced picture of the whole.

The recent development of inquiries and studies of ethnology, archaeology, and positive anthropology makes us conscious of how difficult it is to trace any general outline of the becoming of mankind, whether in old or in recent times, whether in Eastern or Western countries. Nevertheless, the comments of Vico and Marx concerning the so-called oriental or Asiatic mode of production are, for their lasting value, most stimulating, and they deserve the serious attention of those students who do not wish to be engulfed by the shapeless mass of pure facts.

Naturalism in Vico and Marx: *A Theory of the Body Politic*

John O'Neill

> The human mind is naturally inclined by the senses to see itself externally in the body, and only with great difficulty does it come to understand itself by means of reflection. This axiom gives us the universal principle of etymology in all languages: words are carried over from bodies and from the properties of bodies to signify the contributions of the mind and spirit.[1]

Vico and Marx are two of the greatest naturalists. They are, by the same token, two of the great humanists. Today such a claim would seem paradoxical inasmuch as nothing threatens humanism so much as the naturalist methods of the human and social sciences in their embrace of a universal scientism. Yet Vico and Marx rejected both materialism and idealism because of their inadequate conception of man's embodied mind and sensuous history. In the words of Marx:

> But man is not only a natural being, he is a human natural being. This means that he is a being that exists for himself, thus a species-being that must confirm and exercise himself as such in his being and knowledge. Thus human objects are not natural objects as they immediately present themselves nor is human sense, in its purely objective existence, human sensitivity and human objectivity. Neither nature in its objective aspect nor in its subjective aspect is immediately adequate to the human being. And as everything natural must have an origin, so man too has his process of origin, history, which can, however, be known by him

[1] Vico, *New Science,* pars. 236-37.

and thus is a conscious process of origin that transcends itself. *History is the true natural history of man.*[2]

We have shown elsewhere how Marx is indebted to Vico for his conception of "natural man" and a radically historicized account of the development of the human senses.[3] Here we propose to accept Habermas's argument[4] that Marx's naturalism fails to achieve the historical transcendence implicit in it because Marx did not sufficiently distinguish the level of language and communicative praxis from the level of economy. He thereby failed to ground the convertibility of historical experience and historical reflection—*verum et factum convertuntur*— falling into an economistic naturalism alien to his own humanism.[5] But whereas Habermas also considers Vico's naturalism to be wholly underwritten by providence, and thereby deprived of any emancipatory reflection, we shall try to show how Vico's philology may be developed so that we gain a subversive conception of poetic economy, that is, of the body politic.

For Marx, the integral body politic is a pre- and posthistorical phenomenon. Thus, in the historical period Marx's natural man serves rather as a critical principle for thinking and rethinking the foundations of society and political economy. Insofar as Marx's naturalistic methodology focused upon the analysis of the economic process and tended, as Habermas argues, to ignore the level of communicative process, we think that Vico's philological naturalism supplied a corrective. We shall then argue that Vico's philological naturalism avoids the linguistic degeneration that characterizes all scientistic political economy. It thereby preserves the radically subversive language of the body politic as an essential force in the contemporary struggle between humanism and scientism.

Vico grounds the human sciences in the history of the world's body.[6] We cannot sufficiently stress the originality of Vico's giants (*grossi*

[2] Karl Marx, "Economic and Philosophical Manuscripts," in *Karl Marx Early Texts,* trans. and ed. David McLellan (Oxford: Basil Blackwell, 1971), p. 169.

[3] "On the History of the Human Senses in Vico and Marx," in *Vico and Contemporary Thought,* ed. G. Tagliacozzo, D. P. Verene and M. Mooney (Atlantic Highlands, N.J.: Humanities Press, 1979), Pt. II, pp. 179-86.

[4] Jurgen Habermas, *Knowledge and Human Interests,* trans. Jeremy J. Shapiro (Boston: Beacon Press, 1971), pp. 62-63.

[5] For Habermas's views on the relation between Vico and Marx, see especially his *Theory and Practice,* trans. John Vierbel (Boston: Beacon Press, 1973), pp. 242-52.

[6] John O'Neill, op. cit., Pt. II, pp. 179-86

bestioni). It is upon their shoulders that the philosophers stand—whether Plato or Descartes. That is the core of the *New Science* as fundamental anthropology. It is of course inseparable from Vico's philological method, his literary archaeology, whereby he removed the philosophical accumulations of rationalism to reveal an originary materialism as the only possible ground of our civil humanity. Whatever the ingenuity of later thinkers, they stand in a necessary, historical line with the founding ingenuity of that corporeal imagination exercised by the first men whose bodies ruled them as the generative source of all relationships, concepts, and generalizations. This is the historical ground of common sense considered as an achievement that is fundamental to any higher unity of mankind pursued as a reflective enterprise of reason and morals. By the same token this embodied logic furnishes the scientific ground of the *New Science* itself, of its axioms and hypotheses, of its comparative method, of every test of the truths of its postulated ideal eternal history. Therefore our giants are not allegorical creatures. They gave to the thundering sky a great body like their own and made Jove their god, ruler of all men, source of all things. United under Jove's saving rule, they thereby established the first human communities—under vulgar law, religiously, and without the conceits of philosophy. The body politic, therefore, owes itself to these first awkward bodies who scared themselves into being ruled by their own fantastic ideas of frightful religions, terrible paternal powers, and sacred ablutions. To these awkward ancestors we owe the foundation of harmony

    (a) in ourselves, our minds and bodies,
    (b) in our households.

The heroes apprehended with human senses those two truths which make up the whole of economic doctrine, and which were preserved in the two Latin verbs *educere* and *educare*. In the prevailing best usage the first of these applies to the education of the spirit and the second to that of the body. The first, by a learned metaphor, was transferred by the natural philosophers to the bringing forth of forms from matter. For heroic education began to bring forth in a certain way the form of the human soul which had been completely submerged in the huge bodies of the giants, and began likewise to bring forth the form of the human body

itself in its just dimensions from the disproportionate giant
bodies.[7]

All politics are beholden to the corporeal grounds of poetic economy.
In the first case our giants set the mind and imagination above the heart
and the base passions, and being without writing, they founded the arts
of humanity upon invention and judgment in accordance with the
particulars of their experience. Thus all later humanity is indebted to
the vulgar metaphysics of the first incorporation whereby our giants
proportioned themselves to the human frame, educating their bodies
to suit them to the basic institutions of civil humanity—religion, marriage, and burial.

> But these first men, who later became the princes of the gentile
> nations, must have done their thinking under the strong impul-
> sion of violent passions, as beasts do. We must therefore proceed
> from vulgar metaphysics, such as we will find the theology of the
> poets to have been, and seek by its aid that frightful thought of
> some divinity which imposed form and measure on the bestial
> passions of these lost men and thus transformed them into human
> passions. From this thought must have sprung the impulse proper
> to the human will, to hold in check the motions impressed on the
> mind by the body, so as either to quiet them altogether, as becomes
> the wise man, or at least to direct them to better use, as becomes
> the civil man. This control over the motions of their bodies is
> certainly an effect of the freedom of human choice, and thus of
> free will, which is the home and seal of all the virtues, and among
> the others of justice.[8]

Vico preserves the poetic principle whereby man's nature is shaped
and in turn shapes God's nature insofar as man can know anything of it.
Vico's man sings nature from the very beginning. He therefore listens
to being in nature and in himself. This, moreover, is a social necessity.
The sounds of nature are the inspiration for the sounds and songs of
the first men in human society. Language, music, and society are coeval
elements of man's incarnation: "Whence the Roman custom mentioned
by Cicero whereby children learned the law of the Twelve Tables by

[7] *N.S.*, par. 520.
[8] *N.S.*, Ibid., par. 340.

singing it *tamquam necessarium carmen,* as a required song."[9] And earlier the rhapsodes traveled from city to city in Greece singing the books of Homer; for in the *Odyssey* it is said of a good storyteller that he has told the tale like a singer amid the circle men. Homeric poetry, therefore, gathered a community of men who delighted in sonorous buildings shaped to the human ear and voice, as well as to the human eye. For men are truly gathered where other men speak and sing.

Vico rightly gathers the first men under Jove's thunderbolts. Without language or ideas, without priests or philosophers, the first men, "stupid, insensate, and horrible beasts," could only picture thunder and lightning in terms of their own rumbling and shouting. And so they walked the earth—the surest discovery of the *New Science* as a *science,* and not as its mere poetry. The discovery of the poetic origins of mankind is the surest discovery of a renewed science whose incorporate humanity defends it from rationalist anachronisms. The critical, analytic procedures of Vico's philological method separate poetry and science in order to preserve the real history of their unity and distinction as modifications of embodied mind:

> From these first men, stupid, insensate, and horrible beasts, all the philosophers and philologians should have begun their investigations of the wisdom of the ancient gentiles; that is, from the giants in the proper sense in which we have just taken them.... And they should have begun with metaphysics, which seeks its proofs not in the external world but within the modifications of the mind of him who meditates it. For since this world of nations has certainly been made by men, it is within these modifications that its principles should have been sought.[10]

The scientific power of the *New Science* lies in the calm with which it measures and recovers the distance between science and poetry as fundamental modifications of the human mind and senses. For this reason Vico's giants are neither figments of a sentimentalized imagination nor fictions of an objective science for which history is nothing but its own artifact. Rather, they are the natural agents of a history that is intelligible through our effort to read and hear it as our own and that is thereby part of that continuous tradition of eloquence that marks the

[9] *N.S.,* Ibid., par. 469.
[10] *N.S.,* Ibid., par. 374.

best of humanism. Thus Vichian history is itself a civil institution inseparable from man's modifications of his own mind and body that are the history of man making himself. For the same reason we can only recover the corpse of history through the critical-philological method of the *New Science* in which we apprentice ourselves to decoding the "three languages" of man, together with their respective forms of political, legal, and national life:

> To sum up, a man is properly only mind, body and speech, and speech stands as it were midway between mind and body. Hence with regard to what is just, the certain began in mute times with the body. Then when the so-called articulate languages were invented, it advanced to ideas made certain by spoken formulae. And finally, when our human reason was fully developed, it reached its end in the true in the ideas themselves with regard to what is just, as determined by reason from the detailed circumstances of the facts.[11]

Men speak differently in different ages. But those who speak well speak to all ages where there are still men who love eloquence and despise the solitude of soul that inhabits empty rhetoric and mass propaganda. So far from locking us up in a linguistic relativism, Vico's "Roman" rhetoric is the sounding affirmation of collective life, made reasonable and continuous under law.[12] Eloquence is indispensable to true polity, and it is therefore inconceivable that human society could have emerged from the mute fear of Hobbesian individualism or of Cartesian discourse abstracted from civil concerns. Indeed, the modern philosophy of language lives off the very moral capital of rhetorical language which it suppresses yet presumes upon for community. In short, Vico understood that the integrity of civil society rests in the hearts of men and not only in their minds. Therefore language and eloquence are essential to law and politics, and these can never be reduced to sciences. Lacking an adequate philological method, Descartes and Hobbes failed to ground philosophy and law as properly universal sciences of public welfare that are nevertheless not completely transcendent with respect to the contexts and particulars of

---

[11] *N.S.*, Ibid., par. 1045.
[12] Michael Mooney, "The Primacy of Language in Vico," in *Vico and Contemporary Thought*, Pt. I, pp. 191-210.

their own local and natural history. True polity is preserved through the piety of its origins and in a constant retrieval and translation of the past in order to achieve an inhabitable future. In this sense, then, Vico's method is grounded in a situated and embodied naturalism that is thoroughly opposed to the reductive and anachronistic employment of naturalism in the utilitarian and rationalist tradition of law and the social sciences.

Vico's men learn to seek truth before they seek utility. The circulation of truth according to Cartesian rules of clarity is, however, not the same thing as the social and historical acquisition of the arts of learning the truth. Knowledge cannot be reduced to the professional practices of science and logic; it must include all commonsense, legal, and historical modes of reasoning, evidence, conjecture, and refutation. All men are endowed with an ability to learn the truth. This is an historical, legal, and pedagogical task that cannot, without enormously negative civil consequences, be abrogated in favor of the rationalist procedures of philosophy and science—or similarly based social sciences. Thus Vico anticipates a later distinction in the Marxist theory of production—namely, the distinction between

    (a) the social production of utility

    (b) the social production of truth.

Like Habermas and Apel[13] Vico much earlier insisted upon the priority of the society of truth (*societas veri*) over the society of use (*societas aequi boni*). Habermas and Apel have each argued for the communicative a priori as a corrective to Marx's economistic naturalism. Like Vico they now see that the grounds of reason and morals are properly linguistic or rhetorical achievements of the human community and, as such, not reducible to the same allocative principles of instrumental rationality that may govern the economy and its applied sciences.[14] In short, Vico anticipates the contemporary shift of attention to language and practical reasoning as basic human institutions whose analytic reconstruction may provide the grounds of reasonable society.

It should not be forgotten that the *New Science* is intended to have a practical or emancipatory effect. First of all, inasmuch as it is the science of the modifications of our own minds, it enters into the wisdom

---

[13] Karl-Otto Apel, "The Communication Community as the Transcendental Presupposition for the Social Sciences," in his *Towards a Transformation of Philosophy*, trans. Glyn Adey and David Frisby (London: Routledge and Kegan Paul, 1980).

[14] John O'Neill, *Making Sense Together: An Introduction to Wild Sociology.* (New York: Harper & Row, 1974).

of these practices. But not simply as a speculative philosophy of history. That would neglect Vico's "republican" concerns. In other words, the *New Science* is not intended to remain a piece of abstract reasoning divorced from the prudential and moral contexts of civil action and community. Modern science owes its peculiar force to its contravention of common sense.[15] But the human sciences cannot be similarly abstracted from common sense without ruin to the community. Rather, we need to differentiate the communities of human knowledge and to integrate them within a single polity in which the wisdom of the rulers is rooted in the common sense of the people it fosters and relies upon, as the mind and the imagination are rooted in the human body. Today's rulers, however, will not deprive themselves of the technical arm of the instrumentally national sciences. This is to be granted. Therefore we can neither separate nor subordinate in any simple way the human and the natural sciences as discursive achievements of modern polity. What is to be resisted in the ideology or false rhetoric of the scientization of political and socioeconomic life. In short, we need to preserve the classical arts of rhetoric inasmuch as these fostered the capacity for situated judgments with respect to the particulars and generalities of communal experience. The practical side of the *New Science* is therefore the call for a political pedagogy that would foster the fruitful union of reason and common sense across the divisions of expertise and public knowledge.[16] This is the subversive intent of the *New Science* with respect to the modernism of Descartes and Hobbes; it is the basis of Vico's alliance with the *grossi bestioni* against the conceit (*boria*) of the new giants of modern science.

Vico's dynamics of the sociolinguistic transformations of human consciousness have been briefly formulated as follows:

> Put most simply, the analogy states the following generic similarities between transitions in societies and the tropological transformations of speech:
> 1. The transition from metaphorical identifications by naming external reality in terms taken from the most particular and most sensible ideas of the parts of the body and the emotional states to

[15] Edmund Husserl, *The Crisis of the European Sciences and Transcendental Phenomenology*, An introduction to phenomenological philosophy, trans. David Carr (Evanston, Ill.: Northwestern University Press, 1970).

[16] John O'Neill, "The Mutuality of Accounts: An Essay on Trust," in *Theoretical Perspectives in Sociology*, ed. Scott G. McNall, (New York: St. Martin's Press, 1979), pp. 369-80.

metonymic reductions is analogous to the transition from the rule of the gods to the rule of aristocracies;

2. The transition from metonymic reductions to synecdochic constructions of wholes from parts, genera from species, and so on is analogous to the transition from aristocratic rule to democratic rule; and

3. The transition from synecdochic constructions to ironic statement is analogous to the transition from democracies ruled by law to the decadent societies whose members have no respect for law.[17]

The potentially subversive practice in Vico's sociophilological method may be seen if we treat it as critical and reconstructive technique for coming to terms with the dominant formulations of the administration and interpretation of modern society as a science-based community. Thus it is common to all forms of scientism to recollect human history as the growth of scientific, experimental knowledge whose principles of universalism, ability to learn from errors, and essential skepticism are regarded as normative and constitutive features of a liberal and open society. Consistent with this overall scientistic metaphor, it is possible to speak of social reforms as "experiments" and to regard the scientific administration of social reform as an ongoing experiment conducted without any intrusion of values or ideology. Thus the philosophy of science, regardless of any concern with the way it glosses the actual practices of the community of science, is employed to generate a master metaphor of the liberal, open, and experimental society whose health is in its eschewal of all ideological values and misconceptions of knowledge that otherwise drive societies into totalitarianism.[18] In short, critical rationalism may claim for itself an evolutionary status recapitulated in its own narrative history of the subordination of the senses to mind, of homeopathy to allopathy, and the rejection of all particularistic value and knowledge procedures in favor of universalistic, rationally instrumental community of achievement. Extended in this way, the metaphoric and synecdochic employment of the logic of scientific inquiry as a sociologic of the very

[17] Hayden White, "The Tropics of History: The Deep Structure of the *New Science*," in *Giambattista Vico's Science of Humanity,* ed. Giorgio Tagliacozzo and Donald Phillip Verene (Baltimore: Johns Hopkins University Press, 1976), p. 78.

[18] H. T. Wilson, *The American Ideology. Science, technology and organization as modes of rationality in advanced industrial societies* (London: Routledge and Kegan Paul, 1977).

community it presupposes turns into a reflexive irony. Social problems are not definable in the same way as scientific problems; social change is not reducible to the history of science, any more than the latter can be abstracted from the social changes that have accompanied the growth of science. In short, as Vico might put it, there is a barbarism of scientistic reflection that is greater than the first barbarism of our giant ancestors. We need, then, to listen again, to revise our separatisms, to mind our dualisms, and to rethink the body politic in terms of that very bodily metaphor of the union of the members of society and the integrity of all its members regardless of their varying capacity for intellect, sensibility, labor, and common sense.

We consider that our extended metaphor of the body politic provides an initial specification of Vico's two basic axioms regarding the critical hermeneutic of political institutions:

I. Commonsense is judgment without reflection, shared by an entire class, an entire people, an entire nation, or the entire human race.[19]

II. Uniform ideas originating among entire peoples unknown to each other must have a common ground of truth.[20]

Viewed in this fashion, the body politic requires that we construct scenarios for the mutual accountability of the communities of natural and social science within the larger democratic community of commonsense political and legal practice. The metaphor of body politics, in keeping with Vico's own views, would therefore replace the scientistic metaphor in the dominant imagery of the polity. In this way we might restore the public functions of rhetoric in the rational advocacy of knowledge and values that address the three basic domains of the body politic, which we differentiate as follows:

		Levels	*Institutions*	*Discourse*
	(I)	the bio-body	family	well-being
Body	(II)	the productive body	work	expression
Politic	(III)	the libidinal body	personality	happiness

[19] *N.S.*, par. 142.
[20] *N.S.*, par. 144.

Each of the three levels of the body politic is represented in a characteristic institution that is in turn allocated its proper domain of discourse. Although the various institutional and discourse realms of the body politic are only analytically differentiated, they may be said to constitute an evolutionary process in which the congruency of the three discursive orders maximizes the commonwealth.[21] Every society needs to reproduce itself biologically and materially. These needs are articulated at the institutional levels of work and the family, where discourse focuses upon the translation of notions of well-being, health, suffering, estrangement, and self-expression. Here we cannot deal with the variety of social science knowledge and alternative socioeconomic institutions that are generated at these two levels of the body politic. In the later evolutionary stages the articulation of the libidinal body generates discourse demands that impinge differentially upon the institutions of family and work. To date, the institutionalization of these 'revolutionary' demands represents a challenge to all modes of scientistic social and political knowledge. Meantime we can envisage an extension of Habermas's program for the rational justification of the ideal speech community in terms of the specific discursive contexts of the trilevel body politic.[22] It would be necessary to generate a typology of knowledge and evaluation claims with regard to the bio-body, the productive body, and the libidinal body at each appropriate institutional level, with further criteria for urgency, democratic force, and the like.

The bio-body politic represents a way of collecting the interest men have in their well-being, their bodily health and reproduction. The welfare of the family is iconic of the satisfaction of these demands. The productive body politic represents the complex organization of labor and intellect expended in the social reproduction of the body politic. Here, too, we speak of a healthy family. The libidinal body politic represents the complex organization of labor and intellect expended in the social reproduction of the body politic. Here we speak of a healthy person. The libidinal body politic represents a level of desire that fulfills the order of personality insofar as it transcends the goods of family and economy. So long as men continue to be birthed and familied of one another, then the bodily, social, and libidinal orders of living

[21] John O'Neill, "Language and the Legitimation Problem," *Sociology* 11:2 (1977): 351-58.
[22] Jurgen Habermas, "What Is Universal Pragmatics?", in his *Communication and the Evolution of Society*, trans. Thomas McCarthy (Boston: Beacon Press, 1979), pp. 1-68.

will not be separable pursuits. By the same token the body politic cannot be reduced to purely economistic satisfactions any more than to the dream of love's body. A distinctive feature of the metaphor of the body politic is that it allows us to stand away from the systems, i.e., machine, cybernetic, and organization metaphors, that reduce the problem of political legitimacy to sheerly cognitivist sciences. This shift in turn recovers the plain rationalities of everyday living, family survival, health, self-respect, love, and communion. Members are aware of the necessary interrelationships among their familial, economic, and personal commitments. They judge the benefits of their labors in the productive sector of the body politic in terms of the returns to their familial and personal lives. They are willing to make tradeoffs between the demands of family life and the ambitions of their personal and libidinal lives. In short, members have a fairly complex understanding of their corporate life, which is not reducible to the single pattern of utilitarian or decisionistic reasoning that governs calculations in the productive sector.

By differentiating these three levels of the body politic, we further separate ourselves from naturalistic accounts of the political legitimacy problem by introducing a logic of ethical development as the fundamental myth of political life. The three levels of family, economic, and personal life represent an historical-ethical development and also permit us to identify contradictions or constraints and regressions in the body politic. Thus we can identify alienation as a complex phenomenon that affects not only the productive body but also the bio- and libidinal body. Conversely, alienation is not solved merely by satisfying organic needs or by the smooth engineering of productive relations, since these do not meet the demands of libidinal body. By the same token we cannot abstract the dreams of libidinal life from our commitments to familial and economic life. Thus a critical theory of the legitimacy problems of the body politic is simultaneously a constitutive theory of social development and of members' recognition of the places in their lives where this development is blocked and even deteriorating. Members' expression of their experience with the underlying logic of development that sustains political legitimacy will not be limited to official electoral conduct. It will include such subversive practices as strikes, family breakdown, crime, protest, lampoons, neighborhood and street gatherings, music, song, poster and wall art. A critical theory of political legitimacy does not discount the rationality of members' ordinary accounts of their political experience in terms of the vocabularies of family, work, and person. Moreover, it does not presume upon either the found rationality or irrationality of such accounts.

Every political community has to find a symbolic expression of its beliefs concerning the sources, sustenance, and potential threats to the orderly conduct of its members.[23] Thus the language of the body politic, as Vico would have recognized, is a recurring expression of reflection upon the nature of order and disorder in the human community. From the plebeian secession in Rome to contemporary street politics, the human body has provided the language and the very text of political protest and confrontation with the agencies that administer our inhumanity: This rhetorical conception of the body politic, for which I have argued in keeping with Vico's vision, differs from the administrative science of politics in that it remains continuous with ancient political life. That is to say, we argue that the business of politics is to foster citizens capable of the good life. Therefore, political legitimacy must be grounded in prudential judgments exercised in practical contexts of belief and action that regenerate political education without subordinating it to a political science outside the life of the polity. As such, our theory of the body politic constitutes a small step toward a possibility within the *New Science* that Habermas himself has remarked upon.[24]

---

[23] John O'Neill, "Authority, Knowledge and the Body Politic," in his *"Sociology as a Skin Trade. Essays Towards a Reflexive Sociology* (New York: Harper & Row, 1972), pp. 68-80.

[24] Habermas, op. cit., pp. 43-46.

Marx's Relation to Vico: A Philological Approach*

Arshi Pipa

Marx's Letter to Lassalle Mentioning Vico

Marx first mentions Vico in his letter of 28 April 1862 to Lassalle, which comments briefly on Lassalle's *System of Acquired Rights* (1861). A paragraph in the letter reads:[1]

> As to your writing [*System*], which I now have of course read entirely, repeating particular chapters, it strikes me that you seem not to have read Vico's *New Science*. You would not have found in it anything to serve your purpose; but his philosophical conception

---

*The essay is based on the following works: *La Scienza Nuova* (1744) in Giambattista Vico, *Opere*, ed. Paolo Rossi (Milan: Rizzoli, 1959). *The New Science of Giambattista Vico* [Acronym: *N.S.*], trans. T. G. Bergin and M. H. Fisch (Ithaca, N.Y.: Cornell University Press, 1975). *La Science Nouvelle* par Vico; traduite par [Princess Belgioioso] l'auteur de l'essai sur la formation du dogme catholique. A la Librairie Jules Renard...et à la Librairie Charpentier (Paris, 1844). Karl Marx, *Capital* [Acronym: *C*], vol. I, trans. B. Fowkes (New York: Vintage Books, 1977). Marx, *Early Writings*, [Acronym: *E.W.*], trans. R. Livingstone and G. Benton. New York: Penguin Books, 1977). *Marx-Engels Briefwechsel* [Acronym: *M.E.*], 3 vols. (Berlin: Dietz Verlag, 1949-50), reprint of the Marx-Engels, Lenin Institute edition, Moscow, 1935). Ferdinand Lassalle, *Nachgelassene Briefe und Schriften* [Acronym: *B.S.*]. 4 vols., ed. Gustav Mayer. Stuttgart-Berlin: Deutsche Verlags-Anstalt, 1922 (vol. 3, *Der Briefwechsel zwischen Lassalle und Marx* is quoted as B.S. 3). Lassalle, *Gesammelte Reden und Schriften* [Acronym: *R.S.*], 12 vols., ed. Eduard Bernstein. (Berlin: Paul Cassirer, 1920), (Vols. 7 and 8, *Die Philosophie Herakleitos des Dunklen von Ephesos*, and vols. 9-12, *Das System der erworbenen Rechte*, are quoted as *R.S.* followed by the volume number). B. G. Niebuhr, *Römische Geschichte* [Acronym: *R.G.*], 3 vols. (Berlin: S. Calvary, 1873).

Except for *N.S.*, which is followed by the paragraph number according to the division into paragraphs made by the editors, the other acronyms are followed by the volume number (if the works consist of more than one volume) and then by the page number preceded by a colon (acronyms are omitted when reference to the same work is continuous). An asterisk signals a modification, or addition, made by me to the texts translated by others.

[1] The quotations are found together with the comments in the paragraph. I have set off the quotations for the sake of textual criticism. For the same reason I have separated the quotations, which appear in a sequence in the paragraph in question.

of the spirit of Roman law is opposed [to that] of the legal Philistines. Working through the original, which is written not only in Italian, but also in a queer Neapolitan dialect, would be of little help. My advice is that you read the French translation of the work: *La Science Nouvelle,* etc. traduite par l'auteur de l'essai sur la formation du dogme catholique, Paris, Charpentier Editeur, 1844. To whet your appetite, I quote the following sentences:

"L'ancien droit romain a été un poème sérieux, et l'ancienne jurisprudence a été une poésie sévère dans laquelle se trouvent renfermées les premiers efforts de la métaphysique légale."

"L'ancienne jurisprudence était très poétique, puisqu'elle supposait vrais les faits qui ne l'étaient pas, et qu'elle refusait d'admettre comme vrais les faits qui l'étaient en effet; qu'elle considérait les vivants comme morts et les morts comme vivants dans leurs héritages."

"Les Latins nommèrent *heri* les *héros;* d'où vient le mot *hereditas...*l'héritier...représente, vis-à-vis de l'héritage, le père de famille défunt."

Vico contains in embryo Wolf (on Homer), Niebuhr (on the regal period of Roman history) as well as the foundations of comparative philology (even though in a fantastic manner) and a great deal else bearing the mark of genius. I have so far not been able to locate his juridical writings (*L.M.,* 3: 387).

What strikes one reading these comments and quotations is that the two do not fit together, but are at odds. The comments praise Vico as a genius, even though a "fantastic" one, whereas the quotations, taken out of context from Princess Belgioioso's translation, present Vico as almost insane. Niebuhr called ancient Roman history "poetic" because its sources are found in lays and tales. But he added: "They belong, nonetheless, to history" for their "marvelous images are different from dreams; they contain a hidden core of real truth" (*R.G.,* 1: 182). In the paragraph in question jurisprudence, not history, is called poetic, and it is called so because it exchanges reality for illusion and vice versa, "taking the living for dead and the dead for living in their heritages." This does not make sense. If Marx had really wanted Lassalle to read Vico, he would have quoted him otherwise. The quotations as they stand are not likely to whet the appetite. Could they have been chosen for some other purpose?

We shall first give Princess Belgioioso's French texts from which Marx excerpted his quotations.

[1] COROLLAIRE.
L'ancien droit romain a été un poème sérieux, et l'ancienne juris-prudence a été une poésie sévère dans laquelle se trouvent renfermés les premiers efforts de la métaphysique légale. Les Grecs tirèrent leur philosophie de leurs lois.

[2] L'*hérédité* devint pour eux [the heroes] *la maîtresse des choses héréditaires,* et ils croyaient la reconnaître *toute entière dans chacune des choses héréditaires;* et c'est ainsi qu'ils présentaient au juge un *épi* ou une *motte* de terre du champ contesté, en les désignant dans la *formule de la revendication* par ces mots: HUNC FUNDUM. Ils sentaient, quoique confusément, que les *droits* étaient *indivisibles,* et nous avons dit avec raison que l'*ancienne jurisprudence* était très *poétique,* puisqu'elle supposait *vrais* les faits qui ne l'étaient pas, et qu'elle réfusait d'admettre comme *vrais* les faits qui l'étaient en effet; qu'elle considérait les *vivans* comme *morts,* et les *morts* comme *vivans dans leurs héritages;* qu'elle créa un grand nombre de *masques vagues* et *sans sujets,* appelés *jura imaginaria* ou *droits figurés par* l'*imagination;* et qu'elle fit dépendre toute sa *gloire,* de son habileté à trouver des *fables* qui conservassent à la *loi* sa *gravité* et qui prêtassent aux *faits* l'appui du *droit;* de sorte que toutes les *fictions* de l'*ancienne jurisprudence* ne furent que des *verités masquées* ou *déguisées;* et que les *formules interprètes* de la *loi* étaient appelées *carmina,* à cause de *leur mesure rhythmée et du nombre déterminé de paroles* dont elles devaient être composées...

[3] Les *héros* furent appelés ainsi, parce qu'ils étaient les *seigneurs des familles,* par opposition aux *serviteurs,* qui en étaient les *esclaves.* Les *Latins* nommèrent *heri* les *héros;* d'où vint le mot *hereditas* qui signifiait dans le commencemens de la langue latine *famille,* mais qui devint plus tard l'expression d'un *pouvoir despotique.* La *loi des XII Tables* reconnaît, en effet, aux pères de famille le *pouvoir souverain,* ou le droit de disposer par testament de leur avoir: UTI PATERFAMILIAS SUPER PECUNIA TUTELAVE REI SUAE LEGASSIT, ITA JUS ESTO. Le droit de tester fut dit LEGUER; droit qui semble véritablement propre aux *souverains;* car l'héritier se trouve être un *légat* ou *légataire* qui *représente, vis-à-vis*

de l'héritage, le père de famille défunt. Les *enfans* et les *esclaves* étaient compris sous les mots de REI SUAE ET PECUNIAE: ce qui s'explique par la *puissance monarchique* que les pères avaient exercée sur *leurs familles* dans l'*état de nature*...

The quotations (henceforth identified as first, second, or third) are taken from different places in *La Science Nouvelle*. Marx distinguishes them as such (by quotation marks) but presents them as if they were parts of a discursive sequence. The first quotation centers on the "poetic" nature of ancient Roman jurisprudence. The second quotation illustrates the meaning of that term with an example bearing on heritage. The concept of heritage is then explained in the third quotation, where *heres*, "heir," is derived from *heros*, "hero," a manifest case of Vico's "fantastic" use of etymology. The three quotations constitute a discursive sequence describing ancient Roman jurisprudence as "poetic" in the sense of fictional. Is the discourse ironical?

Indeed, the way Marx deals with Vico's texts is not serious—it amounts to manipulation. This consists of two operations: selection of texts of different natures (a title and two comments) and belonging to different loci in the work; and arrangement of these excerpts into a sequence by pruning parts of them that do not fit as well as by sewing the excerpts together. The result is a text conveying Marx's thought by means of Vichian words.

Let us now consider the quotations one by one.

The first quotation is the incomplete title of a chapter concluding Book IV. Marx has omitted not only the term "Corollaire" that precedes (set off in boldface capital letters) the title (in bold type), but also the title's last sentence, "Les Grecs tirèrent leur philosophie de leurs lois" ("The Greeks derived their philosophy from their laws").

The second quotation is the twice-truncated excerpt from a long sentence found in a paragraph in the "Corollaire" chapter. The paragraph explains the genesis of the *iura imaginaria* in Roman jurisprudence. Marx has eliminated the initial sentence on the indivisibility of the inheritance right, thus making the quotation start with a sentence (I retranslate Belgioioso), "Ancient jurisprudence was very poetic," which provides the link between the first and second quotations. And he has also deleted the next sentence, "All the fictions of ancient jurisprudence were nothing but masked or disguised truths," thus making the excerpt stop after the sentence, "[ancient jurisprudence] considered the living as dead and the dead as living in their heritages," which provides the link between the second and third quotations.

The third quotation is an excerpt from a paragraph in the section "Poetic Morals" (Book II). The paragraph explains why the Roman plebs were denied the right of legal marriage (*connubium*), focusing on the "despotic power" of the *paterfamilias*. The excerpt consists of two propositions: The first stresses the relationship between inheritance and heroism, while the other proposition defines the heir as representing the defunct paterfamilias. Quoting the whimsical etymology *heres-heros* sounds ironical. On the other hand, irony seems to be absent from the second proposition, a matter-of-fact historical truth. As they stand, the first and second propositions are not mediated. And yet the two propositions, which constitute a sort of conclusion for the two other quotations, functioning like the major and minor of a syllogism, must be somehow related, the selection-arrangement of the sequence having been done, most likely, in view of reaching that conclusion. What can that relation be? The question posits the selection-arrangement of the sequence as a hermeneutic problem.

This preliminary analysis has provided us with some clues. (a) Since the concept of "poetic" jurisprudence leads to that of inheritance, we can say that the sequence of the three quotations focuses on the concept of inheritance, a concept that, as we shall soon see, is pivotal in Lassalle's legal treatise. (b) Since the paragraph in question is a comment on that treatise, we can safely infer that the selection-arrangement of the three quotations has been made in order to draw Lassalle's attention to that concept. (c) Although the *New Science* is commended for its originality in three aspects—Vico's interpretation of the Roman law, his "discovery of the true Homer," and his pioneering work in comparative philology—all three quotations bear on Vico's ideas on Roman law. The reference to Vico's juridical works in the paragraph's last sentence further suggests that Marx's interest in Vico was mainly of a juridical order, motivated by Vico's ideas on Roman law as "opposed" to those of "legal Philistines."[2] (d) At this point a doubt arises as to whether Lassalle's *System* contains traces of legal Philistinism. The sentence on it— "You would not have found in it [the *New Science*]

---

[2] We shall recall that Marx began his university studies in Bonn as a law student. His first book-length writing after his doctoral dissertation, *On the Difference Between Democritean and Epicurean Philosophy of Nature* (1840-41), was *Critique of Hegel's Doctrine of the State* (1843), followed soon by *Contribution to the Critique of Hegel's Philosophy of Right. Introduction* (1843-44).

anything to serve your purpose; but his philosophical conception of the spirit of Roman law is opposed [to that] of the legal Philistines" ("Nicht als wenn Du zu Deinem bestimmten Zweck etwas darin gefunden haben würdest, aber doch als philosophische Auffassung des Geistes des römischen Rechts im Gegensatz zu den Rechtsphilistern") — is ambiguous and elusive. Indeed the whole paragraph is elusive in that the comment on Lassalle's *System* turns out to be a comment on Vico's *New Science*. Furthermore, the sentence in the paragraph expressing surprise for Lassalle's apparent ("you seem") ignorance of Vico's work amounts to a silent rejection of Lassalle's work.

To probe this assumption a reading of Lassalle's *System* is imperative. But we must first do justice to Vico by quoting him in context, following the standard Bergin and Fisch English translation. We shall give the full text of the Corollary and the pertinent texts of the paragraphs from which the second and third quotations are excerpted. And we shall also quote other paragraphs, wholly or in part, that further explain the meaning of Vico's *iura imaginaria*, while shedding light on the major problem that is this essay's topic: Marx's relation to Vico.

Iura Imaginaria and Commodity Fetishism

[1027] Corollary: That the ancient Roman law was a serious poem, and the ancient jurisprudence a severe kind of poetry, within which are found the first outlines of legal metaphysics in the rough; and how, among the Greeks, philosophy was born of the laws.

1033 The founders of Roman law, at a time when they could not understand intelligible universals, fashioned imaginative universals. And just as the poets later by art brought personages and masks onto the stage, so these men by nature had previously brought the "names" and "persons"* [the family coat of arms and the person or mask of a family father under which were concealed all his children and servants*] into the forum.

1035 On these same principles, because they did not understand abstract forms, they imagined corporeal forms, and they imagined them, after their own nature, as animate. *Hereditas,* or Inheritance, they imagined as mistress of hereditary property, and they recognized her as entire in every particular item of the inherited goods, just as when they presented to the judge a lump or clod from a farm, they called it *hunc fundum* in the formula of *rei vindicatio*. Thus, if they did not understand, they at least sensed in a rough way that rights were indivisible.

1036   In conformity with such natures, ancient jurisprudence was throughout poetic. By its fictions what had happened was taken as not having happened, and what had not happened as having happened; those not yet born as already born; the living as dead; and the dead as still living in their estates pending acceptance ["nelle loro giacenti eredità"*]. It introduced so many masks without subjects, *iura imaginaria,* rights invented by telling tales* ["ragioni favoleggiate da fantasia*"]. It rested its entire reputation on inventing such fables as might preserve the gravity of the laws and do justice to the facts. Thus all the fictions of ancient jurisprudence were truths under masks, and the formulae in which the laws were expressed, because of their strict measures of such and so many words—admitting neither addition, subtraction, nor alteration—were called *carmina,* or songs...

1037   Thus all ancient Roman law was a serious poem, represented by the Romans in the forum, and ancient jurisprudence was a severe poetry. Very conveniently to our argument, Justinian in the poemium of the *Institutiones** speaks of the fables of the ancient law—*antiqui iuris fabulas*. He uses the phrase in derision but he must have taken it from some ancient jurisconsult who had understood the matters we have been discussing. From these ancient fables, as we here prove, Roman jurisprudence drew its principles. And from the masks called *personae* which were used in these dramatic fables, so true and severe, derive the first origins of the doctrine *de iure personarum,* of the law of persons.

513   Juno is called *jugalis,* "of the yoke," with reference to the yoke of solemn matrimony, for which it was called *conjugium* and the married pair *conjuges*...And she is jealous with a political jealousy, that from which the Romans down to the 309th year of Rome excluded the plebs from *connubium,* or lawful marriage. By the Greeks, however, she was called Hera, whence the name the heroes gave themselves, for they were born of solemn nuptials, of which Juno was the goddess, and hence generated by noble Love (which is the meaning of Eros [ἔρως *], who was identical with Hymen. And the heroes must have been so called in the sense of "lords of the families" in distinction from the famuli, who were in effect slaves. *Heri* has this same meaning "lords of families" in

Latin, whence *hereditas* for inheritance, for which the native Latin word had been *familia*. With such an origin, *hereditas* must have meant a despotic sovereignty, and by the Law of the Twelve Tables there was reserved to the family fathers a sovereign power of testamentary disposition, in the article: *Uti paterfamilias super pecunia tutelave suae rei legassit, ita ius esto* ("As the family father has disposed concerning his property and the guardianship of his estate, so shall it be binding"). The disposing was generally called *legare,* which is the prerogative of the sovereigns; thus the heir becomes a "legate" [legatee] who in inheriting represents the defunct pater-familias, and the children no less than the slaves came under the term "estate" and "property." All of which proves only too conclusively the monarchic power that the fathers had had over their families in the state of nature.

The paragraphs are an extension of Vico's theory of poetic imagination to jurisprudence, in keeping with "poetic metaphysics," "poetic morals," "poetic politics," etc. "The fictions of ancient jurisprudence are truths under masks" just as the ancient myths are *vera narratio* of facts of life under the cover of anthropomorphic language. The ancients resorted to "corporeal" images in the form of imaginative universals (*universali fantastici*) to express abstract ideas that they did not understand. One such abstract idea is the right of inheritance. They imagined that right in the form of the mistress of the land. Transmission of the patrimony from father to son was an everyday occurrence. When this fact of life was legalized into a right, the ancients could not view it otherwise than by imagining a humanlike entity, called Inheritance, that would preside over the transmission, along generations, of landed property, a sort of *genius loci* indivisible into parts and lasting as long as the property itself. And since Inheritance does not disappear with the death of the father, nor was she born with the birth of the son, it all happened as if the dead father continued to live and the unborn son were virtually alive through the good services of *Hereditas.* Other basic juridical concepts, such as *Auctoritas, Nuncupatio, Mancipium, Vindicatio,* etc., were imagined in a similar way. In the forum, where business and legal matters were discussed, the discussion must have been like a performance, with *Hereditas, Auctoritas,* and other such entities impersonating, like masked actors in a drama, legal ideas of the ancient Romans.

Now this does make sense, much the more so to a person like Marx, whose theory of the fetishism of commodites has some resemblance to Vico's theory of legal fictions. According to Marx a commodity, once produced, ceases to be a mere product and takes on a life of its own. This happens because the product of labor is taken away from the worker, who then looks at it as something alien, a thing independent from him. It is he who has produced it, with his own hands, through his own labor. Yet the commodity does not belong to him, he must buy it in order to have it, and if he has no money with which to buy it, he simply cannot have it. Thus the commodity becomes an object of his desire, and therefore alien, endowed as such with an existence and worth of its own, a sort of fetish. The consequence is a misconception of the relation between man and commodities: "they appear as the purchasers of persons.... It is not the maker who buys the means of production and substance, but the means of production that buys the worker to incorporate him into the means of production" (*C* 1: 1003-4). Marx sees the phenomenon as an inverted relation. "In the same way, the impression made by a thing on the optic nerve is perceived not as a subjective excitation of that nerve but as the objective form of a thing outside the eye" (*C* 1: 165). Yet there the relation is between physical objects, whereas in the case of commodities

> "it is nothing but the definite social relation between men them-selves which assumes here, for them, the *fantastic* [emphasis added] form of a relation between things. In order, therefore, to find an analogy we must take flight into the misty realm of religion. There the products of the human brain appear as autonomous figures endowed with a life of their own, which enter into relation both with each other and the human race. So it is in the world of commodities with the products of men's hands." (ibid.)

Vico's description of legal concepts as products of human imagination in the form of masked truths that really are "masks without subjects" differs from Marx's description of commodities in that the latter are real objects in which human labor has been frozen or reified. In a note in *Capital,* the same in which Vico's name appears, Marx contrasts the "misty creations of religion," where human relations are "celestialized," with the under-lying economic conditions, according to his materialistic conception of history (we shall discuss the note in due time). Different also are their concepts of fantasy. For Vico, who conceives of fantasy as the only way of

knowledge available to man not yet grown rational, the fictions correspond to facts. To Marx these are mere hypostases of the mind. The
epithet "fantastic" that he attributes to Vico's "foundations of comparative philology" in his letter to Lassalle is silently contrasted with
"scientific."

Vico's text from which Marx took the second quotation explains the
genesis of *hereditas;* the paragraph from which he extracted the seg-
ments of the third quotation centers on the meaning of that concept:
"*hereditas* [I retranslate Belgioioso]...came later to express a despotic
sovereignty." *Hereditas* leads historically to *legare*, the disposing of property by testament. Whence the inference that "the heir becomes a
legate" who can dispose not only of the property, but of the *famuli* and
children as well. This other Vichian sentence closely fits Marx's historical materialism. For if children are, in legal matters, considered just as
the *famuli*, "who were their [the fathers'] slaves," the relations between
father and son and vice versa could not possibly be based on paternal
love and filial piety. Shortly afterward Vico specifies that "until impe-
rial times, sons, like slaves, had only one kind of *peculium,* or private
property, namely *peculium profecticium* [that acquired by their father's
consent]" (*N.S.,* par. 582). And he adds: "In the earliest times the
fathers must have had the power of really selling their children as many
as three times." Consequently the sons must have hated their fathers.
Likewise, "the mothers must have hated their children, for they had
only the pain of bearing them and the trouble of nursing them, without
having from them any joy or profit." (*N.S.,* par. 994). Expressions such
as these could be taken to illustrate Marx's theory that jurisprudence
and morality grow from the base and not the other way around.

Marx has eliminated from the third quote the very parts that would,
one supposes, appeal to him. The political paragraph, in its mutilated
form, has been reduced to a (wrong) etymological statement (the lords
of families called *heri*), and it is followed by another that is a historical
commonplace (the heir representing his defunct father). The arrangement of the dismembered texts has certainly been made according to
design. For what design?

The answer is provided by considering Marx's relation to Lassalle.

Marx versus Lassalle

Anyone somewhat familiar with the history of socialism knows that
Marx, on the one hand, and Lassalle, on the other, represent two
opposed tendencies in the German socialist movement. A brilliant

lawyer endowed with literary skills, Lassalle was also a scholar in his own right. His active participation in the 1848-49 German revolution brought him in touch with Marx and Engels. While his relationship with Engels remained on a polite level, it was otherwise with Marx, whom Lassalle admired and tried to emulate. He read Marx's works eagerly, although preferring Hegel. Their "friendship" had ups and downs, lasting almost to the end of Lassalle's short life (1825-64). The definitive break occurred in May 1863, when Lassalle founded the General German Workers' Association. He was killed the next year in a duel over a love affair. His ideas outlived him; the association he founded developed into the German Social-Democratic party (1865). Lassalleanism can be described as socialism deftly maneuvering between the Junkers and the liberals for a place in society as a third political party. Marx and Engels rejected Lassalle's idea of state socialism—when the state was Prussia and Bismarck the head of the state.

To Lassalle's frequent and extensive letters Marx would respond occasionally with short notes. From 1849 to 1854 Lassalle wrote thirty letters to Marx (and to his wife), Marx only three to him. Discontinued from November 1855 to April 1857,the correspondence was resumed on Lassalle's initiative. Political differences first came to the fore when, during the Italian war, Marx took an anti-Russian, Lassalle an anti-Austrian, stance. When Marx asked Lassalle to be a correspondent for a German-American workers' newspaper, Lassalle answered that he had to concentrate on "great achievements," adding that he was then engaged in a "great work" (letter of April 9, 1860). He tried, when the new emperor granted an amnesty, to bring back Marx from exile. Marx was then in dire financial straits, having lost his job as correspondent for the *New York Tribune,* and considered seriously the possibility of repatriation. He paid a visit to Lassalle in Berlin, where he was his guest (April 1-12, 1861), and Lassalle returned the visit the next year. Before leaving Marx he promised financial assistance. Having also agreed to endorse a promissory note on Marx's behalf to be covered by Engels, Lassalle asked Engels for confirmation in writing. This infuriated Marx, who wrote Lassalle a nasty letter, accusing him of having doubted Engels' integrity (August 20, 1862). Lassalle in turn charged him with a "nest of offensive insinuations." Marx's last letter to him (November 7, 1862) offered reconciliation. It fell on deaf ears. After Lassalle's death Marx expressed his condolences to Countess Sophie von Hatzfeldt, a longtime friend of Lassalle who was also his proxy. In that letter he invites her to console herself with the thought that

Lassalle "died young, in triumph, like Achilles,"[3] hinting that his break with Lassalle had been due mainly to political differences (September 12, 1864).

These differences were, of course, paramount. Yet they were rooted in temperamental differences.[4] Also conspicuous were differences in the field of scholarship. Marx had a low opinion of Lassalle as a scholar. Unlike Engels, Lassalle was reluctant to accept Marx's intellectual supremacy and his established authority as theoretician of socialism. In 1858 Lassalle published a two-volume work, *The Philosophy of Heraclitus of Ephesus,* the outcome of many years of research.[5] In his introduction to the work, Bernstein writes: "In order to do justice to Lassalle's main work, one must be a philosopher as well as a philologist" (*R.S.,* 7: 5). Marx took justice into his own hands when he wrote to Engels (February 1, 1858) that the "compilation" brings "absolutely nothing new" to what has already been written on Heraclitus, adding that the two volumes could well have been condensed on "two printer's sheets" (see note 11). And when Lassalle sent him his drama, *Franz von Sickingen,* Marx subjected it to devastating criticism (April 19, 1859). He first compliments the author as being superior to the playwrights of the time (who were less than mediocre), then adds that he was "strongly affected" on a first reading, making it clear from what he says afterwards that a second reading would be undeserved. He finds fault with everything: the versification is awkward, the topic unfit for the purpose, its treatment deficient. Lassalle has chosen as his "revolutionary" hero a Don Quixote figure, a person who "went down in defeat because he rebelled, as a *knight* and a *representative of a perishing class,* against the existing condition or rather its new forms [the bourgeosie]" (*L.M.,* 3: 173).[6]

One of the reasons Marx was so set against Lassalle was the conviction that publication of his own work, *Contribution to the Critique of Political Economy* (1859), had been delayed as a result of Lassalle's pressure on

---

[3] A Swiss newspaper, *Social Demokrat,* printed the (ironic) sentence as a motto to Lassalle's necrology (December 18, 1864).

[4] In a letter to Engels (August 7, 1862) Marx writes that he and Lassalle disagree on almost everything political (see note 11).

[5] Preface, *R.S.,* 7: 19. The work numbers about 1,300 pages in Bernstein's edition.

[6] Engels responded quite sympathetically (May 18, 1859). The drama "can stand criticism.... No one of the official poets of Germany today is even remotely capable of writing such a drama." Engels' own criticism was that the play could not be staged as it was and that the characters needed to be "more sharply differentiated and their mutual opposition brought out" (*L.M.,* 3: 179-85).

the publisher (the same for both authors)[7] to have his own work on the Italian war come out first. Marx wrote to Engels (May 25, 1859): "I shall never forgive the little Jew this trick" (*M.E.*, 2: 484). And he never did.

Lassalle's *System of Acquired Rights* appeared in 1861. It is, like his *Heraclitus,* a thick work in two volumes (1,528 pages in Bernstein's edition). The *System* represents the first step toward "the total reform of Hegel's philosophy," practically its "negation" (*R.S.*, 9:43), while abiding to Hegel's basic principles and his method (dialectic). Hegel has repeatedly stated in his works that "philosophy equals the totality of experience, its task being none other than study of the empirical sciences in depth" (9:35). What Hegel has only enunciated Lassalle will, time permitting, accomplish with his new Philosophy of the Spirit. The present work lays the ground for what Lassalle intends to achieve: the "reconciliation of the positive right with the philosophy of right" (subtitle of the work). The reconciliation is possible if jurisprudence as a positive science can be seen to evolve from philosophical principles (9: 34). This in turn presupposes that the philosopher will have to delve into the legal sphere, "becoming a jurist himself" (9: 37). Accordingly, in the first volume the author establishes the theoretical principles of his philosophy of right, while in the second volume he proves their validity by investigating a basic Roman institution, the right of inheritance.

Lassalle's attempt to "reform" Hegel by way of jurisprudence cuts across Marx's effort to overturn Hegel by way of economy. Both were intent, at about the same time, on superseding their spiritual father, using as a lever expertise in their specialized fields. Marx was then working intensely on *Capital,* having already published its prolegomenon, *Contribution to the Critique of Political Economy.* Lassalle's *System* must have appeared to him as a challenge; he must have sensed in his "friend" the forthcoming rival.

Marx's evaluation of the *System*, was, as usual, negative. Was his judgment clouded by envy? The work was greeted by many a learned person as a first-rate achievement. Lange, author of *History of Materialism* (1866), praised it as "one of the most significant books in the philosophy of right."[8] Bernstein, who provides the detail, notes that the

[7] Franz Dunckner in Berlin. In a letter to Engels (May 25, 1859) Marx writes: "That cursed vain fool has imposed an embargo [on my book], so that the public's attention not be divided" (*M.E.*, 2: 483-84). In a long letter on his drama to both Marx and Engels (May 27, 1859) Lassalle announces: "Dear Marx, your book will appear in three days" (*L.M.*, 3: 213).

[8] *Süddeutsche Zeitung,* September 23, 1863.

System impressed mostly socialist professors of philosophy (*Katheder-socialisten*), leaving the jurists cool (*R.S.*, 9: 19). Bernstein himself calls the *System* "a grandiose work" that is "a grandiose failure." Instead of explaining a particular right by going back to the socioeconomic conditions of the historical period, "Lassalle wants to prove that the Roman right of inheritance is, unlike its German counterpart, rooted in a very peculiar *Volksgeist*, which he traces to mythology transmitted by the Pelasgians" (9: 12). Engels liked the style as well as the objections to Hegel, but found fault with the rest: "The fellow," he wrote (December 2, 1861), "must be indeed superstitious to still believe in the 'idea of justice'—in absolute justice" (*M.E.*, 3: 57). And this is what Marx wrote to Lassalle (June 11, 1861):

> Thank you for your book...which reached me a couple of days ago. I began to read it from back to front, starting with the [last] chapter on Pelasgian history. From there I moved to [the initial chapter on] the law of inheritance, and am now at page 215. A significant work in every respect. Criticism and judgment and all will follow, after I read the whole thing (*L.M.*, 3: 365).

Marx observed "by the way" that the institution of the testament, "apart from its specifically Roman origin," exists in bourgeois societies (in England from the 1688 revolution) independently from mythological roots (ibid.).

In his reply (July 1, 1861) Lassalle expressed "annoyance" at Marx's manner of reading his book, pointing out that such a reading would result in a "lop-sided" perspective (3: 371).

Marx's letter of July 22, 1861 begins with apologies for his delayed answer, caused by an eye inflammation. He has now read the whole second volume. But "when I intended to tackle the first one, my sore eyes interfered with the reading" (3: 374). The gist of his criticism is contained in the following paragraph:

> You have demonstrated that originally (and even today, if we consider the scientific insight of the juridical experts) the adoption of the Roman testament [as a modern rule for inheritance law] rests on a misunderstanding. But it in no way follows that in its *modern* form the testament—through whatever misunderstandings of Roman law the contemporary experts may be able to reconstrue it—is the *misunderstood* Roman testament. Otherwise it

might be said that every achievement of an older period, which is
adopted in later times, is the *old misunderstood*. For example, the
three unities, as the French dramatists under Louis XIV theoretically construe them, must surely rest on a misunderstanding
of the Greek drama (and Aristotle its exponent). On the other
hand, it is equally certain that they understood the Greeks in just
such a way as suited their own artistic needs, which is why they still
clung to this so-called "classical" drama long after Dacier and
others had correctly interpreted Aristotle for them. Thus, too, all
modern constitutions rest in great part on the *misunderstood* English constitution, for they take as essential precisely that which
constitutes the decadence of the English constitution—which now
exists only *formally, per abusum,* in England—e.g., a so-called responsible *Cabinet*. The misunderstood form is precisely the general form, applicable for general use at a definite stage of social
development.[9]

Marx's criticism of the *System* parallels and completes his criticism of
Franz von Sickingen. He credits Lassalle for having demonstrated that
Roman law, as conceived by jurists, rests on a misconception, and then
takes him to task by proving wrong his conclusion that the modern
testament is the misunderstood Roman testament. Lassalle's conclusion lays bare his own misunderstanding of the historical process, his
incapability to conceive of the development of juridical relations other
than as changes in the mind. Lassalle has not understood that misunderstanding the old is the normal form of historical awareness, since a
set of new socioeconomic factors necessarily generates a new frame of
mind that, consequently, encompasses the cultural heritage only in
such a way as to suit its needs and demands. This is exactly the meaning
of Vico's dictum: "The order of ideas must follow the order of things"*
(*N.S.,* par. 238). Indeed, Vico's theory of the misconception of the
earliest Roman history rests on this very assumption—namely, that
historians have applied their own conceptual frame of mind to that
particular historical period, thus completely misunderstanding the
sensuous and fantastic frame of mind of the ancient Romans.
    Lassalle reasserted his position when he stated (July 27/28, 1861) that
"it is the very misunderstanding which strongly supported the period
of free competition to create a situation that could not have arisen

---

[9] *Marx & Engels on Literature & Art,* ed. L. Baxandall and S. Moravski (St. Louis: Telos
Press, 1973), p. 98.

without that misunderstanding and that is so fully in keeping with that period and satisfies its dearest desires: the modern testament, this legacy without heirs" (*L.M.*, 3: 380).

Ten months elapsed before Marx answered Lassalle's long letter in defense of himself. And when he answered, he advised Lassalle to read Vico. He must have thought that arguing with Lassalle would be wasted time; the man was hopeless.[10] What he thought about Lassalle can be read in his letters to Engels. The sarcasm is venomous, the language vituperative. He calls Lassalle all sorts of names: "animal," "ape" (February 9, 1860), mental "leper" (May 10, 1861), "revolutionary Cardinal Richelieu" (July 30, 1862). The reader who is curious to know more of his style is directed to excerpts from Marx's letter to Engels.[11]

---

[10] Engels's judgment of Lassalle, expressed before the publication of the *System* (February 6, 1861), was similar: "What beautiful ideas he has about the parliamentarian regime and what right and justice mean in that system. The man won't improve. His forthcoming two-volume towering work might deal with only more of the same" (*M.E.*, 3: 16).

[11] The following are, in chronological order, excerpts from Marx's letters to Engels:

February 1, 1858. "Heraclitus the Dark by Lassalle the Bright is at bottom an apish concoction.... The lad seems to have tried to explain Hegel to himself through Heraclitus, which he does by never getting tired of starting the process afresh... One can tell how terrific the lad seems to himself in his philological tinsel, moving around with the grace of a young man who for the first time in his life is wearing *fashionable dress* [English in the text].... He has, as a matter of fact, added absolutely nothing new to what Hegel says in his *History of Philosophy*. The fellow only distributes it at retail, which could have been done well enough on two printers' sheets.... Only a fellow who prints books at the expense of that awful hussy [Countess Hatzfeldt] could dare to feast the world with two volumes of sixty printers' sheets."

May 18, 1859. "Lassalle's pamphlet [*The Italian War and Prussia's Task*] is an *enormous blunder* [in English].... If Lassalle persists in speaking in the name of the party, he must in the future either be prepared to be disowned publicly by us...or...first come to an understanding with the opinions of other people besides himself. We have to absolutely hold fast to party discipline now, lest everything go down the drain."

February 9, 1860. "By the way, and going back to *nos moutons*, i.e., Lassalle...How the guy prides himself morally as against Liebknecht! And this is the same person who has been using the most shameful means and has associated himself with the most shameful people at the service of Countess Hatzfeldt! Has the animal forgotten that, although I tried to get him into the League [of Communists], a unanimous resolution of the Central Committee in Cologne rejected him because of his disrepute? ...And now look at the strutting ape! As soon as he thinks, looking through his eyes colored with Bonapartism, that he has caught us on a weak point, how he swells and blurts oracles and what airs he assumes, even though gracefully."

May 7, 1861. "Dazzled by the reputation his *Heraclitus* has made in certain learned circles and his good wine and cookery in a circle of spongers, Lassalle is naturally in the dark about his disrepute among the public at large. And then there is his pretense of always being in the right, his obsession with the 'speculative conception' (the lad is even dreaming about a new Hegelian philosophy raised to the second power), his infection with obsolete French liberalism, his bumptious writing, his obtrusiveness and tactlessness, etc."

May 10, 1861. "Lazarus the leper is also the 'Ur-type' of Jew as well as Lazarus-Lassalle. Only leprosy has hit our Lazarus in the brain.... He will send to us all his new legal 'Ur-work'

Marxian Irony

The letter of April 28, 1862 containing the paragraph on Vico is inspired by the same phobia. Marx begins by telling Lassalle he has now read entirely his "writing," wondering whether Lassalle has ever read Vico. The author of the *New Science*, unlike "legal Philistines" (an

---

([his] Dharma)."

December 9, 1861. "The second volume [of the *System*] is more interesting because of the quotations. Ideologism is all-pervasive, and the dialectic is wrongly employed. Hegel has never called dialectic the subsumption of a mass of 'cases' under a general principle."

July 30, 1862. The three-page letter written on this date is, except for the first paragraph, all about Lassalle. Written while the latter was Marx's guest in London, at a time when Marx's financial situation was disastrous, Marx expresses his anger at having to play host to a person he despised. I shall translate only a passage, then summarize the rest.

"The Jewish Nigger Lassalle, who fortunately will leave my house at the end of this week, has fortunately lost another 5000 Taler [£750] in a speculation that went wrong. The lad would rather flush his money down the toilet than lend it to a 'friend,' even were he guaranteed interest and capital. He has moreover, persuaded himself he must live as a Jewish nobleman or an ennobled (through the Countess evidently) Jew."

Marx's wife had taken to the pawnshop everything that was not "riveted and nailed down," to make Lassalle's stay more comfortable. Lassalle finds a job for one of their daughters as "company" to the Countess. He has dissuaded Garibaldi from marching on Rome, advising him to march on Vienna instead. The revolution would have been all over in six weeks with Lassalle's leverage (his pen in particular). Mazzini, too, approved of his plan. Lassalle introduced himself as "representative of the German revolutionary workers' class." It was he who frustrated Prussia's intervention in the Italian war with his pamphlet. "*In fact* [in English], he has been guiding 'the history of the last three years.'" He would rage and rave at Marx's quips, finally reaching the conclusion that Marx was too "abstract" to understand politics. The "idealist" is a voracious eater and regularly in heat. The shape of his head and the growth of his hair—and his indiscretion at that—prove him to be a Negro, from those Negroes who followed Moses (not excluding, however, a more recent interracial family affair). His great discovery, that the Pelasgians are officially Semites, he communicates only to friends. Main proof for it: a passage in the Book of the Maccabees.

August 7, 1862. "Itzig [Lassalle] told me he intends to found a newspaper after his return. I told him I would be the English correspondent *for good money*, but free from any responsibility or political partnership—we disagree politically on everything, except for remote objectives."

August 15, 1863. The letter contrasts Marx's painstaking research (he has revised *Capital*, adding a historical part drawn from primary sources) with Lassalle's pilfering of Marx's economic writings, then advertising them as his own. He has otherwise been collecting "in his manure factory the party excrements" that Marx and Engels dropped in their youth, and which will serve "to fertilize world history." The accusation appears in different language in a note in the Preface of the first edition of *Capital* (1867): "If Ferdinand Lassalle has borrowed almost literally from my writings, and without any acknowledgment, all the general theoretical propositions in his economic works, for example, those on the historical character of capital, on the connection between the relations of production and the mode of production, etc., etc., even down to the terminology created by me, this may perhaps be due to purposes of propaganda. I am of course not speaking here of his detailed working-out and application of these propositions, which I have nothing to do with" (*C.*, 1: 89-90).

allusion to Lassalle?), has caught the true spirit of Roman law. The author of the *System* would find in the *New Science* nothing to serve his "purpose" (which is, according to a letter to Engels of May 7, 1861 [see note 11], Lassalle's "dreaming about a new Hegelian philosophy raised to the second power"). Vico's down-to-earth conception of Roman history is at loggerheads with Lassalle's "speculative conception" (ibid.) of history. Marx's advice to Lassalle to read the *New Science* must then be ironical. In his *Contribution to Hegel's Philosophy of Right* Marx explains Germany's backwardness with respect to England and France by the tendency Germans have to live in thought what other nations have lived in reality: "The Germans have thought in politics what other nations have done" (*E.W.*, 250). "German chauvinists by temperament, and free-thinking liberals by reflection, seek the history of our freedom beyond our history, in the primeval Teutonic forests" (*E.W.*, 246). Lassalle seeking the origins of Roman law in the Pelasgian forests is part of the team.

In the historical chapter of his book Lassalle maintains that the Pelasgians migrated from Asia Minor to Italy.[12] According to a myth related by Macrobius, Hercules, while visiting Rome, slept with Acca Larentia, "the noblest prostitute in those times" (*R.S.* 12: 724). She is also Romulus' nurse. Lassalle identifies her with the she-wolf who suckled Romulus because "in Latin *lupa* means both 'she-wolf' and 'whore' " (12: 727). She then gave herself to a rich Etruscan, who married her. After his death his patrimony went to Acca Larentia and, through her, to the Roman people—"*cum decederet, populum Romanum nuncupavit heredem*" (Macrobius): "thus Acca Larentia is nothing but the appropriate self-personification and self-adoration of Rome"[13] (12: 737-38), the outcome of the merger (in Acca Larentia) of the Pelasgians (according to a myth as related by Diodorus Siculus, Hercules is a non-Italic god) and the Etruscans. Lassalle derives *Larentia* from *lar,* the name for the family gods (12: 726), explaining the Etruscan name—based on Plutarch and other writers—as meaning 'prince,' '*Herr*' (12: 699), which he interprets as the enduring subjectivity of will after death (12: 688). And since the subjectivity of will has its most adequate expression in the testament, the ultimate meaning of the Acca Larentia myth, rooted in the cult of family gods, is the institution of the testa-

[12] Niebuhr: "The Trojans also must be regarded as Pelasgians." *Lectures on the History of Rome*, 3 vols., trans. L. Schmitz (London: Taylor, Walton & Maberly: 1849), 1: 18.
[13] Niebuhr: "Romulus is only a personification of Rome." Ibid. 1:7.

ment. Diodorus also relates that Hercules incognito rewarded two Romans for their hospitality by advising them to consecrate their tithes to Hercules, who would then bless and make them happy. Lassalle interprets Hercules' blessing, not as riches and material goods, but as the right to them: "The testament and the right, this is the rich earthly blessing" (12: 738). "The property tithe introduced by Hercules is not a tithe; it is the Herculean principle in the tithe, the transformation into property tithe of the tithe men paid to the underground goods" (12: 735). Plutarch's sentence, that Hercules liberated the Romans from their obligation to pay tithes to the Etruscans, is interpreted by Lassalle in the sense that Hercules "freed the Romans from paying tithes to the Etruscan substance" (ibid.), i.e., the ritual of immolating children to the Lares, a ritual reintroduced in Rome after the Etruscan conquest (12: 706-7).

Niebuhr found "poetic narrative different from but better than bare history" (*R.G.*, 1: 203). Popular or learned poetry idealizes history. Thus, "poor Sabines appear covered with gold" (1: 188) in the fantasy of Roman poets. When Numa Pompilius was elected "king, he divided the lands...[and] instituted the service for guarding the boundaries. All lawgivers, and especially Moses, founded the success of their commandments about virtue and justice and good customs on landed property, or at least made hereditary possession of the land secure for the greatest number of citizens. Only then he [Numa] turned to institute religion" (1: 196). Lassalle finds fault with Niebuhr's earthly conception of history, attributing to him Vichian concepts: "He [Niebuhr] sees in it [Roman history] a heroic song, a Niebelungenlied, born out 'of heroic distress.' But historical saga and myth are never free poetry, and least of all among the Romans. They are mythic elaborations of a very real content of spiritual history.... What we find in those myths is not a heroic song, but the *relic* [emphasis added] of one of the greatest and truest historico-cultural processes and the truthful development of the specific Roman spirit" (*R.S.*, 12: 744-45).

The language is Vichian—not of the Vico who states that "the order of ideas must follow from the order of things"* (*N.S.*, 238), but of the Vico who believes in "an ideal eternal history traversed in time by the history of every nation in its rise, development, maturity, decline and fall" (*N.S.*, 245). Is Lassalle's "spiritual history" his version of Vico's "ideal eternal history" applied to Roman history? Marx's ironical query whether Lassalle has read Vico is to suggest that he has not only read

Vico but has even borrowed from him—not from the genuine, matter-of-fact Vico, but from the Catholic, metaphysical Vico.

A reexamination of the selection and arrangement of the quotations in the light of what has been found so far shows irony to be the *forma mentis* governing the writing of the paragraph in question.

The sentence excluded from the first quotation is, "The Greeks derived their philosophy from their laws." The sentence weighs more than the rest of the corollary, while also being one Marx certainly agrees with. In the preface to *Contribution to the Critique of Political Economy* philosophy appears together with art as the last step in the development of "ideological forms" in this order: "Legal, political,religious, artistic or philosophic." Why then has Marx deleted the sentence? Because here, in the first quotation, he wants to associate Lassalle with the metaphysical Vico: He makes the quotation end with the phrase "legal metaphysics." The phrase formulates Marx's evaluation of Lassalle's *System,* a legal treatise in the spirit of "legal Philistines."

The second quotation begins with the phrase, "Ancient jurisprudence was very poetic." The arrangement brings "legal metaphysics" and "poetic jurisprudence" into rhetorical juxtaposition, suggesting their relationship. The way Lassalle deals with myths in the last chapter is "poetic" much in the sense Vico uses this term. Vico's partial description of ancient Roman jurisprudence as exchanging fictions for realities renders adequately Marx's opinion on the nonscientific value of the *System.* Its conclusive formula of the "intrinsic identity of the Lares cult and the inheritance law" (*R.S.,* 12: 719) seems to echo Vico's sentence (in Belgioioso's translation) that ancient Roman jurisprudence "considered the living as dead and the dead as still living in their heritages." And Marx could be justified for so interpreting Lassalle's "legal metaphysics," for in the *System* one finds: "In death the Roman acquires a right to what he could never dispose of in life. Once dead, his powers grew. Death transfigured him into a lawgiver" (11: 247). The testament made "the dead stronger than the living" (11: 236).

Lassalle is of course aware of this "contradiction." But he uses it to first reject per absurdum the current thesis that the testament in its present form was an adoption of the ancient Roman testament, and then to prove his own thesis that the testament "represents the permanence of the subjectivity of will" (12: 788). In his letter to Marx of July 27/28, 1861 he states that "the testamentary disposition after death is against all *jus naturale,* totally *contra rationem*" (*R.S.,* 3: 379). It could never occur before the institution of the Roman law and without knowledge of the latter. And it became an accepted dogma only through the misunderstanding of the Roman law (ibid.).

And how does Lassalle prove his own thesis? By conjugating Fichte with Hegel. Ancient Roman law, like any other law originally, could not have been but intestate, based on the natural transmission of the father's property to the son(s). There was no need for a testament at the time. The testament came into existence as a possibility for the father to disinherit his son(s) by bequeathing his patrimony to a person of his choice. This entails the emergence of the subject. For only a person able to conceive of himself as an individual, as a subject, as an ego, can make that departure. As a consequence the ego asserts itself as a subject for an object, exercising its will upon a nonego. The heir is supplanted by the legatee through the testament, and the relation between father and heir is superseded by the relation between testator and legatee, representing a higher moment in the dialectic of right. This higher moment is mediated precisely by the contradiction inherent in the intestate inheritance law, implying the paradox of the dead being stronger than the living. But the assertion of the testator's will turns the legatee into an object; he feels identified with his legacy. He must then separate his ego from his property, which he can do only by asserting his own will upon it, by disposing of it at his will. The legatee must become a subject himself. Now he can effect a synthesis between the testator's will and his own will. The testament represents precisely this highest moment in the dialectic of right, the identity of the testator and the legatee, the full subjectivity of will. Hence the conclusion that the Roman testament "represents the permanence of the subjectivity of will, and not a patrimony shift.... Its spiritual significance consists in its being the Roman form of the immortality dogma" (12: 788). Both intestate and testate inheritance laws are rooted in what is the Roman way of conceiving the immortality of the soul, this concept constituting the "genus" of both (11: 324).

One can imagine Marx's repugnance at conclusions such as these. He did, however, agree with part of Lassalle's theory according to which the conception of Roman law as natural law by German jurists was a misconception, the result of a total misunderstanding. How did this happen? Lassalle's explanation almost echoes Vico: "One understands nations adopting alien institutions incomprehensible to them as far as their inner nature is concerned. One also understands jurists abstracting their external legal features and transplanting them into their own institutions.... They have thus construed a natural law which exists nowhere, a natural impossibility" (12: 791). In this case the misunderstanding was twofold. German jurists could not understand why there was no such law in German law. And they were far from realizing the nature of that law in Roman jurisprudence. "Because of these two errors, the jurists elevated to the *proud* [emphasis added] rank of natural law the power of dead will to dispose of heritage, a result of their own *learned misunderstanding*" [emphasis added] (12: 792).

Niebuhr speaks of "family vanity" and "national vanity," referring to "forgeries"[14] perpetrated upon the lays and tales from which arose the earliest history of Rome. But he respects the learned. Lassalle's *gelehrtes Mißverständnis*, alongside other characteristic Vichian terms, seems to derive from Vico. Did he then read the *New Science*? Paragraph 127 reads: "To this conceit of nations is added that of scholars, who will have it that what they know is as old as the world."

One of the reasons Marx praises Vico is because he had pioneered in the field of comparative philology. Lassalle, we saw, was versed in philology (his *Heraclitus*), and occasionally he avails himself of it in his legal work. We have seen examples in his interpretation of myths. We shall produce one more example. With respect to his theory of the identity of testator and legatee, Lassalle quotes the formula for that identification: "*heres mihi esto*" ("you shall be my heir"). Then he writes in a note: "Here the meaning of 'heir' catches one's eye. For *heres* is nothing but *Herr* [lord], *Willensherr* [lord of one's will].... This absolute meaning, unrelated to property, comes clearly out of *herus* and *hera*." (Plautus and Horace are referred to, and *Institutiones* is quoted: "*Heres apud antiquos pro domino ponebatur*".) Then follows a sentence bearing on comparative philology: "[A.T.G.] Passow compares the Greek ἥρως with *herus, hera*" (11: 305). Another note explains that the identification act excludes all relations between persons who are not free, adding: "Here lies the difference from the slave, who is a thing, not a person. On the contrary, children are free Roman persons" (11: 306).

In paragraph 513 Vico quotes and interprets *herus* and ἔρος —poetic form of ἔρως—just as does Lassalle later. And Vico also quotes a Latin formula, "...*ita ius esto*," which is the equivalent of the shorter Latin formula quoted by Lassalle. Yet Vico's political paragraph reaches a conclusion opposite to Lassalle's: Children and slaves were equally considered as property by Roman law.

[14] Ibid. 1: 15

Let us now look afresh at Marx's dealing with Vico's pieces forming the third quotation. He has it begin with, "The Romans called the heros *heri,* whence *hereditas* comes..." and has it end with, "the heir...represents, as to heritage, the defunct family father." The quotation results from cutting off whole sentences from Belgioioso's text. I quote the (retranslated) text, setting off the two sentences forming the third quotation by spacing the letters of those sentences.

> T h e   R o m a n s   c a l l e d   t h e   h e r o s   *h e r i,*   w h e n c e   *h e r e d i t a s*   c o m e s , meaning 'family' at the beginning of the Latin language, but which later came to signify a despotic power. In fact the Law of the Twelve Tables attributes to family fathers a despotic power, the right of disposing by testament of their possessions: UTI PATERFAMILIAS SUPER PECUNIA TUTELAVE REI SUAE LEGASSIT, ITA JUS ESTO ["As the family father has disposed concerning his property and the guardianship of his estate, so shall it be binding"]. The right of disposing by testament was called *legare,* a right that seems to pertain to sovereigns; for t h e   h e i r comes to be a legate or legatee that r e p r e s e n t s ,   a s   t o   h e r i t a g e ,   t h e   d e f u n c t   f a m i l y   f a t h e r . Children and slaves were comprised in the formula REI SUAE ET PECUNIAE ["estate" and "property"], a consequence of the monarchic power exercised by the family fathers on their families in the state of nature.

This text expresses Vico's original idea that the power of the paterfamilias was monarchic and despotic. When Marx writes, "his [Vico's] conception of the spirit of the Roman law is opposed [to that] of legal Philistines," he most likely has in mind Vico's idea of the monarchic authority of the fathers, considering that the sentences omitted in the third quotation discuss exactly that idea. Why, then, has he then omitted them? We saw that Marx has deleted in the first quotation the corollary's last sentence, with which he most likely agrees. And he has also deleted, in the second quotation, the very core of paragraph 1036, the author's explanation of his concept of *iura imaginaria,* which, we saw, presents some resemblance to Marx's own theory of the fetishism of commodities. The quotations, as they stand, introduced by a gastronomic metaphor, look like bones cleared of meat and thrown to a dog—to "whet" his "appetite."

Lassalle's treatment of myth is "poetic" much in the Vichian sense of the word. And it is no coincidence that his interpretation of myths centers on Hercules, just as Vico's does. We also saw that the equation *heres = heros* is common to both authors. The evidence is sufficient, it would seem, for Marx to infer that Lassalle had not only read the *New Science*, but also had appropriated quite a few Vichian ideas. In a note in the preface to *Capital* (1867) Marx charges Lassalle with having "borrowed almost literally from *his* writings, and without any acknowledgement" (see end of note 11). And in a previous letter to Engels (August 15, 1863), he lashes out at Lassalle for his advertising as his own some ideas of Marx and Engels that Marx considers as their youth "excrements" (ibid.). Lassalle's *Heraclitus* distributed Hegel's ideas on the Greek philosopher "at retail" (letter to Engels of February 1, 1858—see note 11). His *System*, Marx must have thought, smuggled Vico's ideas on Roman law.

Lassalle's idea of the Roman testament as originating the modern testament is grounded on his assumption that the institution of the testament implies the emergence of the subjectivity of will, conceived as willpower, as spiritual lordship ["Willensherr"]. Lassalle arrives at this concept by overturning, in an idealistic sense, Vico's matter-of-fact idea that the legatee comes, through the act of *legare,* in possession of monarchic, i.e., full economic and political, power. In the third quotation Marx has left out only the sentences on the monarchic power of the paterfamilias as a result of the act of *legare,* stopping short of the sentence that equates children and slaves with regard to property. He omitted a Vichian sentence he most likely approved of, thus repeating the already known pattern of quoting only sentences he disagreed with and which, he thought, Lassalle had appropriated. But while in the first and second quotations the Vichian texts have been cut off at their extremities (the corollary's final sentence in the first quotation, the initial and final sentences in paragraph 1035), in the third quotation the text has been fragmented. And while the omissions in the first two quotations are not signaled, those in the third quotation are hinted at twice by the typographical sign of ellipsis: "...the heir...represents as to heritage, the defunct family father." Here ellipsis recalls the rhetorical figure of paraleipsis, a way of emphasizing what is understated or briefly mentioned. By omitting the initial sentences on the monarchic power of the paterfamilias as well as the final sentence equating children and slaves with regard to property, Marx points out fundamental differences between Vico and Lassalle. Up to this point he has associated them: Now he opposes them.

We just noted Lassalle's idealistic travesty of Vico's concept of monarchic power. Lassalle also rejects Vico's equation of children and slaves in the Roman family, maintaining that Roman law considers children as persons, slaves as things. Their conceptions of the Roman family are indeed in sharp contrast. Vico conceives of family feelings as originally conditioned by economy, whereas Lassalle traces the institution of the Roman testate and intestate law in which the Roman family is grounded to the dogma of the immortality of the soul. From a socialist point of view a conception of Roman family life as viewed by the old Italian professor of rhetoric is certainly more advanced than that of the modern German lawyer. The ellipsis-paraleipsis functions as a reminder.

But paraleipsis is perhaps not the right word here. Pretermission is, in legal practice, the silent passing over by a testator of a natural heir, such as children in a will. And since the case in question is about inheritance, it would seem that Marx is conveying his message by compounding ellipsis with pretermission. He stopped short of including Vico's sentence equating children and slaves so as not to set Lassalle against Vico overtly. Had he included it, he would have dispelled the atmosphere of irony permeating the whole paragraph. His intention, when he set out to play his insidious game with Lassalle (they were still 'friends' at the time), was to demolish the latter's *System* by way of vitriolic irony. And irony is consistently at work in the paragraph in question, which begins with an imperceptible smile feigning surprise for Lassalle's *apparent* ("you seem" is emphatic: "...*nicht gelesen zu haben scheinst*") ignorance of Vico's work, and culminates with a sneer. Through ellipsis evoking pretermission Lassalle is made an "heir" to Vico "as to [cultural] heritage"—a degenerate heir who misrepresents rather than "represents" his "father."

It goes without saying that Lassalle's kinship with Vico is far from flattering for the Neapolitan philosopher. And this obtains with respect of him as both philosopher and writer. To an expert and sparkling writer such as Marx, the *New Science* must have seemed a mishmash of disciplines as diverse as history, poetics, and philology, the product of a rather provincial writer (his "queer Neapolitan dialect").[15] He deals with Vico's texts as if they were raw writing material for a master to reshape and recast. Not much different was his appreciation of Lassalle's writing skills.

---

[15] Here Marx is following Princess Belgioioso's judgment: "Ajoutons encore que son italien n'est guère qu'un dialecte napolitain rattaché au latin, ce qui forme un langage inintelligible au premier coup d'oeil, pour tout autre que pour un latiniste de la ville de Naples" (op. cit., pp. cxvi-cxvii).

We have seen what he thought of Lassalle as a playwright and philologist; a letter to Engels (May 7, 1860—see note 11) mentions his "bumptious writing." A sentence in the paragraph immediately preceding the one containing the Vichian quotations conveys the same message. There Marx writes, with respect to *Capital,* that the work is lagging behind not only because of his being compelled to "do the meanest manual jobs in order not to starve," but also because of his "peculiar habit" of "totally recasting" what he thought he had already "finished" (*"etwas fertig Geschriebenes...ich es ungenügend finde und wieder total umarbeite"*), something Lassalle was incapable of achieving, due to his nonscholarly mind.

Lassalle, ordinarily very much to the point in his responses, did not mention Vico in his reply. His failure to do so further suggests that Marx's letter had hit the bull's-eye.

Marx's Letter to Engels Mentioning Vico

On the same day that Marx wrote to Lassalle on Vico he also wrote to Engels. His letter to Engels contains the following paragraph: "In his *New Science* Vico says that Germany is the only country in Europe where "a heroic language" is still spoken. Had he had the pleasure of acquainting himself with the Vienna *Press* or the Berlin *Nationalzeitung,* the old Neapolitan would have dropped that prejudice" (*M.E.,* 3: 77).

There are several references to German as a heroic language in the *New Science.* One of them reads: "The first writers in the modern languages of Europe were versemakers and in Silesia, a province inhabited almost entirely by peasants, the people are born poets. And generally the German language preserves its heroic origin intact— even to excess—and this is the reason...Greek compound words can be happily rendered in German, especially in poetry" (*N.S.,* 471).

The paragraph on Vico in Marx's letter to Engels is complementary to the one in Marx's letter to Lassalle—the two letters were written the same day. We just saw that Lassalle associates ἥρως with *herus,* after having equated *heres* and *Herr.* It is quite possible that Marx was thinking of exactly this passage when, in his letter to Lassalle, he quoted the sentence, "The Romans called the heros *heri.*" Lassalle's equation ἥρως = *heres* = *Herr,* equivalent to Vico's *herus* = ἔρος, leads logically to the thought that, like the Greek language, the German language is heroic, as implied in Vico's par. 471. The naiveté of Vico's comment must have amused Marx. And if Marx did, as I think, relate Vico's saying about heroic German language to Lassalle's equation of *heres* and *Herr,* his amusement would have been much greater. For, by dint of his philological expertise, Lassalle had proved property to be the quintessence of German heroism.

The Note on Vico in *Capital*

Marx mentions Vico for the third and last time in a note to the chapter "Machinery and Large-Scale Industry" in the first volume of *Capital*:

> Spinning machines had already been used before his [John Wyatt's] time, although very imperfect ones, and Italy was probably the country where they first appeared. A critical history of technology would show how little any of the inventions of the eighteenth century are the work of a single individual. As yet such a book does not exist. Darwin directed attention to the history of natural technology, i.e., the formation of the organs of plants and animals, which serve as the instruments of production for sustaining their life. Does not the history of the productive organs of man in society, of organs that are the material basis of every particular organization of society, deserve equal attention? And would not such a history be easier to compile, since, as Vico says, human history differs from natural history in that we have made the former, but not the latter? Technology reveals the active relation of man to nature, the direct process of the production of the social relations of his life, and of the mental conceptions that flow from those relations. Even a history of religion that is written in abstraction from this material basis is uncritical. It is, in reality, much easier to discover by analysis the earthly kernel of the misty creations of religion than to do the opposite, i.e., to develop from the actual, given relations of life the form in which these have been celestialized.* The latter method is the only materialist, and therefore the only scientific one. The weaknesses of the abstract materialism of natural science, a materialism which excludes the historical process, are immediately evident from the abstract and ideological conceptions expressed by its spokesman whenever they venture beyond the bounds of their own speciality. (*C.*, 1: 494-95.)

The passage in this paragraph, "Vico says, human history differs from natural history in that we have made the former, but not the latter," both misquotes and mutilates Vico's well-known statement,

> ...that the world of civil society has certainly been made by men, and that its principles are therefore to be found within the modifications of our human mind. Whoever reflects on this cannot but marvel that the philosophers should have bent all their energies to the study of *the world of nature, which, since God made it, He alone knows;* and that they should have neglected the study of *the world of nations, or civil world, which, since men had made it, men could come to know* [emphasis added]. (*N.S.*, 331.)

Marx attributes to Vico a phrase, "natural history" [*Naturgeschichte*], that Vico would not have accepted. Vico's phrase is "world of nature," which he contrasts with "world of nations" or "civil world." Marx is silent with regard to Vico's reason for man's inability to know the world of nature, i.e., because God has made it, and "since God made it, He alone knows [it]." Marx certainly disapproves of Vico's argument that knowledge of nature is God's privilege. The sentence in the note immediately following the sentence in question, "Technology reveals the active relation of man to nature," is an implicit denial of Vico's implied thesis that it is impossible for men to know nature. According to Vico, since nature has been made by God, it falls outside the range of human knowledge, "historical" and "natural" being related in the same way as man is related to God. Marx predicates history to both man [*Menschengeschichte*] and nature [*Naturgeschichte*]; "historical" and "natural" are to him complementary terms. He sees natural history as an extension of human history, nature being the recipient of man's action upon it. True, man has not made nature; he is part of nature himself. Nevertheless, he transforms nature through labor and industry, reshapes it, and in a sense remakes it. Man is *actively* related to nature through technology. The relation is active in the sense that, by remaking nature, man comes to know it. Marx's formulation of the active relation of man to nature is already found in the first of his Theses on Feuerbach: "The chief defect of all hitherto existing materialism (that of Feuerbach included) is that the thing, reality, sensuousness, is conceived only in the form of the *object or of contemplation,* but not as *sensuous human* activity, practice ["Praxis"*], [it is not conceived*] subjectively." (*E.W.*, 421.) Here "subjectively" means *a parte subiecti*, i.e., from the point of view of man as

active subject, as man subjecting nature to his action upon it. By so
doing man comes to know nature and achieves "natural science." The
phrase occurs in *Economic and Philosophical Manuscripts:*

> Even historiography only incidentally takes account of natural
> science which it sees as contributing to enlightenment, utility and
> a few great discoveries. But natural science has intervened and
> transformed human life all the more *practically* through industry
> and has prepared the conditions for human emancipation, how-
> ever much its immediate effect was to complete the process of
> dehumanization. Industry is the real historical relationship of
> nature, and hence of natural science, to man. If it is then con-
> ceived as the exoteric revelation of man's *essential powers,* the
> *human* essence of nature or the *natural* essence of man can also be
> understood.... History itself is a real part of natural history and of
> nature's becoming man. Natural science will in time subsume the
> science of man just as the science of man will subsume natural
> science: there will be *one* science. (*E.W.,* 355.)

Marx's concept of the "one science" in which human and natural
science complement one another is poles apart from Vico's concept of a
"new science" of humanity that excludes the natural sciences. Far from
excluding them from his global science, Marx sees in them the very
"condition" for the emancipation of mankind from its present state of
dehumanization, brought about by capitalism. The natural sciences
promote the development of industry, and this is "the real historical
relationship of nature...to man." Industry is man's natural ally in his
struggle, especially against religious obscurantism (for "divine miracles are made superfluous by the miracles of industry" (*E.W.,* 330).
Deliverance from both capitalistic exploitation and religious obscurantism leads to socialism: "For socialist man the whole of what is called
world history is nothing more than the creation of man through labor
and the development of nature *for* [emphasis added] man" (*E.W.,* 357).
  Socialist man, who will deliver mankind from these two basic forms of
alienation, will humanize nature by making it serve his ends. Human
history and natural history will thus merge into "world history." The
note in question in *Capital* recasts Marx's earlier formulae about man's
relation to nature in phraseology characteristic of Marx's mature
thought. The sentence, "Technology reveals the active relation of man
to nature, the direct process of the production of his life, and thereby it

also lays bare the process of the production of the social relations of his life, and of the mental conceptions that flow from those relations," is a succinct formulation of the theory of historical materialism, as enunciated in the preface to *Contribution to the Critique of Political Economy.*

For both Vico and Marx man enters into a relationship with nature through labor. Vico's concept of labor, however, is quite different from that of Marx, a consequence of their different concepts of the relationship between man and nature. In *Economic and Philosophic Manuscripts* nature is viewed as the extension of the human body, as "man's inorganic body" (*E.W.*, 328). Man "subjugates nature through his labor" (330) and appropriates it. "Taken abstractly, for itself, and fixed in its separation from man, [nature] is *nothing* for man" (398). It becomes what it is through man's labor. Marx's concept of labor is triumphalistic. Vico views nature as God's domain and man as alien in it. Hence his awe and fear when he begins to perceive it as a huge, animated body. Vico's Christian faith combines with Lucretian memories to form his perception of nature. Of course, man modifies nature through labor. Still the modification remains superficial and limited; it hardly goes beyond the stage of domestication. Vico's version of the humanizing of nature is the taming of the wild forest and the domestication of wild animals. The chapter on economics in the *New Science* stops at domestic economy. Its first economic institution, patrimony, is built "through hard and unceasing labor" (*col travaglio e coll'industria, N.S.,* par. 525). Vico views labor as an exacting necessity of life, facing man from birth to death. His type of labor is manual work, done under the spur of great want and insecurity. Primitive man cleared part of the forest with fire and tilled the ground with the plough. Agriculture, which marks the beginning of civilization, remains for Vico the type of all civilization. He has little understanding for trade and industry and, in fact, he denies trade a role in the colonization process of the western part of the Mediterranean. He explains the migrations of peoples leading to colonization as a consequence of only class conflict: "Many leaders of bands of *famuli* which had rebelled and been conquered by the heroes...in order to avoid oppression and to find escape and safety along with the members of their factions, committed themselves to the hazards of the sea and went in search of unoccupied lands along the shores of the Mediterranean" (*N.S.,* par. 20). He is silent about the art of navigation, which would have developed, one thinks, as a consequence of migrations by way of the sea. On the frontispiece table of the *New Science* the rudder, which symbolizes the art of navigation, is found "at some distance from the plough, which is in front of the altar... The plough rests its handle against the altar with a certain majesty, to give us to understand that ploughed lands were the first altars of the gentiles" (*N.S.*, par. 20). Of the four tools found in the frontispiece table as symbols of civilization (all other items are "hieroglyphs"), the plough has priority over the rudder (which ploughs the waters). "The arts," Vico writes, "are imitations of nature and consequently in a certain sense real poetry" (*N.S.*, par. 498). Dante called art God's grandchild, reasoning that God created nature, which art then imitates: "*Sì ch'a vostr'arte Dio quasi è nepote*" (*Inferno* XI, 105). Vico's conception of art (*techne*) is as medieval as Dante's. The heroic bent of his mind—"De mente heroica" (1732) was his last inaugural oration—forecloses to him a view of the modern world. His contemplation of history stops at the Middle Ages, with only sporadic glimpses into modern times. And thus labor has in his work an archaeological aspect, its structure being feudal: "all commonwealths are born from certain eternal principles of fiefs" (*N.S.*, par. 599).

Very telling in this respect is the involution process of his most representative hero. Piecing together Vico's interpretations of the most significant myths related to Hercules, the picture one gets of him as the founder of gentile civilization emerges as follows. The hero begins by clearing the ground in order to make it arable (the Nemaean lion, the Hesperides, the Hydra, *N.S.*, par. 540). He then clears the social ground, "slaying monsters and tyrants...on his civilization mission about the world" (*N.S.*, par. 93). Next he institutes the Olympiads (*N.S.*, par. 371)—*panem et circenses*—measuring years "from harvest to harvest" (*N.S.*, par. 77). "Finally Hercules...struggles with Antaeus (a character of the mutinous *famuli*)...conquers him and binds him to the earth" (*N.S.*, par. 618). "The Herculean knot" marks the point of the parable's descent when the liberator becomes an oppressor. This knot tells the tale of mancipation (the legal act of enslavement) ritualized "by the handing over of a symbolic knot in imitation of the chain whereby Jove had bound the giants to the first unoccupied lands" (*N.S.*, par. 1030). By that legal act the heroes bound to their lands their *famuli* or *socii*, treating them in an inhuman way. Vico illustrates this with literary examples, one of them being "pious Aeneas' killing" of his socius, Misenus, to perform a religious rite (*N.S.*, par. 558). He condemns the heroes' cruelty toward their *famuli* and sympathizes with the gradual emancipation of the *socii*. Yet, at the same time, Vico laments (just as Dante had, though for another reason) the *embourgeoisement* process undergone by the heroes when, as a result of that emancipation, they mixed with their *socii*. This process he finds revealed in the myth of Hercules spinning. "Hercules in his old age becomes effeminate and spins at the behest of Iole and Omphale" (*N.S.*, par. 657). Hence his unheroic end. For, once Hercules has "extended *connubium* to the plebs" (*N.S.*, 658) as a result of becoming involved with plebeian women (Vico sees women as a lower social class),[16] he is bound to die "contaminated by plebeian blood" (ibid.). Vico relates the name of Nessus, the centaur whose poisoned blood caused Hercules' death, to the Petelian law called "De nexu," which released the *nexi*, the insolvent debtors, held in bondage by their creditors.[17] The attribution of womanly and, therefore, plebeian labor to Hercules signifies the end of the heroic era and the beginning of the "human" era, in which reason is found to be the common property of human nature. Vico believes in human rationality, but his allegiance is to the heroic mind. Hercules is dear to him so long as he is heroic and a champion of the plebs ("*parcere subiectis et debellare superbos*"). Vico drops him when he becomes a plebeian and begins to spin: "*lilia non nent.*"[18]

Vico's interpretation of the myths about Hercules contains in a nutshell his philosophy of history. A person more appreciative of technology would have read, in the myth of Hercules spinning, the title of glory for his greatest labor: the invention of spinning, which is such a landmark in the history of civilization. Marx begins the chapter in *Capital* containing the note on Vico with a historical overview of the textile industry, and the note itself begins with a reference to the probable invention of spinning by Italians. Marx writes that "in Germany they tried first to make one spinner work two spinning wheels...that proved to be too exhausting. Later, a treadle spinning wheel with two spindles was invented" (*C.*, 1: 495). "In 1735 John Wyatt announced his spinning machine, and thereby started the industrial revolution of the eighteenth century...it was called a machine 'to spin without fingers'" (493). Finally, the spinning jenny came, which "even at the very beginning, spun with twelve to eighteen spindles" (495).

Marx took over exactly where Vico left off. The opening sentence in *The Eighteenth Brumaire of Louis Bonaparte* (1852) has a Vichian ring:

[16] Likewise, Niebuhr illustrates the social differences between *populus*, the upper class, and plebs with a gender difference: "*populus* and *plebes:* accordingly named in masculine and feminine gender" (R.G. 1: 346).

[17] Niebuhr: "The Petelian law abolished the *nexum*, but not the *addictio* [the legal act by which a debtor was given up as a servant to his creditor]" (R.G. 3: xcii).

[18] "The lilies do not spin" is the motto on the French royal coat of arms, signifying that women cannot inherit the kingdom.

"Men make history, not as they please and under circumstances chosen by themselves; but under circumstances directly given and inherited from the past." Both Vico and Marx view civilization as an historical process, the result of human work. But, whereas Vico associates the *techne* with poetry, Marx relates it to science. Technology is absent from Vico's portrait of human history. Marx begins the chapter in *Capital*, "Machinery and Large-Scale Industry," with a discussion of the difference between tool and machine: "The machine is a mechanism that, after being set in motion, performs with its tools the same operation as the worker formerly did with similar tools" (495).

This is not to say that Vico's sense of economy was deficient or even inferior to that of Marx. Economics permeates Vico's system; one can even say that the economic moment is structural, though not in the same sense as Marx construes the relation between base and superstructure.[19] The difference is in the kind of economy envisaged, domestic versus national, agricultural versus industrial, medieval versus modern. If Marx read the *New Science* attentively, he hardly could have missed the importance economics has in it. Yet Vico's concept of economy would have seemed to Marx, compared to his own concept of it, as folklore is to science. The only time Vico is mentioned in *Capital*, it is as a philosopher of history, not as an economist.

Italian Economists in *Capital*

We can reach the same conclusion by means of a shortcut. Marx mentions many Italian economists in *Capital*. His source is the "Parte Moderna" of a multivolume collection edited by Pietro Custodi.[20] He quotes Pietro Verri's definition, "Money is the universal commodity" (*C.*, 1: 184), adding C. F. Pagnini's remark that in the Middle Ages "it was strictly forbidden to treat money as a commodity" (185). Antonio Genovesi is mentioned for his idea that the merchant always has his eye on his future profit (254). Marx quotes from Italian, "The abundance of wealth of some people is always balanced by the lack of wealth of others." The author, "the Venetian monk [Giammaria] Ortes, one of the greatest economic writers of the eighteenth century," also wrote: "Instead of projecting useless systems for achieving the happiness of

---

[19] See my article, "Economy in Vico's System," in *Vico: Past and Present*, ed. G. Tagliacozzo (Atlantic Highlands, N.J.: Humanities Press, 1981), 2: 144-56.

[20] *Scrittori classici italiani di economia politica* (Milan, 1804).

peoples, I shall limit myself to investigating the reasons for their unhappiness" (800).

Marx's favorite Italian economist is Ferdinando Galiani.[21] In his treatise *On Money* (1750) the Neapolitan diplomat refuted the mercantilistic theory that money has no intrinsic value ("Gold and silver have value before they are money," 185). And in his *Dialogues sur le commerce des blès* (1770) Galiani ridiculed the physiocrats. Writing on the concept of exchange value, Marx notes that "by equating their different products to each other in exchange as values, they [men] equate their different kinds of labor as human labor. They do this without being aware of it" (166). At this point he refers to the Italian economist: "Therefore, when Galiani said: Value is a relation between persons (*la Ricchezza è una ragione tra due persone*), he ought to have added: a relation concealed beneath a material shell" (167). The fetish aspect of commodities is then once more described:

Value, therefore, does not have its description branded on its forehead; it rather transforms every product of labor into a social hieroglyphic. Later on men try to decipher the hieroglyphic, to get behind the secret of their own social product: for the characteristic which objects of utility have of being values is as much man's social product as is their language. (ibid.)

"Hieroglyph" is a rather Vichian word. "The hieroglyphic or sacred or secret language," Vico writes, "[is created] by means of mute acts" (*N.S.*, par. 32). Elsewhere, elaborating on the origin of many a technical word from property relations, he notes that "the originally real terms [or boundary posts] [*termini**] of the fields later became the vocal terms of the scholastics" (*N.S.*, par. 486). "The conclusion to be drawn from the foregoing is that in the time of the mute nations the great need answered by the ensigns was that for certainty of ownership" (*N.S.*, par. 487).

---

[21] Galiani comes first in *Capital* as to the number of quotations, eight, from the Italian economists. He is outnumbered by Malthus (25), Ricardo (24), Smith (19) Engels (17), Ure (15), Sismondi (14), Petty (12), Steuart (10), Storch, Senior, and J. S. Mill (9 each). Galiani outnumbers (listed alphabetically) Bailey, Burke, Destutt de Tracy, Fourier, Locke, MacCulloch, Proudhon, Quesnay, Say, Turgot, Wanderlint, Verri, and Young.

Galiani begins his discussion on the value of money by adopting Vico's metaphorical-metonymical method in explaining the origin of language:[22]

> I propose to begin the discussion on the utility and necessity of money, fixing the right limits of its value, so that human beings, stepping back from that common error that makes them exchange images for things, instruments for works, come to realize that the metal of money is a commodity of luxury and not of necessity, and that money is not wealth but only its simulacrum, as well as an instrument for getting wealth by cheating.... Wealth is the possession of something desired by other people more than by its possessor.[23]

Two more quotations from Galiani are political: "Where equality exists, there is no gain" (*Dove è egualità, non è lucro, C.*, 1: 261). "When the crafts assume a more perfect form, this means nothing other than the discovery of new ways of making a product with fewer people or (which is the same thing) in a shorter time than previously" (431). Elsewhere Marx first quotes Adam Smith's sentence, "Poverty seems favorable to generation," and then comments on it by returning to Galiani: "Indeed, according to the gallant and witty Abbé Galiani, this is a specially wise arrangement made by God: 'God has decreed that the men who carry on the most useful crafts should be born in abundant numbers'" (797).

Compared to the brilliant conversationalist and "witty" economist, "the old Neapolitan" endowed with genius but lacking all sense of humor must have looked to the author of *Capital* as a relic of an archaic age, a latter-day Cyclops, useful for occasionally scaring a "bourgeois"[24] posing as a socialist. All intent to gather evidence in support of his "critique" of capitalism, *Capital* being such a critique, Marx draws from Italian economists, not suspecting that most of them were Vico's disciples in one way or another. He credited Vico for his daring (for one who

---

[22] For Vico's influence on Galiani see Giorgio Tagliacozzo, "Economic Vichianism: Vico, Galiani, Croce—Economics, Economic Liberalism," in *Giambattista Vico: An International Symposium* (Baltimore: Johns Hopkins Press, 1969), pp. 349-68.

[23] *Opere di Ferdinando Galiani*, ed. F. Diaz & L. Guerci (Milan-Naples: Ricciardi, 1975), pp. 119, 120.

[24] "Bürgerlich" is twice attributed to Lassalle by Marx in his letter of August 20, 1862, to Lassalle.

was such a good Catholic) conception of human history as made by human beings. He did this, once for all, in a footnote where he formulates his own conception of human history in terms of historical materialism. He thought he had given Vico his due. What would be his surprise, where he to come back to life, to see the obscure Neapolitan philosopher compared and even associated with him.

Sorel, Vico, and Marx   J. R. Jennings

The work of Georges Sorel (1847-1922) provides an opportunity to assess the comparative influence of Vico and Marx upon one of the most controversial and innovative thinkers of the past century. For the greater part of his writing career, from the middle of the 1890s until his death in 1922, Sorel reflected upon the status and utility of their respective writings. This process gave rise to a series of differing interpretations of their work, the implications of which can be discerned throughout his vast and diverse oeuvre.

Four subjects—the philosophy of science, religion, politics, and its related field, ethics—occupied a dominant position in Sorel's work. In his treatment of each one it is possible to detect the influence of Vico and Marx. What makes Sorel particularly fascinating in this context is that in certain important respects it is the influence of Vico that is the most decisive and enduring of the two; indeed, as we shall see, Sorel turned to the work of Vico as a means of correcting and alleviating the inadequacies and weaknesses that he felt existed within the writings of Marx.

These inadequacies related to three specific issues: the failure of Marx to provide a correct assessment of the significance and meaning of human action, the defectiveness of Marx's account of scientific method, and the inability of Marx to comprehend the epistemological and emotional status of religious faith. Sorel's knowledge of Vico's work was instrumental in his initial perception of these weaknesses in the thought of Marx. The position subsequently adopted by Sorel in respect of each of these three issues—the philosophies of action, science, and religion—was Vichian in the sense that Sorel utilized and accepted the validity of ideas gleaned from a highly original, and not uncritical, interpretation of Vico's work. Consequently, a Vichian interpretation of action, science, and religion permeated the work of Sorel, and accordingly his Marxism cannot be correctly understood without reference to

Vico's ideas. It has to be added, however, that Sorel was always an eclectic thinker and that Vico and Marx were by no means the sole intellectual influences upon his work.

Sorel's earliest writings, written before he became acquainted with the work of either Vico or Marx, disclosed in embryo questions and themes that he was to develop in subsequent works. *Le procès de Socrate*[1] elucidated the "heroic" morality around which Sorel's later moral thinking was to gravitate; the *Contribution à l'étude profane de la Bible*[2] affirmed the central place of belief in the miraculous for religious faith; the various articles published in the *Revue philosophique*[3] and the *Annales de philosophie chrétienne*[4] set out a scientific methodology based upon a rejection of Cartesianism and an acceptance of experimentation, cautious progress, and the claims of tradition.

There can be little doubt that Sorel's earliest writings on Marxism[5]—from 1893 to 1896—represented a distinct phase in the development of his thought. In an initial flush of enthusiasm Sorel adopted a position that he himself was later to describe and repudiate as one of "Marxist orthodoxy."[6] "I take the theories of Marx," he wrote, "for the greatest innovation introduced into philosophy for many centuries...all our ideas must be organized from now on around the new principles put forward by scientific socialism."[7] Marxism alone, he asserted, was able to provide the correct means of approaching and solving questions scientifically, and it was the only theory that could legitimately claim to contain an "exact, absolute science of economic relationships."[8] He was

[1] G. Sorel, *Le procès de Socrate* (Paris: Felix Alcan, 1889).

[2] G. Sorel, *Contribution à l'étude profane de la Bible* (Paris: Auguste Ghio, 1889).

[3] G. Sorel, "Sur les applications de la psycho-physique," *Revue philosophique de la France et de l'Etranger,* XXII (1886): 363-75; G. Sorel, "Le calcul des probabilités et l'expérience," *Revue philosophique de la France et de l'Etranger,* XXIII (1887):50-66; G. Sorel, "De la cause en physique," *Revue philosophique de la France et de l'Etranger,* XXVI (1888): 464-80; G. Sorel, "Sur la géométrie non-Euclidienne," *Revue philosophique de la France et de l'Etranger,* XXXI (1891): 428-30.

[4] G. Sorel, "Les Fondements scientifiques de l'atomisme," *Annales de philosophie chrétienne,* XXV (1891-92): 577-94; XXVI (1892): pp. 5-32; G. Sorel, "La physique de Descartes," *Annales de philosophie chrétienne,* XXVI (1892): 200-17; G. Sorel, "Deux nouveaux sophismes sur le temps," *Annales de philosophie chrétienne,* XXVII (1892-93): 243-63, 301-15.

[5] See especially G. Sorel, "Science et socialisme," *Revue philosophique de la France et de l'Etranger,* XXXV (1893): 509-11; G. Sorel, "La fin du paganisme," reprinted as *La ruine du monde antique* (Paris: Rivière, 1933); G. Sorel, "L'ancienne et la nouvelle métaphysique," reprinted as *D'Aristote à Marx* (Paris: Rivière, 1935).

[6] G. Sorel, "Avertissement," for the 1st edition, *La ruine du monde antique,* op. cit., p. xix.

[7] G. Sorel, *D'Aristote à Marx,* op. cit., p. 94.

[8] Ibid., p. 96.

certain that Marxism was "a science based upon facts"[9] and that all its conclusions were "deduced, scientifically, from observation."[10] Principally, Marxism appealed to Sorel as a doctrine that had escaped the influence of metaphysics and that fully appreciated the claims of science; as a philosophy that did not rely upon subjectivist theories of knowledge and that was capable of achieving an objective understanding of reality.

What is clear is that Sorel's initial acceptance of the scientific status of Marxism had important implications for his work. Firstly, in accepting that Marxism, as science, was able to go beyond "specific circumstances" in order to reveal what was 'fundamental behind appearances,'[11] Sorel concluded that Marx had been able to extrapolate the laws that explained and "determined" economic development. Secondly, Sorel's belief that Marxism was able to provide an objective understanding of reality, that there was an exact correspondence between science and nature, led him to adopt a position that came close to epistemological monism and, thereby, to disclaim the pluralism that had been implicit in his original elucidation of scientific method. Thirdly, Sorel's enthusiasm for "scientific socialism" involved the condemnation of the subjective and, hence, inadequate epistemological foundations of religious faith. Defense of the central place of the miracle in religious faith was superseded by a view that saw religion as either a positive threat to the progress of society or as a complete irrelevance. Finally, as Sorel was imbued with the notion of Marxism as science, it was in the field of ethics that Marxism added least to Sorel's ideas. The "heroic" morality of *Le procès de Socrate* was replaced by a limited number of ethical principles that Sorel believed could be derived from contemporary industrial practice. Taken together, Sorel's indiscriminate acceptance of Marxism as science involved him in a fundamental revision of the positions taken in his pre-Marxist writings.[12]

It is also beyond doubt that the greater familiarity with the writings of Marx that resulted from the desire to clarify their meaning produced an awareness on Sorel's part of certain difficulties in Marx's

[9] Ibid., p. 132.

[10] Loc. cit.

[11] Ibid., p. 113.

[12] Sorel himself later said that his first studies of Marxism revealed "the inexperience of a beginner"; G. Sorel, 'Avertissement' for the 2nd edition, *La ruine du monde antique*, op. cit., p. xxi.

exposition of his argument. In the numerous articles published in *Le Devenir social*[13] Sorel, like many subsequent critics of Marx's work, sought to assess the correct status to be attached to Marx's "laws" of capitalist development. In order to avoid the charge of "fatalism" Sorel was obliged to restrict severely their applicability and generality. It was at this point—as Sorel first detected the inadequacies of Marxist orthodoxy—that he turned to Vico.

Sorel published his "Etude sur Vico"[14] at the end of 1896. At this time Vico's ideas were virtually unknown in socialist circles in France, but through Marx's footnote in *Capital* Sorel had become acquainted with his work.[15] It is not difficult to perceive why Sorel was attracted to Vico's ideas. Marx's footnote had indicated the possibility of writing a history of technology upon the basis of principles derived from Vico's work, and Sorel quickly realized that Vichian philosophy was a repudiation of his subjectivist adversary, Cartesianism. However, although Sorel believed that Vico's ideas provided the foundation for a modern conception of science,[16] "Etude sur Vico" was not principally undertaken as an analysis of Vico's rejection of Cartesianism and its consequences.

"Great men," Sorel wrote, "have the good fortune that their errors are fertile and merit being studied with the greatest care."[17] Consequently, while Sorel felt that Vico's notion of the ideal history— with its reliance upon providence, determinist implications, and lack of empirical basis—had to be rejected,[18] he saw in Vico's recognition that history was not to be regarded as a series of discrete empirical data, but as possessing an "identity of substance,"[19] an outstanding contribution to human understanding.

Vico perceived this identity of substance, Sorel argued, to be a consequence of the existence of *"laws of succession* which defined the evolu-

---

[13] See especially G. Sorel, "Superstition socialiste," *Le Devenir social,* I (1895): 729-64; G. Sorel, "Progrès et Développement," *Le Devenir social,* II (1896): 193-207.

[14] G. Sorel, "Etude sur Vico," *Le Devenir social,* II (1896): pp. 785-817, 906-41, 1013-46.

[15] See P. Ungari, "Vico et Sorel," *Archives de philosophie,* 40 (1977): 267-81; E. Kamenka, "Vico and Marxism," in G. Tagliacozzo (ed.), *Giambattista Vico: An International Symposium* (Baltimore: Johns Hopkins University Press, 1969), pp. 137-43; A. Pons. "Vico and French Thought," in G. Tagliacozzo, op. cit., pp. 165-85.

[16] G. Sorel, "Etude sur Vico," op. cit., pp. 809-17.

[17] Ibid., p. 906.

[18] Ibid., pp. 786-809. In "Was man von Vico lernt," published two years later, Sorel was more explicit. "A very large part of the *New Science,*" he wrote, "is worthless; the principle of the ideal history in the sense to which Vico subscribed can no longer be understood. The *corsi* and *ricorsi* are non-existent": G. Sorel, "Was man von Vico lernt," *Sozialistische Monatshefte,* II (1898): 270.

[19] G. Sorel, "Etude sur Vico," op. cit., p. 912.

tion through which the human intellect passed in a uniform manner from emotional and irrational origins to the intelligible and the scientific."[20] It was impossible, Sorel argued, to accept, as Vico had, that such psychological evolutions took place *en masse* within a society and that once completed they could only recur if the whole historical process began again. Rather, Sorel thought, "we have a tangling up of evolutions, which are not susceptible to any definition, because at a given instant we find them in all the stages of their development."[21]

Vico's "ideogenetic law" that ideas were profoundly influenced by the practices of political life had also to be supplemented by an awareness of the importance of the economic conditions of the various classes, the social relationships between these classes,[22] and by what Sorel considered to be another "ideogenetic law": the role of the family as the primary source of our moral values.[23] Despite these reservations Sorel believed that Vico was substantially correct in asserting that history had to be understood as the history of human ideas[24] and that ideas themselves were to be comprehended through a knowledge of the "laws of psychology" that governed their evolution.[25] Vico also correctly perceived that history had to be seen as a human creation—"it is this conception of the construction of history by man that constitutes the original part of the work of Vico,"[26] Sorel wrote—and, therefore, that the historian ought to concentrate his attention upon what was "specifically human," namely, ethics.[27]

Further, in Vico's emphasis upon class struggle,[28] in his awareness that such struggle could take the form of either an attempt to gain control of the State or to invert the class structure,[29] in his stress upon the importance of the development of juridical principles in class conflicts,[30] and in his reflections upon the development of morality[31] and

[20] Ibid., p. 911.
[21] Loc. cit.
[22] Ibid., pp. 906, 911.
[23] Ibid., p. 925.
[24] Ibid., p. 814.
[25] Ibid., p. 912; "It seems to me," Sorel later wrote, "that the great merit of Vico was to have been more aware than any of his predecessors of the importance of psychological laws"— G. Sorel, "Préface pour une oeuvre nouvelle," *Table Ronde*, 12 (1948): 2132.
[26] G. Sorel, "Etude sur Vico," op. cit., p. 786.
[27] Ibid., p. 1018.
[28] Ibid., p. 931.
[29] Ibid., p. 939.
[30] Ibid., p. 1046.
[31] Ibid., pp. 919-30.

the "logic of imagination,"[32] Sorel saw insights of extraordinary fecundity.

It is noticeable that at the time of writing "Etude sur Vico" Sorel saw in many of these issues Vico's work as a precursor of that of Marx, as an elucidation of an approach to the analysis of human behavior that Marx, with the benefit of perspectives gained through the emergence of industrial technology, was to develop to the full. Sorel also clearly saw Vico's work as a storehouse of novel ideas that, if not completely correct, contained sufficient veracity to provide considerable illumination for the modern mind. Certainly, Sorel was to return frequently to Vico's work for guidance and inspiration, and as he did so, it was increasingly as a corrective to defects, deficiencies, and lacunae that he discerned in Marx's work.

This was most immediately visible in Sorel's discussion of scientific method. As we have already seen, Sorel had readily accepted the scientific status of Marx's work. Marx's theories, Sorel asserted in that context, had been established according to the principles of "la Science rationelle."[33] In the exposition of scientific method contained in "Etude sur Vico" Marx had not even been mentioned. Rather, Sorel had proceeded to elucidate a definition of the epistemological status and methodological practice of science that he felt could be derived from principles to be found in Vico's work. It was this definition of both the status and practice of science—not that derived from Marx—that informed all of Sorel's subsequent writings on the subject.

At the very basis of this Vichian conception of science was a distinction between what Sorel termed "artificial nature" and "natural nature." Principally this distinction arose from the Vichian epistemological criterion that we can only have knowledge of what we have made ourselves: *verum ipsum factum*. It followed that the only form of scientific knowledge we could acquire was that which man had made himself; man would create his own world; it would be an artificial creation. Knowledge of "natural nature" was an impossibility; it did not make sense to talk about acquiring such knowledge. Accordingly there was a need for a fundamental revision of our conception of the ties that connected science to reality. Strictly speaking, Sorel argued, there were no ties at all.

[32] Ibid., p. 1020.
[33] G. Sorel, *D'Aristote à Marx*, op. cit., pp. 96-97.

When we carry out an experiment we do not imitate nature; we employ our own schemes, our own tools; we seek to produce movements which will never be realized in the cosmic world. An experiment is therefore a creation; it belongs completely to the artificial environment; it is at one and the same time fact and truth... We can never truly know the cosmic world; but we can know the artificial world because we create it.[34]

It was incorrect, therefore, to suppose that there was an identity between science and nature.

Several points arise from this. It is important to realize that Sorel had always been conscious that scientific knowledge was in some sense "artificial." He had originally become aware of this through the work of Claude Bernard[35] and Franz Reuleaux.[36] Yet Vico's epistemological criterion of *verum ipsum factum* was crucial to the development of his thought. Both Bernard and Reuleaux, while acknowledging that science involved the imposition of a man-made order upon nature, still retained a realist conception of science. Vico's equation of the man-made with the known effectively broke the connection between science and nature, thereby providing Sorel with the foundation of a conventionalist conception of science. Accordingly the distinction, derived from Vico, between "artificial nature" and "natural nature" informed Sorel's later approval of the conventionalist conception of science presented by Poincaré[37] and the pragmatism of William James.[38]

It also had implications for Sorel's assessment of the epistemological status of Marxism. The attraction of Marxism had been that it claimed to provide knowledge that Sorel now considered to be unattainable— namely, an objective study of reality, a knowledge of what was "real" behind appearances. What, then, was to become of Marx's "laws" of

[34] G. Sorel, "Etude sur Vico," op. cit., pp. 816-17.

[35] C. Bernard, *Introduction à l'étude de la médecine expérimentale*, (Paris: J. B. Baillière, 1865).

[36] F. Reuleaux, *Cinématique* (Paris: F. Savy, 1877).

[37] G. Sorel, "Les préoccupations métaphysiques des physiciens modernes," *Revue de Métaphysique et de Morale*, XIII (1905): 859-89.

[38] G. Sorel, *De l'utilité du Pragmatisme* (Paris: Rivière, 1921). The importance that Sorel attached to this distinction and the place occupied by Vico in his conception of pragmatism is best illustrated by the following statement: "Vico," Sorel commented, "denies to man the possibility of possessing a science of what he has not made. It does not seem that this insight of genius has had a notable influence upon the development of modern thought; but I consider that the time has come to develop the system of Vico"—G. Sorel, *De l'utilité du Pragmatisme* (Paris: Rivière, 1928), p. 336.

capitalist development? Initially, Sorel argued that they had to be seen as excessively abstract generalizations that had enabled Marx to understand the essential principles of capitalism. Marx, he felt, was dealing with an imagined "homogeneous capitalism" that bore little relationship to the more complicated "real capitalism."[39] Subsequently Sorel redefined Marxism as "social poetry"[40] and then as "social myth."[41] Deprived of their scientific validity, the central tenets of Marxism became, for Sorel, sources of nonrational human motivation whose primary value lay not in their empirical veracity but in their ability to inspire men to action. It was in this guise that Marxism was to figure in Sorel's most famous works.[42] Marxism, as befitted its new status as "social myth," was no longer even considered as a possible guide to scientific method.

The connotations of the distinction between "artificial nature" and "natural nature" extended further. In terms of science it meant that Sorel placed himself firmly on the side of experimentation in both the factory and the laboratory and that he rejected all theories that claimed to possess an all-embracing, nonexperimental knowledge of the natural world. It also implied that a definitive knowledge of the phenomena that make up the natural world was impossible. Science had to be seen as being infinite: The most appropriate approach for science, therefore, was one of methodological pluralism. It is obvious that such an account of the epistemological status and methodological practice of science is open to the charge of engendering subjectivism. Sorel was aware of this possibility and went to considerable lengths to prove that this was not the case. In doing so he drew once again upon ideas derived from his reading of Vico.

In the epistemological differences between Descartes and Vico Sorel placed himself firmly on the side of Vico. Descartes' "appeal to individual sentiment, this pretension to reconstruct by personal effort that which previous generations had had so much trouble in building,

[39] G. Sorel, "Sur la théorie marxiste de la valeur," *Le Journal des Economistes*, XXX, (1897): 222-31; G. Sorel, "Die Entwickelung des Kapitalismus," *Sozialistische Monatschefte*, I (1897), pp. 544-47.

[40] G. Sorel, "Préface," to N. Colajanni, *Le Socialisme* (Paris: Giard et Brière, 1900); reprinted in G. Sorel, *Matériaux d'une théorie du prolétariat* (Paris: Rivière, 1919), p. 199.

[41] G. Sorel, "Conclusions aux 'Enseignements sociaux de l'Economie moderne,'" *Le Mouvement socialiste*, XVI (1905): 294.

[42] See especially G. Sorel, *Réflexions sur la violence* (Paris: Rivière, 1908); G. Sorel, *La Décomposition du marxisme* (Paris: Rivière, 1908).

seemed to Vico the means of destroying all science."[43] Science, despite being the creation of an "artificial nature," would perish if it became a subjectivist fantasy. It was not sufficient that science should be able to claim one's personal intellectual support: It was a social activity. One thing struck Vico strongly, Sorel wrote: "science was not born yesterday, it had a history behind it."[44] Past scientific activity defined scientific procedure. "It would not therefore be intelligent," Sorel wrote, "to neglect the authority of tradition."[45] In other words, in Vico's repudiation of Cartesian skepticism, in his consequent emphasis upon the acquisition of knowledge as a social activity and the importance of tradition in this procedure, Sorel felt it possible to accept the equation of the knowable with the man-made and yet avoid the charge of subjectivism. He felt that Vico had provided the foundation of a thoroughly modern conception of science. "It is interesting," he reflected, "to establish how little modern thought has been able to add to the argument of Vico."[46]

The impact of the epistemological distinctions that Sorel derived from Vico was not limited to his extensive writings on scientific method: Indirectly it had crucial implications for Sorel's considered assessment of the status of religious faith. In his treatment of this theme Sorel was to draw heavily upon a series of ideas and perspectives taken from Vico, and in doing so he was to abandon his hostility to what he had regarded, under the influence of "scientific socialism," as the subjectivist premises of religious faith.

Fundamental to this change of position was Sorel's recognition that the progress of science was not incompatible with religious faith.[47] This crucial argument—crucial in the sense that it underpinned Sorel's pluralism—rested largely upon an assessment of the epistemological principles of science that Sorel had drawn from Vico. The most important feature of this assessment was the argument that science could only acquire knowledge of "artificial nature"; it said nothing of the "nature of things." As the scientist was denied knowledge of the essence of

[43] G. Sorel, "Etude sur Vico," op. cit., p. 812.

[44] Loc. cit.

[45] Ibid., p. 813.

[46] Ibid., p. 817; see also G. Sorel, "Vues sur les problèmes de la philosophie," *Revue de Métaphysique et de Morale*, XVIII (1910): pp. 605-6.

[47] See especially G. Sorel, "La crise de la pensée catholique," *Revue de Métaphysique et de Morale*, X (1902): pp. 523-51; G. Sorel, 'La religion d'aujourd'hui', *Revue de Métaphysique et de Morale*, XVII (1909): 240-73, 413-47.

phenomena, so science could provide no conclusions that challenged or refuted religious faith. There are, Sorel concluded, "no decisive arguments for or against the miracle: one accepts or rejects it upon the basis of deep-seated conviction, over which science has no influence."[48]

Sorel's admission of the legitimacy of religious belief reflected, therefore, the modification of his views on science away from the position that he had adopted in his original characterization of Marxism as science in 1894. He thereby provided an assessment of the significance of religious faith that was unlike anything to be found in the work of Marx. Nowhere was there any suggestion that Sorel, like Marx, regarded religion as a false view of the world. No attempt was made to unmask the religious illusion. Consequently, unlike Marx, Sorel did not conclude from his analysis of religion that there was a need for a revolution in the social conditions that produced that illusion. Furthermore it is impossible to attribute this difference of approach to possible ignorance of Marx's work on Sorel's part. He had been on the editorial board of *Le Devenir social* when it published Marx's "Critique de la philosophie de droit de Hegel."[49] It was in this piece that Marx described religion as "the opium of the people" and in which he employed with full force the arguments that he had derived from Feuerbach's *The Essence of Christianity*. The considerable disparity of approach becomes intelligible once the importance to Marx of Feuerbach's religious criticism is realized and when it is perceived that *The Essence of Christianity* is correctly located on the radical wing of a tradition of biblical scholarship—associated with D. F. Strauss, F. C. Baur, Albrecht Ritschl, and Adolf Harnack—that Sorel had despised from the outset: liberal theology.[50] The anthropological approach to religious studies employed by this tradition lent itself to the development of a thoroughgoing atheism. It was this strand of the tradition that Feuerbach and, indirectly, Marx belonged to, and which Sorel, with the aid of Vico, rejected entirely.

In his writings Sorel made many criticisms of this primarily Protestant tradition of biblical scholarship. He felt, for example, that it was

---

[48] G. Sorel, "La crise de la pensée catholique," op. cit., p. 537.

[49] K. Marx, "Critique de la philosophie de droit de Hegel," *Le Devenir Social,* I (1895): 501-15.

[50] *Contribution à l'étude profane de la Bible* was primarily an attack upon the assumptions of this tradition. This critique was continued in "La crise de la pensée catholique," "La religion d'aujourd'hui," and, on a larger scale, in *Le Système historique de Renan* (Paris: Jacques, 1905-1906).

motivated by the desire to destroy religious faith itself, and he remained extremely skeptical of the claims made on behalf of its historical method. Essentially, however, Sorel objected to what he saw as its inability to comprehend the character of religious faith. Given Marx's adherence to a Feuerbachian analysis of religion he could only possibly conceive of religious faith as a form of alienation, but the tradition as a whole was obliged to erase the essentially religious aspect of religion and reduce it to the probable and the possible. Here again Sorel felt that Vico had something to offer. For Sorel, Vico's cyclical theory of decline and rebirth, the *ricorsi,* seemed an adequate explanation not only of the initial emergence of Christianity but also of its continued survival and intermittent rejuvenation.

If one looks closely at Sorel's work, one will notice that despite his at-times open hostility toward the Church and his attachment to Marxism as science, he never denied the importance of belief in the miraculous for religious faith. At no time was the central thesis of *Contribution à l'étude profane de la Bible* rejected. Sorel's acceptance of Vico's notion of the psychological evolution of the human intellect from primitive and irrational beginnings toward intelligible and scientific modes of thought reaffirmed and reinforced his adherence to this position. As we saw in our analysis of "Etude sur Vico," Sorel accepted the accuracy of Vico's description of the development of the human intellect, though he argued that the level of that development could be found at various stages within a society at any one time. This enabled Sorel to accept not only the reality of nonscientific modes of thought—of which belief in the miraculous was an example—but also that such modes of thought could exist at any stage in a society's development. This argument had clear implications for any attempted assessment of the probable future and durability of religious faith. Writing in "Y-a-t-il de l'utopie dans le Marxisme?", for example, Sorel argued that

> In our very complex societies all products of human nature exist in a state of combination. We have seen that Marx thought that religion must disappear in the face of science: experience hardly confirms this view. Religions always find elements of rejuvenation in the mystical. If it is true that on the one hand they develop from sentiment to intellectualism, on the other hand they re-create themselves continuously—so much so that at every period the various stages of rejuvenation and decomposition are mixed.

What is so true for religion is true for every other manifestation of psychological activity.[51]

The central place of the miraculous in religious faith could therefore be affirmed by Sorel, this time within the context of Vico's notion of the psychological evolution of the human intellect. Most importantly, this aspect of religious faith, given Sorel's rejection of what he took to be the determinist implications of the "ideal history," could reappear at any time; therefore, unlike Marx, Sorel was led to conclude that religious faith was not about to disappear.

Vico's theory also offered Sorel an insight into the original character of Christianity itself. Inspired by Vico's notion of *ricorsi,* Sorel characterized early Christianity as a work not of reflection but of instinct. The early Christians thought mythically. They were austere, heroic, capable of pure revolt. The Christian community remained immune from the impurity of the corrupt civilization that surrounded it. Above all, early Christianity was the beginning of a new age, the rejuvenation of a dying civilization.[52] It was that original force and strength of Christianity that liberal Protestant and Catholic theology and even more so Marxism could not understand and that, in seeking to dispel what Sorel took to be the core of religious faith, they sought to destroy forever. It is interesting to reflect, however, whether a reinterpretation of early Christianity in terms of the mythical beliefs of a primitive people was not in fact as destructive of the Christian faith as an attempted rationalistic explanation of religious phenomena. Sorel himself seemed unaware of this possibility. In his opinion the beauty of his own method—and of Vico's—was that it left religious faith intact. It should also be noted that all the qualities ascribed to early Christianity were subsequently attributed by Sorel to the emerging syndicalist movement.

Vico, then, provided Sorel not only with the basic epistemological criterion that justified an acceptance of a duality between science and religious faith, but also an insight into the character and strength of

[51] G. Sorel, "Y-a-t-il de l'utopie dans le Marxisme?" *Revue de Métaphysique et de Morale,* VII (1899): 173-74; see also G. Sorel, *Le système historique de Renan* (Geneva: Slatkine Reprints, 1971), pp. 74-77, and G. Sorel, "La science et la morale," in *Questions de morale* (Paris: Alcan, 1900), p. 6.

[52] G. Sorel, *le Système historique de Renan* (Geneva: Slatkine Reprints, 1971), pp. 187-208, 459-69.

religious faith and the religious mind. Implicit in this was a rejection of the philosophical monism of Marx.

In Sorel's writings on politics the impact of Vico is less noticeable, but equally profound. While in this instance Sorel did not deny the value of the views put forward by Marx, he utilized ideas taken from Vico in order to supplement those of Marx, to fill in what he regarded as "lacunae," and also as a corrective to some of the excesses not only of "orthodox" Marxists but also of Marx himself.

Sorel, as we have already seen, quickly perceived the problems engendered by Marx's "laws" of capitalist development. Marx's historical materialism, Sorel wished to assert, implied neither rigid determinism nor fatalism. In the preface to the French edition of Antonio Labriola's *Essais sur la conception matérialiste de l'histoire*—written simultaneously with the publication of "Etude sur Vico"—Sorel argued that Marx was fully aware of the potentialities of human action, and in this, Sorel implied, he occupied a position similar to that of Vico.[53] In a slightly earlier review of Labriola's book Sorel was more specific about this similarity. Historical materialism, he argued, "applied in the strictest sense the rule of Vico: 'the world of civil society has been made by men' (*le monde social est l'ouvrage des hommes*)."[54] This essentially untenable position provided the term of what was ultimately to be a reinterpretation of Marxism on Sorel's part.

Sorel fully recognized the practical as well as theoretical significance of what he took to be the restoration of human action to the central position it had held in Marxist theory. In place of the determinism of "orthodoxy" the emphasis necessarily had to fall upon the political, moral, and economic development of the proletariat. Socialism was as much dependent upon the psychological evolution of the working class as it was upon the perfection of the productive forces of capitalism. If Marx had not sufficiently recognized the "psychological part," Sorel argued, it was only because "few had comprehended the treasures contained in the work of Vico."[55] It was this basic idea that informed Sorel's later syndicalist writings.

The elucidation of this position involved Sorel not only in the introduction of morality into his own conception of historical materialism

[53] G. Sorel, "Préface," to A. Labriola, *Essais sur la conception matérialiste de l'histoire,* (Paris: Giard et Brière, 1897), pp. 5-11.

[54] G. Sorel, review of "A. Labriola, Del materialismo storico," *Le Devenir social,* II (1896): 762. This point was restated in G. Sorel, review of "A. Fouillée, Le Mouvement positiviste et la conception sociologique du monde," *Le Devenir social,* III (1897), p. 178.

[55] G. Sorel, "La necessità e il fatalismo nel marxismo," *La Riforma sociale,* VIII (1898), p. 728.

but also, it could be argued, into that of Marx himself. Ethics, Sorel now argued, played a crucial, if largely unrecognized, part in Marx's work. In order to establish that this was the case, Sorel was obliged to argue— upon the most slender evidence—that Marx saw socialism primarily as an ethical movement. What Sorel considered the ethical principles substantiated by Marx to be need not detain us; the point is that, given their paucity, Sorel attributed to Marx concepts he had first discerned in his study of Vico.[56] This was most noticeable in Sorel's assertion of the juridical nature not only of the class struggle[57]—Marx, Sorel argued, following Vico, saw the class struggle not as a simple clash of interests but as the occasion upon which each class outlined distinct juridical conceptions—but of socialism in general. The whole idea of the juridical nature of socialism was elucidated in an article entitled 'Les Aspects juridiques du Socialisme.'[58] For Sorel, the development of juridical notions among the working class meant the elaboration of a rigid code of behavior, the growth of an internal moral discipline. Without mentioning Vico by name, Sorel presented an account of the process of *ricorsi* in which he argued that the psychological evolution of the human intellect from instinct to reason was also accompanied by the development of juridical notions. Keeping faith with his earlier voluntaristic interpretation of Vico's "ideal history," Sorel thought it quite possible that the working class might fail to complete the process of psychological, and therefore juridical, evolution. It might yet remain in the domain of instinct. But there can be no doubt that Sorel saw the advance of socialism in terms of the attainment of the highest stage of Vico's *ricorso*: human action guided by the laws of conscience, reason, and duty.[59]

At the very minimum, therefore, Sorel's knowledge of Vico arguably increased his understanding of the fundamental place of human action in the making of history, enabled him to comprehend the importance of the psychological as well as economic evolution of a society, and also gave rise to his notion of the juridical nature of socialism. Each of these ideas was to be of critical importance in Sorel's reformulation of Marx-

---

[56] Sorel also turned to the austere morality of Proudhon.

[57] G. Sorel, "L'Ethique du socialisme," *Revue de Métaphysique et de Morale,* VII (1899): 286-87; G. Sorel, "La crise du socialisme," *Revue politique et parlementaire,* XVIII (1898): 602, n. 3.

[58] G. Sorel, "Les Aspects juridiques du Socialisme," *La Revue socialiste,* XXXII (1900): 385-415, 558-85.

[59] Ibid., pp. 389-94.

ism away from the conception of a predetermined economic collapse awaiting capitalism toward the voluntaristic conception of a moral catastrophe facing bourgeois society.

Yet the impact of Vico did not end there. Sorel's reinterpretation of Marxism involved an implicit acceptance of the fact that even though it provided an adequate explanation of the advance of capitalism—Marxism, Sorel argued, was a form of "Manchesterianism"[60]—it failed to explain how the proletariat would achieve its moral and intellectual development or "consciousness" in the manner that Marx had imagined.[61] Marx, Sorel argued, "revealed himself to be more backward as a man of action than he was as a philosopher."[62] Given Sorel's rejection of economic determinism, it is not surprising that he believed that ideas did not depend exclusively upon economic conditions: They also depended upon the "ineluctable psychological laws" discovered by Vico.[63] What Vico, unlike Marx, could provide was not only an account of why men acted but also an explanation of how they acquired new ideas and sentiments.

According to Vico, Sorel wrote in "Le Syndicalisme Révolutionnaire," a *ricorso* only takes place "when the popular soul returns to a primitive state, when everything is instinctive, creative and poetic." Socialism, Sorel added, "could not claim to renew the world if it did not take the same form."[64] In Sorel's opinion revolutionary syndicalism did take that form, and it is within this framework that he placed both the strike and the notion for which he is most widely known, that of myth. For example, Sorel argued that "each notable strike can become a partial *ricorso*";[65] it was capable of "rejuvenating" the socialist idea and of engendering "the sentiments of heroism, sacrifice and union."[66] Likewise, Sorel argued that theories arose out of "bourgeois reflection," were the products of a society that had reached "the highest level of intellectualism." As such, they ought to be thrust aside by the syndicalist, who should rely upon "instinct."[67] The theories associated with

[60] G. Sorel, "Idées Socialistes et Faits Economiques," *La Revue socialiste*, XXXV (1902): 519-31; G. Sorel, *La Décomposition du marxisme*, op. cit., pp. 43-48.

[61] G. Sorel, "Conclusions aux 'Enseignements sociaux de l'Economie moderne,'", op. cit., pp. 292-93.

[62] G. Sorel, *La Décomposition du marxisme*, op. cit., p. 50.

[63] G. Sorel, "Préface" to F. Peloutier, *L'histoire des Bourses du Travail* (Paris: Schleicher, 1902), p. 32.

[64] G. Sorel, "Le Syndicalisme Révolutionnaire," *Le Mouvement socialiste*, XVII (1905): p. 273.

[65] G. Sorel, "Conclusions aux 'Enseignements sociaux de l'Economie moderne,'" op. cit., p. 298.

[66] G. Sorel, "Le Syndicalisme Révolutionnaire," op. cit., p. 276.

[67] Ibid., pp. 273-74.

Marx's "catastrophic" conception of the collapse of capitalism gained their value solely in this context, as "social myths," sources of inspiration that encapsulated the essence of socialism.[68]

Vico's "psychological laws," therefore, enabled Sorel to perceive that men would only act if they were inspired by clearly defined images or myths, and that the moral and intellectual development of the proletariat would result from instinctive, heroic action.

It would be possible to continue exploring the numerous ways Sorel utilized the ideas of Vico and Marx. Sorel, for example, even spoke of the "literary *ricorso*" brought about by Rousseau's "barbarism"![69] But from this brief discussion it is possible to draw certain conclusions. There can be little doubt that the discussion of the writings of Vico and Marx occupied a central position in Sorel's work from the middle of the 1890s until his death in 1922. During this period he continuously revised his interpretation and application of their work. An examination of this process shows that the initial predominance of Marx in Sorel's work was short-lived and that from "Etude sur Vico" onward he turned increasingly to Vico's ideas for inspiration. We have seen that in two of the most important areas of Sorel's thought—his analyses of science and of religion—he utilized ideas taken from Vico to the exclusion of those of Marx. In his writings on politics and ethics Sorel supplemented Marxist theories with a whole series of Vichian perspectives. In the last analysis Marx was of value for Sorel because he alone had correctly analyzed the mechanisms of capitalism and because the "catastrophic conception" of the collapse of capitalism contained in his writings encapsulated the essence of socialism. Two final points arise. Firstly, it is interesting to note that while Sorel's original adherence to Marxism as science involved him in the repudiation of his earliest writings, the Vichian notions he subsequently adopted were quite compatible with them. Once again he was able to espouse an heroic morality, a pluralistic science, and the legitimacy of religious belief. Secondly, while we have been concerned primarily to assess the comparative influence of Vico and Marx upon Sorel, it is also the case that by doing this we have been able to broaden the picture that has normally been presented of Sorel's work. Sorel is no longer perceived solely as the disillusioned syndicalist. He was, among many other things, preoccupied with the issues and problems posed by science and religion.

---

[68] G. Sorel, "Conclusions aux 'Enseignements sociaux de l'Economie moderne,'" op. cit., p. 294.

[69] G. Sorel, "Jean-Jacques Rousseau," *Le Mouvement socialiste*, XXI (1907): 517-18.

Human Sciences and Philosophy of History Between Vico and Marx
Paolo Cristofolini

(Croce, Labriola, Sorel, and "Philosophy of History")

I

Croce's 1911 essay on Vico contains a statement that has a central significance for his approach and is, in my opinion, still acceptable. Croce maintains that Vico's achievement cannot be understood as "what is called a philosophy of history."[1] It should be recalled in this context that Croce's criticism of "philosophy of history" is derived from Labriola, as it most evidently appears from the first of the essays published in *Materialismo storico ed economia marxistica;*[2] and Labriola had been giving impulse and suggestions since the start of Croce's toils on Vico.[3]

In his movement from Labriola to Vico the early Croce comes to identify two main features of what should be eliminated from philosophical thought under the label of "philosophy of history." (Croce's exposition gradually gains in clearness and systematic thoroughness, until it reaches its final state in chapter IV of *Teoria e storia della storiografia.*) The first of those features is the claim to describe "universal history" (let's call it feature A); the second is apriorism, i.e., the claim to deduct historical development on the strength of natural or mechanical necessity (let's call it feature B). Taking his early stand under the influence of his dialogue with Labriola, Croce sees Marxism, first, and Vico's philosophy, later, as two bodies of thought that are both immune from the taint of "philosophy of history." There is, however, a dif-

---

[1] B. Croce, *La filosofia di G. B. Vico* (Bari, 1911), pp. 145-46.
[2] B. Croce, "Sulla concezione materialistica della storia," *Atti dell'Accademia Pontaniana di Napoli* (1896): see *Materialismo storico ed economia marxistica,* 3rd ed. (Bari, 1918), pp. 10-11.
[3] Cf. A. Labriola, *Lettere a Benedetto Croce 1885-1904* (Naples, 1975), p. 355.

ference in point of view: So far as Vico is concerned, the test of immunity is the absence of feature A,[4] which appears in all evidence to entail also the absence of feature B, although this is never explicitly asserted; on the other hand, Croce admits Marxism to be immune from feature B[5] in the wake of Labriola's *Saggi,* where the concept of "morphological prevision" was the theoretical tool that legitimated a nonaprioristic interpretation of the kind of historical prevision implicit in Marx's "tendency law." Later, Croce's judgment will be fully reversed, again with feature B as the only criterion,[6] and even Labriola's "morphological prevision" will be summarily rejected.[7] In any case Croce will always refrain from evaluating Marxism by the standard of feature A.

Such one-sidedness and imbalance in Croce's evaluations of Vico and Marx, which are worth noting because of the ideological unrest they betray, make a comparison between the two thinkers based on Croce's judgments on them practically impossible. Nevertheless, they should not deter us from working on this comparison with the tools used by Croce in his attacks against the "philosophy of history." If a preliminary but cogent test for this comparison is to be achieved, we shall have to take both A and B into account with reference to both authors, guarding against the delusion or rhetorical device of proceeding *as if* the two features mutually implied or excluded each other.

II

We have already hinted that Croce's attitude toward "philosophy of history" and his early treatment of Marxism were both influenced by Labriola or, to say the least, congenial with Labriola's thought. However, for what concerns Croce's analysis and overall evaluation of Vico, on the one hand we may well register Labriola's granting a certain (by no means unqualified) approval for his having grasped the core of Vico's philosophy within the framework of "a new Philosophy of the Spirit";[8] on the other hand, we must notice that Croce neither appropriates nor develops in any way Labriola's stimulating view of Vico as forerunner of Morgan, a view that he could not but find altogether foreign and uncongenial. In Labriola that was never much more than a

[4] Croce, *La filosofia di G. B. Vico,* p. 145.
[5] Croce, *Materialismo storico ed economia marxistica,* p. 11.
[6] B. Croce, *La storia come pensiero e come azione* (Bari, 1938), p. 137.
[7] B. Croce, *Filosofia e storiografia* (Bari, 1949), p. 274.
[8] Labriola, *Lettere a Benedetto Croce,* p. 355.

rough draft; still, it showed that the themes of ethnological research
could be given ready reception by Marxists (whose interest for Morgan
had been aroused by Engels's famous book[9]); significantly, it was just on
this ground, from inside Marxism, that the theoretical relevance of
Vico's *Scienza Nuova* was coming to the forefront. In Labriola's thought
two components were closely linked together: (a) the rejection of the
tendency, which he detects in philosophies of history, to see a teleological design in history,[10] and (b) the ability to pinpoint and appreciate in
their full worth those moments in modern thought that were leading to
a conception of history as "a process which man achieves by himself, as
it were by a succession of experiments, a process which is a discovery of
language, religions, manners, and law."[11] Hence the positions of Vico
and Marx were linked together in Labriola's thought, but with certain
links that are mainly identifiable within the modern development of
the sciences of man; and Morgan was chosen precisely as the typical
representative of such development.

We should also consider another interpretation that predates Croce's
work on the author of *Scienza Nuova*—Sorel's *Étude sur Vico* (1896).[12]
Sorel wished to see his study discussed by Croce, but, at least publicly,
the latter did not devote to it anything more than a passing reference
fifteen years after its publication.[13] Actually, Sorel's general attitude to
Vico was utterly unacceptable to Croce. Sorel had seen in Vico's "ideal
history" a weak point, something that had to be discarded, being vitiated by apriorism and deriving its ancestry from the Platonic superim-
position of ideas onto facts. A whole series of thinkers, from Plato and
Polybius to Machiavelli and Vico, were guilty of this kind of apriorism,
in Sorel's view; in Labriola's and Croce's terms they had fallen into
"philosophy of history."[14] If we relate Sorel's interpretation to the way in
which Michelet (a source Sorel held in great esteem) had introduced
Vico into France, i.e., with the translation published under the title
Philosophie de l'histoire (a work complementary indeed with the *Discours*

[9] F. Engels, *Der Ursprung der Familie, des Privateigenthums und des Staats. Im Anschluss an Lewis H. Morgan's Forschungen* (Stuttgart, 1884). On Vico as a forerunner of Morgan see A. Labriola, *La concezione materialistica della storia* (Bari, 1965), p. 46; and *Lettere a Benedetto Croce*, p. 72, 74. See also the remarks by N. Badaloni in his introduction to G. B. Vico, *Opere filosofiche* (Florence, 1971), p. lvii.
[10] Labriola, *La concezione materialistica della storia*, p. 80.
[11] Ibid., p. 46.
[12] Labriola, *Lettere a Benedetto Croce*, p. 196.
[13] Croce, *La filosofia di G. B. Vico*, p. 306.
[14] G. Sorel, "Etude sur Vico," *Le devenir social*, II, 10 (1896): 786-87.

sur l'histoire universelle), we shall notice that one of the main traits of Croce's interpretation of Vico is to be seen actually in its remoteness from the French tradition, which, either to extol Vico or to blame him, had imposed upon his work both features (our *A* and *B*) distinctive of a philosophy of history.

Thus, in the very stage when he was developing his coherent critique of "philosophy of history," Croce was actually pursuing a line of research that had originally been proposed by Labriola. So much can be said for what concerns philosophy of history, the interpretation of Vico, and the interpretation of Marx. In the meantime Croce was developing his own general idealistic framework, in the course of which he would take leave from Labriola precisely on the theme of the natural sciences of man, which were for Labriola, but were not any more for Croce, a constant prerequisite for dealing with the three problems we have mentioned above.

All the same, the neat, complete break Croce had accomplished with Sorel's interpretation emphasizes how close Croce—this early Croce, at least—was to another prerequisite of Labriola's Marxism, i.e., the primacy of the factual. It was on the strength of this prerequisite that Sorel's evaluations of Vico and Machiavelli could not be accepted. We cannot ascribe the features of the "philosophy of history" to Machiavelli, not only because feature *A* is simply absent from his thought, but also because feature *B*, which Sorel had thought to detect in Machiavelli's acceptance of the Polybian pattern of ἀνακύκλωσις , is tempered by his appeal to the "effectual reality of things" and to human activity, to the extent that the whole science of politics comes to be identified by him with the science of the counteracting devices that human *virtue* can successfully employ to escape (even in the long run, as shown by the examples of Sparta and Venice) from the natural inevitability of the cyclical decay of commonwealths. This is not the place for an analysis of these aspects; moreover, a vast bibliography is already available. It will be enough to stress that when Sorel brings Vico and Machiavelli together, against the common setting of apriorism and Platonism, he is disregarding Machiavelli's appeal to reality and Vico's principle of *verum ipsum factum*. These traits were, on the contrary, appreciated by Marx[15] (before Labriola and Croce) so far as Vico is concerned, while in regard to Machiavelli it is only fair to acknowledge

---

[15] K. Marx, *Capital,* I, chap. XIII, n. 89.

that, within Marxism, the rediscovery of the Florentine secretary by Gramsci[16] stems from the important hints offered by Croce.

The guidelines provided by Croce allow us therefore to include among the philosophies of history not only universal histories in the manner of Bossuet, but also Michelet's version of the *Scienza nuova*, while they absolutely do not extend to Machiavelli and Vico. We have noticed indeed how unilateral and unsatisfactory is Croce's handling of his own guidelines when he comes down to individual cases, and we have pointed out that Croce's reversal of his own early evaluation of Marx arouses serious suspicions of being ideologically motivated. Croce's evaluation of Vico should therefore be submitted to further verification, and the comparison between Vico and Marx cannot be established without referring to Antonio Labriola, Croce's Marxist source, who gave such comparison a plausible foundation.

III

Such a foundation is given by the sciences of man (anthropology and ethnology), which in Vico's times were still in the stage of a slightly developed embryo. In the background of Vico's conception of man lies a whole set of controversies, spanning the fields from anthropology to theology, on issues such as the Preadamites and the origin of the Americans, which had divided European scholars for two centuries. Vico can hardly be credited with anything more than an approximate, secondhand awareness of La Peyrère's work,[17] yet it is on the debate about Preadamites that Vico's remarks about the "conceit of nations" came to be grafted, as the mature response to an issue that had finally reached a definitive shape. Vico's remarks rest on a comparative method of inquiry, which was in sharp contrast with the method, based on the assumption of the primacy of one people, that sought to deduce the universal history of all peoples from the primacy of that one.

Vico's overt critique is directed against the Chinese, Egyptians, Chaldeans, and Scythians; Jews are excepted, and their priority in time is acknowledged. Nevertheless, Bossuet's scheme is utterly overthrown.[18] Vico's comparative method of historical inquiry turns on the pivot of axiom XIII, where the providence that operates naturally, i.e., imma-

---

[16] See A. Gramsci, *Quaderni del carcere* (Turin, 1975), pp. 1567-76.

[17] Cf. F. Nicolini, *Commento storico alla Seconda Scienza Nuova* (Roma, 1949 and 1978²) p. 35.

[18] See especially: Vico, *Opere filosofiche* (Firenze: Sansoni, 1971), pp. 412, 432-33.

nently, is assumed to be the source of the "common sense of mankind" and consequently of the "common ground of truth" that must exist for "uniform ideas originating among entire peoples unknown to each other." Thus, once the histories and traditions of different peoples have been purged from that transient and inessential fallacy, the Ptolemaic presumption of each people's own centrality (a presumption rooted in sheer "ignorance," according to axiom I), these same histories and traditions convert themselves into precious sources of genuine knowledge.

This outcome could be reached by Vico by virtue also of La Peyrère's attack against monogenism, and of the vast controversy concerning the *Preadamitae*—a controversy recorded, for instance, in Bayle's Dictionnaire—with the result of giving to the polygenetic thesis a far wider audience than the narrow circle of the readers of the condemned book. In regard to that controversy Vico did not rank himself with orthodox monogenism (although he allowed a priority in time to Jews), nor could he in a strict sense be said to side with La Peyrère (although he assumed Adam to be the first of the Jews, and in the second *Scienza Nuova* he never hinted at the principle of the descent of all other peoples from Adam's seed[19]). There is indeed a passage in the *Scienza Nuova* that endorses monogenism, since the biblical notion that all peoples descend from Noah's sons is accepted; yet we find on the same page that Vico conceived of a difference between Jews, who "had a right-sized body from the beginning of the world," and "Gentiles," who were descended from *giants*.[20] It is precisely in passages such as this that the true presupposition of the "new science" comes forth—that is to say, the distinction between the ideal or mythical point of beginning of the world and of man, and the point (not mythical any more, but an object of scientific inquiry) where "the nations as well as the sciences" trace their "beginning": This point cannot be found in the misty regions of theology, but only by exploring the "peoples' public necessities or utilities."[21]

We may therefore conclude that Vico accepts La Peyrère's challenge and gives further development to the most viable hints it offered. The ideological dispute about Adam is set aside (not for reasons of pru-

---

[19] Adam is merely called by Vico the first (*principe*) of the Hebrew people (*Opere filosofiche*, p. 410) and sometimes of the whole of mankind (pp. 384, 735), but he is never regarded as forefather or called with a correspondent appellative.

[20] Vico, *Opere filosofiche*, p. 384.

[21] Ibid., p. 411.

dence alone), and other issues concerning the nature and method of the sciences of man, of philology and comparative linguistics (whose exactitude La Peyrère had already urged against Grotius[22]), come to the forefront. In Vico the varieties of mankind and the lack of communication among peoples throughout the genesis and development of natural law are such that every conception of universal history and law that links (in Bossuet's manner) the brotherhood of all men with the assumption of a common forefather,[23] is placed outside the territory that the new science sets out to explore. A remark made by Bertrando Spaventa in 1875 is relevant on this point: "Antidarwinian philosophers might find themselves in the same predicament against Darwin as a follower of Bossuet would against Vico."[24] In Vico, more than a century before, we can see Darwin's placid and wise prediction fulfilled in advance: "before long, the dispute between the monogenists and the polygenists will die a silent and unobserved death."[25]

IV

The attitude underlying Labriola's suggestion of a link between Vico and Morgan is not very dissimilar from that which prompted Spaventa to his comparison between Vico and Darwin: In both instances we meet with the historiographic bias of an age for which the search for forerunners, even far remote in time, was standard practice.

In both comparisons, however, there is a rational core, which consists of the discovery in Vico of the broad outlines of a science of the evolution of the human forms of life. If we analyze the new science into its structural components, we shall be able to detect a recognition (very advanced for its age) of the interplay between constants and variables. The constants are the natural foundation on which the process takes place (necessity and utility), the direction according to which it moves (providence), and its cyclical rhythm (*corsi e ricorsi*); the variables are the circumstances of time and place by which the different histories of different peoples are conditioned. The *New Science* is enabled to grasp

[22] Cf. *Systema ex Praeadamitarum hypothesi* (s.l., 1655), pp. 246-48 (the work was printed as anonymous at Amsterdam). See also H. Grotii, *De origine gentium americanarum dissertatio altera* (Paris, 1643), p. 15.

[23] See J.-B. Bossuet, *Politique tirée des propres paroles de l'Ecriture sainte*, I, 3d proposition.

[24] Cf. A. Savorelli, "Un frammento inedito di Bertrando Spaventa su Vico e Darwin," *Bollettino del Centro di Studi Vichiani*, IV (1974), p. 175.

[25] See Darwin, *The Descent of Man* (London, 1871), vol. I, p. 235.

such a variety by means of the tools offered by philology, linguistics, physics, etc.; and by applying the comparative method to these disciplines it can interpret the multiplicity of histories and weld them together into a synthesis of ideal eternal history by means of the constants or general laws. Two metaphysical residues are left over, providential finalism and the primacy of a particular history, the history of Jews; but, in spite of such metaphysical residues, Vico applies to the history of Jews the same tools of inquiry and the same comparative method he holds valid for other histories.

If what we have sketched above is Vico's scheme, we cannot but recognize in it some traits common to the type of scientific rationality which is distinctive of nineteenth-century evolutionism.

V

Marx, however, seems to use Vico's hints not so much to establish a continuity between Vico and Evolutionism, but rather to go beyond Darwin's perspective.

The theme in Vico that has attracted Marx's attention is relevant to one of the *Capital*'s crucial points, and is recalled by Marx in connection with Darwin. It is the distinction between natural history, which is not made by man, and human history, which is made by man.[26] But in Marx's view the growth of technology is a historical fact of such significance that by virtue of it man-made history comes progressively to erode the realm of the other history, which was previously impervious to human intervention. Vico's conception of the *verum-factum* is thus for Marx a source of stimulation and a guiding rule even beyond Darwinism.

Returning to the pattern of constants and variables which we have shown above to be a distinctive mark of Vico's thought as well as of evolutionism, we may interpret the widening of the realm open to human activity in the form of technology, as a widening of the realm of variables, while the limits of the necessary process are retreating. We have before us the contrary of that "necessitarian" version of Marxism that held sway in the second International, and the contrary of the prophetic caricature of Marx that obtained credit and currency in Cold War culture.

[26] See now L. Krader, "Evoluzione, rivoluzione e Stato: Marx e il pensiero etnologico," *Storia del marxismo. I. Il marxismo ai tempi di Marx* (Turin, 1978), pp. 213-44.

We shall give here but one example of Marx's attitude—the epistolary discussion with Engels in August, 1866, about Trémaux's book,[27] which they received with contrasting evaluations. The terms of their disagreement are well known[28]: At his first reading Marx found in the book, in spite of "all its flaws," "a remarkable advance in respect to Darwin," because, among other things, it gave a "natural foundation" to passages from one stage to another in human evolution, by ascribing to soil the role of decisive factor.[29] Engels answered, in two successive rounds,[30] with such a savage criticism of the book's flaws that Marx could not but virtually drop the subject altogether; but not before justifying his undoubtedly hasty enthusiasm, by pointing out those traits that to a reader like him, if not to the author of the book, suggested a significant advance in respect to Darwin so far as the interpretation of human progress was concerned. He wrote on that occasion: "although Trémaux does not consider the historical modifications of the influence of soil (while I include among them even the chemical mutations wrought upon the earth's surface by agriculture etc., and the different influence which things such as coal veins exercise in different modes of production), yet his fundamental conception of the influence of soil is in my opinion an idea which only needs to be stated to gain admission into science, once and for all, and without considering at all how Trémaux has stated it."[31]

The most relevant part in this quotation is the passage within brackets, which has little if any relation to Trémaux, apart from the hint that Marx found in it. The problem Marx is coping with here is that of giving room to the rationality of the variables, within a view of historical evolution that embraces Darwinian naturalism and assumes a model based on the interplay between constants and variables. According to Marx, in Darwin variables occur casually; in any case they do not admit of any explanation.[32] Trémaux's suggestion, which should be historically connected with a long French tradition, going back to Bodin and Montesquieu, that emphasized the influence of climate and

[27] See the Marx-Engels correspondence, Aug.-Oct. 1866. The work in question is: P. Trémaux, *Origine et transformations de l'homme et des autres êtres* (Paris, 1865).

[28] For a critical view on Marx's lecture of Darwin, see the recent essay by B. Naccache, *Marx critique de Darwin* (Paris, 1980).

[29] Marx to Engels, Aug. 7, 1866.

[30] Engels to Marx, Aug. 10 and Oct. 5, 1866.

[31] Marx to Engels, Oct. 3, 1866.

[32] Marx to Engels, Aug. 7, 1866.

soil upon history and civilization,[33] induces Marx to consider here the dynamics of human intervention, modifying nature through the use of technique and the employment of resources; an intervention that shows itself to be a modifying factor of nature and of man himself at the same time.

It is in such a context that the distinction Marx so much appreciated in Vico, between a history we make and a history we do not make, can be restated in a form that widens the scope of the former, man-made history.

Out of a self-imposed restraint we shall not venture further in our research of the lines of continuity between Vico and Marx: Apparently the part played by human intervention in forming the variables that Marx sees at work in the historical process lies outside the range of Vico's intuitions; or, in other words, "the realm of liberty" is wider in Marx than in Vico. Nevertheless, those intuitions, exactly because of the way in which they guide the comprehension of the historical process toward freeing itself from the fetters of the "philosophy of history," within the rigor of a unitary reading of the historical process, amply justify Marx's and Labriola's recalling of the *New Science* and their admiration for its author.

Translated by Onofrio Nicastro.

---

[33] See L. Febvre, *La terre et l'évolution humaine*, 3d ed. (Paris, 1949), pp. 2-8.

Vico and the Crisis of Marxism

B. A. Haddock

Serious discussion of Marxism developed rather later in Italy than in the other advanced countries of Western Europe. Whether this lack of interest should be attributed to the relative backwardness of large-scale industry in Italy or to the hostility toward Marxism displayed by the followers of Mazzini and Bakunin or to the preoccupation with national politics in Italy in the 1860s and 1870s is beyond my present concern. The point to stress, however, is that by the time Marx's ideas began to be discussed in the 1880s, Marxism had already become an orthodoxy; and though the orthodoxy had an international flavor, with its much vaunted synthesis of English, French, and German ideas, it had developed independently of Italian traditions.

The first attempts to popularize Marxist ideas in Italy were altogether unhappy. In Loria's various accounts Marxist ideas are presented within the broad framework of the evolutionary positivism associated with Darwin and Spencer, which enjoyed a passing popularity in Italy.[1] And though Loria had pillaged certain of Marx's texts, it can scarcely be claimed that his works fulfilled the basic expository role which was the precondition of an informed discussion of Marxism in Italian intellectual circles.

It was not until Antonio Labriola set himself the task of explaining the genesis of socialism and its leading doctrines, both in his lectures at the University of Rome and in his writings of the 1890s, that discussion

---

[1] See Achille Loria, *La rendita fondiaria e la sua elisione naturale* (Milan: Hoepli, 1880); *La teoria economica della costituzione politica* (Rome: Bocca, 1886); and *Analisi della proprietà capitalista* (Rome: Bocca, 1889). There is an important discussion of Loria's ideas in Benedetto Croce, "Le teorie storiche del prof. Loria," first published in *Devenir social* (1896), and now reprinted in his collection of essays, *Materialismo storico ed economia marxistica* (Bari: Laterza, 1961), pp. 23-56. For a discussion of the general cultural background to the years of positivist supremacy see Benedetto Croce, *Storia d'Italia dal 1871 al 1915* (Bari: Laterza, 1943), pp. 133-51.

of Marxism acquired a firm foundation in a detailed knowledge of Marx's texts.[2] And it is here, precisely where a distinctive Italian Marxist tradition emerges, that the story of Vico's influence begins. Labriola had turned to Marxism relatively late in life, but he had been familiar with Vico through the teaching of Bertrando Spaventa since his student days at the University of Naples in 1861. At this stage of his career, under Spaventa's influence, he regarded himself as a Hegelian, though he remained suspicious of attempts to construct closed metaphysical systems. It was the tendency toward a priorism, and the failure to accommodate the richness and variety of historical experience, that led Labriola to reject Hegel. But he was still intent upon seeing history as a "whole" and had little interest in the fragmented view of the past that was implicit in the approach of philologists, antiquarians, and "professional" historians who refused to allow their attention to be diverted from the narrow field of their special studies. The aim of historical studies was not to acquire an ever-increasing store of detailed knowledge but to understand man as an agent acting in an artificial sphere of institutions and customs that successive generations had fashioned to meet the exigencies of life. Positivism, though it had a theoretical commitment to realism, could not fulfil a unifying role because it failed to make a connection between general evolutionary schemes and detailed historical research. Instead, Labriola turned to Herbart and associationist psychology; but it was Vico who enabled him to establish a link between the theory and practice of history. In 1871 he delivered an important set of lectures on Vico, and Vico would loom large in his later lectures on philosophy of history.[3] When he finally adopted Marx-

---

[2] Labriola's most important writings on Marxism of this period have been collected in Antonio Labriola, *La concezione materialistica della storia,* ed. Eugenio Garin (Bari: Laterza, 1976). For biographical details and a thorough survey of Labriola's ideas in the various phases of his career see Luigi Dal Pane, *Antonio Labriola: La vita e il pensiero* (Bologna: Forni, 1935). Croce's personal account of the genesis and demise of Marxism in Italy is important for the light it sheds on his relationship with Labriola. See Benedetto Croce, "Come nacque e come morì il marxismo teorico in Italia (1895-1900)," in *Materialismo storico ed economia marxistica,* pp. 279-322. See also Benedetto Croce, *Storia d'Italia dal 1871 al 1915,* pp. 153-171. The details of the relationship between Labriola and Croce are considered in Edmund E. Jacobitti, "Labriola, Croce, and Italian Marxism (1895-1910)," *Journal of the History of Ideas,* XXXVI (1975): 297-318. There is a clear summary of Labriola's ideas for the English reader in Leszek Kolakowski, *Main Currents of Marxism,* trans. P. S. Falla (Oxford: Clarendon Press, 1978), vol. II, pp. 175-92.

[3] An outline of the lecture course, "Esposizione critica della dottrina di Vico," is reproduced in Luigi Dal Pane, *Antonio Labriola: La vita e il pensiero,* pp. 508-10. See Dal Pane's comments, pp. 125-28.

ism in the 1890s, he had thoroughly assimilated a theory of history that
he regarded as an improvement upon the abstract ideological schemes
associated with Hegel and Comte. The novelty of his view of Marxism
can be seen in the attempt to interpret historical materialism as the
culmination of a realist theory of history which had been implicit in
much nineteenth-century reflection on philosophy and science.

It should not be supposed that Labriola's studies of Marxism took the
form of an exposition of a fixed and finished doctrine. Too much
contemporary Marxist writing, in his view, repeated the mistake of
idealist metaphysics, reducing the intricate problem of historical development to the terms of an abstract system. For Labriola, Marx represented an advance upon Hegel precisely because he kept the study of
history rooted in concrete experience. If, instead, Marx's writings were
regarded as a definitive philosophy containing final solutions in the
fields of politics, economics, and history, then Marxism itself would
simply become yet another ideology, instructive in its way as a testimony
to a passing mode of thought but without lasting scientific value. In
trying to retain an openness to experience Labriola firmly believed that
he was remaining true to the spirit of Marx's writings. "Our doctrine
does not profess to be the *intellectual vision* of a grand plan or design,
but is only a *method* of research and understanding. Not by chance Marx
spoke of his discovery as *a guiding thread.*"[4] And, of course, Engels had
repeated in a stream of letters toward the end of his life that Marxism
should not be regarded as a substitute for historical research but rather
as a new method that would direct historians to hitherto neglected
fields in their interpretations. In his defense of Marxism against both
its ideological opponents and its narrow-minded defenders Labriola
believed that he was pursuing a line of enquiry that had been specifically indicated by Marx and Engels. "...in our doctrine it is not a
question of translating all the complicated manifestations of history
into economic categories, but it is only a matter of explaining *in the last
resort* (Engels) every historical fact *by means of the economic substructure*
(Marx)..."[5] When the so-called "crisis of Marxism broke," and his own
writings were cited as an example of the dissension that had beset the
Marxian camp, Labriola reacted with a mixture of outrage and dis-
belief.[6]

---

[4] Antonio Labriola, *La concezione materialistica della storia,* p. 85.
[5] Ibid., p. 70.
[6] See ibid., pp. 291-302.

Such feelings are not difficult to understand. Labriola's essays on historical materialism had initially been published thanks to the encouragement and editorial effort of Croce. Indeed, Labriola had come to regard Croce as something of a follower; and Croce records how his interest in theories of history had been sustained by conversations with Labriola.[7] Croce's flirtation with Marxism, however, was brief. While Labriola had expected a further elaboration and refinement of his own arguments to emerge from Croce's studies, Croce was instead led to write a series of essays that were sharply critical of the Marxist theory of history. His two most important essays on Marxist theory in fact took the form of detailed comment on Labriola's ideas.[8] And when Croce's essays attracted international attention, Labriola had the mortifying experience of seeing his own views considered alongside those of Croce as a contribution to the criticism of Marxism. Labriola was at pains to point out that his position was "diametrically opposed" to Croce's.[9] The debate between them, however, is especially instructive for students of Vico and Marx. Both men had been familiar with Vico before they gave their attention to Marx.[10] The attempt to read Marx within the broad terms of the Italian tradition had a lasting impact on the history of Marxism. And their polemical exchange serves to highlight some of the central problems encountered in fashioning a science of society.

Labriola's emphasis on *praxis* as the kernel of the doctrine of historical materialism distinguishes his version of Marxism from many that were current in his day. Suspicion that a determinist theory was incompatible with a view of the freedom and dignity of man had done much to discredit Marxism. But Labriola had long regarded the contrast between free will and determinism as false. His early studies of Spinoza had sought to show how an adequate understanding of the forces that impel men to action was in fact a necessary condition for speaking of freedom at all.[11] The real contrast was not between free will and determinism but rather between a conception of human conduct as arbitrary

[7] For details see Benedetto Croce, "Come nacque e come morì il marxismo teorico in Italia (1895-1900)."

[8] See Benedetto Croce, "Sulla forma scientifica del materialismo storico," in *Materialismo storico ed economia marxistica*, pp. 1-21; and "Per la interpretazione e la critica di alcuni concetti del marxismo," ibid., pp. 57-114. The essays were first published in 1896 and 1897, respectively.

[9] Antonio Labriola, *La concezione materialistica della storia*, p. 292.

[10] Croce had first read the *Scienza nuova* in 1892. See Benedetto Croce, *Contributo alla critica di me stesso* (Bari: Laterza, 1945), p. 24.

[11] See Luigi Dal Pane, *Antonio Labriola: La vita e il pensiero*, pp. 19-25.

(and hence unintelligible) and a view that demonstrated how a given
course of action was intelligible in specific circumstances. In Spinoza,
of course, the circumstantial constraints on conduct are not historically
specific. But Marx (in Labriola's interpretation) had successfully
shown how man was both the creature and the creator of his environment, satisfying his needs through a (more or less elaborate) technology which involved a system of institutions for production and
distribution and a corresponding set of ideas that both explained and
justified such institutions. It is not that technological changes are
always the determining factor behind changes in ideas and beliefs;
rather, economic conditions and prevalent ideologies shared the common form of artificial creations in the struggle for subsistence against
niggardly nature. "History is made by man, in so far as man can create
and perfect his tools, and with such instruments he is able to create for
himself an artificial environment, which then reacts upon him in complicated ways, and thus, as it modifies him, is both the occasion and the
condition of his development."[12] Here is a distinction between human
history and natural history that recalls both Vico and Marx.[13] And if
commentators have sometimes found it difficult to reconcile Marx's
various references to men making their own history with the more
deterministic tone of the preface to *A Contribution to the Critique of
Political Economy,* for Labriola no such problem existed. The need to
work, and the consequent emergence of specific social relationships,
was a theme that unified Marx's apparently disparate writings.

It is important to stress that Labriola did not regard historical research as a confirmation of a theory that Marx and Engels had elaborated in schematic form. The historian was intent upon writing a
narrative account of the past, and while he might have resort to the
resources of psychology, sociology, economics, and statistics in order to
make his account as plausible as possible, these disciplines would always
remain (from the historian's point of view) subordinate instruments of
research. Historical materialism, too, shared the status of a set of
generalizations that might inform a narrative but that did not have
independent theoretical value: "...the proof of its value consists exclusively in the most suitable and adequate explanation of the succes-

[12] Antonio Labriola, *La concezione materialistica della storia,* p. 76.
[13] Specifically, of course, Marx's famous footnote in *Capital* referring to Vico. See Karl
Marx, *Capital: A Critique of Political Economy,* trans. Ben Fowkes (Harmondsworth: Penguin
Books, 1976), vol. I, p. 493.

sion of human events..."[14] In other passages, however, Labriola tends to be equivocal about the methodological role of historical materialism. Thus, while insisting that the doctrine does not pretend to represent the "logic of things," he claims that it is a "realistic doctrine," which portrays historical changes in "the rhythm of their particular development."[15] On the general burden of the doctrine there is no ambiguity. Historical materialism "objectifies, and in a certain sense *naturalizes* history."[16] And this tendency toward historical realism (in Labriola's view) was precisely Vico's contribution to historical thought. In his lectures of 1871 he described Vico as having established "an historical theory (rather than a philosophy of history) based on the concept of a unique and uniform process" which "naturalizes history."[17] And in his essays he referred to Vico's discovery that "Providence does not work *ab extra* in history, but rather through the conception men have of their existence," reducing "all history to a process that man himself accomplishes through his successive efforts and which can be studied in language, religions, customs and law."[18] Marx, it seems, provided further specification and a detailed analysis (at least in the case of capitalist society) of the way historical development was fostered by the conflict of interests between classes. But it is specifically the status of Marx's substantive claims that remains uncertain in Labriola's interpretation.

If Marxism were to be seen as a heuristic device, there would be little to differentiate it from the various sociological, psychological, and evolutionary hypotheses that flourished in the nineteenth century. These, too, might be more or less useful to the historian as he fashions his accounts. But Labriola was careful to distinguish historical materialism from its major competitors in Italy—positivism and the evolutionary theories of Darwin and Spencer. Indeed, he greeted the new French edition of Enrico Ferri's *Darwin, Spencer, Marx* (1897) with scarcely disguised contempt.[19] Any such association of Marxism and positivism, in Labriola's view, disregards the fact that "socialism has its real foundation only in the current condition of capitalist society, and in what the proletariat and the remaining lower classes can achieve."[20] In

[14] Antonio Labriola, *La concezione materialistica della storia*, p. 63.
[15] Ibid., pp. 65, 66.
[16] Ibid., p. 72.
[17] Luigi Dal Pane, *Antonio Labriola: La vita e il pensiero*, pp. 509-10; see also Dal Pane's comments, p. 127.
[18] Antonio Labriola, *La concezione materialistica della storia*, p. 46.
[19] See ibid., pp. 243-45.
[20] Ibid., p. 244.

other words, Marxism is seen as a specifically class-based ideology, and any attempt to describe affinities with positivism would be futile because of the incompatible interests of the proletariat and the bourgeoisie. Labriola is steering a dangerous course here. Having taken pains to show that the theory of historical materialism (*pace* its vulgar adherents) could not be treated as an a priori criterion of truth, he proceeds to dismiss a positivist reading of Marx because such an interpretation would contradict the Marxist view that theories are class-based ideologies. This is not to say that Labriola's other arguments against positivism are not valid, especially those expressed in his elaboration of the notion of *praxis*. But it is indicative of the difficulty he found in separating the formal and substantive aspects of Marxism.

Labriola's problem is perhaps best illustrated by his criticism of the belief in so-called historical factors that seemed to inform so much "professional" history.[21] The vision of history as a complex interplay of political, economic, religious, and moral practices and beliefs, affected in different ways by various philosophical, scientific, and literary ideas, had merely fragmented our view of the past. And such a kaleidoscopic conception, far from presenting an alternative to the theory of historical materialism, could (at best) be regarded as a "semi-doctrine" that left the past as a whole unintelligible.[22] In fact, the proliferation of "points of view" from which the past might be studied was merely the corollary of the proliferation of analytical disciplines that had emerged in the nineteenth century. Each of these disciplines might be of service to the historian, but at the same time they emphasized the need for a general theory of society that would make history intelligible as a process. "The various analytical disciplines, which illustrate historical development, finally evoke the need for a common and general social science, which makes the unification of historical processes possible."[23] It was the "tendency to monism" that distinguished the special role of historical materialism.[24] Labriola was not arguing merely for the addition of a so-called economic factor to the various political, moral, religious, and philosophical factors that historians were currently emphasizing in their explanations; rather, he saw "the materialist doctrine" as the "limit" or "apex" of the unification of the past.[25]

[21] See ibid., pp. 87-96.
[22] Ibid., p. 88.
[23] Ibid., p. 93.
[24] Ibid., p. 232.
[25] Ibid., pp. 88, 93.

Historical materialism, in Labriola's interpretation, was variously a new method of approaching history, a philosophy of history that distinguished the determining factors in historical development, and a set of political beliefs to guide the proletariat in their mission to overthrow capitalist society. And it was the ease with which Marxism could fulfill this synthetic role, relating fields of inquiry that were (on the face of it) distinct, which persuaded Labriola that historical materialism held the key to a coherent theory of history and the social sciences. Marxism (as it were) provided the paradigm that would enable the more specialized disciplines to be seen within a broader context.

To Croce, however, the very search for such a synthesis was suspect. His suspicion stemmed from Labriola's failure to distinguish two quite different kinds of reflection upon history. In the traditional view "the possibility of a philosophy of history presupposes the possibility of a conceptual reduction of the course of history"; and this, in effect, amounts to the reduction of history to suprahistorical categories.[26] Marx had recognized the danger of such an approach in his criticisms of Hegelian and theological treatments of history; but though he claimed to be establishing his theory of history on empirical rather than ideological grounds, Marx himself had an a priori conception of the importance that should be attributed to the different classes of factors. This is not to say that Marx's emphasis on economic conditions might not be more realistic than the grand schemes of Hegel or Augustine; it remains the case, however, that his grounds for asserting the primacy of economic factors in all historical explanations (even if only in the "last resort") could not themselves be empirical. Labriola was aware of the danger and hence insisted that the doctrine of historical materialism be regarded as a method rather than a philosophy of history. But a method could not stipulate which factors would be most important in a given situation, much less that conflicts of a religious or philosophical sort should be seen as manifestations of contradictions in the economic substructure. Marx's exhortation to historians to pay heed to economic conditions was not based on a formal analysis of the problems of historical research but on a conception of the way historical changes actually occurred. Labriola, *malgré lui*, followed his master in error. He had used a schematic account of historical development as a criterion to guide historical research. And in this he had confused speculative philosophy of history with philosophical reflection on the practice of

[26] Benedetto Croce, *Materialismo storico ed economia marxistica*, p. 3.

history. This was a distinction Croce employed to great effect in his later works on philosophy of history. But it was stated explicitly for the first time in his critique of Labriola's view of historical materialism.[27]

Croce's distinction between a methodology of history and a philosophy of history had far-reaching implications for Labriola's position. In particular the claim that historical materialism could be summed up as a "tendency to monism" became meaningless.[28] The historian was faced simply with a concatenation of circumstances—a more or less abundant natural terrain, men arranging their lives through more or less elaborate institutions and customs, with more or less developed technological skills—and "if it is possible to reduce conceptually the various elements of reality that appear in history, and it is hence possible to have a philosophy of morals or law, science or art, and at the same time a philosophy of their connections, it is not possible to elaborate conceptually the specific complex of these elements, or rather the concrete fact, which is the course of history."[29] It is not only that Croce is rejecting Marxist monism in favor of a refurbished theory of "historical factors." Marxism, as a "macro-historical" theory, is systematically addressing itself to questions that do not arise for the working historian. When Marx wanted to establish the details of capitalist production in nineteenth-century England, he consulted the documents that would have recommended themselves to any similarly curious and diligent historian. His larger reflections on the course of historical development, hinting at the ultimate triumph of the proletariat as capitalist society collapsed under the weight of its own contradictory tendencies, were rather an imaginative portrayal of familiar facts than a contribution to a detailed understanding of economic history. The persuasiveness of Marx's teleological view undoubtedly led many historians to pay more attention to economic conditions than had previously been the case, but to the extent that his followers sought to fill in the details of the schematic account in, say, *The Communist Manifesto,* they had ceased to be historians. It is dubious to presuppose that economic factors are always predominant; the risk of distortion is merely multiplied if one has also presupposed how economic factors manifest their importance. In short, for Croce, "historical materialism is not, and cannot be, a new

[27] See ibid., pp. 2-9.
[28] See Antonio Labriola, *La concezione materialistica della storia,* p. 232; Benedetto Croce, *Materialismo storico ed economia marxistica,* p. 6.
[29] Ibid., p. 3.

philosophy of history, or a new method, but it is, and must be, just this: an addition of new data, of new experiences, that become a part of the consciousness of the historian."[30] Economic history was important, had been unduly neglected, was relevant to general treatments of political and cultural history, but, in relation to a broad account of the life of a people, presented no more than a new set of factors to be deployed together with those that historians had traditionally recognized.

By returning to a conception of history as the *Zusammenhang* of myriad forces and tendencies, irreducible to a conceptual scheme and only intelligible in a concrete narrative, Croce had rejected not only monism but also the teleological dimension of Marxism. Hence Labriola's contention that the theory of historical materialism could provide support for the political aspirations of the proletariat was seen to be groundless. "Historical materialism, divested of every remnant of finality and providential design, can give support neither to socialism nor to any other practical trend in life."[31] And with the dismissal of the conflation of theory and practice, so important for Labriola's notion of *praxis,* Croce had deprived historical materialism of the conceptual apparatus that made it a distinctive theory of history.

The view that informed Croce's criticisms had been elaborated in his *La storia ridotta sotto il concetto generale dell'arte* (1893).[32] Having defined history as "that type of artistic production which aims to represent what really happened," it followed that any attempt to see history as a part of a general science of society was merely a confusion of distinct modes of discourse.[33] Scientific methods, designed to disclose general truths, would be of little use to the historian whose concern was to make individual facts intelligible in a narrative. Since Marxism had made no contribution to historical method, and its claim to the status of a general theory of history was spurious, it could be dispatched to a museum of speculative curiosities.

It would be misleading to suggest that Croce's distinction between the spheres of science and art had been prompted by his reading of Vico. Indeed, in 1893 he still classed Vico (along with Herder and Hegel) as an exponent of a speculative philosophy of history that confused reflection on the character of historical knowledge with a

---

[30] Ibid., p. 10.
[31] Ibid., p. 17.
[32] Now in Benedetto Croce, *Primi saggi* (Bari: Laterza, 1951), pp. 1-41.
[33] Ibid., p. 36.

scheme of universal history.[34] But he found his designation of science as
the sphere of universal truths and art as the realm of particular representation confirmed by Vico.[35] More importantly, however, his distinction between two kinds of philosophical reflection on history enables a
contrast to be drawn between Vico and Marx, which is too often obscured when attention is focused on the apparent similarity of their
ideas on specific issues. While it is true that Vico and Marx share a
predilection for portraying broad lines of historical development, it
remains the case that Vico's analysis in the *Scienza nuova* emerges from
a consideration of basic methodological problems. Vico was concerned
to show precisely how historical accounts go wrong. And though his
own argument sometimes seems to take the form of an apparently
random juxtaposition of more or less perceptive obiter dicta, the full
force of his case is only appreciated when attention is given to his
treatment of methodological problems as they arise in, say, interpretations of Homer or Bodin or Dante or Roman law.[36] This is not to say, of
course, that Vico was always in control of his materials in these discussions (his shortcomings as a scholar are legendary); rather, that without
serious consideration of the often cumbersome, careless, and clumsy
accounts that form the body of the *Scienza nuova*, one is apt to forget
that Vico is presenting an elaborate historiographical theory along with
a philosophy of history. Here the contrast with Marx is clear. Croce's
case against historical materialism was precisely that it did not offer a
new method. Marx's argument might stimulate a radical reappraisal of
the importance of economic history, but it depended upon traditional
historical methods for the establishment of details. Vico, on the other
hand, was preoccupied with the problem of history. The details of the
storia ideale eterna might be of little philosophical interest in the light of
the arguments Croce had advanced against Marx, but there remained
in the *Scienza nuova* a core of what might be termed (at risk of anachro-
nism) a critical philosophy of history addressed to the activity of the
historian rather than to the pattern of the past.[37]

Nor is this the only serious disparity between Vico and Marx that the
terms of Croce's criticisms of Labriola suggest. We have seen how

[34] See ibid., pp. 21-22.

[35] See ibid., p. 23, n. 1.

[36] See B. A. Haddock, "Vico's 'Discovery of the True Homer': A Case-Study in Historical
Reconstruction," *Journal of the History of Ideas*, XL (1979): 583-602.

[37] For an important account in this vein see Leon Pompa, *Vico: A Study of the 'New Science'*
(London: Cambridge University Press, 1975).

Labriola's fusion of theory and practice is no longer tenable once the possibility of a teleological theory of history is rejected. It might seem at first glance that Vico's vision of history as an immanent development through the ages of "gods," "heroes," and "men" should share the same fate as Marx's view of history as a series of progressive phases determined by changes in the mode of economic production. But this is to forget that the *Scienza nuova* is concerned with purely theoretical problems. Vico's intention is to elaborate a theory that might assist an historian to understand the practices and conventions of different kinds of society. Having shown how the three great epochs are distinct and (largely) incompatible *Weltanschauungen,* he does not go on to use the specific conceptions of one age as a criterion to evaluate the others. Though he speaks of "fully developed human reason" in the age of men, the rationality in question has very limited practical possibilities.[38] Men are portrayed as narrow, self-seeking egoists, unable to recognize that the pursuit of their own advantage is the fundamental factor driving themselves and their societies to ruin. The relapse into barbarism fosters a simpler and purer morality, lacking theoretical sophistication but certain in its requirements and respected despite its severity. It is the antiquated notion of the *ricorso,* in fact, which ensures that the practices of one epoch will be irrelevant or unintelligible in another. Where Hegel and Marx had both seen history culminating in a qualitative change in the way men approach the world, Vico is content to describe historical development in terms of a rhythm that allows men scant practical satisfaction. Men can take pleasure in coming to understand how the hand of providence manages to sustain some form of human society or another, but they cannot transform this theoretical understanding into a practical wisdom that will enable them to escape the consequences of their own folly. Marx, on the other hand, is committed to a view of a mighty transformation that will bring "the prehistory of human society to a close" and finally make men the masters of their destiny.[39] On this issue, at least, Vico and Marx could hardly be further apart. Vico's doctrine, dominated as it is by the notion of original sin, might be less attractive to modern philosophers than Marx's promethean vision of man struggling against nature to achieve

---

[38] *The New Science of Giambattista Vico,* trans. T. G. Bergin and M. H. Fisch (Ithaca, N.Y.: Cornell University Press, 1968), par. 924.

[39] Karl Marx, "Preface to 'A Contribution to the Critique of Political Economy,'" in Karl Marx and Frederick Engels, *Selected Works* (London: Lawrence and Wishart, 1968), p. 182.

final satisfaction in a society that has cast off the last remnants of social conflict; but it nevertheless hints at a distinction between theory and practice that (formulated rather differently) has been important in recent discussions of history, political philosophy, and social theory.[40]

The problems that dominated fin de siècle discussions of Marxism, then, raise fundamental questions about the character and scope of the social sciences. Croce is perhaps unusual in that his initial association with Marxism was brief and his rejection of historical materialism involved pari passu a rejection of the very idea of a general science of society. His later essays in philosophy of history were in effect a further elaboration of the claim that the historian's role is to interpret in a narrative rather than explain through a theory. And while he could find support for this contention in his (admittedly partial) reading of Vico, Marx assumed the guise of a wrong-headed exponent of a bogus social science. Marx was committed to the view that what men supposed they were up to (at least during the "prehistory of human society") was merely an ideological reflection of fundamental contradictions in their economic arrangements. The manner in which ideas "reflected" material conditions was not itself simple, but the historian was obliged to explain away the religious, moral, aesthetic, and philosophical beliefs that constituted the ideological superstructure. There could be no understanding of agents on their own terms because their conduct was seen to be finally explicable only in relation to economic circumstances of which they were not necessarily aware. All would change, of course, with the triumph of the proletariat, when economy and ideology would be in harmony and men would see their situation aright. In the meantime, however, the history of ideas would be a history of folly and illusion.

Vico, on the other hand, despite the absurdity of some of his more fanciful speculations, was intent upon showing how the bizarre beliefs and practices of primitive peoples would be intelligible if they were seen in the proper context. Here it is not a question of one perspective, that of the triumphant proletariat, being used as a criterion to evaluate the curious beliefs that had once prevailed; rather, the point is that the social world is intelligible from various (mutually exclusive) points of view. We can understand what is meant when it is said that lightning is a

---

[40] For a further discussion of the implications of the distinction between theory and practice for Vico's political ideas see B. A. Haddock, "Vico on Political Wisdom," *European Studies Review*, 8 (1978): 165-91.

reprimand from Jove or that rivers are capricious gods without ourselves subscribing to such anthropomorphic notions. And while in our understanding of nature we might have technological reasons for preferring one set of ideas to another (if our aim is an abundant harvest, certain agricultural techniques are simply more efficient), in the moral sphere there is no criterion outside our practices to serve as an independent standard in their evaluation. Having distinguished the methods appropriate to the study of human conduct from those current in the natural sciences, Vico was content with a panoramic picture of changing modes of thought as a key to understanding the different kinds of society that fell within his purview. To hazard a pecking order of societies on moral, political, aesthetic, or indeed any grounds would be to misunderstand how the various practices of a society hung together and gave significance to actions that, taken in isolation, would appear meaningless. Specific actions are seen to be significant or trivial because of their relation to a world of assumptions that it is the historian's business to recover. By focusing on a form of society as a link in a teleological chain, Marx had effectively foreclosed the possibility of understanding a society from the "inside." Vico's endeavor to reconstruct the original significance of the dramatis personae of the earliest history is, by contrast, an attempt to come to grips with methodological problems encountered in historical research. Reflection on the past shaped the thought of both Vico and Marx, but it is Vico's concern with historical precision for its own sake, rather than as an instrumental guide to political conduct, that divides them.

In the broader context of the history of historical thought the methodological differences that separate Vico and Marx assume a larger significance. When Croce asked himself whether history should properly be regarded as an art or a science, he was returning to a problem that had dominated historical thought since the Renaissance. Where Bacon had asserted that the study of human conduct was "but a portion of natural philosophy in the continent of nature," Vico had claimed that special problems arose in the interpretation of the thoughts and deeds of men that made it impossible to reduce history to the form of a common empirical method applicable to all natural phenomena.[41] Historical materialism seemed to be a part of a general movement in the nineteenth century to establish a science of history on the basis of

[41] *The Works of Francis Bacon*, ed. J. Spedding, R. L. Ellis, and D. D. Heath (London: Longmans, 1858-74), vol. III, p. 366.

methods that had been developed in the natural sciences. In the 1890s, however, it began to be widely felt that either Marxism had been wrongly interpreted or its naturalistic emphasis was out of place in a science of society. Labriola, we have seen, saw the separation of historical materialism from positivism as one of the principal objectives of his essays, while Croce tended to regard Marxism as a contribution to a narrow economic science, more or less useful in the study of production and distribution in capitalist society, but worthless as a general social science. The "crisis of Marxism" was very much a reappraisal of the larger claims made for historical materialism. Whether or not Marxism was in fact an attempt to explain human conduct through the application of naturalistic methods is a question that must be left open here. But the terms in which the disputes of the 1890s were conducted have a general significance for students of the history of philosophy. And it is in relation to such broad questions about the proper methods for studying human conduct that Vico and Marx warrant our attention.[42]

[42] For a general discussion of the place of Vico and Marx in the history of historical thought see B. A. Haddock, *An Introduction to Historical Thought* (London: Edward Arnold, 1980), pp. 60-72, 120-34.

From Vico's Common Sense to Gramsci's Hegemony

Edmund E. Jacobitti

Devoid of any kind of sentimentality, the term "humanism" implies the study of man—man as he is, not as he ought to be, man in history as opposed to man in the abstract. The term inevitably recalls the Renaissance when, liberated from the city of God, man began, with the aid of the pagan Greeks and Romans, to study his own city. The term implies something else, too: the daring suspicion that life is without any meaning save that given it by man in history. Belief in transcendence of any kind is therefore a snare; and the meaning of life, if there is any, is to be found in the study of man, not in the study of Platonic forms, gods Christian or otherwise, or natural laws. This is a powerful thought, which not only orphans us all from the Almighty, but at the same time catapults us to center stage in his place. Orphaned all, mankind turns to its past to discover there its meaning. To know a thing, says Vico, is precisely (and only) to know how it came into being. By studying the origins of the human spirit, its development, humanists hope to discover what traditional philosophers had sought outside man and his history, had sought in the eternal and changeless.

The humanist's credo was stated nowhere so boldly as in Vico's immortal words:

> But in the night of thick darkness enveloping the earliest antiquity so remote from ourselves, there shines the eternal and never failing light of a truth beyond all question: that the world of civil society has certainly been made by men, and that its principles are therefore to be found within the modifications of our own human mind.[1]

---

[1] Giambattista Vico, *La scienza nuova seconda,* ed. Fausto Nicolini (Bari: Laterza, 1953) par. 331, hereafter designated *S.N.* My translations on the whole conform to those of Max A. Fish and Thomas G. Bergin in *The New Science of Giambattista Vico* (Ithaca, N.Y.: Cornell University Press, 1968).

All civil history therefore, and all nations, are the product of our own
ingenuity carved from the void without any model and resting then as
today upon the accumulated wisdom of the past, upon the "modifications of our own human mind." That wisdom Vico calls common sense.
A nation, the *New Science* tells us, is held together by its ethical fabric,
the moral values its citizens create and then hold and demand of each
other. Without this shared way of life, this "common sense," there would
be no nation, for it is from this common sense that a people generates
laws, institutions, magistrates, and heroes. It is from common sense, in
short, that a people, together and without guidance, narrow down the
limitless and open-ended world of human choice. "Human choice, by
its nature most uncertain, is made certain and determined by the
common sense of men." This extraordinary insight comes early in the
New Science and is followed by a definition of common sense. "Common
sense is judgment *without reflection,* shared by an entire class, an entire
people, an entire nation, or the entire human race."[2]

"Without reflection" is the key phrase here, and with it Vico made two
very important points. First, he rejected the existential void opened to
those who "with reflection" see that "the choice" a people make is, after
all, only "a" choice; second, Vico made plain that common sense without
reflection is an unconscious unity of theory and practice. In fact it is
Vico's contention, spelled out in page after page of the *De nostri temporis
studiorum ratione,*[3] that only with the dawn of the era of philosophical
reflection—thought outside of practice—did theory and practice become separated. This was particularly true in the age of the scientific
revolution into which Vico had been born. There, in that age, reason
was radically separated from practice and from common sense, with
monumental consequences reaching down to the present. This change
equated reason—sound reason, anyhow—with exactitude and science,
with physics. In so doing it preempted and dominated the entire field
of "reason." All thought that did not approach the scientific standard
was not thought at all, was mere nonsense.[4] Thus "common sense"—

[2] N.S., par. 142 (emphasis mine).

[3] See G. Vico, *On the Study Methods of Our Time,* trans. Elio Gianturco (Indianapolis: Bobbs-
Merril, 1965).

[4] A glance through the literature and scholarly journals of modern social science, with
their charts, graphs, and cryptic formulae, reveals the heritage of the scientific and Cartesian
revolutions. The modern social scientist aims at rising above the value-laden terminology of
ordinary language or common sense to arrive at the supposedly value-free world of the
modern physicist. Thus Talcott Parsons opened his *The Social System* by noting that "it is
possible to treat such...a system in the scientific sense and subject it to the same order of

which treats of matters that are not, and cannot be made to be, exact, but are more important than those that are exact—was removed from the camp of reason altogether, demoted to the level of the nonrational, the "common sense" of the vulgar herd. This has left social scientists with the choice of vainly pursuing precision in a field where precision does not exist or of resigning themselves to the fact that they are "merely" commonsensical.

A good deal of modern Italian thought, however, has maintained—occasionally unconsciously—the Vichian hostility to the scientific model,[5] and therefore in Italy "common sense"—or "culture," as Francesco De Sanctis called it—is still held in esteem and seen as the true foundation of a nation. For this school of thought "religion," whether sacred or secular, "faith," "culture," and "common sense"—the *superstructure* of a nation, as Marx called it—are all seen as the true *structure*

---

theoretical analysis which has been successfully applied to other types of systems in other sciences."—*The Social System* (New York: Free Press, 1964), p. 3. Likewise, A.J. Ayer chastizes those who "cherish the belief that there are some things in the world which...lie beyond the scope of empirical science. But this belief is a delusion. There is no field of experience which cannot, in principle, be brought under some form of scientific law, and no type of speculative knowledge about the world which is, in principle, beyond the power of science to give— *Language Truth, and Logic* (New York: Dover Publications, 1946), p. 48.

Hear also Heinz Eulau: "It is the function of science to understand and interpret the world, not to change it. A science of politics which deserves its name must build from the bottom up by asking simple questions....An empirical discipline is built by the slow, modest, and piecemeal cumulation of relevant theories and data. The great issues of politics, such as the conditions and consequences of freedom, justice, or authority, are admittedly significant topics, but they are topics compounded with a strong dose of metaphysical discourse. I don't think that they are beyond the reach of behavioral investigation, but before they can be tackled, the groundwork must be laid."—*The Behavioral Persuasion in Politics* (New York: Random House, 1963), pp. 9-10.

Vico reminds us of two elements here. First, our knowledge of nature is pragmatic and approximate rather than absolute. Truth is a function of knowing, *verum factum convertuntur,* and since nature was made not by man but by God, it can only be known by God. Secondly, Vico reminds us that man can know civil society for he alone has made it, but knowledge of civil society does not derive from the application of the empirical method of physics to society, but by an examination of common sense, the modifications of the human mind.

[5] Though Vico gives us the most sophisticated analysis of common sense since, say, Thucydides' *History of the Peloponnesian War,* the idea of treating the modifications of the human mind as the true determinant of a nations' history had deep Italian roots long before Vico. One need only recall Machiavelli's hostility to abstract Christian culture and his attempt to establish a "new order," which guided a nation. But Machiavelli did not spring from a vacuum. Writing of *The Florentine Enlightenment 1400-50* Professor George Holmes noted: "For masterpieces of humanist and historical writing we must wait until the days of Machiavelli and Guicciardini when the classical and native worlds are more completely fused. The essential revolution in intellectual concepts, however, is the work of this [earlier] age, not the age of Machiavelli." (New York: Pegasus, 1969), p. 167.

of the nation, the fertile soil from which all its other institutions and even its individuals spring. The value of this superstructure of "common sense" and "culture" in generating "a civil and individual conduct" as surely as the economic "structure" was keenly appreciated even by Italian Marxists. It was Antonio Gramsci who, as he sat in one of Mussolini's prisons and reflected back on De Sanctis's very Vichian definition of culture, asked (as well as answered) himself:

> But what does "culture" mean in this case? undoubtedly it means a coherent, unitary, nationally diffused "conception of life and man," a "lay religion," a philosophy that has become precisely a "culture," that is, it has generated an ethic, a way of life, a civil and individual conduct.[6]

From this idea of culture it is relatively simple to see how Gramsci proceeded to what is usually regarded as his most important insight and revision of Marxism, namely, his theory of hegemony. Hegemony is but common sense "instrumentalized" so that a minority can, without constant resort to violence, dominate the majority by *imposing upon it* a common sense. Gramsci noted that all states are repressive, that they are but the means for one group to oppress another. The idea that a state might be made up of persons with a common interest or that it is an institution in which all persons might best pursue their own self-interest was foreign to his thinking—and, for that matter, to his experience.

To Gramsci a state was divided into two spheres, the political and the civil, or the political and the "cultural," where the "political" sphere represented the brute force of the ruling class and the civil or cultural sphere represented the cultural domination—the hegemony—of the ruling class.[7] In this hegemony over civil society the ideas, values, institutions, and cultural parameters of the ruling class are imposed upon the oppressed. This hegemony is a subtle form of domination carried out in the educational system, in the arts and sciences, and in the developmental process of each citizen so that the definition of an "education," of "success," of "aspiration" is synonymous with the values

[6] Antonio Gramsci, *Letteratura e vita nazionale* (Rome: Editori riuniti, 1971), p. 20.

[7] These ideas are scattered all through Gramsci, but see in particular *Passato e presente* (Rome: Editori riuniti, 1973), pp. 217-18; *Gli intellettuali* (Rome: Editori riuniti, 1971), pp. 20-21; *Note sul Machiavelli* (Rome: Editori riuniti, 1973), pp. 171-78.

of the ruling class. The oppressed do not therefore know of their oppression: indeed, they have only two categories in which to put their lives—success or failure. This hegemony therefore effectively insulates the political sphere from criticism. Gramsci's awareness of how hegemony and culture so profoundly and unconsciously shape conduct led him to see how it also might be turned against the middle class by "hegemonizing" the proletariat with a revolutionary ethic. Thus "common sense" was here made an instrument of battle.

Gramsci acknowledged various sources for these insights. First he claimed, somewhat elliptically, to have derived the idea from Lenin's distinction between "war of position" and "war of maneuver." "War of maneuver" was equated with the revolutionary assault, the Jacobin coup d'etat, and the collapse of the *political* arm of the state. The "war of position," on the other hand, was the long, arduous struggle to destroy the middle-class hegemony over culture, over the minds of the proletariat.[8] In Russia, Gramsci said, the Bolshevik revolution was simply a war of maneuver, for the Czardom no longer had a cultural hegemony over the masses, no longer had a reservoir of public support that needed undermining. Russia, in short, was an "Oriental despotism." For that reason "hegemony" was put off until after the revolution, when the new revolutionary government turned to the task of "hegemonizing" the masses it had just liberated—turned, in short, to raising them from unconsciousness to consciousness.

In Western states, Gramsci noted, the process might have to be reversed so that the war of position would *precede* the war of maneuver. "In the East the State was everything, the civil society was primordial and gelatinous; in the West, between the State and society there was a just *rapport* and in the trembling of the State one immediately noticed a robust structure of civil society. The State was only an advanced trench behind which stood a strong chain of fortresses and casements,"[9] namely, the healthy civil society. To Gramsci this indicated the resilience of the bourgeois state, the efficacy of a hegemony that led the masses into believing that the ruling class ruled with the consent of the governed.

To deal with the question of revolution in the West, in Italy, required therefore that Gramsci go beyond Lenin's strategy for Russia. In Italy the question was how bourgeois hegemony might be broken and re-

[8] Gramsci, *Note sul Machiavelli*, pp. 94-96.
[9] Ibid., p. 96.

placed with proletarian hegemony, how the "war of position" might be waged either before, or at least in tandem with, the war of maneuver. To deepen his knowledge of hegemony in the West, Gramsci turned to thinkers in the Italian tradition. There, though there was, obviously, no example of proletarian hegemony, there were examples aplenty of bourgeois revolution and bourgeois hegemony. Thus Gramsci examined Italian thinkers like Vincenzo Cuoco, who, following the French example of 1789, had fought to replace the Italian feudal order with middle-class order. Following Cuoco he noted the nineteenth-century Italian Hegelians, who had made the bourgeois *Risorgimento*, and more recently, Benedetto Croce, dean of the Italian Idealists, who at the turn of the present century had carried out a cultural revolution of his own, an intellectual hegemony that was to make him, as Gramsci put it, the "lay Pope" of Italy.

It was to Vincenzo Cuoco that Gramsci turned first. Cuoco was a convinced Vichian—or at any rate he was convinced he was a Vichian[10] —and had made several revisions in Vico's idea of common sense that have become part of the intellectual heritage of a good many Italian intellectuals—and are reflected in Gramsci's ideas in particular. The first of these is the separation of reason from "mere" common sense, a separation that emphasized the gulf between the elite and the mass, or as Gramsci called them, the "conscious" and the "unconscious"; the second was that in a community divided between elite and mass it was the duty of the elite to guide the masses.[11]

[10] See for example Enrico De Mas, "Vico and Italian Thought," in *Giambattista Vico: An International Symposium,* ed. Giorgio Tagliacozzo and Hayden V. White (Baltimore: Johns Hopkins Press, 1969), pp. 157-61; and Edmund E. Jacobitti, *Revolutionary Humanism and Historicism in Modern Italy* (New Haven: Yale University Press, 1981), pp. 24-31.

[11] Were there two peoples in Vico's *Scienza*? Cuoco finds them in the castes of the fathers and the *famuli* (see, e.g., *S.N.,* 555-56). And if, as De Mas implies, Cuoco makes too much of the distinction— "Cuoco's Vico is pre-eminently the author of the sociology of the two peoples, a thinker for whom history is never the creation of the lowest stratum of the population (the plebeians), but is instead the work of a minority." (Enrico De Mas, "Vico and Italian Thought," in *Symposium,* p. 159)—it is not surprising after the 1799 revolution. But there were two peoples in Vico's time as well—and long before. Since at least the Renaissance there have been two peoples and two cultures in Italy, a Catholic culture and a lay humanist culture. The Catholic culture visible alongside—or below—Renaissance humanism had been strengthened by the Jesuits, among others, in the baroque era of Counter-Reformation exaggeration. The lay culture received new sustenance from the Cartesian and later Enlightenment culture, a culture that, however, steered lay thought *away* from its old Renaissance humanist base and toward French materialism and the scientific culture. Vico's *New Science* on the other hand is the true descendant of Renaissance humanism—"the world of civil society has certainly been made by men"—and as such it was opposed to both the

Cuoco's ideas developed, Gramsci saw, as a result of his experiences in the abortive revolution of the republicans at Naples in 1799, a revolution inspired by, and for that matter dominated by, the French. In 1801 Cuoco wrote an account of the failure of that revolution,[12] noting that the overwhelming majority of the population had not supported the revolt and preferred by far to be ruled by their traditional kings, priests, and feudal barons.[13] When the French armies, which had held the population at bay and had propped up the republican regime, were forced to withdraw on account of the formation of the Second Coalition, the populace fell upon the revolutionaries and made a swift and bloody end of their liberators. The hostility of the people toward the revolution, Cuoco said, came from the fact that the "common sense" of the people had been opposed to the "reason" of the philosopher-revolutionaries. The revolution had been doomed because its leaders had failed to enlist the support of the masses, failed to

---

superficial French materialism and—less explicitly, but no less emphatically—to Catholic and religious culture. The Catholic culture was on the whole a passive culture whose center of gravity lay outside this world, while Enlightenment culture, though no less otherworldly with its abstract natural laws, was an active, not to say an arrogant, culture opposed to all that man had done in history. Vico's whole work is a recognition of *these* two peoples—and a firm rejection of both of them. Vico's natural law *was* the history of man disdained by the philosophe and the Church; and Vico's god was mankind, disdained as ignorant and sinful by both philosophe and Church. That Vico made less than Cuoco of the "sociology of the two peoples" seems to stem from the fact that Vico lived before 1799 and that when he was alive the conflict was not between an inert peasantry and an elite, but between two competing elites—the aristocracy and the middle class. Vico was therefore primarily concerned with the arrogance of the middle-class Enlightenment.

[12] Cuoco, *Saggio storico sulla revoluzione napolitana del 1799 seguito dal rapporto al cittadino Carnot di Francesco Lomonaco*, ed. Fausto Nicolini (Bari: Laterza, 1913).

[13] They had not, to use Gramsci's words, been "hegemonized." Republicanism, imported from France, was totally alien to the Neapolitan common sense. The revolutionaries, fittingly enough, named their republic after Partenope, an earlier siren who also lured men to their destruction. The constitution of the republic, Cuoco noted, "is not the best....It seems to me that it is too French and too little Italian"—Cuoco, *Saggio storico*, p. 222. Indeed, as Salvatorelli put it, the constitution was "of the Roman type," complete with "archons, censors, and ephors." The population barely quieted from its huzzahs for the Holy Faith, and San Gennaro "gave but grudging approval"—Luigi Salvatorelli, *A Concise History of Italy*, trans. Bernard Miall (New York: AMS Press, 1940), p. 497. Whether too Roman or too French, it was certainly too abstract. Although Cuoco had participated in the revolution, he had early begun to suspect that the revolutionaries were too removed from the Neapolitan reality, that they intended to leap out of their own particular history and, like the Jacobins they were, start the kingdom over again with the Year I. The republicans, Cuoco said, refused to see that "the residue of customs and government of other times, which is found in every nation, is precious to a wise legislator and ought to form the base of his new order....Those that wish to destroy it, do they not see that they destroy in their way every foundation of justice and every principle of order?"—Cuoco, *Saggio storico*, pp. 220-221.

provide them with a new "common sense." Thus the revolution of 1799 was "passive," said Cuoco.

> Our revolution was a passive one, the only means of bringing it to a successful conclusion being to win over public opinion. But the views of the [revolutionaries] and those of the population were not the same; they had different ideas, different customs, and even different languages...The Neapolitan Kingdom is to be considered as divided into two peoples separated by two centuries.[14]

The cornerstone of Cuoco's thesis rested on the idea of the "two peoples," the Catholic masses, or *sanfedisti,* and the intellectual elite. The former had been "educated" by the Jesuits, the latter by the *philosophes* of France. The revolution of 1799 had proved that any sudden attempt at raising the masses to philosophy "is impossible and dangerous."[15] The elite must rule, but patiently. The "common sense" of the "common people" was, for better or worse, the unalterable foundation of the state, and any who lightheartedly tampered with what was sacred to the masses would not survive. Where "two peoples" are separated by "two languages" and "two centuries," change had to be gradual, and revolution was impossible. "Imagining a republican constitution is not the same as founding a republic.... Liberty is not established save through forming free men. Before erecting the edifice of liberty on Neapolitan soil, there were, in the ancient constitution, in the ancient customs and prejudices, in the present interests of the inhabitants, a thousand obstacles."[16] For Cuoco, therefore, "the political problem is a problem of education."[17]

When Gramsci read Cuoco, he too concluded that the political problem was one of education. Gramsci, however, was an impatient educator and aimed at telescoping the educational process. The revolution of 1799, it appeared to Gramsci, had failed because it had never attempted to activate the "passive" revolution. For Gramsci, in other words, the common sense of a people was not a given, but might *be*

[14] Ibid., p. 90. For Gramsci's remarks on Cuoco's "passive revolution" see in particular the *Note sul Machiavelli,* pp. 96-103; *Il Materialismo storico:* (Rome: Editori riuniti, 1971), pp. 261-65; *Il Risorgimento* (Rome: Editori riuniti, 1974), pp. 95-124.

[15] Vincenzo Cuoco, "Rapporto al re Gioacchino Murat e progetto di decreto per l'organizzazione della pubblica istruzione (1809), "in *Scritti vari,* ed. Fausto Nicolini and Nino Cortese (Bari: Laterza, 1924), p. 7.

[16] Cuoco, *Saggio storico,* p. 87.

[17] Dina Bertoni Jovine, *La scuola italiana dal 1870 ai giorni nostri* (Rome: Editori riuniti, 1967), p. 206.

given, even imposed. Thus, where Cuoco despaired of any attempt to use philosophy "to win over public opinion" and bridge the gap of centuries and languages, Gramsci saw this as precisely the challenge of the passive revolution. If, in short, the passive revolution could be made into a campaign of active propaganda and agitation, could not the passive revolution become the equivalent of Lenin's war of position? Could there not be "an absolute identity between war of position and passive revolution" as Gramsci had now redefined it? "Or at least [cannot] the two concepts...be identified...up to the point where the war of position becomes the war of maneuver?"[18]

The Cuoco who graduated from 1799 was prepared to see the revolution become evolution, to see it stretched out over decades, centuries. Gramsci was not. Yet if he revised Cuoco's passive revolution into a war of position/hegemony, he accepted without revision Cuoco's elitist idea of the two peoples, the view that the conscious must guide and rule the unconscious masses. Cuoco claimed to have derived the idea of the two peoples from Vico, but as Vico was quite opposed to rationalist leadership, Cuoco was simply mistaken. In fact Cuoco had reversed Vico in recommending rationalist leadership, and Gramsci accepted Cuoco's reversal. But where Cuoco had suggested that prudent leaders not unsettle the volatile masses by disturbing their common sense, Gramsci suggested the opposite course. For Gramsci common sense had no value and ought therefore to be eliminated. Common sense "is the 'philosophy of the non-philosophers,' "... "incoherent" and "unconnected.".... "Philosophy is an intellectual order which religion and common sense cannot be.... Philosophy is the critique and overcoming of common sense and...coincides with 'good sense' which is counterpoised to common sense."[19]

---

[18] Antonio Gramsci, *Note sul Machiavelli* (Rome: 1973), pp. 97-98.

[19] Antonio Gramsci, *Il materialismo storico* pp. 6, 139. When Gramsci turned to the Risorgimento, he employed there as elsewhere Cuoco's concept of "the two peoples," the one moved by theory, the other by common sense. Cuoco's analysis of the 1799 revolution should have warned the Risorgimento leaders, Gramsci said, that the masses needed to be led by the reasoned elite. Instead the patriot leaders chose to make the Risorgimento too passive a revolution, chose not to hegemonize the masses but to have a "revolution without a revolution." (See *Il materialismo storico*, p. 218.) "Vincenzo Cuoco's critical formula on the 'passive revolution' was pronounced (after the tragic experiment of the Parthenopean Republic of 1799) [and] was valuable as a warning and should have created a national will of greater energy and of popular revolutionary initiative [but] was converted into a positive conception, into a political program [which aimed at preventing a] truly popular Italian revolution, that is a radical national [revolution]." (See *Il Risorgimento*, pp. 200-201) This was the "betrayed revolution," the "missing revolution," the "*rivoluzione mancata*," which aimed, Gramsci said, at insulating a volatile population from unsettling change and restraining them in docile ignorance.

This "Leninist" separation of the "common sense" of the few from the common sense and nonsense of the many—a separation evident long before Lenin—was sharpened in the nineteenth century by the rapid diffusion of Hegelian thought into Italy. The Italian Hegelians' reverence for *Philosophie* almost automatically cut them off from mundane common sense, so that they shared, with their opponents—the heirs of the Enlightenment—the common view that between elite and mass there stretched an unbridgeable gulf. This was a result of, among other things, the nature of the *Risorgimento* process itself.

For a good part of the nineteenth century Italians struggled to create a state. They were a people at war with feudal despots, papal plots, and Austrian garrisons—but they were also, let us not forget, at war with themselves and, especially after 1848, with their own Catholicism. The *Risorgimento*, like the events of 1799, pitted the intellectual and patriotic elite, especially in the south, against an indifferent and hostile peasantry who, under "instructions" from the papacy, were hostile to the whole idea of a unified Italian state. If Pius IX was the philosopher of these hostile peasants, the "philosopher" of "common sense," then it was Hegel who was the philosopher of the patriot intellectuals.[20]

Hegel's reverence for the ascending historical process, his promise that *Philosophie* (reason) would absorb mere religion and common sense, his conviction that the highest stage of history was the nation state, all ensured for him—in stateless Italy—a warm reception among *Risorgimento* patriots. The equation of reason with the state made the opposition to the state irrational and fraudulent. In the South, where a good part of the population's common sense told them to reject the northern invaders, the Hegelians found such opposition inconceivable. Thus, when the Hegelian Bertrando Spaventa was confronted at Naples with opponents of the new *Risorgimento* state, he was stupefied, he could not believe his opponents were serious. Historical theory, reason, pointed to the nation-state, and therefore the common sense loyalty of the masses to the Church and the Bourbons must be a sham. "They have no faith in anything, [they] are not really Bourbons, nor Italians, but rogues, intriguers, thieves, charlatans, liars, adulators."[21]

---

[20] "The Italian philosophy of the Risorgimento," wrote Bertrando Spaventa, "was German philosophy. Hegel and the other earlier German philosophers were known in Naples before 1848." See Spaventa, *Opere*, vol. 3, *Logica e metafisica*, ed. Giovanni Gentile (Florence: Sansoni, 1972), p. 19. The literature on Hegelianism during the *Risorgimento* is too vast to cite here, but one should start with Guido Oldrini, *La cultura filosofica napoletana dell'ottocento* (Bari: Laterza, 1973).

[21] Bertrando Spaventa, *La filosofia italiana nelle sue relazioni con la filosofia europea, con note e appendici di documenti*, ed. Giovanni Gentile, 3rd ed. (Bari: Laterza, 1926), p. 284.

In their assault upon the religion and common sense of the ordinary man the Hegelians confirmed the subordination of common sense to Hegelian reason and made of the *Risorgimento* a revolution of the rational against the irrational, a revolution of those who understood the course of history against those who did not. The Risorgimento Hegelians had "come to feel themselves citizens of a wider world and they aimed at the reattachment of the Southern culture to the general Italian culture and also to the European culture...[They] meant to bring about the] end of a regime—and not only in the political camp. They were not men of a party...but of a new faith."[22]

It is difficult to exaggerate the impact of Hegel on Italian thought,[23] difficult, too, to exaggerate the consequent hiatus placed by Hegel's adherents between common sense and reason. A measure of how far the Hegelians had come from Vico may be gauged by noting that for the Hegelians the authors of history were the philosophers rather than the early poets. Indeed, for the Hegelians it was the simple poets who now stood in the way of historical progress. It was into this heritage that Gramsci was born.

But into another heritage too: Hegel did not survive intact in Italy, for no sooner had he arrived than, at least in this sense, was he "Vichianized." Even its most enthusiastic followers soon became aware that Hegelianism, for all its benefits in the nationalist struggle, was still a Trojan horse; for within Hegelian thought lay that enemy of Vichian immanentism, the transcendent *Weltgeist*. History to the Hegelian was not the work of man but the work of God; this view contrasted sharply with Vico's message that the "world of civil society has certainly been made by men." This was hegemony of a different kind, not of conscious

---

[22] Luigi Russo, *Francesco De Sanctis e la cultura Napoletana*, 3rd. ed. (Florence: Sansoni, 1958), pp. 26-27.

[23] It is also difficult to weigh its impact precisely. Hegelianism came to Italy not from Germany but from France in the person of Victor Cousin and in the translations of Augusto Vera. The translation of Hegel is not an easy task (see, e.g., the remarks of Guido Oldrini in *La cultura filosofica napoletana*, p. 397), and these translations in particular have received near universal condemnation. (See Guido Oldrini, "Introduzione" to *Gli Hegeliani di Napoli: Augusto Vera e la corrente ortodossa* [Milan, 1964], and Benedetto Croce, "L'Enciclopedia di Hegel e i suoi traduttori," in *Anedotti di varia letteratura* [Bari: Laterza, 1954], 4: 261-65.) The whole problem is further complicated by the fact that the police and the censors regarded (rightly) the Hegelians as revolutionaries (before 1860), and their persecutions made the writings of the Hegelians even more elliptical than normal. See, e.g., the comments of Pier Vincenzo di Luca on the amazing alliance of the Hegelians and the Mazzinians in Alessandro Casati, "Mazzini e gli hegeliani di Napoli," *La Critica*, 9 (1912): 78. On the revolutionary nature of the early Hegelians see Giuseppe Berti, "Bertrando Spaventa, Antonio Labriola e l'hegelismo napoletano," *Società*, 10 (1954): 406-30, 583-607, 764-91.

men over unconscious men—for not even the philosophers were fully conscious in Hegel—but of God and the absolute over the whole of unconscious men. Here man's primacy and responsibility were not confirmed but denied, and Hegel's transcendent vision was challenged long before Croce satirized it.[24] "I am fed up with the Absolute, the ontology, and the a priori," wrote Francesco De Sanctis. "Hegel has done me a great deal of good, but also a great deal of harm. It has been years since I read him."[25]

This immanentism, this rejection of all transcendence, constitutes the hard core of Italian philosophy and the Vichian heritage. Other aspects of Vico might be altered or, as Cuoco had done with the assigned value of "reason" as opposed to common sense, even reversed, but the immanentism and anthropological thrust remained. Man had made this civil world, and it was therefore his to remake.

Nowhere is this theme more persistently stressed than in the works of Gramsci's mentor, Benedetto Croce. Croce's intellectual "dictatorship" over Italy was an astonishing case of individual influence, and the search for any equivalent "hegemony" would send one back nearly a hundred years to Goethe's domination of German culture. "Not since Goethe," wrote H. Stuart Hughes, "had any single individual dominated so completely the culture of a single major European country."[26] Through his journal *La Critica*, through his alliance with the powerful Laterza Press,[27] and through his association with and leadership of a whole generation of discontented intellectuals, Croce was able in less than a decade to transform the culture of his country and impose upon it an idealist philosophical orientation.[28] At the turn of the century, Croce explained in 1918, "the philosopher who enjoyed the greatest fame and following in Italy was Spencer (now almost entirely forgotten) and with him many other positivists and evolutionists... My first critical affirmations therefore took the form of opposition to that disoriented, momentary, and impetuous fad."[29] Croce's presence was soon felt in every area of the humanities and social sciences. Thus Attilio Momigliano noted in 1946, "he who examines the state of stud-

[24] In Croce, *Ciò che è vivo e ciò che è morto della filosofia di Hegel* (Bari: Laterza, 1907).

[25] As quoted by Berti, p. 412.

[26] H. Stuart Hughes, *Consciousness and Society* (New York: Random House, 1958), p. 201.

[27] See Edmund E. Jacobitti, "Hegemony Before Gramsci: The Case of Benedetto Croce," *Journal of Modern History*, 52 (March 1980): 66-84.

[28] Eugenio Garin, *Intellettuali italiani del xx secolo* (Rome: Editori riuniti, 1974), p. 3.

[29] Croce, *Primi saggi*, 3rd. ed. (Bari: Laterza, 1951), p. ix.

ies in 1903 and the present state and examines their development during these forty years will see that philosophy and particularly aesthetics, literary criticism, history and historical criticism, the criticism of art, linguistics, law, have all felt the influence of [Croce]."[30] No one, not Gramsci either, was immune to Croce's influence. "I and...many other intellectuals of that period," wrote Gramsci, "you could say for the first fifteen years of the century, participated entirely or in part in the moral and intellectual reform promoted in Italy by Benedetto Croce."[31]

To Gramsci Croceanism was the Hegelianism of the twentieth century, and any advancement of Marxism would therefore have to be within the Crocean framework just as Marx had advanced within the Hegelian framework. Gramsci wrote,

> It is necessary to make of the philosophical conception of Croce the very same reduction that the first [Marxist] theorists made of the Hegelian conception. This is the only historical possibility which will permit an adequate rebirth of Marxism....For us Italians, to be the heirs of classical German philosophy means to be the heirs of Crocean philosophy.[32]

Thus Croceanism was not to be discarded but distilled so that only the useful essence of his philosophy remained. Distilling Croce's philosophy and fusing it with his own were to take the rest of Gramsci's life, and the critics have been left vainly puzzling over whether the resulting admixture was Gramsci seasoned with Croce or Croce seasoned with Gramsci.[33] It is no wonder, for the multifaceted philosophies of Croce and Gramsci intermesh with each other in various and unpredictable ways, and neither of their philosophies lends itself to easy exposition or

[30] Attilio Momigliano, "La critica," *La rassegna d'Italia,* 1 (February-March 1946): 235.

[31] Antonio Gramsci, *Lettere del carcere* (Turin: Einaudi, 1950), p. 132.

[32] Antonio Gramsci, *Il materialismo storico,* op. cit., pp. 236-37.

[33] A glance through any contemporary Marxist journal will reveal the link between Croce and Gramsci, but one should know, too, that the whole of Gramsci has become a weapon employed by various factions within and without the Italian Communist party. All history is contemporary history, as Croce said. A good introduction to how Gramsci has been used— but from the point of view of the Bordighiani—is Rosa Alcara, *La formazione e i primi anni del Partito Comunista Italiano nella storiografia marxista* (Milan: 1970). Also useful is Gian Carlo Jocteau, *Leggere Gramsci* (Milan: Feltrinelli, 1975). Forewarned and forearmed one may then proceed to *Studi gramsciani* (Rome: Editori riuniti, 1958), *Politica e storia* in Gramsci I, II. (Rome: Editori riuniti, 1977), as well as the scores of other texts on Gramsci too numerous to mention.

synopsis. For our purposes, however, it is enough to deal with one element of Croce's thought that was to have a decisive impact on Gramsci's theory of hegemony—namely, Croce's antipathy to philosophy of history.

As Croce immodestly sifted through the long line of his "precursors" to discover "what was living and what was dead" in their earlier and ill-formed ideas, he invariably found "dead" any semblance of "philosophy of history," any attempt to impose upon history an abstract and predetermined course. To Croce all history was human history, and—particularly for the young Croce, who influenced Gramsci—no barriers or limits prevented man from steering any course he chose. Thus did Croce emphasize the absolute human responsibility for history and set out to navigate with optimism upon Nietzsche's limitless sea. That the destination might have already been fixed by some greater Navigator he rejected out of hand. Thus when Croce took up Hegel, for example, he accepted the historicism but rejected that "philosophy of history" which placed the *logos* outside man and in the World Spirit.[34] Though for Croce only the past might be an object of knowledge, that past told man nothing about the journey that lay ahead. For Croce, too, the owl of minerva flew only at twilight, but its message was only and always of the past. Thus when Croce took up even Vico he accepted that "man had made this civil world" but rejected the *corso e ricorso,* for that seemed to imply that, whatever man attempted, history in the end would compel man to take "the course the nations run."[35] Croce followed the same logic when, on the advice of Antonio Labriola, he took up the study of Marx.[36] In Croce's view the hard core of Marxism was the idea of the class war, and so he called Marx the "Machiavelli of the proletariat."[37] But "Marx the economist and Marx the philosopher," Marx's "philosophy of history," that was so much "fantasy of dreams and poetry."[38] A Marxist revolution had to be made by *men,* not by the

---

[34] Croce, *Ciò che è vivo,* pp. 132-35, for example.

[35] See the whole of *The Philosophy of Giambattista Vico,* trans. R.G. Collingwood (New York, 1913), and *Estetica come scienza dell'espressione e linguistica generale,* 3rd ed. (Bari: Laterza, 1908), pp. 262-63. It was not enough, of course, to throw out simply the *corsi,* for with it had to go the whole phylogenetic concept of distinct "ages" in human history. For Croce, determined above all to preserve man's autonomy, the poetic characteristics of early man—all characteristics of man, for that matter—were eternal and went through no necessary decline. All ages and categories were therefore eternal, according to Croce.

[36] Croce's writings on Marx are now in *Materialismo storico ed economia marxistica,* available in many editions. I have used here the edition published by Laterza at Bari in 1968.

[37] Ibid., pp. 103-04.

[38] Croce, "Due conversazioni," *Cultura e vita morale* (Bari: Laterza, 1955), p. 153.

material forces of history. This idea was to have an extraordinary impact upon Italian Marxism and upon Gramsci, for it not only helped to cut the ground from beneath the materialist reformists like Turati in the Socialist party,[39] it exalted those who, like Sorel, wished to make socialism an act of will, a religious crusade of martyr-zealots. It was precisely what Croce intended: "I admired Sorel; I recognized that socialism, if it was to be, had to be that [of Sorel] and none other."[40]

It was in this context that Gramsci developed his concept of hegemony. By the end of the first decade of the twentieth century the equation of Marx with a rigid historical determinism had become a commonplace. On account of Croce's extraordinary impact on Italian culture, on Italian Marxism in general,[41] and on Gramsci in particular, many persons, including Gramsci, came to feel the need to "humanize" Marx. Gramsci, commenting upon the Bolsheviks having leapfrogged the bourgeois phase of historical development, thus moving directly to the proletarian phase, praised them for having escaped the iron determinism of Marx's *Capital* and reinserting human will into history. Thus he called the October revolution "the revolution against 'Capital'." The Bolsheviks "are not 'Marxists', that's all; they have not used the works of the Master to compile a rigid doctrine of dogmatic utterances never to be questioned."[42]

Whether for philosophical, tactical, or purely "spiritual" reasons Gramsci could not completely abandon Marx, and yet *in* Marx he could find little sustenance for what he conceived Marxism to be. Doubtless he would have welcomed another Marx, would have liked to have discovered, or to have contrived to discover, another Marx in the *Economic and Philosophical Manuscripts of 1844,* but they were not available. He had therefore to turn to the traditions of German and Italian Idealism, to the heritage bequeathed to him by Vico, Cuoco, the Risorgimento Hegelians, and Croce in order to find the true Marx— the true Marx that even Marx had forgotten. True "Marxist thought...represents a continuation of German and Italian idealism...which in the case of Marx was contaminated by positivist and materialist encrustations."[43] This was 1917, but not much had changed,

[39] Edmund E. Jacobitti, "Labriola, Croce, and Italian Marxism (1895-1910), *Journal of the History of Ideas,* 36 (April-May 1975): 297-318.

[40] Croce, "Due conversazioni," p. 157.

[41] See, for example, Giuseppe Petronio, "Problemi della cultura," in *Critica Sociale,* I, ed. Mario Spinella et al. (Milan, 1959), p. cxlv.

[42] Gramsci, *Scritti giovanili* (Turin: Einaudi, 1958), p. 150.

[43] Ibid.

in this respect anyway, by the time of the *Prison Notebooks*. As James Joll put it, "In the purely economic theories of Marx [Gramsci] never seems to have had any great interest. What concerned him above all was the problem of the relations between the structure and the superstructure....It was the visible signs of impending historical change which interested him, and above all, the system of cultural and moral values."[44] In Gramsci Marxism took a step beyond Marx for, in Gramsci's words: "the most recent phase of [Marxism's] development consists precisely in vindicating the moment of hegemony as essential to its conception of the state, and in increasing the evaluation of the cultural fact, of cultural activity, [and] of a cultural front as necessary alongside the merely economic and political fronts."[45] Like Vico, Gramsci too had discovered that civil society rests upon the modifications of the human mind.

Yet if it is now apparent that between Vico and Gramsci there has been a kind of apostolic succession, that with or without Lenin the doctrine of common sense would have yielded up, after Cuoco, the Risorgimento, and especially Croce, the doctrine of hegemony, this should not obscure for us the fact that between Vico and Gramsci there is a vast difference. They differ most clearly in the scope of their ideas.

Some works deal with important issues in a narrowly partisan and political fashion, others in a journalistic fashion, still others resemble the harangue in the piazza, while others seem to transcend the particular problem and rise to a wholly different level of address. In the latter case the discourse treats of an eternal or universal problem. Vico clearly falls into this last category, and yet Gramsci somehow probably does not. The whole of Gramsci's work, with all of its historical analysis, even its cosmological analysis, all its brilliant flashes and insights, remains— as doubtless he would wish it to remain—a political tract, an instrument of battle in the class war. This is not to say that there are not in Gramsci ideas that transcend—or at any rate could be made to transcend[46]—the class struggle. Certainly hegemony is one such concept, which even nonpartisans in the class war can value.

Vico's writings are, however, quite different. Even if one makes the extreme case that all his works were nothing more than an assault on

[44] James Joll, *Antonio Gramsci* (New York: Penguin Books, 1978), p. 38.

[45] Gramsci, *Il materialismo storico*, p. 233.

[46] See, e.g., Valentino Gerratana, "Stato, partito, strumenti e istituti dell'egemonia nei 'quaderni del carcere,'" in *Egemonia, stato, partito in Gramsci*, ed., Leonardo Paggi, Valentino Gerratana, and Biagio De Giovanni (Rome: Editori riuniti, 1977), pp. 37-53.

some ideas of the eighteenth century, it is obvious that the works themselves transcend this, setting out, and not just here and there, a whole new basis for understanding human society. Indeed, not since the classical period of ancient Greece had such an unorthodox—by contemporary standards—and yet wholly "commonsensical" statement about man been made, and made in a way that provides still not only a viable alternative to the scientific study of man but to the approaches taken by Hegelians and Marxists as well.

Just as Gramsci and Vico differ in the style and purpose of their analyses, so too do they differ even more obviously in their theories of history. For Vico history is an *ad infinitum,* the endless cycles repeating themselves as one common sense gives way to another. For Gramsci, however, history is tied to the Hegelian and Marxist view of a *progressus ad terminum,* and it is because the *terminum is* fixed and is fixed as an ethical synthetic a priori—rather than, as Vico saw it, an inevitable and not particularly attractive conclusion to the cycle—that Gramsci's theory of history is inflexible and rigid. For Vico all actions are allowed and accounted for, since all arise out of diverse customs and developing common sense. Gramsci, instead, must impose his hegemony at the expense of common sense. Thus Vico had no need of a Machiavellian political party—a "Modern Prince," as Gramsci called his party[47]—for Vico did not aim at creating a "new order." For Gramsci, on the other hand, the primary responsibility of the party was precisely to create the new order. "The modern Prince must be, and cannot avoid being, the promoter and organizer of an intellectual and moral reform, which means to prepare the terrain for a further development of the collective national popular will."[48] With his fixed view of an historical "ought-to-be" it could have been no other way. The party therefore became a kind of school (*un partito come scuola*) for Gramsci, and as such it was divided into "the conscious" instructors ("captains," "directors") and the "unconscious" pupils (the "soldiers," the "ordinary people") and, for want of a better term, the teaching assistants, or "cadres" (the link between the "head" and the "body" of the movement). Though the masses might constitute the largest element within the party, "they are a force [only] in so far as they are centralized, organized, and disciplined; in the absence of this cohesive force they would be dispersed and annulled into an impotent cloud of dust." The conscious leader-

[47] Gramsci, *Note sul Machiavelli,* p. 23.
[48] Ibid., p. 23.

ship of the party, by contrast, is the "highly cohesive, centralizing, and disciplining force," which, though numerically minuscule in the party, "nevertheless shapes it more than the first element." They are the captains and more valuable because "one can more easily shape a party than a captain."[49]

This elitist conception, of course, stemmed from the fact that for Gramsci the party was not a voluntary organization of men with a common interest, but a group of men who did not yet know of their common interest and would not know of it until they were educated. In short the "ordinary" man was a prisoner of common sense and operated without a theory.[50] It was the task of the party to remedy this. "The philosophy of practice does not aim at leaving the 'simple' in their primitive philosophy of common sense, but instead at leading them to a superior conception of life."[51]

"Leading them..." It is an ambiguous idea, for while a people without leadership is cast back into Hobbes' state of nature, a people led must always worry where leading might leave off and herding begin, where a people's leaders might become its masters. Eternal vigilance seems the only and very uncertain remedy: eternal vigilance on the part of both leaders and led. For Gramsci, however, the issue was a good deal less slippery, for in his view only the leaders were conscious. Any hope of a vigilant population, wary and jealous of its rights, was obviated by the presence of an unconscious people. The success of the Jesuits, the revolution of 1799, these unforgettables testified to a people's innocence, the ease with which they were seduced and the fanaticism with which they clung to the seducer. Because of the startling contrast between leaders and led the heightened responsibilities of the conscious for the unconscious were obvious.

What particularly troubled Gramsci about common sense was, obviously, its divergence from the philosophy of praxis; also, oddly, he found that it "is not a single conception, identical in time and space [but] the 'folklore' of philosophy and as folklore it is presented in innumerable forms."[52] Common sense, custom, and tradition varied according to both time and place and were automatically excluded from the realm of the *verum*. For Gramsci, in fact, common sense obscured the truth and deluded man in his search for wisdom. The

---

[49] Ibid., pp. 42-43.
[50] Gramsci; *Il materialismo storico*, p. 13.
[51] Gramsci, *Gli intellettuali e l'organizzazione della cultura* (Rome: Editori riuniti, 1971), p. 18.
[52] Gramsci, *Il materialismo storico*, p. 6.

search for truth must defy common sense, just as Newton had defied the common sense of his peers to find the cause of the movement of the planets. Could the social scientist do less? Unlike Vico, in short, Gramsci did not see common sense as something to be accounted for and confirmed in a universal theory, but as contrary to theory, contrary to reason. In Gramsci reason was not confirmed in the common sense of men—it was defied there.

In Vico one finds, or apparently finds, a quite different vision. It is necessary, unfortunately, to retain the "apparently" in the last phrase because, though Vico has been used to justify everything from the Jacobins to De Maistre, Vico himself left us only the vaguest political instructions. Nevertheless, some things can be said at least about the implications of the concept of common sense as the determinant of history, and these things do distinguish it from hegemony. As we noted at the beginning, Vico, like Gramsci, envisioned an era where theory and practice coincided—namely, the era before abstract speculation and the present (and consequent) Fear and Trembling, as Kierkegaard called it. This was the era before common sense fell into disrepute; therefore, if a politics is to be found in Vico, it is to be found in the prerationalist world. Obviously, it is not to be found as a result of abstract reflection, for as Vico says, common sense is thought "without reflection." A politics similar to Vico's, it appears, is then to be found in the ideas of Edmund Burke, whose reverence for common law was as deep as Vico's reverence for common sense. Thus, as Burke "reflected" upon the French Revolution and his own common law tradition which had yielded up Magna Carta and the Declaration of Right, he noted that the benefits of such checks on authority were "the happy effect of following nature, which is widsom *without reflection,* and above it." He pointed out that history can never be abandoned for "the human race, the whole, unchangeable constancy" as it moves through the "varied tenor of perpetual decay, fall, renovation, and progression." Therefore Burke counseled men to avoid "the fallible and feeble contrivances of our reason" and consider "our liberties in the light of an inheritance....By this means our liberties become a noble freedom....All your sophisters cannot produce anything better adapted to preserve a rational and manly freedom than the course we have pursued, who have *chosen* nature rather than our speculations, our breasts rather than our inventions."[53]

[53] Edmund Burke, *Reflections on the Revolution in France* (New York: Everyman's Library, 1971), pp. 31-32.

In Vico's and Burke's "wisdom without reflection" and in their concepts of "common sense" and "common law" we can therefore find a kind of "Practic of the New Science,"[54] for both abhor Jacobin abstraction and revolutionary attempts to leap out of history. Both are based on the belief that beneath the common sense and common law of men there lies no "natural law," no "objective," no "structure," but only chaos and the dictator. Both men ridiculed any equation of reason and physics and, while avoiding the later Marxian preoccupation with the linking of theory and practice, made plain that only by avoiding abstract reason could a harmonious society survive. This caution is not surprising in men who suspect that society is held together by something as fragile as common sense, and it leads to a practice quite different from Gramsci's.

For Gramsci the world is to be set right by making practice conform to theory, by bringing the practice of the unconscious into conformity with Marxist theory. It is the answer of the Jacobins, and no less Jacobin because it rejects the static natural law vision of the eighteenth century. To see a future in which the laws of man will conform to the laws of nature and to see it as a result of man's being liberated from the prejudices inculcated by an artificial feudal society was the vision of the Jacobins. To see a future in which the laws of man will conform to the laws of history and to see it as a result of man's being liberated from the hegemony of the ⁹bourgeoisie was the vision of Gramsci. Both imply liberating man from himself and making his practice conform to a vision of theory.

In Vico one would find, instead, not practice being made to conform to theory, but theory to practice. This is so even in Vico's discovery of the concept of the *corsi e ricorsi,* which came as a *result* of his observation of practice. It is true as well of his concept of the prerationalist society, where common sense—the obvious union of theory and practice—is the sole basis of society. Therefore, instead of having practice conform to an abstract theory, Vico urges us to make theory conform to practice, to make law conform not to the natural law envisioned by the seer and made by fiat, but to the common law worked out by man in practice.

Alain Pons has argued that Vico returns us to an age of princes and a prudent elite of advisors and decision-makers.[55] If this be true, it is a

[54] Giambattista Vico, *Practic of the New Science,* trans. T. G. Bergin and M. H. Fisch, in *Giambattista Vico's Science of Humanity,* ed. G. Tagliacozzo and D. P. Verene (Baltimore: Johns Hopkins University Press, 1976), pp. 451-54.

different kind of elite than that envisioned by Gramsci, for it has a broad and popular base, a base that in Gramsci will come only after the hegemony of the party is complete. In Vico we have already a broad and common base because law rests upon common law, the common sense of the people—the people as they already are and not as they ought to be. Rulers in this sense would be but custom and tradition personified, the heroic and poetic innovators who are within the earthly providence rather than without it, who are not enemies of common sense but the very expression of it. That they are innovators we know, for they are "poets," which as Vico says is Greek for "creators." That they are innovators we know too from history, for only thus could common sense be made to change and the obvious growth of man through history take place.

[55] Alain Pons, "Prudence And Providence: The 'Pratica della Scienza Nuova' and the Problem of Theory and Practice In Vico," in *Giambattista Vico's Science of Humanity.* p. 448.

Vico and Marx After Nietzsche

Allan Megill

In seeking to unveil the hidden connections between two thinkers so different as Vico and Marx—thinkers, moreover, who wrote in quite different periods and responded to quite different problems—one inevitably finds oneself stepping back, searching for some perspective, neither Vichian nor Marxian, in the light of which their significance for us, living in yet another historical period and faced by still different problems, can be illuminated. One could, of course, attempt a direct comparison between these two imposing figures—a dialogue of the dead, as it were, carried out with our own necessary assistance (since Vico was unable to comment on Marx, and Marx, as is well known, was not directly influenced by Vico, never found occasion to grapple seriously with his thought, and mentioned him only once in his published writings).[1] But in the present essay I propose a rather different tack. I propose to look at Vico and Marx in the light of the recent tendency to assimilate them (illegitimately, it seems to me) to Nietzsche. This "Nietzscheanization" of Vico and Marx is closely connected with a broad, though still largely inchoate and undefined current in contemporary thought, one whose dominant feature is its predilection for focusing, in its analytical enterprises, on "discourse," as distinguished from the presumed reality addressed by that discourse. Various labels, among them "post-modernism," "structuralism," and "post-structuralism," have gained wide usage as markers for subcurrents within this broader current, and will be familiar to readers acquainted with the

---

[1] See Eugene Kamenka, "Vico and Marxism," in *Giambattista Vico: An International Symposium,* ed. Giorgio Tagliacozzo and Hayden V. White (Baltimore: Johns Hopkins University Press, 1969), pp. 137-43. Marx's only reference to Vico in a published work occurs in the fourth footnote of chap. 15 of the first volume of *Capital,* where Marx refers approvingly to Vico's belief that human history differs from natural history in that the former is made by men; see Karl Marx, *Capital,* vol. I, trans. Ben Fowkes (New York: Vintage Books, 1977), p. 493. The only other references to Vico in the entire Marxian corpus appear in letters to Engels and to Lassalle, both written on April 28, 1862.

newer, discourse-oriented trends in literary criticism. These labels are misleading, suggesting as they do something rather more idiosyncratic and restricted than I here intend. But at the same time they remain useful, even indispensable, for within the territories they designate the issues are posed much more radically and, in consequence, much more clearly than anywhere else. This is particularly true of post-structuralism, whose leading figures, Michel Foucault and Jacques Derrida, raise, albeit in heightened form, important questions regarding the nature of science and of scholarly work in general. As participants in the avant-garde intellectual scene in France, a scene notorious for its lability, the post-structuralists are widely regarded as beyond the pale of legitimate scholarly discussion. Yet, for all that is suspect about them, their reflections converge with the (admittedly much less apocalyptic) views of such Anglo-American figures as Thomas S. Kuhn and Paul Feyerabend[2] and with a great deal else in such varied fields as the history of ideas, political theory, philosophy, and literary criticism.

While a close examination of post-structuralism would lead me too far away from my concern in the present essay with the contemporary interpretation of Vico and Marx, I can at least point out the decisive references underlying the post-structuralist perspective. One such reference is Heidegger, whom I shall leave out of consideration here except to note that the Heidegger in question is less the "existentialist" figure who so influenced Sartre and his generation than the "later" Heidegger, the author of such works as "The Origin of the Work of Art" and the *Letter on Humanism*. As for Nietzsche, the figure to whom these contemporary writers appeal is not the critical demythologizer, still working in the tradition of Voltaire and the Enlightenment, that Walter Kaufmann portrays in his *Nietzsche: Philosopher, Psychologist, Antichrist*,[3] but a rather different Nietzsche, suggested by his assertion in *The Birth of Tragedy* that "it is only as an *aesthetic phenomenon* that existence and the world are eternally *justified*," and by the *Nachlass* fragment in which he characterizes "the world" as "a work of art that gives birth to itself."[4] This Nietzsche is one who views the world not as a fixed and solid

---

[2] See Thomas S. Kuhn, *The Structure of Scientific Revolutions*, 2nd ed. (Chicago: University of Chicago Press, 1970), and Paul Feyerabend, *Against Method: Outline of an Anarchistic Theory of Knowledge* (London: New Left Books, 1975). John Sturrock, ed., *Structuralism and Since: From Lévi-Strauss to Derrida* (London: Oxford University Press, 1979), provides a relatively lucid introduction to poststructuralism and the intellectual context out of which it emerged.

[3] 4th ed. (Princeton, N.J.: Princeton University Press, 1974).

[4] Friedrich Nietzsche, *The Birth of Tragedy*, Preface, §5; sec. 5; sec. 24; in Nietzsche, *"The Birth of Tragedy" and "The Case of Wagner,"* trans. Walter Kaufmann (New York: Vintage Books, 1967), pp. 22, 52, 141; Nietzsche, *The Will to Power*, ed. Walter Kaufmann, trans. Walter Kaufmann and R.J. Hollingdale (New York: Vintage Books, 1968), §796, p. 419.

reality but rather as something created, in a quasi-aesthetic way, by the observer himself. To be sure, such an "aestheticist" view is advanced by Nietzsche only in the most tentative fashion, and its implications and difficulties are not at all explored. In the later Heidegger, however, the notion of the self-creative potential of "art" becomes absolutely decisive; this notion underlies, for example, his assertion in "The Origin of the Work of Art" that "to be a work (*Werk*) means to set up a world."[5] And in Foucault and Derrida, who work under the double impact of these predecessors, the "aestheticist" perspective becomes little short of programmatic. When the absurdist Derrida avers that "there is nothing outside the text [*il n'y a pas de hors-texte*]," and when the quasi-radical Foucault declares that "henceforth, and through the mediation of madness, it is the world that becomes culpable (for the first time in the Western world) in relation to the work [*oeuvre*], it is now arraigned by the work, obliged to order itself by its language, compelled by it to a task of recognition, of reparation...,"[6] they are working within this perspective. In case all this sounds horrendously foreign to anything appearing within the Anglo-American intellectual context, let me note that T.S. Kuhn is pointing toward just such a perspective when in *The Structure of Scientific Revolutions* he avers that "examining the record of past research from the vantage of contemporary historiography, the historian of science may be tempted to exclaim that when paradigms change, the world itself changes with them."[7]

And now to Marx and Vico. There has been a noticeable tendency among writers influenced by the post-modernist current in contemporary thought and criticism toward the assimilation of both thinkers to the "aestheticist" Nietzsche, and more generally to the notion of reality as, in fact, a creation of the observer. The most succinct attempt to suggest such an interpretation of Marx is to be found in Michel Foucault's 1964 essay, "Nietzsche, Freud, Marx." Here Foucault purports to deal with the "techniques of interpretation" of these three writers, who, he argues, have "founded anew the possibility of a hermeneutics."[8] I shall leave Freud out of the picture here and focus

[5] Martin Heidegger, "The Origin of the Work of Art," in Heidegger, *Poetry, Language, Thought,* trans. Albert Hofstadter (New York: Harper & Row, 1971), p. 44.

[6] Jacques Derrida, *Of Grammatology,* trans. Gayatri Spivak (Baltimore: Johns Hopkins University Press, 1976), pp. 163, 158; Michel Foucault, *Madness and Civilization: A History of Insanity in the Age of Reason,* trans. Richard Howard (New York: Vintage Books, 1967), p. 288 (translation slightly altered).

[7] Kuhn, *Structure of Scientific Revolutions,* p. 111.

[8] Foucault, "Nietzsche, Marx, Freud," in *Nietzsche,* Cahiers de Royaumont, Philosophie no. 6 (Paris: Minuit, 1967), pp. 183, 185.

instead on Foucault's account of Marx and Nietzsche. It is clear that in Foucault's eyes Nietzsche is the key figure in the emergence of this "new possibility of interpretation";[9] indeed, in his characteristically overdramatized fashion he declares, in *The Order of Things* (1966), that Nietzsche "marks the threshold beyond which contemporary philosophy can begin thinking again."[10] On Foucault's reading, one finds in Nietzsche a critique of what Foucault regards as an outmoded view of interpretation—the view that interpretation plumbs the depths of "mere appearance" in order to arrive, finally, at the true and solid reality of things. Against this view of depth as "interiority" Nietzsche articulates, according to Foucault, a view of depth as "exteriority," with depth conceived as "an absolutely superficial secret" rather than as a hidden reality that now becomes visible. Whereas previously the process of interpretation came to an end once it had reached the bedrock of reality, it now becomes infinite in its unfolding, a matter of revealing the mask behind the mask, each mask turning out to be the mask for some further reality, which itself turns out to be not a reality at all but yet another mask.[11]

There is much that could be said in defense of the view of Nietzsche that Foucault is here suggesting, but this is not the place to make that defense. Suffice it to say that Foucault has, in my opinion, perceived an important strand in Nietzsche's thought. But what of Marx? Foucault admits that his treatment of Marx is very cursory and that the notion of an "infinity of interpretation" may apply in lesser degree to Marx than it does to Nietzsche.[12] He does suggest that Marx's political economy concerns itself not with relations of production *as fact,* but rather with certain interpretations of economic life which, as interpretations, need to be destroyed; he suggests, too, that in the *Eighteenth Brumaire* Marx "never presents his interpretation as the final interpretation. He well knows, and he says so, that one could interpret at a more profound level, or at a more general level, and that there is no explanation that gets down to base rock [*soit au ras du sol*]."[13] But Foucault provides no analysis of Marx; in particular, he does not confront (though he does recognize) the difficulties presented by the Marxian distinction between base and superstructure, which even on a purely metaphorical level seems an explicit rejection of the notion of interpretation as

[9] Ibid., p. 185.
[10] Foucault, *The Order of Things,* trans. anon. (New York: Vintage Books, 1973), p. 342.
[11] Foucault, "Nietzsche, Marx, Freud," pp. 185-89.
[12] Ibid., pp. 195, 188.
[13] Ibid., pp. 189-91, 195.

infinite. It is quite evident that Foucault is not interested in carrying
out "faithful" textual exegeses and analyses; his real interest is in
exploiting past texts for contemporary polemical purposes. As he has
said in an interview, "the only mark of gratitude that one can give to a
thought like that of Nietzsche is precisely to *use* it, to deform it, to make
it creak and cry out. Consequently it is of no interest when the commentators say that one is or is not faithful."[14] And it is clear why, from the
perspective of interpretation that Foucault espouses, such a view follows—for if there is no base, no final reality, then the text, too, has no
foundational significance and can logically be viewed as only the mask
of a mask.

One should not, therefore, expect Foucault and other contemporary
post-Nietzscheans to give sustained defenses of their interpretations
of, for example, Marx and Vico. What happens, rather, is that such
interpreters ignore a range of questions and concerns that have traditionally, and I think rightly, been regarded as decisive, and instead
focus on the Vichian or Marxian texts in their guise as "discursive
practices" or "rhetorical strategies." The classic instance of this, insofar
as Marx is concerned, is Louis Althusser's *Reading Capital* (first published in 1965).[15] *Reading Capital* stands as an interesting case study of
how one can, in interpreting a work, avoid confronting any of the
important questions that the work raises. As the title indicates, Althusser focuses quite definitely on the "reading" of *Capital* rather than
on the arguments and analyses that *Capital* puts forward. Indeed, he
explicitly avoids asking any economic, historical, or logical questions of
the work; in his words,

> to have read *Capital* as economists would have meant reading it
> while posing the question of the economic content and value of its
> analyses and schemes, hence comparing its discourse with an
> object already defined outside it, without questioning the object
> itself. To have read *Capital* as historians would have meant reading
> it while posing the question of the relation between its historical
> analyses and a historical object already defined outside it, without
> questioning that object itself. To have read *Capital* as a logician

[14] Foucault, "Les Jeux du Pouvoir" (interview of 1975 with J.-J. Brochier), in *Politiques de la philosophie* ed. Dominique Grisoni (Paris: Grasset, 1976), p. 174.
[15] Louis Althusser and Etienne Balibar, *Reading Capital,* trans. Ben Brewster (London: New Left Books, 1970).

would have meant posing it the question of its methods of exposition and proof, but in the abstract, once again without questioning the object to which the methods of this discourse relate.

Instead, says Althusser, "we read *Capital* as philosophers, and therefore posed it a different question....we posed it the question of its *relation to its object....*" Such a reading, according to Althusser, is one that in fact calls "the object" into question; indeed, he suggests that seen from this perspective *Capital* constitutes "a real epistemological mutation of its object," and a mutation, too, of the notions of theory and method.[16]

Viewed negatively, Althusser's rejection of the economic, historical, and logical analysis of *Capital* can be seen as conveniently evading the host of difficulties that confront, or at any rate ought to confront, anyone who seeks to maintain a position of rigid Marxist orthodoxy—and commitment to such an orthodoxy has certainly been a leitmotif in Althusser's career (significantly, he refers to *Capital* not as "the book" but as "the Book," and it is clear that he takes the capitalization very seriously). But here I am interested rather in the positive aspect of Althusser's strategy, for like Nietzsche (at least in his "aestheticist" mode), like the later Heidegger, and like Foucault (whose influence on *Reading Capital* he warmly acknowledges), Althusser wants to attribute to language, and specifically to that piece of language that we know as *Capital,* a mythic, founding significance.[17] To view *Capital* in such a way it is necessary to cease viewing it as something pointing toward a referent or series of referents undeniably "there" in the world outside the book; it is necessary, rather, to view it as a "work of art" in the Heideggerian sense, something that, far from merely representing the world, Orpheus-like creates it. Hence it is not subject to the usual forms of logical and historical analysis, but has accorded to it the appreciative privilege of a "reading"—which itself, as far as the "reader" is concerned, opens up the same liberty of interpretation that

---

[16] Ibid., pp. 14-15.

[17] See, for example, the astonishing assessment of *Thus Spoke Zarathustra* that Nietzsche advances in *Ecce Homo*—an assessment that can be credited, it seems to me, only on the assumption that Nietzsche views *Thus Spoke Zarathustra* as a "work of art" in the Heideggerian sense, somehow bringing into being the reality that it depicts (Nietzsche, *Ecce Homo,* "Thus Spoke Zarathustra," in *"On the Genealogy of Morals" and "Ecce Homo,"* trans. Walter Kaufmann [New York: Vintage Books, 1969], pp. 295-309). For Althusser's indebtedness to Foucault see *Reading Capital,* esp. pp. 45, 103.

we claim for ourselves when we stand, as aesthetic observers, before a work of art in the *conventional* sense. Althusser's particular "aesthetic" stance is that of an orthodox Marxist revolutionary seeking to complete the work that Marx began. The revolutionary activity, in this case, consists in the propounding of discourses—of networks of interpretation—designed to bring into being the reality that on the surface of things the text claims only to represent. No longer, then, is the Marx of *Capital* a mere theoretician; on the contrary, by the very act of writing the Book he has set in train the movement whereby the Book itself will be realized.

Thus, for the moment, Marx. In the realm of Vico interpretation the parallel to Althusser's interpretation of Marx is to be found in Edward Said's treatment of Vico in his *Beginnings: Intention and Method*.[18] (Not surprisingly, Said, too, acknowledges having been influenced by the work of Foucault.) Admittedly, there are important differences between Althusser's account of Marx and Said's account of Vico. Most significant is the fact that Althusser repeatedly insists that Marx, at least the Marx of post-1845, was engaged in a genuinely scientific enterprise, and makes no secret of his belief that this enterprise ought, in a direct and immediate way, to be carried to its completion. Said, on the other hand, makes no comparable claims for the Vico. What Said does argue, though, is that Vico had a remarkably cogent insight into the reality-creating power of language—an insight anticipating that of Nietzsche and his successors. Consequently, in spite of his having written more than two centuries ago, Vico can rightly be viewed as "the prototypical modern thinker."[19] On Said's reading Vico "takes words as his subject": "Every word carries—indeed is—a system of relationships to other words; *The New Science* much of the time is a virtuoso, if not always accurate, display of etymological and correlative explanations."[20] Underlying this interpretive profusion Said perceives something that is in fact essential to the quasi-radical wing of postmodernism, namely, a devaluation of the "signified" and a consequent emphasis on the "signifier," carried out with the intention of disrupting comfortable assumptions about the transparency of representation and about the neutrality of the language that we employ. Said links this aspect of Vico's project to Vico's well-known distinction between

[18] New York: Basic Books, 1975.
[19] Ibid., p. 349.
[20] Ibid., pp. 352, 351

"Hebrew" and "gentile" history: the history of God's chosen people, according to Vico, is different in kind from the history of the gentiles, and he rigorously excludes the former from the ambit of the New Science, which thus concerns itself with gentile history alone. On Said's reading, whereas the history of the Hebrews is characterized by the presence of God, gentile history is characterized by God's absence—characterized, that is, by the absence of the "original" or "transcendental" signified, to use the terminology of Foucault and Derrida. And since the signified (more accurately, the referent)[21] is dead, already in Vico everything is (interpretively) permitted; as Said puts it, "with the discrediting of mimetic representation a work enters a realm of gentile history...where extraordinary possibilities of variety and diversity are open to it but where it will not be referred back docilely to an idea that stands above it and explains it."[22] Thus Vico's "philological" enterprise anticipates the discussion opened up by Nietzsche and continued by his successors, so that, in Said's words, the *New Science* "prophetically suggests terms for comprehending a very modern polemic."[23]

Clearly, each in his own way, Althusser views Marx, and Said views Vico, as an exemplary intellectual figure. Althusser views Marx as exemplary because he is "scientific" (though Althusser's science turns out to be something that creates its own object, and hence has rather the character of myth), while Said views Vico as exemplary because of his sheer interpretive exuberance (*New Science*, par. 1009),[24] which Said sees as providing a model for what he regards as language's *productive* capacity, its capacity, that is, for renewing, revolutionizing, and overturning those ideological habits that help keep us functioning in the existing order (whose nefarious character Said assumes). I do not deny that Vico and Marx, each in *his* own way, are exemplary, but they are here being seen as exemplary for precisely the wrong reasons. They are being tailored to fit something that may well be on the way toward becoming the dominant mentality within Western intellectual life in the late twentieth century. For it seems to me that insofar as a genuine

[21] Foucault, Derrida, and their followers tend to blur the distinction between the "signified" (which constitutes one-half of the signified/signifier couple making up the sign) and the "referent" (to which this signifying couple refers).

[22] Said, *Beginnings*, pp. 11-12.

[23] Ibid., p. 373.

[24] I have used the Bergin and Fisch translation: Giambattista Vico, *The New Science, Revised Translation of the Third Edition (1744)*, trans. Thomas G. Bergin and Max H. Fisch (Ithaca, N.Y.: Cornell University Press, 1968).

intellectual life exists today—and to a large extent it has been destroyed by the barriers of professionalism and subprofessionalism that
many scholars have erected for themselves—it has entered into an
ironic phase, what we might call the phase of "distance."[25] Among those
who attempt to break through the barriers of specialty and sub-
specialty, and who thus find themselves confronted (as those who work
totally within the existing scholarly paradigms do not) by issues of a
genuinely *theoretical* bearing, there has arisen a widespread feeling that
one cannot come to grips with the world of actuality because, in fact,
there *is* no such world, but only a variety of languages that have created
the illusion that such a world exists. Obviously, at the deepest level it is
just such an ironism that underlies and propels the "aestheticist" side of
Nietzsche, with his notion of reality as a mask concealing another mask
and so on ad infinitum; it is central, too, for Foucault and Derrida
(Heidegger is a somewhat different case).

But these are "extremist," "avant-garde" figures, and it is easy
enough to discount their significance. More important, certainly in the
Anglo-American sphere, is the kind of ironism derivable from, e.g.,
T.S. Kuhn. Kuhn's *Structure of Scientific Revolutions* is a complex, even in
some respects confused work, and it is not at all surprising that it can be
used in support of perspectives on the scientific enterprise that are
radically opposed to each other.[26] On the one hand, when the Kuhnian
notion of a paradigm, and his related notion of a scientific community,
are applied to the social sciences and humanities, Kuhn can be seen as
supporting a narrow (but in some ways very productive) professionalism.[27] Such an extrapolation of Kuhn (which, I hasten to point out,

[25] See especially John S.Nelson, "Ironic Politics: Critical Commitment in the Fourth Age"
(Ph.D. diss., University of North Carolina at Chapel Hill, 1977), which, incidentally, makes
extensive use of Vico. The term "phase of 'distance'" is mine, not Nelson's.

[26] In his "Reflections on My Critics" Kuhn goes so far as to postulate the existence of two
Thomas Kuhns, with $Kuhn_2$ on occasion making points that subvert the position outlined by
$Kuhn_1$. See Imre Lakatos and Alan Musgrave, eds., *Criticism and the Growth of Knowledge*
(London: Cambridge University Press, 1970), p. 231. On the confusions that run through *The
Structure of Scientific Revolutions* see, in the same volume, Margaret Masterson, "The Nature
of a Paradigm"; Masterson identifies no less than twenty-two different uses of the term
"paradigm" in Kuhn's book. As Kuhn indicates (p. 234), he largely concurs with Masterson's
judgment on this point.

[27] I note that in my own discipline, history, these notions have received widespread if
largely informal acceptance. This is not surprising, since they are quite close to the older
tendency to view history as a scholarly "craft," yet they add to those older notions a new sense
of scientific purpose and prestige.

Kuhn himself does not countenance)[28] leads in the opposite direction from irony; it leads, rather, to a supreme confidence in the solidity of scientifically established fact and in the validity of the interpretive results derived therefrom. But there is another, highly subversive side to Kuhn, which we have already in part glimpsed. This is the side of Kuhn that wants to insist that "fact"—indeed, "reality" itself—is something that the scientific observer *invents* in the course of his construction of the intellectual grids ("paradigms") by which he seeks to understand that reality. But if, as Kuhn so tentatively suggests, the "world itself" changes when paradigms change, this raises an important question: What happens when there is a conflict between opposing viewpoints? Since Kuhn himself restricts the paradigm notion to the natural sciences, wherein, he finds, the "normal" state of affairs is one in which a single paradigm is dominant, he is able to confine the problem of a conflict between paradigms to those brief and abnormal "revolutionary" periods during which a given science makes a Gestalt shift to a new paradigm. Hence Kuhn is in no way forced to deal with the problem of a *continuing* conflict of viewpoints. Suppose, however, one attempts to apply the notion of paradigm to the social sciences, whose practitioners, as Kuhn acknowledges, do not customarily fall in line behind a single consensus. How, then, will the conflict between opposing viewpoints proceed? The answer, I think, is obvious: given a rejection of the notion that "fact" and "world" exist independently of "paradigm," the conflict will take the form of a battle between opposing rhetorics. On one level this will be an *ironic* battle because its participants, aware of their own Kuhnian epistemological limitations, will recognize that, whatever they may claim in the heat of the moment, the viewpoint that they propound no more corresponds to an objective reality than the viewpoint or viewpoints they oppose. But "ironic" battles are a contradiction in terms, since of all attitudes irony is the one least suited to the battlefield. So the irony must turn into something

[28] In fact Kuhn intends the notion of paradigm to *differentiate* natural scientists, on the one hand, from social scientists, humanists, and artists on the other. According to Kuhn natural scientists address their research only to their fellow scientific specialists, whereas social scientists, humanists, and artists seek a lay audience. Kuhn attributes this difference to the (alleged) fact that natural scientists work within small, well-insulated scientific communities, each of which is tied together by commitment to a common paradigm, whereas those outside the natural sciences do not work within such a context. See *Structure of Scientific Revolutions*, pp. 164 and 174ff.

else; and this "something else," though it may go by the name of science, is in fact myth—by which I mean, in this case, a dramatic story that *demands* our adhesion without feeling the need to stake out a mimetic claim (either "high" mimetic or "low")[29] to being a representation of an extant reality.

And this gets us back once more to Vico and to Marx. To what degree are these thinkers working within an ironic or mythic perspective as here defined? To what degree did Vico see himself as caught on the circling wheel of history, forced to view the human world from the degraded perspective of a late, ironic age that was about to turn back to the mythic consciousness of a renewed barbarism? And to what extent did Marx see himself as making a myth of revolution—a myth that would serve to create an object of knowledge that unfortunately did not yet exist? Or to put it differently: To what degree did Marx and Vico (like the contemporary ironists and mythmakers) see themselves as irremediably cut off from the reality of the human world, so that their only choice was to chronicle ironically that world's degradation or, alternatively, to create mythically and ex nihilo a new, utopian universe?

What is striking about both thinkers is their very strong conviction—entirely foreign to any ironistic battle of rhetorics—that they *were* grasping the "real world," a world quite independent of the observer's perception of it. Focusing on the interpretive profusion—the incredible richness—of the Vichian text, one can certainly misread him in an "aestheticist," post-modern direction, holding, with Said, that in Vico "the ceaseless activity of mind delivers language and is delivered by and in language, Vico's own, and it is precisely this that characterizes Vico's novelty and originality."[30] But this is to underestimate the extralinguistic, referential focus of Vico's enterprise, for his interpretations, exuberant though they may be, converge toward a reality that in his eyes is unambiguous; his "philology," like his "philosophy," points outward to the thing itself—to the social and historical reality that it is his intention to illuminate. To be sure, he insists repeatedly on the difficulty with which this outward, referential activity is fraught, particularly when it is a matter of trying to understand the mind of primitive humanity (see, for example, pars. 34, 338, and 378 of the *New Science*). But to regard

[29]I depend, here, on Frye's theory of modes; see Northrop Frye, *Anatomy of Criticism: Four Essays* (Princeton, N.J.: Princeton University Press, 1971), esp. pp. 31-67.

[30]Said, *Beginnings*, p. 369.

these assertions as qualifying the referential character of the work is to attribute to them a significance that is virtually the opposite of what Vico intends, for his aim in these passages is not to make an admission of theoretical impotence but rather to emphasize the magnitude of his achievement in penetrating, in spite of all difficulties, the dark mists of the human past. Nor is it legitimate to seek to assimilate the Vichian notion of gentile humanity as alienated from God, and as therefore constructing its *own* humanity, to the post-Nietzschean notion of the omnipotence of aesthetic creativity, for in Vico's view (as in Marx's) the construction of humanity is a collective, historical process, not the act of a willful interpreter. Moreover, the process is not one of consciousness *tout court* but rather one in which consciousness is continually coming up against the brute reality of the nonhuman—which contact, in the guise of the initial Vichian claps of thunder, set off the process in the first place. Finally, there is the thorny question of Vico's relation to myth. The reader attuned to a Nietzschean or post-Nietzschean mythopoeia might well think that Vico's intentions must have been mythopoeic as well. But nothing could be further from the truth, for Vico's mythology is intended as a *science* of myth; it is an attempt to avoid myth's "treacherous reefs" (par. 81) by translating the visual, poetic language of the fables into the abstract, conceptual language of philosophy.

Marx's view of the relationship between his text and the object that it seeks to describe is likewise unambiguous. Althusser, following Foucault, argues that the focus of Marx's enterprise is the "symptomatic reading" that he gives of the texts of classical political economy, but Marx himself thought that he was engaged in portraying not previous texts but rather the deeply hidden inner dynamic of capitalism. To be sure, like Althusser he attacks "naive" empiricism; he does so, however, not in order to clear the way for the notion of a "production of knowledge" in Althusser's sense, but rather because he thinks that empiricism, in its concentration on surface phenomena, has failed to grasp the underlying essence of capitalism—an essence that is unequivocally *there* in the world outside the text. The point that I am making here is not an antiquarian one; I am not concerned *simply* with the scholarly task of providing a correct exegesis of Marx on this point. I am concerned, rather, that we ask the right questions of Marx; and given the continuing impact of Marxism on the contemporary world, what needs to be asked is not, "How did Marx produce a new object and a new knowledge of that object?" but rather, "To what extent is Marx's interpretation of capitalism historically and logically correct?"

The point is one that goes far beyond Marx and Marxism. For the issue is this: Are we confined, in our theoretical discourse, to the rhetorical deconstruction of previous rhetorics, so that, e.g., against the Marxian dialectic, here conceived not as a theory articulating how the human world actually develops but rather as a rhetorical strategy designed to undermine bourgeois apologies for capitalism, our response is to articulate rhetorical counterstrategies, *or* is there not a final level of experience, a domain of reality independent of, and logically prior to, our interpretation of it—a bus coming down the road, a clap of thunder, the sex drive, hunger, pleasure/leisure of various kinds, rainfall, a tornado, a nuclear explosion?

One may call everything "text" if one will, but one still has to distinguish between the kind of text that is written or spoken and that other kind of "text" that is the world. Vico and Marx, for all their differences, stand together on this point; for here are two theorists who, in very different ways, sought to penetrate to the bedrock of interpretation, to unveil the mystery of human society. Moreover, unlike the scholarly professionals, they did so on a wide, indeed a breathtaking scale—so that, if nothing else, they reinitiate us into what we are in danger of losing, the openness of learning. And finally, looking at the rhetorizing theoreticians who are now coming on the scene, we have every right to ask which is the more effective rhetoric: the rhetoric of "rhetorical strategy," of "discursive practice," of "symptomatic reading," and of "deconstruction," *or* the rhetoric that claims, for all the difficulties of the enterprise, to be illuminating something that lies *beyond* rhetoric?

Defense of Vico
Against Some of His
Admirers
For Celso Leifer and Rubens Ricupero　　　　　　　J.G. Merquior

---

*Most writers on the emotions and on human conduct (...) appear to
conceive man to be situated in nature as a kingdom within a kingdom: for
they believe that he disturbs rather than follows nature's order, that he has
absolute control over his actions, and that he is determined solely by
himself.*

　　　　　　　　　　　　　—Spinoza, *Ethics,* Preface to Part III

The problem of anthropomorphism and the current image of Vico

*Gli uomini ignoranti delle naturali cagioni che producon le cose, ove non le
possono spiegare nemmeno per cose simili, essi dánno alle cose la loro propia
natura.*[1] Thus works, according to Vico, the primitive physics of illiterate people. To be sure, in Vico's historical anthropology this anthropomorphic drive is not to be derided but, rather, to be understood.
It is presented as a particular instance of the constant propensity of
ignorant minds to see themselves as the measure of the world—hence
the connection between anthropomorphism and the ubiquitous fancifulness of common sense in all primitive societies. Fantastic reasoning
was indeed, in remote ages, "a mental language common to all nations."
As long as reason was still too weak, fantasy, and therefore anthropomorphic projections, reigned everywhere.[2]

　　But the gist of anthropomorphism—naive self-projection—is as little
a privilege of primitives that it is often indulged in, Vico tells us, by
advanced nations and learned people, who assume the mind of the past

---

[1] Giambattista Vico, *La Scienza nuova* (Bari: Laterza, 1967), par. 180.
[2] Ibid., pars. 120, 181, 142, 144, 161, 185.

to have been basically identical with their own. Such is the "conceit of nations" and "of the learned" (*boria delle nazioni, boria de'dotti*) that Vico castigated in the *Scienza nuova* (pars. 123-27), because one of the chief aims of his "new science" was precisely to elicit the truth about the Ancients. That is why he called upon philology to help philosophy in the knowledge of human evolution (pars. 7, 140, 143, 351, 359, 390, 392).

As every reader of the *Scienza nuova* recalls, the conceptual cluster on anthropomorphism occupies a strategic place in the work: It belongs to the very "elements" of the "new science," as listed by the first set of axioms of Book I. But we also know that the *Scienza nuova* was thoroughly innocent of primitivism. There is not a shadow in its pages of that sentimental, preromantic idealization and nostalgia of early man and pristine times. Vico was no Herder, let alone a Hamann; he never pitted a noble primeval *physis* against the corrupt *thesis* of civilization.[3] Consequently, his understanding of anthropomorphism can scarcely be transmogrified into an indulgence toward "humanized," because "poetic," lore beyond the dawn of history. What he tried to *explain* within the ancient mind, as the triple corso of "poetic," "heroic," and "human" stages, he would never dream of *justifying* in terms of modern knowledge.

It is much to be doubted whether we can say as much of modern Vichians. Indeed, there are grounds for contending that what is mostly valued in Vico by contemporary social theory boils down to a humanistic epistemology that unabashedly attempts to vindicate anthropomorphism as the basis of social science. In what follows I propose to show that such a notion is largely mistaken, both as an interpretation of Vico and as an account of sociological knowledge at large.

There are at least two Vicos: the theorist of substantive history and that of historical science, of history as rational knowledge. By and large the one who is again in favor among us is the latter.

---

[3] The difference between Vico and Herder in their attitude to the primitive was aptly emphasized by Erich Auerbach's "Vico and Aesthetic Historism" (1949), repr. in his *Scenes from the Drama of European Literature* (New York: Meridian, 1959), pp. 193-94. See also his previous essay, "Vico und Herder," *Deutsche Viertel Jahrschrift*, 10 (1932). Modern scholars concur: see George A. Wells, "Vico and Herder," in *Giambattista Vico: An International Symposium*, ed. Giorgio Tagliacozzo and Hayden V. White, hereafter GVIS (Baltimore: Johns Hopkins University Press, 1969), p. 94. But Vico's conspicuous lack of primitivist longings was already noticed in Friedrich Meinecke's large study, *Historism: The Rise of a New Historical Outlook* (*Die Entstehung des Historismus*, 1936; London: Routledge and Kegan Paul, 1972), p. 45.

In the first Vico revival, soon after his European discovery by French Restoration ideologists like Chateaubriand, Ballanche, and, above all, Joseph de Maistre—the revival enthusiastically led by Michelet—the famous doctrine of the *corsi* and *ricorsi* was chiefly a casualty. Saint-Simonian liberals such as Jules Michelet and Edgar Quinet had no use for *ricorsi*, and their Promethean creed was pledged to wrestle Vico's idea of man as a self-creator in history from the conservative overtones of his Catholic politics.

Michelet introduced his fellow historian and Saint-Simonian, Quinet, who was already interested in Herder, to Vico's main book. Presumably the French translation of the *Scienza nuova*, which then appeared signed by Cristina, Princess Belgioioso—the notorious Carbonara and necrophile, and a friend of Saint-Simonian artists like Berlioz and Heine—was in fact the work of her lover, Quinet. But the name of the Belgioioso, the future model of the neurotic woman dabbling in radical politics in James's *Princess Casamassima*, is an apt emblem of the distance covered by Vico's European image, from the reactionary praise of a De Maistre to the populist hero worship of the left. Small wonder if, one generation later, we find Vico appealing, however fleetingly, to no less than Marx.

In the *second* Vichian revival, headed by Sorel and Croce, the theory of *corsi* and *ricorsi* was also eventually disparaged, whereas Vico's views on historical cognition were acclaimed. True, Sorel adopted the *ricorso* as a *machine de guerre* against the faith in progress in bourgeois ideology and the Marxist evolutionism of the II International. He longed for the return of barbarism as a repristination of human creativity in the hands of revolutionary trade unions. He preempted the creeping historical Angst of fin-de-siècle revolutionism—Rosa Luxemburg's "socialism or barbarism"—by actually identifying, in a consciously mythical way, the redemptive experience of social revolution with a mystique of violence. However, Belle Epoque Vichianism was far more molded by the peaceful neoliberalism of Croce than by the Sorelian paean of violent historical epiphanies; and Croce demolished *corsi* and *ricorsi* as a hopeless conceptual muddle, an archvulnerable "law" of history; upon which, interest in Vico became focused on his idea of historical knowledge.

Roughly speaking, modern Vichianism may be described as Crocean to the extent that it concentrates on the strictly epistemological qualities of its hero. Modern Vichianism is but a footnote to the *verum et factum convertuntur*, the Christian postulate that Vico borrowed from Augustinian theology and enshrined as the cardinal principle of

human knowledge. Man knows, or knows best, what he did—history—
rather than what he did not make—nature. "Only what the mind has
made does it fully understand," as Dilthey put it,[4] and in his *Life of
Schleiermacher* the founder of modern hermeneutics praised Vico's
"new science" as "one of the greatest triumphs of modern thought." Nor
did the praise remain a monopoly of Lebensphilosophie: It was renewed, for instance, by the most humanistic-minded of the neo-Kantian systems, that of Cassirer. Besides greeting Vico as the true
forerunner of his own theory of myth, in the second part of his *Philosophy of Symbolic Forms* (1925), Cassirer stated in his *Logic of the Humanities*
(1942) that Vico had rescued from Cartesianism the sense of the value
and uniqueness of historical knowledge.[5]

The result of all this was the enthronement of Vico as the main
challenge to Descartes. Human and humane knowledge, such is the
ideal opposed by the Neapolitan's "new science" to the dogmatic rationalism, impervious to history, of the founder of modern philosophy.
Cartesianism was once fought along *naturalist* assumptions largely
shared by itself, as in the British empiricists from Locke to Hume. Now,
thanks to the wide acknowledgment of Vico, it came to be rejected for
the sake of a quite different position. The latter is best called *culturalism*, the belief that not only is the human world a sphere of reality
irreducible to its physical underpinnings, but it also requires a separate
form of knowledge. What is at stake is the acceptance or refusal of
mechanism and materialism as a necessary scientific outlook.

The prevailing tone can be sensed in the introduction of Sir Isaiah
Berlin's *Vico and Herder*: 'Vico's notion of *scienza*...seems to embody a

---

[4] Dilthey, *Der Aufbau der geschichtlichen Welt in den Geisteswissenschaften*, Gesammelte
Schriften, vol. 7 (Stuttgart: Teubner, 1956²), p. 148. For the affinities between Vico and
Dilthey see the essays by H. A. Hodges and H. P. Rickman in GVIS, part IV, and the one by
Howard N. Tuttle in G. Tagliacozzo and D. P. Verene (eds), *Giambattista Vico's Science of
Humanity* (Baltimore: the Johns Hopkins Press, 1976), part III [hereafter: GVSH]. However,
Professor Hodges rightly recalls that the Vichian concern with "laws" in a "storia ideale
eterna" has no parallel in Dilthey's concept of history as a distinctly *individualizing* discipline.
This important point places Dilthey in the company of Herder and Ranke, not Vico. Here the
Herder-through-Dilthey tradition of German *historism* was deeply at odds with *historicism* in
Popper's sense of a search for historical laws; Vico's baroque providentialism was not, or not
so much. For the difference between historism (Historismus) and historicism, as well as the
different brands of historism, see inter alia J. G. Merquior, *Rousseau and Weber: Two Studies in
the Theory of Legitimacy* (London: Routledge and Kegan Paul, 1980), pp. 138-46.

[5] For the kinship between Vico and Cassirer's philosophy of the symbolic see Donald
Phillip Verene, "Vico's Science of Imaginative Universals and the Philosophy of Symbolic
Forms," GVSH, pp. 295-317, rather than the diffuse essay of Enzo Paci in GVIS, part IV.

view of causality which differs from those of Descartes or Hume or Kant or modern positivists..."⁶ The model involved, as Berlin himself makes clear in another book, is an autonomous kind of knowledge, not to be subsumed under any of Gilbert Ryle's species, "knowing that" and "knowing how," because it is closer to the knowledge we have when we feel we know somebody and his or her character; it is an empathy, a participant's knowledge, essentially distinct from impersonal observation.⁷ An introspective, imaginative, even intuitive grasping of motives—such is the gist of the culturalist approach to the uniqueness of individuals, ages, or cultures.

Beyond the common premise of culturalism contemporary Vichians usually part company. Some are content with sticking to the bare declaration of independence of historical understanding, or alternatively to elaborate on it—as does Berlin—by tracing a Counter-Enlightenment tradition stretching from Vico and Herder to de Maistre and Schelling.⁸ Others prefer to fuse the culturalist stance with philosophical tenets originally unconnected with it. Four paths, in particular, seem to attract a growing number of adherents. The first is the phenomenological appropriation of Vico's culturalism, undertaken not by orthodox Husserlians but by florid followers of Merleau-Ponty like Enzo Paci.⁹ The second is the Wittgensteinian reading of Vico—the verum/factum foreshadowing the interpretation of historical life through "language games" reconstructed by philosophy.¹⁰ The third sees Vico as a protostructuralist rhetorician, describing the similarities in the evolution of societies by means of a set of tropological transformations.¹¹ Finally, there occurs a fair measure of assimilation of Vichianism into the more historist brands of western Marxism; Jürgen Habermas' neo-Marxism is a case in point.

Habermas and Berlin on Vico

Habermas prizes Vico's Aristotelian recovery of *phronesis*, or prudential wisdom, in the teeth of the Cartesian primacy of science, or *episteme*.

---

⁶ Berlin, *Vico and Herder* (London: Hogarth Press, 1976), p. xiv.

⁷ Berlin, *Against the Current* (London: Hogarth Press, 1979), pp. 116-17 (on Vico's concept of knowledge).

⁸ Berlin, "The Counter-Enlightenment," originally in *Dictionary of the History of Ideas* (New York: Scribner's, 1968-73), repr. in *Against the Current,* op. cit.

⁹ See Paci's book *Ingens Sylva: saggio su Vico* (Milan: Mondadori, 1949, 1957) as well as John O'Neill's contribution to GVSH.

¹⁰ See for example Emanuele Riverso's "Vico and Wittgenstein" in GVSH.

¹¹ See Hayden White, "The Tropics of History: The Deep Structure of the *New Science*," in GVSH.

He is also keen on the deep rhetorical nature of the new science, an art of topics in defiance of the rationalist Occam's razor.[12] In his opus magnum, *Knowledge and Human Interests,* he goes so far as to put Vico's use of the *verum = factum* topos above Dilthey's attempt to ground it on a Kantian epistemology made of synthetic a priori judgments.[13]

In a way, however, Habermas turns this equation against Vico himself. Visibly put off by Vichian providentialism, he complains that in the *Scienza nuova* man knows history because he makes it, *yet is not its true subject.* We are at a far remove from the next creative reprise of the *verum-factum*: Kant's daring suggestion that prophets know the future because they see to it that it may come true. In short: unfortunately, the liberator of historical reason from the contempt of Cartesianism was less than a Promethean; his knowledge of the historical did not fully realize the self-creation of man through history.[14] What Michelet read into Vico was not his thought, just Hegel's and Marx's.

It is tempting to compare Habermas's criticism with Berlin's picture of Vico as the inventor of *verstehen,* of interpretative knowledge. Berlin discerns in Vico four types of knowledge. There is *scienza,* yielding a priori truths (*verum*) that "one can only have of one's own artefacts or fictions." There is *coscienza,* yielding the *certainty* of outer facts, things and events. There is the knowledge of eternal truths and principles, as in Vico's beloved Plato and, of course, in religious revelation. And there is knowledge *per caussas,* namely, the awareness of motives and intentions, our own or others', which we reach by scrutinizing the "modifications of our mind" (*New Science,* par. 331). Berlin attaches prime importance to the fourth type, the interpretive cognition of human intentions.[15] Vico "virtually invented the concept of the understanding"

[12] Habermas, *Theory and Practice* (London: Heinemann, 1974), pp. 45-46, 73-74.

[13] Habermas, *Knowledge and Human Interests* (London: Heinemann, 1972), pp. 148-49.

[14] Habermas, *Theory and Practice,* pp. 244-46. Habermas's strictures become all the more significant if one keeps in mind that they are by no means current coin in Western Marxism. For Lukács, the most important founder of this philosophical movement, Vico is a Promethean thinker all right, the main discoverer, before classical German philosophy, that men make their own history. See his book *History and Class Consciousness* (1923; English trans., London: Merlin Press, 1971), pp. 112, 145, and *The Young Hegel* (1948; English trans., London: Merlin Press, 1975), pp. 320, 545. What is more, it is Lukács, not Habermas, who is here in keeping with Marx's own view of the matter, as can be inferred from his complimentary reference to Vico in a footnote to the first volume of *Capital* (chap. XV, I).

[15] Berlin, *Vico and Herder,* cit., pp. 105-9. Note that while the book version (1975) of the essay on Vico in *Vico and Herder* speaks of *four* types of knowledge, the 1969 essay "Vico's concept of knowledge," originally published under a slightly different title in GVIS and collected into *Against the Current,* discussed only *two* such types: With platonic knowledge put aside, true knowing and causal knowledge were conflated, and the *certum* opposed to the *verum-*or-*per caussas* type.

because he focused on *acts,* not events—though, admittedly, acts were for him more often than not embodied in past *institutions.*

True, in the eyes of Vico providence is the true author of history. Berlin knows it, yet he reckons this belief as either a theological disguise or sheer inconsistency. Clearly, Vico—the ancestor of "voluntarism," even of the existentialist stress on human action[16]—held men and societies to evolve in response to their own aims. Furthermore, he saw that in this human pursuit of goals there are no fixed, preordained ends.[17] For Vico did not belong to the older of the two main Western traditions of social thought—the one that, from Plato to Comte, invariably rationalistically asserts an ethical monism, an essentialist thesis of human nature and of a summum bonum. Rather, he seems to have been the first thinker ever to work out the bold idea (adumbrated by Machiavelli) that there is no one single universal human goal, high or low. Vico was the first to have made explicit, albeit in his crooked, often obscure prose, Berlin's dearest conviction: the sacredness of ethical pluralism.[18]

But let us return to our dear *verum = factum* topos and notice the difference between Berlin's reading and that of Habermas. The latter rightly found Vico to be wanting in Promethean spirit; accordingly, he confines the *verum-factum* to the epistemological level. Curiously enough it is Berlin, a good agnostic in regard to the logic of history, whose concern is from the start strictly epistemological, who reverts to the stress on Vichian "anthropogony," the theme—which later so impressed the young Marx in Hegel—of the self-constitution of mankind through history.

Homo non intelligendo: Vico as a protosociologist

Who is closer to the Vichian truth, Habermas or Berlin? Do men make their own history or not, in the *Scienza nuova?* Now, while each position could easily gather quotations from the book, some stressing human agency, others, no less numerous, invoking the power of providence, perhaps the best way to solve the problem is to draw attention to another topos in Vico, closely related to his providentialism. This

---

[16] Idem, pp. 109, 114 (in agreement with the Vico expert Max Fisch's rapprochement with existentialism).

[17] Idem, pp. 113-14.

[18] Berlin, *Against the Current,* pp. 6, 37, 67-79, 301.

topos, far less cherished by Vichians throughout the ages, speaks of the *unintended effects* of social action.

Homo non intelligendo fit omnia: Such was, according to Meinecke, Vico's emendation of the rationalist account of society in natural law theory.[19] The jewel in the jusnaturalist conceptual weaponry—the notion of a social contract—portrayed history as an arena of man's rational will: *homo intelligendo fit omnia.* By contrast Vico pointed to the significance of positive unintended consequences of men's acts. Divine providence so contrived events as to put man's selfish behavior at the service of beneficial ends (*Scienza nuova,* pars. 133, 341-42, 344, 1108). Thus marriage grew out of lust because it held the best way to protect children (par. 336); religious awe led men to the experience of law (pars. 177-78); and civil authority profited by the disruptive effects of the strife between patricians and plebeians. Well before Hume and others denounced the logical inconsistencies and empirical weakness of the contractarian idea as historical explanation, Vico shrewdly measured the gap between voluntary action and historical outcome.

Although his conjectures about what actually thwarted men's intentions were often as fanciful as they were pious, like his postulation of the Flood, even so they were, from another point of view, quite felicitous: They helped to discard what would be otherwise overly finalist, too much teleological, explanations. For instance, in Vico's imaginary reconstruction feral men came to abandon promiscuous fornication out of fear of natural forces such as thunder, and took refuge in caves followed by one or just a few women, thereby starting early family life. They therefore arrived at the institution of marriage without any wish to do so, since they had no inkling of its useful implications. In W. H. Walsh's comment providence, not man, did the intending[20]—and, one might add, historical teleology was kept well outside the range of actual social action. The moral is all too clear: Men act with goals in view, yet these do not command the unfolding of history.

By the same token, remove providence from the picture and you get a tale as free from teleological explanations as Darwin's story about the importance of long necks for the survival of giraffes. Darwinian—as distinct from Lamarckian—giraffes do not evolve a long neck *in order to* better survive by easily getting food—they survive because they *hap-*

---

[19] Meinecke, op. cit., p. 43. Vico actually employs such a dictum in the context of the etymological remarks of *S.N.,* par. 405.

[20] W. H. Walsh, "The logical status of Vico's ideal eternal history," GVSH, p. 145.

pened to have a long neck, and the latter proved quite useful in their nutrition. Similarly, Vico's *bestioni* did not marry in order to ensure the survival of their progeny—yet their descendants survived because as defenseless children they were better protected within families. One could say, with Alfred Schutz, that Vico's *bestioni,* frightened by the thunder into chastity, were impelled by a "because-motive," and were not at all self-propelled by an "in-order-to" motive.[21]

We can ignore the fancifulness of Vico's prehistorical hypotheses because nobody reads the *New Science* as a book of history; it is only read as a seminal treatise on the logic of historical knowledge. However, taking it at such an epistemological level means, or at any rate should mean, properly to acknowledge the centrality of the *unintended* in historical change, over and above the role of motives and the understanding thereof. Vico's emphasis on the cunning of providence does not remind one of hermeneutics and the art of imaginative empathy, but rather of a crucial leitmotif in sociological thought: the heteronomy of ends, or the disparity between act and result.

The theme of the unintended and often undesirable effects of human action amounts to a specification of what was for Pareto the chief task of sociology: the analysis of the sense of irrationality, or, in any event, of *complexity,* in human action.[22] It is precisely the pervasiveness of "perverse effects" in social experience, argues their best living theorist, French sociologist Raymond Boudon, that damages the credibility of cybernetic utopias—the idea of a programmed, or likely to be programmed, society.[23]

Significantly, the main paradigms of sociological explanation all deal with unintended outcomes. Let us, with Boudon's help,[24] glimpse at three such paradigms: the capitalists' behavior in the third volume of Marx's *Capital,* that of the French aristocrats as contrasted with their English counterparts in Tocqueville's *The Old Regime and the Revolution,* and that of the Puritans in Weber's *The Protestant Ethic and the Spirit of Capitalism.*

Marx's capitalists, aiming at more profit, invested in new machinery, thus unwittingly raised the proportion of fixed capital in regard to

[21] Alfred Schutz, *The Phenomenology of the Social World* (1932) (London: Heinemann, 1972), pp. 86-96.

[22] On this point see Raymond Boudon, *La Logique du Social* (Paris: Hachette, 1979), pp. 14-19.

[23] Boudon, *Effects Pervers et Ordre Social* (Paris: Presses Universitaires de France, 1977), p. 13.

[24] Idem, chap. VII.

variable capital—in regard, that is, to surplus value; hence a falling rate of profit, and consequently the weakening of capitalism itself.

Tocqueville's French noblemen, attracted by crown offices instead of turning to capitalist entrepreneurship, eventually hardened the hierarchic privileges of old French society, thus contributing to its final breakdown.

Weber's Puritans, earnestly seeking the salvation of their souls, chose the ascetic, money-saving way of life that bred widespread capitalism and its aftermath, secularization, or, in any event, the dwindling of ascetic religiosity in the West.

In all cases events defeated the acts that gave them birth. And mark: none of these famous sociological scenarios tells anything secondary or peripheral; all dwell on major social changes, at the very root of our present world, its economy, its polity, and its social structure.

The kind of explanation couched in Vico's operation of the providence—the broad pattern of what he called "ideal eternal history"—offers the same basic logic: It begins in intention and ends in full irony. In addition, Vico's providential tales (e.g., the origin of marriage) work as a neat illustration of the one among Boudon's sociological paradigms that qualifies as (partly) "determinist."[25] I refer, of course, to the Protestant ethic story. Weber's account is "determinist," where Marx's or Tocqueville's are not, in that it presupposes that the social agents under analysis had their behavior previously shaped by a given pattern of socialization—in this case their Puritan upbringing. The Puritans' action was dictated to them by an explanatory variable not wholly belonging to the present of their acts but stemming from their past and cultural background.[26]

It is my contention that the affinities between the Vichian *storia ideale eterna* and the logic of the sociological explanation of historical change dispose of Habermas's rather doctrinaire embarassment at Vico's providentialism. Nevertheless, in a sense Habermas's Promethean disappointment at the idea of providence authoring history says more about the importance of Vico for social science than does Berlin's infatuation with imaginative understanding. Why? Because the praise of Vico as inventor of *verstehen,* for all its humanistic ranking of "act" well above "event," evinces no real grasp of the true fate of action in real history: a

[25] Idem, pp. 192, 199-200.

[26] This is emphasized, in the context of rival interpretations of what Weber was up to in *The Protestant Ethic,* in J. G. Merquior, *Rousseau and Weber,* op. cit., pp. 178-80.

complex interplay of will and circumstance, which can seldom be explained chiefly, still less solely, in terms of conscious motives. To be sure, history is man's doing, but it rarely corresponds to what men wanted, let alone pursued. Progress itself, even in our days of technological planning, largely remains unforeseen—an unexpected bonus resting on a cumulative growth of wealth and skill that far surpasses the intentions of each of their individual or collective originators.[27]

Marx and Engels, in their youthful Feuerbachian days, revolted against the residual logicism of the Hegelian left. They made clear that history was not the work of a logos, not even of an abstract, generic concept of man. As they wrote in the *Holy Family*: "History does *nothing*,...Rather it is *man*, actual and living man, who does all...who possesses and fights; history does not use man as a means for *its* purposes as though it were a person apart; it is *nothing* but the activity of man pursuing his ends."

But the old Engels knew still better. In *Ludwig Feuerbach and the Outcome of Classical German Philosophy* (1888)—a book intended as a mature reprise of Marxism's settling of accounts with Hegel, Feuerbach, and most of German mid-century advanced philosophy—he preferred to stress how seldom in history conscious design is achieved: "Thus," added Engels,

the conflicts of countless wills and individual actions engender in the field of history a situation wholly analogous to that which prevails in unconscious nature. The ends of actions are willed, but the results that follow are not, or if at the onset they seem to correspond nonetheless to the goal pursued, eventually they have consequences quite different from those which were aimed at.

The *Holy Family* quotation is perfectly right as a reminder against philosophical hypostases of social action. History is indeed no logos—it is just man's doings. But the trouble is that those who extol the powers of *praxis* do not leave it at that. They invariably wish to celebrate human freedom at the expense of the scientific explanation of social conduct and social change (that such explanation often remains none too satisfactory is beside the point, for it does not prejudice the validity of the

[27] For a forceful argumentation of this see F. A. Hayek, *The Constitution of Liberty* (London: Routledge and Kegan Paul, 1960), chap. 3.

attempt). Now from the viewpoint of explanatory social science (and a social science that is not vocationally explanatory is not yet science; it is at most a preface to science) the interesting proposition clearly belongs to the old Engels, not to the earlier, Feuerbachian, one. Nobody denies that history is made up of human will, but unfortunately, this truth is either trivial or false. If it means that history is the realm of intent and design, it is plainly false; if, on the other hand, it means that history is in man's work, not in the hands of any superhuman agency, then it is of course true, but also exceedingly unenlightening as an explanatory road, since it does not even hint at any causal mechanisms for understanding how social action is triggered, complicated, or constrained. That is why *praxis* worship has never been of real help to the rational account of action.

Motive and intention do play an important part in history, but they are far from encompassing the total meaning of most major historical processes. Therefore, while the understanding of past acts and attitudes is a necessary step in historical research, it cannot be a sufficient one. It is a good—in fact, often the most reasonable—starting point, yet in time it must give way, in the course of explanation, to the identification of causal factors of a quite different nature. In a nutshell: If the understanding of the intentional side of social action does not yield to a search for those various determinisms (social or otherwise) abhorred by the humanist mind in its misplaced concern for free will, there is little hope of avoiding the crippling of explanatory social science. Such is the lucid lesson from Weber—but also a fruitful insight in Vico's *Scienza nuova,* shining beneath the theological trappings of almighty providence. That strange Talmudic self-styled Marxist, Walter Benjamin, used to insist that truth lies "in the death of intention"—a fine description of the meaning of history in Vico's weird treatise.

Neither those who, like Hannah Arendt or Habermas, complain that "Vico's philosophy of history remains retrospective,"[28] nor those who, like Alain Pons, think that this belief in the contemplative character of Vico's views deserves serious qualification, seem to realize the centrality of this point. Consequently, in their concern with action in the present and the future they neglect the worthy methodological role of the *actus,*

---

[28] Habermas, *Theory and Practice,* p. 245. Cf. Hannah Arendt, *Between Past and Future* (New York: Viking Press, 1968), chap. 2. The conspicuous influence of Arendt's stress on the value of the *vita activa,* the free space of speech and (political) action, on the work of Habermas can be traced since the latter's first book, *Strukturwandel der Oeffentlichkeit* (Neuwied: Luchterhand, 1962).

of the past act, in Vico's logic of history. Regardless of his swerving or vacillation on the need for giving providence a helping hand—which eventually prevented him from including his 1731 *Pratica* in the third edition of the *New Science*[29]—the truth is that in a view of history dominated by the theme of the gap between intention and result, the analytic focus on action must of necessity privilege the past—the irrevocably done, not the future act. However, this imposition of historical knowledge in no way detracts from the "openness" of the present or, indeed, from the role of prudence in it.

The fetishism of meaning

Ultimately both the overrating of motives and "understanding" and the impatience with the backward-looking thrust in Vico stem from a common source: humanist anthropocentrism. An heir to *historism*— indeed, its best-known paladin in the Anglo-Saxon countries—Sir Isaiah Berlin may rest content with "the motivated" in Vico, for in his own Herzen-like distrust of every ideological despotism, his keen awareness that progress worship often turns into sacrifices to ruthless new Molochs,[30] he has no use whatsoever for Promethean creeds and *historicist* (not historist) "laws" of development. History for Berlin deals above all with the uniqueness of the individual slice of time, which no amount of general laws can ever reproduce. Like Hamann, Goethe, and Meinecke, Berlin subscribes to the motto of historism: *individuum est ineffabile.* Mark the difference between historicism, the concept of historical laws, and historism, the apotheosis of the unique historical *individuum*; we shall return to it shortly. Berlin is the archhistorist among present thinkers.

By contrast, Habermas, coming as he does from the historicist tradition of Hegel and Marx, with its Promethean overtones, cannot help demanding that man's authorship of history be strongly underlined, by Vico as by everyone else. Like Berlin, however, Habermas operates with a humanistic premise: *the paramountcy of human purpose* in matters social. Berlin concentrates on the epistemological level of the premise; Habermas, on its practical side. The trouble is that neither allows what

---

[29] See Alain Pons, "Prudence and Providence: The *Pratica della Scienza nuova* and the Problem of Theory and Practice in Vico," GVSH, pp. 431-48.

[30] Cf. Isaiah Berlin, *Russian Thinkers* (London: Hogarth Press, 1978), pp. 89-92.

they say of Vico to do justice to the most relevant aspect of his thought, as far as social science is concerned.

Croce credited Vico with the belief that our knowledge of history is wholly a priori. Berlin's neoidealism is not so brazen. It does not assert any apriorism. Yet it circumvents a great deal of empirically given historical causality by sticking to the understanding of purposeful action as the specialty of sociological cognition. However, as the accomplished Vicologist Leon Pompa and another Edinburgh scholar, W. H. Walsh, have pithily argued, Vico's epistemology is not to be misconstrued as though the *verum* = *factum* amounted to a glorification of either the cultural relativism of "conceptual" social science or of the humanist myth of a dialogue of souls through the gifted medium of a special kind of interpersonal insight.[31]

To begin with there could not possibly exist any communion of souls in meaning in Vico, for, as he took pains to stress, "poetic," primitive man acted on conceptual schemes widely different from ours. For instance, the *bestioni* heard in thunder a command of Jove—but it is only in *our mind,* not in "poetic" imagination, that thunder and the god are conceptually distinguished. As Pompa impeccably remarks, to this extent *scienza*—Vico's knowledge of the *verum* which is *factum*—is something reserved *to the historian,* emphatically not something shared with him by the human agents whom he studies.[32] Behind the charming cameo of Vico-the-forerunner-of-Dilthey, then, there lurks that old fallacy of hermeneutics: the fetishism of meaning as immediate presence—and also, of course, its attendant extolling of "human" meaning over (natural) cause.[33]

When the true founder of the hermeneutic tradition in social science, Wilhelm Dilthey, first traced the history of the concept of *verstehen,* he set great store by the fact that between Schleiermacher, "the Kant of hermeneutics," and his own day (1860) the art of interpretation shifted focus from sacred or classic texts to human expression in general, holy or profane, so that not only the word but life itself came to be carefully interpreted. With which, wrote the young Dilthey, the mystery of meaning came to be seen to lie no longer in an invisible transcen-

---

[31] See Pompa's "Vico and the Presuppositions of Historical Knowledge," and Walsh, "The logical status...", op. cit., in GVSH, pp. 125-53.

[32] Pompa, loc. cit., p. 132.

[33] On the meaning/cause antithesis and neoidealism in contemporary social theory see Ernest Gellner, *Cause and Meaning in the Social Sciences* (London: Routledge and Kegan Paul, 1973), especially chaps. 2 to 5.

dence, but in the "immediate presence" of the world of human experience.[34]

What Dilthey failed to realize, as he thus beautifully welded the two main themes of his lifelong *Lebensphilosophie* (the *verstehen* plus the *Erlebnis* motive), was that the lay mystique of immediate meaning would prove itself to be no less mythical than the religious truth it came to replace.[35] As such, hermeneutics was bound to pit "meaning" against "cause," "act" against "event," intelligible purpose against impersonal nature—a combat fit for the humanist mind but of little avail to the social scientist. For, as Ernest Gellner wisely put it, "human and social life consists of the interplay of "conceptual" or "intelligible" factors, on one hand, and brute, blind forces, extraneous to the ideas and illusions of a culture, on the other. There is *no* way of telling a priori which kind of factor is crucial at any one point, and no way of guaranteeing a priori (or at all) that we live in an untainted realm of meaning."[36] Curiously enough, unlike today's neoidealists, Vico—who very probably believed in "invisible transcendence"—does not appear to have forgotten these basic truths when sketching his fanciful tales of institution birth.

Furthermore, on close inspection the case against Vico's providentialism, on the grounds that it obliterates human agency, sounds rather overstated. Apart from the fact that Vichian providentalism can be easily translated, as we have shown, into the language of a sharp realization of the ways of history, even in its strictly literal meaning Vico's providence is no busybody. Meinecke's comment seems to me quite perceptive: "[Vico] withdrew the divine hand, as it were, to a

---

[34] Wilhelm Dilthey, "Das hermeneutische System Schleiermachers in der Auseinandersetzung mit der älteren protestantischen Hermeneutik," in *Gesammelte Schriften* (Stuttgart: Teubner, 1966); quoted, and well commented on, by Michael Ermarth, *Wilhelm Dilthey: the critique of historical reason* (Chicago: University of Chicago Press, 1978), p. 243.

[35] I fervently hope nobody is going to mistake my criticism of the mystique of immediate meaning as allegiance to litero-philosophical fads like "deconstruction"—the fruitless and exceedingly arbitrary pedantry developed by Jacques Derrida out of mainly Heideggerian sources. Deconstruction also castigates presence and immediacy, but it conspicuously lacks any true, i.e., logico-empirical, explanatory calling. On the other hand, Dilthey was not of course after *immediate* meaning, but rather after the meaning of immediate presence—the immediacy of Erlebnis, or "life" in the sense of life (and live) experience, experience endowed with rich inner meaning. But Dilthey remained an analyst of texts, not of social processes. It is all the more disturbing to see those who claim to be his followers write as though they would like to reduce sociological explanations to the almost instant seizure of meanings within intentional action.

[36] Gellner, *Cause and Meaning*, op. cit., p. 87.

greater distance from history, though without weakening its control, and gave history its natural freedom of movement."[37]

The uses of contextualism

Ever since the Renaissance, Philology, biblical hermeneutics, and legal history had known how to dissociate texts and monuments from the historical accretions of meaning and to try to restore them to their original cultural environment. Vico raised contextual exegesis into the *via regia* of philological reconstruction. But contextualism could be put to very different uses. On the one hand, Renaissance Gallican jurists like the great François Hotman employed it to deny legitimacy to the primacy of Roman law, in the name of the authority of a context of national mores. On the other hand, Spinoza used it to demonstrate the irrationality of the Mosaic image of God, thus undermining the Calvinist paradigm of a Hebrew theocracy founded on the theology of the Pentateuch. This meant to direct the sense of history *against tradition*.

What about *Vichian* contextualism? There seems to be at least one significant instance of a progressive usage: Ferdinando Galiani's "economic Vichianism." Galiani (1728-87), the Neapolitan "abbé" whose output spans the decades between the second *Scienza nuova* and the French Revolution, was every inch a philosophe. But he was also, in the words of Schumpeter, "the one eighteenth-century economist who always insisted on the variability of man and on the relativity, to time and place, of all policies."[38] His quarrel with doctrinaire physiocratism, in his shrewd and witty *Dialogues sur le commerce des blés* (1769), is as such exemplary. The book had a decisive influence on its editor, Diderot, whose historical sense was broadened and sharpened by Galiani's analyses.[39]

Ever since Fausto Nicolini, Vico's famous Crocean biographer, Galiani's debt to Vico has been highlighted. The link was minimized by Schumpeter[40] but persuasively reasserted (on conceptual grounds

---

[37] Meinecke, *Historism*, op. cit., p. 42.
[38] Joseph A. Schumpeter, *History of Economic Analysis* (London: Allen & Unwin, 1954), p. 292.
[39] Cf. Arthur M. Wilson, *Diderot* (New York: Oxford University Press, 1972), pp. 551-56.
[40] Schumpeter, op. cit., p. 300, footnote.

apart from technical economic theory) by Giorgio Tagliacozzo.[41] Now Galiani's reasoned refusal of dogmatic application of laissez-faire economics to agriculture was not a reactionary move, but a critical qualification of *von oben* reforms (the tandem physiocrats-cum-enlightened despotism, so conspicuous in Turgot) in the name of historical knowledge. Typically, his motto remained a bow to critical reason: "Je ne suis pour rien....Je suis *pour qu'on ne déraisonne pas*".

As for Vico himself, he doubtless sided with plain traditionalist, not revisionist and heretical, contextualism. By the time of devising his "new science," he had become a baroque Burke, as it were, in all matters religious and political. The gulf between Vico's conformism and Neapolitan reformists of the Seicento, such as Pietro Giannone, reminds one of the polemics between the progressive bent of Hegel state worship and the contextualist conservatism of Savigny.

Yet even though the mature Vico was a staunch conservative in his opinions (and the point is still partly debatable), there is no gainsaying that his method, his *philological archeology,* was not. As Piovani aptly observes, his excavation of the roots of authority was at the very least a dubious service to authoritarianism.[42] It must be recognized that Vico's heterodox way of upholding orthodoxy was far from appealing to the religious establishment, in those days of hard-fought struggle between church and state. Presumably Vico, like Marx's Luther, wanted to shake faith in authority just to restore the authority of faith,[43] but the end result was, once again, very far from his intentions.

From historicism to historism

Be that as it may, all the preceding remarks on Vico's beliefs and politics refer only to his *ideology*; they do not address the problem of the *validity* of his insights. As we have seen, some Vichian ideas concerning the nature of historical change and its conceptualization proved to be of lasting value. The joint effect of his views on collective behavior as "occasioned spontaneity" (Funkenstein's phrase) and on the dialectical

---

[41] Giorgio Tagliacozzo, "Economic Vichianism: Vico, Galiani, Croce—Economics, Economic Liberalism," GVIS, pp. 349-68. Cf. also Tagliacozzo, *Economisti Napoletani dei secoli XVII e XVIII* (Bologna: Cappelli, 1937), pp. xvi-xx, xl-lxviii.

[42] Pietro Piovani, "Apoliticality and Politicality in Vico," GVSH, pp. 405-8.

[43] Karl Marx, "Introduction to a Contribution to the Critique of Hegel's "Philosophy of Right," in *Critique of Hegel's "Philosophy of Right"*, ed. Joseph O'Malley (Cambridge: Cambridge University Press, 1970), p. 138.

alchemy of intentions and results constitutes a remarkable anticipation of our soundest concepts of historical processes. For Vico, men are neither the mere puppets of an alleged but unwarranted historical determinism nor the happy masters of the long-run consequences of their own acts—not too implausible a way of looking at things.

I believe it is high time we bring home to social scientists in general a portrait of Vico along these lines, rather than the jaded encomium of him as a celebrator of human creativity or, worse, as the prophet of an uncanny special kind of knowledge, distinct by nature from the causal character of empirical cognition. Perhaps our present idea of Vico is too lopsided in a "humanist" direction, be it "Promethean" or "romantic"; and maybe the lopsidedness is aggravated by the strange phenomenon that plagues western Marxism and, within it, much of the contemporary valuation of Vico—*the supersession, in modern Marxism, of historicism by historism.*

Classical Marxism was shamelessly *historicist*: It offered a logic of history—indeed, a historiosophy.[44] But it certainly was no *historism*: It showed no delight in the historical individuum per se. Of course Marx protested, as he once did in an eloquent reply to the Russian Marxist Mikhailovsky, whenever his theories were misused as a historico-philosophical passe partout, utterly blind to the manifold variety of histor-

---

[44] The concept of historiosophy, forged by the Polish Hegelian August Cieszkowski (*Prolegomena zur Historiosophie,* 1838), has recently been made into a main element of the philosophical characterization of Marxism by Leszek Kolakowski's comprehensive *Main Currents of Marxism* (Oxford: Clarendon, 1978), a critical summa likely to command the field of Marxology for many years to come. The basic meaning of historiosophy is historical theodicy: the justification of history in the name of a logic of ages and events leading to a final blissful state of mankind. Historiosophy posits the eschaton as a goal attainable at the epilogue of a world-story. Roughly, it imposed a soteriological slant on the "philosophy of history," a characteristic intellectual exercise of German theologicians since Lessing. The peak of historiosophy was reached in the system of Hegel. Marx welded the historiosophical framework with an economic version of the class war theme, and by so doing gave a spectacularly dramatic twist to the soteriology built into it: historical bliss was no longer the "Christian-bourgeois" (Loewith) present, but the radiant communist future, to be conquered through violent social revolution. As Otto Hintze used to say, there are two main forms of conceiving of historical movement, comparable to two old rival geological theories: Neptunism sees water as the formative agent, working slowly by sedimentation; Plutonism, on the other hand, claims that the creative force is volcanic activity, explosive by nature. See *The Historical Essays of Otto Hintze,* ed. Felix Gilbert (New York: Oxford University Press, 1975), p. 396. Neptunian theories are evolutionary, Plutonian ones revolutionary. Clearly, Marxism, as compared to Hegel, is historical Plutonism. The historiosophical grounding of Marxism is forcefully unraveled by Lukács in *History and Class Consciousness* (1923).

ical contexts.[45] But he was quite alien to the historist mystique of ineffable historical uniqueness—or else he would never have dreamed, no matter how wrongly, of historical laws or, for that matter, of historical materialism. Above all classical Marxism did not vouch for any claims that historical interpretation ought to be kept out of touch with causal explanations and their inherent mechanist outlook.

Yet living Marxism, ever since Lukács' *History and Class Consciousness,* embarked on quite a different path. As if the failure of revolution in the West had shaken irretrievably their faith in historical laws, Western Marxists turned more and more from historicism to historism—and often, as in the case of the Frankfurt school, to historism with a vengeance; a frantic onslaught on science and its rationality.

The grounds for the supersession of historicism by historism within Marxism were laid when Lukács redefined Marxism as a gnosis of Totality, starkly severed from mechanism, determinism, and ultimately, albeit unavowedly, materialism; materialism, that is, in the rich epistemological sense of a flair to infrastructure, an attempt to uncover the underlying mechanisms of social processes.[46] But the open rejection of historicism came to fruition much later, when even lip-service respect for the main tenets of the founding fathers of Marxism was no longer required, and the need for a critical "reconstruction" of their theory became the prevalent mood.[47]

[45] Cf. Karl Marx, *Selected Writings in Sociology and Social Philosophy,* ed. T. B. Bottomore and Maxilien Rubel (London: Watts, 1956), pp. 22-23. It is perhaps useful to add that Western Marxism has been recently bemused into a quasi-mystical concern with the uniqueness of the historical by the Althusserian school. As Georg Lichtheim was quick to point out—see his *From Marx to Hegel* (London: Orbach & Chambers, 1971), p. 149—the Althusser of *For Marx,* while speculating about contradiction, speaks of the October Revolution in frontal disagreement with the idea of historical laws, based on an attempt at a theoretical generalization of Lenin's well-known remarks about the uniqueness of 1917 as an historical opportunity. No "logic of history" is invoked—just the historical individuum. But what a chasm between Marx's candid warnings about the danger of treating economic determinism as a suprahistorical, ready-made explanation and Althusser's convoluted and unconvincing usage of "overdetermination"—a *flatus vocis* intended to cope with the elusiveness of historical events from the viewpoint of causality. At any rate, "overdetermination" makes of Althusserianism, for all its antihistorist disclaimers (as shown, for instance, in its strictures against Gramsci), a virtuous historism *malgré lui.*

[46] For the crucial place of the theme of infrastructure in a rational epistemology of social science see "Methodological Infrastructuralism: An Approach to the Sociology of Culture," in J. G. Merquior, *The Veil and the Mask: Essays on Culture and Ideology* (London: Routledge & Kegan Paul, 1979), pp. 62-79.

[47] Cf. Jürgen Habermas, *Zur Rekonstruktion des Historischen Materialismus* (Frankfurt: Suhrkamp, 1976), trans. *Communication and the Evolution of Society* (London: Heinemann, 1979), chaps. 3 and 4.

Helmut Fleischer's *Marxism and History* (1969) epitomizes the new look, strongly influenced by the work of Habermas. In the name of "critical theory" Fleischer polemicizes against two Marxist concepts of history: on the one hand, history as a march of the ages toward the full self-realization of the "whole man," the Renaissance *uomo universale*; on the other hand, history viewed as a process governed by objective laws inherent in "a logic of social relations uninfluenced by human intentions."[48] Briefly, the Frankfurt school declares war both on Marxism as historiosophy and on Marxism as historical materialism.

While no one will cry over the Habermasian dismissal of historiosophy (being as we are too much aware of historiosophical Gulags), there are plenty of reasons for regretting the eclipse of historical materialism. Undogmatically conceived as a sense of social determinisms, materialism is very much in decline in social science at large. There is a fine exception—historiography—but even here the tide of unreliable psychohistory is wrecking the sound, spontaneous, epistemological materialism of historians.[49] The collapse of materialism as an epistemological duty is particularly visible in present-day Marxism, especially since its penetration into the social sciences has impressively grown during the last two decades. It is as though historical materialism, undoubtedly the biggest contribution of Marxism to social science, were being reduced to a historians' job, but kept at arm's distance in the would-be Marxist analysis of contemporary society. The sad truth is that, as a sociological language, Marxism is no longer materialist, except in a purely verbal way; nor indeed materialist have been its main rivals in the field: the now much abused structural-functionalism, ethnomethodology, "humanist" sociology, etc. As a whole, Western Marxists have gladly joined the "antipositivist" rage. They gloat over "meaning" in social lives, but they are patently incurious about causal approaches.

So "humanism" holds the field—to such an extent that even the avowed antihumanists, like Althusserian scholastics, pay virtue the homage of vice by dropping in turn the embarrassing economic determinism of the classics, without suggesting any really fruitful alternative for empirical research (but then, we all know that empirical research is not the forte of Althusserians). Can we possibly be surprised if, in such

---

[48] Helmut Fleischer, *Marxism and History* (New York: Harper & Row, 1973), pp. 7-8.
[49] See the sensible criticisms of David E. Stannard in *Shrinking History. On Freud and the Failure of Psychohistory* (New York: Oxford University Press, 1980).

a climate of opinion, old Vico is treated as a founding father of Historismus? Or if, at the other extreme, he is taken to be a clever protostructuralist, a reducer of ages to master tropes—but in any case the author of a grammar of diachrony that is thoroughly severed from social action analysis, and therefore does not even begin to explain historical change?

Back to anthropomorphism

Historism and "structuralism"—history without any logic and "logic" without history—are far from valuing the best of Vico. To begin with he was not a historist. Meinecke was right in seeing his *scienza nuova* as an essentially stunted historism, for it had grasped historical development but not historical individuality. The difference is that we take this verdict as evidence of Vico's sensible universalism. He was as good a "contextualist" as anyone, but he kept his mind open to the role of the general in human mind, hence in history as well.

This positive clinging to a rational ground, from which alone historical diversity can be compared and understood, was a precious legacy to what is probably the sole outstanding instance of Vichianism in the Enlightenment: the economics of Galiani. Significantly, our clever abbé, for all his keenness on the diversity of social contexts, abstained from heralding the economic historism of the "historical school" (Roscher, Hildebrand, Knies) and its silly denial of the possibility of establishing general principles of economics.[50] Like Carl Menger, the great late-nineteenth-century challenger of economic Historismus, Galiani refused to choose "between theory and history." He seems to have realized that if theory without history is blind, history without theory is nonsense.

The net result of both historist and pseudostructuralist readings of Vico is to deliver him right in the hands of an intellectual disease he correctly diagnosed and shunned: anthropomorphism. Which puts us back where we began. Historism is inherently anthropomorphic in that it thrives on an ideal of empathic *description* of historical objects, leaving no room for the inevitable gap that every true *explanation* (of history as of everything else) creates between the self-image of times and groups and their explained reality.

[50] See G. Tagliacozzo, "Economic Vichianism," op. cit., GVIS, p. 362.

Historism perverts the sense of context involved in—indeed, required by—historical analysis into an abdication of the comparative
approach and of the search for common ground between different ages
and places. While such an abdication is ultimately impossible in the
actual practice of the study of history, attempting it seriously damages
the depth of the analysis, maiming, in particular, its explanatory dimension.[51] Once fetishized, contextualism ceases to be an instrument of
sociological explanation and in fact turns against its fulfilment.

Wittgensteinian readings of Vico issue in the same shortcomings:
They, too, are obviously perverse contextualisms. As for "structuralist"
Vichianism, its chief defect is to neglect the sound naturalism of the
Scienza nuova, its keen realization that historical change is prompted by
transformations of the mind *in response to external stimuli,* natural and
social.[52] "Structuralist" tropological interpretations completely blur
this key element of the Vichian picture of change, with the result that
they are left without any proper theory of change. The sequence from
metaphor to synecdoche through metonymy as pivotal tropes and
world-views of each age remains unexplained. "Structuralist" Vichianism gets rid of the fetishism of context but leaves intact the atrophy of
explanation.

Social science is able to escape anthropomorphism because historical
analysis does not imply our full identification with the subject matter,
only our understanding of past behavior predicated on human *universals* and yet permeated by changing collective concepts. When Simmel
wrote that we need not be Caesar in order to understand his actions, he

[51] There has been recently a lively defense of the full description ideal in historiography
(as against explanation), curiously conducted in terms not of the empathic epistemology of
classic historism but of praxeology, i.e., the social-action approach: Paul Veyne's *Comment on
écrit l'histoire* (Paris: Seuil, 1971, abridged ed., 1978). But Veyne's main argument seems
vitiated by the non sequitur of believing that, as one can never explain everything in the
événement, one cannot explain anything well while being faithful to the richness of events.
This view sounds surprisingly pre-Hintzean as concerns the compatibility between the
attention to the historical individuum and the analysis of action with explanatory aims. See
Otto Hintze. "The Individualist and the Collective Approach to History," and especially his
1927 essay "Troeltsch and the Problems of Historicism" (i.e., Historismus, historism—J. G.
M.) in *The Historical Essays of Otto Hintz,* op. cit., pp. 357-421. Hintze skillfully fuses the
Rankean motives of classical historism with two Weberian stances: praxeology, and the
comparative method based on "ideal type" heuristics. On the need for the praxeological
approach in social science see R. Boudon, *La Logique du Social,* op. cit., and also J. G.
Merquior, "Mort de l'homo oeconomicus?" *European Journal of Sociology,* XXI (1980); 190-212.
[52] Outside classical Vico scholarship, the natural determinism element in Vico is acknowledged by historians of sociological ideas. See for example Marvin Harris, *The Rise of Anthropological Theory. A History of Theories of Culture* (New York: Crowell, 1968), pp. 19-20.

was stressing the power of empathy: We need not be Caesar because we can very well feel like him. But Weber retorted that we need *not even* feel like him to grasp the meaning of his acts; praxeology, not psychology, is what is involved in historical understanding.

That is why historical understanding is no irrational (and ultimately impossible) plunge into the past; rather, it is the skillful cognitive management of historical *distance*. As writes Raymond Aron: "if the universe of the interpreter had no kinship with the universe to be interpreted, the interpretation would be impossible. If they were confused with one another, there would be no history."[53] Against this plain, epistemological good sense, the neohistorists claim a "special kind" of intuitive knowledge, by empathy, of other cultures or of the past. Most present-day culturalist epistemologists seem to assume the excellence of that old historist shibboleth, knowledge by total immersion—what Ernest Gellner has sarcastically dubbed "the Baptist theory of knowledge,"[54] an epistemological myth last propped by the cult of field work in anthropology. Now the cultic view of field work—atheoretical, description-monger field-workism—has been vastly undermined by the separate but equally brilliant examples of Claude Lévi-Strauss and Nero Wolfe. It looks rather strange, therefore, to see its mythical idea of knowledge survive. Nevertheless it does survive, if only because the irrationalism of historism has received a lot of new converts from schools that, like Western Marxism, exchanged the historicism of their origins by the historist habit of stubbornly spurning "positivist" causal explanations.

Thus anthropomorphism, once denounced by Vico, has become a motive for exalting him. However, the humanist Vichians should care to ponder over a simple truth, namely, that "the fact that, tautologically, the subject matter of the 'study of man' is indeed *man* does not seem...to entail that the *explanatory* concepts invoked must also be...*human*."[55] "Human," that is, in the sense of being identical with the "warmth" of our ordinary experience. Acquaintance may be indeed "warm," but true knowledge is always "cool," whether you like it or not.

In his philosophy of the mind as "pure act" the main rival of Croce among Italian Belle Epoque neo-Hegelians, Giovanni Gentile

[53] Raymond Aron, "Max Weber and Michael Polanyi," in *Intellect and Hope Essays in the Thought of Michael Polanyi*, ed. Thomas Langford and William Poteat (Durham, N.C.: Duke University Press, 1968), p. 354; repr. in Aron, *Etudes Politiques* (Paris: Gallimard, 1972).

[54] Gellner, *Cause and Meaning...*, op. cit., p. 126.

[55] Idem, p. 73.

(1875-1944), harks back to Vico's *verum* = *factum* as a source of a thorough dissolution of truth into action: "vero è quel che si fa," wrote Gentile, in an exceedingly antiintellectualist vein.[56] As Herbert Marcuse, in his brief Hegelian spell, rightly observed, this was tantamount to the fascist blind worship of action for action's sake.[57] Years before he became Mussolini's secretary of state for education, Gentile had already drawn a distinctly protofascist, action-besotted philosophy, irrationalist in the extreme.

Just as Gentile's Hegelianism meant Hegel's march of the mind shorn of reason, much of today's "Vichianism" means Vico's search for historical contexts shorn of his rational sense of historical distance. Yet it was thanks to this sense, which best encapsulates the rationalist element in the *Scienza nuova,* that Vico was able to understand historical *change* as well as "context"—which is only to his credit.

A heretic finale: the Cartesianism of Vico

The average historist Vichian—Herderian (Berlin), neo-Marxist (Habermas), or phenomenological (Paci)—is terribly concerned with the humanization of knowledge, but quite indifferent to the problem of logico-empirical *validation* in (social) science.[58] As we can see from his wise remarks against anthropomorphic projections, Vico did not share this overall indifference. At first sight it would appear that the humanists hail in Vico a great pioneering epistemologist—the rescuer of historical knowledge from Cartesian malign neglect. On closer inspection, however, things look slightly different. What the humanists wel-

---

[56] Giovanni Gentile, *Teoria Generale dello Spirito come Atto Puro* (1916); (Florence: Sansoni, 1944), pp. 19-21.

[57] Cf. Herbert Marcuse, *Reason and Revolution. Hegel and the Rise of Social Theory* (New York: Oxford University Press, 1941), pt. II, chap. III 3.

[58] This seems to call for serious qualification in the case of Habermas. Yet ultimately Habermas's most cherished kind of knowledge—critical "analysis," as opposed to "information," governed by technical interest, and to "interpretation," led by practical interest—aims at reflexive emancipation through genuine dialogue, for dialogue, and not observation has become for him the main epistemological paradigm (see *Theory and Practice,* op. cit., p. 11). But there's the rub: If emancipatory knowledge does not in the least aspire to the condition of a proper logico-empirical explanation based on the idea of *objective* truth (truth, that is, to be "observed" rather than agreed without an external standard), then the criteria of validation become awfully blurred. To that extent Habermas's dialogical "communicational" validation theory is also impervious to cognitive legitimacy. On this point see J. G. Merquior, "A Marxisant Dilthey: Habermas and the Epistemology of "Critical Theory"" in *The Veil and the Mask,* op. cit., pp. 109-21.

come in Vico's theory of historical knowledge is the adjective, not the noun: They glory in historicalness far more than in *knowledge*. Yet Vico was after a "new science," and this puts him somewhat nearer Descartes, if not vulgar Cartesianism, than it is often realized.

It all depends, of course, on what Descartes you have. If you take the metaphysician, let alone the *contemptor historiae*, the kinship will be naturally nil. But in the end what matters most is the historical role of Descartes. As Ernest Gellner has been forcefully arguing, the basic historical task of Cartesianism was to lead the philosophical legitimation of a momentous shift in "the cognitive history of mankind"—"the shift of authority to the manner, and away from the content, of knowledge."[59] The change meant nothing less than the rise of *critical* knowledge, viz., *science*; and the implementation of such a crucial change implied the triumph of "selector" theories of cognition—theories that, instead of endorsing the stuff of culture, broke it up in order to submit each of its parts to the new filter of critical reason.[60] Accordingly, cognitive selection involved in turn a bold stepping outside one's own culture, an avoidance of the indulgence in the social self-image and its projections.

Descartes' myth of the purified self was just the best-known symbol of it all,[61] the emblem, as it were, of the cognitive revolution of modern science and modern philosophy. As for Vico, it is true that his *practice* as a historian scarcely qualifies as an instance of cognitive selection. By turning early modern philology into fanciful etymology, the *Scienza nuova* fared doubtless badly as concerns critical knowledge. But, remember, the novelty of Vico did not lie as much in his work as historian as in his *concept* of historical knowledge and his views on historical change. And here he *does* qualify as a "selector" epistemologist. He resorted to philosophy precisely to circumvent cultural anthropomorphism, the "conceit of nations and scholars." He put forward an ideally critical theory of the past, built on historical distance, not on the vain hope of empathic identification. Of course, he had to do it against the prevalent Cartesian wisdom, which held history as unworthy of

[59] Gellner, *Spectacles and Predicaments. Essays in Social Theory* (Cambridge: Cambridge University Press, 1979), p. 162.

[60] On the concept of "selector" theories of knowledge see Gellner, *Legitimation of Belief* (Cambridge: Cambridge University Press, 1974), pp. 46-47, 56-58.

[61] Gellner, *Spectacles and Predicaments,* op. cit., p. 149.

rigorous knowledge. But in a way this meant that he had to be anti-Cartesian only in order to become, in a deeper sense, the Descartes of historical science. To be sure, he played this role in a rather sketchy and roundabout way, but his critical intention, if not execution, was on the whole unmistakable. At any rate one thing is certain: Vico was far less of an irrationalist than most of his present admirers.

Contributors

HILLIARD ARONOVITCH. Assistant Professor of Philosophy at the University of Ottawa. Author of articles on philosophy of the social sciences, Marx, and moral theory. At work on a book on *The Primacy of Politics*.

TERENCE BALL. Associate Professor of Political Science at the University of Minnesota. Editor and contributor, *Political Theory and Praxis* (1977), co-editor and contributor, *After Marx* (1983), and author of numerous articles in academic journals. Currently completing a book on the political philosophy of James Mill and another on political theory and the social sciences.

JEFFREY BARNOUW. Assistant Professor of German at Boston University. Author of three other published essays on Vico, as well as articles dealing with Bacon and Hobbes, James Harrington, Leibniz, John Dennis, Trenchard and Gordon, Johnson, Hume, Johann Nicolas Tetens, Schiller, Fichte, Hölderlin and Schelling, Jefferson, Goethe and Helmholtz, and Saussure.

NIKHIL BHATTACHARYA. Associate Professor of Philosophy, Chairman of the Division of Liberal Arts at the Rhode Island School of Design. Author of "John Dewey's Philosophy of Science (1977), "Popper's Theory of the Rationality of Science" (1978), "Psychology and Rationality: The Structure of Mead's Problem" (1979); Co-editor with N. Baron of *Theory and Methodology in Semiotics* (1979).

GUSTAVO COSTA. Professor of Italian at the University of California, Berkeley. Author of *La leggenda dei secoli d'oro nella letteratura italiana* (1972), *Le antichità germaniche nella cultura italiana da Machiavelli a Vico* (1977), and of numerous essays on Vico.

PAOLO CRISTOFOLINI. Professor of Philosophy of History at the University of Pisa. Author of *Cartesiani e sociniani* (1974), *Il cielo aperto di Pierre Cuppé*, with the critical edition of Cuppé's *Le ciel ouvert à tous les hommes* (1981). Editor of Vico's *Opere filosofiche* (1971) and *Opere giuridiche* (1974).

ADRIENNE FULCO. Instructor in the Department of Political Science, Queens College, City University of New York; Research Assistant for the Institute for Vico Studies. Author of articles on Vico.

ERNESTO GRASSI. Professor and Director of the "Centro italiano di studi umanistici e filosofici" at the University of Munich. Author, among other works, of *Humanismus und Marxismus* (1973), *Die Macht der Phantasie* (1979), and *Rhetoric as Philosophy* (1980); Editor of *Rowohlts deutsche Enzyklopädie* and *Rowohlts Klassiker.*

BRUCE A. HADDOCK. Lecturer in Political Theory and Government, University College of Swansea. Author of *An Introduction to Historical Thought* (1980) and articles on Vico and political theory.

PATRICK HUTTON. Professor of History at the University of Vermont. Author of *The Cult of the Revolutionary Tradition* (1981) and of articles in European intellectual history and in French history.

EDMUND E. JACOBITTI. Associate Professor of Historical Studies at Southern Illinois University at Edwardsville. Author of *Revolutionary Humanism and Historicism in Modern Italy* (1981) and articles on modern Italian thought.

JEREMY JENNINGS. Lecturer in French Government and Political Thought at the University College of Swansea. Author of several forthcoming articles on Georges Sorel and of an intellectual biography on the same subject.

GEORGE L. KLINE. Milton C. Nahm Professor of Philosophy at Bryn Mawr College. Editor of *Alfred North Whitehead: Essays on his Philosophy* (1963); editor of, and contributor to, *European Philosophy Today* (1965). Translator of V. V. Zenkovsky, *A History of Russian Philosophy* (2 vols., 1953); translator and introducer of *Joseph Brodsky: Selected Poems* (1973). Author of *Spinoza in Soviet Philosophy* (1952, reprint 1981) and *Religious and Anti-Religious Thought in Russia* (1968).

DAVID L. LACHTERMAN. Visiting Lecturer in Philosophy at Vassar College. Editor and translator of *Max Scheler: Selected Philosophical Essays* (1973) and author of "Vico, Doria e la geometria sintetica," "The Physics of Spinoza's *Ethics*" and other articles. Collaborator on the forthcoming *Sachkommentar* to Vico's *De antiquissima*.

ALLAN MEGILL. Associate Professor of History at the University of Iowa. Author of various articles in the history of ideas. He is completing a book on Nietzsche, Heidegger, Foucault, and Derrida.

JOSÉ GUILHERME MERQUIOR. Visiting Professor of Political Science at the University of Brasilia, and formerly Visiting Professor at King's College, London. Author of *Arte e Sociedade em Marcuse, Adorno e Benjamin* (1969), *L'Esthétique de Lévi-Strauss* (1977), *The Veil and the Mask: Essays on Culture and Ideology* (1979), *Rousseau and Weber* (1980), *As Idéias e as Formas* (1981).

PETER MUNZ. Professor of History at the Victoria University of Wellington, New Zealand. Author of *The Place of Hooker in the History of Thought* (1952), *Problems of Religious Knowledge* (1959), *The Origin of the Carolingian Empire* (1960), *Relationship and Solitude* (1964), *Frederick Barbarossa* (1969), *Life in the Age of Charlemagne* (1969), *When the Golden Bough Breaks* (1973), *Boso's Life of Alexander III* (1973), *The Shape of Time* (1977).

JOHN O'NEILL. Professor of Sociology at York University, Toronto and Affiliate of the Center for Comparative Literature, University of Toronto. Editor of the *International Library of Phenomenology and Moral Sciences* and the international quarterly, *Philosophy of the Social Sciences*. Author of *Perception, Expression and History* (1970), *Sociology as a Skin Trade* (1972), *Making Sense Together* (1974), *Essaying Montaigne: A Study of the Renaissance Institution of Writing and Reading* (1982), and *For Marx Against Althusser* (1982).

ARSHI PIPA. Professor of Italian at the University of Minnesota. Author of *Montale e Dante* (1968), *Hieronymus De Rada* (1978), *Albanian Folk Verse: Structure and Genre* (1978), and articles on Italian literature and aesthetics, and on Albanian literature and folklore.

LEON POMPA. Professor and Head of the Department of Philosophy, University of Birmingham. Author, among other works, of *Vico: A Study of the 'New Science'* (1975). Editor, with W. H. Dray, of *Substance and Form in History* (1981). Editor and translator of *Vico: Selected Writings* (1982).

ALAIN PONS. Professor of philosophy at the University of Paris X—Nanterre. Translator into French of Vico's *Autobiografia* and *De nostri temporis studiorum ratione* (1981). Author of articles on Vico, on Diderot's and

D'Alembert's *Encyclopédie*, on utopia, and on various topics of political philosophy.

EMANUELE RIVERSO. Professor of History of Philosophy, University of Naples. Author of *Il pensiero di Bertrand Russell* (1958), *Il pensiero di Ludovico Wittgenstein* (1964), *Natura e logo* (1966), *La filosofia analitica in Inghilterra* (1969), *Individuo, società e cultura* (1971), *Riferimento e struttura* (1977), and *Filosofia analitica del tempo* (1979). Editor of *Leggere Vico* (1982).

TOM ROCKMORE. Associate Professor of Philosophy at Fordham University. Author of *Fichte, Marx and the German Philosophical Tradition* (1980), Co-author of *Marxism and Alternatives* (1981). Author of numerous articles in academic journals.

LAWRENCE H. SIMON. Assistant Professor of Philosophy at the University of Notre Dame. Author of articles on Vico, Marx, Habermas, and the problem of explanation in the social sciences.

GIORGIO TAGLIACOZZO. Founder and Director of the Institute for Vico Studies (1974). Founder of the periodical *New Vico Studies* (1983). Author of *Economia e massimo edonistico collettivo* (1933) and *Economisti napoletani dei secoli xvii e xviii* (1937). Coeditor with Hayden White of *Giambattista Vico: An International Symposium* (1969), with Donald P. Verene of *Giambattista Vico's Science of Humanity* (1976), with Michael Mooney and Donald P. Verene of *Vico and Contemporary Thought* (1979). Editor of *Vico: Past and Present* (1981). Author of articles on Vico.

DONALD PHILLIP VERENE. Professor and Chairman, Department of Philosophy, Emory University. Editor of *Philosophy and Rhetoric* and coeditor with Giorgio Tagliacozzo of *New Vico Studies*. Coeditor with Giorgio Tagliacozzo of *Giambattista Vico's Science of Humanity* (1976) and with Michael Mooney and Giorgio Tagliacozzo *of Vico and Comtemporary Thought* (1979). Editor of *Symbol, Myth, and Culture: Essays and Lectures of Ernst Cassirer 1935–1945* (1979). Author of *Vico's Science of Imagination* (1981).

NAME INDEX

(Page numbers in *italics* refer
to foot notes)

Abrams, M. H., *3*
Acosta, J., 265
Adorno, T., *1*
Allen, D. P. H., *219*
Allen, W. L., *264*
Althusser, L., 392–395, 399, *419*, 420
Amerio, A., 122–123
Apel, K.-O., 283
Arcara, R., *379*
Arendt, H., *43, 60, 89, 90,* 103, 412
Aristotle, 3, *40,* 45, 47, 52, 54, 85–86,
    131, 183, 185, 188, 304
Arneson, R. J., *219*
Aron, R., 423
Aronovitch, H., 138–139, *219*
Assoun, P. L., *158*
Auerbach, E., *402*
Augustine, 2, 24, 85, 180, 359, 403
Augustus, 8
Avineri, S., *80,* 107, *108, 131,* 137, *146,*
    151
Axelos, K., *41, 91, 140*
Ayer, A. J., *369*

Bacon, F., 1, *44, 100,* 181, 192–197,
    200, 202, 204, 365
Badaloni, N., *20, 121, 344*
Bailey, S., *323*
Bakan, M., *43*
Bakunin, 352
Balibar, E., *392*
Ball, T., *78, 86, 93*
Ballanche, P. S., 402
Barnouw, J., *96, 97, 100*
Bauer, B., 152
Baur, F. C., 335
Baxandall, L., *304*
Bayle, P., 347

Beaufret, J., 234
Belaval, Y., *121, 127*
Belgioioso, s. Cristina di Belgioioso
Benjamin, W., 412
Bergin, T. G., *5, 39, 115, 119, 141, 200,*
    295, *367*
Berkeley, G., 114, 192
Berlin, I., 5, *9, 10, 14, 38, 53, 78,* 82,
    84, *85, 87, 89, 127,* 139, 190, 207,
    208, 404–407, 410, 413–414, 424
Bernard, C., 332
Berlioz, H., 403
Berns, L., *44*
Bernstein, E., *290,* 301, 303
Berti, G., *377*
Bertoni Jovine, D., *374*
Bhattacharya, N., *192, 193, 198, 204*
Biasutti, F., *53*
Binswanger, L., *17*
Bismarck, O. v., 300
Blakeley, T. J., *115*
Bloch, E., *150*
Blum, A., *45*
Boccaccio, G., 243–244
Bodin, J., 350, 362
Bossuet, J. B., 346, 348
Bottigelli, E., *154*
Bottomore, T. B., *418*
Boudon, R., 409, *422*
Boyle, R., 204
Brancato, F., *153*
Brenkert, G. G., *219,* 223, *225*
Brombert, B. A., *153*
Buchanan, A., *219*
Bulmash, K., 131
Burke, E., 385–386
Burke, P., *1, 323*

Cabet, E., 29
Callicles, 25
Cambon, G., *85*
Campbell, D. T., *12*
Campbell, R. H., *272*

Cantelli, G., *49*
Caponigri, R., *58*
Carver, T., *42*
Casati, A., *377*
Cassirer, E., *7*, 245, 404
Castoriadis, C., *45*
Chateaubriand, F. R., *402*
Chesneaux, J., *17*
Child, A., *46, 193, 202*
Cicero, *80*, 280
Cieszkowski, A., *418*
Cohen, G. A., *13*, 98, *111, 171*, 174–176, 220, *221*
Cohen, M., *219, 221*
Colletti, L., *44*
Collingwood, R. G., *56, 121*
Comte, A., 354, 407
Cooper, L. N., *3*
Corsano, A., *53, 85*
Cousin, V., *377*
Crick, B., *98*
Cristina di Belgioioso, 152–155, 159, 162, 253, 291–292, 299, 309, 312, 314, 403
Cristofolini, P., *40, 47, 266, 269*
Croce, B., *5, 38, 53,* 54, *118,* 120–123, *151, 153, 154,* 179, 342–346, *352, 353,* 355, 359–366, *377,* 382, 403, 414, 423
Crosby, J. F., *44*
Cuoco, V., 372–375, 381–382
Curtius, E. R., 243
Custodi, P., 322

Dal Pane, L., *353, 355, 357*
Dante, *85,* 257, 320, 362
Darnton, R., *1*
Darwin, C., 39, 62, 78, 97, 251–252, 316, 348–350, 352, 357, 408
Davis, J. C., *1*
De Giovanni, B., *40, 46, 49, 382*
De Maistre, J., 385, 402–403, 405
De Mas, E., *372*

Democritus, 116
Derrida, J., 389, 390, 395–396, *415*
De Sanctis, F., 369–370, 378
Descartes, R., 1, 3, 44, 54, 84, *90,* 120–121, 127, 178–191, 192, 233–234, 247, 279, 282–284, 333–334, 404–405, 424–425
Destutt de Tracy, A. L. C., *323*
Dewey, J., *88,* 193, 198
D'Hont, J., *42*
Diaz, F., *324*
Diderot, D., 416
Dilthey, W., 403, *404,* 406, 414–415
Diodorus Siculus, 307
Doz, A., *42*
Draco, 90
Dunckner, F., *302*
Dupré, L., *45*
Durkheim, E., 82

Easton, L. D., *97, 145*
Eliade, M., *156*
Ellis, R. L., *365*
Engels, F., *13, 29,* 30, 32, 33, 36, *39, 43, 79, 82, 91, 92, 93,* 116, 118, *135,* 151, *152,* 154, 157, 187, *201, 220,* 253, 300–302, 305, *306,* 313–315, *323,* 344, 350, 354, 356, *388,* 411–412
Epicurus, 116, *118*
Ermarth, M., *415*
Euclides, 54
Eulau, H., *369*

Farr, J., *78, 93*
Fassò, G., *40*
Febvre, L., *351*
Fellmann, F., *46, 59*
Ferguson, A., *1*
Fernandez de Oviedo y Valdés, G., 265
Fernbach, D., 220
Ferrari, G. A., *40,* 153, 162

Ferri, E., 357
Feuerbach, L., *43,* 92, *93,* 108, 115–
116, 131, 147, *151,* 152, 158, 160–
161, 200–201, 317, 335–336, 411–
412
Feuerlicht, I., *151*
Feyerabend, P., 389
Fichte, J. G., *43,* 152, 181, 310
Finch, H. L., *195*
Fisch, M. H., *5, 39, 80,* 84, *87, 99, 115,*
119, 121, 141, 151, *200, 252,* 295,
367, 407
Fleischer, H., 419, *420*
Flora, F., *153*
Foot, P., 217–219, 232
Foucault, M., 389–396
Fourier, C.-F.-M., 21, 29, *323*
Frank, M., *43*
Frankena, W. K., *209,* 211, *214*
Freud, S., 13–14, 167, 390
Freye, N., *398*
Fubini, M., *153*
Furth, P., *116*

Gadamer, H.-G., *86*
Galiani, F., 323–324, 416–417, 421
Galilei, G., 1, 192
Gandy, D. R., *156*
Gardiner, P., 206
Garibaldi, G., *306*
Garin, E., *5, 353, 378*
Gellner, E., *414,* 415, 423, 425
Gendrom, B., *109*
Genovesi, A., 322
Gentile, G., *5, 115, 119, 368, 376,* 423–
424
Gerratana, V., *382*
Giacco, B. M., 60
Giannone, P., 417
Gianturco, E., *368*
Gilbert, F., *418*
Gillispie, C. O., *1*
Giovannino da Mantova, 243

Giuliani, A., *120*
Goldman, A., *210*
Goldmann, L., *150*
Goethe, *3, 11,* 378, 413
Gramsci, A., 33, 346, 367–387, *419*
Granel, G., *41*
Grassi, E., *38, 147*
Grisoni, D., *392*
Grotius, H., 181, 348
Guddat, K. H., *97, 145*
Guerci, L., *324*
Guicciardini, F., *369*

Habermas, J., *38, 40, 43, 45, 88, 90,*
91, 278, 283, 287, 289, 405–407,
410, *412,* 413, 419–420, 424
Haddock, B. A., *17, 78, 87, 362, 364,*
366
Hamann, J. G., 402, 413
Hampshire, S., *89*
Hardy, H., *82*
Harman, G., 210–218, 223–224, 230
Harnack, A., 335
Harriot, T., 265
Harris, M., *422*
Harrison, A., *84*
Hatzfeld, S. v., 300, *305*
Hayek, F. A., 411
Heath, D. D., *365*
Hegel, G. W. F., *3,* 5, *7,* 9, 12, 14, 30–
32, 36–37, *42, 43, 45, 71,* 81, 103,
106–107, *108, 111,* 114, 118, *121,* 122,
124–125, 127, 152, 155, 158, 170,
181, 184, 189, 192, 233–234, 246–
247, 275, 300, 302, *305, 306,* 307,
310, 335, 353–354, 359, 361, 363,
376, 377–380, 406–407, 411, 413,
417, *418,* 424
Heidegger, M., *40,* 233–250, 389–390,
393
Heimann, P. M., *1*
Heine, H., 403
Henry, M., *41, 42, 45*

Heraclitus, 236, 239, 301, *305*
Herbart, J. F., 353
Herder, J. G., 3, 361, 402–403, *404,*
    405
Hildebrand, A. v., 421
Hill, M. A., *43*
Hintikka, J., *84*
Hintze, O., *418, 422*
Hobbes, T., 3, 48, *53, 100,* 192, 282,
    284
Hodges, H. A., *404*
Hölderlin, F., *3,* 239
Holmes, G., *369*
Holmstrom, N., *219*
Homer, 14, *17,* 88, 281, 291, 294, 362
Horace, 311
Horkheimer, M., *1, 38,* 179
Hotman, F., 416
Houghton, W. E., *153*
Hughes, H. S., 82, 378
Hume, D., 75, 170, 192, 195, 198, 404,
    408
Hunt, E. K., *151*
Husami, Z. I., *219, 225*
Husserl, E., 182, 184, *284*
Hutton, P. H., *11*
Huyghens, C., 1

Immerwahr, H. R., *3*

Jacobelli, A. M., *60, 151*
Jacobitti, E. E., *353, 372, 378, 381*
James, H., 403
James, W., 332
Jay, M., *79*
Jocteau, G. C., *379*
John, P. M., *151*
Joll, J., 382
Jordan, Z. A., *63, 64, 68*
Josa, M., *45*
Justinian, 296

Kamenka, E., *13, 39, 62, 79, 200, 202,*
    253, 329, 388

Kant, E., 5, 9, 11–14, 74, 97, 114, 116,
    180, 183, 189, 192, 195, 199, 206,
    222, 404, 406, 414
Kaufmann, W., *5,* 389
Kautsky, K., *274*
Kelley, D. R., *52*
Kepler, J., *1*
Kennington, R., *44*
Kibiehler, Y., *153*
Kierkegaard, S., 385
Kim, J., *210*
Kline, G. L., *115, 118, 124*
Knies, K., 421
Kolakowski, L., 30–31, *149,* 171, 264,
    353, 418
Körner, S., *84*
Kosik, K., *41*
Koyré, A., *83*
Krader, L., *264,* 273–274, *349*
Krois, J. M., *86, 262*
Kuhn, S., 389, 390, 396–397
Küng, H., *140*

Labriola, A., 81, 159, 338, 342–346,
    348, 351–363, 366
Lachterman, D. R., *120, 121,* 123, 124
Laet, J. van, 265
Lafargue, P., 81, 154
Laing, R. D., *17*
Lakatos, I., *396*
Lamarck, J.-B., 408
La Peyrère, I., de, 386–388
Langford, T., *423*
Laplace, P.-S. de, 83
Lasch, C., 81
Lassalle, F., *39,* 79, 151–154, 253, 290,
    294, 295, 299–316, *388*
Laud, J. P. N., *120*
Lee, E. N., *125*
Lefort, C., *156*
Leibniz, G. W., 48, 192
Lenin, 33, 114, 371, 375–376, 382, *419*
LeoGrande, W. M., *151, 155*

Lescarbot, M., 265
Lessing, G. E., 3, 10, *418*
Lévi-Strauss, C., *7*, 423
Lévy-Bruhl, L., *7*
Lewin, H., *161*
Lichtheim, G., *82*, *149*, *418*
Lieber, H.-J., *116*
Liebknecht, W., *305*
Linschooten, H. van, 265
Livet, P., *41*
Livy, 104
Lobkowicz, N., 86, *87*, *91*
Locke, J., 3, 10, *157*, 192, 198, *323*, 404
Lorenz, K., *12*
Loria, A., 352
Louis XIV, 304
Löwith, K., *46*, *85*, *147*, *156*, *418*
Lubbock, J., *274*
Lukács, G., *13*, *41*, 122, 179, 180, *406*,
    418, 419
Luther, M., 417
Luxemburg, R., 403
Lycurgus, 27, 88, 90
McBride, W. L., *219*
MacCulloch, J. R., *323*
Machiavelli, N., 23, *98*, 344–346, 369,
    380, 407
McLellan, D., *45*, *79*, *221*
McMullin, E., *46*
McMurtry, J., *40*
McNall, S. G., *284*
Macrobius, 307
Maine, H. S., 274
Malthus, T. R., *323*
Mandelbaum, M., *124*
Mansfield, H., *45*
Manuel, F. E., *156*
Manuel, F. P., *156*
Marcuse, H., 239, 423–424
Mas, Enrico de, *1*
Masterson, M., *396*
Masterson, P., *151*
Mastroianni, G., *153*
Mathieu, V., *58*, 229

May, R., *17*
Mayer, G., *290*
Mazzini, G., *306*, 352
Meek, R. L., *4*
Meinecke, F., *4*, *402*, 408, 413, 415, *416*
Meisel, J. H., *98*
Menger, C., 421
Merleau-Ponty, M., 405
Merquior, J. G., *404*, *410*, *419*, *422*,
    424
Mészáros, I., *151*
Michelet, J., 153–155, 344, 346, 402,
    403, 406
Mignet, F., 152
Mikhailovski, N. K., *418*
Mill, J., *43*, *45*
Mill, J. S., 268, *323*
Miller, R. W., *70*
Momigliano, A., 379
Mondolfo, R., *160*
Montesquieu, *3*, 350
Mooney, M., *17*, *38*, *49*, *60*, *128*, *139*,
    260, *278*, *282*
Moore, S., *70*
Mora, G., *119*
Morawski, S., *304*
More, T., 21
Morgan, L. H., *274*, 343–344, 348
Morris, J., *161*
Morrison, J. C., *46*, *52*, *58*, 83, *130*, *140*
Munz, P., *5*, *6*, *7*, *9*, *10*, *13*, *17*
Musgrave, A., *396*
Mussato, A., 242–244
Mussolini, 370, 424

Naccache, B., *350*
Nagel, T., *219*
Napoleon, *83*
Napoleon III, 14
Nelson, J. S., *396*
Newton, I., 1, 6, 11, 385
Nicolini, F., *39*, *46*, *115*, *119*, *151*, *152*,
    153, *154*, *226*, *346*, *367*, *368*, *374*,
    416

Niebuhr, B. G., 154, *290*, 291, *307*, 308, 311, *321*
Nietzsche, F., 13–14, 25, 103, 380, 388–400
Nielsen, K., *219*
Nino, 271
Nisbet, R., *1*
Novalis, *3*
Numa Pompilius, 308

Oldrini, G., *376*, *377*
Ollman, B., *138*, *151*, 263, *275*
O'Malley, J., *42*, *108*, *112*, *417*
O'Neill, J., *38*, *278*, *283*, *284*, *287*, *289*
O'Rourke, J. J., *115*
Ortes, G., 322
Otto, S., *46*, *54*, *58*

Paci, E., *404*, 405, 424
Padover, S. K., *140*, *152*
Paggi, L., *382*
Pagliaro, A., *49*
Pagnini, C. F., 322
Panizzi, A., 153, *154*
Parekh, B., *43*
Pareto, V., 409
Parmenides, 236, 239
Parsons, H. L., *157*
Parsons, T., *369*
Passow, A. T. G., 311
Peirce, C. S., *86*, *88*
Peloutier, F., *340*
Pelz, W., *6*
Petronio, G., *381*
Petrovic, G., 249
Petty, W., *323*
Phear, J. B., 274
Piaget, J., *7*, *119*
Pier Vincenzo di Lucca, *377*
Piovani, P., *417*
Pipa, A., *79*, *322*
Pius IX, 376

Plato, 3, 11, 20–23, 25, 28–29, 31, 33, 35, 55, 60, *86*, 181, 188, 198, 279, 344–345, 367, 406–407
Plautus, 311
Plutarch, 308
Poincaré, J.-H., 332
Polybius, 344–345
Pompa, L., *10*, *46*, *169*, 188, *226*, 227, *232*, *269*, *362*, 414
Pons, A., *60*, *329*, *387*, *412*, *413*
Pontano, G., 245
Popper, K. R., *11*, 192, *404*
Poteat, W., *423*
Prawer, S. S., *157*
Previtera, G., *245*
Proudhon, P. J., 36, *323*
Pythagoras, 121

Quesnay, F., *323*
Quine, W. V. O., 189
Quinet, E., 403

Rabelais, F., 21
Rader, M., *131*, *156*, 208
Ranke, L. v., 24, *404*, *422*
Reinhold, K. L., 189
Reuleaux, F., 332
Ricardo, D., 203, 272, *323*
Riccardo Waitbornio, s.
    Withnourne R.
Richelieu, 305
Rickman, H. P., *404*
Riedel, M., *45*
Ritschl, A., 335
Riverso, E., *5*, *89*, *266*, *405*
Rockmore, T., *43*
Romulus, 88, 307
Roscher, W., 421
Rossi, P., *290*
Rousseau, J.-J., *7*, 152, 341
Rubel, M., 80–81, *418*
Russo, L., *377*
Ryle, G., 405

Said, E., 394–395, *398*
Salomone, A. W., *119*
Salutati, C., 244–245
Salvatorelli, L., *374*
Sanderson, J. B., *111*
Sartre, J.-P., 389
Savorelli, A., *348*
Say, J. B., *323*
Scanlon, T., *219*
Schacht, R., *151*
Schelle, G., *16*
Schelling, F. W. J., *43,* 405
Schiller, F., 152
Schilpp, P. A., *12*
Schleiermacher, F. D. E., 414, *415*
Schmidt, A., *44*
Schouten, J., 265
Schopenhauer, A., *12*
Schumpeter, J. A., 416
Schutz, A., 409
Scultenio, G., s. Schouten J.
Seliger, M., *135*
Severino, E., *46, 57*
Shakespeare, W., 254
Shaw, W. H., *16, 156*
Simmel, G., 422
Simon, L. H., *38, 229, 232*
Sismondi, S. de, *323*
Simpson, T. K., *61*
Skinner, A. S., *272*
Smith, A., 10, *45,* 203, 271, *272, 323*
Socrates, 23, *60,* 206
Sohrawardi, S. Y., 267
Solon, 27, 88, 90, 100
Sophocles, 239, 240
Sorel, G., 81, 82, *98,* 326–341, 342–
    346, 381, 403
Spaventa, B., 348, 353, 376, *377*
Spedding, J., *365*
Spencer, H., 352, 357, 378
Spicker, S. F., *44*
Spinella, M., *381*
Spinoza, B., 23, *53,* 118–120, 355–356,
    401, 416

Stanfield, J. R., *151*
Stannard, D. E., *420*
Steiner, G., *14, 15*
Steuart, J., *323*
Stevenson, W. T., *141*
Stirling, J. H., *120*
Storch Sr., H. F., *323*
Strauss, D. F., 335
Strauss, L., *83*
Sturrock, J., *389*
Swingewood, A., *131, 137*

Tacitus, 181
Tagliacozzo, G., *5, 13, 17, 20, 38, 39,*
    40, 46, 49, 52, 58, 60, 62, 78, 79, 85,
    86, 89, 96, 127, 128, 139, 147, 166,
    169, 198, 200, 204, 229, 253, 260,
    266, 278, 285, 322, 324, 329, 372,
    387, 388, 402, 404, 417, *421*
Taylor, C., 176
Thomas Aquinas, 85–87
Thrasymachus, 206
Thucydides, *369*
Tocqueville, 409–410
Todd, W. B., *272*
Trakl, G., 239
Trémaux, P., *350*
Trollope, T. A., *153*
Trompf, G. W., *156*
Trotsky, L., 81
Tucker, R., *131, 156, 160, 170, 173*
Turgot, R. J., 16, *323,* 417
Tuttle, H. N., *404*

Ugone Linschotano, s. Linschooten H.
    van
Ulmer, K., *40*
Ungari, P., *329*
Ure, R., *323*

Vaughan, F., *83*
Vera, A., *377*

Verene, D. P., *17, 20, 38, 40, 46, 49, 51,*
  52, 58, 60, 89, 94, 128, 139, 147,
  229, 254, 260, 278, 285, 387, 404
Verri, P., 322, *323*
Veyne, P., *422*
Vloten, J. van, *120*
Voltaire, *3,* 389

Wackenheim, C., *140*
Wagner, A., *45*
Walsh, W. H., *46,* 408, 414
Wanderlint, M., *323*
Weber, M., 6, 409–410, 412, 422
Wells, G. A., *402*
White, H. V., *13, 39, 40, 62, 79,* 85, *89,*
  120, 127, 128, 137, *200, 253, 285,*
  372, 388, 402, 405

Whitehead, A. N., 119
Williams, B., 218
Wilson, A. M., *416*
Wilson, E., 83
Wilson, H. T., *285*
Withbourne, R., 265
Wittgenstein, L., *89,* 422
Wolf, C., 291
Wolfe, N., 423
Wood, A. W., *219,* 220, 222–223, 225
Wyatt, J., 251–252, 260, 321

Young, A., 323

Zasulich, V., 37, 274
Zeno, 120, 121